ISBN 978-1-333-70903-7
PIBN 10524270

FB &c Ltd, Dalton House, 60 Windsor Avenue, London, SW19 2RR.
Company number 08720141. Registered in England and Wales.

For support please visit www.forgottenbooks.com

THE

LAND WE LOVE,

A MONTHLY MAGAZINE

DEVOTED TO

LITERATURE, MILITARY HISTORY, AND AGRICULTURE.

VOLUME V.

MAY---OCTOBER, 1867-'68.

CHARLOTTE, N. C.
PUBLISHED BY D. H. HILL.

1868.

INDEX TO VOLUME V.

A

B

C

D

E

F

G

H

I

J

L

M

N

O

P

POETRY.

FAMILY OF HON. JEFF DAVIS.

Eng^d by R Whitechurch for
"THE LAND WE LOV

THE LAND WE LOVE

[illegible] VOL. V.

[illegible] GENERAL S. D. RAMSEUR.

MAJOR [illegible] RAMSEUR was [illegible] the village of Lincolnton [illegible] 31st of May, 18[illegible] was the second child of [illegible] and Lucy M. Ramseur. [illegible] arents were members [illegible] Presbyterian church, and [illegible] was bred under religious [illegible]. The circumstances of [illegible] childhood, were those best adapted to develop his character [illegible] favorably. His parents [illegible] ample means [illegible] give them [illegible] then all necessary [illegible] and [illegible] tual advantages, [illegible] lieved [illegible] the one hand [illegible] poverty, while on [illegible] preserved them [illegible] ng and corrupt- [illegible] an artificial [illegible]. Having re- [illegible] mentary education [illegible] of Lincolnton, and [illegible], in his native [illegible] an appointment [illegible] Academy, at [illegible] in this ef- [illegible] freshman [illegible] llege, N. C.

At this institution he spent about eighteen months, but he had early chosen arms as his profession, and the opportunity again recurring, he determined to apply again for a Cadet-ship. Encouraged and aided by General D. H. Hill, at that time Professor of Mathematics, in the College, and who recommended him to the notice of the Hon. Burton Craige, he succeeded in gaining the eagerly desired appointment.

At West Point he remained five years, an additional year having been added to the course, while he was a student there. He was graduated in 1860.

By his courtesy, high-toned integrity and sterling worth, he made many warm personal friends, both among his brother cadets and in the professional staff. Of the branches of the service left to his choice, he preferred the Light Artillery, and in this was commissioned second Lieutenant by brevet.

It will be seen that the young

THE LAND WE LOVE.

No. I. MAY, 1868. Vol. V.

SKETCH OF MAJOR GENERAL S. D. RAMSEUR.

Major General S. D. Ramseur was born in the village of Lincolnton, N. C., on the 31st of May, 1837. He was the second child of Jacob A. and Lucy M. Ramseur. His parents were members of the Presbyterian Church, and he was bred under religious influences. The circumstances of his childhood, were those best adapted to develop his character most favorably. His parents possessing ample means to give their children all necessary social and intellectual advantages, relieved them on the one hand from the ills of poverty, while on the other, they preserved them from the enervating and corrupting allurements of an artificial and worldly life. Having received his elementary education in the schools of Lincolnton, and the village of Milton, in his native State, he sought an appointment in the Military Academy, at West Point. Failing in this effort, he entered the freshman class, in Davidson College, N. C. At this institution he spent about eighteen months, but he had early chosen arms as his profession, and the opportunity again recurring, he determined to apply again for a Cadet-ship. Encouraged and aided by General D. H. Hill, at that time Professor of Mathematics, in the College, and who recommended him to the notice of the Hon. Burton Craige, he succeeded in gaining the eagerly desired appointment.

At West Point he remained five years, an additional year having been added to the course, while he was a student there. He was graduated in 1860.

By his courtesy, high-toned integrity and sterling worth, he made many warm personal friends, both among his brother cadets and in the professional staff. Of the branches of the service left to his choice, he preferred the Light Artillery, and in this was commissioned second Lieutenant by brevet.

It will be seen that the young

Lieutenant was in the United States army but a short time before the breaking out of hostilities between the North and South, and this period—from June, 1860, to April, 1861—he spent in the performance of his duties at Fortress Monroe. In April, 1861, after the bursting of the storm-cloud, Lieutenant Ramseur resigned his commission in the army, and tendered his services to the newly-formed government at Montgomery. On the 22nd of the same month, he was commissioned 1st Lieutenant of Artillery, and ordered to the Mississippi. But whilst on his way to his new post, he recieved a telegram announcing his election to a captaincy of the "Ellis Light Artillery."

This was a battery composed of the first young men in his State, and was then in formation at the capital.

Captain Ramseur now repaired with all haste to Raleigh, where, by his energy and activity, he soon secured the requisite number of guns, horses and other equipments necessary for a thoroughly-appointed battery; and in a very short time he had his full complement of men. At "Camp Boylan," near Raleigh, he drilled and practiced his battery for some time, and brought it to such a state of perfection that it became the pride of our State.

But the people began to ask why he did not go to the front.—Troops from all the Southern States had been passing through Raleigh, and hastening on to Virginia, but the "Ellis Artillery" was still going through its daily drills. The citizens, who had not become well acquainted with the young commander, began to think that this was a holiday company, and one of the papers published at the Capital, spoke somewhat derisively of Captain Ramseur's artillery, as the "Parlor Battery." Inquiries were made by the authorities at Richmond, to which place the seat of the Confederate Government had been removed, as to when the battery would be in readiness. No definite answer could be returned—Captain Ramseur said that his command had not yet attained the proficiency which he desired, and the drilling and reviewing continued. Some of Ramseur's friends thought that he had been tardy in resigning his commission in the old service, and they now thought him censurably slow in taking the field. In both of these opinions they were wrong. In the one case, before giving up his commission, the young officer was determined to wait until every effort of the South to avert the strife had proven futile; and in the other, now that he had drawn his sword in our cause, he was as fully determined that when he went to the contest, its prowess should be recognized. And the record of the "Ellis Light Artillery" affords a favorable comment on his decision of purpose.

At last he was ready, and late in the summer of 1861, his battery proceeded to Virginia. He was stationed near Southfield on the South side of the James, and spent the fall and winter months in camp at that place, or in occasional movements to and from Norfolk.

At all of the reviews of the army in the department of Norfolk, this battery was the cynosure of attraction; and its beautiful evolutions and proficiency in drilling gained for the youthful commander many encomiums from the reviewing generals.

In the Spring of 1862, when Richmond was threatened by McClellan's advance, up the Peninsula, Captain Ramseur was ordered to report, with his battery, to General Magruder, at Yorktown. It had the honor, therefore, of forming a part of that little army of about 7,000 or 8,000, which, by the masterly activity of its General, was made to represent such a formidable front, that the opposing force, (which has been variously estimated at from 40,000 to 160,000) was deceived into a halt, which continued until the arrival of the "Army of Northern Virginia," under Jos. E. Johnston.

General Magruder had known the meritorious young officer when they were both in the service of the United States; and he, therefore, detached him from his favorite battery, to place him in command of the artillery of the right wing. It was here that Major Ramseur, who had now been promoted, saw his first active service.

Before any serious fighting occurred on the Peninsula, Major Ramseur was elected to the Colonelcy of the 49th North Carolina infantry, and although he regretted to dissever his connection with the artillery, he accepted the new promotion. The "Ellis Artillery," however, under the gallant leadership of Captain Manly, a short time afterwards, at the battle of Williamsburg, won its first laurels, which continned to brighten till the close of the war.

The regiment of which Colonel Ramseur now took command, was composed altogether of new men, men who had just enlisted. But, by the exercise of his knowledge of infantry tactics, the young commander, at an early day, had it prepared for the front. The 49th belonged to Ransom's brigade of Huger's division, and saw its first service in the skirmishes which preceded the opening battles before Richmond. Encouraged by the fearless intrepidity of its commander, this body of men, from the very outset, rendered most signal service. It went through the series of battles memorable as the "seven day's fighting," and in the last of these, at Malvern Hill, on the 1st of July, whilst leading a victorious charge, the young Colonel was wounded. He was shot through the right arm, above the elbow, and that night, after the battle, was borne to Richmond, and carried to the house of Mr. M. S. Valentine. Here he met with every possible kind attention, but the nature of his wound was such, that more than a month elapsed before he could travel to his home in North Carolina.

Whilst at home, and before he had sufficiently convalesced to return to the field, Colonel Ramseur received his commission as Brigadier General. He now thought that promotion was coming too rapidly, and felt seriously disinclined to accept this newly offered compliment. But at the earnest request of his friends, who had a higher opinion of his capacity, than he himself had, he reluctantly accepted the increased rank. It is a commentary both on the innate bravery of his regiment, and the fearlessness of its commander, that this officer was promoted immediately after leading a new command into its comparatively first fight.

In October, 1862—though unable to use his right hand, even in writing—he repaired to Richmond in order to make a decision in regard to the brigade which had been offered him. He called on President Davis, and explained to him his delicacy in accepting the exalted rank that had been conferred upon him, but the President insisted that he should take the commission, telling him, at the same time to return to his home until he was entirely restored to health. But General Ramseur, instead of returning to North Carolina, sought out the army, and took command of the brigade which had been left without a general officer, by the death of the gallant George B. Anderson. His arrival at his new command, was thus spoken of afterwards, at a meeting of condolence, held in Lincolnton, on the 31st of October, 1864. It is an extract from a speech delivered by Colonel Bynum:

"Assigned to a command in which I served, I knew him well. He succeeded the lamented Gen. Anderson, an officer of great abilities, and well skilled in the art of war, commanding the love and confidence of his men. His was a place not easily filled.

"General Ramseur came to the brigade, a stranger, from another branch of the service; but he at once disarmed criticism by his high professional attainment and great amiability of character, inspiring his men, by his own enthusiastic nature, with those lofty martial qualities which distinguish the true Southern soldier."

This brigade, composed of the 2nd, 4th, 14th and 30th North Carolina regiments, then attached to Jackson's corps, was commanded by General Ramseur at the battle of Chancellorsville, where he was again wounded in the foot by a shell, whilst leading a successful charge upon the enemy's works. This second wound did not take him from the field, but he continued with his brigade, and shortly afterwards accompanied it through the Pennsylvania campaign. In the battle of Gettysburg he acted with conspicuous gallantry—his brigade being among the first to enter the captured town. Here he won, by his courage and military deportment, the highest esteem and warmest admiration of the division, corps, and army commanders.

After the return of the army from Pennsylvania, and when there seemed to be a peaceful lull in the terrible war, and when the division to which General Ramseur's brigade belonged was preparing to go into winter quarters, near Orange Court House, he obtained leave of absence for the purpose of being married. He had long been engaged to Miss Ellen E. Richmond, of Milton, N.

C., and on the 27th of October, 1863, they were united in marriage. Spending some time at the house of his wife's mother and at his home in Lincolnton, he again repaired to his brigade.

The winter of '63 and '64 was spent in comparative quiet, but Grant having taken command of the army of the Potomac, the struggle was renewed in the spring with increased fury. Following the fortunes of the corps to which his brigade belonged, the next general engagements in which he bore a part were at the Wilderness and Spotsylvania Court House. The following extract from the "London Morning Herald" affords a vivid picture of the action of this brigade. Having been written by an English gentleman, who had familiar access to Gen. Lee's Head Quarters, it must needs be more impartial than if it had been written by any one connected with the army. It is a description of the battle of the Wilderness, fought on the 12th of May, 1864, and is dated at Richmond, on the 25th of the same month. After recounting the skirmishes which preceded the battle, and describing the commencement of the battle itself, this correspondent thus alludes to the recapture, by Ramseur's brigade, of a most important salient from which another portion of the army had been dislodged:

"The Federalists continued to hold their ground in the salient, and along the line of works, to the left of that angle, within a short distance of the position of Monoghan's (Hay's) Louisianians.—Ramseur's North Carolinians of Rode's division formed, covering Monoghan's right; and being ordered to charge, were received by the enemy with a stubborn resistance. The desperate character of the struggle along that brigade-front, was told terribly in the hoarseness and rapidity of its musketry. So close was the fighting there, for a time, that the fire of friend and foe rose up rattling in one common roar. Ramseur's North Carolinians dropped in the ranks thick and fast, but still he continued, with glorious constancy, to gain ground, foot by foot. Pressing under a fierce fire, resolutely on, on, on, the struggle was about to become one of hand to hand, when the Federalists shrank from the bloody trial. Driven back, they were not defeated. The earthworks being at the moment in their immediate rear, they bounded on the opposite side; and having thus placed them in their front, they renewed the conflict. A rush of an instant brought Ramseur's men to the side of the defences; and though they crouched close to the slopes, under enfilade from the guns of the salient, their musketry rattled in deep and deadly fire on the enemy that stood in overwhelming numbers but a few yards from their front. Those brave North Carolinians had thus, in one of the hottest conflicts of the day, succeeded in driving the enemy from the works that had been occupied during the previous night by a brigade which, until the 12th of May, had never yet yielded to a foe—the Stonewall."

At Spottsylvania Court House, General Ramseur acted with his accustomed gallantry. In this battle he was shot through his already disabled arm, and had three horses killed under him; still he never left the field, but led on his brigade to the gathering of fresh laurels for himself and forces. General Ramseur's career as a brigade commander was an uncommonly brilliant one. He never led the brigade into action that he did not add to its reputation. It was noted at Chancellorsville that he drilled it under heavy fire, and led it in a charge when others refused to advance, his men absolutely running over portions of a recusant command. An officer describing his appearance as he stepped up to Gen. Rodes and offered his brigade for the charge said, "he looked splendidly."

For his services at Spottsylvania, on the occasion referred to, by the correspondent of the London *Herald*, Gen. Ramseur was complimented on the field by Generals Ewell and A. P. Hill, and sent for by General Lee, that he might receive, in person, the thanks of that noble commander.

While General Ramseur infused his own daring impetuous nature into his men, they almost worshipped him. They seemed to feel the same kind of personal enthusiasm towards him that the corps felt toward General Jackson. He could lead them anywhere; if he was guiding them, they never distrusted, never hesitated, never quailed. Their hearts beat with his high courage and responded to his heroic intrepidity. They had the most unbounded confidence in his daring, skill, and military resource.

In June, 1864, he was promoted to a Major Generalship, and assigned to the division formerly commanded by General Early.

Early's corps, composed of Gordon's Rodes' and Ramseur's divisions, was shortly afterwards detached from Lee, and sent to repel Hunter, who was threatening Lynchburg. General Early reached Lynchburg in time to save the city, and after the repulse of Hunter, he marched, for the third time, into Maryland. No serious fighting occurred during this campaign, until the army reached Monococy bridge, where Ramseur and Gordon defeated the forces commanded by General Wallace. The army of the valley then marched to within five miles of Washington city, and but for the timely arrival of troops from the Department of the Gulf, might have captured the Federal capitol.

This addition to the enemy's army caused General Early to retreat to the lower valley, where, with various successes and reverses, he remained until ordered to rejoin the army before Richmond.

At the battle of Winchester, on the 19th of September, General Ramseur's division sustained the brunt of the fight, from daylight until nine or ten o'clock, when the other divisions came to his relief. It was in this fierce conflict that the gallant Rodes gave up his life; and with the departure of his spirit, our army lost one of its noblest commanders. Gen. Ramseur was transferred from Early's old division to the division which was left without a Major General by the fall of Rodes. He commanded this but one month, when he, too, died the gallant death of a soldier, at the battle of Cedar Creek.

In what esteem Major General S. D. Ramseur was held by his immediate superiors the following extract will show. And the cause of the letter, from which the extract is taken, gives a faint indication of the love entertained for him by his troops. Lieutenant General Early wrote as follows to Brig. General Bryan Grimes, who, at the request of the division lately commanded by Generals Rodes and Ramseur, had asked for a suspension of military duties for one day, that it might duly honor these noble captains:

"Head Quarters, Valley Dist.,
Oct. 31, 1864.

GENERAL: Your request for the suspension for to-morrow in your division of all military duties which are not indispensable, in order to carry out the purposes of the resolutions of the officers of the division, in honor of Major General R. E. Rodes and Major General S. D. Ramseur, is granted. I take occasion to express to the division, so lately commanded in succession by these lamented officers, my high appreciation of their merits, and my profound sorrow at their deaths.

* * * * * *

"Major General Ramseur has often proved his courage, and his capacity to command; but never did these qualities shine more conspicuously than on the afternoon of the 19th, of this month, when, after two divisions on his left had given way, and his own was doing the same thing, he rallied a small band, and for one hour and a quarter held in check the enemy, until he was shot down himself. In endeavoring to stop those who were retiring from the field, I had occasion to point them to the gallant stand made by Ramseur with his small party; and if his spirit could have animated those who left him thus battling, the 19th of October would have had a far different history. He met the death of a hero, *and with his fall, the last hope of saving the day was lost.*—General Ramseur was a soldier of whom his State has reason to be proud—he was brave, chivalrous and capable

Respectfully,
J. A. EARLY,
Lt. Gen.

Brig. Gen. BRYAN GRIMES
Com'd'g. Div.

Mortally wounded on the afternoon of October the 19th, 1864, after having participated in one of the most brilliant strategic movements of the war, he was captured, and died in the hands of the enemy, next morning, about 10 o'clock. Some of his friends, in Winchester, procured his body, had it embalmed, and sent through the lines to his family. To Major Hutchinson, his Adjutant General, who was captured at the same time, the family of General Ramseur are indebted for some additional accounts of his last moments. His wound was through the body, and of a very painful nature; but he had occasional periods of ease, and during these, he conversed very calmly. He knew that he was fatally wounded, but was not unprepared to meet death. To General Hoke, who had been an old schoolmate, and friend, from childhood, he sent this word: "Tell General Hoke, I die a Christian, and have done my duty."

He had heard, but the day before the battle in which he was to give up his life, of the birth of his little daughter. He spoke most tenderly of his wife and little child, and sent them many loving messages. The last words he whispered were for her: "Tell my darling wife," he said, "I die with a firm faith in Christ, and trust to meet her hereafter." For his father, brothers and sisters, also, he had words of peace and love.

General Ramseur was a Major General only for the period of five months, commanding first, Early's division, and after the death of General Rodes, taking his command. But during this short time he maintained his high military character, and the entire confidence of his superior officers and brother Major Generals. There was only one occurrence in the whole of General Ramseur's military career to which it is possible to attach any blame, or make him the subject of censure, and even if it be a blunder or mistake, what commander has not, at some time, made one false step.

It is thus spoken of by General Early in his narrative of his campaign in the Valley.

"On this day, (19th of July,) I received information that a column, under Averill, was moving from Martinsburg, towards Winchester, as the position I held left my trains exposed in the rear, I determined to concentrate my force near Strasburg. This movement was commenced on the night of the 19th; Ramseur's division being sent to Winchester, to cover that place against Averill. Vaughn's and Jackson's cavalry had been watching Averill, and on the afternoon of the 20th, it was reported to General Ramseur that Averill was at Stephenson's depot, with an inferior force, which could be captured, and Ramseur moved out from Winchester to attack him.

But relying on the information he received, General Ramseur did not take the proper precautions in advancing, and his division, while moving by the flank, was suddenly met by a larger force, under Averill, advancing in line of battle, and the result was, Ramseur was thrown into confusion, and compelled to retire, with the loss of four pieces of artillery, and a number in killed and wounded. The error committed on this occasion, by this most gallant officer, was nobly retrieved on the subsequent part of the campaign."

It is very doubtful if any blame should be attached to Gen. Ramseur for this affair. The cavalry command, mentioned, had been in his front all day, for the special purpose of watching Averill, and reporting from time to time. A General commanding, must rely on his subordinates for much information; he cannot possibly attend to everything himself. Gen. Ramseur had secured no information that the enemy were nearer than Stephenson's depot. Those whose duty it was to inform him, reported such as the fact. It was a mistake, therefore, that under the circumstances, might have happened to any general. Certain it is that General Early did not *censure* Gen. Ramseur, at the time, and General Rodes did not for one moment lose his confidence in him.

General Early thus speaks of General Ramseur in his account of the battle of Cedar Creek:

"Major General Ramseur fell into the hands of the enemy, mortally wounded, and in him, not only my command, but the country suffered a heavy loss. He was a most gallant and energetic officer, whom no disaster appalled, but his courage and energy seemed to gain new strength in the midst of confusion and disorder. He fell at his post, fighting like a lion at bay, and his native State has reason to be proud of his memory."

General Ramseur was a noble specimen of a man; though distinguished as a warrior, and possessing marked abilities for military success, yet his greatest excellence was his *character as a man.* He had all those qualities that excite the love and admiration of friends, and the respect of foes; no dishonorable thought, word, or act stains his bright name. In all the relations of life he was a model, as a son, brother, husband, friend; he was without reproach. His friendship elevated and ennobled, for the whole tone of his character was lofty. He had developed in a remarkable manner two elements necessary to the highest type of man, viz: a humanly tenderness of feeling, united with the most manly courage and self-reliance. His courage was the theme of the whole army, he seemed perfectly fearless, absolutely devoid of any sense of fear. It seems strange that one so affectionate, so almost womanly in his feelings, should have been so completely at home amid the dreadful scenes of the battle field. But he absolutely reveled in the fierce joys of the strife, his whole being seemed to kindle and burn and glow amid the excitements of danger. He was spoken of by one of the Virginia papers as the Chevalier Bayard of the war. His courage was marvelous—danger seemed to draw him as by a strange fascination,—and he could pardon everything but cowardice. Yet all this was not because he was indifferent to human life and suffering, he would expose himself to shield his staff, and his eyes would fill with tears as he reviewed his broken ranks, after the engagement was over.

General Ramseur was remarkable for his love of children; he would devote himself to them wherever he met them and seemed to take the greatest pleasure in pleasing them. From childhood he himself had been a most devoted child to his parents, and no sister ever had a brother more affectionate, no wife a husband more entirely her own. His whole nature was self-denying—open-hearted—generous; no mean envies, no base jealousies were found in him. He never sought promotion, it always came unasked by him.

In person, General Ramseur was of medium height, his figure was slender but well proportioned, very erect and of fine martial bearing. His brow was large, prominent, well rounded—his eye large and black and the whole expression open, winning and striking. His face indicated in a most remarkable manner loftiness of character and purity of sentiment. He was a fine horseman, sitting his horse with grace, and managing him with skill.

Gen. Ramseur was a member of the Presbyterian Church and died expressing his hope in Jesus as his Saviour.

The writer of this sketch passed the last two years of the war in close intimacy with General Ramseur. He saw much of his Christian character, and had many conversations with him on religious subjects. During this period he always expressed himself as trusting in Jesus. He read his Bible, and was regularly at church, and always promoted religious observance among his troops. The last winter of his life Mrs. Ramseur spent with him in camp.—He had prayers regularly in his family, and read religious books. He spoke particularly of his enjoyment of Jay's "Christian Contemplated," a book on the Christian character. He also read his Bible a great deal, and his faith gradually became brighter, more fixed and calmer. The last sermon he heard was in New Market from the text "To him that overcometh will I give to eat of the hidden manna and will give him a white stone." He enjoyed it and spoke of his satisfaction in it.

His last words to Mrs. Ramseur were an expression of assured hope in Christ.

A high-toned and chivalrous gentleman, a gallant soldier, an humble Christian. We may apply to him the words of the great Poet of our language

"In war was never lion raged more fierce,
In peace was never lamb more mild,
Than was that young and princely gentleman."

THE REALM OF ENCHANTMENT.

We live in a fairy region,
And everything rich and rare,
Floats down on the wings of wishing,
And circles about us there

The light of the land falls faintly,
With radiance mellowed fine,
A diamond sun beams shimmer
On pearls of the pale moon-shine.

Four seasons, in one united,
The best of their gifts display;
October emulates August,
December melts into May.

We pluck off ambrosial roses,
And powder their pink with snow,
Or dash away clear icicles
From branches, where ripe grapes glow.

Age has the vigor of childhood;
Youth, the experience of age;
The merriest mind is monarch,
The lovingest heart a sage.

Here honor, and faith, and duty
Are old, yet forever new.
Here manhood is grandly noble,
And womanhood purely true.

All ages and aims commingle,
All tempers and times disport;
The Sages of Greece give greetings
To Wits of Queen Anna's Court.

Here Homer hovers round Shakespeare,
And Milton merges in Moore;
Boccaccio is fused with Browning,
Cervantes and Sappho soar!

Lancelot lays off his laurels,
Ivanhoe tilts on the plain,
While Cleopatra wanders
With the Lilly Maid Elaine.

Love is the law of the kingdom,
And Virtue is nurse to Love;
But whether an earthly Eden,
Or Scintillant Star above,

Be site of our fair dominion,
We know not, nor greatly care.
We know we are very happy,
All we, who are dwellers there!

FANNY DOWNING.

THE STATE OF FRANKLIN.

SUCH was the condition of affairs when the North Carolina Legislature met at Newbern, almost simultaneously with the adjournment of the Franklin Convention.

The parent State had not been inattentive to the growing alienation and defection of her Western citizens. Exhibiting the same kind and conciliatory spirit as had been manifested by Governors Martin and Caswell, the Legislature, in the preamble to their action on this subject, says: "It was, and continues to be, the desire of the General Assembly to extend the benefit of civil government to the citizens of the Western counties until such time as they might be separated with advantage and convenience to themselves; and the Assembly are ready to pass over, and consign to oblivion, the mistakes and misconduct of such persons in the above mentioned counties, as have withdrawn themselves from the government of this State; to hear and redress their grievances, if any they have, and to afford them the benefits and protection of government, until such time, as they may be in a condition, from their numbers and wealth, to be formed into a separate commonwealth, and be received by the United States as a member of the Union."

The act then grants pardon and oblivion for all that had been done in the revolted counties, on the condition that they return to their allegiance to North Carolina. They also appointed officers, civil and military, in place of the incumbents under the Franklin dynasty, and empowered the voters to choose their representatives otherwise than by the then required forms.

It is not known how many of the several counties participated in the provisions thus made by the parent State for a return of the Western citizens to their allegiance. In Washington county disaffection to the Franklin Government began to manifest itself. An election was held at the Sycamore Shoals and Col. Tipton was chosen Senator, and James Stuart and Richard White were chosen as members of the House of Commons in the Legislature of North Carolina. These gentlemen had been members of the Convention of Franklin, and in other ways had participated in its administration. Their well known influence and weight of character rendered their present position, of ill-omen to the future fortunes of the new government. Many, in Washington county especially, influenced by their example, accepted the terms of accommodation held out by North Carolina, and enrolled their names in opposition to the new State. From this period resistance to or refusal of its authority assumed a more systematic and determined form.

In the year 1786 was presented

the strange spectacle of two empires exercised at one and the same time, over one and the same people. County courts were held in the same counties, under both governments; the militia were called out by officers appointed by both; laws were passed by both Assemblies, and taxes were laid by the authorities of both States; the conflict of opinion between the adherents of both parties became every day more acrimonious.—Every fresh provocation on the one side, was surpassed, by way of retaliation, by a still greater provocation on the other. The Judges commissioned by Franklin held Supreme Courts twice a year at Jonesboro. Col. Tipton openly refused obedience to the new government. There arose a deadly hatred between him and Governor Sevier, and each endeavored by all the means in his power to strengthen his party against the other. Tipton held Courts under the authority of North Carolina, at Buffalo, ten miles above Jonesboro,—which were conducted by her officers and agreeably to her laws. Courts were held at Jonesboro in the same county under the authority of the State of Franklin. As the process of these courts frequently required the Sheriff to pass within the jurisdiction of each other, to execute it, a rencounter was sure to take place. Hence it became necessary to appoint the stoutest men in the county to the office of Sheriff. Whilst a county court was sitting in Jonesboro Col. Tipton, with a party of men, entered the Court House, took away the papers from the desk, and turned the Justices out of doors. Not long after, Sevier's party came to the house where a North Carolina court was sitting and took away the clerk's papers and turned the court out of doors.—Similar acts were several times repeated during the Franklin Regime. In one case the papers of the Franklin Clerk, after being recaptured, were taken to a cave for better concealment and safety.—The same scenes were also enacted in Greene county, but less frequently. The two clerks in all the counties issued marriage licenses and many persons were married by virtue of their authority. Wills were admitted to probate, and letters of administration were granted on both sides.*

Notwithstanding the defection of some of its early advocates, and the neutrality of others of its friends, the government of Franklin continued to exercise its functions in the seven counties now constituting its sovereignty. County and Superior Courts were held, the militia was mustered, and disciplined, and civil and military elections took place under its authority. Not only were the frontier settlements protected and defended, but Gov. Sevier with his volunteers, often invaded the Cherokee country and laid waste their villages. His administrative ability was not less in military than in civil affairs, conspicuously exhibited. He early adopted the policy, heretofore ascertained to be the most effectual, of penetrating at once, with his mounted men, into the heart of

* Haywood.

the enemy's country, securing thereby, the immediate return of the hostile Indians to the defence of their towns and their homes.

In one of these invasions he crossed the Tennessee at Island Town and marched over the Unaca Mountain, to the Hiwassee. Here three of the Cherokee villages were destroyed, and a number of their warriors killed.

The effect of this bold invasion was most salutary. Few aggressions were, for some time after, made against the frontier. But it was considered by each of the sovereignties claiming jurisdiction over the country, a wise and necessary policy to adopt further methods of conciliation and security.

North Carolina had sent Col. Martin on a mission of peace into the interior of the Cherokee Nation. Governor Sevier was not less attentive in the meantime to the relations of Franklin with that tribe, and in the exercise of one of the highest attributes of political sovereignty, be appointed Commissioners to negotiate a second treaty with the Cherokees. The conference began at Chota Ford, July 31st, and was concluded at Coiatee, August 3d, 1786.

The difficulties with the Cherokees being thus adjusted, and provision having been made for co-operating with Georgia against the Creeks, it remained for the Franklin Authorities to reconcile conflicts nearer home. The *imperium in imperio* condition of things, threatened anarchy, or misrule — perhaps disaster and ruin to all parties. The people in some of the revolted counties, had sent forward their members to the North Carolina Assembly, which met at Fayetteville. They were in like manner also represented in the Assembly of Franklin. Taxes were laid by both governments, and collected by neither—the people not knowing, as was pretended, which had the better right to receive them: and neither government was forward in overruling the plea, for fear of giving offence to those who could, at pleasure, transfer their allegiance. Previous attempts had failed in securing from North Carolina, consent to the separation of her revolted counties. Disaffection had already manifested itself against the authority of Franklin, and some of those who were at first most zealous and clamorous for the separation, were now opposed to it in their legislative capacity, at Fayetteville. Every day brought new embarrassments to the administration of Governor Sevier, who, with the Assembly, was devising plans by which to extricate the new government from impending danger. One of these was the appointment of General Cocke and Judge Campbell, as Commissioners to North Carolina, to negotiate a separation. Each of them was well suited for the purpose of his mission. The former was identified with the new settlements, by an early participation in the privation, enterprise and danger of pioneer life. More recently, he had taken an active part in founding the new State—had been appointed its Delegate to Congress—commanded a brigade of its militia, and held other positions implying confidence in his talents and address. His colleague had also a minute acquaintance with every question relating to either of the parties—held the highest judicial station in the government, from which he was accredited, and by his private worth, was entitled to the respect of the one, to which he was now sent.

To secure to his embassy the greater consideration and weight, the Governor of Franklin addressed to the Governor of North Carolina a communication conceived in respectful and lenient terms, yet manifesting, at the same time, earnestness and determination in maintaining the rights and advancing the interests of his State. He reviewed the course that had been adopted from the Act of Cession—its hasty repeal, and the confusion which had resulted from it,—vindicated himself and his countrymen from the aspersions that had been cast upon them, for the action which had been taken in the premises, and expressed the hope that the Assembly of the parent State would not involve in further ruin the late citizens who had, at King's Mountain and other places, fought and bled for the defence, and who were still ready to die in the support of freedom and independence. "Your constitution and laws," said he, "we revere, and consider ourselves happy that we have been able to establish them in Franklin. We do, in the most candid and solemn manner, assure you that we do not wish to separate from you on any other terms but those perfectly consistent with the honor and interest of each party: neither do we believe there is any amongst us who wish for a separation did they believe that the parent State should suffer from it any real inconvenience. We would be willing to stand or fall together under any dangerous crisis whatever, and, though wanting to be separated in government, we wish to be united in friendship, and hope that mutual good offices may ever pass between the parent and infant State."

Such was the calm and pacific tones of Governor Sevier in introducing to Governor Caswell the embassadors from the State of Franklin.

Judge Campbell, on account of ill-health, was unable to attend in person at Fayetteville; but desirous of effecting the object of his embassy, "a ratification of our Independence," he forwarded to Governor Caswell his written argument in support of it. "Is not your State," said he, "when connected with this part of the country, too extensive? Are we not then one day to be separate people? Do you recieve any advantages from us as now situated? or do you expect ever to recieve any? I believe you do not. Suffer us then to pursue our own happiness in a way most agreeable to our situation and circumstances.—Can a people so nearly connected as yours are with ours delight in our misfortunes? It was not from a love of novelty, or the desire of titles that our leaders were induced to engage in the present revolution, but from pure necessity. If we set out wrong, or were too hasty in our separation, this country is not altogether to blame; your State pointed out the line of conduct which we adopted. We really thought you in earnest when you ceded us to Congress. If you then thought we ought to be separate, or if you now think we ever ought to be, permit us to complete the work that is now more than half done. Suffer us to give energy to our laws, and force to our councils, by saying we are a separate and independent people. Nature has separated us; do not oppose her in her work. By acquiescing you will bless us and do yourself no injury. You bless us by uniting the disaffected and do yourself no injury because you lose nothing but people who are a clog to your government, and to whom you cannot do equal justice by reason of their detached situation."

Such was the plain common-sense and well tempered written argument of Judge Campbell.—But notwithstanding these earnest representations made in behalf of the people of Franklin, the Assembly of North Carolina, disregarding their protests and memorials, continued to legislate for them—establishing new counties and appointing new officers, civil and military. It had also taken into consideration the measures necessary to be adopted in relation to the revolters, in Franklin. At this moment, General Cooke, the other Commissioner from the State of Franklin, appeared in Fayetteville, and at his request, was heard at the bar of the House of Commons. His speech has been preserved, in which he pathetically depicted the miseries of his distressed countrymen, be traced the motives of their separation to the difficult and perilous condition in which they had been placed by the Cession Act of 1784; he stated that the savages, in their neighborhood, often committed upon the defenceless inhabitants, the most shocking barbarities; and that they were without the means of raising, or subsisting troops for their protection; without authority to levy men; without the power to lay taxes for the support of internal government; and without the hope, that any of their necessary expenditures would be defrayed by North Carolina, which had then become no more interested in their safety, than any other of the United States. The sovereignty retained, being precarious and nominal, as it depended on the acceptance of the Cession by Congress, so it was anticipated, would be the concern of North Carolina for the ceded territory. With these considerations full in view, what were the people of the ceded territory to do, to avoid the blow of the uplifted tomahawk? How were the women and children to be rescued from the impending destruction? Would Congress come to their rescue? Alas! Congress had not yet accepted them, and possibly never would. And if accepted, Congress was to deliberate on the quantum of defence which might be afforded to them. The distant State would wish to know what profits they would respectively draw from the ceded country, and how much land would remain after satisfying the claims upon it. The contributions from the several States were to be spontaneous. They might be too limited to do any good, too tardy for practical purposes. The powers of Congress were too feeble, to enforce contributions. Whatever aids should be resolved on, might not reach the objects of their bounty, till all was lost. Would common prudence justify a reliance upon such prospects? Could the lives of themselves and of their families be staked upon them? Immediate and pressing necessity called for the power to concentrate the scanty means they possessed, of saving themselves from destruction. A cruel and insiduous foe was at their doors. Delay was but another name for death. They might supinely wait for events, but the first of them would be, the yell of the savage throughout all their settlements. It was the well known disposition of the savages to take every advantage of an unpreparedness to receive them, and of a sudden, to raise the shrieking cry of exultation over the fallen inhabitants. The hearts of the people of North Carolina should not be hardened against their brethren, who have stood by their sides in perilous times, and never heard the cry of distress, when they did not instantly rise and march to their aid. Those brethren have bled in profusion to save you from bondage and from the sanguinary hands of a relentless enemy, whose mildest laws for the punishment of rebellion is beheading and quartering. When driven in the late war, by the pressure of that enemy, from your homes, we gave to many of you a sanctified asylum in the bosom of our country, and gladly performed the rites of hospitality to a people we loved so dearly. Every hand was ready to be raised for the least unhallowed violation of the sanctuary in which they reposed."

"The act for our dismission was, indeed, in the winter of 1784, revoked; what then was our condition? More penniless, defenceless, and unprepared if possible, than before, and under the same necessity as ever to meet and consult together for our common safety. The resources of the country all locked up, where is the record that shows any money or supplies sent to us?—a single soldier ordered to be stationed on the frontier—or any plan formed for mitigating the horrors of our situation? On the contrary, the savages are irritated by the stoppage of those goods on their passage, which were promised as a compensation for the lands which had been taken from them. If North Carolina must still hold us in subjection, it should be at least understood to what a state of distraction, suffering and poverty her varying conduct has reduced us, and the liberal hand of generosity should be widely opened for relief from the pressure of present circumstances: all animosity should be laid aside and buried in deep oblivion, and our errors should be considered, as the offspring of greater errors, committed by yourselves. It belongs to a magnanimous people to weep over the failings of their unfortunate children, especially if prompted by the inconsiderate behavior of the parent. Far should it be from their hearts to harbor the unnatural purpose of adding still more affliction to those who have suffered but too much already. It belongs to a magnanimous people to give an industrious attention to circumstances in order to form a just judgment upon a subject so much deserving their serious meditation, and when once carefully formed, to employ with sedulous anxiety, the best efforts of their purest wisdom in choosing a course to pursue suitable to the dignity of their own character, consistent with their own honor, and the best calculated to allay that storm of distraction in which their hapless children have been so unexpectedly involved. If the mother shall judge the expense of adhesion too heavy to be borne, let us remain as we are and support ourselves by our own exertions; if otherwise, let the means for the continuance of our connexion be supplied with that degree of liberality which will demonstrate seriousness on the one hand and secure affection on the other."

General Cooke's speech was heard with attention, and he retired.

The General Assembly continued to legislate for the revolted counties and by an act of that session, pardoned the offences of all persons who had returned to their allegiance to the State of North Carolina, and restored them to all the privileges of other citizens of the State, as if the said offences and misconduct had never existed. But they continued in office all officers who held and enjoyed their offices, April 1, 1784, and declared vacant the offices of all such persons as had accepted and exercised other offices and appointments, the acceptance and exercise of which were considered to be a resignation of their former offices, held under the State of North Carolina; and directed that such vacant offices, should be filled with proper persons to be appointed by the General Assembly, and commissioned by the Governor of North Carolina, as directed by law.

The latter provisions of this Act produced great dissatisfaction amongst the people upon whom it was intended to operate. The old office holders were capable, they had been faithful, and their experience and attention to official duty had secured universal confidence and approbation. Those upon whom the new appointments were conferred, were, many of them, non-residents, inexperienced and not reliable, selected by the favoritism of some functionary in the old State, and for that reason odious to the people. Their appointment was denounced by, and drew forth the bitter condemnation of some of both parties. The temper of the complainants is seen in a further letter of Judge Campbell, to Governor Caswell, after the adjournment of the Legislature. "The majority of the people of the State of Franklin" said he, "proclaim with enthusiastic zeal against a reversion to your State. Indeed, I am at a loss to conjecture whether your Assembly wished us to revert: if so, why did they treat the old faithful officers of this country with contempt? Officers who have suffered in the common cause, who have been faithful in the discharge of the trust reposed in them, have been displaced without even the formality of a trial. If the old officers, who were the choice of the people, and under whom they have long served, had been continued, I doubt not but all things would have been settled here, agreeable to the most sanguine wishes of the General Assembly; but such infringement on the rights and privileges of a free people, will never be attended with salutary consequences. I also blame the law, enabling the people here to hold partial elections. If it was intended to divide us, and to set us to massacreing one another, it was well conducted, but an ill-planned scheme, if intended for the good of all." * * * * *

"You mention that if the people here could be brought to agree in making a general application to the Legislature, the desired object might be easily brought,about. Human nature is the same in all countries. To expect to bring a people cordially and unanimously to adopt the most salutary measure, is not to be expected, and they will most assuredly be refractory to doubtful and exceptionable plans." "The people here dread the idea of a reversion. They say if North Carolina is in earnest about granting them a separation, why not permit them to go on as they have begun, and not involve them in inextricable difficulties, by undoing the work of two or three years." And again he says respecting a reversion: "Many who were formerly unknown are now flaming patriots for Franklin. Many who were real Franklinites, are now burning with enthusiastic zeal. They say that North Carolina has not treated us like a parent, but like a step-mother; she means to sacrifice us to the Indian Savages: she has broke our old officers, under whom we fought, and bled: and placed over us men unskilled in military achievements, and who were none of our choice. I have no doubt, but your Excellency will use your influence to bring matters to a friendly and advantageous issue to both parties. Nothing that the love of humanity can inspire me with, shall be wanting on my part."

North Carolina, in the meantime, adopted a further measure of conciliation, viz: the relinquishing to the revolted citizens, all the taxes due, and unpaid, since 1784. This, with the act of pardon and oblivion already mentioned, had the desired effect upon a part of the disaffected. Commissions were sent to, and accepted by justices of the peace, in Washington, Sullivan, and Hawkins counties, and under the authority of the old State, Courts were held by them, and law administered as though the State of Franklin did not exist. In Greene county, and the new counties below it, men could not be found willing to accept the offered Commissions. There the authority of Franklin was supreme, and there was no conflict of jurisdiction. It was very different elsewhere, and especially in Washington county.

Previous to the revolt, Courts had been held at Jonesboro', and had afterwards been held at the same place under the new government. Now, when the sentiment of allegiance to North Carolina had become, in some measure, general, the newly appointed magistrates opened, and held, the Courts at Davis' ten miles above Jonesboro'. The partisans of one government quarreled with those of the other. The officers of each, in discharge of official duty, came into conflict with the authority of the rival government. The animosity thus engendered, became the more acrimonious, as this county was the residence of Gov. Sevier, and also of Colonel John Tipton, who, though at first, a leader in the revolt, had now become prominent at the head of the Old State party. These two, alike, brave, ambitious, patriotic, and champions of their respective adherents, kept the people in a constant tumult, each, alternately, breaking in upon, and interrupting the Courts and jurisdiction of the other. The horrors of a fratricidal conflict seemed inevitable. Measures were adopted by both parties to allay the agitation, and restore quiet. General Rutherford had introduced before the Legislature of North Carolina, a measure of conciliation, that would have been acceptable to the malcontents beyond the mountains, but it had been instantly rejected. The mission of General Cooke, and the pacific overtures of Judge Campbell, had been abortive and unsuccessful. Franklin and North Carolina stood — not upon the edge of a precipice over which both might have been precipitated and engulphed, but upon the brink of a volcano, whose crater was yawning to receive, or whose fiery lava, was ready to inundate and overwhelm both parties in a common ruin. The patriot sighed for some mode of escape from the threatened catastrophe, while the statesman anxiously contemplated the impending crisis, and devised the best plan to avert the storm, or to mitigate its violence. What mode of *Reconstruction* did wisdom suggest, or patriotism provide, to meet the present emergencies, and to save the political fabric from further wreck and ultimate ruin and annihilation? Fortunately there was then, both wisdom and patriotism. There were, then, in those pure and infant days, of each republic, not only true patriots, but wise and sagacious statemen—inspired may we hope, for the exigencies of the momentous occasion. As a final resort, negotiation was attempted to reconcile the conflicts of interests and of feeling between the two States. But who should be the negotiator to harmonize the antagonistic forces? An officer of the old State? The opposition to such an one, was at one time a mere prejudice, it had now become a sentiment of inappeasable malignity, and no offers of compromise from him could be, for a moment, entertained. Policy dictated that the negotiator should be selected from the Western people themselves, and that he should be one who, from his past position, was identified, in all his sympathies and interests, with the West. General Evan Shelby, high in the confidence of his countrymen everywhere, remarkable for his probity, candor, good sense, and patriotism, was requested by Governor Caswell to undertake this delicate negotiation, and in conjunction with others, whose assistance he solicited, met a Commissioner from the State of Franklin, at a private house, on the 20th March, 1787. At this conference, Gov. Sevier represented his own Government, aided by such of his friends as he chose to invite.

Time and space will not allow the writer to give in detail the results of this important conference. Let it suffice here to say that a temporary quiet succeeded this compromise, and the people having by it secured the right of paying their taxes and of owing allegiance to either of their rival governments at their own option, the jurisdiction of both was for a time coördinate. No better proof need be adduced that the inhabitants of the disaffected country were honest, law-abiding, just and peaceable, than their demeanor under this unwonted condition of questionable allegiance. Any where else than amongst this irascible though virtuous community, anarchy, misrule, tumult and violence, would have followed. Prevalent sentiment was amongst these primitive people, essentially the law, and had the validity and force of legislative authority. Popular opinion was radically sound. It was in favor of right and justice. The people bowed to its supremacy, and paid allegiance to its mandates. They needed no other tribunal.

Still a wound had been inflicted upon the dignity of the parent State, and there were not wanting men in the country willing to appease her wrath and make an atonement for the indignity and injury she had recieved. These finding fault with and condemning the acts of the new State, reported its wrong doings to Gov. Caswell. They were clamorous about trespasses committed upon Cherokee territory by the intruding "Franklinites," and foreboded, what really took place, a renewal of Indian aggression upon the settlements, if they were not restrained. By one Governor Caswell was advised to remove the intruders by an armed force, and the writer expressed his apprehension that "the contention will end in blood." Gov. Caswell received another letter of still more portentous import, from an accredited agent, who had been sent to spy out the real condition of affairs in his trans-montane territory.—In his tour of observation, he seems to have detected, not only infidelity to North Carolina on the part of the people of Franklin, but "a tendency to dissolve the Federal bands." He is the first to advise "the interference of government" to suppress the insurgents by arms.

POOR TOM.

"*A'cold.*"

"TRUE! OH! KING."

Years of his Freedom—TWO!
And a shivering phantom stands
With the firelight flickering through
His gaunt and wasted hands.
"Home!"—and he bowed his head
With a low and wailing cry;
Ah! not for shelter and not for bread,
Only a place to—DIE!

To die at the master's feet,
Out of the scourging storm
Where the winds might never beat;
Where Tom lay ever warm;
Till Freedom, the pitiless
Fell from the cruel sky,
And the bitterness of his nakedness
Made TOM so glad to—DIE!

Oh! had these arms the pith
Of just *two years* ago,
Wrecked in the wrestle with
You wilderness of woe!
TOM'S love would bring the light
Back to his master's eye
But the blood in his heart is cold to-night,
And he only comes to—DIE!

Was it *ever so many years*,
Or only yesterday,
That master, among his peers
Went bravest, with TOM, the gay?
Before the "locust" and "hail,"
Or only an hour gone by,
That Freedom fell with a flail
On TÔM, and made him DIE!

Of the dear old days, so sweet
  Does *master* dream as he sits
Till the weariness of his *feet*
  Seems—wandering in his wits;
Till yesterday seems so dim,
  And the far-away, so nigh,
That his head goes all a'swim.
  And his heart is faint to DIE!

POOR TOM!—For a *hundred years*
  Your blood has coursed by *mine*,
Were there warmth in bitter tears,
  There should not lack the brine;
DYING!—I know it well,
  As I know the signs on high;
The tokens that grimly tell,
Out of the STORM, 'twere well
  BOTH of us, TOM, to DIE!

INDUSTRIAL COMBINATIONS.

COMBINATIONS for the prosecution of industrial pursuits are the characteristic of our age. They now enjoy almost universal favor, and are extending themselves, in old and new directions, every year. In the delight which is inspired by their efficiency for money-getting, people seem unsuspicious of the extensive changes and disasters which they are probably destined to introduce into modern society. The successive curses which have blighted the hopes of civilized man so often, have usually proceeded from some institution, valued and approved, (because useful in its place) but unexpectedly prevented. The disposition to favor chartered corporations, so prevalent in the European family of nations, finds its explanation in their history.—Corporate rights were not unknown to the Roman Civil law.—But their value grew into its present appreciation in the feudal ages. When the ancient order of the Roman world fell before the Gothic and Teutonic hordes, there was, for a time, a total prostration of civic rights, before the armed violence of the nomadic and military barbarians. For a time Western Europe was a chaos, "without form and void," presenting no settled rights, or distinctive social order. At length, as the stormy and seething elements subsided, the *feudal system* was seen to emerge, the crude rudiments of which had, perhaps, been brought by the Teutons from the German forests. This was a military organization of society: in which the main feature was the tenure of the lands, not in fee simple, but as tenants for life, on condition of certain military service to be rendered to the noble land owner. The tie which connected the vassal with his immediate suzerain was thus made the most close and efficient, which existed in civil society. Each Barony thus became a sort of military clan, directed by the sovereign will of its lord, and practically irresponsible to king and constitution. For the vassal, there might be some rights and franchises, guaranteed to him by the compact of his fief, on condition of his homage and service: but for all those who did not belong to the military caste, for the artizan, the merchant, the citizens of towns, there was practically no right, and no protection. The neighboring feudal chieftains were, as to them, irresponsible plunderers. The King, the nominal chief magistrate, was himself but the chief suzerain of the inferior laborers, wielding no other authority over them, but that of feudal compacts. It was, of course, vain to hope that a regal authority, resting only on a feudal basis, could be exercised to repress the excesses of the great feudatories. The consequence was, that plunder was the order of the day: and so far did the disorder proceed, that arts and commerce were well nigh banished from many States of Western Europe.

The industrial classes at length began to find, in the 11th and 12th centuries, this expedient. Living mainly in towns and cities, they combined to procure from the military barons who claimed authority over them, *charters*, conferring certain stipulated immunities upon them, by the jealous preservation of which, a part of their rights and property at least, was secured from spoliation.—These charters were sometimes bought with money, sometimes bestowed in return for some valuable service: and sometimes extracted by the good right arms of the sturdy burghers, by hard blows. Kings, perceiving in these corporations, probable make-weights to counterpoise the power of the great feudatories, who were, practically, almost independent, soon found an interest in favoring these charter institutions, and in proposing themselves to the corporations as umpires and patrons. Thus was laid the foundation of the modern social order, before which feudalism has virtually disappeared from Europe and America. Chief magistrates protecting and employing the chartered communities against the feudal barons, found, in the former, elements of support by which they were gradually enabled to consolidate their people, before little more than clusters of independent and discordant fiefs, into true nations.

Corporate immunities sanctified, by charter-stipulations, were thus, the very fountains of all the rights and prosperity of the commonalty. It is not strange that they were cherished as precious and admirable; and that the disposition prevailed to extend them, as a shield of protection against military violence, over every species of interest. The monastery, the dean and chapter of the diocese, the very parson and wardens of the parish, aspired to become corporations in law, and to assert their chartered rights to their endowments, against greedy barons. The different trades and professions in the towns were organized into "guilds," governed within themselves, by strict by-laws, and guarding their common privileges with jealous public spirit. Just as among the military caste, every tenure had assumed the form of a fief, so among the industrial classes, every franchise sought the sanction of the corporate charter.

Now this tendency to favor incorporations, and to exalt chartered rights, has been inherited by us, in full force, after the state of society, which presented the rational basis for these feelings, has been totally displaced. Feudalism has long been dead. The organization of modern society is no longer military, but civil.—The law, before which all classes in the State are equal, is in theory, supreme. The chief magistrate, in enforcing the law, acts directly upon individuals, and no longer upon fiefs. The State itself has become the comprehensive "guild," whose charter, (the constitution and laws) extends abundant protection, if fairly executed, to each citizen, no matter what his rank or pursuit. It is manifest that after this revolution of the social order, the ground for attaching the former value to the usage of incorporation, as the bulwark of individual rights, is all reversed. Yet the prejudice and the usage still continue! Thus, out of this mediæval expedient of the commonalty, is now rapidly growing a new aristocracy, which is acquiring, by the perversion of an institution which should have passed away with the occasion for it, class privileges, and exclusive powers, more odious than the feudal-chartered corporations were justly valued as a *protection* of the weak against irresponsible baronial power. No such power now exists. These privileges have become, virtually, the expedients for arming favored individuals with powers of *aggression* against their fellows.

Is it demanded then, that society shall exist without corporate combinations? This question will be asked, in a disdainful tone of incredulity, by an age inordinately devoted to material acquisition, and fully instructed in the advantages of combination. Men find that "union is strength." The wondrous power evolved by large combinations of capital and labor, now especially that the material arts have furnished industry with so many appliances for expediting its work, which are at once costly and efficient, set men all agog, to extend this system more widely than ever before. There is no likelihood that the excesses of it will be surrendered. In the din and turmoil of successful avarice, the warning of history will be scouted by the interested few, who gather the spoils of the system, and neglected by the many, who are the victims of the abuse. The overthrow of the liberty of the 19th century, by this unsuspected cause, appears therefore inevitable. But it is done the less, the duty of the philosophy to leave her warning on record.

There are only two cases which present any fair pretext in the constitution of free society for incorporating a part of the citizens with special privileges not common to them all. One is where the work or function to be performed demands more means than can be ever found in the possession of an individual. One man is not found rich enough to build a whole railroad. Yet railroads are useful. The other case is, where the perpetuity of the function requires the retention of the means and management under the same direction for more than the life-time of one man. The railroad again, may be an instance. The rich man who began one as an individual enterprise, might, in some cases, expend his natural life without more than completing it. Hence, the law creates the artificial person, which never dies, a corporation to retain and manage so enduring an interest. Now, for the prosecution of such enterprises, there are but two alternatives. Either chartered corporations of some citizens must be formed with special privileges, to execute them: or the State must execute them all herself, through her own numerous officials; and thus make herself at once civil government, and the universal corporation.—The Commonwealth which should act out this scheme would become, literally, the το παν of human combinations, and her multifarious functions would cover all the forms of associated human action, except the family. The action of the British government, in recent times, does indeed approach this conception: for we see Parliament concerning itself, through its different classes of State officials, with every conceivable function, from teaching the population christianity, down to draining the marshy lands of the country.—The government, by thus making itself the only corporation, would, indeed, seem to guard effectually against partial class privileges.—But it would be only in seeming. The aggregate of business, money and power thus combined in the hands of government, would be too great for any administration except that of an omniscient mind. It would result in boundless official mismanagement and peculation. And it would convert a free government into a species of Chinese despotism. Modern States, then, must have some corporate combinations of a part of the citizens, for executing these useful ends.—But obviously, the principle we have developed requires that they shall not be causelessly multiplied; that their privileges shall be jealously limited to such as will enable them for the useful works designed: that they shall be made to wear, as nearly as may be, the character of mere business firms; that the corporation, as an artificial person, shall have no privilege whatsoever, which does not belong to every citizen, as a natural person, by the constitution and laws.

Now, does the legislation of the American States regard these necessary cautions? Does it not madly disdain them? Combinations protected and privileged by law are the order of the day for everything. The material spirit of the age deliberately postpones everything to money; and it is enough for men to perceive that in the art of acquisition the old adage usually holds true, that 'union is strength.' The old prejudice in favor of chartered associations is loudly claimed, after every condition of society has been reversed, which gave them legitimate value; with the view of wielding peculiar privileges for selfish ends. We have corporations for everything: corporations to teach the arts and sciences to young men; corporations to teach children; corporations to construct railroads and canals; corporations to carry parcels on the vehicles of these other corporations; corporations to navigate ships and steamers; corporations to manage the alleys and pigs of our villages; corporations to spin; corporations to make clocks and watches; corporations to peg shoes; corporations to make a nail; corporations to lend money and play Shylock for the community; corporations to insure our lives; a corporation to paint bank-notes for other bubble corporations; corporations to shake carpets, and associated companies to wash the linen of the "great unwashed." The picture of the excess to which the institution is carried by American society would be extremely ludicrous, were it not too alarming.

In explaining the dangers which have been intimated, let us begin with that which is, in itself, least important; the pecuniary evils attending the abuse of this system. These may be quickly perceived by the answer to the following question: why do the persons who have capital and skill for a given business, prefer to pursue it under one of these powerful chartered associations, rather than as, each man for himself, individual adventurers? Obviously, because they know that they shall get more gain for the use of their capital and skill. Then of course, the rest of the people who employ them pay more for the service, than they would if served by individuals. The evasion is, that this does not follow; because the combination of many men and much means enables the association to carry on that business so much more skillfully and efficiently that thereby, the public is served more cheaply, and the association is better rewarded for its outlay. In most cases, this evasion is false. If there is an extensive improvement, which, on the one hand, costs many times as much as any one rich man possesses, and on the other hand, will, when completed, perform its appointed work as much more cheaply than any other possible agency, as its cost has exceeded them, in this case the plea may be good. Such is the truth as to some railroads, when compared with existing country roads. But in a multitude of cases which claim to be similar, the advantage is utterly illusory: the public, after giving the chartered privileges, gives more for the service than it had paid before. And in all cases where the business is one within the scope of individual wealth, the plea carries falsehood on its face. Why does the money-lender prefer to lend through a bank? Money-lending is a function which may be, with equal facility, accommodated to any amount of capital, large or small! His motive is, that by the power of a banking corporation, he is enabled to get more usury than he can legally get as an individual.—So the Yankee manufacturing capitalist, who has means abundant to build one adequate cotton mill usually prefers not to do so as an individual adventurer, but to have a certain number of shares in some vast corporation owning a whole city of mills. Why? Because he aims at the power of a monopolist, to a certain extent.—A ship owner possesses plenty of money to build and sail a steamer between New York and Charleston. But he prefers to put in his money as member of a "Steamship Company." Why? He has his eye on a monopoly of the coasting trade between the two ports: the meaning of which monopoly is, to oppress the trading public, and plunder them in the shape of measured freights, by excluding competition. But perhaps the most glaring instance of the plunder of a monopoly is that presented by the great "Express-forwarding Companies:" chartered associations preposterously created to do the duties of "common carriers," on the vehicles of other companies designed by their very existence for the very same function, and which, if they are not fully competent to it, should be punished as delinquents. What reason on earth is there, that so humble and plain a function as the forwarding of parcels, and that too, where another agency had already been provided to execute it should be armed by law with the power to levy gains so immense on the business of the country? See their pompous palaces in all our cities: their armies of sleek, pampered horses and officials; their share-holders dividing fabulous dividends, and rolling in wealth equal to that of a nation's revenues. What is that exalted function, for the performance of which modern society rewards them so splendidly? Only that which was performed for our forefathers by sturdy, simple wagoners and ship-masters! Truly, we are a wise generation! This picture betrays the pecuniary results of this perverse system: as being, in the main, extortionate and wasteful, and forming a frightful and iniquitous tax on the productive industry of the country.

That these combinations for industrial pursuits are, in most cases inimical to public wealth, is very plain from these facts: that they uniformly employ more costly and wasteful means of administration, than individual enterprise would. The monopolist power which they wield, to rake together large piles of money, surely tempts the successful manipulators and their families, and dependents, to wasteful luxuries of living; which are all unproductive consumption; and thus devour the public means, while they corrupt the morals of all concerned.

2. *Money is power.* Have men forgotten the maxim which our wise fathers taught us, from the lessons of historical experience? that "*where power is, thither power tends.*" Need we repeat here the proofs and illustrations of this almost self-evident postulate? As long as man's heart is what it is, this centripetal tendency must exist. Our fathers taught that in order that a republican equality of rights may exist among the citizens, no great inequality of wealth must be encouraged among them. Hence they felt that, in order to perpetuate republican government, they must needs abolish the rights of primogeniture, and thus provide for the redistribution of property, and its equal division among the citizens. But we insanely create an aristocracy of active capital, equipped moreover with organizations and armies of trained officials and servants, tenfold more dangerous to the common liberties than a landed aristocracy. We arm them, under the pretext of facilitating industrial pursuits, with the power of getting at once immense wealth and influence.—Must not the natural arrogance of wealth suggest the lust for more power? The power of organization already possessed, is employed by them, first to enlarge their advantages and opportunities for getting more inordenate gains in the pursuits for which they were

incorporated. It is for this purpose they at first enter the arena of political manœuvre, and measure their strength with party leaders and factions. Will not their success in this object suggest the thought of using their power also for further ends? The experience of the States with these associations has just now passed through this stage, and is approaching the next. The seniors among us can well remember how a mongrel corporation, in Philadelphia, once challenged the whole force of the government of the United States, in the attempt to evade the surrender of its financial monopoly, and almost came off conquerors. Cotemporaries are not strangers to the influences which powerful railroad corporations exert every winter, at Albany, corrupting and controlling the government of the great State of New York. There is a corporation in Maryland, whose revenues and resources are far larger, and whose employés are more numerous and devoted than those of the Commonwealth. In the provisional government of Virginia, this corporation of another State has actually wielded a power equal, or superior to, that of the true people of that once powerful and jealous Commonwealth. It is now no longer a strange thing to hear shrewd men explaining the action of legislative bodies, by the outside influences of powerful corporations. And, for a reason which will be unfolded anon, corporations may be expected to employ, for controlling rulers and legislators whom they wish to use, much more corrupt means, than their sense of decency would allow them to employ in support of individual applications. Thus the virtue of the government is contaminated, while its powers are perverted.

The eager longing of this age is for republican equality before the law. The people had suffered so much in the 17th and 18th centuries from the tyranny of kings and landed nobles, and had seen the evils of the old privileged classes so painfully, that their passion in the early part of this century has been for the abolition of feudal privileges, and equality before the law. Their craving is destined to be disappointed, through their own shortsightedness; and the enemy by which the great popular movement of the age is destined to be overthrown, is corporation. Out of these associations will be developed a new oligarchy, a hundred-fold more ruthless and insatiable, as it is a hundred-fold less respectable and venerable, than the landed aristocracy which the spirit of the age has swept away. The forms of the American commonwealths are extravagantly democratic; but already the true spirit of their government is that of oligarchy. Thus do extremes meet and generate each other. The assurance of this calamitous disappointment of the hopes and labors of a whole century is to be seen in this fact: that deceivers and deceived alike, monopolists and victims, are so devoted to mere material good, as to disdain an admonition drawn from higher considerations. The whole force of our argument, and of all similar ones, better uttered by others, will undoubtedly be neutralized by the single assertion that these associations seem to present a more ready way to make money.

3. One prime motive of business men for preferring corporate to individual enterprise is, that the laws of these privileged associations authorize them to make the industrial adventure, and incur pecuniary obligations, without making their own property responsible therefor. Only the capital stock of the association is bound for the debts of the association: the corporators, acting in their combined capacity, may deliberately incur liabilities far beyond the assets of the association, and yet, under the plea of the distinction between their corporate, and their personal possession, may retain their wealth, while their just creditors demand their dues in vain. So licentious and flagrant has the legislation of many States become, that not content with incorporating these privileged plunderers by special act, in almost countless cases, they have even enacted general laws, by a sweeping clause enabling any persons to associate themselves into a firm or co-partnership, for the ostensible purpose of pursuing any business; to which firm the simple form of advertising gives this odious privilege of contracting debts without becoming responsible for their payment. The excuse is, in part, that the law requires them to advertise their capital stock; so that the business public is informed of the extent to which the firm is bound: and if they trust them farther, the fault is their own. The answer is, that if the privilege is unjust, as will be shown, the excuse is wholly inadequate. How audacious is the sophism, that the wrong of a transgressor may be made right by its publication beforehand? Besides, the legal person in these quasi corporations, to which the responsiblility for debt is limited, being purely artificial, when its visible assets are exhausted, there is nothing else against which the creditors can have their just resort. There is no actual person: *stat nominis umbra.*—Whence it is plain that this publication is not a fair and adequate protection of the business public.

The other plea is this: that it is an encouragement of enterprise, to enable some adventurous men to make experiment of efforts which may result in general advantage, without risking more than a definite part of their means. Were the privilege only granted to new and untried enterprises, this plea might be a little more plausible. But we see it extended to a thousand lines of business, as old as civilized society; in which, if any where, any man who is fit to meddle with them, can ascertain the prospects beforehand.—But the more full answer is, that such encouragement ought not to be given. It is neither for the financial nor moral advantage of society. The proper encouragement for enterprises which promise general advantage, and yet are hazardous because of novelty, is a cautious system of bounties, paid at the common expense. In all other cases, business adventure, more reckless than a prudent regard for the adventurer's own private estate will justify, is mischievous, and only mischievous, and should be repressed, instead of stimulated. The interests of commerce loudly demand just the guarantee against reckless enterprise which is presented by the jeopardy of the adventurer's own estate. The thirst for adventure is always in excess: it is one of the keenest and most active propensities of the human heart.—When an ill-considered enterprise is carried on to disastrous results, if the adventurer is protected, other men are plundered of the means expended in the abortive experiment. He who made the blunder should pay the cost.—Otherwise it is iniquity: it is a radical injustice, which no considerations of policy can justify.

This suggests the moral effects of all these special privileges to business enterprises. These are deplorable in every aspect. The system, as we have seen, fosters recklessness, which is always akin to, and almost always gives occasion to dishonesty. It familiarizes the minds of all parties to results, which we have shown, are essential iniquities. The legalized plunderer, if he has a conscience, lives self-degraded by the retention of wealth which, he feels, belongs to his injured fellow men: they are tempted by the natural sense of indignation, to meditate redress by similar means; for has not the law itself, the very exponent of justice, countenanced them? Hence, in part, that growing absence of commercial integrity, that frightful dissolution of moral principle, of which we hear so much complaint, and which, we are told, has rendered the commercial marts of America like dens of wolves ravening for mammon.

4. One more evil influence of this system upon the virtue of society remains to be explained. Business combinations acting through officials have now been carried so far, that scarcely anything is done by men in their individual capacity. Do you want a parcel carried, by sea or land? It is not done for you by any individual ship-master, or carrier, acting under the moral restraints of a personal conscience and responsibility; but by an Express or Navigation "Company." Do you buy a pair of shoes? You do not get them from the shop of a shoe-maker: but of some "shoe-company," in Yankee land. Do you need a handful of nails? Some Iron company must be invoked to produce them. Do you wish your person transported? You commit it to a railroad company. So it is, to the end of the chapter. Now it was remarked by Sir Edward Coke, that "corporations have no souls," and the proposition is true in another sense than that of the legal abstraction which he meant to express. They have no moral sense: no conscience. Their own legal personality is artificial; and the moral responsibility of their acts is so sub-divided among the actual persons who compose the body, that it is felt no where. The executive hand of the body is a set of hired officials. These also divest themselves of moral

responsibility for the official acts: for are not these the acts of the corporation, which employs them as inanimate tools? The only influence which personal conscience has in them is to produce official fidelity to the interests of the corporation. Thus, the business code of all these associations has come to be as utterly heartless as though the world recognized no God, or right, or hell. Every shrewd man understands perfectly, when he has dealings with them, that they are to be expected to treat him no more justly than actual necessity, or selfish policy may dictate. The man who should hope for more at their hands, would be laughed at as a soft fool!

Thus this system of privileged combinations is an ingenious artifice, (as efficacious for the purpose as though invented for it,) for banishing conscience and hearty integrity out of the world. But our duty to God sets this interest of virtue in the first place. The very existence and well-being of society depends on its virtue. Or has the "cuteness" of this Yankee age exploded this, as a delusion of the dark ages? At all events, we find that Madison, Calhoun, Jackson, Washington, and Solomon believed it to be true. Hence the true statesman will, for this high and solemn consideration, always prefer individual to corporate action, where he is not driven to the latter by absolute necessity.

The crowning objection then, to this prevalent system is, that it is unfavorable to the virtue of society. It swells the volume of that flood of dishonesty, which threatens to dissolve the very foundations of the age, and plunge it into another chaos of barbarism. And this is the chief influence, by which the system manifests itself to the thoughtful mind, as the appointed destroyer of the constitutional free governments, and of the civilization of the 19th century. A little reflection, following out the hints given above, will convince the reader, that without the influences of this system at the North, the recent revolution, by which that people have destroyed the constitution of the United States could not have occurred.—Hitherto, the agency of the industrial combinations has been to promote, by manifold influences, political centralization. This is Act I. of the tragedy.

THE SEVEN PINES.

Fancied voices, as of ghosts speaking, when, of late, I heard the night-winds sweeping through the trees on the battle-field.

A SPIRIT.

Sad-hearted Southron, as you stray,
Like Sorrow's Ghost o'er fields of glory,
Where spectral forms, in weeds of gray,
Stand in your path or cross your way,
And wail, in witch-like voice, a story—
Why do you pause? 'Tis but a seeming—
A sigh of pines, or dead men dreaming!

1ST PINE—THE UNDAUNTED.

Pale pilgrim, list my sigh alone—
A dreary ceaseless monotone,
But, like the Surge on Sumter's shore,
It speaks where glory spoke before,
As unseen mortals who implore
From tree and flower and stone!
A hushed complaint is in the air—
Not told to men who do not dare
But to the winds which will be free
Despite of storm and tyranny!
'Tis whispered everywhere—
"Say not our cause is lost—was vain—
Or ghostly troops shall sweep the plain—
We'll fight the battles o'er again!
There's nothing lost where men will give
Their lives in honor's cause to live:
No tyrant can the dead control—
Who breaks the heart can't rule the soul!"

2ND PINE—THE CAUTIOUS.

'Tis man to man is most unjust,

And brother least his brother knows—
E'en those who say, "In God we trust,"
Their lying littleness disclose—
Man's nature leads him, right or wrong,
And oftimes "right" means "we are strong,"
Therefore beware our foes!

3RD PINE—THE COWARDLY.

Good pilgrim, there's no Summer air
Can still the voice that in me dwells,—
Its cry is all of dark despair,
And many a gloomy hap foretells,
All of the old "I told you so,"
Which turns to anguish every woe,
 And not a cloud dispels.

4TH PINE—THE REPROACHFUL.

The craven cry of time who feels
The lesser woes of little life—
The coward's wailing, which reveals
The cause of war—the loss of strife—
The nothings, who, with failing hearts,
Invite the woes which tyrants give—
Who lack the honor which imparts
The claim to manhood—right to live—
Who fear to speak—who dare not die,
And shrink from kind Eternity!

5TH PINE—THE CHIVALROUS.

Who cannot suffer, cannot dare!
Misfortune may be everywhere,
But, while a free heart holds its home,
A spirit-glory makes sublime
Each stony road o'er which we roam—
It leads us into honor's clime—
Each noble deed it sanctifies
And makes the mind a paradise!

6TH PINE—THE SUFFERING.

Ah, kinder winds from Norway blow

Than o'er the constant Northern snow—
E'en Lapland lying like a ghost,
With pine trees singing her to sleep,
And night prevailing on her coast,
Awakes in tears when others weep!
And dreamy Egypt, in her bed,
With Love's-witch toying in her hair,
And love awake, and joy not sped,
Would, when she heard the cry—" Despair!"
Refuse her wild desires to leave—
Rush from her love-couch quick to save—
Weep out the passion in her eyes
O'er others dreadful destinies,
And arm her lover for the grave!

7TH PINE—THE HOPEFUL.

The stars, which seem like angels eyes,
So full of love and light and hope,
Still, hold their watch in quiet skies,
And though in murky clouds we grope,
Bright day shall streak the night above,
And, as our foes shall act in love,
So shall our hearts resistance cease—
Hope smile, and Heaven accord us peace!
Not distant is that better time,
When all the orbs above shall seem
To light lost reason to each clime
And carry North the dead men's dream!

CHARLESTON, S. C. JOHN TEMPLETON.

MARY ASHBURTON.*

A TALE OF MARYLAND LIFE.

OUR breakfast was a silent, gloomy one. With difficulty I swallowed a cup of coffee. Even father ate in silence and with less appetite than usual. Mother bustled about providing for my comfort in her homely way, even laying up a store of her cake and biscuit, to be sent with my clothes to the Grove, supposing that the change would be felt less keenly with these little softenings. I remember noting how the clock ticked that morning on the high black mantel, the bright china ornaments and agricultural specimens that decked it also, the gay carpet with the rainbows running up and down, even the fire that crackled 'good night' upon the hearth; they all wore such a meaning look.

I think my parents felt this thing very deeply then. When first mentioned they had not realized it, and in the ambition of seeing their daughter mistress of the Grove, bearing the aristocratic Chauncey name, they had lost sight of the attendant unhappiness that such exaltation must bring with it to their child.

In his heart I believe my father anathematized the hour in which he had referred the matter to myself, to my judgment which he had assisted as he thought by his own opinion,—and mother's eyes were swollen with tears as she moved about, impatiently handling her much prized treasures. Father was fretful and cross, more so than I had ever seen him.

I almost swooned when mother's trembling hands arrayed me for the ceremony. My dress was a plain, gray silk, for I wished to look as little like a bride as possible, not to taunt him there at the altar with a raiment that would remind him of her who was to have stood beside him, whom his aching heart yet called for with outraged, yet clinging, intense adoration. I wore a mantle and bonnet of the same hue, a delicate blue wreath around the face.

"You look very pale, daughter," said father, "don't be frightened, my dear child."

He said nothing more, but I could see that he was moved in his blunt way. That was his way of showing grief always; an effort to conceal it under a rough, blunt manner, which, unconsciously to himself, softened into tenderness on this morning.

When the carriage was at the door,—only the sight of their almost angry reluctance gave me strength to enter it—my inward agitation was terrible.

I looked around me. It was a showery April morning, alternately sunshine and a light, sprinkling rain that did not always obscure the sun-beams which shone through it in glimmering, broken radiance as pleasure and sorrow so

---

* Continued from page 504, vol. 4.

near together in our human life; the washed sky coming out fresh and blue after the weeping process.

I never heard the birds sing more sweetly, or loved the violets as well. As I passed to the carriage I trod inadvertently upon a daffodil that moved a little farther than the rest in a clump, and crushed it to the ground. Almost weeping—I didn't want *them* to see me weep—I stooped to put it in its place again, supporting it among the others, for it grieved me that my last act at home was to crush the life from one of my innocent friends.

Seated in the carriage I glanced back into the dear bright old *home* room. The fire was smouldering on the hearth, the ashes had rolled down between the sparkling brass and were scattered over the bricks,—mother's great horror.—The tea-pot yet simmered among them, the coffee sent up a faint steam from the dear old pot that my hands had rubbed so often; the table standing just as of old, and the great sideboard beyond. All those dear simple objects I noted as father took his seat and the carriage rolled away, just catching a farewell glimpse of the clock, pointing to half past seven, the table and the china between the portals of the door, as we wheeled around and rode off.

We were to meet them at the church. It was a melancholy looking procession; my parents with me, the boys in another carriage. I have no space to linger over the details, the remarks of that morning; my little brothers' opposition and wondering surmises, the servants' also; it would make my story, which I wish as simple as possible, too long. I had bidden them a hasty adieu, too hasty to listen even to their well wishes, or their expressions of surprise which they had understood from the first that I did not desire.

Very few remarks were made during our ride; mother alone interrupting the silence by some motherly warnings about my health, my wardrobe and other little matters that a mother alone would think of, caring for me in a way that made me more conscious than I had ever been of the love she bore me and I her. When we have blessings, the usual ones that God gives us, how little conscious we are of their value, till they are removed from us—a hackneyed remark, yet ever new as long as the world stands—they are so wound about our being, so entangled in our heart-strings that we scarcely know of their possession till the strings are broken and the loved object withdrawn. Ah! no one cared for me as she did, though no congeniality and scarcely a tie save that of parent and child, existed between us.

When the town drew in sight, I trembled and sank back in the intense desire for escape, and when mother said, "The Grove carriage is there," I could have torn open the door by me and run through the fields away; anything to escape seeing him then.

My eyes were closed!—oh! if I could only keep them so. I knew when the carriage stopped where we were. I heard father help mother out.

"Come, Mary, get out," my father took hold of me with unusual tenderness in his touch, "child, you *must* get out."

I had grown very faint, but I allowed him to help me; I knew that the other gentlemen were near, but they thought that father would do best just then, I suppose, at least the elder one did, and alighted at the gate where Adéle had done before me in her splendor of dress and beauty.—Mr. Chauncey saluted me, then took me up to Alfred, who stood a pace or two off.

Did he speak to me? I do not know. I knew only that he was there, that Mr. Chauncey released my hand and placed it in Alfred's arm, who could not fail then to perceive my extreme agitation.—I felt him look down at me; he was not lost, as he deemed himself, to all human feeling.

"Poor child," he muttered, with an accent of pity in his dry, hollow tones, "I am most truly sorry for your fate."

Agitated as I was I could scarcely keep the tears from flowing.—But he had spoken kindly to me, and suddenly I was wonderfully supported. Like a drooping plant I revived under this drop, and entered the church with a firmer step. One furtive glance at Alfred's face showed me his wild, despairing eye, his wan, ghastly visage. It will be mine to draw him from this, I whispered to myself, though this scene adds to his torture now. Oh! my Father, give me strength, trembling and awed as I am.

There was no one in the church; the early hour and the secrecy with which it had been conducted preventing all intrusion. The clergyman was already there, standing before the chancel rail in his white robes. It was no time for thought. Like an automaton I moved with him up the aisle, banishing feeling which would have broken down all composure; he equally lifeless from a writhing sense of mockery he was engaged in.

But a few steps and we stood before the altar—a few words, was it possible?—pronounced us man and wife.

Bewildered, I left the altar with him, was rejoined by our parents, received their silent kisses

"Good-bye. God bless you, my child," said Mr. Chauncey, embracing me cordially. "Take care of my boy," he whispered, "bear with him for a while; your sweetness and skill cannot fail to bring him around. Farewell."

He stepped into the carriage, that was waiting to conduct him to the boat, and was gone.

It was scarcely a farewell from my parents, our homes were so near, when they placed me in the Grove state carriage. How strange!—the same that had so often held the queenly Mrs. Chauncey and her fashionable guests.

We were alone then. I looked up in his face when I had gathered courage. It was stern and gloomy, his brows contracted, his eyes looking far away through the window, as if he saw nothing around him in his absent gaze.

The ride was but a few miles. Once he glanced towards me, his eye softening at the expression of my face as I sat trembling and timid at his side, and he spoke, again with that accent of pity in his tone.

"Poor child! you chose unwisely. I wish for your sake that it had been otherwise."

He seemed to regard me but as a child, and I felt unable every way to correct the impression. I had no power to move or show vitality at that moment, for the passiveness of a dream had come over me and I quietly suffered everything, went through every form in that state of half-unconsciousness. Such a bridal pair! I looked from my window, he from his. I noted the woods, the waving wheat fields, the sloping banks and the meadows as we rode along, thinking that each one as it appeared brought us to our destination. I was glad, for I longed to be rid of this oppressive silence and stiffness and to be about my duties.

At last it came in sight. I mind the stately avenue well, the waving poplars and chestnuts, sweeping over the roof of the carriage as we drove under their overhanging boughs, the bold sweep of the lawn up to the imposing portico.

There was no one to welcome me; all had a silent, gloomy, deserted air, lacking the life-giving presence of a mistress. Desolation appeared to have swept over the scene, leaving the objects there, but taking away the life from them. I remember noting as we drove up that one of the shutters on the cupola, hung loose in its hinges and slammed to and fro in the breeze, a sign of decay.

With the courteousness he would have shown to a stranger, nothing more, Alfred assisted me to alight, conducted me up the steps into the hall, where one or two of the old family servants, who had not been dismissed met us.

"Where is Melissa?" asked their young master of these.

They went to summon her and presently a bright looking mulatto woman of middle age presented herself.

"Show this lady her apartments," he said to her, "and see that she has every comfort and attention."

"Your servant, missy," she replied with a low curtsey, "I'll show you the room that old master had fixed for you."

"Pardon me," said Alfred to me in a low tone. "I—I go to make some arrangements. See that you are obeyed and cared for, and—be as happy as you can." He turned away choked with emotion.

Do not fear for me," I found voice to say, "I will take care of myself."

He looked relieved and turned away. I followed the old woman up the broad staircase, my feet seeming to tread upon air as I ascended by such easy grades, accustomed as I was to the narrow, winding stairs at home, with their short, stumping steps.

A broad, handsome passage, with the doors from various apartments opening upon it, received me at the head of the strairs.

"Master had this room prepared for you, madam," said Melissa with old time courteousness. She opened a door as she spoke and introduced me into a large, elegant apartment, stately in old fashioned furniture.

"This room was ——?" I asked and hesitated.

"A company room, madam," she curtseyed again, "Missis' room is locked up now and master gave me the key to give to you."

She produced it as she spoke, and I took it half hesitatingly as if I had no right for it to be surrendered to me, internally marveling at the strange chain of circumstances that had given me such right in Mr. Chauncey's house, the right to hold that key as Alfred's wife. My face I felt to crimson at the thought as the old domestic looked at me, and I wished most earnestly to be alone that I might recover from the confusion I was afraid of showing in her presence.

She was too well trained, however, to intrude long, and interpreting my diffidence, I suspect, showed me the various conveniences of the apartment, offering to unpack my trunks and arrange the dresses in the wardrobe; showed me the bell, then with another curtsey asked my permission to retire. I must have shown myself most unsophisticated, for in answer to her inquiries concerning this and that thing to be done, I could hardly conceal my ignorance, with difficulty understanding her terms.

Old master, she said, had ordered dinner at such an hour today, would I have it always at that time? and did I like this thing or that thing? she went through the whole vocabulary of French cookery till I was bewildered.

Most relieved was I to be left alone, to be allowed time to breathe and collect my thoughts.

The servant had disposed of my bonnet and mantle, so there was nothing for me to do but to think.

Think! how could I do that? In his house—alone there with him! Where was he? and what was he doing now that his unwelcome, unloved bride was there?

His coldness—did it hurt me? No, no, I could expect nothing else. I clasped my hands over the aching heart and walked about the room.

Rich silk curtains swept over the windows. Putting one aside, I looked out over the lawn, trying to catch a glimpse of him without whom I cared for nothing there.

He did not appear and the hours grew long and wearisome. I had nothing to do, was tired of the same room, yet too shy to show myself alone in the lower apartments, to be stared at by the servants, or perhaps encounter my—my husband—I could not whisper the word to myself as yet—for I dreaded meeting him as if I was an intruder or a spy upon his grief, interfering with his privileges of home.

Noon had advanced and I was sitting disconsolately at the window, my hands folded upon my knee, when there was a knock at the door. Upon my giving permission to enter, Melissa came in with a waiter of refreshments.

"Young master says, wont you have something to eat, Madam?" she said, dropping her usual curtsey.

"He? did young Mr. Chauncey

send you here?" I asked eagerly.

"Yes, Madam, he rang the bell to see if you was properly attended to, Miss, and I told him how I'd see to you."

"Where is he?" I asked breathlessly, "I thought—" here I checked myself in what I was about to add.

"In his own room, Madam."

Now that I knew I could hear the distant beat of a restless foot pacing the floor.

"Is he not coming out?—does he want nothing?" I asked, too eager for information to observe my usual taciturnity where he was concerned.

"No, Madam, he wants nothing. I begged him to eat, but he just waved me off with his hands and I daren't say another word, so jest come out."

"Did he—did he look sick, or very badly?"

"Well, Miss, he didn't look no worse than he has done ever since —these times."

"He ordered this, you say?"

"Yes, Miss, he rang the bell and I went to see what he wanted, 'cause I was his nurse and loved him like my own child. He stopped in his walk and said, 'Let the young lady want for nothing. See that she is attended to, and take her some refreshments,' then waved me off and I had to come."

I painfully swallowed a morsel. "Take this away," I said and walked again to the window that she might not witness my emotion. When alone I indulged in a burst of tears. I longed to go to him. Why could I not? I had the right given me that morning by the priestly sanction. Ah! the offer of the universe could not have tempted me to invade the privacy of that chamber. Oh! those long dreary, sickening hours! I wanted to see home and parents, my dear little pets and flowers—yet still that closed door contained what was more precious to me than all, and the right of being there was enough to make me happy of itself.

I suddenly resolved not to remain there a prisoner any longer; and hearing a singular beating sound outside my door, I went and opened it. To my surprise, Leo, our old house dog, sprang up and greeted me with a joyful bark, putting his paws on my shoulders and rubbing his shaggy head against my dress.

I was pleased and affected, delighted at seeing a familiar, loving face in my strange, cold home. I constituted him at once my companion, and felt protection from strangers in his affectionate society, so putting my hand on his rough head, we went solemnly down stairs together to survey the premises. I had gathered some courage to move about now that I was certain of not encountering Alfred who was in his room and not being considered an intruder.

When we got down stairs I timidly opened the dining-room door. It was as it had been when I supped there in childish years. Melissa was there arranging some glass on the sideboard.

"Would'nt you like me to show you where the things is kept, madam?" she suggested.

"Yes," I replied, "I partly came for that."

She showed me the great sideboard with its handsome contents, where the silver was kept, its various arrangements,—then took me in the parlor. How grand it looked to my unsophisticated eyes! Many a rich piece of needlework was there, embroidered by the hands of the late unfortunate lady of the house. The rosewood furniture with their seats of royal purple velvet were covered with linen, but the splendid carpet of so many brilliant, beautiful dyes that it was hard to distinguish the predominating one, save the rich background of shaded purple, gave the room a lively look. In the corner were marble statuettes and on the low, pure white mantel were lofty alabaster vases of the Etruscan shape. In the centre of the room stood a table of peculiarly rich workmanship, the legs of which formed a lily with the broad leaves folding so as to support the slab of marble at the top. On the centre of this stood an alabaster vase with carved lilies arising from its brim, so exquisitely delicate and pure that I was lost in admiration of its sculpture. A golden goblet with Alfred's name stood on one side, a purple velvet Bible with golden clasps on the other of this beautiful ornament. Melissa had thrown the windows open for me to see. It had not been done before, she said, since Mrs. Chauncey's death.

"To tell the truth," she added, "we didn't take much care of nothin. We heard old master was broke, and all we had to be scattered, so we thought the house, furniture, and everything belonging here, would be done just so by, so we let the things go."

"Are you glad that it is not as you expected?" I asked.

"Yes, miss, I am. 'Cause it's hard to be driven from your old home where ye expect to end your days, to go along of strangers. We was all glad when old master told us to let things go on as usual, that we was not to go. We all love Mars Alfred, and like to live with him—for he's a mighty good young man, for all that—treated him so. Then old master told us yesterday who was comin', so we was glad of that too, for we thought, maybe it'ud save young master, and make him forget that—"

At these blanks she shook her head till her bright turban almost fell off, expressing indignation and disgust so strongly as her features were capable of.

I went to the low window where that young, beautiful pair stood seven years ago, he with his boyish admiration, she in her loveliness and girlish coquetry. What changes had passed over them—over us all since. I, who had watched them so wistfully then, so insignificant in my plainness beside the budding beauty, the elegant heir, was now the mistress of that home, saved by my patrimony from the hands of the law. But—alas! I was insignificant still—a bride who had not seen the bridegroom since directly after the ceremony. I felt no exultation, but so thankful that my money had saved it. I looked from the window on the noble scene, the smooth, green turf of the lawn just below with the trunks of the stately trees arising from it at intervals, to the iron trellis-work that formed the entrance to the garden, some forty yards distant, and I loved it all for his sake. If he but loved me, I sighed, how happy I would be, here, with so much that is beautiful to gratify my tastes. To see this, and do for him what I can, is all that I can have for comfort. But—oh! so much sweeter than that life-long desolation I feared.

"Would'nt you like to see the pantry, missy?" asked Melissa, who had been uncovering some things.

"To think of missis' work bein' sold," she added reflectively, looking on the result of her operations.

"It would have been a sorrowful thing," I replied, "I am ready to look elsewhere now."

We went to the store-room, where my practised eye discovered much that was wanting, and which I inwardly resolved to supply from our own abundant one at home, to the pantry, a small china shop in its way, with splendid glass and porcelain, ranged on its shelves down to the homelier and more useful articles for furnishing the table, to the dairy, (I suspect she thought I felt myself at home there for the first time) to the ground rooms where various articles were stored away, showing me the use of each, and familiarising me with them.

There were many things amiss which must be rectified in the future, I thought, and addressed her several observations which proved my competency, in that respect, at least, for assuming the post of mistress,

Then Leo and I took a walk on the lawn and about the garden.—How vivid it all was—the scene of the past. Adéle and her boy lover.

But it was too painful and I would not let my thoughts dwell upon it,so I turned them as quickly as I could.

The garden was sadly neglected;—many of the vines had fallen down and were trailing about the paths destitute of leaves, and the rose bushes were scraggy where the branches showed themselves through a wilderness of beauty blushing around them.

I paused before some magnificent pinks of every hue, from crimson to white spotted with rose color and hyacinths, to pull up the weeds that were choking their growth. This I did in several places, feeling greatly relieved at having something to do. Then we wandered about the walks, up and down the violet banks, shaded with a grove of horse chestnuts, firmly bound together with gigantic grape vines, that ran network along the border for some space on the left garden boundary. It was a queer garden when you left the first, regularly planned borders, surprising you with quaint little nooks where the vinework formed a most unexpected arbor, or a rill gushed out at the base of a flowery, sloping bank. A great, thick hedge of yews formed its termination, between the stems of which now torn asunder and sadly neglected, I could see a field of wheat beyond. Here the rill dashed from a stone basin into this part of the garden, rippling away half concealed until it joined that nearer the centre. I washed my hands, soiled with the earth I had shaken from the plants, and Leo and I proceeded to the lawn.

The slanting rays of the sun were gilding its rich, green surface, or sinking into luxurious softness where the long shadows of the trees lay. I felt no longer alone as I drank in nature's beauty; while lingering there the sunbeams warmed me into love for it all, and my heart turned with redoubled affection to the poor, lonely sufferer above.

The old waiter that I had seen before, came out just then with his white apron on and the tray under his arm as he had done seven years before to so different a party.

"Dinner is ready, madam," he said with great solemnity.

Will *he* be there, thought I, as I retraced my steps to the door. Surely I shall see him now. Yet, though my heart beat with intense anxiety to see him, I felt afraid to encounter his eye and shy of meeting him as the mistress of his house. To sit at the head of his table—oh! I should sink through the floor.

As my foot touched the bottom step, a hand reached forward and raising my startled eyes, I met Alfred's dark, stern gaze.

"You have been lonesome?" he said questioningly. "I pity you, but know of no consolations to offer."

He console, when he looked as if he had been wrestling with despair! Oh! he did not know that the inability to console him was my greatest trouble, what was my loneliness to that!

I did not tell him so but stupidly stammered, "I—I—did not care."

His face grew darker still. "To be tied to such a woman with neither sense nor feeling," no doubt was his reflection. He turned off with an air which I interpreted. "But then it's better as it is," and took his seat at the foot of the table, while I timidly took the other seat, placed for me at the head.

For the first time I presided over Mrs. Chauncey's table. The old waiter stood there to serve, I uncertain whether to be glad or sorry for his presence. Alfred helped me with an absent, though courteous air, placed something upon his own plate which he scarcely touched, then seemed lost in thought, from which he started once or twice to say something to me, the attempt failing him before the words were formed upon his lips. When all the courses had been gone through with, the old waiter placing and removing them with equal solemnity, he arose, perceiving my hesitation and came near me.

"Will you go out on the porch?" he said offering me his arm. "The resources of your house, you know, are at your own command, for whatever you want or desire to do."

Oh! that miserable timidity! I was so nervously in awe of him that I could scarcely speak. I could not act with the dignified courtesy that he did and his coldness sealed my lips from all expression of my feelings. So I took his arm and suffered him to lead me out on the porch, the sun just disappearing behind the forest trees as I took the seat he handed me.

He remained with me, but looking so gloomy with his brow still contracted, his lips compressed as ever and his arms folded as if to still some tempest that was raging in his breast.

"I wished it was in my power to show you greater kindness," he said at last without relaxing his brows, "but my gloom and my desolation are all I have left in this world."

Surely I could say something now, when he looked upon it all as mine, relieved by *my* money, could tell him that it was his thrice over and would still be were I a beggar for his sake, but no ——.

Glancing towards the lawn, I saw my parents approaching the house. A look of intense disgust and aversion came over Alfred's face. "Coming to take possession in right of the newly married daughter and act the parents-in-law already," it seemed to say.

But he descended the steps and met them with cold, grave courtesy; that of a gentleman, nothing more.

I think mother was chilled at the outset; she certainly did not make herself at home, and appeared somewhat fidgety. I met them affectionately, but my own manner was restrained in Alfred's presence, so that none of the party were at ease except father, whose own free manner was partly put on, I believed.

"Fine grazing ground, Mr. Chauncey. Going to turn your cattle in there?" he asked, referring to a field he had just passed by.

"I do not know, sir," replied Alfred, haughtily, "it has not been a subject of consideration with me at all."

"Then I'd advise you to be seeing about it. It's time if you're going to do any thing with your place this year."

I could see that Alfred writhed in an agony of impatience at this infliction, and to spare him, I engaged them both in home matters which successfully diverted father from his attack. He darted at me the first grateful glance I had received from him, and, unable to endure his torture longer, he disappeared before they had missed his presence. I longed to follow, to go to him and try to comfort him in my feeble way! I felt almost that I had the power just then, my love and sympathy were so intense. I hated too to be alone with my parents who I knew would question me on the most delicate point.

"Why, Mary, that husband of yours is'nt much like a groom," commenced my father, leaning forward.

"You *must* be lonesome here," observed mother, significantly, looking through the door into the hall.

"I'm afraid he's not a going to do much with my money," pursued father, "I could'nt get a word of sense out of him. What *does* he intend to do?"

"He need'nt make himself such a fool over that girl," responded mother, "she was a heartless jilt and I know my Mary will come up to her in many things, and two or three times her worth besides." She shook her head decidedly.

"Oh! never mind him now, mother," I besought her tearfully, "he loved her so, and suffered so dreadfully."

"Plague on it all!" exclaimed father, shaking the ashes from the pipe he had been indulging in since Alfred's departure, "but if ever a woman had treated me so when I was a sharp young blade, I'd a seen her to Jericho before I'd a wasted all my days crying over her. There's an old saying about crying over spilt-milk, which it seems your young man has'nt learnt yet, Mary."

To hear him spoken of in this fashion! My blood tingled with mortified indignation. What had I, or my family, to expect of one who had honestly told me the consequences of accepting him! Then the indelicacy of discussing his affairs as if I had been a chosen wife, and of assuming the air of a father-in-law over him who had not made the slightest acknowledgement of his right to that title.

If he had overheard him—and I was miserably afraid that the open doors and windows of a warm Spring evening would convey the sound to his ears—I believe he would have fled the premises forever,

"Well, husband, it's getting late, and I must get home to see that the cows are milked," said mother, rising. "Mary, child, come home every day, it is'nt likely but what you'll be lonesome here. Well, never mind," she added, seeing how I shrank back, maybe he'll come round in time, after while."

I said nothing, but bade them both an affectionate farewell.—Then they left me, walking along in their quiet, sober way, and, no doubt, talking about Mary's present forlorn prospects.

I saw no more of Alfred that evening. He had fled, locked and double locked himself up in his own apartment. The evening air was chilly, so I went in the house after my parents left, and staid in the dark, lonely parlor, till night came with its gloomy shadows that fell on the walls and the sombre furniture till it looked like the ghosts of those who had once been there.

The portrait of Alfred's mother stared out from the darkness, the moonlight as it fell upon her proud, handsome features, seeming to give them life till I almost fancied she looked at me, the plebeian usurper of her rights, frowningly. If she had lived, this would never have been, I could not help thinking. She would have said, "come poverty, come privations, but no alliance of our proud blood with that of common clod-hoppers, my head shall be loftier than ever, for my pride is the last thing left me." Alfred was a blended likeness of both parents, deriving his dark eyes and short upper-lip from his mother, his light hair, and complexion, from his father.

A chill crept over me as I gazed at her face, I fancied she would speak to me, her eyes appeared to follow me so, and the long black shadows around the wall seemed to creep nearer. I longed for some living creature to be near. Even Leo had trotted off after mother and father. I was so entirely alone. Not a sound disturbed the silence, save the distant echo from the kitchen, or the cry of some fowl as it went to roost.

As quickly as my trembling limbs would take me I ran from the parlor, closed the door on its ghostly occupants, on the darkness and gathering gloom, and sought for relief in the fresh air. They had closed and barred the front door, so I did not disturb it. The moonlight was streaming in at one of the great windows. I stood there gazing out till I heard footsteps approaching. It was Melissa with a light in her hand.

"Here's your lamp, missy," she said, "I've just been filling it with oil or I'd a brought it to you before. What time do you want breakfast, to-morrow?"

"What time does Mr. Chauncey usually have his?"

"Laws a massy! miss, he don't keer, if it's Mars Alfred you mean. He comes any time or no time."

"Let it be at nine then to-morrow."

I took the light from her and went to my room. For a long time I sat at one of the windows, watching the play of the moonbeams on the scene, and thinking of my life—what it was to be. I could not see at present, what my duties were, what I must do, or could do. To be sure that was but the close of the first day, a most dreary one, but were all to be like that—nothing to do, weariness and vacuity? Time would develope and I must patiently wait. In the meantime I was at hand for whatever should be needed, there to tend and soothe if I could, or work for him in other ways should his present condition require it. With that consolation I retired to rest.

But I did not rest. All was quiet—so quiet till, wearily tossing upon an uneasy couch, I heard a sound.

Was it the wind? It grew louder. No, it was a human voice, as in agony; deep, terrible sobs and long drawn sighs as if a heart would break at each.

This was maddening; I could endure it no longer. Wringing my hands in passionate sorrow, I sprang from my bed and opened the door. His room was several doors from mine. I could hear him pacing the floor with rapid steps. Throwing myself on his sill, I sat there wringing my hands and weeping bitterly as I listened to agony, for how could I rest upon my couch while he, whom I loved better than all the world, was enduring such suffering? How he must have loved her! and I did not wonder, for her every look or movement was fascination. Such a passion as she could inspire must be intense. Then to be discarded so, after her professions of attachment, to be deceived where he had placed every hope in life, received by an attachment that was more than hopeless; everything about him connected with her image, it must have torn up his heart's roots to sever them from her. To be without her he had to live life over again; to crush her intoxicating loveliness from his soul, to begin a new existence divested of all thought of her. How miserably impossible that was, I knew—alas!—by bitter experience. I felt too that on that particular night his misery was intensely aggravated by the day's occurrences; how scornfully he was picturing to himself the plebeian, senseless bride, that his father had brought him, her vulgar old parents who could come so conveniently and intrude upon his grief, almost taking possession in right of the wrong they had spent upon the home of his ancestors; so different from the beautiful, high born bride, the elegant, cultivated circle of friends and connections that he would have lived in with her, she dispensing the honors of his house as an accomplished lady, what I never can be, I thought, weeping sorrowfully, I am so shy and so very, very timid.

So I set there and listened to the heavy step pacing backwards and forwards, starting with terror as he approached the door, fearful that he would open it suddenly and discover me there; longing to go to him and whisper consolation, yet doing all I could—weeping with him.

At last he threw himself exhansted on a couch; nature had resumed her sway and I could perceive by his deep breathing that he slept the sleep of weariness. Then I crept back to my room and slept till daylight. When I awoke the next morning it was with a disposition to look from my little window at home to see the sun's rays mantling the east with the warm blushes of sunrise, but the light coming in broadly from a different direction, I turned my startled eyes and saw it stealing through the embroidered curtains of four lofty windows. I lay for some time looking around me, wondering to find myself there and unable to realize that it was all true, that this was Alfred's home, and mine also now—*our* home, but no blissful dual unity as of a married pair. Alas! no "we" and "our" existed for us; so near and yet so far apart were we. I arose, threw on a white morning wrapper and went down stairs. A desire to do something for *him* overcame my timidity and I resolved to venture upon my prerogative as mistress at once.

(TO BE CONTINUED.)

"TELL THE BOYS I'M COMING SOON."

BY J. AUGUSTINE SIGNAIGO.

I was just well enough to leave the hospital to repair to my command. In passing out I stopped to bid a sick comrade adieu. I found the poor fellow was dying. He took my hand in his, and, with a last effort, whispered: "Tell the boys I'm coming soon!"—*Letter from Atlanta*, 1864.

Where a hundred sick and dying
  Groaned in agony and pain,
While the whizzing shells were flying
  Fast as comes the pelting rain,
Was a soldier quickly straying
  Into death's remorseless swoon,
Still he woke up firmly saying—
  "Tell the boys I'm coming soon!"

"Did you hear it not? the rattle
  Of the canister—the crash!
Hear the furious peals of battle,
  See the cannon's lightning flash!
God of Heaven! my bosom's swelling,
  Beating to the bullets' tune!
Listen to their distant yelling—
  'Tell the boys I'm coming soon!'

"Have they fought another battle?
  I must be with them—I must!
God! there's music in its rattle
  As the foemen bite the dust!
Tell the boys to strike for freedom!
  'Tis of Heaven the priceless boon,
Tell all freemen that we need 'em—
  'Tell the boys I'm coming soon!'"

Fast the soldier now was sinking,
  Like the setting of the day,
Still his mind was dreaming, thinking,
  Of the boys who wore the grey;
And with one strong effort sighing,
  Ere he fell in Death's last swoon,
Still he said as he was dying—
  "Tell the boys I'm coming soon!"

Coming quickly, coming blandly,
  Rising up beyond the skies,
Marching onward, marching grandly,
  To the gates of Paradise!
Tell the dead who've gone before him
  He has won the holy boon,
Tell the saints who still watched o'er him—
  Tell all Heaven he's coming soon!

MODEL HOUSEKEEPING,

OR

NELLY RANDOM'S DINNER PARTY.

"HALLOO! NELLY, come down, quick, sweetheart, I want you in the parlor"—and Frank Random, standing at the foot of the stairs, turned up his handsome, flushed face, as if expecting to see "Nelly" running down at once, obedient to his commands,—but he looked in vain for she did not come. Now Frank was not the most patient individual alive, so he did not wait long, but taking four steps at a stride, was soon at the door of his wife's room, muttering, as he dashed on this headlong course up stairs.

"No wonder she cannot hear me through that infernal din in the nursery. Nelly, where are you, child?"

And he slammed open their chamber door, but she was not there. Slightly ruffled at this unexpected chance of missing her when he was in haste, for his friends must leave in half an hour on the noon train—and Frank being very proud of his handsome young wife, wanted this old college chum to have a glance at her *en passant*—he broke through the nursery where Betty was shrieking "John Brown's body" to the baby.

"Confound it all!" he shouted "*can't* you stop that yelling for a moment and tell me where your Miss Nelly is?"

Poor Betty stopped with her mouth half open, and stared at him aghast—for, being generally good natured, she wondered what had happened to put "Massa Frank" in such a fret—and then stammered out—

"I b'leves Miss Nelly's in de kitchen, sir. I's ben a singin de baby to sleep, and never heered you callin."

"Singing! the devil you were. Why don't you know such an infernal noise as that is enough to keep *forty* babies awake, let alone one? Halloo! Posey! glad to see papa, aren't you?" and he tossed the plump rosy thing until she laughed and crowed with delight! "Come little one, let's go to the parlor. Where's master Eddie?"

"In de kitchen long a his ma, I spec—he follered her down dar."

"And what in the thunder is your mistress doing in the kitchen?"

"Don't know, Massa Frank," and Betty grinned. "She's took a monstrous likin to de kitchen lately, peers like she's heap fonder of it den she was—shill I go and tell her you wants her?"

"No, I'll go for her myself.—Come, let's hunt up mama, Posey," and off went Frank, with his baby, down stairs, through the diningroom and pantry to a little back passage adjoining the kitchen, where a most unexpected, and, to his refined taste, not very pleasant tableau was presented to his astonished gaze; for, being summer, the kitchen door stood open; and there was his beautiful Nelly, with sleeves rolled up, scouring away at something, he could not tell whether it was tin, pewter, or silver, and he did not care, for the mere fact of his wife, a lady born and bred, doing menial work, set Frank Random's aristocratic blood in a fever of indignation, and he called out in a tone of voice less gentler than she had ever heard from him before—

"Nelly, my child, what *are* you about? Come quickly to the parlor, an old friend of mine is waiting there to see you, and must be off in a few moments."

"Mercy, Frank, don't look so cross, I am only helping Aunt Cloe to clean up a little; stop Eddie, you'll tear mama's apron, just let me go and smooth my hair, and I'll be all right for the parlor." And Nelly pulling down her sleeves, and wiping the moisture from her flushed face with a delicate cambric handkerchief, smiled at her husband as she passed him to go up stairs.

"All right indeed! no you won't, he replied, clucking her under the chin. Your face is as red as blazes, go on though—it can't be helped now, we will discuss this kitchen freak of yours anon young lady.

"Aunt Cloe" as soon as Nell was out of hearing—"what brings her here?"

"De Lord knows, I spec sum of dem tarin down old housekeepers bin got after her, Mas Frank, I wish de debble had um, and I's mighty glad you disproves of it sir, for she bothers me mightily, dese here *raal* quality ladies (like Miss Nelly,) don't know nothin on de Lord's earth about work, dey always hinders us niggers when dey pertends to help! yah! yah! yah! it makes me laugh to see sich a putty creetur as dat fussin round and tryin to do what dem old hard reasoned house-keepers tells her she ought to do—last-ways, I spec dey dun it, can't say for sartin, she's jist took to it dis las week!

"Very likely, said Frank" as he nodded to Aunt Cloe, and walked off—"but I'll put a stop to it."

Nelly smoothed her hair, and was a little provoked that the flush did not disappear the moment she looked in the glass, but after giving her cheeks and forehead two or three gentle taps with the powder puff, and laughing her light careless laugh, at the memory of Frank's troubled look, when he caught her in the kitchen—away she ran to the parlor.

"Well, what do you think of my Nelly, Bob?" said Frank Random, as they turned off from his pretty cottage home.

"Very handsome! by George, she *is a stunner!* but I was somewhat astonished to find her so *florid;* you told me she was pale!"

"And so she *is*—curse such luck—as white as a lily, scarcely ever has a tinge of color, or if any, just enough to be *perfect*, but when we came in, where do you suppose I found her?

"Don't know, working with the baby, I suppose, that is generally the occupation of feminines when there's a baby on hand."

"No indeed—worse than that—she was actually in the kitchen, my dear fellow, scrubbing and tearing away at some infernal old tin pot or another. I'm afraid one or more of these fussy old house-keepers have been tampering with her innocent ignorance of such matters, and inoculating her brain with the neatness mania—*confound* such meddlesome old frumps say I, they are a nuisance in any community, cramming every young house-keeper they meet with their absurd notions of rubbing and scrubbing and sweeping and scouring, from Monday morning to Saturday night. I swear, it makes me perfectly savage to think of my elegant, refined, beautiful Nelly, having all her elegance, refinement, and beauty, coarsened by the horrible housekeeping disease, well nigh as fatal to good looks as the small-pox, and which too often transforms our young American ladies into coarse, middle-aged women, with rough red hands, no longer fit for the piano, or harp, or to dress and adorn their children for that matter. A lady should confine her usefulness to lady-like duties and employments, not coarsen herself by menial labor, unless poverty compels it, and then, of course, one must submit to the annoyance of seeing a diamond, or pearl, or ruby (as the case may be) sullied with smut and dust, consoled by the hope that if it be a real gem, and no sham, the dirt will not stick to its perfect polish!

"Halloo! Frank," said his friend, laughing, "you are turning lecturer—don't fret about your Nelly, she is a real *jewel*, and won't collect much dust: refined natures are not easily coarsened, and by analyzing the composition of those fussy, fretting, hard-working housewives (or young ones either for that matter) you would be very apt to discover a strong run of vulgarity near the surface, the vulgarity of *birth* which neither association or education can ever entirely refine. Your Nelly is more the real lady in the kitchen, scrubbing tin pots and pans, with sleeves rolled up and apron on, aye, even with a flushed face and soiled hands, than the tiresome old body who incited her to such absurd proceedings—robed in royal velvet and lounging in a splendid drawingroom. Yet I agree with you that it's very provoking to see a young beauty spoiling her hands and complexion by doing kitchen work, when there is no necessity for it, and I would put a summary stop to such proceedings!"

"By George!" exclaimed Frank, "I think this infernal hot weather ought to put a summary stop to Nell's foolish kitchen craze, but now that I've caught her at it, old Mrs. Fiddle-faddle, or the Lord knows who, may whistle up her new pupil in vain; when Random meets Particular, 'then comes the tug of war.' I don't mean to have my authority set at naught by a nest of fussy old gossips, and will route old Fuzzle-guzzle or die for it—whip her in a fair fight if necessary, and you shall hear the results. *Au revoir.*" And Bob Moore was whistled off on the express train while Frank sauntered home vowing vengeance against meddlers as a class, and one in particular, he did not exactly know who, but intended to find out; yes that he would!

CHAPTER II.

"Lord bless my soul, but ain't I glad massa Frank done been here and called Miss Nelly out of *my* kitchen?" exclaimed aunt Cloe, fanning her big, black, good-natured self with a tin plate, and haranguing the house servants as they ate their dinner on that memorable day. "Pears like she's took a mighty notion to help me dis las week. I wonder what's got into her? I'll bet a tater, a big sweet tater too, dat sum of dem hard taren down old housekeepers bin knowed her ebber since she's bin born, put my young mistiss up to spilin her putty little white hands, Lord knows d'arn is red and big enough! I'd stood it jist as long as I could, and had done made up my mind to tell her how dat de kitchen ain't no place for a lady-born. I was tryin to git up sparit enough to speak out to dis inference when de master come, and, Lord! how I did chuckle when he hollered at her like he was kinder mad, and yet she's so putty he couldn't scold her, and no wonder, for I'd been scourin and cleanin away and rollin my eyes round ebery now and den to see what she was about, and termined to burst out and say: 'Now Miss Nelly, what you think your blessed Ma would say, if she could put her head in dat dar door, like she used to peep in de old Grange kitchen, and see you wid your lily-white hands scourin away at dat dratted old cake mould? You ought to go out of here, in fact you ought, Miss Nelly, its no place for de likes of you,' and my heart kept kinder fillin up inside of me like a tater in a pot, and I kep swellin and sweatin mightily, but I couldn't speak as I oughter; and when Massa Frank come along and blow'd her up, I could a hugged him, fore de Lord! I could, and I b'leves he's put a *vetum*, as my ole master use to say, on her comin here to bother me agin. Jehol-ikins! but ain't it hot?—Come, hurry up your dinner;—you niggers takes heap longer to eat dan you did fore freedum broke out!" and aunt Cloe went about her afternoon work with a vim that hurried up her audience to a speedy prosecution and completion of their dinner operations; for aunt Cloe was queen of the kitchen, and not to be trifled with or interfered with—no, not even by "Miss Nelly," and aunt Cloe was right!

"Now, come, my darling, and tell me candidly what ever put it into your pretty little head to turn kitchen maid? Your mother never did such work, so far as I know, and certainly mine never does. Who has been tampering with your lady-like notions of housekeeping, causing you to place kitchen work high up—nay, perhaps to head with it your list of daily duties?" And Frank Random drew Nelly down besides him on a tete-a-tete sofa, near the library window, after tea, when the children were asleep, and there appeared a fair chance for uninterrupted chat.

Nelly laughed at his business-like manner, and replied jestingingly—

"You talk as if I had been guilty of some grave offense, Mr. Inquisitor, its precious little of anything in the shape of work I've ever done, not half as much as I ought, it seems—for Mrs. Noah Scrubbinwell"—

"There!" exclaimed Frank, springing up and standing before her as if to do battle then and there, "I knew it—I forgot her name, and called her old Fuzzle-guzzle to-day, but knew it to be her doings all the same, meddlesome, tiresome, fussy old gossip! She's been here, has she, teaching you your duty? just let her try it again, and if I don't raise the devil's delight for her benefit, my name's not Frank Random!"

"Do stop," said Nelly, when she could speak through her laughter, "don't pitch into the poor old thing like that—she meant no harm; but always having heard of her as a model housekeeper, I thought best to profit by her advice, for she called here last week, and this is the way it all come about. I was saying how much more forgetful and negligent the negroes were, or the generality of them, at least, than in the days of slavery, when she replied:

"Well, maybe its so with them that don't *see* after their servants, but mine are always up to time; for I go along and work with them. You'll find, my dear, that even aunt Cloe—and she used to be a first-rate nigger in your mother's day—even she will be spoiled entirely if you don't see after her every day. I consider it the duty of every housekeeper to go into her kitchen and even help the cook if necessary, after she is through helping in the dining-room. Our Jemima rubs the silver an hour, at least, every day, for I'm bringing her up to be *real useful* and none of your fine ladies that's afraid of spoiling their hands."

And she glanced at mine, which you know, Frank, don't look *much* used up, and I had on *all* my rings, too!"

"Confound her for an old dragon," said Frank, "go on."

"Mercy," I exclaimed "Mrs. Scrubbinwell, I never help with any kind of work but only look after the servants to see that they do it properly. My mother never worked, and never taught me to, (except the pleasant work of making ices, jellies, etc.,) and I don't *know how.*"

"Oh, my dear, your good mother lived in the days of slavery, which abomination I'm happy to say has been done away with. Then there was not quite so much need of our helping by hand, as well as by word of mouth—besides, Nelly, dear, though your poor mother was one of the kindest and best of women, she never was considered a model housekeeper."

"Damn her lying old tongue!" roared Frank, wrought up to a perfect pitch of fury by Nelly's story, "I'll teach her to come sticking her ugly red nose into *my* domestic arrangements; she's a perfect old nuisance, and I'll tell her so for a second provocation."

"Gracious goodness, Frank! how you made me jump, shrieking out like that, and saying such dreadful words too—if you don't stop getting so mad at old Fuzzle-guzzle, as you are pleased to call her, I wont tell you another bit of our conversation; whereas if you'll be reasonable and stop swearing, you shall hear it all, and its worth hearing."

"I beg your pardon, Nell, for swearing, and did not mean to, but am so terribly hot-headed, and it did make me infernally mad to hear of that impudent old frump daring to underrate your lovely mother's housekeeping, when the Grange was always so proverbial for good, nay, luxurious living, and open-hearted hospitality—just to think of such a vulgar old thing as Scrubbinhard——"

"Oh, mercy, Frank, not *hard, well*, you are *too* funny."

"Hard as well makes precious little difference, its all she's fit for, but go on, what else did she have to say?"

"Oh, poor old thing, she praised my dear mother very much, and only said she was not quite as particular as she might have been, or as housekeepers are expected to be now-a-days."

"I'll be bound," cut in Frank, "damning with faint praise.—There's a rhyme, Nell, go on."

"And then she said as I was young and inexperienced she would take great pleasure in telling me just what my routine of daily duties should be."

"'By the by, my dear,'" she continued, "were you ever in Mrs. McSweeper's kitchen?" I shook my head, saying I scarcely knew Mrs. McSweeper well enough to be initiated into the mysteries of her kitchen. "Then you have missed a great treat, for it is the very perfection of neatness; such pans and plates! just like silver, and you might eat off of her kitchen tables, they are so clean.'"

"Oh, mercy, thinks I to myself, what would she say to eating off aunt Cloe's tables as a general thing? And, Frank, do you know, on hearing all this, I felt condemned as a miserable, careless housekeeper, and determined to reform, turn over a new leaf, become bustling, energetic—yet as these thoughts flashed through my mind I was too proud to own up to my domestic delinquencies and replied:

"'But, Mrs. Scrubbinwell, I don't see the need of having tables always in a condition that one might eat off of them without plates, and if used constantly, as kitchen tables must be, how is it possible?'"

"I wish you could have seen her horrified look, and how she bristled up like a porcupine about to do battle, while answering:

"'My dear, 'cleanliness is next to Godliness,' and a lady's kitchen should be as clean as her parlor. The fact is, even Mrs. McSweeper's back yard is always so exquisitely neat that I would not mind eating off of her pavement.'"

"'Oh, mercy, you don't say so—that is wonderful!' I exclaimed, looking, doubtless, very incredulous, for a vision of *our* pavement with Sancho, Tass, and little Lee, the puppy, eating their daily mess there, or with the old bones, rusty tin pans, and black Bob's worn-out shoes, and other unsightly things flying round flashed before me, and then—Oh! horrors, Frank!—would you believe it—I got into one of my absurd ways, and burst out laughing; for close on the heels of this dog tableau rose another, of old Scrub, on all fours, taking her dinner with the canines; well, this was rather natural, for she had suggested the idea of dining on Mrs. McSweeper's bricks, why not on *ours?* and I wondered if it would taste less savory than from that model housekeeper's model back pavement!"

"What amuses you, Nelly?" she asked in a very dignified manner, bristling up again.

"Nothing I said, in a state of visible alarm. I was only thinking how unpleasant it would be to take my lunch or dinner off the bare bricks in our yard, for with dogs about, and Frank is so fond of hunting he keeps two setters, and a young one coming on, to say nothing of children, white and black. I scarcely think it possible to keep the back premises in such a *perfect* state of neatness, do you?"

"Well, my dear," she answered, slightly mollified. "I can't agree with you there, for energy can accomplish almost anything, and I think the fault of your house-keepers, generally, is a lack of energy, they lie in bed too late, you should rise at the crack of day, to bring all things in proper order and perfectly neat, not meaning, to be personal, of course, child, and her keen, searching, prying eyes, glanced in a most expressive way round the dining-room, where we happened to be, and where one of the curtains was tied up in a knot, for you know, Frank, you *will* fix it so, when you are mad at the room for being dark, or at me for being given to curtains, I don't know which, and Eddie's gun, and one of the baby's old shoes were tossed on the table, to say nothing of my gloves and veil on the side-board, and little Posey's finger marks all over both the window sashes, especially that one under the knotted curtain, and down by the hearth was one of your slippers which the puppy had dragged in, and I intended to take back to its place, but forgot all about it."

"I'll warrant you," said Frank, tapping Nelly's fair cheek, "my careless pet is not famous for remembering such little matters, and I'd rather have her so, than a second edition revised and improved of old Scrub, or that model house-keeper, Mrs. Ephriam McSweeper!"

"Well!" continued Nelly, "she searched the room with her eyes, while saying she meant no personality, which caused me to remark apologetically, 'don't scrutinize this room, please, for people, wilh babies, cannot emulate either yourself, or Mrs. McSweeper, who have no encumbrances of the kind, for yours are grown up and out of the way, and she never had any.'"

"Ah! that is a great mistake dear, for in my youth, with three or four little children, I was a famous house-keeper, and kept my children beautifully clean too, and Mrs. McSweepers would be a model if she had a dozen; and look at Amanda Overnice, Nelly,' *there* is an example for you, six young ones, a baby always on hand, keeps only one servant besides her cook, and those children always look as if they had just come out of a band-box, she is a model mother as well as a housekeeper."

"Mercy, I ejaculated mentally, as the thought of Eddie, dirty as a pig, up stairs, presented itself. I hope he's asleep, or, at least, that he will *stay* up stairs, but he was'nt asleep, and he did *not* stay up stairs, for just as the words, "model mother," came out, precise and hard, to the ear, as words cut out on a slab of granite would look, in rushed the little scamp, more outrageously dirty than usual, smeared from ear to ear with molosses candy, and black as the back of the chimney! I wish I could have seen the old lady *rear* up for an instant, and then *shrink* as far as possible, within her capacious silk wrappings like a great fat snail trying to disappear within its shell, as after flinging himself on my lap a moment, and peeping up at the stately dame, as a mouse might be supposed to survey the highest of Egyptian pyramids, the little fellow made a dead point at her Niagara fan which has a bird in the center, and was just about seizing it, when, in a fit of despair, saying, 'come go to Betty and get your face washed.' I laid hold of the young invader, and hurried him from the room, without one word of apology or explanation, with regard to his appearance, half inclined to give master Eddie a small dose of my old slipper, and wishing Mrs. Scrub in Joppa! When I returned, she looked severe and dignified, but went on, without any allusion to Eddie's appearance. 'The secret lies in *energy;* you must rise early; *I* am up at the first crack of day, and always have been.' "

"Yes, thinks I to myself, you look hard and old and puffed up and keen, as if you had been on the look out for dust and cobwebs and all sorts of dirt ever since you were married! A chief-of-police infesting the high-ways and by-ways of domestic life, to observe, detect, and bring to light the short-comings of lazy, young house-keepers, and I suppose, Nelly Random; you must be dreadfully lazy and trifling and good-for-nothing, in comparison with such veterans as Scrub, Overnice & Co. And, then and there, Frank, beneath the searching eyes of that domestic inquisitor, that chief of house inspectors, and under the spell of her alarming eloquence, I determined to reform, that is, as far as possible, not that Aunt Cloe's tables can ever emulate Mr. McSweeper's, or our back-yard her back-yard, not that I can ever be up at the 'crack of day,' except to tend the children, for after fussing with baby half the night that is scarcely possible; but then I might do better, and I will, if its in me, which is extremely doubtful; but my intentions are good, you see, for ever since your poor Nelly has been doing penance, by helping in the dining-room and kitchen both, till you caught me at it this morning; and I really believe Aunt Cloe was glad to see me defeated, driven off from her premises, for though silent, her discomfiture at my presence has been evident and visible in the roll of her eyes, and groans of disapprobation as I went about rubbing here and polishing there! But, Frank, when 'model house-keepers' pitch into you like that, what is a poor lazy one to do?"

"Do? why do nothing—at least in their line—for stupid old cases who choose to offer up their lives a sacrifice on the altar of 'model housekeeping' don't deserve either to be admired or emulated—the kitchen should be their sphere of action, for it suits both their tastes and capacities. Look into their parlors, and what do you see? Tables, chairs, everything bolt up-right, looking as if they had been there from the beginning and would be till the end, adorning a small temple of uninhabited splendor,—where photograph albums and other unreadable books look at you from the centre-table as if stuck there with Spalding's glue! Just fancy one's pitching at such a thing as that and tumbling the books, etc., down on the floor, or piling them on the windows, and then transforming said formidable looking centre-piece into a card-table! as *we* do oftentimes in *our* parlor. Oh! Jupiter Amon! I would as soon dare displace the gifts on some holy shrine, or worse still, throw a snow-ball at the bows on Mrs. Scrubbinwell's cap!—Now, Nell, I am going to defeat old Scrub, route the enemy, and put an effectual stop to this meddling. My wish is, that you shall always do your duty, viz: keep house as nicely, and easily, and comfortably as you now do, and to my perfect satisfaction, I don't want to eat off of kitchen tables, or back pavements *a la* Overnice or Scrub or McSweeper, as long, at least, as we have dining tables and plates. Be the unselfish and devoted mother you always are, and if the children do look a little piggish at times, I shall not have the neat-shivers, and am sure you wont either, but one thing I forbid, Nelly, and that is your entering the kitchen for two weeks upon any pretense whatever."

"Two weeks?" cried Nell, "why that's longer than I ever missed going in yet. What's your fancy now, Frank?"

"No matter; my reasons are good; you may look in, but don't cross the threshold for a fortnight, as at the end of that time I want you to invite Scrub and Overnice to dinner."

"Oh, mercy, Frank—to dinner? *We* invite two model housekeepers to *dinner?* I should absolutely die of alarm even at the prospect of such an ordeal."

"No you wont, Nell; my mind is made up, so don't protest. I will furnish the supplies for a first-rate dinner, which aunt Cloe shall prepare without your assistance; the defect you can fuss about to your heart's content in the dining-room, that is pies and cakes, the pastry shall come forth puffy and perfect as usual from aunt Cloe's ebony fingers. It shall be a dinner calculated to transfix these two model housekeepers with wonder—especially when informed that you have not been inside the kitchen for two weeks, which startling piece of intelligence I shall present in due form for their august consideration."

"No, Frank, you could not be so cruel as to tell such a scandalous thing on your poor Nell? Why it would ruin me with all the nice housekeepers in town!"

"I don't care a ——!"

"Gracious, Frank! don't swear again; you are *too* bad."

"Swear I'm not swearing; why don't you let me go on? I only meant to say I don't care a cent for all the nice housekeepers boiled up in a mess as unsavory as that concocted by the witches in Macbeth! My mind is made up about the dinner, and I want two or three of our set invited to enjoy the fun. Don't fret yourself. Everything will go off *splendidly*, and then to see two model housekeepers routed, beaten, by George! what grand sport it will be."

And Frank went off to smoke his pipe, leaving poor Nelly half amused at his freak, and half tormented at the terrible ordeal awaiting her. There was some comfort in the reflection that she could consult Mag. Parker and Nannie Danvers, who were her dearest friends, and kept house in her style, that is, without pretending to be *models*, and who, like herself, cared not one rush about the condition of their neighbors kitchens, or back yards!

CHAPTER III.

"What do you suppose ever possessed Nelly Random to invite *us* to dine there?" said Mrs. Scrubbinwell to her neighbor, Mrs. Overnice, as they sat over their tea, the evening before Nelly's long anticipated agony was to be accomplished.

"Can't imagine, I'm sure; do you know it strikes me as almost *impertinent* for a lazy, careless thing, like Nelly Random to invite two such good managers as you and myself to a dinner-party. *I* am just going out of curiosity, for I know there won't be one thing fit to eat; she leaves everything to that saucy old nigger, Cloe, who, in my opinion is no part of a cook, and such a kitchen as she keeps! they say it's a perfect disgrace, but no wonder, what can you expect from *fashionable* people who lie in bed till 9 o'clock? In the winter they never breakfast till after nine; for a nigger that lived there last year told me so, and then such pigs of children! Why, Tilly McSweeper told me that their faces were never washed more than twice a day, and sometimes only once, just think of it!"

"I believe that," chimed in her companion, "for the other day when I was calling there, Eddie came tearing into the room, looking like a chimney-sweep, *stiff* with molasses candy, and a streaming nose! After pitching head-foremost into his mothers laps, and peeping up at me, every now and then, as if I were a dragon, the young monkey made a dead set on my beautiful new Niagara fan, and was about to seize it with his filthy paws, when Nelly had sense enough, for a wonder, to take him out of the room. Oh! but did'nt I give her a piece of my mind that day, about laziness, etc., perhaps its been of service, and out of gratitude she's going to give us the benefit of her improvement in the house-keeping line."

"Well, maybe so, but I doubt it," said Mrs. Overnice, "depend on it, she's too elegant, too fashionable, and worse than all, thinks herself too handsome ever to be a good house-keeper, or useful in any way! Her mother, my dear, was *literary*, and I never knew a literary woman who was fit for anything, let alone keeping house and bringing up young ones! but we'll see to-morrow, I expect to come home half starved!"

After the first panic of alarm

passed off, Nelly rather enjoyed the idea of having two such veteran old house-keepers to dinner, especially, with an equal balance of her own clique, to participate in the fun of seeing them *routed* by Frank.

The silver, china and glass shone, the damask was spotless, and everything in keeping. No baby shoes, old veils, gloves, or slippers, tossing about; Frank being particularly amiable, we had coaxed him to let the window curtains alone, after she had arranged them, and little Posey's finger-marks were all washed off the window glass! Mrs. Scrubbinwell gave Mrs. Overnice a look of exultation when they entered the dining room, as much as to say, "See the wonders effected by my lecture!"

"What delicious gumbo, Nelly," said Mag. Parker, "I would like the recipe."

"I dare say aunt Cloe will be proud to give it to you," she answered, telegraphing Frank with her eyes, "it is mamma's old recipe—the Grange gumbo was famous, you know."

"I thought you had succeeded in obtaining Mrs. McSweeper's recipe—*she* makes the *best I* ever tasted," snapped in Mrs Overnice, tucking in her gumbo with her spoon held very far down, and her soup-plate tilted the wrong way."

"I never tasted her's," said Nannie Danvers, "but this is by far the most delicious gumbo I ever did taste. Mag, we must flatter up aunt Cloe and try to get the exact proportions."

"Mrs. McSweeper knows the *exact* proportions of everything on *her* table. I never asked how to make anything that she could not tell within a thimble full the precise quantities. That's what *I* call good housekeeping—don't you, Louisa?" turning to Mrs. Scrub.

"Yes, of course I do; one cannot be too particular in such matters."

"Dear me," said Nelly, "it would keep my poor head in an everlasting whirl—worse than unhappy Mrs. Raggs, if I were to dot down in my brain so many proportions of butter, eggs, flour, etc., etc., pertaining to cakes and custards, but as to soups, meat-dishes, and all that sort of thing, my taste might help me, but my memory never!"

"The pastry of this veal pate is perfect, Nelly, said Nannie Danvers, "I know you made it with your own fair hands," looking at her young hostess with a speaking twinkle of the eye, which was intended to say "now is your chance to stun the two model housekeepers, go ahead," for a sketch of the conversational programme had been drawn off beforehand

"I am happy to say," replied Nell laughing, "that my 'fair hands,' as you are pleased to call them, are not much given to such laborious species of amusement, and as I have not been inside my kitchen for two weeks, Aunt Cloe must have all the credit, if there is any due to my culinary department."

If a bomb-shell had fallen and exploded, then and there, in the middle of the table between Mrs. Overnice and Mrs. Scrubinwell their looks of consternation could not have been greater, or their countenances wore a more horrified expression. "Two weeks!" almost, shrieked Mrs. S., "two weeks!" shrieked a half-smothered echo from Mrs. O's capacious mouth, which was over-full of the delicate pastry, and both models gave a little bounce off their chairs, as if seated on gum-elastic cushions.

"Nelly Random, my dear child, how you do talk! it is well we are all friends here, and know your funny way of exaggerating and how much to believe of this most improbable assertion; for, if such a thing should get out in town, it would ruin your reputation as a house-keeper forever, just suppose Mrs. McSweeper should hear it!"

"Well, as I don't keep house to please Mrs. McSweeper, individually, or the town collectively, and only for my husband and true friends, it makes very little difference what estimate is placed upon my house-keeping, by the town, and if all reports be true, regarding Mrs. McSweeper's perfections in that line, she ought to be too constantly occupied with her own kitchen and back-yard to care how often I visit mine!"

"Nelly does not exaggerate either, I assure you ladies," said Frank, turning with his most insinuating smile to Scrub. "She has not been in the kitchen for a whole fortnight, I know, for having caught her there two weeks ago, and actually at work, I put a positive injunction on all such unlady-like proceedings, and as a punishment, forbade her entering Aunt Cloe's domains for a specified time, no matter how long."

The two astonished dames turned the full battery of their eyes upon poor Frank at this critical juncture, and Mrs. S., bringing her tongue to bear at the same instant, said in her most caustic style.

"Really, Mr. Random, you are severe upon those who consider it a necessary part of good housekeeping to look after culinary arrangements!"

"Not at all," responded Frank, blandly, "and there can be nothing personal to the present company, in my remark, for I am very sure such famous managers as we have here, can never find it necessary to frequent the kitchen, save at rare intervals, simply to encourage the cook in a neat and orderly style of conducting matters, or to prevent anything monstrous, such as making up bread in a wash-bowl, feeding chickens off the biscuit-board, or making a dog kernel of the kitchen floor!"

Nelly thought of Aunt Cloe's "style," though guiltless of such monstrous improprieties, and said inwardly: "Well, Mr. Frank, you certainly possess no small share of assurance to turn the tables on two veterans in that fashion," for, so completely astonished were the models, and those of the Random school also, at his audacity, that a dead silence reigned for several minutes, broken at last by Mr. Scrubbinwell.

Now Mr. S. was a small man, with small locks of iron gray hair, branching out in prim comical manner on each side of his small head, adding to the extreme look of apprehension which pervaded his countenance, for his small, dark eyes were always darting round with an apprehensive expression, as if in perpetual terror of something disagreeable turning up. The fact is Mr. S. was a man of small qualities, qualifications, and capacities generally —there was but one great sensation in his composition, viz: his immense apprehension of Mrs. S., and no wonder, for her wrath was prodigious! and quite sufficient to keep several small men apprehensive. He was always on the lookout for clouds on the matrimonial horizon; and having been weather-beaten by storms setting from that direction for a large portion of his life, it was no matter of astonishment to the friends of little Mr. S. that he endeavored to steer as clear of these domestic tornadoes as the very diminutive compass of his small wit would allow! But, on the present occasion, Mr. S. had been indulging rather more freely than usual in some fine old sherry, and felt, under its warming influence, very fine himself, and so bold that his boldness reached the verge of temerity, for the table was between himself and Mrs. S.—to say nothing of the wine—so he came suddenly to the determination of advancing an opinion, and did so, in his own little, peculiar, apprehensive way, looking full in the face of his matrimonial horizon.

"Bless my soul, Polly, I think Miss Nelly—I beg pardon—Mrs. Random is quite right to keep out of the kitchen in such savage weather!" and Mr. S., switching out a small silk handkerchief, wiped the small drops of perspiration from his small forehead, and then to bolster up his small, and rapidly declining courage, gulped down another glass of sherry, poured out by Frank, in expectation of rising storms.

"Mr. S.!" snapped out the extreme indignation of Mrs. Scrub, "You know if there is anything on earth I hate, it is to be called 'Polly.' My name is Mary Louisa—I prefer the latter, and presume that is the reason you always choose the former, vulgarized, for I do think Polly is the vulgarest name on earth." And the capacious breast-works of outraged Mrs. S. heaved with such a prodigious swell as to threaten destruction to all restraining surroundings, such as stays, hooks, etc., as she proceeded. "The weather is never too warm for me to attend to my domestic duties!"

Now the last glass of wine had done wonders with the small man's declining courage, and he replied, through a little facetious laugh: "Well! well, Polly used to be your name in old times when I courted you, my dear, maybe that's the reason I like it, and as to the kitchen, you see, old seasoned timber can stand heat better than new, and Miss Nelly, excuse me, Mrs. Random, you're quite right not to spoil your pretty white skin over the fire; you know,—Polly, God bless my soul, there I go again—Mary, I should say, when we were young, I used to beg you not to fuss so about cooking and such things," and again, Mr. S. looked his smiling tempest full in the face. The first bomb-shell was a squib to this last stunner, and the electrified little speaker (to whom the over-powering effects of his audacity were beginning to be reached) seized the decanter of sherry once more as the cloud burst with a vengeance, for a button flew off and struck his plate as giving another visible swell of offended dignity, the majestic model spoke.

"I don't remember your interfering, at any time or in any way, with my domestic arrangements, Mr. Scrubbinwell, but if you did once, I fancy you never dared a repetition," and looking unutterable things at her frightened little man, she attempted a sarcastic smile, which was a failure, and faded off in a sort of green pallor, ghastly and portentous like the sea-green hue of a thunder cloud!

"Bravo! Scrubbinwell," exclaimed Frank, before the words of wrath were fairly uttered, "you are a trump and I hold you on my side."

"Trumps are not always the winning cards, however, Frank, and as you gentlemen are not expected to know much about the duties of house-keeping, you had just as well yield with a good grace," said Nelly, making a move to adjourn to the drawing-room.

"No we won't give up either, we are the best judges of what our wives ought to do, as they are supposed to study our comfort, and I shall take care to keep you regulated now, Miss Nelly, before you become 'seasoned timber,' to quote from the most eloquent remarks of Mr. S.," and he made a bow to her offended Scrubship, who went sailing out through the dining-room door under a full press of indignation!

"Very well," said Nelly with her light laugh, "manage your own affairs as you will and let other people enjoy the same privilege."

"That's just what I want, Miss Nell," he answered, "so remember you are to keep house to please your husband, *a-la* Random, and not to please the town, *a-la* McSweeper, or any other model in that line," and he smiled a bland expressive smile at the two models, so-called, present. "Don't you think I am right, ladies?"

"Certainly, we do," quickly replied Nannie Danvers,—the two insulted dames were by this time, past speech—"for after such a dinner, Nelly must take a high stand among the models of even a severer school of house-keeping than that supported in this severe town. Let me give you some coffee, Mr. Overnice," and the two defeated feminines were glad to seek an antidote for their warm feelings, in the steaming Mocha. Mr. S. having taken refuge in a corner, as far from his amiable spouse as possible, was looking rather more apprehensive than usual, perspiring freely over his coffee, and still more so over the thought of that storm of wrath which Mrs. S. was nursing diligently to keep it warm. He had ventured an opinion in opposition to Polly under the inciting influence of sherry! May it be long before he indulges in a like quantity of sherry again! and his apprehensive side-long looks over the frail bulwark of a small coffee cup from his corner of refuge, in the direction of danger, expressed as much, and more; and we venture to say, Mr. Scrub will be less intemperate in future, as regards the consumption of old or new wine, and also presumptuous in launching bomb-shells at "Polly!"

"Oh! but wont he catch it, though?" said Frank, so soon as they were alone after that memorable dinner, "and didn't I beat old Fuzzle-guzzle in a fair fight? She wont dare to open her mouth to you about housekeeping again, I fancy. What fun it was! and then to think of weak little Scrub's coming to the rescue! Who would have thought it? Hurrah! for my fine old sherry—how it did sharpen both his little wit and his little courage! I say, Nell, aren't you glad its over, and that we whipped the enemy?"

"Yes, I'm glad its over, but the enemy wont stay whipped. Model housekeepers are not to be extinguished by bomb-shells, either foreign or domestic! Poor little man! how I do pity him getting into such a scrape for me—its too bad. Just imagine how wretchedly he will feel when the sherry dies off, and 'Polly' comes on in full force to the attack. Oh, dear! its dreadful, and I do wish the small idiot had held his stupid little tongue, don't you, Frank?"

"No indeed, it was such fun, and a blowing up wont hurt him a bit, he's used to it. Mercy, how the two old women bounced when the 'two weeks' bomb-shell exploded, didn't they? It was as good as a play! Go up to the baby, Nelly, Betty's roaring 'John Brown's body' in his ear again, and she'll be as deaf as a post before long if you don't stop it. By George! it's enough to split the ear of a Rhinoceros! I'm going to smoke and write to Bob about my triumph over old Fuzzle. *Au revoir.*"

And off went Frank to the library, and Nelly to her baby, both well pleased with the success of a model dinner-party *a la* Random.

AN ALPINE PICTURE.*

(AFTER RUSKIN.)

Ferny pastures, beetling rock,
  Slopes half islanded by streams,
  Glisten in the amber gleams
Of the sunshine,—gleams that mock
Shadowed field, and cool, grey rock.

Farther up, the sobbing pines
  Hold their uncontested sway,
  Shutting out the winsome day
With their sullen, serried lines,
—Mournful, melancholy pines!

Through them, with eternal roar
  From the glaciers, thunder deep
  Torrents, whose terrific leap
Pales them, plunging evermore
Shuddering through the twilight roar:—

Filling with their misty cold,
  All the gorges in their fall,
  As athwart the granite wall,
Which they loosen from its hold,
Down they shiver, blanched with cold.

Thread this craggy mountain path,
  Fringed with ferns that shun the light,
  Climb the ridgy, rugged height,—
Stand within the arch that hath
Bounded in the curving path.

Dark against the whitened foam,—
  Rises a rude cross of pine,
  Whose mysterious, sacred sign

---

* See Modern Painters, page 313.

Points the thoughts that wandering roam,
Skyward, through the eddying foam.

From the lichen'd niche we gaze
  Out upon the pale, far sky,
  Where the peaks that stretch so high,
Catch the tender, dying day's
Last, faint flushes, while we gaze.

Drop your vision fathoms down
  Yonder cavernous abyss,
  Where the waters seethe and hiss,
And the jagged snow-crags frown—
Drop it like a plummet down.

All along the laboring steep,
  Where the traveler's alpenstock
  Needs must pierce the ice-bound rock,
Let your straining glances sweep,
Scanning all the toilsome steep.

Then, look up!—See how the cross
  Casts its symbol-shade sublime,
  O'er the wrack and roar of time
O'er its fret, and moil and loss:
So!—we'll rest here—at the cross.

MARGARET J. PRESTON.

THE TOMB OF NAPOLEON—THE GRAVE OF MARSHAL NEY.

"I desire that my remains should repose on the banks of the Seine, in the midst of that French people I have loved so well."

Such were the words the dying Emperor appended to his last will and testament, as amid the storming and convulsion of the elements, on the lonely and barren Isle of St. Helena, his great spirit separated from its tenement of clay. They are peculiarly touching and sublime. They are not so much the wishes of the man who had once been the pride and glory of the French nation, who, out of chaos, had brought order, and began for them a new career in the race of nations: as the outworkings of a feeling that mingles with the longing of every soul, that realizes the numbering of its days on earth. It matters not how great our hatred towards, or how justly we believe ourselves to have been wronged by, our native land, we all imagine our dust will rest more quietly "'neath our parent turf," and we prefer an enemy rather than a stranger to tread over our tomb.

There was little prospect at the time of the utterance of these words, that the prayer of that spirit, borne down with anguish, would be fulfilled, and that after being guarded for eighteen years by that ceaseless tramp of an English sentinel, those remains would no longer be tossed by the wild waves of the Atlantic, but be laid to rest on "the banks of the Seine," amid the grandest and most heartfelt pageant the fickle population of Paris ever accorded their once beloved Idol.

Such are the overturnings and upheavings of the political world. The Power that contributed more than any other to the restoration of the older and more aristocratic branch of the Bourbon family, was the first to acknowledge the success of the *Citizen King*, seeing not, or caring not that in time to come Louis Philippe would give place to the representative of the man that England "feared and hated."

Though the mortal part of Napoleon was reposing beneath the friendly willow in the green valley of the Atlantic Isle, his name and the glorious memories of his genius continued to agitate the hearts of his people, and the plebeian Bourbon, more sagacious than the rest of his family, who would neither learn nor forget, determined to make himself capital from the bones of his ancestral enemy.

Time, in a measure, had softened even the English nation, and as no good purpose could be served by a refusal, they were willing to grant the demands of the French Monarch, and restore the ashes of the man they had been watching so carefully for nearly a score of years. To give still further significance to the affair, in 1840 an expedition was dispatched under the son of the King to bring the crumbling dust to its natural place of rest, and to pay the last sad offices to departed greatness. When the remains had reach Paris and were carried to the Hotel des Invalides, a *Bourbon King* received the ashes of Napoleon "in the name of France" and, in behalf of her people, welcomed them to their place of repose "on the banks of the Seine in the midst of that French people he had loved so well."

For eleven years, the honored remains rested in the chapel of the Hotel des Invalides, while a tomb was being prepared worthy the nation's hero. The work was completed in 1853, and under the auspices of a Napoleon, imposing ceremonies marked the change to a monument magnificent, but only temporary, as the Napoleons are to forego the past, and sleep the long sleep beside the Bourbon, at St. Denis.

The Hotel des Invalides was built by Louis XIV. at the request of his War Minister, Louvois, in 1671. It is for the reception of old and disabled soldiers of the French armies. Three thousand monuments to the ravages of war dwell here. In its discipline and management are still retained the military regulations, and each of the veterans must have been a pensioner of the Imperial Treasury, and served in some branch of the army for thirty years. The Governor is a Marshal of France. This hospital is one of the noblest works of which the country can boast, for whatever may be said of the French people, among those charges cannot be enumerated the neglect of those who have contributed life or strength to the military renown of this war-loving race. The recollections of past glory are not allowed even here to pass away. On an esplanade in front of the building is a battery of captured guns in which most European nations are represented. The church is decorated with the flags taken during the wars of Napoleon.—Once they numbered three thousand, but most were burnt before the occupation by the allied armies, and now only 34 worn and dirty emblems remain of so vast a multitude. In the vaults beneath are long lists of names that fill one with awe, comprehending that array of soldiers that shed so bright a lustre about the memories of the First Empire, and which, during the beginning of the present and the close of the past century, made France the terror of Europe. We select at random such as Berruyer, Lannes, Eblé, Kleber, Jourdan, Mortier, Grouchy, Bertrand, Oudinot, etc.

There are two churches, an ancient and modern one. Above the former, approached from the Place Vauban, rises a dome which, for beauty and grandeur, surpasses anything of the kind in existence. It is three hundred and twenty feet high and combines the result of thirty years' toil, by one of the most celebrated architects France has ever produced. Beneath this dome rests all that is mortal of the illustrious Emperor.

"The dome measures sixty one yards on the four sides. The portal consists of a triple building with a flight of fifteen steps.—Fourteen columns decorate the principal entrance. There are also fifteen other columns, among which are seen too niches containing white marble statues of St. Louis, and Charlemagne.

"Above the Doric entablature rises a story supported by columns of the Corinthian order. There are also three figures representing Temperance, Fortitude and Prudence. The escutcheon of the arms of France is in the pediment of the portico, and at the summit is a cross, with two figures representing Faith and Charity.

"The principal front is of incomparable richness. Forty composite columns decorate the elevation of the dome, and eight piers support thirty-two columns, on the outside. The inside is lighted by stained glass windows, crowned with heads of angels and cherubim. Twelve windows with semi-circular arches form the attic above. A stone balustrade is placed above the eight large composite piers."

On the cornice above the large piers are plinths supporting candelabra, behind them rises the dome, the form of which calls for all one's admiration. Trophies of arms, in bas-relief, ornament all the largest sides. The dome is supported by four enormous piers. At the four cardinal points are four chapels. The roof of the nave forms four arches. In the pendentives of these arches we see the figures of the four evangelists, admirably painted by Delafosse.

Between the pilasters of the basement are twelve windows which light the drum of the dome. Above, alternating with pannels. are arches on which are painted the twelve Apostles, by Sowvenet.

The cupola that surmounts this dome, contains a splendid painting, by Delafosse, representing "*St. Louis* offering to the Saviour, the sword destined to combat the enemies of the religion of the true God."

Although the Chapel of St. Louis was designed before the genius of Napoleon Bonaparte had developed itself, yet, no place could have been more fitting for his tomb, certainly none grander in its conception, or more exquisite in its execution. Art has here exhausted its powers, yet grandeur and simplicity are so combined, as to produce the most powerful effect. The tall cross pointing Heavenward—God's emblem to man—bespeaks the holy character of the building. Here the emotions of religion and military glory are combined, the feelings that act most effectively on the French heart.

In through the lofty portal, with uncovered heads, the multitude pass. On either side the entrance, are monuments to Turenne and Vauban, which contain their mortal remains, "each a masterpiece of art." They were mighty and unsurpassed as Great Captains, in their day, but the brightness of their genius has dimned before the later hero, and they guard the door of his sepulchre. Passing over a floor of magnificent Mosaic, you reach a white marble balustrade, surrounding a depression, twenty feet deep, under the centre of the dome. Beneath you is the sarcophagus of Napoleon I.

The tomb is only open on Mondays and Thursdays. All day

long eager crowds gather here to pay honor to the venerated dust. Hour after hour the stream passes by, yet, there is no diminution to the vast concourse, and no lessening of that feeling of sacred awe that fills every mind. Above the matchless work of human skill: beneath, enclosed in stone, the mouldering form of him whose name will live while there is an appreciation of heroic daring, or unequaled genius. A soft and gentle light falls around, so delicately shaded, as to appear reflected through mother of pearl. No brilliant light enters here. It comes as if awed by some unseen power, and hangs about the tomb as if unwilling to dispel the sad solemnity of the spot.

Just in front of the depression is the altar of St. Louis. It is a gilt canopy, supported by four twisted columns of black marble, twenty-three feet high, each made from a single block. The altar is surmounted by a figure of Christ, in white marble, attached to a gilt cross. The sides are faced with green marble.

The altar has been raised and a passage opened under it to the Crypt. On either side are marble steps leading down behind the altar, terminating in the gallery, which is adorned with numerous statues. The light is here veiled, and is in harmony with the whole spirit of the place. On the sides of the corridor stand the tombs of *Bertrand* and *Duroc*. The former, after following Napoleon in Egypt, and all his campaigns, both North and South, who bore the exile at Elba, mingled in the dangers of Waterloo, and comforted amid the sufferings of St. Helena, stands as a sentinel at his master's grave. Duroc, whom the Emperor loved as a brother, who shared his triumphs and defeats from 1797 to 1813, and who finally died a soldier's death, in Silesia, divides with the faithful Bertrand, the solemn duty of watching at the gates of his sepulchre.

Beside the door of the Crypt are two colossal bronze statues of stern and forbidding aspect, holding an Imperial crown and sceptre. One personates the civil, the other the military power. Above the door, placed in a block of black marble, is the inscription,

"*Jé désire, que mes cendres reposent sur les bords de la Seine au milieu de ce peuple Francais que J'ai tant aimé.*"

Placed in the middle of the Crypt is the sarcophagus. It is thirteen feet long, six and a half wide, and thirteen high. It is made of a red granite, brought from Finland, is the hardest marble known, and when exposed to the atmosphere defies, unchanged, the lapse of centuries. It is formed of four blocks, and stands on a plinth of green Russian marble. There is a second coffin made of Corsican stone, which encloses the two caskets originally used in St. Helena. The sarcophagus is plain, though beautifully polished, a work which was so difficult as to demand the use of steam.

The pavement around the sarcophagus is of rich Mosaic, in the form of a Roman laurel wreath, with rays of light emanating from every point. In the Mosaic are inscribed the words, *Rivoli*, *Pyramids*, *Marengo*, *Austerlitz*, *Jena*, *Friedland*, *Wagram*, *Moscow*. The circular walls are adorned with bas-relief figures, representing the most remarkable events in the history of France, during Napoleon's reign, while the ceiling is supported by twelve pillars of white Carrara marble, each of which is a large figure, facing the tomb, and holding symbols of as many victories under the First Emperor. These were executed by the distinguished artist Pradier, who died before the last monuments of skill had taken up their proud position. Around the open part of the Crypt, are hung twelve lamps, made from models discovered at Pompeii. Even their light is softened by shading, and they are only used upon the anniversaries of remarkable events which occurred in the life of the illustrious dead.

A small sanctuary leads off the Crypt, called the Chapelle Ardente. It is closed by an iron door, and in it are deposited, the sword used by the Emperor at Austerlitz, the golden crown presented by the city of Cherbourg, the insignia he wore on grand occasions, and seventy flags captured by the French armies. It is dimly lighted by a lamp, and through the grating is seen, in one corner, a statue of Napoleon in his Imperial costume.

This monument to Napoleon, as was said before, in a remarkable degree combines the religious and military element, and to this fact is attributed the selection of the designs by Visconti. The work is not yet completed. The Court or entrance is to be filled up with statues of the twelve Marshals created when the Emperor gave new life to "that institution of the old monarchy." In the centre on a rich pedestal is to be a statue of Napoleon, in military costume, as he appeared on the field of battle. "Thus we have outside, the man—inside, his apotheosis."

Notwithstanding all this beauty and grandeur, the ashes of the great warrior are not to remain here. Louis Napoleon has chosen, as the last resting place of his family, St. Denis, where, for sixty generations the Bourbons have been gathered to their fathers. Whatever may be the fate of the present government, whatever may be the destiny Paris imposes upon France, the name of Napoleon will ever live in the hearts of this people. For a time after his fatal defeat, at Waterloo, and the subsequent occupation by the Allies, when the nation was burning under the shame and ignominy of foreign domination, his name lost its charm, and for a season, allegiance to his glories grew cold. Yet, as the recollection of these has passed away, and his family have again brought France to a proud place in the European Confederation, the bonds that bind them are stronger than ever, tried as they have been in adversity, and the fame of the First Emperor will ever be in the eyes of Frenchmen, their proudest legacy.

THE GRAVE OF MARSHAL NEY.

MEN are generally judged by the manner in which they live, yet sometimes by that in which they die. Whatever may have been the merits or demerits of Ney's conduct, no one can deny that there was, in his death, a sublime heroism which demands admiration. The necessity or even the policy of political executions will remain to the end of time a disputed question. Upon whichever side individual opinions may be, it cannot destroy the veneration of mankind for the soul which, sustained and encouraged by its moral innocence and the justness of its intentions, fights, undaunted, the last great struggle.

Fifty-two years ago Marshal Ney died appealing "to Europe and posterity," and though the *Chamber of Peers* pronounced him guilty of treason, posterity, as he predicted, has reversed the verdict and acquitted him of the crime.

Truly there was some thing sublime in the character of the man who chose "to die a Frenchman rather than live a Prussian." Who, although given, by the Government that executed him, a passport to leave the confines of France, when in sight of a foreign land, gave up the prospect of safety, and preferred to bear all that might follow rather than have his name tainted with a breath of dishonor.

It was on the 7th day of December, 1815, that the fatal sentence was carried into execution. Carried from the Palace of Luxembourg into the adjoining garden he gladly gave the signal that was to end his then burdensome life. The darkness and gloom was in keeping with the sadness of the scene then being enacted. Facing, unblinded, his own soldiers, he fell, in the gray dawn of that December morning, a victim to the broken faith of England, pledged through her representative, the Duke of Wellington.—Hence he was carried to the heights of Pére La Chaise, the city of the dead that overlooks the gay Capital of France.

The manner of his death brought with it no disgrace in the eyes of the people he had so nobly served, and his dust moulders alongside the monuments that record the proudest names in the category of illustrious Frenchmen.

In keeping with a sentiment that pervades everything connected with the death of Ney, not even a cross or a stone marks his grave. Around it on every side are costly monuments and chapels (fitted up as for the living) but among them is one (at least in this sense) unhonored grave.

A small circular space, surrounded with a hedge, and planted with beautiful flowers which are sedulously cared for, is the only material record to the man, whose name was once the watchword of the brave, and whose chivalry was the pride of a chivalrous nation. Few can stand by the spot unmoved. The old guide, who passes by it a score of times daily, sheds tears as, with mingled sorrow and pride, he points, and in broken English exclaims: "There sleeps the bravest of the brave."

DEMORALIZED WEEKLIES.

No one can reflect a moment and fail to see the vast influence of the newspaper press in America—an influence already almost unlimited and growing day by day in power of working good or evil.

In a reading—if not a Red—Republic where "the people is king," there must be some power to govern the sovereign; and with us that unseen influence comes from clean type and white paper.

Though the daily press, especially in great metropolitan centres, leads public opinion—when it does not make it—still the work done by the weeklies is too important to be despised. For these weeklies, in some sort, off-shoots of the dailies, in some sort share their influence with a class of readers, less numerous perhaps, but more important because more thoughtful.

The great daily finds its way at early morning into the hands of the broker, the merchant and the politician. It is hastily turned over for a glance at the news, the markets, or for skimming the political leader: and then it is thrown upon the floor of the horse-car, descends to the servants'-hall, or does duty round a parcel from market. Or perhaps its possessor is a working man, a detrimental do-nothing, or one of "the Fancy." In the first case there is a laborious spelling of the local news and the price list; in the second, a glance at the critiques and a careful study of the Paris letter; while the last reads with delectation of the late "mill," picks the plums from the police report and looks at the advertisements of sport, dog-trainers and rat matches.

But in any case the great daily is born for an object, accomplishes it and then—like the fabled *Ephemeron*—dies before the morrow's sun sees a fresh birth take its place.

It has found its way into some hundred thousand pairs of hands; it has sent through some hundred thousand pairs of eyes into some hundred thousand brains—more or less fruitful—some particular seed best suited to the soil, there to germinate, perhaps.

But the weekly—of equal ability and tone—meets its reader at dinner, or tea, after the business of the day is done; or else it is pocketed carefully till leisure offers for a calmer reading.

The weekly appeals to the mental appetite with just the same difference from the daily as there is between the varied, plentiful but jostled dinner of the steaming *table d' hote* and the substantial, plain, but thoroughly comfortable dinner at home.

While the daily touches boldly, graphically and sometimes thoughtfully, the vital topics of the hour, the weekly has time to collect the cream of many dailies and give it—in a calmer and more scholarly article—dessicated and condensed so as to be readily absorbed and thoroughly nourishing.

The daily appeals to the masses; is the barometer by which they measure the fluctuations of party, of morals and of money.—But the considered utterance of a journal like the *Nation* or the *Round Table* appeals to the few who think for the masses; and thus reacts upon them.

Reflecting therefore upon the important mission to be performed by the weekly journalism of America, we cannot too deeply regret the base uses to which it has come at last:—to pander to the prurient indecency of the great cities, or to the still more base passions of sectional bitterness.

Though the march of demoralization has been wofully rapid, and hurtful, in compound ratio, even to its rapidity, we can clearly trace its commencement to the birth of the mania for popular illustrations. While the organs of Thought and of Reason were, doubtless, a power still, thinkers and reasoners were too few to make them paying investments; and while the number of readers increased immensely, the number of thinkers remained a constant quantity. Thousands of readers clamored, weekly, for something amusing—for something "light."

And then Progress, with the big P, put her tax-stamp upon every publication, and descent began. Now they have something "light" in the moral, as well as the mental balance.

Pictorial illustrations—appealing to the eye and to no deeper sense—naturally attracts many to whom a thoughtful article were Sanscrit, or a humorous sketch utterly incomprehensible. Publishers, finding the quantity of buyers increase as the quality decreased, had little hesitation about reducing the pabulum offered to the level of the greatest majority of palates.

Facilis descensus: and the downward movement, beginning slowly, soon degenerated into a tumble. Papers entirely lost any claim to control, or even to elevate, public taste. They strove solely to cater to that of the greatest number, let it be never so low; and as a result, became simply a budget of pictures, to which the reading matter was loosely adapted.

And yet we have never had a first-class illustrated paper become a great and undeniable power in America. Nothing is more common than the expression of surprise that we never had an American *Punch*.

There is no cause for wonder. Even granting that in the excessive numbers of American readers, there are more thoroughly appreciative of keen and pointed humor than in England, still the fact is undoubted, that the vast majorities here prefer the broad to the delicate. The early death of three or four rather good imitations of *Punch* has satisfied the paper men, at least, of this fact.

A few papers—like the two named above—have, to their great credit, resisted the popular clamor. They have resisted Progress, and repudiated her tax, preferring to force their way by pure strength into a permanent position of utility, rather than grasp a spurious prosperity that only dazzles by the phosphorescent gleams from its own putridity. There can be little doubt which will be better off when the good fight is fought, and common sense is herself again; but, meantime, all honor to the staunch few that battle in it for principle and decency.

Let any one, who doubts the mission of the illustrated weeklies, glance over the almost endless list on the shelves of any newsman in the Union.

He will find political pictorials of every shade of politics, of which the chief attraction is gross caricature of the better—because more prominent—men of every party. Lacking, equally, point of conception and ability of execution, these pasquinades seek "raciness" and novelty; and in the vain search for this, they pry into the private life of public men, drag their misfortunes into flaming publicity, and not infrequently manufacture, wholesale, the grossest and most revolting libels.

He will find the "comic" weeklies worse, if possible, in mechanical execution than the political: and perhaps even beneath them in ability of their subject matter. For their sole object is to amuse—Heaven save the markl—and it is a sad reflection, in turning over the pages, dismal with bald trash, that in thousands and thousands of cases that object is accomplished. But the strictly "comic" weeklies are rarely broadly indecent. Weak as is their attempt at fun, futile as is their strife after point, they yet tend to debase the mental rather than the moral man. Appealing to a class of readers far from eclectic, they seek solely for palpable hits and make up in broadness their woful deficiency in ability of any sort. But, as a rule, they are low rather than ımmoral—coarse rather than indecent.

Next to these upon the counter lie heaps of fashion papers—meet organs of that fashion that is gauged by dollars and diamonds and that has reached the "German" stage on the high-road to *Can-can*. *Fiat justitia*, however. The harm the fashion papers do is rather influential than direct, in stimulating still further aimless rivalry and unwarranted extravagance. Adapted for the rose-tipped digits of upper-tendom they are more tasteful than their plebeian neighbors on the shelf. Their plates are more artistic and their reading matter is of the delicate mush-and-rose-water description that cannot taint the highly perfumed atmosphere of fashion into which they penetrate.

They are not "food for strong men;" but there may be grave doubts if they are yet tonics for very weak women.

But the most pretentious, while

surely the most influential school of weekly literature, is that which assumes to instruct while amusing. Edited with considerable ability, filled with careful engravings of really good drawings and, above all, claiming for themselves a high moral tone, these journals penetrate into every household from the St. Lawrence to the Rio Grande. Not confined to any particular class of readers, they naturally blend the characteristics of the three foregoing grades, and the *mélange* thus offered to the intellectual appetite, might be satisfying, if it were not sometimes sickening.

And their field is so large and varied, that they have become, in some instances, a real power, which we may regret, but cannot afford to despise. Their attractive pictures catch the eye of thoughtless youths and yawning do-nothings; they are a momentary relaxation for thought to wearied men of business. Some special article demands attention even from the solid thinker, or Madame, on the Avenue, must have the next chapters of the vigorous sensational novel. Even straightest laced moralists may find some excuse for cutting the leaves, innocent, perhaps, that a very cunning fox—if not a dangerons wolf—may lurk under the very lamb-like fleece.

Foremost in this school are *Frank Leslie's Illustrated Newspaper*, and *Harper's Weekly*, which is just what it modestly claims to be, "*A Journal of Civilization.*"

There is little in either paper to offend the taste, however much there may be in one of them to shock the prejudices. The former numbers its readers by the hundred thousand, reaches into the South and South-west, as well as the North; and is even reproduced in German and Spanish. It is a source of sufficient revenue to its proprietor to warrant his devoting to it—and to its dozen monthly and weekly off-shoots—an immense building which is a perfect hive of artists, engravers, writers, readers, printers, binders, folders—in short of every one of the busy bees that hum and buzz about a great newspaper. From this machinery each week turns out a dozen varied publications, with the "Illustrated newspaper" as their centre; these are distributed to every corner of the Union and even beyond it; they meet hundreds of thousands of readers of every age, class and position; and to many of these they naturally become an authority.

"*Harper's Weekly*" strives to reach a higher level of literary and moral usefulness, as is the duty of a "Journal of Civilization"—even in its present state. Backed by the capital of the most enterprising firm in New York, and by the influence of the still popular "Magazine," it still finds many readers and many blind believers, although its popularity is monthly waning before the Reconstructed "*Leslie.*"

Newspapers—especially illustrated newspapers—are rarely published for a more philanthropic purpose than to make money; and to accomplish this they must —even if they lead it—bend somewhat to the popular opinion.—

During the war the Southern field was shut to both these, in common with all Northern publications.

It became necessary to make up the lost Southern readers by getting fresh ones at the North.—"*Harper's Weekly*" reveled in a perfect carnival of Southern atrocities, slave-drivings, prisoner-butcherings and all that pleasant school. Upon this, like Jeshurun's ass, it "waxed fat and kicked" to a degree to bring its rival to a like course. "*Leslie's Illustrated*" thereupon produced many pictures of fearfully tattered and painfully emaciated Rebels passing under the yoke to apparently well-fed and certainly well-clothed Federals; nor was it behind hand in showing up in very deep lines and peculiarly black ink the horrors of Andersonville and Belle Isle;—albeit we see no illustrations of Camp Chase.

All this was very natural. The papers were meant to sell and this sold them: and no one can quarrel with Interest for beginning at home where Charity sets the good example. We would think very little of the butcher who insisted on giving his patrons pork when they showed a marked preference for veal; or of the shoemaker who insists on a gentleman wearing pointed toes if he declared for square.

But since the war "*Harper's*" has become a dangerous and incurable lunatic on the radical question. It has out Heroded the Herod at the Capital in more than once striving to slay the male children of the South and the mothers that bare them as well. Latterly, it has worked off the furions paroxysm, however, to that degree that its wild ravings have sunk into impotent gibberings.

"*Leslie*," on the other hand, having had a much slighter attack—he was only inoculated by his neighbor and never took the rabies naturally—may be considered as completely cured. If drunken with the success of his loyal pictures, the generous display of reeling Helots in Washington has quite sobered him now: and his tone each week shows a deeper conviction that a country is better than an anarchy.

Equally able as its strongest rival in literary ability, in originality and in excellence of illustration, it reaches a more widely diffused class of readers, and the evil worked by many numbers of *Harper's* is neutralized by one such cut as that of "The bones-and-banjo Congress"—the point and inspiration of which come from a deeper source than the lines on the wood-block.

Of another school—in fact of its own school—is Bonner's *Ledger*, which is the unique organ of proper sensation. Eschewing politics, and not particularly strong in any way, but novelty; it certainly outstrips all competition in that. Though there is seldom any thing startling in the *Ledger*, there is never anything shocking; and if not possessing the unhealthy vigor of *Harper's*, it is at least—

> "Weak without rage, without o'er-flowing full."

From its inception, Mr. Bonner has believed that one dollar judiciously spent in advertising, would bring in two; and he has literally advertised his paper into such a paying circulation as will enable him, in his own language, "to buy the best of everything."

Upon this principle, he lately bought the great trotter "Dexter," for his private wagon; and he moreover purchased the brains of Mr. Beecher for a very flat novel, and the wonderful memory of Mr. Greeley, whose "Recollections of a Busy Life," date back some *two hundred and forty years!*

But Mr. Bonner's last card is the life of General Grant, by his father. And though we are prepared for a war upon Lindley Murray, that may be vigorously waged "all summer," doubtless, the author of his existence is the best person to describe it. No doubt the *Ledger* would print next, the early days of Thaddeus Stevens, if the oldest inhabitant could be found to remember them.

But with all its clap-trap, the *Ledger* is just the paper for the masses—not above their comprehension, and never verging upon the boundaries of impropriety. Its owner justly described it in saying:—

"I never print anything that an old lady would be afraid to put in the hands of her little girls when she goes out of an afternoon."

This—and his persistent advertising of unique sensations—has made the paper, perhaps, the greatest pecuniary success of all the Weeklies.

But if your news-dealer is a respectable man—if he have a family, or a reputation—it may be that you will have to remove a goodly pile of literature before coming to the substratum of veritable "Demoralized Weeklies." These may be classed as comprising the journals of the prize-ring, where all its brutal and degrading features are exaggerated in sad caricatures of the little that is human in this inhuman pastime: of the *Police Gazettes*, in which we find the most obscene and revolting chapters of criminal low-life displayed in flaring pictures, and described in unctuous—if ungrammatical—exactitude; and, finally, of the plenipotentiary, and fully accredited organs of open debauchery.

These latter, have, within a short time, come to play so important a *role* in our journalism as to deserve more than a passing notice; if, indeed, such very filthy pitch could be touched without defilement. They search the lowest foreign publications, and extracting from them the vilest pictures of depravity, broaden their outlines and deepen their tints. They dive into the loathsome purlieus of our own cities, and fishing up their reeking filthiness, spread it openly before a public, who snuff up with distended nostrils the savor, as that of a feast. They glory in being the gazetteers of fashionable brothels; and seek to drag to a still lower level, the indecencies of the naked ballets in which our Northern cities riot to-day.

In short, they are receptacles for every species of moral filth that cannot find sewerage through other channels; are the records of most brutalizing acts that transpire in those nameless haunts—

> "Where Satan shows his cloven foot,
> And hides his titled name."

Vilest among those that are all vile;—very Arch-Bestials in a carnival of beastiality are the latest born among them—"*Stetson's Dime Illustrated*" and the "*Last Sensation.*"

These twins—for born near the same time, they are of the same size, have the same debauched features, the same imbecility—leave nothing more to be desired by the Low-Priests of depravity. They exceed the wild prayer of those who asked "An Anti-Slavery God;" for, in the vilest terms, they

> "Preach the Gospel of Murder and pray for Lust's
> Kingdom to come!"

They are veritable "Bibles of Damnation;" and their "Genesis" would bring a blush to the cheeks of those filthy monsters that Gulliver saw, as slaves to the brutes.

Such, in unvarnished English, are some of the illustrated weeklies, one finds upon the shelves of every book-man in this patent republic of free thought and free speech. And they sell with a rapidity that makes us wonder while we grieve.

"I have done my best," said one of the first metropolitan dealers: "I have written to the Chief of Police, stating that some of them are unfit for exhibition anywhere, and that they should be at once suppressed. He does nothing, my customers demand them and I sell hundreds of each."

There are two very cogent reasons why the chief of Police "does nothing." The dealer gave the first in a nutshell, when he said "my customers demand them." It is a sad truth that popular taste—fed so long on the very highly spiced diet of sensation—has become so morbid as to crave this peculiarly putrid food. There are thousands of readers who, beginning on the very antiphlogistic "*Ledger*," passed thro' the intermediate courses of the "*Phunny Phellow*" and the *entremets* of the "*Police Gazette*" till they now can relish nothing more wholesome than the "*Last Sensation.*" And these gourmets are not confined, as one might suppose, to the dregs of the reading population. Solid looking men, decent looking boys and even quiet seeming girls elbow and jostle each other in the struggle to get late numbers, still damp from the press.

I am informed that many of them find their way into the most fashionable quarters of every Northern city, where they give a zest to Madam's early chocolate, or share the sacred privacy of Miss's own chamber. Public taste, on both sides of the Atlantic, has been educated down to a low grade by a judicious course of Miss Braddon, Ouida, *et id omne genus.* With us on this side, the course has been generously illustrated with the nude drama and the numberless criticisms thereof, good, bad and worse—but all couched in the very plainest of plain English. Our Police machinery, too, lacks somewhat that precision of action characterizing that of Europe; and its officials become most opportunely deaf, or conveniently blind, when occasion demands.

Here then are the two reasons.

A vitiated and morbid public craving,calls for such publications and their sales are immense. The profit tempts some influential or wealthy publisher to do in reality the work, and reap the benefit from it, while some unknown individual is the ostensible head.—Without *knowing* anything of the sort, one may make a shrewd guess that the Chief of Police, or his subordinates, must receive some equivalent—whether in money, in influence or in political assistance matters little—for carefully ignoring the fact that papers are daily exposed under his nose that far exceed the point of illegality. But with a public crying "bread and bestiality"—as the old Spaniard cried "*Pan y Toro*"—and a police that tacitly echoes the cry, there is no telling to what depth literature (so-called) may not be dragged down.

But one fact comes nearer home to our Southern people than this. We have long looked to the North for a large proportion of our books of amusement and instruction.—With the far more capable machinery that the North had at command for their production, this was but natural. She got up far better picture papers, too, than we could and at a much less cost. Therefore these papers penetrated into the heart of our territory; and it was only when they were forced out by the blockade that our people ceased to read them. Even the gross libels upon Southern men and manners, that coined money for "*Harper's Weekly*" during the war, have not sufficed to expel it altogether since its close.

But if we must have the literature of the North, there is no reason why we must have its immorality as well.

Crushed, ruined and conquered as our people are, they can only be degraded by their own act.—Living in small congregations and with almost every thought concentred on the struggle for bread, our people are removed from the temptations of the festering masses of every great city. They have but little time and no taste for indecent displays on the stage; and the naked Drama would find few admirers in a trip from the Potomac to the Gulf.

Why then do they permit the introduction from the North of a poison more subtle and more dangerons because forging the name of literature and put in a shape attractive to the young, the thoughtless and the weak; even while dressed with the scantiest drapery of propriety that

"Gives all it can and bids us take the rest"

The writer had late occasion to travel through an intelligent portion of the South. In every train, in every town, and at every station he had a sight, or a sound of "*Stetson's Dime!*"—"*La-ast Sensation!*" from the Newsboys.—These latter were in most cases indigenous to the wood-nutmegiferous corner of the Union. Born in the shadow of Plymouth Rock and weaned on the east wind, their wits are as sharp as their features; and—with a splinter of the Sacred Stone in breeches pocket—they have wedged their way into the South and vend the products most congenial to them.

"La Crosse Democrat and Leslie sell well; and Harper sells a little," answered a very sharp-faced specimen to a query—"*But, Lord! I sell ten Stetsons' and ten Dimes for one of anything else I have!*"

And this boy's information was endorsed wherever I made the inquiry.

If these new publications—still in their infancy—have already acquired a foothold in the South, they cannot fail to have a future, fraught with infinite evil. It matters not what portion of our people are the buyers. We might as well stop to enquire if it was the freedman, or Yankee emigrant only, who had the small-pox, or the plague. The poison has certainly made an entry, and the virus must spread. Actual cautery is the only remedy; and it is a hard case if there be not local law enough, left in the South, to summarily stop the sale of such broadly indecent sheets.

It is the plain duty of the press to promptly and fully expose their true character: of every newspaper to warn its readers of their vicinage, as they would of the appearance of the tobacco-worm, or any other foul vermin.

This done; and there is little doubt that the strong innate love of decency our people possess, will,—if it do not drive them entirely out—at least, prevent much harm from the visits of the "Demoralized Weeklies."

THE HAVERSACK.

In the Spring of 1861, when the Confederate and Federal forces were stationed at Pensacola and Fort Pickens, and before the secession of the State of Virginia, the United States steamer "Wyandotte" lay between the opposing forces, floating a flag of truce. Then, civilities between the two armies were not uncommon, and the death of Captain Berryman, Federal Commander of the Wyandotte occurring, permission was obtained to inter his remains in the cemetery of the "Marine Hospital," then in our possession. A Naval procession from the Federal fleet, outside the bar, brought the remains to the wharf, and by invitation, the Confederate officers united with the Federal in the procession, thence to the grave.

A Federal "Officer of the day" was arranging the officers, irrespectively, according to rank, as the "Regulations" required. It was before the adoption of the Confederate uniform, and our officers were dressed as fancy, or convenience, suggested to the various companies that composed our command. The Quarter-master of the —— Alabama regiment, a whole-souled patriot and gallant soldier, was present, in the uniform of the volunteer company of which he was a member before the war. This consisted of a coat of blue cloth, single-breasted, a "navy cap," with broad band of gold lace, a small, straight sword, with white bone handle and brass scabbard, and the whole surmounted by a pair of epaulettes, *borrowed from a Major General of militia.* The officer of the day seemed "spiced with a little humor," and as his eye fell upon our Quarter-master, he at once carried him to the rear of the column; soon he returned and carried him to the front; again in passing along the line he removed him to the center, and with an air of anxious solicitude, remarked,

"Sir, if I fail to assign you your proper place in this procession, you must really excuse me, but you will appreciate the difficultics under which I labor, when you remember that you have on a Commodore's cap; a Major General's epaulettes; a Captain's coat, and a Sergeant's sword."

A wounded Irishman at Shiloh refused to be carried to the rear, saying that he wanted to see "the prasoners." He took out his short pipe, filled it up, struck a light and began to puff like a loyal editor. As the prisoners filed past, including General Prince, he kept inquiring every minute, "I say, boys, what State are you from?" No one deigned a reply, all strode along in sullen, not to say majestic, silence. At length, one of our Northern brethren, being led along in durance vile, turned upon Patrick and cursing him bitterly said, "I'm from Ohio, you impertinent Irish rebel."—Pat, without taking the pipe out of his mouth and without a moment's hesitation, answered, "and a good deliverance it was to the State of Ohio when you joined the Yankee army!"

When we look around and see the number of graceless fellows at the South, who have turned their backs upon friends and country, and joined the ranks of the enemies of the white race, not to say of mankind, we are disposed to echo Pat's sentiment and exclaim, "and a good deliverance it was to the South when you joined the Radical party."

H. T. J. sends from Roxboro, N. C., the two following anecdotes:

I have just been rummaging your "Haversack," which, by the way, I find supplied with much daintier viands than our haversacks were of late wont to be filled with, and have concluded to pay for what I have had, by dropping a bone or two of my own into the capacious receptacle. "Of moving accidents by field and flood" you have had a rich abundance. I propose to vary the repast now by two of different characters; for I see that your *Haversack* is like Littleton's pudding, wherein "is not commonly put one thing alone, but one thing with other things together."

And first, as apposite to these times of rampant "loyalty," let me take you back to the super-patriotic era of Know-nothingism. Two men, whose initials only I will give, to wit: H. C., a Democrat, dyed in the wool, cut out with Democratic shears and made up with Democratic needle and thread, and G. W., a Know-nothing fresh from the furnace, and red-hot with enthusiasm, met in our town and straightway fell into the inevitable political wrangle. They *jawed* each other by the hour and neither was convinced, because each, intent only upon what he was saying himself, paid no attention to what the other said. At last W., whose *forte* was the fervor and brilliancy of his charge, becoming weary of the Grant-like, dogged obstinacy of his adversary, brought up his reserve, determined to end the fight and the foe together. "What, sir," said he, "did General Washington say? Didn't he say 'put none but Americans on guard to-night?'"

"What if he did?" said Hardy, "everybody knows he was nothing but *a durned old tory!*"

It is useless to add that *Grandison* was routed.

My next is an incident of prison life:

It was my fortune to spend the last twenty-one months of the war at that delightful Summer resort, and favorite retreat, of Confederate officers, known in "the bills of mortality," as Johnson's Island. (And hereby hangeth a tale which I could unfold, were it in place here, that would startle some of the sanctimonious and sanctified haters of the late "hell-born rebellion." Of them, though in their own time. It is a great consolation to know, that if they never get their deserts, on earth, they will in ——.)

I had for a mess-mate, Lieutenant B. of the 55th North Carolina. One night, a couple of the prisoners made their escape, and the next night the prison yard was alive with men, crawling and creeping about, trying to "follow suit." None, however, succeeded. On the return of my roommates, they told the following on my friend, George:

George, they said, was getting on finely, crawling on hands and knees, down a ditch, which served as a screen, when to his sudden dismay, looking up, he found a Yankee within six feet of him, with his "piece" at a "ready," and, apparently, about to blow my friend's brains out.

"Don't shoot!" yelled George, springing up; "Don't shoot. I surrender!"

No answer from the Yank, and George, walking up, found that he had surrendered to a pump.

In a skirmish near Corinth, Thomas McCulloch, a private in the regiment of Colonel (afterwards General) J. H. Clanton, received a wound in the right arm, which so shattered it, that it was plain, amputation would be necessary. His Colonel, observing the wound, said to him as he was retiring,

"I am sorry, Tom, that you have lost your best friend."

With a smile on his face, the wounded man replied,

"Never mind, Colonel, it was lost in a glorious cause."

This noble fellow is now living in Montgomery, Alabama.

Captain Owen Finnegan, a gallant Irishman, now living in Mobile, Ala., was the Captain of a steamboat on the Alabama river, in the days of the Confederacy, so-called. After the surrender, Captain F. received an order to carry down to Mobile, the dead bodies of the Federals who fell at Selma.

"I never liked your people when alive, and I don't think that I will like them any better when they are not smelling good," said Captain F. in reply to the order.

In a few hours, a Federal officer, with a squad of soldiers, came to the steam-boat, and said to Captain F.,

"I have come to compel you to carry the bodies of the Union soldiers from Selma, to Mobile, as it has been reported that you refused to obey the order."

Captain Finnegan. "I didn't refuse to obey the order. How are the bodies to be taken?"

Federal Officer. "They are all in boxes."

Captain Finnegan. "So far from refusing, it would be a great satisfaction to me, to carry in boxes, the last one of the Yankee army."

S. T. F., a late captain in the so-named 24th Texas regiment of infantry, in the so-called Confederate army, sends from San Antonio, Texas, the following:

Shortly after the evacuation of Atlanta, Ga., by Hood, and while our forces lay on the Atlanta and Macon road, it was announced that President Davis had arrived at Head Quarters, and would soon review the army. It was also reported that the late Governor of our beloved Texas was one of his Excellency's Staff.

The day for review arrived and the army was displayed in line of battle, several hundred yards in rear of the breast-works, while the reviewing party rode in front. The President and Staff approached our division, and of course, recognized Cleburne's well-known flag. The Governor dropped back and reined up in front, as he supposed, of a Texas regiment, but he was really before the notorious 5th Confederate regiment, composed of all nationalities, but particularly of Irish boat-hands and railroad employées from Memphis, Tennessee and Helena, Arkansas. The distinguished civilian raised his hat very solemnly and remarked loud enough to be heard by the whole regiment, that he was "Governor —— of Texas, but that out of respect to the President, he did not wish any loud cheering or unusual demonstration." Whereupon a big specimen of Irish rebeldom cried out in a loud voice, "Who the bloody h—ll is Governor —— of Texas, and who the divil cares for ye?" There *was* an unusual demonstration, but not exactly of the kind expected by the eminent statesman.

Colonel J. G. C., of Huntsville, Alabama, gives us the name of another hero in the ranks.

Private Moses Long, of the

19th Alabama regiment, threw a burning shell out of the intrenchments, on Kennesaw Mountain, during Johnston's retreat from Dalton. We wish to preserve a record of all such deeds of heroism.

The gallant Colonel gives, also, an incident in his own military experience.

"The afternoon before the battle of Murfreesboro', or Stone River, witnessed a terrific artillery duel between the opposing armies. Night came on, damp and cold, but all fires were forbidden on the advance lines, though permitted in the rear. I was in command of a brigade, and while adjusting my line for the night, a member of my Staff reported that he had found a lime-stone sink where a fire could be built, without exposing the light. After I had completed the arrangements for the night, I went to the sink and let myself down. It was about eight feet deep and ten feet in diameter. A match was applied to some dry leaves and cedar brush, and I soon recognized the smell, and soon after the explosion, of a fuse. It proved to be a 12-pound Schrapnel shell, but by a singular protection of Providence, the shell itself failed to explode. *We left the pit.*"

The life of the bravest of the brave, as well as the truest of the true, was thus miraculously preserved.

We suppress the name of the principal party in the annexed Court Martial incident and give a fictitious one to the witness:

A poor fellow, moved and instigated by the Father of all mischief, had Butlerized some property not belonging to himself.—He was brought before a Court Martial, and having failed to establish an *alibi*, he next resorted to the expedient, so often practiced, of proving "previous good character." Jerry O'Flynn was called upon to prove the integrity of the Confederate Butler. Now it so happened that Jerry did not know any thing particularly good about the accused, and his conscience was too tender to permit him to swear an untruth to save an afflicted friend, though his kindness of heart prompted him to say all that he could consistent with the obligation of his oath. He stood, therefore, scratching his head with a perplexed air, when the prisoner proposed the point-blank question: "From your previous knowledge of my character, don't you believe me to be an honest man?" Truth and conscience were on one side, friendship and good feeling were on the other. Jerry was sorely puzzled. At length, a bright thought seemed to strike him, and with a happy smile and relieved expression, he exclaimed, "faith, an you would be an honest mon, Jock, ef there was nothing to stale!"

We sometimes hear even Southern men trying to excuse the *diabolism* of the Radicals, upon the ground that they mean well and are *honest* in their intentions. At such times, Jerry O'Flynn's testimony *will* recur to our mind and we are constrained to reply, "they would be honest if there was nothing to stale!"

One of the saddest comments upon human consistency was to be found in the vast number of Irish rebels in the Federal service fighting against the rebellion, and of Germans in the same service, who were exiles from home for outbreaks against their own government. The rebellion could never have been suppressed, had not the Federal army been swelled to its vast proportions by these foreign rebels. Irish rebels in blue uniforms lay thick upon Malvern Hill, Marye's Heights, Chickamauga, and in fact, upon every battlefield of the war. They fought everywhere with the characteristic courage of their nation upon whatever side they happened to be, and with characteristic faithfulness to the banner under which they had enlisted. When the fortunes of war made them prisoners to either party, they were treated with great kindness by their own countrymen in the ranks of the conqueror. We have heard one of them in our service tell how he was saved from starvation in that Andersonville of the "loyal North," known in Dixie as Johnson's Island, by the generous exertions of one of his own people in the Federal ranks.

Sometimes, however, captors and prisoners revived their old religious, political or domestic feuds and had a regular set-to in the old Tipperary style. Col. O., of the 4th N. C. regiment of infantry gives us an incident of the latter kind at Manassas, in the first year of the war.

Pat was one of the famous Tigers of Wheat's battalion, and was well known for his frequent confinement in the guard house, at Manassas station, while the troops were quartered at that point. The confiement seemed to have been the result of Pat's native fondness for anything, and everything, of a stimulating character, and which he seems to have possessed the faculty of finding and obtaining, however faithfully preserved by Surgeons as "hospital supplies," or by Commissaries, for "bad weather," and "extra duty," and when once it was found, all his shrewdness and cunning were soon obscured, or forgotten, in a glorious state of intoxication.

On one occasion when our hero was paying the penalty for some such breach of "good order and military discipline," a couple of prisoners, who had been captured on the picket line, were committed to the "Bull-pen," where Pat was recounting to a dozen comrades, in a most amiable and amusing manner, the adventure which had brought upon him his present trouble. The cry of "fresh fish!" "fresh fish!" attracted his attention, as the two new comers, in blue blouses, were introduced. Pat, who it seems, had been an old Tar on the Mississippi river, at once recognized an old acquaintance, with whom he had taken many fisticuffs, in former times, and who had joined the other side.

"Halloo, Mike! you here! and its meself that made ye cry quarthers minny a time afore, and its meself that can do it agin if ye are not objecting," said Pat as he squared himself to receive an attack.

The prisoner replied:

"Arrah, it's you, is it, you blatherin dog, that would be afther another licking sich as you got afore, when I use to know ye. An it's that is it? Thin, by the powers, jist let my loving honies here, with the grey jackets on, clear the deck, and it's Mike that'll taich you how to welcome a friend."

With this, he gave the hero of the whiskey raids a blow that landed him on his back in the midst of his companions.

"Fair play!" "fair play" rose from a score of by-standers, and in an instant a ring was formed for the old acquaintances. Pat was on his feet in an instant, and returned his friend's greeting in a most cordial manner, and at it they went in the most professional style. For full ten minutes the conflict raged, the result seemed doubtful, and more than once Mike's friends (a dozen of whom had been previously captured) raised a shout of triumph, as the contest seemed to be in his favor, but at length he roared, "take 'im off, take 'im off! I surrender, I give up, and by my soul, I'll niver harm a hair of your head agin, and will iver call ye the politest gintleman in all Tipperary."

A Chaplain sends us, from Lexington, Virginia, the anecdote below:

Your incident of the race between the "Big Preach," and the "Little Preach" reminded me of an incident which occurred at Cedar Run Mountain, and in which your correspondent must confess to have been an *active* participant. Just as a certain brigade was going into action, the Chaplains and Surgeons belonging to it rode up on a high hill, on the flank, which commanded a splendid view of the field. They were enjoying the grand panorama, not a little, when a Yankee battery came into position, and—perhaps mistaking the party for some General and his Staff—opened on us with four pieces. The missiles came shrieking through the air, falling dangerously near; we unanimously concluded that we "had no business there," and, accordingly, left, without "considering the order of our going." One of the Surgeons had a negro boy, mounted on a fine horse, who led the party to the cover of the hill. When the Doctor came up with him, he began to abuse him for being so much frightened, and for riding his horse so hard. The boy meekly replied:

"I didn't like the whizzing of them things any better than the rest did—and I don't think you ought to blame me, Doctor, 'cause my horse can beat yours running."

An explosion followed, for it was evident that the Doctor, as well as the rest of us, made the best time he could.

Col. M. T. P. sends from Bolivar, Tennessee, the incident below:

I send you an account of an actual fact, showing with what dread the children and women regarded the troops of the United States, who "occupied" this District. In 1863, this town was under command of a dirty scoundrel from Springfield, Illinois, named Brayman, who disgraced the uniform of a Brigadier General, U. S. A., and whose command did unlimited stealing. My neighbor's three-year old girl, talking to her mother, said, "Mamma, will General Brayman and his Yankees go to Heaven?"

"I hope so, my daughter," replied the mother.

Little blue eyes exclaimed "Oh! mamma, please don't let them, I am afraid they will steal God!"

You can judge the mother's feeling when the child expressed her little *feeling*, and upon my word Brayman deserved the dread of the child.

During the campaign of General Early, in the Valley of Virginia in 1864, and while his army was in position on Fisher's Hill, near the town of Strasburg, the Federals made a flank movement across North Mountain, thereby turning General E.'s left, which caused a general stampede on the right and centre.

During the confusion, amid the bursting of shells and rattle of musketry, General E. was endeavoring to rally his men, when a *slightly demoralized* reb came running by the General, minus hat or gun, and in reply to the General's order to rally, exclaimed, "how in the h—ll can a man rally without a hat or gun?"

G. B. M.

Trion Factory, Ga.

EDITORIAL.

We have all along based our opposition to the Reconstruction Bill, upon the ground that it puts the life and property of the South at the mercy and control of ignorant and irresponsible negroes, who must necessarily become the dupes of the vilest and basest of mankind. Nothing has so effectually demonstrated the utter unfitness of the negroes to exercise the elective franchise, as the selections they have made of candidates for office. They have chosen as their champions, negro-traders, slave-drivers of the most brutal type, or men whose life-record had been hatred of the Union. The trafficker in flesh and blood, the brutal master and Yankee hater are now the standard bearers for "the man and brother." Hunnicutt, of Virginia, embodies in his own proper person, the three qualifications, which seem to be the most popular with the deluded negroes. Holden, of North Carolina, is a life-long nullifier and secessionist. He raised a hue and cry against

Professor Hedrick, of the University of North Carolina, and had him driven out of the State, for advocating Fremont for the Presidency. He succeeded in banishing H. H. Helper for a similar offence. He signed, with his own gold pen, the Ordinance of Secession, which took North Carolina out of the Union, wiped the pen carefully and said "that he intended to leave it as an heirloom in his family." He, for weeks and months, declared, through his paper, his "unalterable opposition to negro suffrage." This man is now the negro candidate for Governor of North Carolina!! All the negro pets in the State are men of precisely the same type.

The Raleigh *Register*, a "truly loyal" Radical paper, published at the Capital of the State, gives the following pen-and-ink sketch of the negro leaders:

W. W. Holden is a disfranchised traitor, by the laws of the United States, and he could not take his seat if elected.

He has also declared that his object in wishing to stop the war was to "*save slavery.*" He has declared, since the war, that opposition to negro suffrage was the most conspicuous of "Union landmarks." He tried, during the war, it is said, to put his negroes into money.

D. A. Jenkins, of Gaston, is the Holden candidate for Public Treasurer. He was a notorious slave driver and negro trader, and is "charged with having *hung a negro woman* by the neck until dead."

Samuel W. Watts, of Martin, is the Holden candidate for Judge in the Sixth District. He was in Franklin county, during the war, hunting fugitive negroes *with dogs.*

John V. Sherard, of Wayne, is the Holden candidate for Solicitor in that District. Col. Jenkins states, in his public speeches, that, when he was Attorney General, he prosecuted Sherard, in Johnston Superior Court, for "*whipping an old negro man to death*, and convicted him of *manslaughter.*"

This is a precious picture! The man who drove Prof. Hedrick out of the State, (though one of the most gifted and patriotic men in it) on account of very mild anti-slavery views, is now the adored idol of the negro race, in North Carolina.

The negro pet, in South Carolina, was banished from all decent society, in Columbia, for his brutality to his negroes. We have heard one of the most prominent citizens in that State relate a most revolting instance of this fiend's cruelty. His joining the negro party is due to his hatred of respectable people, for the contempt with which they treated him, on account of his outrageous treatment of his negroes.

In Georgia, the man most confided in, by this ignorant class, next to Brown and Bullock, was once an overseer, noted for his heartless severity. The *loyal* Governor Brown himself, is the very same individual, who ordered the seizure of Fort Pulaski, on the 3d Jan., 1861, *some weeks before the Secession of Georgia.* He was so extreme in his zeal for the Southern cause, that he could not wait for the action of his State. With the same hot zeal, he seized, in the Port of Savannah, private vessels belonging to parties in the North. But he is now a loyal man, because he favors negro equality; while Ben Hill, who always opposed Secession, is branded as a traitor. Truly, we have fallen upon strange times!

In Alabama, the negro idols are of the same class as in the four States alluded to. We learn from the *Metropolitan Record* that General Jas. H. Clanton, of Montgomery, had an interview with General Meade, in which he gave full-length portraits of the negro leaders in that city, which have their counterparts in every city, town and village of the South

Gen. M.—I have been informed that armed white men waylaid and deterred negroes from going to the polls.

Gen. C.—Gen. Meade, I pronounce your informants liars and scoundrels, and am responsible, personally and every other way, for what I say. The frauds were against, and not by the Conservatives. I cannot give you a better idea of the character of the white Radicals in Alabama who managed the recent election, than by informing you who they were in this city. At one box, "Norcross," not a citizen of Alabama, but of Pennsylvania, and correspondent of Forney's *Press*, presided. He is a brother-in-law of Keffer, who is candidate for Commissioner of Internal Resources in this State, and don't claim a vote here. The second box was presided over by one John Cloud, a most notorious character for his age. The third year of the war, when only about fifteen or sixteen years of age, and not liable to conscription, he volunteered and joined my brigade, and was mustered into the service of the Confederate States, taking a solemn oath to defend and bear true allegiance to the same. He remained in the company to which he was attached until he was driven out of camp for being guilty of all manner of villainy, such as obtaining money under false pretences, stealing from his messmates, &c. Passing himself off as an officer, he traveled through Georgia, living by his villainies. He was published in the newspapers of the State as a most notorious scoundrel and swindler, which charges were uncontradicted by him or his friends, if he had any. I can prove him to be a thief by men in this city who were born North, who reside here and were Union men during the war. As manager of the election, he took the iron-clad oath, I suppose, with impunity. A brother of his, who was in the Confederate army as a volunteer, was a manager of another box. I heard the former, while acting as manager, haranguing the negroes around the polls, and advising them how to vote. I have it from good authority, that he took votes out of negroes' hands which did not have "Constitution" upon them, and substituted others.—The father of these young men was an enthusiastic Confederate, and a surgeon in the army, though past the conscript age. He was the Radical candidate for Superintendent of Education in the recent election. At a third box, one Wynn presided as manager, who, from the best information I can obtain, is a robber. Since the war, I am informed, he was one of a band who at midnight went to the house of an old citizen about seventy-five years of age, residing near Wetumpka, Ala., and hung him to the joist by the neck until life was nearly extinct, to extort from him gold, which was supposed to be hid about his place. His stepfather, was also a Radical candidate at the recent election. If such men, General Meade, were selected and permitted to manage the election in such a city as Montgomery, how must it have been in the interior?

The negro idols in Florida, Mississippi, Louisiana, Arkansas and Texas, all have a similar record. They are, with few exceptions, Yankees of the Bureau school of corruption (and the world has never had a worse in any period of its history,) or when Southern-born they are old negro traders, brutal masters or fire-eaters of the most ferocious type. Banished from decent society because of their brutality, or disappointed in their hopes of political preferment, they hate, with a bitter hatred, the culture, the refinement and the virtue of the land of their nativity, and seek to drag down to their own level, those of better birth and purer morals. Hence, they have naturally sought an alliance with an ignorant race, who are easily deceived and betrayed.

Starting out with uttering a known falsehood about the insecurity of life and property at the South, the Reconstruction Bill has developed an amount of baseness, which the world had hitherto supposed to be impossible, in a civilized nation. So much bungling, too, has been shown in the provisions of the Bill, and so little skill in its details, that the Satraps have been constrained to proclaim Conventions to be called, which had been defeated, and Constitutions to be accepted, which had been rejected. But for the active exertions of the military commanders, the whole thing would have been a farce and a failure in all of the ten States.—Policy required that those alone should be counted in opposition, who took a decided stand against Reconstruction, but by a singular blunder, the most efficient way to defeat the iniquitous scheme was to do nothing at all. There is nothing which the "loyal North" so much despises as want of *cuteness*, and the Radicals have specially plumed themselves upon the possession of that delectable quality. But, surely, they showed a great lack of this essential element of wicked success, when they failed to frame the Bill, so that all not voting against it should be counted as endorsing it. The Alabama Constitution was lost by this stupid mistake. The Report of the Committee sets forth piteously that there was a big rain on the *day* of election, which kept thousands away from the polls, while ignoring the fact that the election lasted five days. We are not surprised at the insinuated falsehood in the Report; that was in keeping with the celebrated Preamble to the Bill. But we are surprised at the Jacobins for not adopting the good old rule of "silence gives consent." Still better, they might have required the negroes to continue to vote day by day, until the elections were carried. Or still better, they might have required the military commanders to report them as carried. A little tact and management would have saved them a world of trouble and annoyance. It is melancholy to reflect how much perjury has been necessary to counter-balance this want of tact, how witnesses have been compelled to swear that the rivers of Alabama were choked up with ice! and how a poor negro on his way to the polls was crushed by an iceberg!

His Majesty (we'll not name him) must have been greatly grieved at the want of cunning in his children. He himself is distinguished for his subtlety (Genesis III, 1,) and he has a right to expect the same characteristic in his descendants.

But if the provisions of the Bill show want of address and cunning, the whole Bill itself betrays want of wisdom and statesmanship. There is no folly like the folly of temporary expediency. The Jacobins, in the hope of present gain of strength to their party, by the negro vote, jeopardize the very interests which they wish to subserve. The negro is not too low in the scale of intelligence to learn that the cotton tax is an injury to him, that the tariff is an injury to him, that the bounty on fish is an injury to him, that the restriction on the coast-trade is an injury to him, and that the interest on the bonds of the Government is an injury to him. In less than five years, he will be a repudiator, and a violent opponent to the whole New England policy of selfish aggrandizement. The most prominent feature, in all the Constitutions framed by the Fetich Conventions, is that of repudiation—the so-called measures of Relief. They expect by this one provision alone, to array on their side the bankrupt, the insolvent, the dishonest and the baser sort. Can it be expected that men, who have tasted the sweets of relief at home, will be willing to wear burdens abroad? The Jacobins are not merely playing with edged tools, they have actually made and then sharpened the tools for their wicked sport! They lack wisdom, they lack statesmanship, they lack even cunning. Surely, their great Progenitor has reason to be ashamed of them!

The Hon. Charles Sumner was, probably, at no time a very amiable man. But he has been so soured by the chastisement inflicted by Brooks, and the desertion of his beautiful wife, that every utterance is now a sneer, or a sarcasm. His last fling at General Grant is peculiarly unkind. "We must have a *stable* Government," says he, in his bitter, ironical matter. This thrust at the hero of fast trotters and "horse-talk" is very ungracious at this juncture of affairs.

A SINGULAR MISTAKE.—The Hon. Thad. Stevens, in July last, thus taunted the Republicans in Congress:

He begged the House to consider that the Senate was several furlongs behind the House in the march of reform—perhaps he ought to say Radicalism. Senators were coming up sidelong, but had not yet got quite squarely up. What he had just mentioned was an illustration of that. Some fragments of the old shattered Constitution had struck, perhaps, the kidneys of some of the Senators (laughter.) and troubled them at night. When they tried to progress, the ghost of the past Constitution was found in their way, and obstructed them.

It is always expected of great Parliamentary leaders to know the temper, disposition, and moral character of their followers.—Walpole, Chatham, Fox, Pitt, Peel, Palmerston—have all been distinguished in that way. Our own Clay, Calhoun, Webster, Benton, &c., have shown equal skill in understanding the men with whom they had to deal. How then is it that Mr. Stevens has fallen into the singular delusion, that his party would be troubled with any scruples of conscience about violating the Constitution? Nothing in their past history can warrant such an absurdity. Nothing in their moral character can justify such a wild assumption. Is Mr. Stevens, then, really ignorant of his party? We are too charitable to entertain such an opinion, and make such a reflection upon his shrewdness. This unjust taunt to the men of great moral ideas was, doubtless, due to a momentary out-burst of temper, (to which he is subject) and which may have been caused by thinking about his property in that furnace which the rebels burned, or his property in that *other* burning furnace, which the rebels are not disposed to dispossess him of.

We observe in our esteemed and highly valued contemporary, the *Chronicle and Sentinel*, of Augusta, Ga., the following significant notice:

To Our Subscribers.—Stealing money from the Postal Department has become so frequent, that we are compelled thus publicly to warn our subscribers, not to send any more money by mail without a money order. If this cannot be procured, have the letters registered in every instance. Whenever convenient send it to us by express.

We had supposed that the P. O. Department had as efficient blockaders around the Port of Augusta as in any other part of the world, and that it was as difficult for an adventurous greenback to run the gauntlet there as it was possible to be elsewhere. But as the Head of the blockading squadron has turned his attention towards the Capitol of the nation, we had hoped that there would have been a relaxation of vigilance.

To Contributors.—No serials, or articles of such length as to require division, need be sent by voluntary contributors. Our arrangements have been completed for the Poetic Department, and we will confine ourselves to regular contributors.

THE LAND WE LOVE.

No. II. JUNE, 1868. Vol. V.

SKETCH OF GENERAL JUNIUS DANIEL.

Although the writer had learned to place the highest estimate on the character of General Daniel, before its greater development during the progress of hostilities, he greatly fears that he must fail in presenting it to the reader, in all that excellence which was so manifest to himself, as it could be properly appreciated only by those who were intimately acquainted therewith, and had thus the opportunity of knowing the principles and motives which entered into its formation. The record of his military life is but the history of the most unselfish devotion to the cause which he espoused, and which was so dear to his heart. From the time he volunteered in the struggle of the South for independence, until he received his death wound, his entire action, all his aims and aspirations, were concentrated on one object—the deliverance of his country. A simple narrative of facts will best attest the truth of this assertion.

General Daniel was the youngest child, and last surviving issue of the Hon. J. R. J. Daniel. He was born in the town of Halifax, N. C., on the 27th day of June, 1828, and at the age of three years, met with the irreparable loss of an admirable mother. His youth was passed at the best preparatory schools, and through life he acted upon the principle, so constantly impressed upon him, in his early training, "An utter abhorrence of lying, dishonesty, and every low and degrading vice." About the year 1843, he entered the excellent school of J. M. Lovejoy, Esq., at Raleigh, and there remained until admitted to the Military Academy, at West Point, in 1846, as one of the Cadets at large, under the appointment of President Polk. Whilst engaged there in artillery practice, the gun carriage to which he was attached was upset, and the gun thrown upon him, inflicting a severe spinal injury. His course, retarded one year by this accident, was completed in 1851, with a highly respectable standing for deportment and scholarship.

He entered West Point with the bona fide purpose of giving his services to the country, as a soldier. When he graduated, he was ordered, after the usual furlough, to Newport, Kentucky, as acting assistant Quarter-master. In the fall of 1852, he went in charge of a company, or detachment, to New Mexico, where he remained four years, stationed, successively, at Forts Albuquerque, Fillmore, and Stanton, spending his time in charge of scouting and exploring parties, in ascertaining the topography of the country, and in keeping in subjection, the Indians, with whom he had many skirmishes.

In the early part of 1857, he returned from New Mexico. His father having purchased a large body of land in Louisiana, he was induced to resign his commission in the army for the purpose of aiding in its cultivation and improvement. In this new sphere, he exerted himself with great energy and effect, reducing his scientific knowledge to practical tests. He always insisted that the education obtained at West Point, or the pursuit of a similar course of studies, is much better adapted to ensure success in the actual affairs of life than one confined principally to the classics; experience, it would seem, confirms this testimony.

In October, 1860, he married Ellen, a lovely and accomplished young lady, daughter of John J. Long, Esq., of Northampton Co., N. C., and immediately returned to his plantation in Louisiana, where he was engaged, devoting his energies to agriculture, when "Sumter fell."

Upon the inauguration of hostilities, he was offered a position among the Louisiana troops, but preferring to serve in his own State he hastened hither, and tendered his service to Gov. Ellis. That devoted son of the South highly appreciated his worth, but there was no position vacant commensurate with his abilities. General Daniel was no politician; he had never interfered in mere party contests, but he was an ardent supporter of the Constitution of the United States, as he understood it; and in drawing his sword for the Southern Cause, he believed that he was defending the, now obsolete, principles enunciated in that instrument. Nor was he misled by the enthusiasm of the day. He despised alike the vaporing of those at the North who professed their ability to conquer the South in ninety days, and the rhodomontade of such among ourselves as prophesied a bloodless victory. He clearly foresaw the nature of the coming contest, frequently predicting to his friends and the writer the long and terribly exhausting struggle before us.

In tendering his services to his country, General Daniel was free from personal ambition. He had no selfish ends to gratify. He had no children. Yet, at the very first hostile movement, he tore himself away from a home filled with every other endearment that can touch the heart of man, and with the hope of no other reward, than the satisfaction arising from duty performed. Such, indeed, was his determined patriotism, he would then have entered the service had it been revealed to him, that the first step would be to his grave.

Immediately after the tender of his services to Governor Ellis, he was elected colonel of the 4th, afterwards 14th, regiment North Carolina volunteers, with which he remained until nearly the expiration of its twelve months' service. He was then elected to the colonelcy of the 43d and 45th regiments, both of which had enlisted for the war, and, about the same time, was tendered, by Gov. Clark, that of the 2nd North Carolina cavalry. In accepting the command of the 45th, he showed, as in all other matters, the utmost disinterestedness, declining that of the 43d, which had several companies from his own county, in favor of a promising young officer, who had given decided evidence of ability, and that of the 2nd cavalry, in favor of Colonel Sol. Williams, saying, with the frankness of the true soldier: "Williams is a better man, for he is, par excellence, a cavalry man, so put him there."

The writer has received interesting accounts of Gen. Daniel's military career, from officers who served with him, and had resolved to incorporate them in this sketch, but the limits of a magazine article compel him to forego that pleasure, and he must content himself with this acknowledgment, and a synopsis of their contents.

As an organizer and disciplinarian, General Daniel had no superior, and the troops which had received the benefit of his training, especially the 43rd and 45th regiments, were never known to falter, or even to hesitate, whilst under his command; and they retained their *esprit du corps* throughout the gloomiest days of the Confederacy. He first served as colonel of the 45th, under General Holmes; in a few days that officer discovered his fine qualities as a soldier, and recommended him for promotion, asking that he might be assigned to duty under himself. The Government, however, had been so very liberal in rewarding politicians, that it had more brigadiers than brigades, so the application was denied; but an officer of that grade was tendered to General Holmes, who declined his services, saying: "You can keep your generals, I can get along with my colonels." From this period until he received his commission as brigadier, he served under three different departmental commanders, each of whom urged his promotion at headquarters, and, failing to secure it, refused to turn his command over to general officers. He organized three brigades, two of which were taken from him, and given to "Generals without a command." The third he commanded for twelve months as senior colonel, and when it was rumored that this too was about to be assigned to another, he did not complain of the government, but simply remarked to one of his officers: "I would certainly dislike to give up the command of these troops, now that I have had all the trouble of training them, and have become attached to them. I do not seek the distinction of rank for position merely, for were the war to close to-morrow, the offer of the highest could not induce me to remain in the army. I have other obligations to fulfill; but whilst this war lasts, here in the field will I be found—my whole soul is in the cause, and my life is at my country's service. If the government does not choose to give me command of my brigade, I will stick to my regiment and make no complaint."

About June, 1862, commanding his brigade as senior colonel, he was ordered to Petersburg under General Holmes. Although not actually engaged in the field during this period, an incident occurred too characteristic of the man to be omitted. It is thus related by an eye witness.

"At the battle of Malvern Hill, our brigade was on the extreme right of the line, and, although not actually brought into action, was exposed to a converging fire from three points, vastly more trying to troops than actual fighting. On one flank, in full view, at a distance of about a third of a mile, three gun-boats, lying in the James River, were playing upon us with shell, two parks of artillery, one from the famous Malvern Hill battery, were throwing their missiles into our ranks. Our troops were raw, few of them had ever before been under fire. Just at this time some cavalry, which had been sent to the front, came dashing down the road in disgraceful haste, riding down all who did not get out of their way. Immediately some artillery, for a cause never explained, acted in like manner, and the danger of a general panic was evident. Gen. Daniel almost instantly threw a regiment across the road, halted a piece of artillery, placing it in command of an officer who afterwards won his spurs, and ordered him to fire upon all who did not halt. This prompt action restorted order so speedily, that the confusion was unknown to any other part of the army. Whilst thus engaged, his horse was shot under him, and he had a very narrow escape."

In October, 1862, General Daniel was commissioned as a brigadier. He was assigned the 32nd regiment, commanded by Brabble, who was killed at Spotsylvania, then by Cowand; the 43rd, by Keenan, wounded and captured at Gettysburg, afterwards by Cary Whitaker, killed in the last days at Petersburg; the 45th, first by Morehead, who died at Martinsburg, Va., then by Boyd, who was wounded and captured at Gettysburg, exchanged and killed at Spotsylvania; the 53rd, by Owens, killed at Winchester, and the 2nd N. C. battalion, by Lieut. Colonel Andrews, killed at Gettysburg. What a sad record, and how eloquently it speaks to our hearts of the bravery of those devoted men! By impugning the memory of all such, some among us may earn an unenviable notoriety, but it is not in these days of calamity and humiliation, we can cease to venerate their heroism. Even should the despotism to which we are now consigned become the permanent condition of the country, the spirit of the South shall never utterly sink, while she looks back with redeeming pride upon "the martyr band," whose glorious achievements will be to her for a testimony, that her bondage did not arise from any want in her people of those high qualities, which give victory and freedom.

It is somewhat remarkable, and is, perhaps, the highest evidence of General Daniel's capacity, that, at this period, no officer of his grade, had acquired a higher reputation for soldierly qualities, although he had had no opportunity to distinguish himself in the field. He excelled, in many things essential to a great commander. "Reticence," says one of his officers, "he possessed, in an eminent degree, vigilance also. I regarded it as impossible for him to be surprised, and on one occasion, particularly, I know that the wing of the army to which he belonged, was saved from disaster thereby. Well might the lamented Rodes so often exclaim, during the Valley campaign, 'Oh if Daniel were only here now!'"

In attention to the wants of his men, in a thorough acquaintance with details, in his ability as an organizer and disciplinarian, as already stated, and in his skill in handling troops under fire, as proved at Gettysburg and Spotsylvania, he was equal to any man in the army of Northern Virginia. From the very first, he saw the necessity of discipline, and required from officers and men, the strictest attention to duty. He never relaxed, never exacted of others and spared himself; frequently, when in command of the division, has he been seen, at midnight, at the utmost limits thereof, seeing for himself, that his instructions were being properly carried out. At first, both officers and men chafed under his rule; but when it became manifest that he was actuated solely by a sense of the responsibility resting upon him, when his rigid impartiality, and high sense of honor, became known, when his brigade was seen to move under fire with the same accuracy as if on parade, he gained the hearts of all. Indeed, he was singularly gifted with the power of securing the warmest attachment, and the highest confidence of his subordinates, as testimonials, in the writer's possession, amply prove. This has always been considered as a high merit, in some of the greatest commanders.

Had he seconded the applications of his superiors in rank, by his personal efforts, or by those of his friends outside of the army, he would, doubtless, have speedily attained higher promotion, but he scorned all this as beneath the dignity of a true soldier. The writer has been informed, upon good authority, that, at the time of his death, his commission as Major General was made out, a tribute solely to his merits. Singleness of purpose characterized all his actions to the very last. Believing the South to be right, the voice of patriotism and the sense of duty urged him to subordinate all his powers to the effort for her success. Hence, he never even murmured at that severest trial of the deserving military man, the placing of persons inferior in ability and service, over his head. On some reference being made to this subject, he remarked to the writer: "The promotion of others does not excite in me either envy or discontent. I care not who receives the honors, provided we gain the fight."

General Daniel spent the Fall of 1862, with his brigade, at Drewry's Bluff. In December of that year, he was ordered to North Carolina, under command of General D. H. Hill, to meet a diversion of Foster, in favor of Burnside. Here he received, from one of his regiments, the significant sobriquet of "Old Blockhouse," which he ever afterwards retained. Shortly after the battle of Chancellorsville, he was transferred to Lee's army, Rodes' division, attached to Ewell's corps, during the Pennsylvania campaign, the division being the advance column. At that time, General Ewell had, as his head-quarters' flag, the only regular Confederate flag in the command. When Carlisle, the extreme point of the advance, was reached, General Ewell made a speech to his men, congratulating them on their successes, military bearing, and subordination, then, turning to Daniel's brigade, but recently attached to his corps, he said: "They had shown themselves so obedient to all orders, so steady and regular in their march, and so well disciplined, that he entrusted to them the charge of bearing the 'corps flag,' confident that its honor could never suffer while in keeping of such troops."

The writer has in his possession, General Daniel's report of the movements of his brigade during this period. It is an admirable paper, and may yet be published as a valuable contribution to the history of the campaign. The following extract, referring to its action in the battle of Gettysburg, is all that can be inserted here:

"I cannot, in justice to the officers and men of my command, close, this portion of my report without recording my earnest conviction that the conduct, of none of the troops who participated in this engagement, will furnish brighter examples of patient endurance than were exhibited by them. Entering the fight on the first day at 1 P. M., and hotly engaged until 4 P. M., constantly driving before them a superior force of the enemy, and losing nearly one-third of their number and many valuable officers. Exposed, during the afternoon of the second day, to a galling fire of artillery, from which they suffered much, they moved at night, in line of battle, on the enemy's strong position, after which, with less than two hours' rest, and having made a fatiguing night march, they reported to General Johnson, and entered the fight again at 5 A. M. on the third day, and were not withdrawn until between three and four in the afternoon—their skirmishers remaining engaged until 12 at night, and the whole line being constantly exposed to, and suffering from, the enemy's fire. Shortly after 12 at night, they were required to repeat the march of the preceding night, and to re-occupy the position from which they had driven the enemy on the first day. Nor was there exhibited, by any portion of the command, during the three days in which they were engaged, any disposition to shrink from the duties before them, or any indication of that despondency with which men, similarly exposed, are often affected."

The conduct of Gen. Daniel at Gettysburg, the first real opportunity he had had to display his ability in handling troops under fire, won for him the very highest place in the estimation of his fellow soldiers of every rank. His brigade never faltered for a moment upon that disastrous field, but moved under the direction of its leader, with the precision of clock work. This is well attested by the declaration of Gen. Ramseur, an honored rival. Referring to the first day's battle, when the brigade lost over six hundred men, "I watched," said he, "the corps flag, and I never saw troops move with more precision on parade, than the troops who bore it, when ordered to change their position under the full fire of the enemy." No higher encomium could have been passed upon officers and men. The friends of General Daniel, both in the army and out of it, were greatly chagrined at his failure to receive that promotion which he so eminently deserved. During the retreat, General Daniel, in command of the "rear guard" of the army, acted with admirable skill, coolness and discretion.

The space already occupied, compels the writer to pass, at once, over the intervening period, to the closing scene—the battles of the Wilderness and of Spotsylvania Court House. The following statement is based upon the authority of gentlemen of the highest sense of honor, who were eye witnesses of the events referred to.

The morning of May 5th, 1864, was, perhaps, the proudest moment of Gen. Daniel's military life. He was then in reserve, supporting the Stonewall brigade, Doles' Ga., Battle's Ala., and J. M. Jones' Va. brigades. General Jones was killed, and all gave way before the charge of the enemy. At this critical moment, "when to hesitate was to be lost," he appeared the very impersonation of heroism. Of fine personal appearance, admirably proportioned, vigorous, muscular, and singularly erect, seeming to have increased in stature, his fine grey eye flashing fire, he appealed to his brigade by name, in that stentorian, sonorous voice, which could animate the most timid, and was now heard loud above the din of battle: "Attention, Daniel's North Carolina brigade, forward, charge!" The advance of the enemy was almost instantly checked, and they were driven in a steady retreat. Their officers rallied them in a gully about three feet deep, forming an excellent substitute for a breast-work, and right across Daniel's line. At the approach of his men, they arose and fired almost in their very faces, then resumed their retreat.

Daniel halted his line, dressed it, fired by rank at the word of command, then charged. General Gordon, having taken the enemy on the flank about the same time, the rout was complete, and the slaughter very great.

To General Gordon is, generally, attributed the credit of retrieving the fortunes of the day, on this occasion, whilst General Daniel is, rarely, if ever, mentioned in connection therewith. It is very difficult to reconcile conflicting accounts from the battlefield, but the evidence, both verbal and written, which has been presented to the writer, warrants him in insisting on all that he has claimed in this matter for General Daniel. Were it not for his prompt and decisive action, we must, in all probability, have chronicled an inglorious defeat instead of a great victory.

On the night of the 5th, Daniel's brigade was moved to the extreme right of the line, and was almost constantly engaged in the contest of the following days. On the 8th, the construction of the works known as the "Horse Shoes," were ordered, against General Daniel's protest, as they were flanked on both sides. They proved to be a lamentable mistake, and were held only at a terrible sacrifice. It was at this point, on the morning of the 12th of May, that General Daniel fell. Grant had driven Edward Johnson's division out of the salient. Ramseur and Harris had gone in to retake the works, the enemy were trying to break Lee's second line, as they had broken the first, pushing the right of Daniel's brigade very heavily. He was a few paces in the rear of the 45th regiment, his staff officers on various parts of the line, and while giving orders to one of his gallant young couriers, he fell forward on his face, struck in the abdomen by a Minnie ball.

He was carried under a shower of shot and shell to the rear, and at first, was of the opinion caused, doubtless, by the fact, that the point of exit of the ball alone gave him pain, that he had been shot by one of our own men, who was too cowardly to be well up, and too frightened to take aim. When made aware of his error, he seemed to entertain no hopes of life, but these revived, somewhat, when the Surgeons hesitated to pronounce the wound to be mortal. During his remaining hours, his thoughts constantly turned to the great events passing around him, to the fate of his beloved South, to that home where his happiest hours had been passed, and to her whose image lay enshrined in his heart. But let the incidents attending the last moments of the patriot and the hero, be told by one who witnessed them.

"General Daniel was wounded about 9 o'clock, a. m. About three in the afternoon, General Ramseur, who had left the field to have a wound in his arm dressed, came into the tent, shook General Daniel's hand warmly, expressing his deep sympathy and sorrow. They had been true friends, and two more gallant men never fought side by side. General Ramseur remained but a moment, and, about to hasten to the front, he took General Daniel's hand within his own, saying, whilst tears filled the eyes of both, 'Daniel, we will hardly meet again in this world, may God Almighty bless you, my friend.' 'God bless you, Ramseur.' Such were the parting words of two as noble and brave men as ever died in a holy cause."

"On Friday, the 13th, I felt satisfied that he could not long survive, and so informed him, in answer to his enquiries. He had the Surgeons called in, that he might ascertain whether his wife could reach him ere he died. This being impossible, he spoke of her in the most endearing terms, directing Major Badger, who was present, to place his watch in her hands, saying it was 'Ellen's watch,' or 'Ellen's gift,' and to ask her to provide for his boy, William, who had been a good and faithful servant, and 'tell Bill,' said he, 'to take good care of old John,' the noble old war-horse that had carried him through more than one bloody field. Occasionally, he would exclaim, 'Oh, that I could have lived to have seen Grant defeated!' And then would enquire of his brigade, how the men had behaved, and whether they had suffered."

"A short time before his dissolution, the Doctor informed him that he was dying, and asked if he might call in a minister of the Gospel. He readily assented, a minister was brought in, spoke a few words, and knelt down in prayer. During prayer he was very quiet, and as soon as it was over, he requested us to raise him up in bed; when we had done so, he breathed once or twice quite freely. 'Now lay me down,' he said, then folding his hands across his bosom, and closing his eyes, he immediately expired."

A mournful sight was presented in Halifax on the day when General Daniel was borne to his grave. Some of the most gallant sons of the county had fallen in the struggle, and now the true and tried soldier, in whom the citizens most prided, and from whom they hoped the most, struck down in the midst of the carnage, lay cold in death before them. Many of those present had known him from his infancy; all had loved him; a few days before their hearts had bounded with exultation at the recital of his achievements—but "he had fought his last battle."

He was buried amidst the venerable oaks in the old church yard of Halifax, where his deceased relations, and the dust of many other honored dead, lie interred. The taste and sympathy of woman, whose heart instinctively turns to the beautiful and true, and whose devotion, equally with the blood of its martyrs, sanctified the Southern cause, spread upon the hero's bier the richest floral offerings, emblematical of her grief and his virtues. Let not the people of his native county and town forget what they owe to him and themselves. No one brought more honesty of purpose to the cause than he, no one loved it more earnestly or served it with more fidelity. His daring valor, his stainless integrity and devoted patriotism, entitle his memory to all honor and affection, and the suffered to sleep in a forgotten ashes of such a man should not be grave.

NATURE'S LESSON.

A SONNET.

Pain is no longer pain when it is past:
And what is all the joy of yesterday,
More than the sunshine that has died away,
Leaving no trace across the landscape cast,
Whereby to prove its presence? The rude blast
That bowed the knotted oak beneath its sway,
And bent the lissome ash, the forest may
Keep some slight note of,—since strewn leaves out last
Quick caught-up sunbeams.—Be like Nature, then,
Calmly receptive of all sweet delights,
The while they soothe and strengthen thee; and when
The wrench of trial shakes thy soul again,—
Think of the still progressive days and nights
That blot, with equal sweep, both joy and pain.

Lexington, Va. MARGARET J. PRESTON.

UNPUBLISHED CORRESPONDENCE OF WASHINGTON.

WE are indebted to Mrs. M. F. Pritchard, of Carrollton, Mo., for the following letter from Col. Woodford, and the reply of Gen. Washington. Mrs. P. made exact copies of the original letters, still in the hands of the descendants of Colonel Woodford. The spelling, punctuation, &c., have been carefully followed.

It is a wonderful proof of the laboriousness, as well as kindness, of the Father of his country, that he could find time, amidst his arduous duties, to write an autograph letter to a subordinate officer. The gentle, courteous, tone of his letter shows, moreover, that the great General never forgot the *gentleman*. As everything emanating from Washington must have an enduring interest with the American people, we feel sure that we can present nothing that would be more acceptable to the readers of THE LAND WE LOVE.—Editor.

WILLIAMSBURG,
JULY 6th, 1776.

DEAR SIR:

I was favored with yours of the 10th of November and should long ago have thanked you for your kind advice therein contained, together with your polite assurance, of your thorough approbation of my appointment, but supposing you too much engaged in your important office, I feared I might be troublesome; this, and not want of respect alone occasioned my silence. Have ever since made the subject of your letter the line of my conduct, how far the common cause has been benefitted by it, becomes not me to say, but this I venture to affirm, that I have at all times exerted my best ability in the service.—I am sorry to trouble you with complaints, but give me leave Sir to say I feel myself much hurt by the late promotion of my very worthy friend Col. Mercer, and to request your patience to hear my reasons in the best manner I am capable of giving them, with that freedom, which I flatter myself will not be taken amiss by you.—

When the military establishment of this colony first took place, I offered my service in any post the convention thought proper to appoint me to, without soliciting any one man of that Body for his vote or interest before the ballot began, I informed the House of which I was at that time a Member that I wished to serve under that Gentleman, and desired no person would vote for me in preference to him, notwithstanding all that could be said he was rejected, and my appointment confirmed. When the Honorable, the Congress, took out troops upon the Continental Establishment, a few months ago, I again expressed my wish that Colonel Mercer might be appointed to a higher office, their wisdom directed them to make the arrangement otherways, and I looked upon the army as firmly established in such a manner, that every officer would rise in his turn, unless some fault could be laid to his charge. I have the same good opinion of that gentleman I ever had, but what I complain of is the impropriety as I conceive of the appointment, and that the promotion of an officer at that time serving under me, (however well he may deserve it) reflected dishonor upon myself, and will be attributed by the world to some misconduct in me, or at best inability to fill a higher office. I am informed from good authority, that a similar promotion is now in contemplation in favor of Col. Stephens. From the above reasons, I must request your permission to retire, not with any intention to promote any disturbances either, in the army, or country, but on the contrary to do any future service in a private way, to my country, and the common cause, to which I feel myself as warmly attached as ever. Before I conclude I will take the liberty to appeal to your own feelings as an officer, upon such an occasion, and to ask you what light I must be looked upon in the army for the future. My opposition to a popular military Officer, and my exertion to introduce some discipline among those infant troops, has gained me enemys, who I can see exulting in the late promotion, though they hate the man. Wishing you all happiness and success in our Glorious cause, I have the honor to be with the greatest respect,

Your Excellency's

Most Obt humble Servant,

WM. WOODFORD.

NEW YORK
30TH JULY 1776

DEAR SIR

Your letter of the 6th Inst came to my hands a Post or two ago and the answer delayed longer than I intended from the multiplicity of business in which I am engaged.—

I am sorry you should consider Genl Mercer's late appointment as a slight put upon your services, because I am persuaded no slight was intended.—Whilst the service was local, and appointment of Officers affected no other Colony than that in which they were raised, the Continental Congress discovered no inclination to interpose in the appointments, But when they were to be chosen for more extensive service each member then concieved his own Colony to be affected, and that it was his duty to make choice of Gentlemen for Genl Officers whose former Rank (as they were to be placed over Officers that have commanded Regiments since the commencement of these disputes, and many of the field Officers in the last war) would give them the best pretensions, and those over whom they were to be placed, least offence—Upon this principle therefore I knew it was that Genl Mercer got appointed, and upon this principle also it will be that Col Stephens is, if such a event should take place; upon a revision therefore of the matter I cannot think you will find any just cause of complaint notwithstanding you stood foremost in the appointments of Virginia; which, as I observed before, were local, and whilst they regarded no other Colony, were unattended to by the Congress; but you should consider that Col Mercer, Genl Lewis, and Col Stephens were Field Officers in the same service, and at the same time, that you acted as subaltern, and that in general appointments by the Congress, regard must be had to the troops here, as much as elsewhere, the Officers being equally tenacious of Rank; and only reconcilable to Mercer's coming in over them on acct of his former Rank in the army.

Upon the whole, I am sorry to hear you mention a resignation on any account, and hope upon a Reconsideration of the matter you will change your sentiments and continue in the military line you are now in—every rub, and difficulty of this kind impedes the service—hurts our cause—and encourages the Enemy.—However, if after what I have said, and could say upon the occasion you are still resolved not to continue in the service, I must refer you to the Officer commanding in the southern department to receive your resignation, or the person from whence you derived your commission, for as I never have interfered in any matter relative to the southern command I would not wish to begin with a resignation that I would wish to be instrumental in preventing.—I am with much respect esteem and regard

Dr Sir Yr most Obt Servt
GEORGE WASHINGTON.

THE STATE OF FRANKLIN.

BUT the patriot statesman at the head of the government of North Carolina, could not be moved from his propriety. After the adjournment of the Legislature, he communicated directly to Governor Sevier, the proceedings of that body, in reference to the revolters. His letter is marked with good sense and a pacific tone. His words are, "the people are not yet of strength and opulence sufficient to support an independent State. The Assembly wish to continue the benefits and protection of the State towards them, until such time as their numbers and wealth will enable them to do for themselves, when the Assembly are free to say, a separation may take place. In the meantime, the most friendly intercourse between the people on the Eastern and Western waters, is strongly recommended, and your people, as they have received for the past two years, no benefit from Government, are exempted from the payment of the public taxes." In answer to this letter, the Governor of Franklin writes respectfully, but firmly, expressing his disappointment that the separation of the two States had not been assented to by the Assembly, and closing with the declaration on the part of Franklin: "We shall continue to act as independent, and would rather suffer death in all its various and frightful shapes, than to conform to anything that is disgraceful."

The firm and decisive tone of this letter, was in accordance with the present temper of Sevier and his adherents. The compromise entered into by the contracting parties on the 20th March, was found to be, in some of the counties, of little avail.—"It is agreed and it is recommended" were terms sufficiently explicit and strong to be obligatory on the masses, and their "regard to peace, tranquility and good decorum" led *them* to respect the provisions of the agreement made by Gen. Shelby and Gov. Sevier. But in those counties, where the recent Act of North Carolina had vacated certain of the offices, and where commissions under her authority, had been accepted and acted under, a spirit of faction and discontent developed itself. The *ins* and the *outs*, as is sometimes seen with more modern politicians, quarreled. A question arose as to the *powers*, who had negotiated the late "agreement and recommendation." By common consent, the office-holders considered them invalid and irregular. The truce was ended. Governor Sevier determined that he and the other officers of Franklin would "act as independent." But still to this declaration, Gov Caswell replied in a very friendly and conciliatory spirit, favorable to separation on the conditions previously specified. "If the violent passions of some men among you," said he, "are not restrained, if they are suffered to break out, it will be putting the day farther off, and perhaps the separation may not be effected without bloodshed. This, I am sure, neither you nor any other man capable of reflection, would wish to see, if it can be avoided by justifiable means. You may rely upon it that my sentiments are clearly in favor of a separation, whenever the people think themselves of sufficient strength and abilities to support a government."

General Shelby, the other diplomatist, proposed, in the meantime, to the Government he represented, the adoption of more energetic and efficient measures, and asks that troops and ammunition should be sent to restore order and enforce the laws in Franklin, and suggests that aid for that purpose might be obtained from the contiguous counties of Virginia.

At this alarming crisis, in the affairs of the two communities most interested in it, Colonel A. Bledsoe, of Nashville, and a gentleman of great personal influence and weight of character, aided by his presence in the disaffected counties, in keeping down any violence or outbreak. He also addressed to Governor Caswell a letter rather seconding the views of General Shelby, but suggesting that the Governor should once more address the people, advising them of the necessity and advantage of returning to their duty once more, and of the danger and evil consequences of further attempts at independence, and expressing his belief that such an address, from the Governor, would have a very good effect upon the principal people in the revolted party.

The moderation and good sense of Governor Caswell seem to have been never at fault, and at no time to have forsaken him. To the suggestions of General Shelby, of maintaining the authority of North Carolina, by an armed force, the Governor replied negatively and adds, "that it would be very imprudent to add to the dissatisfaction of the Western people, by showing a wish to encourage the shedding of blood, as thereby, a civil war would be brought on, which, at all times, should be avoided, if possible." What profound wisdom—what ardent patriotism are here exhibited. Let the virtue and ability of Caswell ever be revered by North Carolina, by Tennessee, and by the country at large! In the same letter, the Governor goes on to say: "I must therefore recommend to you, the using of every means in your power, to conciliate the minds of the people, as well, those who call themselves Franklinites, as the friends and supporters of Government. If things could be dormant, as it were, till the next Assembly, and each man's mind be employed in considering your common defence against the savage enemy, I should suppose it best, and whenever unanimity prevails amongst your people, and their strength and numbers will justify an application for a separation; if it is general, I have no doubt of its taking place upon reciprocal and friendly terms." The Governor, at the same time, forwarded through Gen. Shelby, a long address to the disaffected inhabitants, in which he says: "that although the behavior of some of the refractory might justify coercive measures, yet of the consequences that must ensue from them, and I am willing to hope, that upon reflection, and due consideration—a moment's thought must evince the necessity of mutual friendship, and the ties of brotherly love being cemented among you." He concludes this long and most conciliatory communication thus: "I will conclude by once more entreating you to consider the dreadful calamities and cousequences of a civil war. Humanity demands this of me. Your own good sense will point out the propriety of it; at least, let all animosities and disputes subside till the next Assembly; even let things remain as they are, without pursuing compulsory measures, until then, and I flatter myself that that honorable body will be disposed to do what is just and right, and what sound policy may dictate."

Nothing yet had occurred between Franklin and North Carolina, so well calculated to heal the breach and effect a reconciliation between them, as this letter of Gov. Caswell and the action of the North Carolina Legislature communicated in it. The origin and cause of the separation, at the time it occurred, was the Cession Act. That had been repealed. The great object of the secessionists, now was independence of North Carolina, so as to avoid a reënactment of the repealed law. The apprehension of that objectionable and inadmissible policy was removed in the minds of some of the earliest and most steadfast friends of Franklin, by the assurances of the Governor and Legislature of North Carolina, that at the proper time, a new State should be formed, and their cherished wishes for independence should be gratified, if the malcontents would return to their allegiance. The argument was forcible, to many perfectly satisfactory and irresistible. It inflicted a vital stab upon the new government, which, within the next year, caused its dissolution.

Under the Franklin Treaties, new lands had been acquired from the Cherokees. To these a flood of emigrants flowed in rapidly, and the Franklin settlements extended to and embraced the country East and North of the Little Tennessee. Coming thus in close proximity to the territory and people of Georgia, an alliance between the latter and Franklin was considered as mutually advantageous and desirable. Gov. Houston accordingly commissioned Gov. Sevier as a Brigadier General in the service of Georgia, in order to secure the assistance and coöperation of the Franklin soldiery, in the occupancy and defence of the projected settlements in the great bend of the Tennessee River—now North Alabama. Gov. Sevier was not unwilling to accept this evidence of the confidence and friendship of Georgia. He was sensible of the opposition Franklin had encountered, and the growing discontent and difficulty yet to be encountered, from some in the new State and from the government of North Carolina. His Cherokee neighbors, and their allies, the Creeks, were ready at any moment to take advantage of the necessities of the infant government, and involve it in a general war. He took the precaution, therefore, to assure himself of the good feeling and coöperation of the Georgians, and to identify that people with his own in the common cause of self-defence and self-protection. With many of their leading men, he had become acquainted in the Revolutionary war. Some of them had been at his side on King's Mountain and other battle-grounds of that struggle. Some of them at its close had followed him to the West and adhered to his fortunes in every vicissitude. The countrymen of Clarke, Pickens and Matthews, all knew his gallantry, and were his steadfast friends. Under these circumstances it is not strange, that the authorities of Georgia made an engagement with those of Franklin to suppress the hostilities of the Creek Indians, and to bind the two communities in the bonds of a common brotherhood.

Such a fraternization had now become, with Sevier, a pressing necessity. Some of the causes for separating the Western counties from the parent State, had either ceased to exist, or operated now, upon the minds of the people, with less intensity, and it had become evident that a very formidable party, in Franklin, was now opposed to a further continuance of the new Government. Appointees, of North Carolina, now held regular sessions of their courts in Washington county. In other counties, the authority of Franklin was so far extinct, that of North Carolina so fully recognized, that elections for the Greeneville Assembly were not held, but representatives were regularly chosen for the old State, to meet in Tarboro'. Of those thus elected, several had been the steadfast friends of separation and independence, and had been the principal functionaries of the new Commonwealth. Even Greene county, which had heretofore refused to permit commissions emanating from the old dynasty, to be accepted and acted under, within its boundaries, had partaken of the general defection, and elected to the Tarboro' Assembly, as Senator, the presiding Judge of the Franklin Bench, and as members of the House, Daniel Kennedy, one of the Franklin brigadiers, and James Reese, Esq., recently a member of its Legislature.

Washington county, in like manner, was represented now, by members who had been the first to propose, and the most active in carrying into effect, the insurrectionary movement. Sullivan county, too, had chosen for representatives to the Tarboro' Assembly, gentlemen, who had been original supporters of Franklin, and advocates of separation.—Sevier and Caswell counties, alone, maintained their allegiance to the new State, and adhered to Sevier and his fortunes; and even in these, there were not wanting men, whose position was equivocal, and who hesitated not to dissuade from further resistance to the current, which now set so strongly in favor of the mother State. Harassed by the difficulties that surrounded his official position, and perplexed by the duties and responsibilities devolving on him as a patriot, Governor Sevier instituted a further embassy to Georgia, with the hope of extricating himself and his government from accumulating embarrassments. As a dernier resort, he invited the mediation of Georgia,* between North Carolina and Franklin. This embassy, however, was followed by no practical benefit to Franklin. The authorities of Georgia, while they eulogized the spirit of the Franks, and expressed the hope for their success, did nothing in the proposed mediation. They, however, renewed the plan of co-operation by Franklin and Georgia, in the conquest of the Creek Nation. Dispatches containing the proceedings at Augusta, and the alliance between the contracting parties, were forwarded, by express, to Governor Sevier. This intelligence was hailed with joy by his adherents, and was not unacceptable to that part of the people, who had transferred, or were prepared to transfer their allegiance to the mother State. The object of the alliance—the conquest of the Creeks,

* For a further account of the negotiation between Franklin and Georgia, see "Ramsey's Tennessee," page 376 to 399.

and the occupancy of the country below them, on the Tennessee,—accorded exactly with the martial spirit of the Western soldiery, and comported well with their character and taste for adventure and enterprise. Small as was their number, remote and inaccessible as was the theatre for the contemplated campaign, difficulty and danger only stimulated them to the undertaking, and they longed for the opportunity of carrying their victorious arms to the country above Mobile Bay. Rumors had reached them of the occlusion of the Mississippi, and they already cherished the design of opening up, by their own swords, a channel of commerce with the world, in despite of Federal indifference or foreign diplomacy and injustice.

If the people of Franklin rejoiced at this intelligence, it may be easily supposed that Gov. Sevier received it with the highest gratification. He was too sagacious, not to have observed that the new State was at the point of dissolution—the crisis was at hand which it could not probably survive. Elections had not been holden of members for a succeeding session of the Franklin Assembly. His gubernatorial term would expire in a few short months. He was, himself, ineligible and a successor could be appointed only by a vote of the legislative bodies. The only chance of preserving the integrity of his government was that the projected campaign would silence the clamor of the malcontents, and restore harmony and concert to the distracted members of his little republic. This hope was fallacious and illusory; but the Governor's perseverance was indomitable, and by a circular to each colonel of all the counties, he made an appeal to the chivalry of the country to rally to his standard and volunteer for the distant service. This appeal by Gov. Sevier to the gallantry of his countrymen was responded to, in their usual warlike spirit. An army of volunteers was at once recruited and only waited for the promised aid of Georgia to commence the campaign. The expedition was afterwards abandoned on account of a treaty with the Indians under authority of Congress. This delay, and the consequent disappointment of the militia of Franklin, baffled the hope its Governor had cherished of harmonizing the people, in support of the new government. The volunteers were restless, impatient and disappointed. Employment suited to their taste—danger, with which habit had made them familiar—victory, which had ever followed them and their leader—conquest, which they never doubted—renown, which they deified—achievement, which they idolized,—and fame, for which they sighed,—had suddenly vanished and eluded their grasp. Not a word of censure was uttered against their gallant commander-in-chief, but the soldiery remained, in sullen silence and discontent, at home.

Pending negotiations for obtaining auxiliaries from abroad, the new government was every day losing an adherent at home, who, by transferring his allegiance to North Carolina, sensibly diminished the influence and authority of Sevier. In 1787, there scarcely remained in the Commonwealth of Franklin vitality enough to give it a nominal existence; its substance and strength were absolved into the Carolina *Regime*, and the pangs of political annihilation having thus come, little more of the skeleton of the government was left than its head. That, still, under all the debility which affected the body, retained its wonted vitality and vigor. The Council of State had participated in the general disaffection, and some of its members had accepted office under North Carolina, while others had failed to meet their colleagues in the Board, or had formerly withdrawn from it. The judiciary, in its highest department, was annihilated by the election of Judge Campbell to a seat in the Tarboro Legislature, and his appointment by that body as Judge of the Superior Court at Jonesboro. The Legislature of Franklin suffered also from the prevalent disintegration, and manifested a strong tendency to dismemberment. From some of the old counties there was no representation, while the delegates from others exhibited indecision or discordance.

In September, of this year, a quorum was got together, and constituted, at Greeneville, the last Legislature of Franklin. Its legislation was unimportant. The Governor was scarcely able to secure the passage of an act to provide for descending, with his troops, the Tennessee river, and taking possession of its Great Bend. This bill was passed by a compromise. The *quid pro quo*, given to the dissentients, was the appointment of two delegates, to make to the Legislature of North Carolina, such representations of the affairs of Franklin as might be thought proper.

The Legislature, however, failed to elect the State Council, and the Governor was thus left "alone in his glory." Some of the old Board, though no longer his constitutional advisers, dissuaded him from further effort to perpetuate the new government, and advised him to yield to the necessity that portended its fate, and threatened to overwhelm its executive. Vestige after vestige of Franklin was obliterated; its judiciary was gone; its legislature reduced to a skeleton; its council effete, defunct, powerless; its military disorganized, if not discordant; and its masses confused and distracted, with no concert and unanimity among themselves.

Distraction extended, likewise, to the lower judicial tribunals of Franklin. The possession of the Court Records was, of course, desired by the rival parties: a scuffle would ensue, ending sometimes in a general fight. Scenes of disorder took place, which were generally sources of merriment and pleasurable excitement, rather than causes of settled malice or revenge. The parties separated, and soon after were friends. In Washington county, however, the dispute became acrimonious, and at length generated a feeling of inappeasable malignity between the leaders of their respective parties. From the commencement of the revolt, this county had been the seat of a central influence, which, while it remained united, was able to repress any opposition to its authority. That central power was represented by two very numerous and very respectable families, the leaders of which were John Sevier and John Tipton,—each alike, brave, patriotic and ambitious. Each had been distinguished by martial exploits, and patriotic services in civil life. They had conquered together at the defeat of Ferguson, and coöperated together harmoniously in all the incipient measures of the insurrectionary government. On one occasion, as has been mentioned, when Sevier hesitated and dissuaded from separation, Tipton was decided in support of that measure. Tipton became an officer under the new government. After the repeal of the Cession Act, the former returned to his allegiance to the parent State and was now a member of its legislature—the latter maintained his opposition to it. They were now implacable enemies. Each of them had political adherents and personal friends. Neither of them had a personal enemy. Each of these leaders, it is reasonable to suppose, felt the ambition to supplant his rival, and prevent his supremacy.

In the midst of these rivalries there was still no outbreak or tumult. The Legislature of North Carolina, at its sessions of 1787, continued and extended its conciliatory policy towards the revolters. The former acts of pardon and oblivion were reënacted, and those, who availed themselves of the advantages specified therein, were restored to the privileges of citizenship. Suits were dismissed, which had been instituted for the recovery of penalties or forfeitures incurred by a non-compliance with the revenue laws.—These pacific and satisfactory measures were suggested and supported by the late revolters, but now members from the Western counties, and went far to remove the remaining discontent and quiet the complaints of the citizens. But the Governor of Franklin still retained his elastic and sanguine temper, and as late as January 24, 1788, continued to inspire his adherents with hope. To one of his Generals at that date he says: "I am happy to inform you that I find our friends very warm and steady—much more than heretofore." Very warm and steady were indeed the friends of John Sevier, but not of the Governor of Franklin, now tottering into ruins. In little more than one month, Franklin had ceased to be.

UNDER THE LAVA.

Far down in the depths of my spirit
  Out of the sight of man,
Lies a buried Herculaneum
  Whose secrets none may scan.
No warning cloud of sorrow
  Cast its shadow o'er my way,
No drifting shower of ashes
  Made of life a Pompeii.
But a sudden tide of anguish
  Like molten lava rolled,
And hardened—hardened—hardened
  As its burning waves grew cold.
Beneath it youth was buried,
  And Love, and Hope, and Trust,
And life unto me seemed nothing—
  Nothing but ashes and dust.
Oh! it was glorious! glorious!
  That past with its passionate glow,
Its beautiful painted frescoes,
  Its statues white as snow.
When I tasted love's ambrosia
  As it melted in a kiss,
When I drank the wine of friendship
  And believed in earthly bliss;
When I breathed the rose's perfume,
  With lilies wreathed my hair,
And moved to liquid music
  As it floated on the air.
To me it was real—real—
  That passionate blissful joy,
Which Grief may encrust with lava,
  But Death can alone destroy.
'Twas a life all bright and golden,
  Bright with the light of love,
A past still living though buried
  With another life above.
Another life built o'er it,
  With other love and friends,

Which my spirit often leaveth
  And into the past descends.
Though buried deep in ashes
  Of burnt out hopes it lies,
Under the hardened lava
  From which it ne'er can rise;
It is no ruined city—
  No city of the dead—
When in the mid-night watches
  Its silent streets I tread.
To me it changeth never,
  Buried in all its prime—
Not fading—fading—fading—
  Under the touch of Time.
The beautiful frescoes painted
  By Fancy still are there,
With glowing tints unchanging
  Till brought to upper air.
And many a graceful statue
  In marble white as snow,
Stands fair and all unbroken
  In that silent "Long Ago."
It is not dead but living
  My glorious buried past!
With its life of passionate beauty
  Its joy too bright to last.
But living under the lava,
  For the pictures fade away,
And the statues crumble—crumble—
  When brought to the light of day.
And like to Dead Sea apples
  Is Love's ambrosia now,
And the lilies wither—wither—
  If I place them on my brow.
And so I keep them ever,
  Things from this life apart,
Under the lava and ashes
  Down in the depths of my heart.

PERSONAL RECOLLECTIONS OF EMINENT MEN.

COLONEL THOMAS H. BENTON.

As Colonel Benton was a native of North Carolina, I thought some notice of him, in a magazine published in his native State, may be acceptable.

His public life I leave to history which, I hope, when divested of party rancor, will do him the justice denied by contemporaries.

Of his early career, I know nothing, personally. He was favorably introduced to my notice by his friend and fellow officer in the army of 1812, Gov. James P. Preston. He afterwards married Governor Preston's niece, Miss McDowell, my friend and relative. I thus came to know him intimately, and take pleasure in testifying to his many virtues in private and domestic life.

Owing to the reports which had reached them, Miss McDowell's friends were rather opposed to her marriage, and he was, perhaps, coldly received by them—but such feelings were soon changed by his constant tenderness to his wife, and uniform respectful attentions to her relations; this lasted through life, and it was impossible not to love and admire him as a friend.

For several years before her death, Mrs. Benton was so paralyzed as scarcely to be able to speak. During the whole of this affliction, the Colonel's attentions were never remitted, never faltered, and he required his household to pay her the same respect, she had been accustomed to command when in health. It was touching to see her sitting at the head of her table with honorable guests surrounding it, and he, with the most delicate tact, dispensing those courtesies, which, under other circumstances, were her duty. The Colonel's letters, after her death, were full of expressions of the greatest admiration of her character, and his after-life showed his tender devotion to her memory. Mrs. Benton was endowed with great natural abilities, cultivated by constant intercourse with the best society of our country, and was always considered an ornament to it. She was the sister of Governor McDowell, of Virginia, and near relative and attached friend, from childhood, of Colonel William C. Preston, of South Carolina. During the long political estrangement between Colonel Benton and Colonel Preston, Mrs. B. never forgot the dignity of the wife, nor the kindness of the friend. Their reconciliation was a relief to both, and productive of much pleasure.

Every one knows the amount of work Colonel Benton accomplished in his public capacity—but, perhaps, few are aware of the labors of his private and domestic life. This was his routine one winter. After the late dinner usual in Washington, he retired to his chamber and took a short nap, then rose and taught his children until 10 o'clock, then accompanied his wife, or any young lady who might be under his protection, to some private party, returned at 12, slept until 4, then arose, read Spanish with his teacher for two hours—then his refreshing early walk and breakfast prepared him for the public duties of the day. Such was the system that procured for him the character of the most laborious man of his time. Col. Benton was tall and inclined to corpulency, fair haired, blue eyed and rather pale. His constant labors told on his complexion—not handsome, but would be remarked in any crowd as a fine looking *gentleman.* His manners were uniformly respectful to ladies, and I never saw anything but the utmost courtesy in social life, although I knew he was accused of rudeness in the Senate. He had some little peculiarities of manner, at which his friends laughed. Such, for instance, as repeating a sentence several times, 'How do you do, how do you do, how do you do,' or asserting, 'that's so, that's so, that's so, yes, yes, that's so,' nodding his head every time. Sometimes there was a little ebullition of vanity, excusable in one who had risen so high, and who was constantly receiving honors and adulation.

Speaking of Col. Benton recalls to my mind his brother-in-law, Gov. McDowell, of Virginia. I will, therefore, give a slight sketch of him, as I knew him from childhood—and I never knew a purer man. His youth was moral, his after life religious, and the high sense of honor he inherited from his ancestry, shone forth in every action of his life. He was a native of Rockbridge county, Virginia—a county that has the honor of having given birth to more distinguished men than any other county in the State, and in every department in life; from the Rev. Archibald Alexander, President of Princeton College, nearly a century ago, to Cyrus McCormick, who has just received the highest honors in England and France, as the best machinist in the world. Settled at first by hardy Scotch Irish Presbyterians, they at once set themselves to work to erect churches and schools, and verily they have been rewarded in their moral, industrious, intelligent descendants, who have lately illustrated their good taste and appreciation of worth, by inviting to, and cherishing in their bosom, the most beloved and honored one of our State, whose name will go down to posterity associated with that of the Father of His Country.

Mr. McDowell was born October, 1795, and at an early age was placed in the family of the Rev. Samuel Brown, of Providence church, Rockbridge, not too far from home to be exempt from its blessed influences. When old enough, he attended the schools in Lexington until prepared for college. He was first sent to Yale, but becoming dissatisfied there, with his father's consent he removed to Princeton, where he soon established an enviable reputation as a student and speaker, and graduated with honor.—He studied law but did not come to the bar. Having an ample fortune and marrying early, he preferred the quiet pursuits of literature as a country gentleman—but his talents and worth could not be hidden from the discerning community around him, and he was soon called to serve the interests of his county and *party* in the Legislature. Mr. McDowell was a decided Democrat of that day, but liberal to all. Soon after his election as Governor, a leading Democrat called on him to remonstrate on his retaining Capt. Dimmock as Superintendent of the armory. "Why not, he is better suited to the place than any one I know." "But he is a Whig," said the gentleman. "That makes no difference if he does his duty," replied the Govcruor. "Then, sir, you cannot be sustained by your party." "I am here to serve the State." He never afterwards seemed to have any respect for that gentleman, although a prominent leader of his party. He was scrupulously conscientious in his public as well as private life. I have seen him walk the floor in almost an agony of feeling, his strict sense of justice conflicting with his tender sensibilities, when applied to for pardons. I remember one occasion particularly, when a *young lady* came as a wife only could come, to petition for her husband, who was convicted of forgery—her overwhelming misery was almost too much for the Governor, and he faltered, but after a while stern justice conquered. "If it had been the first offence," he said, "but unfortunately the act has been committed several times, and shows the want of principle."

As an orator Mr. McDowell had few superiors. His action was classical and fluent—his manner graceful and dignified. I have been told his announcement to Congress of the death of the Ex-President, J. Q. Adams, was the most touching effort ever made on the floor of Congress—and when he repeated the old familiar lines,

"'Tis not the whole of life to live,
Nor all of death to die."

there was a thrill throughout the house. It sounds a little ludicrous to us now, that several gentlemen came up and asked him where he got that beautiful quotation. Notwithstanding his reputation as an orator, of which he must have been conscious, it was often with difficulty he overcame his natural diffidence, and it always cost him an effort to appear before a strange audience. He was in Cambridge in '46, the day of Commencement. By some means it was found out he was in the Hall, and he was immediately sought out and conducted to the platform and seated between President J. Q. Adams and Governor Winthrop. Mr. Sumner made a speech—the subject—a eulogy on Judge Story and Bowditch. I do not remember how he brought in abolition and the South, but I can't forget Mr. McDowell's amused and sarcastic look, as he raised his eyes to where I sat in the gallery. After the ceremonies were over Mr. McDowell attempted to join his party, but the officials accompanied him and insisted on his going to the dinner. He made many excuses—among others he had to escort a lady returning to the South to the steamboat. Gov. Winthrop turned to the lady and politely asked her to excuse him. "Certainly," she replied, "I can easily defer my departure till to-morrow," and he was carried off in triumph. That evening, I spent at Abbot Lawrence's. A number of gentlemen came in full of the treat they had had in Mr. McDowell's dinner speech. His style, his manner, his personal appearance were enthusiastically praised; and above all, the extreme modesty and dignity of his demeanor.

If Mr. McDowell had lived in more eventful times he would have been a prominent man, but, fortunately for him, he entered into the rest that remains for the people of God before our troubles commenced.

FARMER BUMBLEBY.

"ALL WOOL."

I.

This is the Legend of what befell
Farmer Bumbleby—down a well.

II.

Farmer Bumbleby. One of those,
Broad of shoulders and square of toes,

That never lose, of their lives, a day,
Nor know of a debt that they cannot pay.

With a "hundred" arms and an eye that scanned
Every finger of every hand.

"Briaerius—Argus!" one to keep
A Bank account with his bees and sheep.

In short, of that natural "order" which
Ripens at forty and ripens—rich!

Rich and rosily, ripened he!
My burliest, busiest—Bumbleby.

III

Farmer Bumbleby digged a—wait!
Mutton! We won't anticipate.

Farmer Bumbleby owned a Ram,
Black as Egypt, begot of "Ham."

Sire, (such was the Squire's delight,)
To flocks with never a fleck of—"white."

Name of Legion! and *now* it fell
That Farmer Bumbleby digged his well.

IV.

Forty feet from the surface, sheer
To gravel, tokening water near.

A picket-paling that rambled nigh
Veiled the pit from a careless eye.

Not too high for the running leap
Of an average fool of a frightened sheep.

V.

"Something hinders the curb inside."
Something lacking to cause it slide.

"Master's hand is the oil," said he
Down he went like a Bumble-Bee,

Sent it home with a rumble, when—
What *did* enter those black sheep then?

VI.

Ham, and the whole of his colored kin,
Seized at once by the sire of sin!

First a frolic and then a fright;
A headlong, diabolic flight

For the little picket, established nigh
The present quarters of Bumbleby.

VII.

Front the lightning! and, if you will,
Turn Niagara up the hill!

Cross the hurricane's path! but keep
Your chivalry clear of a charge of sheep.

VIII.

Here they come, with a stamp and stare!
Over the fence, and a foot to spare!

Wooly cataract! first the sire
And then the progeny, high and higher.

Mutton-torrent; and every sheep
Mad for the highest and lowest leap!

Over the wall with a demivolt,
Down the well, like a catapult!

Endless? nay, for the pit is full;
Up to the windlass, a well of wool.

IX.

'Twas August! The first went down at day,
The last came up when the skies were gray;

Night, when Bumbleby reached the air,
A Picture! *Paint* him! I might despair,

But Black, *the* color, is close and cheap,
And *there's* his likeness upon a sheep!

Deftly done! but a bolder sleight
The Fuller's that ever *un*-paints him, white!

X.

Enough! may never your hands expel
Such a sick man from such a well!

XI.

We laid him out on the grass to cool,
And he fainted, faltering "d-a-s-h all wool!"

He lived but dwindled, the wretched man,
From fat and rosy to gaunt and wan.

A double horror oppressed his soul—
A mutton-mountain and *that* "black hole."

No peace his days; and his nights no sleep;
Ever his morning-and-night-mare—Sheep!

All wool became, and we banished it,
Another name for—"another fit!"

XII.

At last we saw in his waning eye
That either the man must change or die.

We called the Doctor; he came, in cloth!
And ordered, mortally, "mutton-broth!"

XIII.

HAVE you an uncle? Whose name is Sam?
Has your uncle a pet black Ram?

Kind, I think, of his kin to tell
Your uncle of Bumbleby and his Well.

MARY ASHBURTON.*

A TALE OF MARYLAND LIFE.

GOING in the kitchen, I startled its numerous occupants at my unexpected and untimely presence in their dominion. They evidently had the sway there, to judge from appearances. Mother would have been horror-stricken at the sight of a biscuit-board on the floor, trodden by the feet of numerous little dark, sleek urchins that ran and hid themselves behind their mothers' gowns, when they saw me, screaming "The new mistis! the new mistis!"

The floor was stained with dirt, the stove rusty and streaked with grease, while the pans that hung, some on the wall, others strewn about in every direction, were dim and obscured from their natural glory, as I had never seen pans before. "Plenty for me to do," I thought, as I surveyed it all quickly and made my resolutions.

"Good morning," I said with calm dignity, "I have come to see about breakfast. What does Mr. Chauncey like?"

A broad stare was my only reply, until I repeated my question, when two or three voices essayed to answer.

"Which is the cook?" I asked.

"I'se cook, ma'am," replied one black as 'the ace of spades,' for want of a comparison, yet with a keen, bright eye and an air of briskness that betokened considerable smartness, more frequently exerted in eye-service than in the minor details of an

* Continued from page 50.

orderly kitchen, cleanly cooking utensils—more from the need of a mistress' presence, I suspected, than from a natural lack of energy.

Here shall begin my work of reformation, I inwardly decided; there's enough for me to do for the present,—and all this enormous family of servants, how can they be supported now, reduced in means as he is, they having nothing to do at present, and yet swallowing up all the profits.—Mother's training was not lost upon me, and I was too much interested in Alfred's welfare not to be thoroughly alive to everything of a practical nature.

I closely questioned them as to what he liked or disliked, desirous of consulting his tastes in all that was done.

"He don't like nuffin now," remarked the cook, with an accent of discontent in her tone, "he don't hardly eat nuffin."

"What is that? an omelette you are going to prepare for breakfast? Is that what you give him every morning? Let there be something else this morning."

"Dunno what it'll be then, miss," she replied sullenly, "he will eat that as soon as anything."

I did not stop to parley with her, but quietly proceeded as I intended, and when she declared her ignorance of such a dish, I bade her procure me the materials and set to work myself.

She had had pretty much the sway there since Mrs. Chauncey's death, as the housekeeper had left immediately after that had occurred, and, I suppose, had anticipated something of the kind from the unsophisticated girl that was to assume the post of her former mistress. I quickly showed them, however, that they had nothing to expect from that.—Calmly and quietly, I assumed my post as a lady and mistress of the household, and with native quickness and tact she changed her manner at once. From a look of sullen, ill-concealed displeasure, and a disposition to pertness in her tone, she suddenly became very brisk and attentive, bringing me the things I wanted with alacrity, and growing complimentary if not flattering.

"You *is* a smart young lady," she expressed as her opinion. "You do things so nice. Why, I spec as how you can do a'most anything. I think as how ladies oughter come in their kitchen."

This was said very wisely and sententiously, as if delivering herself of some precomposed address she deemed would be agreeable to my peculiar inclinations.

"If it is kept clean," I answered quietly, and keeping her at a distance, for she was too much disposed to familiarity. She looked confused, and muttered something about the children.

"Have they no other place to stay?" I asked.

"There's the quarter, miss, but they don't like to stay there."

"Why?"

"The glass is broke out the winders and they're cold."

"I will see to having it repaired and made comfortable."

"They'll sot it on fire by theyselves."

"I will see also that they are attended to."

So I busied myself for some time, ascertaining their wants and arranging some little delicacy, I hoped would tempt my dear one's lost appetite.

When my little preparations were ready, the table neatly, tastefully arranged with the windows opened just enough to let a cheerful brightness into the room, I had him called to breakfast.

"Mars Alfred says, madam," said the stately waiter, coming back from my mission, "wont you be pleased to excuse his absence, as he is not well and will keep his room."

If the man had not been there I should have burst into tears, I was so disappointed and distressed. I wanted to see him and when would I have the opportunity?—Not for hours—and my work all thrown away. I felt faint and sick ; it seemed so useless to try, but suddenly taking courage again I determined to make another effort. So rising, I took the prettiest silver waiter I could find, arranged the delicacies I had prepared in fine porcelain, and crowned the whole with a bouquet of choice, lovely flowers.

This time I sent by his nurse, thinking that she might have some influence perhaps to induce him to partake of it—and—my heart also whispered a secret hope that he might know—that she might say, perhaps—who had so zealously cared for him—at least she might let him know that I thought of him. She soon returned with the waiter untouched.

"He wouldn't let me in," she said with indignant anxiety, "I don't know what's to become of him at this rate. I'm afeared for his life. Does he mean to starve hisself to death for that critter?"

"Oh!" I exclaimed in extreme distress, "what can I do for him."

"Nothing at all, miss, but trust in the Lord that it'll come right somehow. He's often shut hisself up that a way since—since she treated him so scandalous.—Mebbe now he's got another one here, he'll come out of these ways."

"Order one of the boys in the garden with me," I said quickly, flushing crimson to my temples.

I spent the morning there working in the borders, rooting up weeds, pruning vines with my scissors, training them in the proper direction, where they had burst from their support and trailed along the ground. Working energetically I got some of the squares in order before the midday sun had rendered it time for me to cease from out-door labors, and to seek the refreshing coolness within.

Then I busied myself about the house; there was much to be done, and the numerous servants were set to work in all directions—yet not noisily—I would have him disturbed by no housekeeper's bustle, but as quietly as possible, and as far from his room as the space would admit.

He was there all day. I made another effort, and in much fear and trembling sent him a cooling drink.

"Yes, miss, he drank it," replied Melissa, in answer to my look of inquiry, "he seemed burning up with thirst."

He appeared at dinner, looking

ing feebler than he did the day before, but he ate more and that was some comfort.—He was even more silent than yesterday, and did not make the slightest effort to entertain me, thinking, perhaps, that I had made myself more at home than he felt, since another's money had redeemed the old place from strangers. Unconquerable shyness in his presence kept me still from saying anything to him. I could not utter commonplaces to him, nor insult him with expressions of the sympathy he did not seek and proudly avoided.—Like a timid child I looked on him with awe, and felt crushed into nothingness before him, his mien was so dark and stern, he seemed so much older than I, and so far removed from me in every way. Indeed his youth seemed to have fled, so different was he from the joyous, brilliant young man of a few months since, all the elasticity belonging to his years gone, life darkened into a tomb.

In the evening he went away, directing his steps to the forest as I could see, then I lost sight of him, for my straining eyes could discern his figure no further. I make the house intolerable to him, I thought. Then I took a walk myself, wending my way to the fields in which I discerned a broad, tempting pathway.

"Me gwine along o' oo," I heard behind me as I started. A sleek little chubby-faced darkey with a roly-poly figure, very much bow-legged, and with a blue domestic slip on, was toddling along behind me.

"Where did *you* come from, and what's your name?"

"I'se Rose, I is, and dars mammy in de skitchen."

"You'll get tired if you walk with me. Those fat, little feet can't carry you far."

Upon that she surveyed her four year old feet with wonderment, as if for the first time conscious of their possession.

"You had better go back to your mother."

"No, no," she shook her head persistently, and approaching closer took a piece of my gown in her hand to hang on to and assist her progress with.

"Then come along, Rose, you may walk with me."

"Whar you gwine? to uncle Pete's?"

Signifying my ignorance of this venerable gentleman, she informed me that he lived in such a direction, the way we were pursuing at present.

I had started from the kitchen door and pursued the path through the yard belonging to it till I reached the farmyard gate. It was not fit for a lady's feet to tread, and I picked my way along with difficulty through the filth till I came to an immense pile of it near the gate, where a rooster clapped his wings and crowed lustily. My strange appearance, too frightened away a whole flock of turkeys that were roosting around a well, which was partly broken down and much dilapidated otherwise. It is a blessing to have something to do, I thought. What would I do here without it?

Going through the gate I entered the green field. There also destruction had commenced its work, for a whole drove of pigs were busily rooting there, and the cows had broken through the fences.

A bad prospect for wheat this year, and I shook my wise head. There's no time for you to sentimentalize over its verdant beauties, Mary. Life is becoming yet more practical to you, and the dreams of youth are fulfilling themselves strangely, in the ueeessity of real life.

Here Rose deserted my gown and ran after a squealing pig, which she caught and brought to me, struggling in her arms. This aroused the mother, who ran snorting terrifically towards us. I seized the child, who had let the pig go, and ran swiftly down the path to a small tenement I perceived at its termination, reaching the door just in time to close it on the angry animal. Looking around to see where I was, I found myself in a small cabin dim and obscure with smoke. Two ancient negroes were shaking with the ague by the fire, while a third paused in the act of placing a stew pan on the coals to stare at me. A great high bedstead occupied one-half of the room, nearly, and with three wooden chairs, a clock and a small table constituted its furniture. Two or three old ragged garments stuffed in the window to supply the place of the broken glass, but imperfectly kept the wind out. I knew what it was,—Mr. Chauncey's cabin for the superannuated servants belonging to the estate.

"Sarvent, missus."

"So you live here? Are you comfortable?"

"Marster was very kind and always had us seen to, but since these times, all's out o' sorts, and we wid 'em, so we gets along bad now."

"I will have you attended to. Come up to the house for what you want and you shall have it."

"Casy won't give us nuffin; she's mighty cross and gin me broomstick tother day."

I could scarcely forbear laughing as the picture of the cook pursuing the poor old creature and his lugubrious countenance with a broomstick presented itself, but it was shamefully cruel conduct in her, and should never be done again, I determined.

I sent one of them out to survey the premises, and ascertaining that the dangerous object had left for other parts and was quiet ly rooting in the meadow below, I ventured out again with the attendant Rose.

"Uncle Pete's potater patch," she informed me. Behind the house sloped their little vegetable garden down to the meadow, where cabbages and potatoes enlivened the yellow bank that descended just there, a heap of clay in the surrounding verdure. A stagnant pool, over which swarmed myriads of green flies, greeted my nostrils on turning in that direction, accounting very plausibly for the prevalent ague and fever.

"Where does that come from?" I asked, turning to the door again and pointing to the offensive object.

"Dat! oh! dat's the slops, miss. We pours 'em out dar."

"Did you always do it?"

"No, marm," replied uncle Pete, who was spokesman, his face as wrinkled as a withered apple, his head as white as a sheet. "Marster was mighty perticler afore dese times, and used to come round 'ere 'amost ebery evenin' to see 'bout us. Den we didn't have der ager so nuther, but we got sick and all got wrong togeder, so I spose we'll die now, our time's cum, praps."

"However that may be," I replied smiling, "there is no use to hasten it, when proper measures can be used for making the place healthier. The filth around the door must be cleared away and I'll see that you have proper food. Come and ask me for whatever you want."

"Thank you, missus." Uncle Pete made me a profound bow, informing me that uncle Jake and uncle Eben were equally obliged but could not express their thanks, on account of the chattering of their jaws at present. So I left, pursuing my walk around the field, finding everywhere much to be seen to, and wondering how I could get it done. To speak to *him* I was afraid, yet I did not like to pursue my plans without his knowledge or concurrence. I knew so well how they could be done, and now was the time to reclaim the place from ruin. What would he say, were I to ask him about these matters? Would he consider it presumption, usurpation of his rights, or an indelicate assumption of authority on the strength of the money expended by my father? Whatever he thinks or says, I must nerve myself to the effort, if I am to do him any good, save him from ruin.

I finished my walk around the field, and returned to the house through the park, then seated myself in the front porch with Rose on a step below me. The child seemed to have taken a fancy to me, and I was glad of it; anything like affection to the lonely, unloved bride was welcome to her then.

I sat there wondering what he would say to me if he came. Would it strike him painfully that a stranger sat there as if awaiting his return, where *she* would have sat had she gone there, welcoming him with her beautiful smile and winning grace, and receiving his warm kisses after an absence that was all too long for him, separated from her? With this thought at each figure that appeared to be approaching, I shrank back nervously, and the sight of him nearing the house, would have made me rush in and hide my unwelcome presence from him.

However, it was midnight before he came, and I heard his door close upon his footsteps. He was weary, and the cries and groans of the preceding night did not smite upon my anxious, listening ear as then. When I sent up to tell him that breakfast was ready, the next morning, the old waiter whose name was Tom, replied,

"He's comin' down, madam, will be here directly."

My heart beat violently as it always did when he approached, when I heard his foot on the stair.

He came in and bowed to me with ceremonious politeness, and then took his seat at the table. He looked so wretched; it almost maddened me to see him so. It was as when you witness the dying agonies of one tenderly beloved; in such mortal suffering, yet skill has failed, love has nothing more to do, nothing but to look until your own anguish equals that of the dying. We ate in silence. How could he utter commonplaces when his heart was broken? and I fully entered into his feelings in all things.

Yet I must make that dreaded effort for his own sake. I cannot make improvements without consulting him. As he arose from the table, I did so too and arrested his steps as he was leaving the room.

"Mr. Chauncey,"—my heart failed me, and the words died upon my lips.

He heard me and turned around quickly.

"Did you speak to me?" with his stern eyes full on my face.

I *must* speak then. "I wished to consult you about something. There is much to be done here, but I do not like to attempt it without your concurrence"—

"Do as you please," he replied quickly, interrupting me, "It's all your own; do with it as you will."

"Not mine, but yours,—yours—all yours." I cried. But he was gone, did not even hear my last words. I threw myself in a chair and indulged in a passionate fit of weeping.

So he would regard all my efforts for his welfare as selfish, vulgar pretension upon my own account. It seems so useless to work,—but cheer up, Mary, nerve your arm for duty, and leave the rest to God.

Receiving strength and comfort, I set to work again. He was out of the house all that day, so I could do much without fear of disturbing him, and drove thought away in vigorous effort to restore the Grove to its former state of neatness and elegance.

In flitting along the passage up stairs, I passed his door. It was slightly ajar, and for the first time, I hesitatingly ventured in. Half frightened, I withdrew my steps, then, growing bolder, went in farther, until I stood in the centre and looked around me.

It was a commodious apartment, elegantly, tastefully furnished, a mother's hand plainly seen in the comforts of its arrangement, and his own refined taste in the selection of its ornaments. Two or three exquisite paintings hung upon the walls, besides innumerable engravings and statuettes; books lay scattered about in the disorder of these later times, when, what had pleased his eye and gratified his taste, had become indifferent to him. An exquisite writing-table, inlaid with mother-of-pearl, occupied one corner, but it was stained as if an ink-stand had been suddenly thrown down, and the contents emptied over it, while the paper and pens were strewn carelessly about as if he did not care what became of them, now that the charm had departed from his existence. I moved about lightly among the treasures of his youth, picking some up from the dusty floor, and tenderly wiping the dust from them, restoring others to their places, as far as I dared, for I was fearful of his noticing the change, and being angry at the intrusion. Such little things as I could do for his comfort, I accomplished, so that he would not see what had been done, yet be benefited by it: such as smoothing his pillow, putting clean, cool linen upon it, and arranging articles upon his toilet table.

I trembled for fear he might return and find me there, darting to the door at every sound and looking anxiously down the passage; almost equally afraid of being caught by the servants,—there in Mr. Chauncey's room.

As I went out I met Melissa at the door, and flushed crimson as she looked at me in a startled way, but quickly recovering myself I said quietly,

"Mr. Chauncey's room is somewhat disordered. Would he let *you* clean it, Melissa?"

"He wouldn't let none of us go in thar, madam, 'cept to make his bed sometimes, that is, when he's in it. When he's out he don't keer what we do; he don't keer for nothin'."

"Would he mind, do you think, if I had it fixed?"

"Laws-a-mercy, madam, I don't think he'd know it even; he don't notice nothin'. I wish poor young marster was like himself."

"Aye," I sighed, and left her, having been drawn into this conversation more as a relief to my embarrassment than because I desired or had intended it.

Thus passed one day after another. Since he had waived all interest in his affairs and had left me to do as I pleased, I proceeded with energy to repair the damages that ruin had wrought in that formerly highly cultivated place. Consulting my father, I drew much information from his experience, and acted upon his advice which was invaluable to me at that period. A sufficient time had not elapsed since the elder Mr. Chauncey's careful superintendence of the farming operations, for us to be irremediably behindhand, and a vigorous hand might do much for next year, and some little for this. As much of the ground as I could, I turned into a garden for late vegetables, resolving, with a secret blush at the expedient I was obliged to resort to in giving the proud name of Chauncey such associations, to sell my crop at the county market town. The need of ready money perplexed me much. It was time that the servants had their summer clothing prepared, and all was yet to be done; no money to do it with. Then many of them were a dead expense upon the property—able to work, but there was not work enough for them to have suitable employment, where the family was so small and required so little at their hands.—They lolled about listlessly all day, sleeping in the sun or playing with the children. This was the puzzle—how to get rid of them. I could hire them out, but what would Alfred say? What would he think of my sending his old family servants out from their old home upon the mercy of a world they knew nothing of? yet he could not stand it. I could make nothing, not even the ends meet, while a number of idle, useless people were supported on the estate—a part of which only had been redeemed from debt, while it was my hope and special ambition to save the rest from being partitioned off from us, leaving but a third of what had once belonged to the Chauncey property.

Upon consulting mother, she said:

"Why don't you ask Mr. Chauncey about it? He could hardly object where it's so much to his advantage."

There was the stumbling-block between mother and myself. I could not enter into explanation, and she would not tacitly understand, so I did not go home often on account of that. The subject that was upon the lips, in the hearts of both uppermost when we met, was a sealed one between us, so there was mutual restraint. The moment I perceived those dreaded questions approaching, questions about Alfred and his present state of mind, whether he noticed me or not, I arose to go, or quickly changed the subject, so I was seldom troubled with them, though he was always in our thoughts when we were together. Nor did my parents go often to the Grove. Mother had more to do now that I had left home; then I think she was afraid of Alfred and dreaded meeting him even in her very occasional visits.

"I wonder what he'd a done," she said in a tone of indignation, "if all this had happened after his marriage, and he'd a had a fine lady wife on his hands."

"He would have worked and supported her," I replied gravely.

"Much good she'd a done him, then," answered mother, contemptuously, "I wonder if she'd a tried as you have, nor would'nt a known how, if she had."

As Destiny had directed matters differently, I could not reply, but could not help wondering with her, what the superb Adéle would have done with a poor husband. I will not be uncharitable,—it might have called her out from self and given a new and loftier bias to her character. I did ask him about the servants, for I could not tell what to do. He was entering the hall door, his hair hanging wild and loose, under a slouch hat that half concealed his features, as he came in dripping with rain.

"Mr. Chauncey, I wished to speak with you about something."

He took his hat off and bowed. I had, with difficulty, raised my courage up to the required height, but when he looked at me in that way, those dark, searching eyes of his, between the long hair that fell, in wild, tangled curls almost to his shoulders, I was confused at once, and unable to express myself as I wished. I never *will* be able to make him think better of me, I thought bitterly.

"Mr. Chauncey, indeed, I don't like to do these things without asking you about them—that is—I mean to say—I—I—was thinking"—

"Well," he said with a slight curl of the lip, and gesture of impatience as if wishing to go, "did you wish to speak to me?"

"I was going to say that there were a great many servants here, so many more than I know what to do with, or can find clothes for, while they eat up all that is raised here, and—and, I was going to ask you about it,—if I might hire some of them out. I do not like to do it, as they are your old family servants, but under present circumstances, would you object?"

He had fixed his steady gaze upon me, to my great discomfiture, while I made this speech, but when I ceased, he merely smiled a sort of scornful smile, waved his hand as if to say, "I told you before to do as you pleased with your own, why trouble me about what does not concern me? only do not disturb me on these matters again; I have nothing to do with them," then proceeded on his way up stairs, where I heard him close, and lock, the door upon himself presently.

Useless! I sighed, I must proceed without him, then. How wet and cold he looked, poor Alfred.

I had a fire made in his room, against his return, and had drawn an arm-chair with a dressing gown thrown over it, before the cheerful blaze, hoping that he would notice these little attentions to his comfort and think,—perhaps,—that it was *my* work, that the unloved one had cared for him as far as her poor hand could.

So I crept up to the room near his, and listened to his movements, to see if he, at least, made use of the articles I had arranged for his comfort, and if he had thrown aside those dripping garments.

All was silent except an occasional start or so. As I could ascertain nothing concerning the source of anxiety, I left the neighborhood as noiselessly as I had approached it.

The first Sunday after my marriage,—I remember it so well—as we sat at the breakfast table, the old waiter said something about its being Sunday morning.

"Sunday?" exclaimed Alfred, quickly turning around, "so it is. Are the horses in good condition?"

"Yes, sir. Perhaps the lady would like to go to church," said Tom, with his stately, old-time courtesy.

"Did you wish to go?" and Alfred looked at me.

"Yes," I replied hesitatingly, "and you—will you go?"

"I! no, no," he answered quickly. "Stay—yes, I cannot permit you to be subjected to such remarks as would necessarily follow my absence. I will go."

"Don't mind the world for me, if it causes you pain to go there," I replied, but so low that he did not hear me, and was gone before I had finished speaking.

With that same courteousness, he handed me in and out of the carriage, ever mindful of the gentleman, even when most distracted with sorrow, and maintaining a grave, dignified, demeanor in church.

How I was stared at! I felt the steady gaze that was directed at me even through my downcast lids, but left immediately with him after church, before they had had time to gratify their curiosity further. I felt so strangely in the Grove pew, seated where Mrs. Chauncey had been so short a time before, with her fashionable guests. Certainly it was not comfortable. Had *he* not been there I should much have preferred my old seat with my parents across the aisle, beneath the window, where I had looked at him when a boy, my wandering eyes attracted into steady admiration by his remarkable beauty. I glanced at him furtively to notice the contrast between him, as he now was and then. Alas! a great change had taken place. In lieu of the boyish frankness and ingenuousness of countenance, smiling kindly on all the world, a grave, weary looking man sat, worn with trouble, and frowning gloomily upon life and everything connected with it.

As I came out leaning upon his arm, a strange sensation thrilling at my heart as I did so, two or three pressed forward to congratulate us with well-meaning or officious kindness. But upon looking in our faces, they drew back with the words half uttered, half frozen upon their lips. Alfred looked like a cold, gloomy statue; I hung, trembling and timid, upon his arm, and though I smiled and held out my hand there was not ease or warmth of manner sufficient to justify further familiarity.

I thanked him in my heart for the self-denial that had taken him out of himself to think of me at that time, but was almost equally uncomfortable as though he had not gone and I had been subjected to whispered wonderings and unfavorable comments. These he had spared me by his thoughtfulness; but from internal discomfort he was not able to save me the suffering of *his* suffering and knowledge that for all the love I bore him, he not only was indifferent to me, but most probably regarded me with aversion as one who had taken, all unsought, the place that should have been occupied by one loved and honored.

(TO BE CONTINUED.)

THE AMERICAN CONFLICT.

HORACE GREELEY.

THAT future historians may know the truth, Mr. Greeley gives a table, purporting to be the statistics of the numbers and proportions of men furnished by the individual States, during the war of 1776. This table is in exact accordance with all that he and all his associates, such as Helper, Draper, and others have usually presented to the world, when on the subject of slavery, or any question to which the North and South were parties. I will not dissect this frame, but only say that the number he gives to South Carolina, for the whole seven years' war, was actually raised in that State at one single call of General Rutledge, at the beginning of the war! With this, as sufficient, I dismiss this caricature of statistics.

Mr. Greeley says of the fugitive slave clause, "there was nothing mutual in the obligation it sought to impose. Nor could any one gravely insist that the provision for the mutual rendition of slaves was essential to the completeness of the Federal pact. The old Confederation *had known nothing like it.** Here are three distinct assertions. 1. That there was nothing *mutual* between the North and the South, requiring the Fugitive Slave act. 2. That such act was not necessary to the completeness of the pact. 3. "The old Confederation had known nothing like it." We shall now show that all three of these assertions are totally untrue. Mr. Greeley* had just quoted from the Articles of the Ordinance of 1787, by which the North-West territory was ceded by the South, to the United States, showing that it was the "charter of compact," and "*shall stand as* FUNDAMENTAL CONDITIONS *between* the thirteen States, and those newly described UNALTERABLE, but by the *joint* consent of the United States, in Congress assembled, and of the *particular* State within which such particular alteration is proposed to be made."

Though these pacts were not passed then, he says they were afterwards, i. e., 1787, with little alteration. But when they were passed, our author says, the act concludes with "six *unalterable* Articles of *Perpetual* compact between the above parties. In it, he says, was *the Fugitive Slave Law.* He is right, as every one at all read in those matters knows. It was adopted, Mr. Greeley says, with a unanimous vote of the States present. This was at the very time the famous Convention was framing the Constitution. Mr. Greeley emphasizes the words, that this compact was "PERPETUAL" and "UNALTERABLE" to show the wrong of *secession.* Very well. Yet this compact had two express stipulations: 1. That not more than *five* States should

* Vol. 1. 47.

* Vol. 1. 39.

be made out of the territory ceded. 2. That all fugitive slaves in the territory or States (after their admission) should be returned to their owners. See now what follows. They proceeded at once to carve out *ten* States, in utter violation of this "unalterable" and "perpetual" compact. They failed to complete this, and finally did carve out *seven* States. That compact, he says, stipulated that fugitive slaves should be returned. It was "perpetual" and "unalterable," quotes Mr. Greeley. In making the Constitution, they simply incorporated that already existing "perpetual" "unalterable" article of pact. They were under solemn obligation to retain that ordinance. Yet, Mr. Greeley says, Mr. Butler, of South Carolina, introduced it as a *new* and *unjust* claim. Nay, he says the Confederacy had never known such an act! Yet, he had shown in the same volume, at length, that it was an express and leading part of their "perpetual compact." Now, who will say Mr. Greeley is not the man to write history—yea, and to collect and transmit the proper materials to the future historian, by which future ages may have a fair and impartial view of "the great conflict?"

Says Mr. Greeley, in the *Tribune* of September 1867—"We always distrust the logic which is based on a *falsehood.*" That was a strange and new freak that suddenly passed over the philosopher of the drab coat. Our historian italicises a number of words as the strongest proof of the perpetuity of the Union, in article 1. of the Ordinance first proposed—"they shall *forever* remain a part of the United States"—"perpetual compact." Yet, he knows that they *were* altered, then abolished. That the "perpetual compact" and "forever," all went by the board in less than half a year—in three months' time! Very short and uusubstantial "forevers" "perpetuals" and "unalterables" were they. We could quote fifty pages from the Madison Papers, from the speeches of the framers of the Constitution, to the effect of the following, had we the space.—"Mr. Gerry, of Massachusetts, urged the indecency and pernicious tendency of *dissolving*, in so slight a manner, the solemn obligations of the Articles of Confederation. If nine out of thirteen can dissolve the Compact, six out of nine will be just as able to dissolve the new one hereafter."* Nine did dissolve it, and it perished. So all of Mr. Greeley's italics and arguments, on that point, with the Drapers, Motleys and Bancrofts, are trash and balderdash, and Greeley knows it.

Let us see now if Mr. Greeley really "suspected the logic founded on a falsehood" touching his precious idol—the slavery question. That will try him indeed, as Dogberry says, "if there be *any* allegiance in him"—to truth. We will give him a fair hearing here also.

Mr. Greeley declares that concurring circumstances and the new principles evolved 1776 "had pretty thoroughly cured the North

* Madison Papers, 3. 15-38.

of all attachment to, or disposition to *justify* slavery before the close of the Revolutionary war."* Of the "framers" he says "their judgments condemned, and their consciences reprobated it" (slavery)‡. "Slavery would have found no lodgment in it (the Constitution;) but already the *whip of Disunion* was brandished [Greeley is such an Addison or Livy in style, these classic beauties must be endured,] and the fatal necessity of compromise made manifest. The Convention would have at once and forever prohibited, as far as our country and her people were concerned, the African Slave Trade; but South Carolina and Georgia were present. . . . 'No slave-trade, no Union!' . . . Virginia and her more *Northern Sisters* were *more than* willing to *prohibit* AT ONCE the further importation of slaves."§ It is not too much to say that the writer of that, Mr. Greeley, *knew* that he was penning a deliberate untruth. But we shall see. He adds: "The conscience of the *North* was quieted by embodying a promise that Congress might interdict the foreign slave-trade after the expiration of twenty years."† We shall soon see how that conscience was *soothed*, but by a motive, an opiate as different from the above, as the spirit of heaven is from the feelings of the scoffing fiend that scowled about the walls of Eden. He also tells us that slave traders in the North, 1787 (eighty years ago) "were never held in good repute."*

To quote all the speeches of the leaders of the North in that Convention, when framing the Constitution, that stamps all the above as utterly false, would be to fill whole chapters. Before going to that Convention, let us quote a few leaders of an earlier date, while fully baptized in the spirit of 1776. On Friday, July 12, 1776, only eight days after the Jubilee over the *Declaration of Independence*, Chase observes "that *negroes are property*, and as such cannot be distinguished from *lands*, &c., held in those States where there are few slaves"—Northern States.† He then compares the matter to "taxing as . . . cattle." "The negroes in fact should not be considered as members of the State, *more than cattle*, and that they have no more interest in it."‡ Did Justice Taney's Dred Scott decision equal *that?*

John Adams—(*et tu Brute!*) observed "that it was of no consequence by what name you call your people, whether by that of *freemen* or *slaves*. . . . In some countries the laboring poor . . . were called slaves. . . . That the condition of the laboring poor in most countries—that of the fishermen, particularly, of *the Northern States* is *as* abject *as that of slaves*."§ That is the famous Puritan, John Adams, 2nd President of the United States, the son of Massachusetts

* Conflict, 1.37.
Ibid, 43-4.
Conflict, 1,45.
Ibid 45-6.

* Ibid, 255.
† Madison Papers, 1. 28
‡ Madison Papers, 29.
§ Madison Papers, 1, 29 30.

Pennsylvania's great light, Jas. Wilson, afterwards, her ablest man in the Convention of 1787, feared "the Southern Colonies would have all the benefit of slaves"—the North have to bear the "burden of defence." He spoke of "other kinds of property," while the famous "Doctor Witherspoon," of New Jersey, answered, "It has been objected (by the North) that negroes *eat the food* of freemen, and therefore should be taxed; *horses*, also, eat &c., and should be taxed."* Yes, yes; they were against negroes, because they had mouths, and ate food. A Yankee knows what money and expenses mean.—Finally, John Adams cries out, "Reason, justice, and equity never had weight enough on the face of the earth to govern the councils of men. It is INTEREST ALONE which does it."† Thus talked the great Northern sages of '76. Let us now hear how they talked in 1787, while framing the Constitution.

Mr. Rufus King, of Massachusetts, that colony of "conscience," was careful to tell that Convention that "*Revenue* was *the* object of the General Legislature."‡ Mr. Gorham had said the same thing—being of the same State. On the same page with this Messrs. Butler and Pinckney moved to require "fugitive slaves and servants to be delivered up like criminals."

Mr. Wilson (leader of the Pa. delegation.) "This would oblige the Executive of the State to do it, *at the public expense.*"

Mr. Sherman, (of Connecticut,) "saw no more propriety in the public seizing and surrendering a slave or servant, than a *horse.*"* So ran the debate—this being the exact report. Previous to this, speaking of the slave trade, Mr. Sherman, though opposed to it on *economical* grounds, as they had argued that "as the *public good* did not require it to be taken from them—right to import— . . . he thought it best to leave the matter as we find it."† Ellsworth, the next greatest light of New England there, argued that they could not consider it "in a *moral* light. . . . Let us not intermeddle." Gerry, of Massachusetts, thought "we had nothing to do with the conduct of the States as to slaves."‡ Dickinson, of Delaware, then counted a Northern State, said, "The true question was, whether the *national happiness* would be promoted or impeded by the importation."§ Rufus King, of Massachusetts, afterwards, 1819, U. S. Senator from New York, and author of the Higher Law doctrine, (though he was but its expression as the *type* of New England life) "thought the subject should be considered in a *political light only*. . . . He remarked, on the exemption of slaves from duty, "whilst every *other import* [negroes regarded simply as 'chattles and other imports'] was subjected to it, as an inequality that could not fail to

* Madison Papers 1. 32.
† Madison Papers 1. 36.
‡ Madison Papers, 3, 1447.

* Madison Papers, 1447-8.
† Madison Papers, 3, 1390.
‡ Madison Papers, 1394.
§ Madison Papers, 1394.

strike the *commercial sagacity* of the Northern and Middle States." Gouverneur Morris, of Pennsylvania, thought "these things may form a *bargain* among the Northern and Southern States."*—Again, said Roger Sherman: "Let every State import what it pleases. The *morality* or wisdom of slavery are considerations belonging to the States themselves.—*What enriches* a *part enriches* the *whole.*"† These were the remarks made, this the light in which they viewed it. Let us now see the vote of this great body on the slave-trade. Some were for stopping the slave-trade at once—Col. Mason, Madison and others from the South. Some were for letting it alone, some for regulating it as a revenue, and some for a limited extension of it. It was proposed to let it go on till 1800, then it should cease. It was moved to extend this limitation eight years—to 1808. Madison, of Virginia, opposed this very earnestly, as did Mason also, contending that to 1800 was too long. But when it was proposed to add eight years more to the time allowed for the trade, "Mr. Gorham, of Massachusetts, seconded the motion."‡ On the motion, which passed in the affirmative,—(they stood thus—for extending the Slave Trade to 1808.) New Hampshire, Massachusetts, Connecticut, Maryland North Carolina, South Carolina, Georgia, aye—7. New Jersey, Pennsylvania, Delaware, Virginia, no—4."§ New York and Rhode Island were absent. (Maryland is omitted 'in the vote, but page 1429 on same issue, she appears, and the figure 7 shows she was accidentally omitted.) Thus the whole body of New England States present—and only one was absent—voted to prolong the slave-trade, purely as a *commercial interest*, while Virginia, Delaware, and a number of the delegates of Maryland and North Carolina, voted against it and opposed it. "Mr. King, of Massachusetts, and Mr. Langdon, of New Hampshire, considered this ['property in man'] as the *price* of the first part."* Col. Mason, of Virginia, wished to tax the slave-trade so heavily as to discourage it. But Sherman, of Connecticut, observed that "the smallness of the duty showed *revenue* to be the object, *not the discouragement* of the institution."† As a confirmation of this, it was *unanimously* voted to make the tax ten dollars, so as not to discourage importation. Nor did these men of soothed consciences stop here. The whole New England delegation present—and only one was absent—voted for the fugitive slave law in Congress, 1793, when the new government was put in operation. There was not a word or hint against it in all New England. Sherman, of Connecticut, was on the Committee that reported that law. Gerry, of Massachusetts, voted for it. Only five votes were cast against it from the whole body of Northern members in Congress. Madison, King, Gerry, R. Morris, O. Ells-

* Madison Papers, 1396.
† Madison Papers, 1399.
‡ Madison Papers, 3, 1429.
§ Madison Papers, 1427.

* Madison Papers, 1429.
† Madison Papers, 1429.

worth were of that Congress. The Supreme Courts of Massachusetts, of New York, and of the United States all sanctioned the same law.*

It was after King, Wilson and G. Morris failed to carry some of their favorite commercial "advantages in return," and "preferential distinctions in commerce," as King said† that "the admission of slaves was a most grating circumstance to his mind."‡—Gouverneur Morris, of Pennsylvania, now became terribly wrought upon, as to his conscience, and its qualms "horribly shook his disposition." He suddenly had ghostly visions of chained negroes all crowded together in the holds of miserable ships, and it so harrowed up his soul, that he discovered slavery to be "a nefarious institution." He never could "concur in upholding domestic slavery." He cries out in holy disgust—but his words take us back as effectually as the—"*we are all poor critters,*" did the widow Bedott—"And what is the proposed *compensation* to the *Northern States*, for a *sacrifice of every principle of right, of every impulse of humanity?*" He then finds that the great evil is, they are to aid in bearing a part of the expenses that insurrections and troubles, South, may incur.§ Col. Mason and Madison, of Virginia, were the men who looked at the question from a moral and humane point of view, and assaulted slavery, and the trade, with a zeal unknown in the North in that day*.

In view of all this, had Mr. Greeley possessed one particle of honesty as a writer, when compiling so large a work, and finding time to devote whole chapters to obscure individuals, he would have at least mooted the question of the propriety of, in whole or part, compensating the owners of slaves, or reasoned about the condition of things after venturing to let loose four millions of slaves, degraded, ignorant, and helpless. Any man that had a particle of moral honesty as a writer, or any respect for the intellect and heart of his readers, would have fully discussed these points. He would have looked the question fairly in the face. To unsettle the whole social and political system of an empire, derange the whole machinery of government, society and commerce, were to Mr. Greeley, questions of not one-tenth the importance that attaches to some horse-thief, or scoundrel, who, in addition to other crimes, should murder a family to rescue a negro. He never thinks it worth while to consider what was to be done with such a multitude, in setting them free. He never makes a particle of allowance for the *only* maxim, that is universally settled in political science, that *interest* governs a State, and to which no people on earth ever cling with such tenacity as the North, nor any political leader as unwaveringly as Mr. Greeley himself.

* Southern Review, 1867, Baltimore, by Prof. A. T. Bledsoe, LL. D.

† Madison Papers, 2. 1056.

‡ Madison Papers, 3. 1261.

§ Madison Papers, 3. 1263–4.

* Madison Papers, 3, 1390–1.

Nor does he ever hint at the infamous Indian Slave Trade the Puritans carried on for so many years, while professing to give a full history of slavery in this country. He never gives the South a particle of credit for the well known fact that thousands of the owners of slaves would have gladly given up their slaves, if they could have seen where they could be as happy as they were at home. And he never names or hints another fact of infinite importance here, namely, that the negro slave at the South was infinitely more happy, elevated, and blest, than he was in Africa. After all the light that Livingstone, Baker, and a host of others have thrown upon that benighted region, where ignorance and slavery are at their depth, it becomes evident that Southern slavery was a Paradise of bliss in comparison. Honest historian! "Upright judge!" Pardon us, Mr. Greeley, but "we *always* distrust the logic which is based on a falsehood." "I thank thee, Jew, for that word."

And who could have suspected that this renowned knight of the goose-quill would write such a cold, useless and contemptible a falsehood as the following? for here we may well adopt the Poet's thought—this was no game his arms to exercise. On the meeting of the Convention of 1787, Mr. Greeley says: "Franklin, then over eighty-one years of age, *declined* the chair (as President) on account of his increasing infirmities; and, on *his* motion, George Washington was unanimously elected President."*—

* Conflict, 1. 43.

Small as is this sentence, it has several falsehoods in it, and is, besides, most contemptible.—Franklin was not present, in the body, that day, and could not have either declined a nomination that was *never proposed*, nor could he have nominated, "on *his* motion," Washington, when he, himself, was *not there* to do so. On account of his eminence, he would have been the next most proper person to be President, had not Virginia's son been there. But even then it could not have been proper altogether: for the Convention had been first proposed, first called, set on foot, by Virginia alone. She had, through Madison and Washington, 1781, first hinted and proposed such a measure. Then she was, by far, the largest and most important State. She was, therefore, entitled to the honor of the Presideney. But the facts settle the matter. "Mr. Robert Morris, of Pennsylvania, informed the members assembled, that, by the instruction, and in behalf of the deputation of Pennsylvania, he proposed George Washington, Esq., Commander-in-Chief, for President of the Convention."* In a note it is said, "the Doctor (Franklin) was himself to have made the *nomination* of General Washington, but the state of the weather, and of his health, confined him to his house." Accordingly his name does not stand on the roll as called that day. If Mr. Greely will resort to such mean little falsehoods as that, where he had all the facts open before him, and if for *such* a purpose,

* Madison Papers, 2 722.

and about such illustrious men, what can we expect of him on the great issues of the conflict?

He says, Jefferson, being ambassador abroad, during that time, took "no conspicuous, or decided part either for or against the Convention, in its infancy." On the contrary, he took the deepest interest, and his correspondence, as well as that of Madison, Mason, Randolph and others, shows the deep interest he took in its formation, and how he urged some of the very measures that were added as amendments.

Again, says this Nemesis of Historians—"Mr. John A. Quincy . . . of Boston . indulged in what *resembled*, very closely, a *menace* of *contingent* secession." Of the Hartford Convention he continues—it "evinced its discontent . . by a resort to *rhetoric*, which was denounced as *tending to disunion*, but which does not seem to warrant the imputation."* "Resembled." Here are Quincy's words: "If this bill pass—admitting Louisiana as a State—it is my deliberate opinion that it is a virtual dissolution of the Union; that it will free the States from their moral obligation, and, as it will be the right of all, so it will be the duty of some, definitely to prepare for separation, amicably if they can, *violently* if they must." Mr. Plumer, (who had been in public life years before, being United States Senator from New Hampshire, 1803, Governor for two terms consecutively after this, and who prepared to write a history of the United States,) himself at the time an ardent Federalist, adduces an array of proof that fills half of a huge volume about the size of Mr. Greeley's, bearing on the secession designs and plots of the New England States at that time. He shows beyond the powers of cavil that they openly spoke for secession, and passed resolutions looking directly to a withdrawal from the Union. And that we may see what Quincy meant in the above declaration in Congress in 1811, the Puritan Plumer says it was their intention "to forcibly resist the laws of Congress."* He gives us the following from "the Federal Convention, held March 31, 1811, in Boston, which resolved that the non-intercourse law, just then passed, 'if persisted in, *must* and *will* be resisted.' 'Resistance,' said Dr. Parist, April 11, 1811, 'is our only security.'" He then quotes Josiah Quincy's speech above noticed.† Mr. Bradford wrote to Gerry at the same time that if the Congress persisted, "the New England States will rise in their wonted strength, and with the indignant feelings of 1775, *sever themselves* from that part of the nation which wickedly abandons their rights and interests."‡ He then analyzes the Hartford Convention, and shows beyond the shadow of a cavil that it deliberately resolved on secession, unless its demands were granted. If we had space, we could adduce, from this high New England authority, a long array of facts on these issues. Yet Mr. Greeley smoothes

* Conflict, 1. 85-6.

* Life of Plumer, 385.
† Life of Plumer, 385.
‡ Life of Plumer, 386.

over all these things in a stretch of twelve or fifteen half-column lines, treating it all as a little rhetorical flourish.

But we are not done with this Achilles of the American press. He insinuates that our fathers consolidated the government, and rehashes the thousand-and-one times demolished sophistry of Northern federalist writers and speakers, that the preamble implies it, though the preamble was not made till all else was agreed upon, and a bare accommodation to the manner of ratification, since to say "we the States," enumerating them as was the plan drawn up, was liable to insuperable difficulties, as some might not ratify. He quotes the words of P. Henry, who, in a heated speech, tried to deter Virginia from ratifying the Constitution, and made the bold declaration so constantly quoted by consolidationists, but which Madison and others who framed the instrument showed at the time to have no such meaning.—Yet Greeley and his associates regard it as legitimate argument and unimpeachable logic, that when a body of able, learned, and cautious men frame a document, and make it so very different from what a consolidationist would, that it drives Hamilton out of the Convention in disgust, and arouses the wrath of Read, Wilson and King, to a furious pitch, it is still a consolidation, because one man who was not there at all, in his enthusiastic fury uses every weapon a fiery orator can command, and seizes this among them to alarm the people. Nay, they think a man of Henry's very limited education, who never was given to rigid analysis, and who was not present, knew far better what the instrument was, than the astute Madison, Randolph, Hamilton, Pinckney, Wilson, Sherman, Ellsworth, and Martin, with their illustrious compeers! Greely ought to write "full and impartial histories!"

He then quotes one more—Washington—who said the end was the "*consolidation* of the Union." But Washington did not have a thing to do with its framing. He sat as its President, and never opened his mouth but once,* till all was done, and the Constitution had then been finished and engrossed. But aside, a "consolidation of the *Union*" was infinitely different from a consolidation of the States, the point Greeley contends for.

But what will the reader say, when he learns that this whole thing is a sheer fabrication of Mr. Greeley's. In his note he says this language occurs "in the address of the Federal Convention, signed by Washington, as its President, September 17, 1787."† Yet, on that day, they positively refused to have any "address" prepared, and a motion to that effect, was lost. They had formerly voted to allow the Committee of eleven to draw up an address, but it was not done. But the fitness of Mr. Greeley to write "a full and fair" history, will strike the reader with greater force still, as he advances. To prove consolidation, he quoted Hamilton, Wilson, and Madison,

* Madison Papers, 3. 1600 and note.

† Conflict, 1. 82.

in the Convention of '87, where the first, with Read also—a most inferior member—was for wiping out—"swallowing up" the State governments, Wilson for encroaching more on them, while he declares the one made would be encroached on by the States, while Madison urged a modification of Wilson's view mildly for a while, then gave it up. Yet, Mr. Greeley knew, if he ever read their proceedings, that when such hints were dropped, as repeatedly they were, a burst of indignation from the whole body of the Convention smothered it out. Four-fifths of the members, and every State would have indignantly repudiated any action that contemplated such a possibility. The adoption of such an article would have dissolved the Convention as a mob. And no State was so fierce in denunciation of such hints, as New York, Maryland, Connecticut, New Hampshire, and Delaware. He knows, also, that there could not have been found a corporal's guard of able men in any State of the Union that would have ratified the Constitution, had any such principle been engrafted into it. Greeley says, in the face of these facts, that "History teaches . . . that it was the purpose of the framers of the Constitution to render the inhabitants of all the States, substantially, and *perpetually* one people, . . . known to the rest of mankind, by a common national government." We know that this was the *desire* of some. But we know that it was not the faith of the framers of the Constitution. We can quote three hundred pages from their debates that shows the above statement to be devoid of a particle of truth. They all agreed that there were inseparable obstacles to a unity of interest, even among the little squad of thirteen States. The fierce encounters and efforts of each section, the one to obtain power over tariffs and commerce, the other to make secure her enjoyed rights, as well as the efforts of New England, and Pennsylvania, to crush the prospects of the West, show, beyond cavil, that they felt they were *not* one people. As to "national government," he knows that the Convention, with a unanimous vote, rejected the term. Yet, says Mr. Greeley, as "my plan does not contemplate the INVENTION *of any facts*, I must, &c." Alas, for it, *had* he contemplated such invention then! Mr. Greeley makes a series of statements about John C. Calhoun, that set honor, truth, and honesty at utter defiance. He says, Calhoun was "the most thorough-going champion" of those loose constructions of the Constitution that clamored for national improvement at the public expense, high "Protection, Tariffs," &c. This is utterly false. He did give his influence for the tariff of '16, as he explained, to remove our national debt, and happily and incidently, it would protect our oppressed manufacturers, for he was always most generous and broad in his views. But when in 1824 it was demanded as a *bonus*, when we needed no high tariff, being quite out of debt, and yet still higher in 1828, it was infinitely different.—

But Greeley is not satisfied with such slanders on the South as he weaves in with this question—he must glorify Massachusetts at the expense of the records of Congress, the simplest facts of history, and the declarations of the "great expounder" of that noted State. "The Tariff of 1828—the highest and most protective ever adopted in this country—was passed by a Jackson Congress," of which, Greeley tells us, Van Buren, Silas Wright, and "the Jacksonian leaders of Pennsylvania and Ohio were master-spirits."* *This* is true. "And thereby hangs a tale." That is, that the North, whether as Democrats, Whigs, Federalists, "Know Nothing Americans," or Abolitionists, *always* consolidated against the South in solid array, when ever any land, money, or any interest of the pocket was concerned. The record of Democracy North is little better than Whiggery where ever Banks, Fisheries, Tariffs and admission of Southern States was on hand. "I thank thee, Jew, (I must repeat) for *that* word." "This Tariff imposed high duties on Iron, (to aid Pennsylvania, but mainly to get her vote,) Lead, (to fool Missouri, and do her not a doit of good as it proved,) Hemp, (to wheedle Kentucky, with the same result as in Missouri,) Wool, (to substantially aid Ohio, but mainly to plunder the South, by preventing foreign competition, as the negroes were the main consumers of wool, with the poor of the West, who were seduced by the lead and hemp delusion.) He says, as the result of this tariff, "the country exhibited a rapid growth." On the contrary the records show that the South was utterly prostrated.—Men worth millions of real estate, and hundreds of thousands in lands and negroes, were unable to do more than clothe and feed them. Benton, the fierce enemy of slavery, shows, in vol. 1, of the United States Senate, that they were in a deplorable condition.—The figures and array of general statistics, adduced in Congress by Calhoun, showed this beyond controversy, although Clay had the brazen effrontery to say the South was prospering under it! And while Jackson had the effrontery to publish to the world that the South had no cause of complaint, yet in secret cabinet they admitted her wrongs were grievous and irritating. Honest coercionists! But we have a record Greeley should respect. In his Almanac of 1862, (if I remember its date—it is not now by me,) and in Helper's "Crisis," edition of 1860, ("compendium") we have two tables or plates showing the relative increase and decrease in the wealth and prosperity of all the States. Now, though these men deny that tariffs impoverished the South and made the North, how happens it that the tables of Greeley and Helper exactly agree in showing that the Northern States, especially East, bend or curve upward—the opening of the angles of the lines determining the degree of prosperity *as it occurred*—and rush up with prosperity from the very years the Tariffs were put on! Right at the years 1824 and 1828 they start suddenly up,

* Conflict, 1. 91.

and make a larger angle at 1828, the enormous tariff, than at 1824. But at those very angles the cotton and tobacco States bend (relatively) right down, showing why it was they drooped and lagged behind. Yet their decline is attributed by these cunning Shylocks to *slavery*, and their prosperity to their sagacity and frugality. True it was a sagacity that in the formation of the government, they would not enter the Union, unless provided with a Northern majority in both branches of Congress, avowing its design at the time to hold the commerciai interests in their hands, as they fully and repeatedly declared in the federal debates. Yet Greely says, "there is no evidence that their condition (South's after 1828) was less favorable, her people less comfortable than they had been." It is at the most fearful cost of Mr. Greeley's head that any one can suppose his heart honest in such declarations. But these are not all the blemishes of this *one* single page of his "fair" history. "It," (tariff of 1828,) says he, "was opposed by a majority of those (States) of New England," and he singles out that immaculate State of the Puritans, saying it was "obnoxious to Massachusetts and the States which, on either side, adjoined her."* Verily a man of utmost coolness has need to pray if he would have the grace of quiet, calm forbearance in reading this tissue of slander and falsehoods. Not only did the States around her, but Massachusetts voted for that Tariff with a relish she never had felt before. And Greeley is the less to be excused for this untruth, because that fact was made the more notorious when Col. Hayne, of South Carolina, tantalized Webster, the Senator of Massachusetts 1830, for his desertion of his former course, as in 1824 he had not only voted against the high Tariff, but made one of the most powerful speeches against it, for which Hayne so highly complimented him, as bearing off, on his Atlantian shoulders, the very pillars of the Constitution. Webster explained that in 1824 his State had most of her capital in the carrying trade—I quote from memory, but any who will read his famous reply to Hayne will see it—and it was against her interest to have a high Tariff. But that the government having given such inducing bounties since then to manufactures, his State had gone largely at it, hence his change of principle. He made this explanation in that most eloquent and famous effort of his life. Does Mr. Greeley yet "suspect the logic that is founded on a falsehood?" Indeed this venomous man cannot relate the smallest circumstance, without falling into the temptation of slandering the South. He tells us "Mr. Van Buren *supplanted* him (Calhoun) as Vice President in 1832, sharing in Jackson's second and most decided triumph." Here he says Van Buren supplanted Calhoun. It is false, and he knew it. Next he writes it so as to leave but one impression—no other can he draw, viz: that owing to Calhoun's bad conduct as a Nullifier, he could not be elected.

* P. 91.

It is on the very next page after the above that Greeley says "Mr. Calhoun *resigned* the Vice Presideney when he had three months still to serve, and was chosen to the Senate to fill the seat vacated by Mr. Hayne."* He had been twice elected Vice President, and all knew he would be elected President, as he was the most popular statesman in America, but he deliberately resolved to sacrifice all such honors in defense of his own State

Mr. Greeley says the Dred Scot Decision was "for the purpose of ousting Congress and the people from all right or power to exclude slavery from the Federal territories, organized or unorganized. Congress had repeatedly, and from the very origin of the Government, legislated on the subject, and to this end." But he does not give a single instance, though combating the decision of the Supreme Court of the United States in its most famous decision. Happy serenity! On the contrary, it is utterly untrue. The North West territory was declared free, as he shows, by Virginia, and the South, ere ceded, and that was the essence of the stipulation. Hence, it was not the Congress accepting the donation, but the States ceding, that incorporated the act of exclusion, just as France had stipulated by Article 3, of the Treaty of Cession of the Louisiana territory, that their property, which, by their laws, included slaves, should be protected. But he not only says Congress had repeatedly legislated on this subject, but says it was "to this end"—to exclude it from all the territory that should seek admission into the Union. And this was from the beginning, he tells us. Yet, Kentucky and Tennessee were admitted under Washington's term, and no such legislation was ever heard of. Mississippi, Alabama, and Louisiana followed, and yet there was no such legislation. Nor was there any such, in any form, shape or way, such as he speaks about, till Missouri sought admission, 1819-'20. Surely Mr. Greeley was doing, as ecclesiastics say, a work of supererogation, when he went into the blustery pages of Pollard, for filth, with which to bespatter the South. His own trunk had absorbed enough of that from the foul pools of falsehood, long before the "hot head," of Richmond, opened his hand to his want. And no one can accuse Pollard of such grievous faults as Greeley's.

Though Mr. Greeley's logic has been rent to fragments, yet, it has not been by direct attack on his logic; but his pretended "*facts.*" Let us test his logic a moment. He says of the Convention that made the Constitution, 1787, when Article 16, Section 2, was under consideration, entitling "citizens of each State" to be citizens of any other, "the delegates from South Carolina moved to amend by inserting the word "*white*" between "free" and "inhabitants," which was emphatically *negatived*. "So it was determined that States had, or might have, citizens who were *not* white, &c."* That they refused to enact a propo-

* P. 93-4.

* Conflict. 178.

sitiou offered thus, he considers a guarantee of the reverse. Now, in some cases, this is true, but not necessarily: for many things were defeated by a like vote, wherein the opposite was not established, but members would explain, that for various reasons they were opposed to voting for a measure, when the converse was not established, at all, by such a course. The discussions present so many such examples, it is useless to cite them. That on slavery, in its several shapes, is one. Webster, in his famous seventh of March (1850) speech, utterly refused to vote for the measures proposed to admit free States to the exclusion of slave States. Yet, he vowed, at the same time, his unalterable purpose never to vote to admit a slave State. A word in a certain form was often seen to be liable to other objections, or to cause embarrassments on other articles, and rejected in view of such effect, and not on its merits in such connection.

But there is a nice test of Mr. Greeley's honesty in logic. Mr. Greeley knows that it was proposed, three different times, to incorporate an article, giving the Federal Government the right and power to coerce a State, in case of rebellion, or insurrection, within her borders. This touched directly on the sovereignty of the States. He knows it was negatived twice—the third time it was withdrawn without coming to a vote. There is no equivocation here. It was a direct issue. The possibility of rebellion and insurrection was freely discussed, and regarded as probable—as most likely to occur. Yet, they refused to grant the Federal Government the power or right to judge of it, or intermeddle. Will Mr. Greeley stand by that logic, founded on *facts?* Section 4, of Article 4, of the Constitution, guaranteeing to each State a Republican form of government, and protecting each against invasion, proceeds—"and, *on application* of the Legislature, or of the Executive, when the Legislature cannot be convened, against domestic violence." As first proposed, it read, "to subdue a rebellion in any State, on the application of its Legislature."* "Pinckney moved to strike out, "on the application of its Legislature." "G. Morris seconds. L. Martin opposed it, (striking out) as giving a *dangerous* and unnecessary power (to the Federal Government.) *The consent of the State ought to precede the introduction of any extraneous force.* Mercer supported the opposition of Mr. Martin. Mr. Ellsworth proposed to add, after Legislature, 'or Executive.' G. Morris, of Pennsylvania, "*The Executive* (*Governor of State*) *may possibly be at the head of the rebellion.*" *The General Government* should enforce obedience in all cases where it may be necessary. Mr. Ellsworth, of Connecticut, "In many cases the General Government *ought not to be able to interpose*, unless called upon. He was unwilling to vary his motion to read, 'or without it, when the Legislature cannot meet.' Mr. Gerry, of Massachusetts, was against LETTING LOOSE THE MYRMIDONS *of the United States*

* Madison Papers, 3. 1349.

on a State without ITS OWN CONSENT." In this we have given the discussion verbatim. It continued, Randolph maintaining Martin and Ellsworth's side; G. Morris declaring that it was treating the General Government as if they wished "to tie his hands behind him."* "On the motion to add, 'or without it, (application) when the Legislature cannot meet,' it was agreed to,—New Hampshire, Connecticut, Virginia, South Carolina, Georgia, aye—5, Massachusetts, Delaware, Maryland, no—3, Pennsylvania and North Carolina divided." "On the clause as amended—New Hampshire, Connecticut, Virginia, Georgia, aye—6, Delaware, Maryland, North Carolina, South Carolina, no—4; Massachusetts and Pennsylvania absent. So it was *lost.*" This occurred August 17th.—August 30th they resumed that clause again. *Another* effort is now made to strike out the clause the semi-coercionists wanted as a last hope, having failed fairly three times on its own merits, before this insidious effort we are now noticing.

"Mr. Dickinson moved to strike out, 'on application of its Legislature, against.' He thought it of essential importance to the tranquility of the United States, that they should in all cases suppress domestic violence (substituted that word for 'rebellion' in a State,) *which may* proceed from the State Legislature itself, &c. Mr. Dayton mentioned the conduct of Rhode Island, as showing the necessity of giving latitude to the power of the United States on this subject. On the question—New Jersey, Pennsylvania, Delaware, aye—3; New Hampshire, Massachusetts, Connecticut, Maryland, Virginia, North Carolina, South Carolina, Georgia, no,—8."*

"Mr. Dickinson moved to insert the words 'or Executive' after the words 'application of its Legislature.' The occasion itself might hinder the Legislature from meeting. On this question, New Hampshire, Connecticut, New Jersey, Pennsylvania, Delaware, North Carolina, South Carolina, Georgia, aye—8; Massachusetts, Virginia, no—2; Maryland divided." Finally as completed—it passed—nine for—two against—Maryland and Delaware being against.† Here then was the whole discussion, the various votes, and the parties offered their reasons. The coercionists said they must have power to put down rebellion in the States. It might be alarming and dangerous to the whole government.—The Federal Government must, in their view, be judge of such danger, and be empowered to "crush the rebellion." Not so, thundered back quite three-fourths of the States present, it is a dangerons power, we will not have it. Hence they overwhelmingly voted, and framed the Constitution of the United States so that the Federal Government had no right nor legal power in any way to march "its myrmidons," as Gerry called them, into any State to put down rebellion or domestic

* Madison Papers, 3. 1350–1.

* Madison Papers, 3, 1466–7.

† Madison Papers, 3, 1467–8

violence, unless applied to by the Executive or State Legislature.—And had New York and Rhode Island been represented there, they would, as all knew, have voted with the majority, since two of the three delegates from New York left the Convention because disgusted even with what power *was* granted, and for fear of such powers Rhode Island would not attend.

Hence who was for *the Constitution*, Calhoun, who clung to these principles, or those who have always held that instrument as "a covenant with death?"—And if Mr. Greeley were honest, as a writer, why does he not give the Southern people the credit they have such an indubitable right to, yea, and cling to in the midst of the ruins that surround them, as the only proud legacy they have left—that of having clung to the right—to those rights their fathers had sought to bequeath to them, and died thinking they had done so. We have no patience to notice more of Mr. Greeley's sophistries and untruths, save a passing one on his treatment of secession. He has not a clear idea on the subject one way or the other. He is muddied, befogged, and gropes in utter darkness. He tries to think with Jackson. He tries to think with Webster. He tries to think with Jefferson. He does not stand with either. We will not follow him, but strike at the heart of his position. He gives Clay's illustration of the Union as a marriage, "which is either indissoluble at the pleasure of one or both parties, or else no marriage at all." This is a silly conceit. People marry under law—acknowledge its supremacy, and before witnesses, and in case of abuse have direct recourse to the law for redress of grievances. But sovereign States have no such umpires. They do not, in entering a compact, contract under defined and established laws—have no laws—no superiors. Hence the analogy is an ignorant conceit,—the quintessence of clap-trap. But still, since it is adduced, we could ask: Is it a desirable union of man and wife where they quarrel, fight, hate, and ever more prate of abuse? And has not either party a right to secede, if his or her case be felt to be intolerable, and there *be no* redress?

Mr. Greeley says J. Q. Adams had spoken in favor of the right of a people to *revolutionize*. That a people may *modify*—but leaves out those words "*abolish*," "*separate*," "*dissolve the political ties*," &c. Greeley says: "The people may, from time to time, modify their forms of government. . . . . This right has been set forth, with remarkable clearness and force, in the preamble to the Declaration of Independence, and by many of our patriot sages.—John Quincy Adams had distinctly affirmed it in a speech in Congress."* He says, Mr. Lincoln had contended for it in Congress. That he himself believes in it.—Indeed! And that is the boasted *new* principle our fathers discovered, and with whose praise we have filled the world, and mobs, senates and churches vociferated till they almost split their throats

* Conflict, 1, 357.

—all for *the right of revolution!* Wise Americans! to become frenzied with ecstasy, and froth and foam with fiery enthusiasm at the discovery of a principle, that no fool or madman had ever entertained in the history of the world. Adams, Greeley, Lincoln—all our public men, "with remarkable clearness and force," show a principle, a right, that all know has been exercised for six thousand years. Had not Europe been the theatre of such revolutions for centuries? Do not they reach as far back into her annals as history runs? So of Asia. If Greeley and Webster be right—for he assumes that ground—then the Americans of '76 have made themselves the most barefaced and egregious asses the world ever saw.

By *right* of revolution, Webster and Mr. Greeley do not mean *right* at all, but *might* of revolution. Jackson talked the same kind of puerile twaddle in his South Carolina Proclamations, 1832.

Now Mr. Lincoln took the broad ground of secession as his platform in the two speeches he made in Congress 1848. They are too long for quotation, and are well known. Aside from the addresses of J. Q. Adams, 1839, in which the doctrine of secession is advocated in clear and unequivocal terms, December 12, 1837, after having been President of the United States—1825—1829—he, with the consent of his colleagues from Massachusetts, presented to Congress a Memorial against the annexation of Texas to the Union, and (for he was a member of Congress now) said: "In the face of this House, and in the face of Heaven, I avow it as my solemn belief that the annexation of an independent foreign power (Texas) to this government, would, *ipso facto*, (of itself) *be a* DISSOLUTION *of the Union*." He "had presented one hundred and ninety petitions on this subject. . . . His colleagues had presented collectively a large number." Adams had made slavery the sole ground of his course—i. e. its effect in securing Southern votes in the Senate, thereby holding high tariffs in check. January 24, 1842, "Adams presented a petition to the House (of Congress) praying for the adoption of measures peaceably to *dissolve the Union*, assigning as one of the reasons, the *inequality of benefits* conferred upon different sections." At that time, the high Tariff had expired—that very year, February 24, 1842, J. R. Giddings offered one of a like nature, and it received twenty-four Northern votes. The largest abolition volume ever published, not excepting Mr. Greeley's, 1857, copied the above resolutions and their speeches, to show the zeal of abolitionists.—Yet Mr. Greeley would palm all that off, with volumes of a like character, as a clear reason for modifying our forms of government! He then quoted from his somewhat famous articles of 1860 and 1861, in which he declares "The right to secede may be a revolutionary one, but it exists nevertheless; and we do not see how one party has a right to do what another party has a right to prevent." That is good, but poorly expressed as to the first words. "And when ever a *considerable section* of our Union shall *deliberately* resolve to go out, we should resist all coërcive measures designed to keep it in. We hope never to live in a Republic, where one section is pinned to the residue by bayonets."* This is tolerably well said. But, though reiterated several times, he tried to explain it away afterwards by assuming, as in this volume, that the secession acts were *not* "*deliberately*" passed. That the people of those States did not act with *unanimity*. That he stood for the Declaration of Independence. Well, now, let us see. He stands by the Declaration principles that a people have the right to secede. But who is to determine *when* they *are* acting with "*unanimity*" or "deliberately?" Either themselves, or those from whom they withdraw, of course.

But if left with their oppressors to determine *these* points, you give up all: for they would always say it was hasty, unjustifiable, and rash. Can Mr. Greeley be so very obtuse as to fail to see this, although he may impose such stupid nonsense on his Northern people? If an oppressed people have the right to secede or revolutionize either, with that right goes necessarily the right of determining for themselves when they *are* aggrieved, and to suit their deliberations to themselves. A ten year old boy can see that. If Mr. Greeley's dodge be allowed, how stood it with our fathers?—Pennsylvania and several States at first refused to vote for the Secession of the thirteen Colonies in 1776. One or two States did not vote for it. It was barely possible to get a majority in several of the leading States. So the great Secession document had but little unanimity, and by Mr. Greeley's rule was altogether wrong. But Mr. Greeley's dodge is unfortunate at every turn. All the framers of the Constitution habitually spoke of the dissolving of the old Union—the "perpetual Union" whose "*forevers*" and "indissolubles" our author italicises so much in his work. The States one by one seceded from it, and entered the new Union. Was it with "deliberation and *unanimity?*" Far from it. Connecticut, New York, New Hampshire, Rhode Island, Delaware and Maryland, most persistently opposed it. A majority of the States opposed it. But the three large States, as they were then, Virginia, Pennsylvania, Massachusetts, were bent on it, and the others had to yield. They told them right out they *would* act for themselves, as the others also said they would remain in the old Union, and seek *foreign alliances.* Connecticut led in that threat.—But not only were the States not unanimously inclined, nor deliberate, but the people were equally so. Greeley says in the very page preceding that above quoted, (page 356,) the people "vehemently and formidably opposed it, and its adoption, in several States was, for a time, successfully resisted." "There was manifest danger of its failure in New York, as well as in two other great leading States, Virginia and Massa-

* Conflict, 1, 359.

chusetts. To the New York Convention, sitting at Poughkeepsie, the people had returned a *majority* of delegates hostile to ratification." That is true of several other States, especially Virginia, in which a very large majority—overwhelming—was against it. Greeley proceeds: "The friends of the Constitution, in New York, were constrained to resort to delay, to policy, and to propositions of amendment, to overcome or *wear out* the resistance they had to encounter."* Indeed! And what becomes of that farce of an argument, always the text book of the Websters, and Storys, and Greeleys—"We, the people," and the "one nation" consolidation theory? The truth is *the people never did* ratify the Constitution at all. New Hampshire followed New York, and Virginia. Her people voted against it; and it was by after-trickery they were led in. Rhode Island and North Carolina stood aloof altogether. In a word, when the Constitution was framed over the ruins of the old "*perpetual*," "*eternal*," "*forever*," "*indissoluble*," and "*unalterable*" Constitution of 1777, an overwhelming majority of the people of the thirteen States voted against it, and never did vote on the subject again. As they had no resort without revolution, they submitted. What now becomes of the dodge of Webster, of Jackson, of Story, and of Greeley?

Jackson showed himself stupid enough to write a huge parchment of sophistry against the right of secession; then, as did Clay, in one sentence, undermines it all. He admits in a stroke that "a State, or any great portion of the people . . may have a natural right . . . to absolve themselves," and he would not deny it. "The existence of this right, however, must depend on the *causes which justify its exercise*." But who, again, is to determine when the seceding party has sufficient cause? the party seceding, or the enemy from whom they secede? But, Jackson, and Greeley, and their followers, seemed never to dream of the sternness of such inexorable logic. They preferred a logic "founded on falsehood." It is a misfortune that Greeley has a bad memory. It is said—no inuendo intended by this—that liars ought to have good memories. He sneers at the repeated declarations of "Southrons," that if they withdrew, it would "whelm us (the North) all in bankruptcy and ruin." He repeatedly sneers at their folly for so thinking. Yet, who has forgotten their, and his cries about "the life of the Nation"—"destroying the nation" and all that gibberish? Nay, in the introduction to his second volume ("Explanatory,") he set out on the first page to tell us, that had the South succeeded in gaining their Independence, nearly every State North would have gone to it, adopting slavery as a condition! Wonderful historian—he quotes it as proof absolute, that the "Southrons," as he calls them, were hot-headed fools, and blustering, self-elated numskulls, then turns right round, and says

* Conflict, 1. 353.

twice as much as they ever dreamed of! But we forbear. To expose all his slanders and misstatements, would be to go over every page in the huge volume. These are samples of the rest. It is a disgrace to humanity—a foul slander on the race, and his offense is so rank, it smells to heaven. If the Pythagorean doctrine be true, Mr. Greeley's soul, evidently, once was the animating power of a buzzard—the scavenger of birds. He revels in the foul and base. But he has a dual nature. He is philanthropist, and he is the foe of man. He is patriot, and tyrant. In his *Tribune* he is alternately changing persons. In every other column, or paragraph, he comes with a vase full of flowers, and a barrel of soothing syrup by him. In every other one he "is piled up high"—we quote a great authority with him—with carrion, and has virus enough by him to stagnate the life of the ocean, and make it a dead sea of corruption. His vocabulary is that of the meanest of Puritans, such as the "tuned in their nose full swetely," as Chaucer said of the "nonne." Now he berates the North for harsh epithets, urges the discontinuance of offensive words, and in the next column, by himself, or the next editorial, he pours forth his epithets as if he had been at a feast of treason, and gathered up all the scraps. He is in his element when his tongue is overflowing with rebels, traitors, slave-holders, autocrats, oligarchy, slave-breeders, whip and lash—whip of secession, malignants, discontented malignants, unreconstructed traitors, massacres of Fort Pillow, of New Orleans and Memphis.

He need not fear, however, that his venomous character will ever be known to posterity. He knows the Northern mind—that part of the North that thinks with him. (Of course I always mean that class in using the term North.) The artificial Greeley will live in form. The *real* Greeley will perish at once. Of his private character we care nothing. The meanest and most infamous tyrants that ever cursed the earth, have been warm and generous in domestic and social life. Their impulses have been exalted and magnanimous.—Claverhouse, Robespierre, and St. Just were so. They say Nero was so. Undoubtedly Cæsar and Alexander were so. Unquestionably Mr. Lincoln was a warm, generous-hearted man—full of the milk of human kindness. But such men are often instrumentally made to be the worst of all tyrants, being used by Stantons, Butlers, Sumners, as the soft-hearted Charles I. was by his sycophants.

From Greeley's writings, all that makes him kind, generous, noble, will be recorded by biographers—all the infinitely more voluminous part that makes him a tyrant, will die. Posterity will, therefore, see Greeley the saint, while his cloven foot will be inclosed in silver, and sheltered by a saintly cassock, though the one will be "As great Alcides' shoes upon an ass," and the other as unsightly as "a giant's robe upon a dwarfish child." The world should say—"doff it for shame, and hang a calf-skin 'round those recreant limbs."

"There n'is yevis no serpent so cruel,
When man treadth on his tail, ne half so fel,
As Greeley is, when he hath caught an ire;
Veray vengeance is than all his desire."

[*Chaucer's Canterbury Tales.*

NOTHING TO EAT.

BY ROSA VERTNER JEFFREY.

Nothing to eat,—Oh great God!—what a cry—
To go up from the heart of a city—
Circled with plenty, and splendor,—to die
Without love, without home, without pity.
Starving!—while Fashion is feasting in there,
Feasting, dancing,—in reach of her call,
Freezing!—while snow-flakes, and icicles glare,
With the glow, from that sumptuous hall.

"Don't beg,—go and work"—repeated all day,
Cruel words!—they were seared on her brain,
"Feed me"—she cried—"I will work—let me stay,
I can stitch, scrub"—all pleading was vain.
"A beggar! to work for a lady so grand"—
Oh! sweet Charity!—where shall we go
To seek thee?—When wealth shuts his royal, right hand,
And fair children die—out in the snow!

Rich dainties, and rare—costing marvelous sums,
Were heaped there—in her famishing sight,
Starving!—yet might have been saved with the crumbs
That will fall from that banquet to-night.
"Nothing to eat!"—amid plenty and waste—
Oh dear Christ—at *thy* banquet, above,
Of those thou hast bidden—how few there shall taste,
Here, so wanting in brotherly love.

"Starving!"—they heard—but the great door shut fast!
In this wide world, Oh where could she go?
Homeless, and friendless!—unloved, an out-cast,
With—"nothing to eat"—but the snow!
The çity was vast,—she turned to the east,
Clutched a snow-drift—sank down;—in the light
Of a Heavenly banquet, fair girl, thou shalt feast,
While they starve—who are feasting to-night.

Lexington, Ky., 1868.

ONLY SON OF HIS MOTHER.

"He was the only son of a Widow."—*Monck Jendwine.*

CHAPTER I.

I knew Winsmeede Fallon and admired him for manliness of person and character. He had fine eyes, hair, beard and teeth.—Grace, color and stature combined to make him pleasant to look upon. The first time I ever saw him was in a room crowded with youth and beauty. His mother leaned upon his arm. The one young and handsome, the other old and feeble; both were beautified by the contrast. A lady at my side remarked—

"Winsmeede Fallon will never marry, he is absorbed in his mother."

"She is a quaint looking old lady," said I, "but very attractive."

'Very, there is such harmony in her dress, person, and gentle ways."

"And Winsmeede?" queried I.

"He is a southern gentleman of the highest type. How could he be anything else with such a mother?"

"Did you see that young lady in the reception room?" asked I.

"*That* young lady! Why, my dear sir, there were at least twenty."

I had seen only one, and would have seen her among a thousand. Again she passed before me, a servant following with a trunk, on which I read—"R. Annesley, Petersburg, Virginia."

My companion was still speaking.

"What a pity he has volunteered!"

"Who? Annesley?" asked I, looking towards the door.

"Pshaw! I am speaking of Winsmeede," said she impatiently.

"Ah—yes—no—I mean; not for our cause," rejoined I.

"I was thinking of his mother," continued she, "he is the only son of a widow."

I learned that evening that she had buried her husband and four children in one year. Love had been her idol; Death drew her unto the Cross, and the last child was spared. In perfect trust and resignation lay the loveliness of her old age. Afterwards I said to young Fallon—"How will your mother bear this parting?"

"You do not know my mother," answered he proudly, "she is a dove-hearted woman, but her soul is a tower of strength. She is a patriot and a Christian."

I did not appreciate the force of his words, until I met her the morning he went away, and saw a sweet, patient smile on her face.

CHAPTER II.

READING THE LIST.

A few days after the disastrous battle of ——— a pale anxious throng might have been seen crowding around our village post office. Mrs. Fallon leaned on her cane apart from the crowd, while the list of dead, wounded, and missing was read. The sun was hot, her walk had been long, so her feet ached and the cane shook in her hands. She was growing old very fast. The man inside the office read on.

Killed: John Lanham,
Martin Smith,
Jas. Thompson,
Winsmeede Fallon.

Those within heard no cry, and those without were listening too attentively to notice her, though they said, "Poor old lady!" "Poor Mrs. Fallon!" "Who will break this dreadful news to her?" With her head drooping a trifle lower than was wont, she tottered away voiceless. A mist came before her, and she groped her way home, feeling before her, as one does in the darkness. She was found sitting on the steps of her own door, with her hands clasped together around her knees, rocking herself to and fro. The shock had numbed every faculty, and she submitted like a docile infant, to our ministrations, without any apparent desire for anything, save to lie quite still, her eyes fixed upon the portrait of her son. She did not speak for days, and we feared this dumb grief preceded second childhood, or death. Day after day, exhansted by exertion, oppressed by the stillness, we sat watching and waiting. We sat thus one morning: my arm rested on the window-sill, where I leaned, glad to be near a pet mocking bird, who dipped his beak in a basin of water, twittering and chirping as he stroked his feathers. Mrs. Fallon loved birds. They were never caged, and yet this one had been taught to pick crumbs from her hand, or nestle in her bosom. Winsmeede possessed the same power over horses and dogs, it must have been through gentleness. I held out my hand, the bird hopped upon it, and from thence to the vine against the window, turned his little, sharp, blinking eyes heavenward, and sang his first song. Mrs. Fallon's eyes left the picture, and rested on the bird. When his rich, wild melody changed to a low quivering strain, she spoke: "It is the voice of my son. Vorls never sang before." I passed my hand over my eyes, the ladies wept, she smiled. How wondrous are the ways of God! The Comforter spake, through the song of a little bird.

CHAPTER III.

"Entreat me not to leave thee, or to return from following after thee."

About sunset, in the month of October, a stranger dressed in mourning came to our village inquiring for Mrs. Fallon. The following Sabbath, she attended church, supporting the old lady as her son had done before he died. She was pale and delicate featured, lacking only health and spirits to be handsome. After that day, they were always together. It was Ruth Annesley.

She was very gentle with Mrs. Fallon—walked slowly beside her, chose pleasant paths, folded her shawl carefully about her, and cared for her in hundreds of thoughtful ways. If Winsmeede's devotion to his mother had been pleasant to see, this was beautiful. A visitor asked naturally enough, "Are you related to Mrs. Fallon?"

"No," replied Ruth.

"An old acquaintance, I presume."

"No, I never saw her until I came here."

Finally the story came out, that she went straight to Mrs. Fallon's house, on the day of her arrival, sat down beside her, took her hand and asked—"Are you Mrs. Fallon?"

"Yes," was her reply.

"Did you know Winsmeede Fallon?"

"Winsmeede? My boy? I am his mother—he is dead!"

Both faces quivered; the young woman put her hand to her white throat, sank down at the old woman's feet, and laid her cheek against her hand, as they groaned piteously together.

"What are you to him? asked Mrs. Fallon, as she felt the hot tears drop heavily into her palm.

Ruth lifted her white face, blanched by a grief that had never before been spoken, and answered—"I would have been his wife!"

"Poor thing, poor thing!" repeated the mother, stroking her hair and face tenderly.

From that hour they loved each other dearly.

Miss Annesley gathered about her a few pupils, and officiated as organist in one of the churches. How she played and sang! There was an indescribable under current of sadness and sweetness in every strain. I have watched, with half-closed eyes, the glimmering sunlight through the chancel window set its gorgeous coloring on her face and hair, and wished she might play on forever, that my dream of heaven and angels might never end. To this day, I never hear 'Te Deum Laudamus,' but her frail form and deep lustrous eyes come before me. One evening I heard her sing, "Nearer, My God to Thee"—I have felt nearer and nearer to Him from that hour. She came down smiling, and passed out of the shadowy church, into the red light of evening. As she vanished among the pines, she seemed a part of the golden glory of the day passing westward into the night.

CHAPTER IV.

"Destroy, destroy! Leave not a chimney for a crow to rest upon."—
[*General Sherman, U. S. A.*

Mrs. Fallon's house was on fire! A white fear flew from face to face, for the two women living there alone. The news spread quickly through the place, but alas, it had come too late—we found only a heap of smouldering ruins, slowly whitening in the morning sunshine. A few articles of clothing, a single trunk, and Winsmeede's picture, were in sight. Close by, Mrs. Fallon was reclining in a kind of stupor, with her head resting on Miss Annesley's lap. Both were in their night dresses. Ruth's cheek was parched red, her hands and arms blistered, her long, fine hair burned half away, but she actually smiled in my face—

"See, Doctor, we are safe, thank God! It is a sad thing, but we are *both* alive," said she softly, emphasizing *both*, and pointing to Mrs. Fallon.

Had she wept hysterically, I might have been more calm, but I turned away, choking with wrath and bitterness.

"I fear her eyes are injured," continued she, "You know her sight was failing, and the smoke and flames were terrible. See, her lashes are burned, and her cheeks seared dreadfully." Nothing was said of her own cheek and beautiful hair, until I spoke.

"Ah, that is a trifle," she answered, "I can wear it short awhile—God has been very good to me!"

True, God had been good, but I thought of those who had not—she said not a word against them, and my bitterness died away unspoken. Mrs. Fallon started while we were speaking of carrying her to a cabin near by.

"Ruth, dear, is it not nearly dawn?"

"Yes, mother, it is day," answered Ruth.

Mrs. Fallon held her hands before her eyes, closer and closer, then dropped them heavily, saying, "Ruth, I am blind." Her tone was subdued and she clasped her hands patiently. We looked at each other, and for the first time I saw Miss Annesley's eyes moist with tears. They refused all invitations to neighboring homes. Mrs. Fallon said, "I am too old to change, let me stay here."

"Yes," added Ruth, "let us stay here."

As she spoke her grey, earnest eyes were fixed upon the distance, as if she were waiting.

"Ah," thought I, "she will wait here for some one whom she loves."

However they accepted little kindnesses gratefully, and before another night came, were domiciled rudely enough, in a humble cabin formerly occupied by their servants. We moved Mrs. Fallon there that morning, and spent the day in making it at least a safe shelter. Miss Annesley was almost merry in their humble home; she was here, there and everywhere, helping us all with her little, busy hands and brave spirit. She laughed at her scorched, uneven hair, when a lady held it before her, and with more spirit than usual, bade her cut off the rest for bow-strings for her countrymen. But the flush died away before night came, and I saw the effects of exposure and excitement already, in the slender frame which held so strong a soul. Mrs. Fallon was now almost helpless, and Miss Annesley loved her the more for her dependence upon her.—Through the day she toiled for their support, and at night kept watch, with her hand in hers, that the slightest movement might arouse her. Now that Mrs. Fallon was blind, there was no restraint upon these constant sacrifices. She stinted herself in food until her eyes were sunken and her thin nostrils almost transparent—in dress it was the same. I saw it all one day when she asked me to prescribe for her cough.—She was neat and looked well-dressed in anything, for the strip of linen round her throat was spotless, and she wore her faded mourning with infinite grace, but I was pained to see her shivering without a shawl, and still more grieved to see her thin, white face. I told her she was killing herself, and remonstrated with her; she promised me to eat more and work less for Mrs. Fallon's sake. That night I carried my prescription for her cough, and with it a shawl—but I dared not carry it in the house—twice I took the bundle in my hand, and as often laid it back in my buggy. I carried it back to the village with me next day, and back again by Mrs. Fallon's the following night; the wind was blowing, she could not hear me, so I stole to the door like a robber, and laid the shawl on a shelf under the latticed awning. When we next met I could not look her in the face—I had avoided meeting her, until I heard a little girl say, "I am so glad Miss Ruth has a warm shawl, she doesn't shiver with cold now, when she hears my lesson"—then I went by to see how they were getting along.

"Doctor, don't be afraid that I am angry," said she kindly, "I am a proud woman, and kept this shawl a week to return it, but I am not a cold one, for I could not pain so good a heart; I tried, but could not wound you in return for kindness—I will wear it for your sake."

"For my sake?" The words hurt me more than wounds.

Through winter, spring and summer, she worked on, paler and thinner every day, until the warm days brought a fluctuating color to her cheeks, painful to see. She faded away, but the bird sang among the flowers and vines her hands had trained about the door, and within, her presence beautified the humble walls. A feverish restlessness possessed her, she seemed forever on the watch, earnestly gazing far away. On pleasant evenings she walked to and fro, in sight of the cabin where the blind woman sat under the lattice, talking in low, endearing diminutives, to the bird which stirred the hop vine with his slender feet, and broke the stillness, with a weird mockery of every passing sound. She was walking thus one evening, when I lifted the latch of the gate. She turned swiftly in the path, and almost ran towards me, with her hand pressed to her throat—it seemed as natural there as the linen band, and scarcely less white. Seeing me, she tottered where she stood, and the blood came and went in her face, like a wild wave slowly rocking itself down and down, to rest into the smooth bosom of the sea. Her hand felt like ice in my burning palm when we met—she did not explain her manner, but I knew it was the effect of her failing health, and it —— ah, me, she was one of those victims of love who had grief for her portion, and grief was stealing her life away!

CHAPTER V.

WHO GOES THERE?

Returning home that night, I ran against a man and knocked his pipe out of his mouth. I apologized. He said nothing, filled his pipe and relit it from my cigar. The light shone on his face—it was haggard, scarred and thin. His eyes met mine vacantly. Crime or insanity, I thought, and hurried on, occupied with my own thoughts. Once only, I paused and looked back at him. The speed of his heavy, wavering steps increased, he staggered up the hill, paused for an instant, and disappeared in the direction I had come. Such miserable pedestrians were common after the surrender, so I fell asleep to dream, not of him, but Ruth Annesley. I saw her choked by a highwayman with a thin white hand. Both of my arms were tied down—I could not help her, nor cry for help—my voice died in my throat, and the blood fell drop by drop, from her lips to her bosom, until her eyes closed, her head drooped, and she fell dead before my eyes!

CHAPTER VI.

THE PEDESTRIAN.

Ruth first broke the silence which followed my departure—"Mother, are you thinking of *him?*" The soft withered hand pressed hers gently. A chill wind fluttered the curtain and put out the light. As Ruth closed the window she saw a man's figure shadowed by the moonlight on the ground. Instead of dropping the curtain, she fastened it back securely, kindled a light on the hearth, and returned to her place. There was no sign of nervousness or fear, save the old movement of placing her hand to her throat, whenever she looked that way.

"Ruth," said Mrs. Fallon, "I forget sometimes, and look for him. When I hear a sudden sound, I listen for his voice. When the sun shines brightly, I can see shadows pass before me—my heart then leaps up in my throat, and I lean forward to clasp him in my arms."

"I am glad of that, mother, glad that you forget and look for him—I sometimes feel that we will meet again."

"Aye, in Heaven, dear," said Mrs. Fallon, moving her head slowly, and clasping her hands in the touching way that had come with her blindness.

"Mother," began Ruth, but she grew excited, and laughed strangely as she continued, "I am often so glad for a moment, that I want to laugh and dance and sing, *I feel that he lives!*

"What did you dream last night when you sobbed beside me, Ruth?"

"I dreamed that I went to a battle field, where women had

lifted Our Dead and laid them gently down to rest. These graves were strewn with flowers. Some kind hand had hung a wreath upon a wooden cross by which I lay. Under the wreath I found our loved one's name. Ah, mother, the brown, cold sod was sweet to my lips, and the flowers hung heavy with my tears-it makes you weep, mother."

"But speak on, child," replied Mrs. Fallon, "you are so near to me through my son, you have loved him so well!"

Ruth kissed her hand and continued—

"While I lay there sobbing, with my face pressed to his grave, something lifted my head, and *I saw his dear face, above the mound, smiling upon me!* I wept aloud for joy! The sound of my voice awoke me, then the chill hand crept down on my heart again, and I drew near to you shivering—it was so cold! I did not know you were awake."

"Yes, dear, when you fell asleep again, I put my hand on your face to wipe the tears away, but it was hot and dry—you do not weep like other women, Ruth."

"No, mother, I can seldom weep for sorrow—when he comes, I will weep." Her eyes were on the window again, as the old lady shook her head and spoke: "Ruth, since he died"—

The other shuddered until her teeth chattered as if with cold—

"Are you cold, child?"

"No, mother,—say, since he went away, please!"

"Since he went away," continued the elder, "I feel the second childhood coming on—you know there is a second childhood."

"Yes."

"I remember so much of long ago, not seeing what is passing now, I look back and live in the old time. What are you looking for, Ruth?"

"For him, mother—go on, I am listening."

"Are you tired, my daughter?"

"Oh, no! Talk, mother—I should never grow tired of hearing you speak of him, or his father, or his little brother and sisters who died—they are all mine, you know, I love them all."

"I was saying, of late days the past is so clear, and the present dim. I cannot see my wrinkled face and hands, nor my gray hair, so I forget and think they are soft and fine like yours. Just so, I forget to think of Winsmeede as the man he was when he went away—he seems to be a little boy again, who used to climb on the back of my chair, with his yellow curls brushing my face. I feel his little dimpled hands over my eyes, and hear a child's voice bantering me to guess his name. My husband seems to me now, as my boy looked when he went away. Do you think he was handsome, Ruth?"

"Yes, mother—when he marched into Petersburg, barefooted, cold and hungry, he looked like a prince to me."

"And you loved him then?"

"Oh, no," said Ruth smiling faintly, "not until I knew him to be all he seemed to be."

"I want to be doing little

things for him," continued Mrs. Fallon, following her train of thought to his boyhood. "Last Christmas I wanted to hang a little sock by the chimney. I want his plate by mine at the table every day—it is foolish, but that is the way old age comes on—we turn back to children's ways.

"His place is always ready," said Ruth, "I place a chair for him every day. He might come, oh, he might come!" She spoke vehemently, and drew a chair close beside her.

"Ah, child!" sighed the other, as she took the quivering hands between her own. "Poor thing, poor thing! It is harder for you than for me, for I will soon be gone!" Ruth's quick ear heard a step, she laid the kind hands tenderly back in her lap, and walked to the window, steadying herself by the table, bed, and chairs as she passed them. Holding both hands against the small pane of glass and looking fixedly through them, she saw what seemed to make sunlight dance out of the depths of the night!—Winsmeede stood before her!—There was a sound of shivered ringing glass, as if a hurricane had hurled the sash from the casement, and she fell forward into his arms. They were alone. Only the eye of God was upon them, and His Holy angels were sentineled around that golden sand of time in silence.

"Where are you, Ruth?" they heard Mrs. Fallon say as she felt her way about the room.

"Break it gently to her, darling!" whispered Winsmeede, as he lifted her noiselessly within the room.

"Here, mother!" answered Ruth, going towards her, but she turned back with stifled weeping to touch his face, hands, lips and eyes, to assure herself it was no dream.

"I was afraid you had fainted, child—did you fall?"

"Yes, but I am not hurt"—Ruth's arm was then around her leading her back to her chair; but she, who had been so strong, trembled with the weight on her arm.

"You are not strong, dear, are you ill?"

"No, mother, I am so well, and so—"

She checked herself and looked with her fond smiling face and shining eyes at Winsmeede, who stood with his hand on the door, his foot set forward as if he would spring to her side.

"Ruth, you are weeping now," said Mrs. Fallon, "what has made you so glad?"

"I *feel* glad," answered she, tremulously, still looking towards the door, "you know how I have talked to-night, how I always look and pray and hope for him to come."

"Yes, child."

"The hoping and praying has made me so glad, I am joyous to-night! And you want me to weep like other women, see here." Ruth pressed her wet face against Mrs. Fallon's cheek and hands. "Tears are so sweet, they heal my heart, I thank God I can weep at last!"

"It is late, and you are feverish, Ruth—we have talked too

long to night. If he were to come —if such a thing could be—"

"It can be," interrupted Ruth.

"Hush, it would kill you, poor child!"

"Kill me! Oh, mother! And you? How would you bear it?"

"I? ah, me!" Ruth sprang from her chair and sank back with her hand at her throat.

Winsmeede started forward, but she motioned him back again.

"What is the matter, Ruth?"

"I am as glad, as glad as—if—he—had—come!" answered she, gasping for breath. "I want you to pray, mother—let us pray for strength to bear all things the Father sends. She sank down at Mrs. Fallon's feet as she had done the first time they had ever met.

"She has left it to God," thought Winsmeede, as he listened with eyes fixed yearningly on the two who to him were dearest of all the world. Mrs. Fallon prayed—Ruth lifted her head saying "Amen!"

"Amen!" echoed near them.

"It seemed to me, Ruth, two voices spake!"

"So it seemed to me, mother."

Winsmeede came and laid his head in his mother's lap. She ran her fingers swiftly over his face, tracing each feature—then she whispered, "Is this dying? Ruth, am I dying? Or have I died and met my son in heaven?"

'Oh no, dear mother, *he has come!*"

"Speak to me, my son!" Her voice was very weak, and she shook like one palsied in his arms—his was scarcely less low and tender as he repeated Ruth's words—"Dear mother, he has come!" She lifted her sightless eyes to Heaven and murmured, while he kissed her face, "The lines have fallen unto me in pleasant places, yea, I have a goodly heritage!" Ruth clung to both with fond caressings. Her voice rang its changes through sobs and laughter, her little hands were busy, they passed over and over Winsmeede's face, touched the scar on his temple tenderly—her lips did the same, and she smiled brightly as she wound his empty sleeve about her throat and nestled against the rough and faded grey jacket, as if it were the softest Mechlin lace. The darkest hour had rolled away and she clapped her hands like a happy child in the rosy light of morning.

CHAPTER VII.

"POST NUBILA, JUBILA!"

They were married. Three shining faces passed before me. One was old, two were young—all were beautiful. The central figure was an angel in a mist of floating white. His hand and hers touched mine—I wished them joy, and said—"Ah, Winsmeede, my friend, had you indeed slept in the low thick ranks sown on the field of glory, you would still have been blest in the love and grief of such a woman!"

ORANGE CULTURE.

THE ORANGE is the greatest fruit of commerce. It is the only tropical fruit which can be eaten in the perfection of its freshness, in every part of the world, and at almost every season of the year. The pine-apple and banana must be gathered for transportation before they are ripe, and thus lose much of their flavor and fragrance, and even then, perish quickly—foreign grapes must be treated in the same manner, or dried into raisins; figs and dates must also go through the drying process: the guava must be made into jelly—the cocoa-nut consolidates and becomes indigestible; but the orange carries its tropical perfume and exquisite flavor to St. Petersburg and to Stockholm. To protect it from the effects of heat and cold, it is furnished with a thick, soft rind—to protect it from the attacks of insects this rind is coated with an acrid, aromatic oil. During transportation, it is necessary to guard the fruit from bruises and moisture, and it should be well ventilated.

The cultivation of the orange requires but little labor and expense—fine crops being often obtained from the most neglected orchards. The trees bear abnudantly and attain great age. There is one still living and vigorous in the orangery at Versailles, which is well ascertained to be over four hundred years old. It is called "le grand Bourbon," from having belonged to the celebrated constable of that royal name, in the beginning of the 16th century, and was confiscated to the crown in 1522, at which time it was one hundred years old. A crown is placed on the box in which it stands, with this inscription "Sown in 1421." Some trees at Cordova, in Spain, are said to be greatly older than this, however—not less than six or seven hundred years of age. It is claimed that those at Hampton Court, England, are three hundred years old.

The orange family includes the sweet orange (*Citrus aurantium*) and of this, the Italian gardeners enumerate forty different varieties;—the Seville, or bitter orange (*C. vulgaris*); the lemon (*C. limonum*); the lime (*C. limetta*); the shaddock (*C. decumana*) and the citron (*C. Medica*); all different species with the same general habit.

The last is valuable for its use in being formed into a sweetmeat. The shaddock is a large, showy fruit, of but little value, and so named from a Captain Shaddock, who introduced it into the West Indies, from China. The lemon is hardier and more easily cultivated than the orange, and its value is well known. The Seville, or bitter orange is supposed to have been brought to Florida by the Spaniards, and has become so common, as to appear indigenous. Audubon observes: "Whatever be its native country, the wild orange is, to all appearances, indigenous to many parts of

Florida, not only in the neighborhood of plantations, but in the wildest parts of that wild country, where there exists groves fully a mile in extent. The wild orange is a much more vigorous grower than the sweet, and for this reason, is used as a stock for budding and grafting the sweet orange upon. In Spain, the Seville orange is much cultivated for its fruit also, and forms extensive orchards, which constitute the wealth of many monasteries. The fruit is too bitter to be used in its raw state, but for culinary purposes, and for making wine, it is excellent. The best marmalade, and the richest wine, are made from it, and from its flowers, the best orange water is distilled. But it is to the sweet orange (*aurantium*) that we desire to direct particular attention, for its culture does not receive one tithe of the care, time, and expense which is its due, as *the* great fruit of commerce.

The quickest and easiest way of obtaining an orange orchard, is to select one of the natural orange groves, which are scattered so abundantly over "the wildest portions of this wild country" of Florida, and thin out the trees to about eighteen or twenty feet apart. Saw off the heads of the remaining trees in the winter, and they will throw out strong shoots in the spring. Upon these, bud in the following August, and in three years you will have a fine bearing orchard, if the soil, seasons, &c., are favorable. If any other fruit can be obtained with less labor, and in less time, we would be glad to know what it is. Where a natural orange grove is not available, the next method of growing an orchard, is to select wild stocks from open localities, where they have had room to form an abundance of fibrous roots, and transplant them into rows, the proper distance, eighteen or twenty feet, apart. These stocks should not be more than two or three inches in diameter, and should be budded two feet from the ground, in order to form low, branching heads.

The third, slowest, and *best* mode of forming an orchard, is as follows: Select the most perfect, and perfectly ripened wild fruit, and take out the seeds, which plant in light, rich earth, at the depth of half an inch. Give them the care and attention which you would young peach, or apple trees, and when they have attained the size of a goose-quill, or rather more, they are ready for receiving the buds, which should be selected from sound, plump, young shoots, of such trees as have a free growth, and are in a state of bearing. Seedlings may be expected to produce in seven years. The tree in Florida usually grows about twenty feet high. In its native countries its maximum height is fifty feet.

The Azores produce the most delicious oranges in the world.—On one of the islands, St. Michael's, is a tree which is said to have yielded, in one year, twenty thousand perfect oranges, exclusive of the imperfect or abortive fruits, which they there call curacoa oranges, from their being used in the manufacture of curacoa.—

The variety known as St. Michael's is a small fruit, the skin pale yellow, the rind thin, the pulp juicy, lusciously sweet and often seedless.

Before the great frost in 1835, there was a tree in St. John's, Florida, which produced ten thousand, and in 1829, Mr. A. Alvarez is said to have gathered, from one tree, six thousand five hundred. This frost killed trees that were forty feet high, and with trunks which measured from twenty to twenty-seven inches in diameter, and were supposed to number more than one century in age. At St. Augustine, it was stated, there were at least thirty thousand standard trees, and the crop at this place alone was estimated at from two to two and a half millions of oranges annually. The port here formerly presented quite a commercial aspect, there being frequently in it from fifteen to twenty vessels at a time loading with fruit. At this period, the owner of one hundred standard trees, might safely rely on a yearly income of $2,000, sometimes $3,000 and even $4,000.—

The orange succeeds best in a warm, fertile soil, composed principally of sand and loam, or sand and clay, not too dry, or too much exposed to strong winds. In Italy this fruit is grown to perfection in strong, yellow clay, highly fertilized. With regard to the usual quantity of fruit per tree in Florida, a recent writer remarks: "Their estimates vary from one to ten thousand per tree. I saw no tree which had upon it so many as the latter, though in several instances, I should judge there were upon the trees as many as two thousand." The same writer, in speaking of the orchard of Dr. Snell, on Sarasota bay, says: "We obtained here the most delicious oranges I ever tasted. The man who has the orchard in charge, pays no attention to it, except to gather the fruit as it is called for; and even that labor he seems to consider a peculiar hardship. When we were there in December and again on January 11th, the lemon trees (one-fourth of the orchard consisted of lemon trees) were bent to the ground with their immense loads of fruit, many of them being nearly ruined by the breaking of the limbs; and yet the ground was almost covered with as nice looking fruit as that which still hung upon the trees. The orange trees were not so heavily laden, and many of them had been injured by the gale of October last. During the last five years these trees have had no care." Other orchards he speaks of near Fort Myers, and adds: "With a reasonable amount of care, this might be made one of the most beautiful as well as remunerative places I have seen in Florida. The trees are young and thrifty, and the soil in this vicinity seems particularly adapted to their growth; and, notwithstanding the want of care, and hard usage these trees have received, they give promise of being exceedingly fruitful in a year or two."

The orange plantations of Florida have suffered greatly from the scale insect, (*Coccus hisperidum*), which, in some cases, have destroyed them entirely. Many remedies have been tried for the extirpation of this pest, such as fumigating the trees with tobacco smoke, washing them with lime, soaps &c., but the gardeners of England have found the "best remedy the use of the common Chamomile. It is said that merely hanging up bunches of fresh chamomile amongst the branches destroys the scale insects, and planting it at the roots of the trees has also an excellent effect. When the bark and leaves are much infested, a strong decoction of the chamomile should be applied with a garden syringe. Another excellent remedy is said to be the *gas liquor* of the gas works, largely diluted with water and showered over the trees with a syringe or engine. As this liquor varies in strength, and is sometimes very strongly impregnated with ammonia, it is difficult to give a rule for its dilution. The safest way is to mix some and apply it to the leaves of very tender plants; if too strong, it will injure; if properly diluted, it promotes vegetation and destroys all insects."—(*Downing's Fruit Trees.*)

Oranges can be grown to advantage in Florida, Louisiana, Texas and California. It has been said that wherever the orange begins, the apple ceases, but to California at least, where "the nights of the temperate zone are married to tropical days," and where they have no winter, this remark does not apply. There the orange and the apple grow side by side. A committee appointed by the California Agricultural Society to visit farms, gardens &c., in that State, visited, amongst many other places, that of Mr. Wm. Wolfskill, in Los Angelos county. The orange grove of this gentleman was eighteen years old, trees twenty-five feet high—five feet higher than the average in Florida—and the yield per tree, from a thousand to fifteen hundred. One year he sold the produce of a single tree for $120. Mr. Wolfskill had also large bearing orchards of apples, pears and peaches, and a beautiful grove of sixty English walnuts, fourteen years old, which had been bearing four years.—This tree seldom bears until ten years old. In his nursery were young orange trees which had been budded and had made a growth of *eleven feet from the bud the first year!* And this was in 1857, an unusually dry year. In this nursery were also a number of three year old lemon and lime trees, growing finely—some of them having made a growth of nearly six feet from the bud this year.

Downing says that the orange, with a very slight protection, in the winter, might be grown as far north as Baltimore. "It is not the freezing which destroys them, for they will bear without injury, severe frost—*but the rupture of sap vessels by sudden thawing.* A mere shed, or covering of boards will guard against this mischief. Accordingly, towards the south of Europe, where the climate is pretty severe, the orange is grown in rows against stone walls, or banks in terraced gardens, or trained loosely against sheltered trellises; and at the approach of winter, they are covered with a slight movable frame of boards. In mild weather the sliding doors are opened and air is admitted freely—if very severe, a few pots of charcoal are placed within the enclosure.—When we consider the extreme beauty of the orange, beauty of foliage, flower, fruit and tree, its extreme productiveness, and length of life, this seems a small amount of care to bestow upon it." In speaking of the perfume of the blossom, Du Tour in his "Dictionaire d' Histoire Naturelle," grows quaintly eloquent. "The odor of the orange flower is the standard of perfection of its kind. It has not, like that of many flowers, a deceitful sweetness, which pleases only to injure. It is not faint, like the scent of the jasmine and the rose; it does not affect the head like the narcissis or tuberose; it does not weaken the nerves, but rather strengthens them; it is a salutary odor, which refreshes the senses and enlivens the brain. In fine, it has no rival and is as salutary as it is delicious."

A FEW THOUGHTS ON GOETHE AND SCHILLER.

It was the darkness before the dawn, which was to burst in such regal splendor, over Germany;—she slept, as the princess in one of her own beautiful legends,—aye, she slept, till the depths of her great heart should be stirred, and the weird tones of her wondrous soul-music wake to thrill all Christendom.

Long centuries had made for her, a past of warrior-heroes; and though the German knights had proved their valor, on a hundred fields, and the German soldier brightened a hundred triumphs; though her emperors and kings, led on by glory and the greed of power, had inscribed for later ages, that strong arms, and numbers, achieve more than law or right;—though her vast territory had increased, and her fair expanses showed prosperous cities, towns, and hamlets,—yet her grand old language remained unappreciated;—the strength and beauty of its rich illustrative words,—thought-pictures, wonderfully set in speech,—organ sounds that roll, and vibrate, as the full, deep cadence finds its home in the heart;—all this, to the world, was uncared for, and unknown.

The language of the Germans has been called by them, *Teutsche*, or *Deutsche*, derived from the old Teutonic. The word has, also, been thought to originate from *Theut*, or *Deut*, signifying "the people."

The improvement of the early barbaric melange of provincialisms, and an incongruous foreign jargon, was first essayed by Charlemagne; but the earliest written effort, from which German literature dates its birth, is a translation of the Gospels, by Bishop Ulphilas, as far back as A. D. 360, three hundred years before the time of Charlemagne;—and this little book claims the honor of preceding any attempt in either of the modern languages.

Charlemagne tried a grammar of this motley Mosaic of native and foreign words, and his reign really witnessed the first faint glimmering of that mysterious, and all wonderful German genius.

But the only vestige of the warlike poems, and stirring ballads of this period, has come to us in a fragment of a song of Hildebrand, given to us by the brothers Grimm. Afterwards a change came over the rugged Teutonic; for intercourse with Italy, and France, introduced innovations which softened, and improved it. Then too the fiery zeal and devotion, which united all Christendom under the cross, rolled on the ear the myriad tongues, which rung the alarum for the holy sepulchre,—and this also contributed to soften the harsher original. Later the Hohenstaufens swayed the sceptre, and their cultivation, and taste for art, fostered improvement. The Barbarossa, or red-bearded Frederick, had for a time dwelt in sweet Provence, and from the land of Troubadours, glided the soft music of their poetry. In these, the golden years of Germany's past, arose the Minnesingers, the poets of Love, as the name implies;—and their light, graceful effusions, refined and spiritualized the sturdy old Gothic.

And so the centuries swept on, and the words of strength grew stronger, as they chanted German valor,—and the warbled lore was softer as it sang of the fair, golden-haired frauleins by the Rhine, and thus the grand old language gained in majesty and beauty.

The enthusiasm subdued, and not *vif*, as in the French,—not passionate as the Italian, nor gloomy as that of the Spaniard, demanded soul-food,——therefore poetry and music became necessities, and from the twelfth to the sixteenth century, the prelude only, of what was to come, had sounded.

This strange, metaphysical, poetical, yet stolid race, were struggling in the twilight, grasping after the unattained, yet yearned for,—and on the threshold only, of the brilliant beyond.

After Luther's time, German literature declined;—the "Thirty Year's War" desolated the country,—and pedantry and affectation crept into the mystic circle.

Learning languished during the fierce struggles that succeeded, and though the cry of the soul was still for "light!—more light!" there was misty darkness and shrouding silence, till the eighteenth century heard the music of Klopstock, when his great "Messias" was born; and then the lesser spheres sounded, and the prince-master took his place.

The old city of Frankfort on the Maine, claims the birth of Johann Wolfgang Von Goëthe, August 28th 1749. Sprung from the aristocracy, nursed and petted by his beautiful child-mother, his bright, sunny childhood passed.

Impressionable and fiery we find him, while yet a boy, agonized by the intensity of his first love.

But the heart that through a long life was only to dispense successively, did not break; though the boy-love has, with the boy-faith, so exquisitely idealized the heroine's name, in that Faust which thrilled all Germany. Despite the ethics of the poem-drama, which the "rigid righteons" so vehemently decry, the sweet, girlish trust, the faith and pathos of Margaret's love, hold the heart against all judgment.

The pretty poetry of Mignon's episode in Wilhelm Meister pleases, and the refrain of her child-sorrow is still echoing in our hearts, as she pleads for her return to that sunny land, where "the gold-orange blooms;" but, Margaret, man's spiritualized earth-love, attracts with a sad, sweet witchery, which holds us spell-bound, as only Goëthe's genius can;—lifts us far above the fault, and wrong, and sin, though the hard world thundered its code, as the organ rolled the "Dies Iræ," and faint and weary the broken lily fell at the cathedral gates.

But the perfection of Goëthe's womanhood is seen in his conception of Clara,—the Clara of "Egmont." Here again the characteristics, rather than the morale must appeal!—aye the strength of the passionate devotion of this Amy Robsart of Germany, wakens for her an all-absorbing interest. In Margaret the trust, and clinging, girlish love, are most prominent; the development born of the dangerous guile, of the accomplished man of the world; but in Clara it is Egmont's inspiration,—the passion called to life by the gallant soldier, brilliant noble, and impetuous lover. Her little songs are exquisite; breathing sometimes a witching coquetry, and always her unselfish devotion. In this drama, less metaphysical than Faust, the scenes are graphic, and the stirring history of the revolt of the Netherlands, moves almost as a living spectacle.

Some of Egmont's soliloquies rise into all the grandeur of the truly majestic German, and the famous prison reflection is unsurpassed by anything which even Shakspeare has left to us.

An English writer, comparing the Juliet of Shakspeare with Schiller's Thekla, has remarked that in Juliet is found an "infinity of love," but in Thekla "an eternity," and in truth the womanly characteristics are wonderfully developed in this rare gallery. Sweet, trustful Margaret pleads her faith-love, for even when dying her lips fashion the name of her beloved;—Clarchen, with more of the strength of passion, exhibits the fathomless depths of her intenser nature, while Thekla—Schiller's pure, self-sacrificing girl-patriot, passes away in the music of her broken heart, as she murmurs her exquisite farewell, in the sweet, sad line,

"Ich habe gelebt, und geliebet!"

And this his earliest, and most spirituelle creation, recalls another of the great lights, which brightened the eighteenth century.

John Christopher Frederic Von Schiller, was born on the tenth of November, 1759, at Marbach on the Neckar. And what a contrast his infancy and boyhood present, when compared with the cloudless happiness of Goëthe's life. Born in poverty, and educated at a military-monastic school, he was restricted from all intercourse with women; for Charles, duke of Wurtemberg, thought it most conducive to the intellectual development of his beneficiaries, to allow only the visits of mothers, and very young sisters. Heart-food, and brain-food were alike dusty books;—and we find the talent, which, in the future, was to give us Don Carlos, Marie Stuart, Thekla, and the thrilling drama of William Tell,—diligent in the study of physic and jurisprudence.

But the soul of the thirsting neophyte panted for its native element, and we watch him through the stolen hours of the night, reveling in what was to make his fame, throughout the world.

And now the student life passes away, and we find the independent German spirit, boldly and bravely struggling for freedom of thought; and unwilling to submit to the sway and espionage of his old patron, he escaped from the army, and then appeared "The Robbers,"—the first born of that wonderful intellect,—and a drama of rare talent, and marvelous power.

Afterwards came Don Carlos, Marie Stuart, Wallenstein, and Piccolomini, Revolt of United Netherlands, and as the last effort, and crowning glory, "William Tell." The story of Don Carlos, as told by Prescott, in his simple and beautiful English, is familiar to all;—but the grace and eloquence of the love-passages in the drama, require all the fiery imagination of this grand old master. Marie Stuart as portrayed by Schiller, has all the womanly dignity, with which we love to associate the beautiful queen of Scotland. The garden scene has become world-renowned, since Ristori's perfect rendering, and gentle accents have thrilled two continents with their eloquence.

In preparing himself for Wallenstein, and the Piccolomini, Schiller collected material for "The Revolt of the United Netherlands," a period with which we are now well acquainted, through the researches of the terse, and elegant Prescott, and tireless Motley.

Schiller's life differs entirely from that of his great compeer;—for Goëthe, with his rare beauty, seemed born to happiness;—while his joyous, expansive heart, ever life-giving, received, and gave forth, without ceasing, emphatically an absolvent, and whirled on by destiny, he dispensed what might be called, his life-charities;—receiving always a more costly recompense, as Gretchen, Frederica, and a hundred others answer to the roll-call of his unresisting, and irresistible heart.

But of all the many,—the history of Frederica, the timid, shy, yet loving maiden, stands conspicuous in her sweet forgiving sorrow;—a mute, appealing rebuke to the faithless poet. Through long years of neglect and forgetfulness, still she clung to this grand passion of her life; and when wooed, her reply was,

"The heart that has once been Goëthe's, can never be another's."

Schiller, differently situated, had life's hard realities to struggle against, for poverty, with its iron grasp, had seized him, and he had little time for love's dalliance, or its joys; in fact, his early isolation from women, told plainly in his writings, and his heart-impressions were neither many, nor inspiring; therefore, we are not suprised at his friendship—love-marriage. Whether the heart of this mighty German could have been otherwise wakened, remains a mystery, but certainly the perfection of womanly passion, has never been evidenced in his heroines.

Schiller generally wrote at night, strengthened by very strong coffee:—this was the habit of a life time,—and to and fro, through the cold German midnights, would he pace his room, while the grand conceptions of his magnificent intellect were dreamed into realities.

But the battle, the toil, and the wear of a troubled existence told upon him, while yet in the flush of his manhood. An earnest spirit, disdaining the mean and the sensual, his strivings were after the pure, the true and the good; and as his last born, his farewell benison to his fatherland, he bequeathed his great drama of William Tell.

Who that has read this does not feel his pulses quicken, as the splendid talent of the author does noble battling for the Right?—and, as the last flush on the Rutli dies along the Swiss heavens, we feel Schiller's spirit floating upward in its light.

As the one illustrates the German genius, so the other stands colossal as the German talent.

Even the personal appearance of the men, seem to speak their especial characteristics. Goëthe was tall and majestic—the handsome man of Germany;—with that marvelous beauty which lit every lineament with the reflex of his soul;—and Schiller, towering in his rugged outlines, large featured, and irregular, yet always bearing the impress of the great intellect, that swayed him with imperial rule.

But they both have passed, where to use Schiller's own language,

"Word is kept with Hope, and to wild Belief, a *lovely truth* is given."

And the old German is singing still their echoes—the delicious thrilling minor, and the vibrating heart-stirring bass;—a grandly weird symphony, born in the wild German mountains, and nursed by the blue, rippling Rhine.

Again we listen to the sweet Minnesingers, and again we bow in reverence to the magnificent hymns of the seventeenth century:—now the spell of Goëthe's genius lures us,—and anon Heine's silvery music wilders, as did his own beautiful Lorelei. The soul-chants of Schiller waken, and vibrate to the very depths of the spirit,—while Kremer, fiery, impassioned, freedom-loving Kremer, shields us with that last hymn,—born, while his immortality hovered on the brink of Destiny.

And so the mighty host passes onward, — onward! — marshaled into the far eternity; but, their teachings remain forever in our hearts, and as an inspiration from them echoes the sentiment,

"Whoever with an earnest soul,
Strives for some end, from this low world afar,
Still upward travels tho' he miss the goal,
And strays—but towards a star!"

THE HAVERSACK.

We suppose that the ideas of discipline were not very rigid, in either of the hostile armies, at the beginning of the war. Unfortunately for us, the Federal army, having with it the nucleus of the old army, was constantly improving in character and tone, while we rather declined than improved in essential particulars. Some very crude notions, however, were corrected, and from Gen. Jas. H. Clanton we get an illustration of a change for the better

Enlightened Constituents.—Gen. Bragg had the organization at Pensacola of the first troops in the field. His views, as is well known, were very strict, and those of many of his subordinates very loose. One day, he was giving a certain Colonel "a blowing up" for certain conduct subversive of "good order and military discipline," when the irritated Colonel replied:

"Sir, I am not responsible to you for my behavior, I am accountable only to my enlightened constituents, who elected me Colonel of their regiment!"

This is precisely the view taken of the situation by the Radical chiefs. They are responsible neither to the Constitution, nor to the country, only to the enlightened constituents, who put them in power.

We are indebted to Col. Grayson, of Henderson, Ky., for the annexed incidents.

A SCENE ON THE OHIO RIVER DURING THE WAR.

In the summer of 1864, Gen. Buford, of the C. S. A., commissioned Capt. Ollie B. Steele to enter Southern Kentucky, and recruit for the South. In accordance with his commission, he entered the State, and during the summer, raised a considerable force. He, and his men, early in September, started for the South, and on the 14th of the month arrived on the banks of Cumberland river. Just before they entered Eddyville, on the banks of the river, they met a man coming from the village, who assured the Captain that there were no Federal soldiers in the town.

The Southern boys moved in haste to look for a crossing place, the night was very dark—no sooner had they reached the ferry than to their great surprise, they encountered a large force of "Yanks," belonging to Colonel Burgess' command, concealed under the bank—there was also a portion of Colonel B's. men ambushed in their rear. In a moment, Captain Steele and nearly all his men were taken prisoners—a few of them effected their escape, under cover of darkness. They lost about forty thousand dollars in horses, ammunition, arms, &c., &c. Captain Steele was taken into a room, searched, and divested of all his papers, and pen-knife, then, in order to secure his agreeable company for the remainder of the night, they tied him, hand and foot. Early the next morning his arms were pinioned behind him, and he placed upon a mule, minus saddle or blanket, and hurried off to Princeton, (a small town not far distant) to Colonel Burgess' headquarters. Here they took him to a hotel, and fastened him, at full length upon a plank which was in the bar-room—in this attitude he remained all day. Nearly all the citizens called to see him—some seemed to rejoice greatly, while others looked on with pity and sorrow. The following day, Captain Steele, two of his men, and eleven of General Adam Johnson's command were placed on board the steamer "Colossus," under charge of Lieut. Higgins, with eight well armed soldiers, and started for Louisville, the head-quarters of Gen. Burbridge, who had an *insatiable* thirst for Southern blood. Captain Steele was aware that Burbridge had issued an order to execute him whenever caught, and that his order was in the hands of Colonel Glenn, commandant of the Post at Henderson.

Therefore, Captain Steele determined to regain his liberty or lose his life in the attempt—what was to be done? to go to Louisville, death awaited him and his men, should he fail to rescue himself from the guard on the boat, the same dreadful fate would be the result. Under these circumstances, he conceived the idea of rushing upon the guard and disarming them. This plan was disclosed to his men. Only six out of thirteen consented to aid him. The plan was this: When you see me (said Captain S.) commence to button my coat, plant your feet for a spring upon the man you have singled out. The project was now well understood. On the morning of Sept. 17th, the perilous moment arrived—six of the thirteen men stepped out and remarked to the Captain, that they would live or die with him. All the guard were now on duty, with the exception of one, whose gun was across his lap, and he, apparently, asleep. Capt. Steele commenced buttoning his coat—the last button is now in the button-hole. The attack is made—the struggle is fearful for a few moments, it is doubtful who will be master of the arms. Captain Steele succeeded in getting into his possession one musket—in one moment more his antagonist had received its contents, and fell dead at his feet; he then threw the gun down, and seized a revolver which was attached to the body of the dead man. One of the guard, an exceedingly stout man, rushed forward, grasped the pistol, and endeavored to wrench it from Capt. S. After struggling for some time, he succeeded in getting the Captain's head between his knees, both holding on like "grim death" to the revolver. In this perilous situation, one of the prisoners sprang forward, seized the discharged musket, and thrust the bayonet through the Yankee, killing him instantly—another prisoner succeeded in getting possession of the gun of one of the guard, and shot one arm quite off at the shoulder. At this juncture the remainder of the guard surrendered—having lost three men out of eight. During the little conflict, Lieut. Higgins was no where to be seen. After a cessation of hostilities diligent search was instituted for him; he was finally discovered snugly ensconced under the bed of the chamber-maid—a very cordial invitation was extended to him to come out, as Capt. Steele wished to behold the light of his countenance. As he approached the Captain, he fell on his knees and *besought* him to spare his life. Capt. Steele assured him that he would not harm him, but told him, that he must give a correct statement of the whole affair.

The boat was landed at Weston, on the Kentucky side. All the government property was taken off. There were sixteen thousand dollars on the boat belonging to private individuals, which was unmolested. At that time Capt. Steele was only twenty years of age.

WM. P. GRAYSON.
Henderson, Ky.

From a member of the late 5th South Carolina regiment, of the so-called Confederate army, we get the two incidents below:

At the battle of Seven Pines, after the 5th South Carolina regiment had taken a line of entrenchments from the enemy, the regiment was formed in them, so as to front a dense mass of brush and felled timber. A considerable number of federal stragglers had collected in this abatis, and while we were occupying their former position, poured a pretty heavy fire into us, which made it quite dangerous for any one to raise his head above the works. About that time, private A. Spears, of company H. had his attention attracted by a very large, fine horse, which seemed to be hitched to a snag at the end of the abatis, and fully two hundred yards in front of our line. Without orders from any one, he crossed over the works, in the midst of the firing from both sides, and moved forward towards the horse with the intention of capturing it. As he advanced, nearly the whole regiment ceased firing, and watched his movements with almost breathless silence. At length he arrived within about ten paces of the horse, when he was suddenly halted by one of the federals, who was lying behind a log very near the horse, and who, until then, had been entirely concealed. Nothing daunted, however, Spears immediately came to a ready, and ordered the blue-coat to surrender, which was no sooner said than done. The brave fellow then loosed the horse—which, by the way, was a superb animal—and deliberately marched back to our line with both his prizes, amidst the hearty cheers of his comrades. His success in the adventure was, however, quite remarkable, as I was told afterwards that, while in the act of cocking his gun, the cap dropped off, which, of course, left him at the mercy of his prisoner—though fortunately the latter was not aware of it, and quietly submitted to the orders of his captor.

—

Almost every one is familiar with the tremendous crash made by a brass band at the commencement of certain pieces of music. I once saw it have quite an amusing effect upon a Confederate soldier in Virginia. When the Washington artillery, of New Orleans, was removed from the 2nd South Carolina brigade, in '61, the band of our regiment—the 5th South Carolina—decided to give them a serenade on the night previous to their departure. Accordingly, the band, accompanied by a considerable crowd of the 5th, went over to the artillery camp. It was a calm, clear night, all the noise of the camp had died away, and with the exception of one or two here and there, the whole section was fast asleep. The musicians took their stand between one of the caissons and a large spreading oak, at the root of which, stretched out upon his blanket, lay one of the artillerymen quietly taking his repose, and utterly unconscious of anything that was going on around him. At last the entire band, *both* drums, cymbals, horns and all, struck up some lively air, with a crash equal to the discharge of a twenty-four pounder—away they went, blowing most furiously, and entirely ignorant of the immense excitement they had created in the mind of the poor fellow lying under them, who, at the first sound of their instruments, bounced into the air like an India-rubber ball, and apparently without moving a single muscle—it seemed as if the sound of the horns had tossed him up, without changing the horizontal position of his body. He lit on his feet, however, and still half asleep, with the most ludicrous expression of horror on his face, exclaimed, or rather gasped out—"Great Heavens! has the whole d——d battery blown up?" He was agreeably surprised when informed that only the horns, and not the battery, had been blown up.

E. R. W.

—

Dr. I. E. Nagle sends the next anecdote from New Orleans, La.

At the battle of Lebanon, Tennessee, the 11th Texas cavalry belonged to John Morgan's command. It was made up of a set of brave and reckless men, thoroughly acquainted with all the peculiar accomplishments of their section, including the use of the lasso. Their skill with the lasso was often made available in procuring them certain luxuries, such as fat pig, fat turkey, and fat chicken. On the day of the battle, one of the 11th lassoed a Dutch cavalryman in the Yankee service. He was a fat, thick-set, surly fellow, with a stolid countenance, and as he sat squarely on his horse, giving a grunt of dissatisfaction, when a playful twitch was made on the rope round his neck, he presented a spectacle of intense interest to the surrounding rebs. Approaching General M., the Texan saluted him respectfully, and told him that he had *captivated* the Dutchman at the end of his line.

Dutchy blurted out, "Ish you General Morgans?"

The General replied in the affirmative.

"Vell den, vot sort of a tam vay is dish of vitin? You lets your mensh ketch a feller mit a hell of a r-r-ope rount mit his neck, so like a tamt tog. Dish is von hell's of a vay of vitin mit a tam r-r-ope!"

General Wilcox sends an anecdote of Captain Davy Crockett, of Arkansas, the grandson of the celebrated Crockett, of Tennessee and Texas.

The Captain was going home on a leave of absence, accompanied by a soldier, during the last days of the so-called. He had ridden all day, and hungry and weary, he stopped at night-fall at a house by the way-side, and asked for lodgings.

"Can't take you," said an old man, at the door, "got nothing to eat. The rebels, they comes along and eats up all we got, and then the Yankees, they comes along and they eats up the balance!"

"Very well," says Crockett, "I am too tired to go any farther. Let my horses stay in your lot, so they can't get away, and I will sleep here on the ground."

The old man looked long and inquisitively at him, and then said, "pears like I ought to know you, what mout be your name?"

"I am Captain Crockett, and this is my friend, Robinson Crusoe, from Selkirk's Island."

"Is you enny kin to Davy Crockett of the Western Deestrict of Tennessee?"

The Captain replied, "I am his grandson."

"Get down, Captain, and come in. Here, old woman, is the grandson of our old neighbor, Davy Crockett, of the Western Deestrict, and this is Mr. Robinson Crusoe. We knowed the Captain's granddaddy powerful well, but we wos'nt so well acquainted with the kinfolks of Mr. Crusoe!"

Hendersonville, Mississippi, is responsible for the next anecdote.

During the battle of Seven Pines, the 14th Mississippi was thrown out on picket, with orders to fire on any one coming in front.

Private McIntire, being on the extreme right of the regiment, and seeing a man advancing, unarmed, from the front, fired, and killed him. On creeping up to him, and carefully examining his person, he found that he had been discharged from the Yankee service, the day previous, for being *non compos mentis*, and having been left in camp (as was supposed) by the troops who were then fighting on our left, he had strayed to our portion of the line, and was killed, as above related. After the fighting was over we buried, decently, the man, whose name proved to be John Deal.

A well known *private* of the regiment placed a head-board over the grave, with the following inscription, rudely carved, on it, with the point of a knife.

Here lies a *Yankee*, by name John Deal,
Who was never known, *by us*, to steal:
But for the want of a gun to fire,
Was killed by the *rebel* McIntire.

TATT P.

From a former member of Semmes' brigade we get an anecdote of one who did *not* believe in the Maine liquor law.

A few days before the battle of Seven Pines, Kershaw's South Carolina brigade was moving to take position on the right of Semmes' Georgia brigade. As the South Carolinians came in front of our brigade, they gave three cheers for "the gallant Semmes of Georgia." Not to be out done in courtesy, we roared lustily back "three cheers for the chivalrous Kershaw of South Carolina." The last lingering notes had hardly faded on the breeze, when a voice from far down our line was faintly but distinctly heard, "three cheers for me, boys, and I am d——d drunk at that." There is but a step from the sublime to the ridiculous. The South Carolinians were soon out of sight, but not out of hearing of the laughter following the burlesque upon the scene of the "mutual admiration societies."

An old reb, who has wandered to the loyal town of Elizabeth, New Jersey, tells us of different styles of running.

In July, 1864, a portion of Carter's battalion of artillery, A. N. V. A., was stationed below Richmond in the neighborhood. The river was closely patrolled by Yankee gunboats, and owing to their watchfulness, extensive fields of wheat on Turkey Island and Strawberry Plains could not be harvested, and were lost to a country suffering for food. It was part of the parental discipline inflicted by the best government the world ever saw, "to starve out the rebellion" and restore wandering prodigals to the dear old homestead.

The men being heartily tired of corn meal, were eager to get flour, and numbers of them went into these fields, and with their pocket knives, cut down as much as they could carry. This was threshed in a rough way and ground into flour at an adjoining mill. Men of all arms of the service soon swarmed over the fields, and thus supplied themselves with an article which had become a great luxury.

One day, late in July, I was sent down to ascertain the position and number of the gunboats, and stopped where about a hundred men were reaping with their pocket knives. Private John T. Mills, of Page's battery, was one of the reapers. He was one of the best soldiers in the army, and the bravest of the brave, but the incident I am about to relate will show that he could run too. A party of about fifty marines had landed under cover of the river bank, and when first seen, were only about 60 yards from the reapers, who were wholly unarmed. The marines opened a rapid, but harmless fire, and then charged forward, firing as they advanced. Mills and your correspondent retired promptly, without regard to the order of our going.—Being mounted, your correspondent used his spurs with vigor, and he flatters himself, with effect.—Mills being on foot, started off at a speed which would not have done discredit to the Olympic races.—Looking over my shoulders, I saw him stop, coolly inspect his pursuers, and then started at a run again. When I had reached a place where I could talk with him without danger of unreasonable interruption from our "Northern brethren," I waited till he came up, and inquired,

"Mills, what on earth did you stop for, right in the hottest of the firing?"

"Well," replied he, "I wanted to *gauge my running*, and I stopped to see whether it was cavalry or infantry after me. I was running on the infantry schedule, but if it had been cavalry behind me, I would have run on the cavalry schedule, and gone a little faster!"

We have heard that a man named Schenck, at a place called Vienna, ran on the cavalry schedule, and that no impediments might obstruct the vigor of his speed, he dispensed with his hat and coat.

Our next comes from Napoleon, Arkansas:

While we were at Grenada, Mississippi, a young lieutenant, who felt his position more than his position felt him, had a very peculiar cap. It was made of a coon skin, and really looked very well, though rather- *coonish*, as the tail was left hanging behind. This youngster had occasion one day to ride through Price's infantry, and a more noisy, roaring, mischievous set of fellows could not be found, the whole world over. It was raining very hard, and the young lieutenant met the men returning, hastily, from the drill-ground. He was not long in hearing, "here's the same old coon." "Get out of that coon-skin, I know you ar thar, see your little legs a stickin' out." Another began to whistle, and call for dogs, saying, "boys, we'll catch the varmint and, have a mess of coon-meat." "No," replied another, "it's too *green* to eat." 'Taint none, it's been killed long enough to smell a little already." "Spiled (spoiled) by its elevated position," suggested another.—These jeers were too much for the dignified lieutenant, putting on an important air and blustering manner, he bawled out defiantly, "do you know who you are talking to!"

A little sallow-faced, pumpkin-eating Arkansian replied,

"Yes, we does, we are talking to spiled (spoiled) meat."

The *spiled* meat had sufficient vitality left to wheel his horse, dash his spurs into the poor animal and gallop away.

D. H. C. M.

Halifax, N. C., gives a characteristic anecdote of the generous and lamented Branch:

By a contribution in a late number of THE LAND WE LOVE, in which a chivalric comparison is instituted between Sir Philip Sidney and Bentiago, I am reminded of two acts of nobleness, worthy of Southrons, which equal, if not eclipse, the historian's praise of Sidney, and Lockhart's pompous verse, lauding Bentiago.

As the late, lamented, General L. O. B. Branch was covering the retreat of the Confederates from the battle of Newbern, in 1862, the enemy approaching rapidly, he observed some soldiers dragging slowly along in a blanket, some one badly wounded. Inquiring whom they had, he was told, Captain M——. General Branch immediately said, "here, Captain, take my horse, and make your escape.

The Captain says: "No, General, you are more valuable to our cause, I am only a Captain, go on."

General Branch would not leave him until he had given directions concerning his comfort, and a shorter route for them to take him. He however, was captured, after a long time recovered, was released, and did good service: while General Branch, whom his country mourns, fell, on the Potomac, in the spring-time of his glory. And when the time shall come, as it will, for us to honor properly, his peaceful grave, let us not forget this act of unalloyed humanity. M. T. D.

Memphis, Tennessee, tells of an incorrigible rebel:

In Shelby county, in this State, there lived, during the war, a rich specimen of the unreconstructed. During the Yankee occupancy of the county, he was arrested as a "rebel sympathizer," and ordered to take the oath. Some days of confinement, however, served to "develop his latent Unionism," and he sent for the Yankee commander, and expressed his willingness to "swallow the nasty thing." He, however, probably expressed the opinion that he would throw it up again, and inquired whether he would be released even if he should throw up. Being assured that he would be released upon taking the oath, without regard to the nausea that might be produced, he began to *swallow* the words of the oath after the officer. But the formula was not half through, when he cried, "Stop, Mr. Yank, I want to puke." He went to the window, and did actually throw up, and then came back and swallowed the rest of the oath. Again, he returned to the window and relieved himself, and declared that it had all come up, and tasted "powerful bitter." We have heard of "a new way of paying old debts:" but certainly this was a new way of relieving one's conscience.

A crowd of wounded boys were sitting around the stove in the Bragg Hospital when heavy jokes and left-handed compliments were passed on different Southern States. The manners, customs and language were freely discussed and freely criticised. Some sharp and telling things were said by an Alabamian about East Tennessee. A Tennessean took up the defence and said:

"Well, boys, I admit that there is too much ignorance in East Tennessee, but some of her neighbors have not much to boast of. I got my first bad wound in '62, and as my home was in the Yankee hands, I was furloughed to go where I pleased, and I went to Alabama. I took up my abode with an old lady, who was a fire-eating hater of Yankees, and had as little toleration for a blue-coat as for the Queen's English. One day, when the conversation turned rather gloomily upon the prospect of the final success of the Yankees, she flew into a great passion and cried out, 'never, never, they may captivate all the men, they may arrogate all the women, they may fisticate all the land, but they can never congregate the South, never, never, never.'"

The old lady did not dream of the congregate relations which the school marms would establish with "Afric's chosen race" in the congregated South.

Born in the Dark of the Moon.—Spite of the teachings of men of science to the contrary, many persistently insist that vegetables and cereals should be planted according to the phases of the moon. Root crops are to be planted in the dark of the moon, and other crops from new to full moon. A Dutch farmer would consider it the height of folly, and a gross disrespect to the memory of his fathers to neglect the state of the moon, when planting time had come.

Major —— of the —th Texas, *foot*, was remarkable for the size of his lower extremities, and it was thought that he had appropriately chosen the *foot* service, when he entered the army, as a lieutenant of infantry. He never mired down on the worst roads, and trod over the worst slosh as calmly, and as majestically as though on a Macadamized road. In time, the casualties of war and the gallantry of the man brought about promotion, and the lieutenant was changed into a Field Officer. But his elevation on horseback, like many other elevations in life, only revealed the Major's defects. Those enormous feet (and they were enormous) were the occasion of many sarcastic remarks, often in the gallant Major's hearing. One day, a discussion arose as to the cause of the tremendous pedal developments, when a philosophic reb explained, by saying, "the Major was born in the dark of the moon and all run to root!"

BURIAL OF GENERAL MORGAN.

We copy the following from the Louisville (Ky.,) *Courier*.

In all the land of the captive there is no spot more sacred than the cemetery which the Virginians call Hollywood. It looks upon the James, which runs toward the sea to mingle its waters and its glories with those of the Potomac. On the banks of these two rivers there lived the noblest of their race. By their gurgling waters there now sleep better men than those who live. In that hallowed ground heroes rest, who saw the splendor of the Wilderness, and who escaped the honorable misfortune of the Appomattox. The trees were assuming their new livery; the grass was growing, a few flowers were struggling to add their beauty to the holy scene, and, while spring was leaping from the lap of winter, all that remained of the most attractive tenant of Hollywood was taken from its noble society to be returned to the State that bore him. If Virginians regret to see such a superb monument removed from the Holy City, let them receive consolation from the reflection that there are still sleeping there, in silent graves, heroes sufficient to fill the history of twenty nations with examples which ere long may urge the captives to break the chains that bind them and strike once more for freedom.

As the solemn cortege moves today beneath the shadow of Clay's monument, and by the grave where Hanson sleeps, bearing the dead body of the knightliest horseman who ever drew sword to guard his own and his country's honor, braver than all men—more generous than brave—more merciful than generous—followed by men who had often before followed him where danger was—curious thoughts will arise in the minds of Kentuckians there.—Why is this man dead? Flattered by nature with every grace to adorn his person, with the power to charm alike manhood and beauty—no rank too high—no society too refined—no place in which he would not have been an ornament—why was this man killed? Were there Kentuckians who guided foreign regiments across the State to pillage Virginia, and to murder Hanson, Sidney Johnston, and Morgan? Perhaps it is well they are dead; but remember that there was no price upon their sword. High rank did not allure their virtue, nor did bribes win their arms to enslave their State. Army commissions covering a foreign scheme to pillage their own people, were spurned as gentlemen spurn dishonor. Better that they had not lived to see the disgrace of the country they loved and served so well. By the aid of Kentuckians a false Virginian now domineers over once free Kentucky. The voice of eloquence is softened into a whine of complaint. Tones of defiance are hushed into a whisper of cowardice. Timid men sit in high places with too much selfishness to abdicate, and too little courage to execute. With Joab's friendship, these timid men counsel those who obeyed Johnston, Breckinridge, Buckner, Hanson, and Morgan, to confess that they are ashamed of the flag they followed. Ashamed of what? The fact of defeat and of humiliating conquest is admitted. But ashamed of what? Ashamed that we refused to act with dishonor? Refused to aid foreigners to conquer our own people? Ashamed because bribes could not allure, nor danger intimidate? Never! never! never! Never, by the glories of Stonewall Jackson and of Lee; never, by the grand and picturesque death of Sidney Johnston ; never, by the ashes of Hanson and of Morgan; never, by the untarnished sword of Breckinridge will we confess that we are ashamed of the flag we followed!

Let the cortege move on with its dust. The body was killed in war, but I defy the conqueror to suppress the name that rises from the grave. Tradition will tell it, history will perpetuate it, and song in sweetest music will pour forth its glory from the lips of children, and in the feeble utterances of age. The knightly horseman will be the first picture which the father will paint for his boy, and the strongest example to urge manhood to honorable action.

Farewell, friend of my youth, companion in life, brave, generous, merciful comrade, farewell. Upon the turf that covers you, fair hands will strew *immortelles*. Beautiful word, for it accords so well with Morgan's name. I will go often to your grave, and I may feel your spirit there, and many more will go with me. Farewell. Let the cortege move on. The tears that flow down the cheek from eyes not used to weeping come from men who never wept in battle. Let the brave soldiers weep over their dead chieftain.

HOWARD.

EDITORIAL.

A loyal editor in Dixie does not repose upon a bed of roses. Some of his labors may be judged of by a plain statement of the kind of letters received at this office, and we give a real, and not a fancy picture. Inquiries about a situation for an old man, for a young man, for an old lady, for a young lady; inquiries about Scuppernong vines, about the price of land in the South, about the water-falls of the South; inquiries about a missing soldier, about a stolen watch (referred to loyal men every where,) about the best kind of milch cows, (none as to calf,) about the worst desolated portion of the South, (referred writer to Maj. Nicholls' "March to the Sea.") Next, inquiries about Reports of Battles, (referred to Printing Department of Confederate Government); inquiries about the authorship of a book, of a story, of a poem; inquiries about the address of certain *litterateurs*, of certain Generals of the so-called, of members of the Confederate Congress. Here we may mention that we actually received a letter from a Mississippi soldier asking us to find out the given name and Post Office of his sweetheart! We set about this interesting investigation with as much energy as Butler or Stevens on a mission from their great leader below, and we learned that the young lady had plighted heart and hand *to another man.* Sometimes we have a variation in the shape of complaints against book-keepers, complaints against loyal post-masters (from some unrepentant rebel), complaints against printers, complaints against proof-readers. Again, comes the curt, challenge-like demand "what has become of my wife's poem?" or "what have you done with my article?" Worse than all, more vexatious than all, more perplexing than all, more unendurable than all is the unceasing flow into the sanctum of poetry that *won't* flow. Fainting on the dusty march, freezing in camp, starving on short rations, fighting yankees—all are positive enjoyments compared with the daily duties of the loyal editor in Dixie.

Maj. Gen. Butler, U. S. A., boasts that he has been always in advance of his party, in his grand ideas of progress, emancipation, arming the negroes, impeaching the President, &c., &c., and that the Republicans followed slowly and painfully his leadership for a while, but at length came squarely up abreast with him.—We think that the illustrious hero presents his claims too strongly, or that he does injustice to his party. He may have led the way in his peculiar views about *meum* and *tuum*, but surely he wrongs the Republicans in saying they were slow in adopting his ideas and imitating his practice. The great warrior says nothing about his persistent, persevering vote for

Jeff. Davis as President of the United States. He was in advance of his party in that vote.—As he thinks that it is a mere question of time as to the ultimate carrying out of all his schemes, does he expect the Radicals some day to press the claims of Mr. Davis for the Presidency?

We copy from the Memphis *Appeal*, a flat contradiction of the cock and bull story of Hon. Simon Cameron, of Pennsylvania. We are glad for the sake of the great fame of the illustrious hero, that the falsehood has been exposed. Our able contemporary has done right in thus vindicating the truth of history. General Lee and Hon. Simon Cameron are not so well known abroad as they are at home; and probably, an uncontradicted slander might be believed in the next generation. The source, from which the story came, would render it very doubtful in the minds of all men living in this year of grace, 1868; the personage, to whom the story refers, makes it not merely improbable, but impossible. The *Appeal* says:

A Proud Name.—A writer in one of the leading British Reviews, during the progress of the war, said the truth of history depended upon the dispatches of Gen. Robert E. Lee. As much as to say, he did not prevaricate, he did not extenuate, he alone, was free from exaggeration and misrepresentation. One of our exchanges says, in reference to a slander perpetrated by the notoriously corrupt Cameron, of Pennsylvania:

General Lee.—A correspondent of the Louisville *Courier*, writing from Lexington, Va., has thought it worth while to deny the slanderous statement of Cameron of the particulars connected with the tender of the United States army to Gen. Lee, when the war upon the Southern States was about to be begun. After reasoning upon the inherent and inferential improbability of Cameron's story, the writer says, in italics, "General Lee says the charge is untrue." The denial was altogether unnecessary.—There is something about General Lee that repels the thought of dishonor, that forty thousand Camerons could not fasten the slightest suspicion on him.

What more conclusive evidence is wanted of Cameron's falsehood than the simple denial of Robert E. Lee? There is a moral grandeur in the thought.

When Sumter was fired upon, a howl of indignation went up from the loyal North, "the old flag had been insulted, rebels must be put down, the Union must, and shall be preserved." The fiercest and loudest among the Union shriekers were the men, who had been striving, for a quarter of a century, to break it up, and who had, during all that period, denounced the Constitution as "a covenant with death and a league with hell." Inflamed by the fiery calls to arms from these new converts to Unionism, millions of men sprang forth to crush the rebellion. The old enemies of the Union, now become eloquent patriots, and stern advocates of war, did not themselves take the field, they were needed at home "to fire the heart of the nation," and their precious lives might be taken by ruthless and indiscriminating rebels. So they hired substitutes, took the non-taxable bonds of the government, made contracts, delivered bellicose orations and—shunned the nefarious rebels.

Well, the insult to the old flag was avenged in the best blood of the South, and in the ruin and degradation of a once happy people. When this great and glorious object had been accomplished, a Sergeant of the Federal army, who had been fighting for the Union, while these men were making contracts and speeches, travels alone, and unarmed, all over the rebel South, with the old flag flying over his head. He is received every where kindly, cordially, *enthusiastically*, till he gets to the Capitol of the nation, and comes into the very presence of the men, who shouted so fiercely in '61 about "the insult to the old flag." Here, for the first time is he snubbed, and his flag, the *national* flag—treated with contempt!

How conclusively does this prove the hypocrisy of these Jacobins, when they talked about the insult to the old flag, in 1861. 'Twas hatred of the South and not love of the Union, which made them champions of the old flag. Now as then, hatred of the South is the controlling motive in all that they do. This it is, which prompts them to impose upon us their wicked schemes for our degradation.

Believing that the whole Abolition movement had its root in hatred of God's Word, and contempt of its teachings, we have never doubted that He would, in His own good time, vindicate His authority before the Universe. The vindication has come sooner than we expected. It has come in the demonstration before the world of the *utter* falsehood of all the pretexts set up by the Jacobins for drenching the land in blood. No one in his senses can be made to believe that the men, who have been cursing the old flag for twenty years, could, in a single day, undergo so total a change as to regard it with religious veneration, ornament pulpits with its graceful folds, put pictures of it in bibles, and anthems in its praise in prayer books and hymn books. While the old flag madness pervaded all classes, this glaring inconsistency was not commented upon, perhaps not noticed even. But now, men can look around more calmly and reason more dispassionately; when, therefore, they see the old traitors manifest their contempt for the national colors, they remember that hatred of the Constitution and the Government of our Fathers dates back with this class, for full a quarter of a century.

The emptiness of the other pretext for the war—sympathy with the oppressed negro—has also been satisfactorily demonstrated. The States, which furnished most of the volunteers for the war, have put a social and political ban upon the poor African. The *few* of the afflicted race in their borders are denied those privileges, which the South is *required* to extend to *millions* of these unfortunates. It is easy to pity the poor negro in the rebel South; it is hard to sympathize with him in the loyal North. It is so easy to mourn over other people's sins, it is so hard to repent of our own!

We were disposed to regard the journey of Sergeant Bates as one of those numerous sensationals, which the loyal North has a passion for, such as trundling a wheel-barrow from Bangor to Boston, walking so many miles in so many hours, a prize fight between McCoole and the English bully, freezing all night around a ticket office to get the first chance to hear Mr. Dickens, getting divorces, running after Japanese Tommy, admiring Barnum, adoring Beecher, deifying John Brown, &c., &c., &c. But we now look at the Sergeant's movement from a different stand-point. It will do good, it has already done good. We were fast drifting towards Gen. Grant and the *stable* Government. The unveiling of the Jacobins must have a happy effect. Nothing, too, is so well calculated to revive love for the old flag in the South as the knowledge that it is bitterly hated by the old traitors, Stevens, Phillips & Co.

SOUTHERN FERTILIZERS.—A prejudice has arisen in the minds of many against artificial manures, because of the ignorant and unscientific manner in which they have been used. In some instances, too, the results have been unfavorable through the unpropitiousness of the seasons. But no intelligent man will doubt that the true policy of the Southern farmer is to cultivate less land, and have the less quantity better prepared and better manured.—The English farmers are the most successful in the world, chiefly because they pay so much attention to manures. A like attention on our part will make the waste fields of the South blossom like the rose.

Enterprising men at the South are proving true benefactors to their unfortunate section by providing real, bona fide manures, which are not shams, but possess substantial value for the *purchaser*, as well as the *seller*. The Editor has visited in person the manufactories of G. Ober, Esq., of Baltimore, and of Wm. C. Dukes, of Charleston, S. C., and saw enough to satisfy him that they conducted their establishments upon fair and honorable principles. The manures of Mr. Ober have been most successfully used in this county, (Mecklenburg) and very largely at many points in Georgia, particularly in that fine agricultural section, Hancock county.

Mr. Dukes has the largest establishment in the South, and is putting up a splendid article.

Our old friends, Willis & Chisolm, of Charleston, S. C., are importing the celebrated Rodunda guano, one of the very best fertilizers known. The interests of the farmer will be regarded by them, and only a valuable article will be furnished.

The Southern Fertilizing Company, of Richmond, Virginia, is well and favorably known. Col. Wm. Gilham, late State Geologist of Virginia, is connected with it, and there is no abler chemist in this country.

The Pacific Guano Company,

and the Patapsco Guano Company, of Baltimore, have both a well merited reputation.

Those who wish THE LAND WE LOVE, must remit funds by Express, Check, Post-office order or registered letter. We are only responsible for losses when money is sent in one of these four ways. Persons, however, who wish to give contributions to the loyal Postmasters, may enclose greenbacks to our office and have not the slightest apprehension that the loyal Postmasters aforesaid will not receive their contributions.

BOOK NOTICES.

THE CENTURIONS OF THE GOSPEL. By Rev. W. A. SCOTT, D. D. New York: Anson D. F. Randolph, 1868.

WE have read this book with great interest. The Publishers have done full justice to the learning and piety of the distinguished author.

Our Saviour found no such faith any where, as he found in the Centurion of Capernaum. The Centurion of Cesarea was the first one of the Gentile world, to whom the Gospel was preached. With these two great facts as the basis of his argument, Dr. Scott contends that the profession of arms is not inconsistent with the Christian life and conversation.

We could go farther than this, and show that the self-sacrifice necessarily required of the soldier, is favorable to the development of religious sentiment. Sin is nothing more nor less than an expression of selfishness. "Deny thyself and take up the Cross," is the cardinal doctrine of Christianity. Every victory over self is a victory over sin. As no profession demands such a complete abnegation of self as does the military, there is none that is so favorable to religion, so far as that one element is concerned. On the other hand, there is much about the army, well calculated to turn men into brutes, especially if the commander is himself a brute. The "March to the Sea" must have had a fearful influence upon all connected with it.

Dr. Scott's style is as clear as crystal. You are never at a loss for his meaning. Now when the whole world seems to have run mad after some novelty, Beecher-charlatanry or Cheever-ranting, it is perfectly delightful to find the old Gospel-truths presented in intelligible language.

In striking contrast with the simplicity of Dr. Scott's style, is the mystic bombast of many recent publications. We have a book before us, which has, as the heading of a chapter of mysterious and extravagant verbiage, "The soul a Prayer, whose answer is God." The writer, in order to say something new and striking, is impudently profane. Another chapter is headed, "Hints respecting a nebulous region in the soul." We have never seen any satisfactory distinction between the mind and the soul. But we feel sure that there is, at least, a nebulous region in one mind—that of the novelty-seeking writer. Beecher, in hunting up a new sensation, never stumbled upon any thing more absurd.

THE ROCK OF SALVATION. By W. S. PLUMER, D. D. American Tract Society.

Dr. Plumer is a living refutation of the reflection upon Southern indolence. He has given many books to the world, not crude, ill-digested, hastily prepared productions; but books of solid merit, full of mature thought, and above all, glowing with a genial, warm-hearted piety. He teaches, too, the old and glorious truths of the Gospel, unmixed with new-fangled theories and wild extravagancies.—The aim of the writer is to win souls to Christ, and not to show his own learning and originality of mind. Profound reverence for the great Jehovah pervades his pages, and we find none of that prying, impudent familiarity with holy things, which makes us loathe a certain class of writers, while we shudder at their blasphemy.

When we reflect upon the prodigious labors of Alexander, Thornwell, Baker, Elliott, Pearce, Plumer, Gilmore Simms, Smythe and hundreds of others, we have reason to believe that Southern men can do as much work as any other class. With a sterner necessity now imposed upon them, for more active exertion, we may hope to see richer and more abundant fruits crown their toil.

FOUR OAKS. BY KAMBA THORPE, New York. Geo. W. Carleton & Co.

This is a very entertaining and instructive novel, by a gifted daughter of Alabama, one of the most talented in our grievously oppressed section. The style is good, the sentiments pure and elevated, the moral of the story healthy, and the incidents simple and natural. The lovers of fiction can scarcely wish for a more attractive volume.

THE SOUTHERN BOYS' AND GIRLS' MONTHLY is a charming periodical—all that can be desired for our children. It is really wonderful that a monthly, with 40 pages of reading matter and four or five wood-cuts in each number, can be issued for $1.50 per annum. It is regarded as a rich treat in every household it enters, and parents can put it with safety in the hands of their children, feeling assured that while it contains much to instruct, there is nothing to corrupt the taste or injure the morals. In these degenerate times of *beastly* pictorials and wicked sensational stories, of how little can it be said that this is safe reading. Address Baird & Brother, Richmond, Va.

THE LITTLE GLEANER, published at Fredericksburg, Va., is a very attractive monthly, for children, containing 16 pages, neatly printed on clean white paper. Every effort to build up a pure, native literature that can be put, with safety, in the hands of children, deserves the approbation and encouragement of all good people. The wisest of men has said, "train up a child in the way he should go, and when he is old, he will not depart from it." Many parents, who have the welfare of their children at heart, are wholly regardless of what they read. The child, who would be guarded against mixing in vicious company, is allowed to read immoral tales and obscene anecdotes. The foolish parent forgets that temptation much more frequently comes through the eye than through the ear. The warning of the Saviour was, "if thine eye (not thine ear) offend thee, pluck it out." It is the very height of folly to forbid bad company and permit bad reading. The most powerful agents of Satan are bad books and bad periodicals. Mighty for good and for evil is the Press. Let parents keep a wise supervision over what their children read, as well as over the associations they form. The Little Gleaner is safe reading, and its low price, $1 per annum, puts it within the reach of all.

MINDING THE GAP AND OTHER POEMS. By MOLLIE E. MOORE. CUSHING & CAVE, Houston, Texas:

This little collection of Poems is like a beautiful bouquet, gathered under a tropical sky. Each one is a genuine, perfumed, rain-nursed, dew-kissed blossom.—Mollie Moore takes her place as a Southern poetess, in the hearts of the refined, intellectual, and pure. We give, below, just a stanza or two, as a specimen of her "færy work." The first of her "Mes Amis" commences thus,

"Now surely he upon a Sabbath-day
Was born, with "God bless all men!" on his tongue;
For all his looks are blessings, and his "nay"
Cheers more than "yea" from cold abundance flung.

Her exquisite appreciation of Nature is seen in the following:

"Tall, odorous grass and rustling reed
Waved idly by a broad lagoon;
And there the hunter reined his steed:
The shadows of a broad mid-noon
Were short and round beneath the trees,
Whose beard-like moss hung calm and still,
As sails of ships upon the seas
Where winds are charmed by evil will."

THE LAND WE LOVE.

No. III. JULY, 1868. Vol. V.

COMPARATIVE GENERALSHIP.

A few months after the capture of Gen. Lee's army, in 1865, a writer, in the editorial columns of a widely circulating New York journal, asserted that the achievements of Gen. Grant surpassed those of Alexander, Hannibal, Julius Cæsar, Gustavus Adolphus, Marshal Turenne, Prince Eugene of Savoy, Marlborough, Frederick the Great, Napoleon, and the Duke of Wellington, all combined! The journal in question is so much addicted to quizzing, that we felt at a loss to determine whether this stupendous panegyric was uttered in good faith, or whether it was merely an echo of the popular exultation, which at that moment very nearly approached the borders of frenzy. Napoleon, in his review of Jomini's "Art of War," tells us that a great soldier cannot be made by books of that sort—that the "art" is best taught in the field—that the best substitute for the field is the careful study of eighty-four campaigns which he mentions, viz: the eight of Alexander, seventeen of Hannibal, and thirteen of Cæsar, in ancient times; the three of Gustavus, sixteen of Turenne, nineteen of Eugene, and eleven of Frederick, in modern times. He did not, of course, include his own and those of Wellington. The panegyrist of Gen. Grant, however, includes them in his summary. In order that the reader may see the enormous character of this eulogy, we propose to glance at the career of each of these great captains, before sketching a brief outline of Gen. Grant's.

Alexander the Great, with a force 34,500 strong, invaded the Persian empire, the mightiest, at that time, upon which the sun had ever shone, extending from the shores of the Hellespont to the banks of the Indus, from Memphis on the Nile, to the great mountains of Northern Asia, embracing all those vast kingdoms which played parts so memorable in the early history of mankind, as we find it recorded in the Bible, peopled by innumerable nations, able, at any time, to send a million of men into the field, divided into many provinces, each governed by a satrap equal in power and wealth to the greatest king. In three campaigns, and in three great pitched battles, and two memorable sieges, he struck down the power of this vast monarchy, and assumed the crown of Asia. In five other campaigns, and in innumerable battles, he subdued those wild and warlike tribes around him, which the whole power of the Persian monarchs had never been able to subjugate, and but for the refusal of his troops to follow him farther, would undoubtedly have anticipated Clive and his successors by two thousand years, in making India a province of an European power.

Hannibal, with an army of 26,000 men, arrived on the Italian side of the Alps, with the avowed purpose of overthrowing the Republic of Rome, the most powerful government, at that time, existing in the world. Not only his numbers, but his arms, and the quality of his troops were vastly inferior to those of his enemy. The latter were collected from all quarters; twenty different languages were spoken in his camp, while the Romans were homogeneous. After the battle of Thrasymene, he made his troops arm themselves with the weapons of the dead Romans.—In eighteen months, and in three pitched battles, remembered to this day for the skill with which they were planned, and the vigor with which they were executed, he not only *defeated*, but absolutely and literally *destroyed*, five Roman consular armies, and shook the Roman power to its very foundation. Exhausted by his very victories, denied all reënforcements from home, shut up in the foot of the Italian boot, with no allies but the fierce and intractable Breethans, his numbers waning every day, for fourteen years he defied the whole power of Rome to drive him out of Italy. Never, in his most triumphant days, did his genius shine so brightly as it did in this gloomy season. He left Italy at last, only in consequence of orders from home.

Julius Cæsar, when he took possession of his government of Gaul, found himself at the head of six legions, about 24,000 men, which he recruited to about 60,000 before commencing operations.—In the course of nine years he was victorious in between forty and fifty pitched battles, carried by storm or took by siege eighty fortified places, subdued 300 nations or tribes, forming an aggregate of 20,000,000 of souls, fought in pitched battles or sieges 3,000-000 of men, took 1,000,000 of prisoners, and slew as many fairly in the field. Besides this, he made several expeditions into Germany, and twice crossed over to Britain, where he fought two battles. In the civil war, in a single pitched battle, he destroyed the power of Pompey, in another totally subdued the revolted Egyptians, in a third routed Pharnaces, on which occasion he wrote "*veni, vidi, vici*," and thus made himself master of the Eastern world. In a fourth he struck down the power of Pompey's followers in Africa, and in a fifth put the finishing stroke to his works by destroying the army of Pompey's sons in Spain. He certainly is a very wonderful military man. Who can be called superior to Julius Cæsar?

Gustavus Adolphus made his first campaign in Poland, where, after defeating the King in several battles he compelled him to make peace. The Emperor of Germany was at that time waging the cruel and unjust war, known as the "Thirty Years' War," with his Protestant subjects. His progress, through the skill of his generals, Tilly and Wallenstein, had given alarm to all Europe, Catholic as well as Protestant.—Gustavus espoused the cause of his Protestant brethren. He landed in Pomerania, and made himself master of that province, after having defeated the forces of the Emperor in a bloody battle, and stormed all the strong places in it. He then proceeded south carrying all the fortresses, for which Germany is so famous, as fast as he came to them. Tilly was sent to arrest him. He attacked him and received a bloody repulse.—Gustavus followed up the blow, and attacking Tilly at Leipsic, a great battle ensued, in which Tilly lost half of his army. Gustavus marched on, crossed the Danube, invaded Bavaria, carried every fortress before him in spite of Tilly, and when that officer attempted to stop him at the passage of the Lech he almost annihilated his army, and Tilly himself was killed. He had gone as far on his conquering progress towards the Rhine as Ulm, when he was recalled to Saxony to face Wallenstein. He came in contact with him at Lutzen. After a bloody battle, in which he gained a signal victory, he was, unfortunately, killed. One month more and he would have been in Vienna.

Eugene first commanded in chief in the campaign of 1697 against the Turks, which he rendered memorable by defeating Mustaphe II., in the battle of Zenta, killing, wounding, or taking 20,000 men, and all his artillery, baggage, &c. This ended the war. In the "War of the Succession," he was sent to Italy, where he completely defeated Catinat, and afterwards Villeroi, taking the latter prisoner at Cremona. Called to Germany in 1704, he united his army with that of Marlborough, and the two gained the overwhelming battle of Blenheim. Returning to Italy, although he was at first foiled by Vendome, yet he carried Turin by storm, and virtually put an end to the French power there. He then penetrated into France, and laid siege to Toulon, but was not successful. Withdrawn from Italy, he was sent to Flanders, to command the Austrian forces acting in concert with Marlborough. He participated in the two great battles of Oudenarde and Malplaquet, in 1708 and 1709. In the war with the Turks, be fought the battle of Peterwardein, with greatly inferior force, routed the Turks with great slaughter, and captured Belgrade; which exploit led to peace. He was at the head of the army of 1733 with Poland, but no battle was fought. He commanded in eighteen pitched battles and gained them all.

Marlborough was one of the most fortunate generals that ever lived. It was said of him, that he never drew his sword that he did not conquer. We know of no other general of whom the same can be said with truth. In 1704, when the French marched an overwhelming army into Bavaria, and united with the Bavarian forces, were about to push on to Vienna, he made a sudden and rapid march from Flanders, united his forces to those of Eugene, and gained the tremendous victory of Blenheim, in which the French lost 40,000 men out of 60,000. The way was open to Paris, and Marlborough and Eugene wished to take it, but the Dutch deputies refused their consent. Besides this battle, Marlborough also gained the great victories of Ramillies, Oudenarde and Malplaquet, and took all the fortified towns of Flanders, besides several in the North of France. When Marlborough first landed in Flanders, Louis XIV. was the most powerful monarch that had reigned in Europe since Charlemagne. Marlborough brought him almost to the dust. Another campaign and he would have been suing for peace on any terms, when a faction at home overthrew the great general and caused him to lose his command.

When the Seven Years' War commenced, Russia, Sweden, Austria, France, Saxony, and Poland, with standing armies, numbering 600,000 men, were united against Prussia, which had only 160,000. The combined population of these countries was 100,000,000. The population of Prussia, 5,000,000. England, however, was with Prussia, and sent an army to Hanover, which, with her German subjects and allies, it was thought would protect Prussia on the south. The allies lay at great distances from each other. Frederic lay in the centre, and had a chance to strike them in detail. He commenced the war by overrunning Saxony, seizing Dresden, besieging the Saxon army, 17,000 strong, in the camp of Pirna, leaving a sufficient force to blockade the camp, marching into Bohemia, and totally defeating Marshal Brown, who was approaching to raise the siege, at Lowositz. In the spring of 1757, he attacked Brown before Prague, waiting for Daun to join him before advancing into Saxony, and defeated him with a loss of 24,000 men, he, himself, losing 18,000. Part of the defeated force shut themselves up in Prague, part fled to Daun.—Frederic left a part of his force to blockade Prague, and with the rest, on the 18th June, the same day with the battle of Waterloo, fifty-eight years after, attacked Daun and Brown, at Kolin, and was terribly defeated. But as Daun made no use of his victory, he was soon in the field again. In the meantime the Duke of Cumberland capitulated to the

French army, which being now at liberty, marched to invade the south of Prussia. Silesia was in possession of a powerful Austrian army, and the Russians were in the Northern provinces. Placed in a central position, Frederic was enabled to strike right and left. He marched with great rapidity on the French, and gained a glorious victory over them, at Rossbach, on the 5th November, came back on the Austrians, and in a battle, (fought 5th December,) which Napoleon calls a master-piece, (Leuthen) defeated them utterly, killing, wounding, and taking 27,000 out of 60,000, and in the spring inflicted a terrible defeat on the Russians, at Zorndorf.—But on the 14th October, 1758—the same on which Napoleon prostrated the power of Prussia, fifty-eight years afterwards—he was surprised in his camp, and defeated by Daun and Laudohn, at Hochkirchen, losing 13,000 men. In 1759, the Austrians being in possession of Saxony, and the Russians of the country bordering the Oder, the two united, and Frederic attacking them at Kunersdorf, where they were strongly intrenched, suffered a terrible defeat; the worst he had ever sustained. Out of 50,000 men, he could rally that evening but 3,000. But the allies grew jealous of each other and did not improve their victory. The next day he had rallied 18,000 men, and in a few weeks had an army 30,000 strong. At the commencement of 1760, the enemy were in possession of Berlin, but Frederic gained a great victory over Laudohn at Liegnitz, and another great victory over Daun at Torgau, which restored things to their old condition. In 1761 there was no battle. The Empress of Russia died, and her successor immediately made peace, clothed all the Prussian prisoners in new suits, and sent them back to Frederic, entering at the same time into an alliance with him. England and France made peace soon after. Austria left by herself was not long in following the example. Frederic relinquished nothing whatever. The united exertions of this mighty alliance had been unable to wring any thing from him.

The career of Napoleon is so well known that we shall make our summary as brief as possible. In his first two campaigns, 1796 and 1797, in Italy, in the course of ten months he was victorious in fourteen pitched battles, and seventy combats, destroyed five Austrian armies, took 100,000 prisoners, and killed and wounded as many more, captured six hundred field pieces and two thousand heavy guns, drove the Austrians entirely out of Italy, and forced a peace in sight of the steeples of Vienna. All this he effected with an army of less than thirty thousand men,—the reënforcements he received never covering his losses. In the campaigns of '98–'99 he carried the French arms to the ancient Scripture lands of Egypt and Syria, and won battles on spots renowned in the earliest history of mankind, at Alexandria, the Pyramids, Mount Tabor, Jaffa, (Joppa, the port of Jerusalem,) and was obliged to raise the siege he had laid to Acre, already immortalized in the history of the crusaders. Returning to Egypt, he drove a whole Turkish army into the sea at Aboukir, returned to France, seized the government, and had himself proclaimed first consul.—All his conquests, except Genoa, had been lost, and the Austrians were besieging that, when, in 1800, he crossed the Alps, took possession of Lombardy and Piedmont in their rear, cut off their communications and forced them to fight the battle of Marengo, by which he recovered all the French had lost, in one month from the time he left Paris. In 1805, he destroyed the Austrian Grand Army at Ulm before it could unite with the advancing Russians, and at Austerlitz destroyed the Russian army likewise. In 1806, he destroyed the Prussian army at Jena before the Russians could join, and pursuing it from one end of Prussia to the other, in a fortnight captured all the fortresses and 140,000 prisoners. In 1807 he fought the great battle of Eylau, and repulsed the Russians with great slaughter, and of Friedland, in which the Russian army was almost annihilated. In 1808, he swept over Spain like a whirlwind. In 1809, in four great battles, fought in four consecutive days, he defeated the Archduke Charles of Austria, and drove him over the Danube, leaving the way open to Vienna. He took that city after a slight cannonade, crossed the Danube and fought the bloody and indecisive battle of Essling or Aspern, retired to the Isle of Lobau, recrossed and utterly defeated Charles at Wagram. In 1812 he fought the terrible battle of Borodino, seventy miles from Moscow, in which the Russians lost 52,000. The fire at Moscow, and the frost and snow, destroyed his great army, and all Europe rose against him. In the campaign of 1813, his struggles were gigantic. He fought and gained four of the greatest battles recorded in history; Lutzen, Bautzen, Wurchen, and Dresden. But the numbers of his enemies constantly increased, until at last, at Leipsic, they overwhelmed him. In the campaign of 1814, in France, with 40,000 men, he opposed for weeks a force of 300,000, formed into five armies, which he (moving on the chord of an arc while they moved on the circumference) kept asunder, with infinite skill, fighting a battle every day. He would have succeeded at last, had not Marmont treacherously given up the city of Paris to the invaders. In 1815, at the head of 122,000 men, he marched into Belgium against Wellington and Blucher, whose armies, amounting in the aggregate to 220,000, were quartered separately. He thrust himself between them, beat Blucher, sent Grouchy in pursuit of him, ordering him to keep between Blucher and the main army. He then pursued Wellington, attacked him at Waterloo, and was on the point of beating him, when first Bulow and then Blucher came up.

Wellington landed in Portugal in 1807 with about 30,000 troops. The troops of Junot were dispersed all about the neighborhood of Lisbon. He had about 21,000 in all, but could assemble only 9,000. With these he attacked Wellington at Vimeira, and was, of course, beaten. His whole army capitulated a few days after, and the English had undisputed posession of Portugal. In 1809, Wellington, by a sudden march from Lisbon on Oporto, forced Soult to retreat. He next marched upon Madrid, and fought the bloody battle of Talavera, with doubtful result, it seems to us, since he did not obtain his object, and was forced to retreat back to Lisbon. In 1810, Massena invaded Portugal with 80,000 men.—Wellington had the better in the battle of Busaco. He retired to the lines of Torres-Vedras. Massena, unable to force them, lay before them until he lost half his army. He then retreated, and Wellington following, the battle of Fuentes d'Onore was fought, the English claiming the advantage. In 1811, Wellington took Ciudad Rodrigo by storm. In 1812, he stormed Badajoz—Napoleon having called a great part of his forces from Spain, Wellington took this opportunity to march into it. He attacked Marmont at Salamanca and completely defeated him, but was compelled afterwards to fall back on Portugal. In 1813, Napoleon, in consequence of his losses in Russia, was compelled to abandon Spain. The army under King Joseph was retiring in perfect disorder, laden with plunder, and every way demoralized. When Wellington attacked them (1813) they scarcely made a show of fight, but ran and endeavored to save their treasure. This shameful affair is called the battle of Vittoria, though in truth it was no battle at all. In 1814, Wellington entered the south of France, and fought several battles with Soult, at Bayonne, Orthes and Toulouse. In 1815, he commanded in the battle of Waterloo, which, we suppose, is what chiefly gave him his reputation.

Let us now take a brief glance at the campaigns of Gen. Grant. At the very outset we observe a remarkable contrast between the circumstances under which all his operations were conducted, and those under which the generals to whom he is preferred, conducted theirs. They, in nearly every instance, took the field with inferior numbers; he never moved without an enormous numerical superiority. They generally fought against men whose resources of every kind were at least equal to their own; he *never once* encountered an enemy who was not greatly his inferior, not only in numbers, but in arms, stores, provisions, clothing, medical appliances; every thing except skill and valor. That he was right to make all he could out of this species of superiority, is certainly true. He fought for an object, and it was his duty to obtain that object. But the fact detracts very considerably from his praise as a commander. Napoleon says, that the greatest general is he, who, with the smallest number of men in the field, can bring the greatest number to bear on a given point. This definition is perfect, and so palpable that the unskilled can see its correctness as well as Hannibal could. But where a general operates with three or four to one, he deserves no credit for bringing a superior force to bear on one given point. Napoleon's definition is true, where the parties are equal, or where the manœuvering party is slightly superior. At Eckmuhl, for instance, the armies were equal—90,000 each. Napoleon contrived, by his superior skill, to throw 80,000 men in full weight, upon 40,000 of the enemy, while with 10,000 he kept 50,000 at long taw; and this, he said, at St. Helena, was the most skillful manœuvre he ever executed. Had the French army been greatly superior—had it been, for instance, 130,000, he would have deserved no high degree of credit. He might have thrown the 80,000 upon the 40,000 on the important point, and he could still have held the other 50,000 at bay with a power equal to their own. Instances of this kind abound in his history. General Grant's numbers were always so enormously superior, that he could throw half his army at any time, upon one point, and still have a force of two to one to oppose the rest of his enemy's army. For example. He had, at the Wilderness, 160,000 men; Lee had 47,000 all told. Suppose Lee to have held a vital position with 30,000 of these men; a position which if carried must insure the destruction of his army. Grant could throw 120,000 men upon it and still retain 40,000 to make head against the rest of Lee's army, amounting to but 17,000. Victories gained in this manner, by overwhelming odds, are quite as useful as any other victories, but they are hardly so creditable to the victorious party.

THE RHINE.

(*From the German of F. A. Krummacher.*)

BY MARY BAYARD CLARKE

When grand St. Gothard stood complete
  And Nature's noble work was done,
She smiled upon its heart of ice
  And to the mountain gave a son.
" 'Tis meet that goodness should proceed
  From greatness such as thine,
Thy garnered strength have wider scope,
  Thy gathered waters form the Rhine.
Go forth," she said, " oh noble youth,
  Well worthy of thy lineage grand,
And roll thy Heaven-born waters from
  The hollow of thy Father's hand."
The stream obeyed and tore his way
  Through rocks and crags with wanton force,
Parted the waves of Bodenlake
  And boldly held his onward course.
Now smiling vineyards mark his path,
  The turbid race of youth is run,
And bright luxuriant beauty crowns
  The manhood of St. Gothard's son.
A hundred streams rich tribute yield,
  He lays his vine-leaf wreath aside,
Bears noble ships upon his breast
  And calmly rolls through cornfields wide.
By many a branch he seeks the sea,
  But wheresoe'er his waters pour
Men honored him as " father Rhine,"
  Whom Nature to St. Gothard bore.

THE DECAY OF RELIGION IN THE SOUTH.

MUCH as we may regret the political and household ruin of a whole people, every Christian must deem the decline and corruption of religion among them a far greater evil. But any one, who does not close his eyes to unwelcome yet obvious facts, may now witness the progress of this decay in the Southern States, but more especially in those containing the bulk of the negro population.

We would point out the indications, and trace the causes of this decay ; but in order to measure its progress, we must first state what was the religious condition of the South up to the year 1860. What we have to say is most applicable to the more southern of these States; but especially to those, in which negro slavery, having existed for generations, approached what may be called its normal condition.

From the first settlement of the country, the Christian missionary had trodden close on the heels of the pioneer in the wilderness; and for generations there had been few families which did not, in some form, profess the Christian faith. From the nature of the country, farming and pastoral pursuits engrossed the cares of the bulk of the population, a very small portion dwelling in towns. A necessary result from this, was, that literary education was generally superficial, and by no means universal. In a sparsely peopled country, most households must be remote from schools; and the support necessary to the maintenance of a school, of high order, can be found in few neighborhoods. Indeed, in many poor and thinly settled parts of the country, it would be difficult to collect twenty scholars from as many square miles. It was thus often less easy to bring the young within the reach of the means of education, than it might be in a Tartar horde, or an Arab tribe, which, migrating in a body from pasture to pasture, still always keeps the household composing it, near neighbors to each other; and the schoolmaster would naturally accompany them in all their migrations.

Yet, however thinly settled many parts of the South were, few neighborhoods were without one or more religious societies. A christian church of some kind was habitually frequented by the bulk of the people, although many families had to make almost a journey to worship there. From the fewness, and the defeets of other sources of education, a large part of the instruction received was of a religious character. The Bible was, practically, the chief school book, and the church the chief school of young and old; but this was not always under the charge of a competent teacher.

Yet, from causes which we need not here trace, it is notoriously true that religious impulses and speculations have shown, in the South, little of that tendency to run into the extravagancies of faith, so often and so variously manifested in the Northern States, in the shape of Unitarianism, Universalism, Quakerism, Shakerism, Spiritualism, Mormonism, Free-love doctrines, and other aberrations, from simple heresies in dogmatic theology, down to the utter perversion of all the principles of Christianity.

More than twenty years before 1860, there had been a marked deepening and widening of the current of Christian faith in the South, and a corresponding increase of effort to bring the truths and obligations of Christianity home to the hearts of all in the land. More especially did this zeal show itself in a deepening sense of the responsibility of professed Christians to labor at the religious instruction of the negroes, a duty which had hitherto been much, but not altogether, neglected. All branches of the Church were moved by this impulse; the effort of some were peculiarly successful ; but we might do injustice to others in singling out any as having shown peculiar zeal. The labors of many clergymen, and not a few laymen, in this field, have been worthy of the high and pure motives which prompted them; nor will they lose their reward.

But the Christianizing of any people is up-hill work; and the difficulties increase with the depth of their ignorance, and yet more with the intellectual narrowness of the race. While Christianity, viewed in its merely earthly aspeet, is the most powerful agent in promoting civilization, there is no doubt that civilization opens the door for the entrance of Christianity. Probably some measure of it is essential among any people, if not to the reception, at least to the spontaneous preservation of the faith. For instance: For more than a century the Moravians have maintained missions in Greenland, and have made converts of many of the natives, who, we are quite willing to believe, are devout members of their Church. But, should these missions be withdrawn, and all intercourse with Christendom cut off, does any sane man believe that these people, who are but Esquimaux, and, from the very nature of their country, cannot rise above the pursuits and habits which characterize that race—would they preserve, uncorrupted, for generations, the learning, Church organization, and mutual control, essential to the permanent upholding of the sacred truths and institutions planted among them? We might point out many other countries in which the planting of a self-sustaining Church would be quite as hopeless. It is true that most missionaries, laboring among the heathen of the more degraded types, would have us believe otherwise. But, although the common saying as to traveller's tales is a rare example of a false adage, originating far more in the narrow ignorance of listeners, than the falsehood of travellers, yet, it is no where more justly applicable than to missionary narratives. The mere traveller may be an unbiased observer, seeking only truth, with no prejudged conclusions to uphold. But the missionary, relying on help from on high, readily believes all he hopes, and magnifies the conversion of every doubtful proselyte into a manifest widening of the Kingdom of Christ. Blinded by his zeal, misled by his hopes, he deceives others by being self-deceived.

As one people, from the physical conditions under which they live, may be cut off from taking the first steps in civilization necessary to enable them to maintain the Christian faith, after it is introduced among them: so another people, not from external causes, accidental conditions, but from the low order of their mental and moral endowments, may be equally unable to uphold the civilization and Christianity acquired through their relations with another race.

The negro, out of Africa at least, has always proved a docile proselyte. The race is highly susceptible of religious emotions, and prone to devotional observances. Accordingly in the South great success followed missionary labors among them. This success appeared greater than it was; for the negroes are peculiarly an imitative race; and it is easier to imitate the externals of devotions, than to understand its objects and enter into its spirit. It was soon obvious that those branches of the Church in which the habits of worship afforded the readiest vent to devout excitement by external manifestations of religious enthusiasm, and gave the greatest facilities to taking an active part in public prayer, exhortation, and in the dicipline of the congregation, took the strongest hold upon them. The negro, constitutionally, loves excitement and a crowd. He is by nature loquacious; instinctively given to oratory.—We have often had occasion to observe that, with him, no amount of ignorance or of mental obtuseness, proved the slightest bar to the impulse to exhort, to instruct, to dogmatize, or to lead in public worship.

Their knowledge of the negro convinced most of those who interested themselves in their religious condition, that both their Christianity and their civilization could only be upheld by their constant intercourse and contact with a superior and dominant race.—Even in the heart of cultivated communities, the oldest towns in the South, negro congregations under negro pastors showed a perpetual tendency to glide into a sensuous religion, into debasing superstition and corrupt practices. The negroes are prone to preserve and even to revive rites worthy of the grossest paganism. We will give an example of this: In the earliest settled part of South Carolina, on a plantation which had been in the possession of the same family for generations, the proprietor found that, when a negro died, his family, for many nights after his death, would place a dish of food on his grave; and finding the dish empty in the morning, were fully convinced that their dead kinsman had enjoyed the repast they had provided. In a Christian country, among negroes calling themselves Christians, it cost their master frequent expostulations, much explanation, and repeated prohibitions, before he could slowly eradicate this heathen rite.

The negroes, in the country especially, shunned the observation of the whites in their religious and funeral services. This shyness of remark originated both from the fear of ridicule, and of prohibition of some of their proceedings. The writer of this artiele, although living habitually the greater part of the year on the plantation just spoken of, did not often pry into their mysteries, yet took an occasional opportunity of observing, unobserved, the proceedings of a funeral. On the plantations the funerals usually took place at night, in order that friends from other plantations might attend. We will give an account of one we witnessed unobserved. The night was dark and somewhat rainy. The bier, preceded and followed by more than three hundred negroes, many of whom bore torches of pitch pine, was borne from the negro village to the plantation burial ground in the heart of a cedar grove. We took our post, hidden by a large tree, while the blazing torches lighted up the undulating ground, and the trunks, branches and foliage of the woodland scene. The crowd assembled around the grave with the torches blazing over their heads, and a heavy column of smoke soon formed a canopy over them, while a prayer was offered up and a discourse delivered by one of the head men of the plantation with fluency and fervor, and indications of no little knowledge of Scripture. So far all was well. But when the preacher had concluded his address, the men still stood grouped around the grave, while the women, more than a hundred, drew aside a few steps to a level spot. Here one of them began a very peculiar chant, and all the others were soon circling around her in a wild yet monotonous dance, at every pause she made, repeating by way of a chorus what she had last uttered. She sung in a *contralto* voice, and was plainly an *improvisatrice*, what she said referring either to the individual dead—lamenting his death, or dwelling on some trait in his character, or else alluding to local and contemporary matters. She displayed, amidst her extravagances, some range of sentiment, command of language and rhythmical powers, and was vociferously seconded by her dancing body-guard and somewhat bacchanalian chorus. All evidently enjoyed the occasion for venting their animal spirits under the guise of religious emotions. The whole concert accorded so ill with the *preceding* mournful occasion and the preceding solemnities, as to exhibit a revolting mixture of heathen and Christian rites. Yet most of the negroes were Methodists, many were Baptists, and others habitually catechised and preached to by a clergyman of the Episcopal Church. At the end of these ceremonies the blazing lights were thrown on the ground and extinguished, nor could one of the negroes have been afterwards induced to apply these consecrated torches to any secular use.

From all that we have seen of the religious tendencies, we had almost said instincts, of the negro, we have been forced to assent to the conclusion of an able and learned minister of the Presbyterian Church, not a native of America, who assured us that those clergymen who had devoted themselves to the instruction of congregations composed exclusively of blacks, had mistaken the mode of promoting the Christian progress; this end being best secured by bringing them into the church as adjuncts to the congregations of whites. This he had found the only means of tempering and controlling their bent to superstitious and corrupting observances.

It was constantly remarked that a strong profession of religious zeal was far more common among the negro men than women, while the reverse is the case among white people. But this, among the blacks, was almost always accompanied by an eager desire to assume, however ignorant the party might be, the character of a teacher, exhorter, and leader among his people. With some marked exceptions, it was but too evident that the hope of acquiring influence and personal advantage was the corner-stone at the foundation of their zeal. It may be that their subject condition narrowed the field of action open to the designing and ambitious; but what ever was the cause, no where else could be found, among the teachers of any class of Christians, so many wolves in sheep's clothing.

A tendency to corrupt Christianity is common to all mankind; but among the negroes it was found peculiarly difficult to abolish and keep out superstitious practices, to suppress a mere noisy manifestation of religious excitement, to impress upon them the permanent nature of the marriage bond, and to convince them of the impossibility of divorcing godliness from righteousness. A thorough knowledge of the negro made it plain that both their civilization and their Christianity were dependent upon their intercourse with and subjection to another race.

We do not mean to imply, by any thing that we have said, that the people of the South had acquitted themselves of their obligation, as Christians, to evangelize the negroes among them and under their control. The greater part of the people of these States, like the bulk of the population of every country in Christendom, are not truly followers of Christ.—Even using the term, Christian, in the lowest sense, there were still among the whites, as well as the blacks, throughout the South, large fields for apostolic labor almost unoccupied. But we can truly say that for many years the labors for the religious instruction of the negro, were far more general, more earnest, and apparently far more successful than strangers to the South, and the unobservant there, have imagined.

So much on the religious condition of the South up to 1860.—We now come to the indications and the causes of the decay of religion since that time. That the change has been great and the downward progress rapid, can be made obvious to all. This is owing to certain material, as well as moral, causes. Of their material causes we will speak first.

In a country at once Christian and rich, the very Mammon of unrighteousness is made a powerful agent in advancing the glory of God. Even men, careless of the future, and base in their morals, often give freely of their superfluities to the building of churches, the support of ministers, the extension of missions, the publication of religious books, and the education of those destined to become instrumental for enlarging the kingdom of Christ. All history tells us that there is a close connection between the civilization and prosperity of a people, and their religious condition. We need but look at the degraded churches, and the corrupted faith of the Christian population of the first seat of our religion, and of the nations around it, now the servants of the Turk. Christianity was yet new on earth when its corruption was hastened by the wars and devastations, the decay of commerce, arts, learning, and civilization, that followed the dismemberment of the Roman Empire. At this day we see the Church of Rome every where identical in dogmas, discipline, and rites, yet widely varying in different countries in its practical nature, in its results on priest and laymen, according to the character and condition of the people of each land. It is one thing in Germany, France, and England; quite another in Spain, Portugal, Mexico, and South America.—Here at home, within the pale of other Churches than that of Rome, we can mark wide differences in the Christianity professed and practiced in the more enlightened and more ignorant parts of the world.

The people of the Southern States, after a strenuous effort to defend their political rights, and social organization, and ward off the ruin impending at the hands of their more numerous and domineering confederates, suffered an overthrow more disastrous to their material prosperity, than nine out of ten of the conquests recorded in history, ever proved to the vanquished people. For this conquest, and the social revolution resulting from it, destroyed the very elements of prosperity. The Norman conquests of England did not stamp sterility upon the soil, or paralyze the laborer's arm. The Russian conquest of Poland did not sweep away the elements of fertility, or the means of making them available. We might summon in witness a long array of conquests, which left the material resources of the conquered regions unimpaired. But the overthrow of the South, and of its social organization is surely, and not slowly, converting its most productive territories into barren wastes, hastening to return to the wilderness from which they were laboriously won.

For these States are fertile only in a certain sense, and it is not the labor of every race that can make that fertility available.—The climate, in most parts below, and many above the thirty-fifth degree of latitude, is ill-suited to the winter growing grain crops, which furnish the chief food of civilized man. Here the yield is most uncertain, and always small. The summer's sun parches up the pastures and cuts short the produce of the meadows, so that little profit is derived from cattle and the products of the dairy. The South is dependent for food on summer-growing crops, requiring frequent tillage during their growth, most of it by manual labor, during the hottest and most unhealthy season of the year.

But if the climate, and perhaps the soil, of the southern part of this continent, and those of the adjacent islands have been found ill-suited to the ordinary crops of the farm, they are admirably adapted to some great agricultural staples, which at once become the basis of a world-wide commerce ; for, while they can be grown to advantage, only, under peculiar climates, they are easily transported to, and eagerly sought after in, every land.

A great field was here opened for agricultural enterprise, industry, and skill. But, from the first settlement of the country, it has been found that, on the more productive soils of this bountiful region, the man of Caucasian race followed the labors of the field at the cost of health, and the hazard of life. He cultivated summer-growing crops, unlike the crops sowed from their first germination, in autumn, and growing through the winter, they struggled for air and soil with a host of rank-growing weeds. They can only be preserved and protected by frequent tillage, during their growth, chiefly by manual labor, at the hottest season of the year. We hear sometimes of great returns to farming with white labor in the South. The instances are few, are confined to peculiarly healthy spots, and the success grossly exaggerated.—What says the experience of two centuries? The constitutions of few white men long stand the wasting effects of the climate, when laid open to its worst influences by the fatigue and exposure of the husbandman's toil under our almost tropical sun. The country was settled at a frightful cost of human life. Families of European laborers either ceased to toil as they were wont at home, or died out. Every one who has witnessed the amount of toil undergone, the year round, by the hard working peasantry of England, Scotland, Ireland, and Germany, knows that in the productive parts of the Southern States, such a class neither does, nor can exist.

But this was not the result with all races. The negroes brought hither from Africa, by the ships of old and New England, found a climate and country congenial to their nature, differing indeed somewhat from their native land, but, perhaps, more favorable to them. This we may infer from their speedy multiplication by natural increase, and their improvement in efficiency, intelligence and civilization; or must we attribute these effects, not in part to country and climate, but altogether to their improved social condition? Less than three hundred thousand Africans, the first of whom were brought to the English Colonies in North America since the middle of the 17th century, and most of them a hundred years later, were represented, in 1860, by more than four millions of their offspring. Certain it is that, in numberless regions of the South, the same air that breathes pestilence and death to the white man, wafts health and vigor to the black.

If the experience of two centuries proves that no great and profitable return can be looked for from the soil of the South but through negro labor, the experience of the three years which have elapsed since the emancipation of the negroes—backed by the results of negro freedom in Hayti, Jamaica, Cape Colony and in the Northern States—equally proves that, with few exceptions, the negro, as a free man, is unprofitable to himself, and as a hireling, worthless and ruinous to all who employ him. In 1790, French St. Domingo exported $25,000,000 in sugar and coffee alone—the Empire of Hayti has taken its place, and exports—nothing worth naming. Its people are truly '*fruges consumere nati*,' for their scanty diet is little else than fruit, the spontaneous gift of the soil. Chronic revolution seems to be the only other production. In Jamaica the strong hand of Great Britain has failed to sustain industry; and after thirty years of experiment, it has been found necessary, to enforce order and protect life, by abolishing the local legislature, and putting the Queen's authority in its place. Such is the testimony of Hayti and Jamaica. Every witness from abroad tells a similar tale. Here in the South, except in small farming in the least fertile, and therefore more healthy parts of the country, where white men can labor without ruin to their health, agricultural labor has been so far annihilated that the outlay on almost every agricultural enterprise, and indeed on all undertakings requiring much unskilled labor, has far exceeded the returns. They must all be abandoned. The planter reaps only ruin. The people of the South find themselves poorer and less hopeful year by year. Many, formerly wealthy and still holding large landed property, once of great value, are reduced to absolute want. Their land is worthless, for the only labor that can render it productive can hardly be said to exist. The few fields cultivated yearly shrink within narrower bounds. The idleness and consequent destitution of the negroes drives them to depredate on the crops before they are harvested or even ripe—and are a yet more fatal obstacle to all pastoral industry; for live stock of all kinds rapidly disappears before the nocturnal enterprises of these hungry marauders. Already, in some parts of the country, the impulses of desperate want, guided by the emissaries of evil sent among them, gather them into armed bands, in open day light, and drive them to acts of wholesale plunder, violence and outrage. These may be local and temporary; but the destruction of the agricultural and pastoral prosperity of the country is permanent, and involves the utter loss of value in all fixed capital there.

The mass of the people of the South, formerly so prosperous, are stinted in the necessaries of life. Many neighborhoods have been almost deserted by the educated, the influential, and the once wealthy classes. There is not now in the South remunerative employment for a fifth of those whose professions imply a liberal and costly education. The greater number of them must seek new homes, where their skill and knowledge may be valued and rewarded—or remain to starve on incomes falling short of the wages of a ploughman. This falls with peculiar weight on the clergy. Although their calling relates chiefly to man's interest in another world, they must be fed, clothed, and housed in this; for 'the laborer is worthy of his hire.' But, when the wants of this life come to press heavily on a needy people, men begin to retrench by dispensing with the services of a profession whose duties refer to a life yet to come. The minister is starved out on a curtailed and often unpaid salary. Soon he must neglect dispensing 'the bread of life' to earn that bread which feeds the body. 'For he, who provideth not for his own household, hath denied the faith, and is worse than an infidel.'—Churches are closed and not reopened, they decay and are not repaired, they crumble to the earth and are not rebuilt. Even churches richly endowed are no better off, for their glebe lands become valueless like all other property in the country.

Upon those branches of the church, like the Episcopal and Presbyterian, which require of their ministers a high standard in education and social position, the evil falls soonest and heaviest; but it has gradually a ruinous effect on all. Even the church of Rome, in which, from the celibacy of the clergy, a high standard of education is maintained at comparatively a small cost, will be slowly starved out.

Now though numbers of mankind pass through life apparently without a thought beyond the bare and fleeting objects of this world, yet, by his very nature, man is prone to some kind of worship; and by his fallen and corrupt nature he is prone to the gradual degradation of the mode and object of that worship. No people are long without religious teachers; for their's is a post of power, the greater in proportion to the ignorance of their flock, often too great to measure that of the pastor. Nor is it mere ignorance that takes the place of knowledge. Error in its most corrupting forms, soon fills the place of truth. We can only shut out from the church gross imposture, groveling superstition, revolting rites, and mad fanaticism through the labors of an educated class of men especially devoted to the study and teaching of the word of God. But throughout large portions of the South the people have no longer the means of maintaining this class, indispensible as their services may be.

But besides the causes originating in the poverty and ruin of the country, others of a moral nature are exerting an evil influence on the religious faith of too many in the South.

The people of these States entered on secession with a good conscience, and defended their rights, in arms, with undoubting faith, fully believing it to be not only their right, but their duty, to break off all partnership with their Northern confederates. This conviction, which had been growing on them for years, sprung into action at the new light, thrown by late and startling developments, on the true character and designs of the mass of the Northern people.

The people of the Southern States felt that they had a civilization worth preserving, and that it was altogether dependent on the maintenance of their political and social organization. Observing and reflecting men, among them, had long foreseen, and proclaimed that the triumph of the Northern policy and machinations must at once bring down political and moral degradation on the South, with its economical ruin; and condemu the negro to barbarism, godless superstition, and ultimate extinction.

When denounced and anathematized by the Northern abolitionists, the Southern slave-holder had looked to the North to ascertain the true motives and character of his vituperative assailants, and the condition of the negroes living among them. He at once saw that there was no accord between the words and actions of the Northern people. The negro there was but a masterless slave, needing, but destitute of, an individual protector; the *pariah* of the community, thrown off to find for himself the necessaries of life, yet excluded, by a social excommunication, from every profitable and reputable calling. Although recruited by occasional fugitives from the South, the negroes there were dwindling in numbers, and dying out from destitution. For the working classes at the North, universally treated the black man as an interloper, standing in the way of the whites; and if he attempted to follow any trade or craft, which the former found it profitable to engage in, the mob soon taught him, by club law, to repent his presumption. We will give a single illustration of this feeling: In a Northern city, a negro fugitive from the South, where he had been bred a bricklayer, obtained employment as a hodman on a house, then building, on one of the principal streets. When the workmen went to dinner, the negro, who had no dinner to go to, thought he would try if his hand had lost its skill, and began to lay a few bricks. This attracted the notice of some workmen passing by, and a group of them gathered together, the exclamation was soon heard, 'Look at that damned negro pretending to do a white man's work!' A shower of brick-bats at once drove him from his trowel, and obliged him to seek refuge within the building, to escape a fracture of the skull.

It was easy to see that there

was mingled with the Northern hostility to negro slavery, a large amount of hostility to the negro. There were, in fact, two classes of Abolitionists, one seeking to abolish negro slavery, the other to abolish the negro himself, as a nuisance and obstruction in the white man's way. Many who professed to be of the former class, really belonged to the latter. Southern men saw so many proofs, both open and latent, of this animosity against the blacks, that they were forced to recognize in themselves, as the masters, the only real friends and protectors of the race. In the day of secession we doubt if there was a single secessionist who believed that the negroes would be as well off in freedom as they then were. The belief of that day has now ripened into knowledge.

We might bring forward a thousand proofs of the hollowness of the anti-slavery sentiment. A few will suffice. This same people of the North, while they proclaim the universal equality of man, in their animosity against the whites of the South, are moving heaven and earth to give the negroes the control of the local governments there; yet, at home, among themselves, they deny all social and political equality to the black, shut him out from all share of power, all lucrative and creditable pursuits. Again: All remember the immense success at the North, of Helper's 'Impending Crisis,' a book written to rouse the people there to tear down the barriers of the Constitution, in order to abolish negro slavery. Its object and sentiments procured it the public endorsement of a large portion of the Northern Senators and Representatives. The book was but a tissue of abuse of the South, except in its shallow and blundering attempt to prove to Southern men who had no slaves, that slavery was a debasing obstruction to them, while the slaveholders, not one-twentieth part of the whites in the South, alone, drew profit and power from it. Insidious as his reasoning was, few in the South were misled by it, and its utter falsehood is now known to all. But his aim is attained; the work is accomplished; the negro is free. And Helper now writes a second book to prove that the negro is an encumbrance and curse upon the land, and must be driven out, or exterminated. Are these the vagaries of a madman? No. They are the successive and well-timed strokes of a concocted policy. Now, as in 1860, Helper finds readers and approvers in crowds. His book is the manifesto of a party. He is a representative man.

For years the world has rung with clamorous anathemas against the enormities perpetrated by the slave-holders in the South. Listen to the Abolitionists, and negro slavery was the only shape evil assumed on earth. All the world was an Eden, and this the black and crawling viper which poisoned its innocence, polluted its zephyrs, and desolated its fruitful groves. They raked up every fact and falsehood that could illustrate their history of 'The Great Iniquity.' But they chose their facts like that unimaginative painter, who sketched each distorted limb and feature he got sight of, in order by combining them, to paint his monster.

We have no wish to deny that, in this, as in other cases, the possession of power led to instances of brutal tyranny. We might add thrilling incidents to 'Uncle Tom's Cabin,' perhaps more authentic than those found there, but liable to the same objection, that they represented the rare exceptions, and not the rule. Nor would we perpetuate the blunder of making the negro and mulatto the superior race. But we could quite as easily make up our fagot of social horrors in the free communities of London and New York.

There are two or three broad facts, which no man can deny, yet which give the 'lie direct' to the oft-repeated assertions as to the cruelty of the Southern master, and the misery of the slave.

The rapid multiplication of the negroes throughout the South, and their increased efficiency over native Africans, is, itself, sufficient proof that they were not in an unnatural or disadvantageous condition. Being chiefly occupied in rural labors, they were spreading over the country even more rapidly than the whites, fast as they grew in numbers. This slave population, so assiduously pictured, by the Yankee and English anti-slavery press, as bowed down and worn out by unceasing toil, and ruled with brutal severity, was, in general, well provided for, not over worked, and easily controlled by their masters, among whom oppression and harshness was the exception, and not the rule. It is a libel on human nature, contradicted by all experience, to assert that the exercise of power engenders the desire only to oppress, and not to benefit those under our control. In this case the result proved its falsehood. A natural, and therefore general, though not universal, union of selfish interests and kindly feelings led the master to take care that his negro should be fed, and not hungry, clothed and not naked, sheltered and not houseless; that he should seek comfort in a house, and not fly as from a prison; that he should be, not a beast goaded on under the yoke, but a laborer to be employed; not an enemy to be watched and feared even in his bonds, but a dependent who could be trusted. And that these objects were not only aimed at but attained, is proved by undeniable facts. The natural docility of the negro, a certain sluggishness of body and mind, a sense of inferiority lead him to look beyond himself and his own race for guidance and command, and render him the most easily governed and most incapable of ruling, of all people. All the intrigues and machinations of the Northern Abolitionists failed to throw the negroes into a rebellious or even discontented mood. Nothing can more conclusively prove this, and that the negroes were in a natural and comfortable condition, than the absence, not only before, but during the war, of insurrection or even insubordination; even when, in many parts of the country, the greater number of the few masters were absent on military service, leaving the women and children surrounded by, and to the protection of, large gangs of negroes, whose only change of conduct, as time passed on, was a gradual slackening of industry for the indulgence of the indolence so natural to them. Even in the midst of the war, at points not remote from the enemy, but daily reverberating with the sound of their cannon, many negroes were habitually entrusted with fire-arms, as plantation watchmen, or when sent in pursuit of game, and no ill consequence ensued.—In every part of the South it required the actual presence and exhortations of the enemy to induce them to throw off what had been constantly pictured as a grievous and galling yoke. What the negroes sought, when left to themselves, was not freedom, but exemption from that labor which is the lot of man. To the end of the war it was starvation and impressment, not voluntary enlistment that filled the ranks, constantly thinned by desertion, of the negro regiments raised by the United States Government in the South. It was only when goaded on by the counsels and exhortations of the Northern agitator that the negro, when freed, exhibited feelings of hostility against the Southern man, and generally least of all against his former master. These feelings were not found in their hearts, but had to be sown and cultivated there. There were of course, exceptional cases. Four millions of people can be no where found who do not include characters of every kind. But of the negroes as a class, the whites, as their former masters, had no cause to complain. The same nature makes him worthless as a hireling, which made him so useful as a slave. Of all races he alone accepts servitude as a decree of nature and not of necessity.—But spontaneous industry seems foreign to his constitution. When free, laziness is his master. He must be trained to systematic labor by authority, example, and some penalty on indolence, nearer at hand and more definite than the mere prospect of want.

STORM AND CALM.

BY HENRY TIMROD.

Sweet are these kisses of the South
As if they dropped from maiden's mouth;
And softer are these cloudless skies
Than many a tender maiden's eyes.

But, ah! beneath such influence
Thought is too often lost in sense;
And Action, faltering, as we thrill,
Sinks in the unnerved arms of Will!

Awake, thou Stormy North! and blast
The subtle spells around us cast;
Beat from our limbs these flowery chains
With the sharp scourges of thy rains!

Bring with thee from thy polar cave
All the wild sounds of wind and wave,
Of toppling berg and grinding floe,
And the dread avalanche of snow.

Wrap us in Arctic night and clouds,
Yell like a fiend amid the shrouds
Of some slow-sinking vessel, when
He hears the shrieks of drowning men.

Blend in thy mighty voice whate'er
Of danger, terror, and despair,
Thou hast encountered in thy sweep
Across the land and o'er the deep.

Pour in our ears all notes of woe
That, as these very moments flow,
Rise like a harsh, discordant psalm,
While we lie here in tropic calm.

Sting our weak hearts with bitter shame,
Bear us along with thee like flame;
And show that even to destroy
More godlike may be than to toy,
And rust or rot in idle joy!

THE STATE OF FRANKLIN.

At the return of the members from Tarborough, in July, of 1788, it was announced that the parent State had no intention of acceding to the views of those who favored the establishment of the Franklin Government. A fit opportunity soon after occurred of testing the supremacy of the old and new dynasty. We copy or condense from Haywood an account of it. A *fieri facias* had been placed in the hands of the sheriff of Washington county to be executed against the property of Sevier. The sheriff, acting under the authority of North Carolina, seized Sevier's negroes and removed them for safe keeping to the house of Col. Tipton. Sevier was, at this time, on the frontier providing for the defence of the inhabitants against the Indians. Hearing of the seizure of his negroes, by virtue of an illegal process, as he deemed it, and by an officer not legally constituted, he resolved to suppress all opposition to the new government. He raised a hundred and fifty men and marched directly to Tipton's house, near to which he arrived in the afternoon. Not more than fifteen men of Tipton's party were then with him. Sevier halted his troops two or three hundred yards from the house, on a sunken piece of ground, where they were covered from annoyance by those in the house. Tipton had gained some intimation af Sevier's approach and barricaded the house against the expected assault. The Governor presented himself and his troops, with a small piece of ordnance, took post in front of the house and demanded the unconditional surrender of Tipton and of all who were with him.—Tipton sent word to Sevier to "fire and be damned." Sevier then sent a written summons.—This, with a letter calling for assistance, Tipton sent immediately to Col. Maxwell, in Sullivan county. For some time Tipton would not permit any communication with Sevier. Early next morning, however, he consented that one of his men should correspond with Sevier. This correspondence resulted in nothing, only allowed time for Tipton's expected reïnforcements, which did arrive, and by their junction with the besieged, infused fresh vigor into their resolutions. Elholm, who was second in command to Sevier, in order to make short work, and to avoid the danger of delay, proposed the erection of a light movable battery, under cover of which the troops might safely advance to the walls of the house. In the mean time, those coming in and going out of the house, were fired upon and one man was killed and another wounded. Col. Maxwell, with one hundred and eighty men, had, at night, reached nearly to the camp of Sevier, and avoiding his sentinels, approached Tipton's house and awaited the dawn of day to raise the siege. As soon as objects had become visible, the snow falling, and Sevier's men advancing on the house, the troops under Maxwell fired a volley and raised a shout which seemed to reach the heavens, and communicated to the besieged that deliverance was at hand.—From the house they reëchoed the shout and immediately sallied out upon the besiegers. In the midst of these loud rejoicings a tremor seized the dismayed adherents of Sevier; and they fled in all directions, through every avenue that promised escape from the victors. Tipton and Maxwell did not follow them more than two hundred yards. Within one hour afterwards Sevier sent in a flag, proposing terms of accommodation. One man had been demortally wounded. Among the prisoners were two of Sevier's sons. Tipton forthwith determined to hang them both, but by solicitations of some of Tipton's party, with whom the young men were at good understanding, he desisted from his purpose

This is the account usually given of the affair between Sevier and Tipton. It is believed to be mainly correct. The declaration put into the mouth of Gov. Sevier, that he intended to suppress all opposition to Franklin by *force*, needs confirmation, or ought to be qualified. From the commencement of the difficulties between the parent State and her revolted counties, Sevier had determined to avoid, and did prevent, violence and bloodshed.—His moderation and his good temper, have been attested by the narrative of every pioneer this writer has had the opportunity to examine. The Governor in every instance dissuaded from violence, or even tumult. His own letters private and official, breathe the same spirit. In one of them he deprecated pathetically to Gov. Mathews, a resort to force, and speaks of the mother State with affection and regard—indeed in a tone of filial piety, which cannot be too much admired. His conduct during the siege of Tipton's house, and until he withdrew from it, demonstrates what is intended here to be said, that Gov. Sevier did not intend to maintain the authority of Franklin by force. It is known that in order to recover his property, then in the custody of Tipton's adherents, and confined in the house, the determined spirit of that brave man defied Sevier. Major Elholm advised an immediate assault, and offered to lead it. The Governor restrained the ardor of his Adjutant and declared, that not a gun should be fired. Elholm renewed his application for leave to storm the house, when he was silenced by the remark that he came not there to kill his countrymen, and that those who followed him had no such wish or design. Sevier himself, and most of his adherents, were too patriotic not to be dissatisfied with the position which surrounding circumstances had forced him to assume, and which he now most reluctantly occupied, at the head of the insurgents, and prompted to engage them in a fratricidal warfare. His sword had been often drawn for his country—his heart had never quailed before its enemies. Over these he had often triumphed; but now he refused to imbrue his hands in the blood of patriotic countrymen and friends. The patriot prevailed over the officer, the citizen over the soldier. The sternness of the commander yielded to the claims of duty, and of a common citizenship. His demeanor during the siege, and especially on the night before the assault, is represented by those of his party who served under him, before and after this occasion, to have been very different from that which he usually manifested. The men under his command exhibited the same altered behavior. In all their campaigns, ardor and enthusiasm attended the march—care and vigilance the bivouac,—the mirthful song and the merry jest were heard in every tent. On these occasions, it was the custom of Sevier to visit every mess and to participate in their hilarity. He spoke of enemies and dangers before, and of friends and home behind them. He was thus the companion and friend and idol of his soldiery. But now the camp of the Governor of Franklin was dreary and cheerless. No merry laugh was heard—nor song—nor jest. Little care and less vigilance was taken in placing out his sentinels.—Sevier was silent, appeared abstracted, thoughtful, and at this time only in his whole public life, morose and ascetic. Elholm's vivacity failed to arouse him. He communicated little to that officer, he said nothing to his men. He took no precaution, suggested no plans, either of attack or defence. The enemies of his country were not before him, and the patriot Governor repressed the aspirations of the "Commander-in-Chief of the army of the State of Franklin." In no other instance can be found a livelier exhibition of the true moral sublime of patriotism.

The example of Sevier was contagious. The energy and skill of Elholm effected nothing. Even he could not convert American citizens into fratricides.

A similar spirit actuated the adverse party. Their courageous leader acted only on the defensive. When the siege was raised no immediate pursuit was made. The besiegers and the besieged were soon after friends and peaceable neighbors. It is still strange, under all the circumstances, that so few of both parties were killed or wounded. This has sometimes been ascribed to, and accounted for, by the heavy snow storm which occurred during the siege, and especially at the assault.—One of the besieged, the late Dr. Taylor, may explain it in his own words: "We did not go there to fight. Neither party intended to do that. Many on both sides were unarmed, and some who had guns did not even load them.—Most of us went to prevent mischief, and did not intend to let the neighbors kill one another.—Our men shot into the air, and Sevier's men into the corners of the house. As to the storm of snow keeping the men from taking sure aim, it is all a mistake. Both sides had the best marksmen in the world, who had often killed a deer, and shot it in the head too, when a heavier snow was falling. The men did not try to kill any body. They could easily have done so if they had been enemies."

Of the same import is another authority. "Col. Pemberton ordered a general discharge of the rifles of his party. The discharge was made intentionally to avoid shooting any of Sevier's men."— Other testimony to the same effect might be given, all confirmatory of the position that is here taken, that both parties, leaders and adherents, were alike indisposed to shed blood.

The date of this affair was the 28th of February, 1788. Agreeably to the Constitution of Franklin, the duration of Sevier's office as Governor continued no longer than the 1st of March, and as the Assembly had failed to make a new appointment of a successor, as Sevier himself was ineligible, he was now without office and authority, and a mere private citizen. During the time he had administered the affairs of Franklin, little disturbance existed from the Indians on the frontier. The Cherokees had learned, by past experience, the danger of hostilities with the Franklin people, when commanded by an officer of such vigor and capacity, as in all his campaigns, had been manifested by Sevier. But during the short absence of such of the riflemen as had gone from the lower settlements to the camp of the Governor near Tipton's house, a Cherokee invasion occurred. Messengers were immediately dispatched from the frontier after Sevier, urging his immediate return.— These he received just after his fruitless siege of Tipton's house, and when the disasters of the day hung like a pall around him, and ulcerated his wounded spirit. In a moment Sevier was himself again; elastic, brave, energetic, daring and patriotic. At the head of a body of mounted riflemen, he was at once upon the frontier to guard and protect its most defenceless points and to chastise the enemy in their distant villages.

General Martin who now commanded the brigade of North Carolina militia west of the mountains, continued the policy of conciliation which had so long characterized both of the contending parties. He wrote to General Kennedy, late a Franklin brigadier, and an adherent of Sevier, begging "his friendly interposition to bring about a reconciliation. You well know this is the only way to bring about a separation, and also a reconciliation for our worthy friend (meaning Sevier) whose situation at this time, is very disagreeable. I most sensibly feel for him, and will go very great lengths to serve him. Pray see him often and give him all the comfort you can. Tell the people my object is reconciliation, not war."

There were few—perhaps none—even of the adherents of the old State, whose feelings and wishes, in reference to Sevier, were not in exact consonance with those expressed by General Martin in this letter. Its tone, its moderation, its wisdom, its sympathy for a soldier and a patriot, constitute the highest eulogy upon his own good sense, his patriotism and his kind feeling. They cannot be too much admired or too closely imitated. They saved the country from further tumult and violence, and all opposition, on the part of Franklin to North Carolina, ceased. Still there were not wanting in the West, extra loyal men—the simon pures of a later day—ultra-patriots, who represented to Governor Johnston (the successor of Governor Caswell) that the conduct and motives of Sevier were *treasonable*. Instructions were accordingly sent by Johnston, to Judge Campbell, to issue a warrant for his arrest and confinement in jail, as guilty of high treason. Sevier was now really a private citizen, without command or authority, and yet he was constantly at the head of troops—volunteers, who selected him as their commander, and who followed his standard and obeyed his orders, as fully and as cheerfully as if he were yet in power. The frontier people knew that they could not be safe, but by their own exertions and military services. They needed a leader to combine their strength, discipline the troops, project expeditions, secure their exposed stations, expel their Indian enemies, and give quiet and safety to a scattered and defenceless people. This responsible duty they imposed on Sevier. He could not decline the position thus assigned him by acclamation. He assumed it cheerfully and executed its duties well.

The order for the arrest of Sevier was not obeyed by Judge Campbell. The past relations of that officer with the Governor of Franklin, and his own agency in several transactions of that Government, made him unwilling, if he was not otherwise incapacitated, to execute that duty. But Spencer, another of the judges, issued the warrant against Sevier, for the crime of high treason.

Sevier, in the mean time, after his return from his Indian campaigns, appeared openly in all public places, and was present at Jonesboro when a council of military officers was held. During the day, some of the officers and Sevier had an altercation, which revived past difficulties between them and the ex-Governor. They had separated and left town.—Next morning Tipton and a few of his friends pursued and arrested Sevier a few miles in the country, and brought him back to Jonesboro. From here, under guard, he was sent for trial, across the mountains to Morganton where he was delivered to Wm. Morrison, the then Sheriff of Burke county. The guard with Sevier, had passed through the McDowell settlement, two of whom had experienced his hospitality when refugees on Nollichuckee, and had seen service with him at King's Mountain.—These became sureties for the appearance of Sevier at Morganton, and he was allowed a few days' absence. He returned punctually as he had promised, and was afterwards still further enlarged by the Sheriff. In a few days his two sons, and other friends from the west, came into town singly and were with the people generally, without suspicion. At night when the court broke up and the people dispersed, they, with the ex-Governor, pushed forward toward the mountains with the greatest rapidity, and before morning arrived at them, and were beyond the reach of pursuit.*

Morganton had been selected for the trial of the prisoner as being the most convenient and accessible court in the State, and beyond the limits of the late Franklin jurisdiction; the authorities wisely concluding that at home Sevier could not be successfully prosecuted. The change of venue, however, operated nothing in favor of the prosecution. Burke had been a strong whig county, and no where were whig principles, whig sacrifices, and whig efforts held in higher esteem or more properly appreciated. The McDowells, McGinsies, Alexanders, and all the whigs of that neighborhood had witnessed, and still gratefully recollected, the timely succor and substantial aid rendered to them and their cause, in the hour of trial, by Sevier and his countrymen. He was now a prisoner in their midst, charged with the highest offence known to the laws; they knew him to be a patriot, in exile and distress; they felt for his sufferings, and sympathized in his fallen fortunes. These noble patriots of North Carolina, while sensible that the majesty of law had been offended, were yet unwilling that its penalty should be enforced, or that Sevier should be made its victim. They stood around the court yard in approving silence, witnessed and connived at the rescue, and discountenanced pursuit.

* An account of the arrest and romantic rescue of Sevier is given in Ramsey's Tennessee, page 425-429.

The capture and brief expatriation of Sevier served only to awaken, in his behalf, the higher appreciation of his services and a deeper conviction of his claims to the esteem and consideration of his countrymen. His return was every where greeted with enthusiasm and joy.

The Assembly of North Carolina again extended the Act of pardon and oblivion to such of the Franklin revolters as chose to avail themselves of its provisions. But it was at the same time distinctly provided "that the benefit of this Act shall not entitle John Sevier to the enjoyment of any office of profit, of honor, or trust in the State of North Carolina, but that he be expressly debarred therefrom."

An enactment of this kind may have been due to the supremacy of law. It was in exact conflict, however, with the wishes and voice and decision of the people. Pubiic sentiment, even in high places, demanded its immediate repeal. Technically, Sevier was an insurgent. In all respects, however, he was a lover of his country, and had entitled himself to its highest honors, and its richest rewards. His countrymen could not spare him from their military service; they would not refuse him employment in their civil affairs. At the August election of the next year, after the legislative infliction of these disabilities, the people of Greene county called upon Sevier to represent them in the Senate of North Carolina. He was elected, it need not be added, without difficulty. At the appointed time,

November 2, 1789, he attended, at Fayetteville, but waited a few days before he took his seat. During this interval, the Assembly repealed the clause of the Act excluding him from holding office. Sevier then took his seat after the usual oath of allegiance to North Carolina was administered. Some days after, General Davie introduced a resolution, to enquire into the conduct of the Senator from Greene. It was well known that the proposition would not be favorably received, and to the great satisfaction of the mover the motion for enquiry was laid on the table.

But the work of entire conciliation was not yet completed, on the part of North Carolina, and by the appointment of the Assembly, Sevier was rëinstated in the command he had held before the Franklin Revolt, of Brigadier General for all the western counties, and laws were passed confirmatory of administrations, granted by the Franklin courts, and legalizing marriages, celebrated under the authority of that government. The magnanimity of the Assembly went further in providing for the wants, and promoting the interests of the western people. They laid off a new Congressional District, embracing all her territory west of the Alleghanies, now constituting the great State of Tennessee. From this District thus provided for his laudable ambition, his invaluable services, and his great abilities, John Sevier was elected, and he is thus probably the first member of Congress from the great valley of the Mississippi. "Wednesday, June 16th, 1790, John Sevier, another member from North Carolina, appeared and took his seat."*

VINDICATION OF FRANKLIN.

This may be considered as the finale of Franklin. In speaking of it, in the preceding pages, terms have been used requiring qualification, which, without interrupting the current narrative, could not be elsewhere given.—Insurrection, revolt, dismemberment, defection, as here used, need to be explained, when applied either to those of the Western people, who separated from the parent State, or those of them who afterwards renounced the new government. In either case, the action of the parties need not be ascribed to fickleness of purpose or bad faith, much less to disloyalty to their proper rulers, or insubordination to regular government and law. In vindication of those who once appeared on the side of Franklin and now appeared on the side of North Carolina, it has been well remarked by Haywood "that the face of affairs was quite different at the time of the Convention which resolved on Independence, and in the Autumn of 1786. Before this juncture there was no governmental head, to which the people of the Western counties could carry their complaints. In 1784, it is true, the assembly which passed the Cession Act, retained the sovereignty and jurisdiction of North Carolina in and over the ceded territory,

* Annals of Congress. Vol. 2, page 1,640.

and all the inhabitants thereof, until the United States, in Congress, should have accepted the Cession. Yet, in reality, so long as the Cession Act continued unrepealed, North Carolina felt herself as much estranged from the inhabitants of the Western counties, as she was from any other State or territory in the Union, until induced by the bonds of Federalism and a common interest, so far as concerned their external relations with the other nations of the globe, but wholly unconnected, so far as regarded their internal regulations and engagements. And as any one State was not obliged, by the nature of the Federal duties, to advance monies, for the maintenance of another in the possession of her rights, but through the intervention of all in Congress assembled; so neither did North Carolina conceive herself bound to exert her strength and resources for the defence of the Western counties, unless in the proportion for which she was liable to other Federal contributions. It was in vain, then, to solicit her interference in behalf of the Western counties, so long as the Cession Act subsisted, but when that was repealed, and the precipitancy of the Western people obliterated, it cannot be a matter of surprise, that well meaning and intelligent people should, thenceforward, deem it their duty to return to their dependence on North Carolina.

In behalf of those who sustained their separation from North Carolina until 1788, it may be further added, that in withdrawing from the parent State, and establishing a separate government, the secessionists believed that the course adopted by them, would, at *least imperfectly preserve quiet and order*, under the circumstances in which the Cession act had placed them. Their course was pacific and conservative, and at first, united and harmonized all. Nothing destructive or revolutionary, much less belligerent, was intended or contemplated. In 1784, the Confederation had demonstrated the inadequacy of that organization, as a permanent system of General Government. The transfer, by North Carolina, of her western counties to Congress, at that time imbecile and powerless, even over the original Confederated States, and the novelty of the experiment, had produced alarm, excited apprehension, and aroused a deep discontent in the new settlements. And, perhaps, these could have been quieted and appeased as effectually, in no other way, as the temporary assumption and exercise of the power of separate and distinct self-government.

Again. Heretofore, no instance had presented itself of the formation of an independent State from the territory embraced within the boundaries of a political sovereignty. The process of separation, and the mode of accomplishing it, were all new and unattempted, alike by the people and the State and General Goverments. Now, when the creation of these new political organizations has become matter of frequent occurrence, and plain and easy by its successful trial and repetition, little or no cause can be seen why the subject should then have been viewed as embarrassed with inherent difficulties. But let it be remembered that "in the Articles of Confederation, no provision was made for the creation or admission of New *States*. Canada was to be admitted of right, on her joining in the measures of the United States, and the other *colonies*, at the discretion of nine States. The eventual establishment of new States, seems to have been entirely overlooked by the compilers of that instrument."* The inconvenience of this omission, in the Articles of Confederation, was most apparent, and it may be well questioned whether the Congress of the Confederacy, could, without an assumption of power, have given to the people of the territory, ceded in 1784, a form of State government, such as was guaranteed to them by the provisions of the constitution of North Carolina.

Under this view of the subject, it is not strange that the Cession Act was followed by dissatisfaction and revolt in the Western counties. Their people had been represented in the State Convention of 1776, and it had been probably at the instance of their own delegates in that body, that the provision was then made for "the establishment of one or more governments westward of this State, by consent of the legislature." Indeed, it may be well questioned, whether with this provision of the Bill of Rights, preceding the Constitution itself, the Act of Cession was not unauthorized and invalid.

Be that as it may, the Cession of her Western territory by North Carolina to Congress, as it was, under the Articles of Confederation in 1784, was obviously inexpedient and impolitic. And it was not till the adoption of the Federal Constitution in 1788, that this measure became either wise or practicable. This did not escape the discernment of the malcontent but virtuous and patriotic people of Franklin when the new State ceased to be and they returned to their allegiance to the mother State. This event was not unexpected by its most steadfast friends and supporters, nor were its effects to be deplored. It resulted from no legislative error or want of executive skill, no fickleness of popular sentiment, no defect of public virtue.

Every review of the conduct of both parties in the disaffected counties, from 1784 to 1788, reflects honor upon their patriotism, their moderation, their love of order and their virtue. No other instance is recollected in which two antagonistic governments, existed so long over the same people with so little anarchy, so little misrule, so little violence. A period of nearly four years was passed under two political systems of government, each having its separate Executive, State Council, Legislature and Judiciary, each its own county and military organizations, its own partizans and adherents. And amidst all the rivalry and conflict, personal and official, which must have arisen from this unexampled

* Mr. Madison in the Federalist.

condition of things, the annalist of these early times, has recorded but two deaths, almost no bloodshed, and little violation of property. Private rights were held sacred and inviolable. If, in the collisions between the officers of the two governments, an occasional feat of pugilism did occur, resulting in a trifling mutilation of one or both of the combatants, there followed less of acrimony, unmanly revenge and pitiful spite, than is produced by the disreputable squabbles of the aspirants and functionaries of the present day — members of the same government, and united under the same constitution and laws. In all that was done in Franklin, it is impossible to detect any tendency to radicalism. In their warmest aspirations for self-government and independence, there cannot be found one feature of modern agrarianism or the prostration of all law, but only a disposition to protect themselves from violence and aggression, and possible danger to their rights. This is no partial judgment. It is sustained by the testimony of competent tribunals, east and west of the Alleghanies. Their decisions may be briefly stated.

The formation of a new State was only a question as to *time*. In all the letters, manifestoes, and proclamations of the Governor of the parent State, the *separation* is spoken of as not only right in itself, but desirable, and, at the proper time, expedient. So general was the sentiment, even in North Carolina, in favor of the separation, and so little inclination was there to prevent it by legislative interference, that the General Assembly, though convened by the proclamation of the Governor and Council, "failed to meet." Such was the decision of the people and authorities of North Carolina, east of the mountains, on the abstract question of a new State, west of it. The same opinion was entertained by Dr. Franklin—by three of the Governors of Georgia, and by other statesmen.

As to the *time* and *mode* of a measure of such magnitude, there could not be expected to be entire unanimity—there never is—there never will be. Those adopted in 1784, at first, as has been seen, gave very general satisfaction, and harmonized the community most directly interested, as being the best time and manner of providing the least objectionable measures to quiet the discontented and aggravated citizens of the ceded territory. Was the Revolt of 1784 justifiable—was it wise—was it patriotic—did it prevent greater evils—would a different policy have secured greater good, or produced better results? may be questions of difficult solution. However these may be answered, the verdict of the contemporaries of the Revolters has ever been in their favor, vindicating their patriotism and asserting the integrity of their motives. Those most active and determined and steadfast in the revolt, were, and never ceased to be, the greatest favorites of their countrymen everywhere. General public sentiment is seldom wrong, it never condemns the innocent—it rarely vindicates the guilty. While it scorns the wilful offender, it excuses or palliates unintentional error. It always sustains good intentions and wise purposes, and rewards the faithful public servant. This was emphatically true of the Franklin leaders. We have already mentioned the election of Sevier to Congress. So soon as the western counties became the "Territory of the United States, south of the Ohio," Sevier and his Captains became prominent among its officers. The Territory becomes the State of Tennessee, and the Ex-Governor of Franklin is at once called upon to become its Chief Magistrate, in which office the partiality of his countrymen continned him for twelve years, when being no longer eligible, he is transferred again to Congress—is appointed to a distant service by President Madison, and while absent on that duty, by the continued confidence of his constituents, is elected again to Congress, without opposition, and without his knowledge or consent.

The associates of Gov. Sevier, in the Franklin Government, also received through life similar attestations of public regard and confidence. During the Territorial Government, and that of the State of Tennessee, they filled the highest offices, implying ability, probity, efficiency and zeal in the public service and high personal character. Pioneers of the State of Tennessee in all the varied phases of political organization, through which her people passed, these evidences of trustworthiness, capacity, and patriotism were never withheld from them. They not only held offices of honor and trust, but discharged their duties to the entire satisfaction of the people and of the authorities of government.—Revolters in 1784, they were nevertheless, the purest patriots and the best men of their day. It is singular and well worthy of remark, that not one of the master spirits of Franklin—perhaps not one of its officers, in a long life of usefulness and distinction afterward, ever forfeited the esteem or lost the confidence of his countrymen. A beautiful comment upon the purity of their principles and the loftiness of their love of country—a fit tribute of respect for their public services and their private virtue.

The subject is by no means exhansted. But this is not the place for extended comments; and still the occasion is neither inopportune, nor inappropriate, for a few closing remarks.

The time at which the occurrenees, which have been narrated, took place, was emminently auspicious for their pacific termination. The two communities chiefly concerned in the Revolt of 1784, were then in their infancy, as self governing Associations. *The consent of the governed* was then admitted to be the very genius of Republicanism—the essence of free government. As with individuals, so also with political organizations, *youth* is the period of greatest innocence, purity and virtue. Age, in the latter especially, produces rivalries, corruption, venality, selfishness, faction, ambition, discontent and crime. In those days of primitive simplicity, the great Christian rule of doing to others as we wish others to do to us, formed a prevalent public sentiment, which had all the validity and force of law—affecting alike the rich and the poor, the enlightened and the ignorant. To do justice and right was the law, to violate them was the exception, in the pure days of these infant Republics. Had the rulers of that early period—unlike Martin and Caswell—assumed the language of menace and the tone of authority and dictation, and issued their Pronunciamentos of defiance and revenge against the best men and patriots of any time and place; had they usurped a power unknown to the Constitution and laws of the land; had they fulminated their bitter anathemas—full of reproach and censure, and defamation and falsehood, denouncing them as outlaws and traitors "against the best government the world ever saw;" had they levied troops to enforce obedience at the point of the bayonet; had they marched them to the distant theatre of the Revolt and involved their remote countrymen in all the nameless atrocities of invasion, banishment, confiscation and disfranchisement; had they imposed penalties, forfeitures, and unusual oaths, upon a brave and patriotic people; had the rulers done all this, could the benign work of the Reconstruction of 1788 have been consummated?

Or had a low demagogue, or an upstart politician, from one of the revolted counties, ingloriously deserting his former sentiments, and discarding his faithful constituents, and allying himself with the enemies of his section, denounced in his seat in Fayetteville, the men who had confided to him their interests and had given him his present elevation; had he denounced these as Rebels, and incited against them all the horrors of civil war; had he stood in his place and prated with Sophomoric wisdom and self-complacency, the weak sophistries and puerile truisms and the sublime virtues of the Coërcive policy which he advocated; or had a weak and wicked colleague in the Lower House, joined him in the strange and unnatural opposition to the benignant policy of compromise and negotiation through a Peace Conference and thus urged an incantious and brave constituency into an internecine war—a war of tyranny, spoliation, oppression, subjugation; had all this been done, could the difficulties between North Carolina and Franklin have ever been pacifically settled? Could the old State find a general so lost to all the pleasant charities of life, so unmindful of the high and noble sentiments of the soldier and the gentleman, as to consent to become the instrument of the low revenges of his government against noncombatants, or of outrage and insult to unprotected woman? Such an officer could not have been found in North Carolina—thus to disgrace his epaulets and degrade the honorable profession of arms.—On the contrary, General Rutherford himself introduced in the Legislature of the State he had so efficiently served in war, the first

Act for reconstruction and peace. The entire people of the State heartily sympathized in the same sentiment. The Legislature, when called by the governor to take into consideration the State of public affairs "failed to meet". The statesman-patriot, Governor Caswell, even dissuaded from coërcion and advised to "let things remain as they were."

Such was the course pursued by North Carolina in quieting the rebellion. How was it in the disaffected counties amongst the Revolters themselves? The same moderation and forbearance characterized their conduct. No lawlessness, no radicalism, no disfranchisement, little violence or tumult—no burglary—no incendiarism, no invasion of private rights. The principal rebel, Gov. Sevier, consented to negotiate. Compromise quieted the insurgents, and laid the foundation of a permanent pacification and reconstruction. Both parties were sincere. It was easy to be so. Each was just, and intended to do justice to its rival. The pacification was perfect and complete. No lingering animosities were left to ulcerate the proud spirit of the respective partizans of the Old North State. There were no unmanly triumphs—there were no bitter reproaches. It is still difficult even now to decide which was successful—or which the vanquished party. Each succeeded. North Carolina attained her primary object—the integrity of her government. Franklin was not put down by force, and Sevier himself, at Philadelphia, officially witnessed the cession of the late revolted country, to the Federal Congress—its separation and its subsequent independence of North Carolina. The cradle of the infant Hercules he had watched over and protected. It soon after, under the same gallant chieftain, became the *giant Tennessee.* Each countryman of his, has already erected in his heart, a cenotaph to his memory. It is still a problem, which, most to admire, the magnanimity, forbearance, moderation and wisdom of the parent State, or the manly self-reliance, enlarged patriotism, and filial piety of her daughter in the wilderness. In each of these communities their Solons and Aristides, were their leaders, and their rulers. Their *Work*, is the highest eulogy upon the skill and virtue of the Reconstructionists of 1788.

Happily, as in the material creation, so, also, in political economy, the conservative is stronger than the destructive principle.

In the vegetable kingdom we see a branch of a tree rudely torn from its trunk. The spontaneous action of nature, unaided by man, reproduces the limb. The beauty and gracefulness of the tree is preserved and no mutilation—scarcely a scar is left. A man is wounded, his surgeon pronounces the case incurable unless he amputates or applies the actual cautery. Another surgeon, less incautious, perhaps more timid, dissuades from the more heroic treatment, makes use of cooling and emolient remedies—the wound heals by the first intention—the vis conservative nature has restored the patient. So in the body politic there are medicable wounds, often rendered incurable and deadly by the charlatanism of political empyrics and noisy demagogues. As in the one case the *nimia diligentia medicorum* destroyed the patient, so the officious zeal of the unfledged politician in the other, often inflicts an immedicable wound upon his country. It prescribes amputation, caustics, irritants, and escharotics. The country is ruined and her liberty destroyed. The refrigerant and soothing policy would have saved both.

On this subject ancient Profane History has taught a lesson which this Christian Republic should study well. "When Latium, a Roman Province, revolted, and the revolt was suppressed, the question arose in the Roman Senate, what shall be done with Latium and the people of Latium? There were some who cried, disfranchise. Then others said, confiscate their property. There were none who said, subject them in vassalage to their slaves. But old Camillus, in that speech which revealed his true greatness, and made his name immortal, said, 'Senators! make them your fellow-citizens, and thus add to the power and glory of Rome.'"

(CONCLUDED.)

THE SOLDIER SON.

BY L. CARY WILDEN.

An old man sat on his door step low,
Watching the shadows come and go,
The shadows that were creeping fast,
Over the roof on the trailing grass;
And his heart grew sad with its own refrain,
When he asked of it with inward pain,
"Will my soldier son come back again?

"He went away in the prime of life,
In the vigor of youth he went to the strife;
Will my child the dreadful missiles spare?
They'll pity sure my silvery hair;—
Will I hear him whistle in the glen?
Will I see him o'er the ripe sheaves bend?
His face behold but once again?"

His good dame sat with her knitting by,
Watching the needles glance and fly;
She tried to talk of happier days,
And thus her husband's hopes to raise·
But anon the tears come in her eyes,
And the restless needles idle lie,
For tho' she asks, there's no reply.

She sees the tasseled ranks of corn,
Without a martial drum or horn;
Before her is the unreaped field,
With its bending wealth of golden yield;
And the meadow, though in verdant dress,
Seems to feel a loneliness,
As if it too bore some distress.

Soon the news comes from afar—
News comes from the dreadful war.
A desperate battle had been fought;
A victory gained—by much blood bought.
One side had failed—the other won;
And the dead, alas! there was many a one,
And 'mongst them was the old man's son.

He hears the tale—but, lo, no tears
Come to those eyes, so dimmed with years.
The neighbors shake their heads and say,
"I thought he'd take it in a different way,"
Then leave him in his grief alone,
And pass out sadly one by one,—
He heedeth not that they are gone.

They come again—still in his chair
The old man sits as unaware;
They take his hand, but drop their hold,
For stiff the fingers are and cold;
His arms hang by his side like lead,
And motionless his snowy head,
With pulseless brow—the old man's dead.

The good dame looks from the window sill,
On the lonely meadow lonelier still,

For unreaped grain still waves in the breeze,
The birds still sing in the apple trees,
But she heaves a sigh of secret pain,
And the tears that she cares not to restrain
Fall down her withered cheeks like rain.

MARY ASHBURTON.*

A TALE OF MARYLAND LIFE.

CHAPTER IX.

THUS passed the summer. The lonely, unloved bride was devoted entirely to his service; to anticipate what I supposed might be his wishes; to consult his former tastes, to minister to his comfort in every way that I could; to win him back to life by all the humble means in my power; was my hourly study. It seemed to produce no effect,—I do not think he even noticed my efforts, for I made them so unobtrusive that he, restless and wretched as he was, could not have known who was instrumental in this, without inquiry. He spent whole days away from home, wandering, I know not whither, and making me doubly anxious about him in the terrible possibilities my uneasiness suggested; that he would be brought home a corpse or perish for want of food, in some unfrequented woods

He was always restless, his foot seemed never to weary of that constant motion. When at home, I could hear his steady tramp, tramp up and down his room, ceasing for a few moments sometimes when his weary frame would sink upon a chair, to be resumed almost immediately when an agonizing reflection would cause him to start up and continue his restless movements.

When I knew him to be out, I would venture in his room, arrange a thousand little things that needed repairing, restore the ornaments to their pristine glory; wipe the dust from the books and papers, carefully cleanse the statuettes, sometimes timidly open his drawers and search among their contents for rents and missing buttons, very tremblingly, and in mortal dread of his sudden return, to find me among his secret treasures. When I grew bolder, I ventured upon various little improvements;—once a new dressing gown that my own hands had made, and placed it in his room, on his easy chair; then breathless with fright when he returned, lest he should notice it and wonder at the liberty I had taken; keeping out of his way from the dread of meeting his eye

* Continued from page 185.

after my unprecedented boldness and longing, when I saw him coming, for time to rush up and seize it away before he could enter and see it there. I put it there several times before I had the courage to let it stay. I need not have troubled myself as to his discovery of my agency in it, for when I went up in his room afterwards, I found it thrown in a corner with some other things that had stood in his way as he walked to and fro across the floor. I picked it up with a sigh and just fixed it all over again.

Then I embroidered him a new pair of slippers, seeing that his old ones were beginning to wear, and placed them conspicuously where he might see them. They were not even touched, remaining there day after day, unnoticed and unused. Disheartening as this was, I persevered; it was the post I had assumed voluntarily, and as its fulfillment depended upon my own efforts, unaided but by Providence, I bowed beneath the burden and worked again, rejoicing that it was at least my privilege to work for him I loved, woman's highest honor and crowning glory.

But father did not approve of this condition of affairs. He regarded the neglect of his daughter with resentment, and the neglect of his monetary affairs, also, a sort of breach of honor, being incapable,—poor father,—of considering a mental trouble greater than the emptiness of purse.

One evening he came through the fields wandering hither and thither, with an air of dissatisfaction, which was further expressed upon his arrival at the house, where he scarcely returned my warm salutation with more than a frown of displeasure.

"I don't like the way things is conducted, Mary," he said as he came in, "this is not what I intended doing with my money, to throw it away in this style. Why, it'll go to the dogs at this rate.—No improvements; nothing doing but the little you can do 'round the house; all goin' to waste; my money gone, my security given for the rest. It'll ruin me as well as him. I can't stand it no longer. I must speak to him."

Father, don't." I had listened to this resolution in speechless horror.

"Don't?" my father broke forth, "What do you mean, you fool? Do you think that I'm goose enough to be goin to stand this? Never in the world. I can't see my hard earnings, that I got by the sweat of my brow, befoodled off in this style. We shall all go to the dogs together in no time. Where is he? I must and will speak to him about it, or him and me will have to part. Where is he? I'm a goin to him; you need'nt try to bamboozle me any longer. Don't say a word. I stay here till he comes in if he isn't. If he is, I go to him at once and have it out."

"Father!" To my terror I heard Alfred in his room. He turned to me then. I had fallen in a chair and was wringing my hands in an agony of supplication. "Oh! oh! oh! what *shall* I do?"

"What's the matter?" he answered crossly, compelled to pity in spite of himself.

"Just hear me for one moment. You will kill me if you persist in this."

"People are not so easily killed," he muttered.

But just stop one moment, father. I love Mr. Chauncey,"—the acknowledgement which had never been made aloud before, was wrung from me at last by circumstances—"better than anything in the world."

He eyed me with an expression indicative of so little abatement of his resentment, that I was compelled to throw off my reserve once more.

"If I had not loved him, I should never have married him"

"Queer," he muttered, "to love a chap that takes no more notice of you than an old shoe, better than us who have sheltered and cared for you all your days."

"Dear father, I cannot help it. I love you and mother, but then it's so different. I married Mr. Chauncey for love, nothing else. You know he loved another lady; he can't help that. I want to win him from it, and am trying by all in my power. If you talk to him this way, you'll drive him from me forever, and only seal my misery, indeed you will. Oh! please let him alone now. Let's see together what can be done. Mr. Chauncey says I can do what I please. Then let us, you and I, manage together. You direct me, and I'll show the servants what to do."

"What are you going to do with *him* then," father asked contemptuously, "put him in a 'sylum for mad people, for I think *he's* mad if no one ever was."

"He does not care now, father. Please don't speak of him, or say anything about him. Let's carry out our plans and we'll get along, never fear, dear father, won't you? Your money shan't be thrown away, I promise you."

He eyed me again, then softened the hard lines about his face a little. "Well, well, we'll see about it, but I've no notion, let me tell you, of losing my money."

"We won't lose it, father, can't you cultivate some of the fields with your own?"

"If Chauncey don't object, I'll see ——"

He will *not* object."

"Then perhaps I can manage it, upon a stress. I have much to do already."

"Indeed you have, dear father."

"And I don't feel as much like work now as in my younger days."

"Yes, but you'll have so many more servants."

"True, though they make the work too. But I'll undertake it for the present. I'll do it for your sake anyhow."

I threw my arms around his neck and kissed him, which unusual demonstration affected him more than he wished me to see, putting me from him with a—

"Well, that'll do, child. I promise to do what I can."

And he did. With our combined management the Grove blossomed soon almost as of yore. I journeyed busily around the farm, renewing the fences, having caps put on the posts where the cattle could remove the rails and jump in the fields, seeing that breaches in the out-houses were nailed up, while father overlooked the agricultural department and saw that the servants did their work properly. The wheat had not been attended to, so there was little to expect from harvest, but for next fall we discussed our arrangements in a most business like manner. I waged destructive war with the enemies of the poultry yard, when the servants informed me that much of the young brood had disappeared mysteriously, though the elders of the flock paraded about the premises with their wonted dignity. Proper attention paid to the condition of their houses and yard, soon remedied that, and—shall I confess it?—before the summer was over, a trusty messenger seated in a wagon well loaded with baskets of protesting feathered creatures, conveyed them to market, whence he returned with a goodly result, which I received with a pleasure that the lovers of romance and sentiment would have scoffed at. But it was so much towards redeeming my loved one's patrimony, and was carefully laid aside till the addition of similar sums should make it something of importance.

Then there was the dairy—my only source of pleasure. This was not like that at home, being larger and had once been most elegantly arranged; but from careless usage since Mrs. Chauncey's death, was now much out of repair. The well sweep behind it was broken, and the stone trough through which the water had been wont to flow around its semi-circular floor, had been removed for some purpose—I believe to water the horses—while the poultry roosted immediately around it to the destruction of all cleanliness.

In a short time the sweep was mended, the trough replaced by a temporary wooden one, the fowls driven away and new lattice-work erected by which they were securely kept at a distance, while the richest, most golden of butter was turned out from it in such quantities that the proceeds were soon laid beside that from the poultry yard.

How eagerly I hoped for the time when I could show a sum of such importance that it might go far towards disburdening the estate, and freeing it from the claims of importunate creditors.

Letters came from old Mr. Chauncey to father and myself—I never saw his to Alfred, of course—bidding us let a portion of the land go towards satisfying the claims upon the estate. The farm consisted of twelve hundred acres, one-third of which had been purchased in my name, so that four hundred were in reality all we owned. It grieved me to see any portion of what had belonged to them for generations, the land that their titled ancestors had bought when they first came and settled in this country, go into the hands of strangers; yet I knew that, work as I might, it would take years, a lifetime to reclaim it all, so it had better go. It cannot bring happiness, the possession of all the land on the earth, I sighed; so it was done as Mr. Chauncey had bidden, Alfred merely saying when he was referred to, "Let it be as my father desires. It is all alike to me." It took a load from my shoulders, for I could more easily manage now that the size of the farm was so much reduced.

Outwardly, affairs looked more prosperous than when I went there; the grounds around the house neat and orderly, the house itself freshened and renewed, no longer with shutters slamming on broken hinges, the wind and rain beating through shivered panes. But though I worked on, my hands were often numbed, a faintness stole over me, while a quick pain shot through my aching heart, as the conviction would flash upon me with sudden force that I was as far as ever from my goal, that these efforts brought me no nearer to him, I was as unloved, as unheeded as ever. Indeed I saw less of him; for the native kindness that had not entirely deserted him upon my first arrival, had led him to attempt the courteousness he would show to a stranger; but after a while I seldom met him even at meal time, inclining his head gravely when we met, but seldom speaking.

Oh! how I longed for a word of some kind from him; even anger would have been preferable to this steady indifference. With it all too he was so exceedingly handsome, even thin and worn as he now was. I toiled for him when absent and trembled nervously when he was present, the poor, shy country girl that he must look upon with scorn, still loving him passionately, yet extremely in awe of him.

Mr. Chauncey wrote to me several times such kind, fatherly letters, full of anxious inquiries about his son, and with delicate hesitancy entreated me to care for him, now that there was no one else.

Useless admonition! I smiled bitterly over the letter, thinking of my work—its forlorn results. He that I was to care for seldom ever looked at me. But—I silenced my heart's pleadings—what could you expect? You have what you humbly prayed for. Be content and forget thy poor self. What is there in you to replace what he has lost? Do thy task patiently still unto the last. He needs thee without knowing it, and some time may thank thee at least.

I had no visitors. Once or twice an old acquaintance ventured to see me, but though I treated them kindly, they did not seem to find the atmosphere of the Grove congenial and did not come again. Of all the Chauncey friends, but one benevolent lady, who lived nine miles from us, called to see me during that first summer. I was glad that even curiosity did not subject me to an intrusion I should have been obliged to sustain alone, our affairs a prey to vulgar remark, his absence noted and inquired into.—My own old acquaintances I had kept at a distance—not from pride, but to save myself so much annoyance from their questions; while the few in the country that the Chaunceys had visited hardly regarded it as worth their while to call there, now that such gloom prevailed at the old place, the owner ruined, and his promising heir united to a common country girl. So my days were spent busily and quietly, my evenings in a resort to the extensive library that formed my great recreation when the work of the day was over. There I had my choice of all I desired in literature, and a great intellectual feast it was, enriching my mind at a time when my heart was starving for affection.

So passed the summer; the autumu came on, when one day it happened—oh! I shall never forget the bitter humiliation of that day!—that a party of fox-hunting gentlemen, who had been in the habit of dining at the Grove once a year, to be joined afterwards by the proprietor and his guests, came down from a neighboring county, and, as usual, directed their course to their old hospitable place of entertainment.

I heard the shrill whistle of the bugle, the trampling of the many horses' feet, and looking from an upper window, near which I stood at the time, saw a company of twenty gentlemen with dogs herding around them, advancing up the avenue.

I called Melissa to know whence they came. She told me that it was an established habit of her old master's friends.

"They is perfect gentlemen," she said, "and mistress always entertained 'em herself."

I wondered in my heart what Alfred, who fled the face of man, would do at this juncture. He was in his room, had returned pale and exhausted the evening before, and I had seen him but for a moment.

"Will he meet them, do you think?" I asked of the old woman.

"I dunno how he can get out of it, madam, they're here, and see him too, ketched him down there arter all."

They had made much noise before the door, as no sign of a master appeared about the premises. They asked the servant, who went to the door, if the gentlemen were at home. He answered that his old master was away, and that his young master—here he muttered something confusedly.

"Stand aside, Tom," called out an authoritative voice, and as the startled servant turned around, Alfred stood there to welcome, with his cold, calm dignity, his father's friends.

The clanging of the horses' feet ceased, and the trampling of the dogs, as their bark echoed from the distant stable yard, indicated that they were disposed of as usual.

There were many voices below stairs, and mindful of my duties, I descended by a private stairway to the kitchen to make preparation for a suitable entertainment, determining to be equal in this respect at least to their former hostess.

"Mars Alfred says, madam, would you like to come in the parlor?" asked Tom, appearing at the door of the pantry when I was surrounded with various dishes, the contents of which I was arranging for the cook. Appear before those strangers in my nominal character of the young wife and mistress? How could I? and yet how could I do otherwise than appear? how account to them for my absence? Then Alfred had not forgotten me. I understood his message to mean, the lady of the house should appear before the guests that his mother had been wont to entertain so elegantly.

"But she had ladies with her," I said, doubtfully.

"No, madam, not always," replied Melissa, who was helping me. "Since they were first rate gentlemen, she did not care for that, and always sat at the head of the table."

How bitterly I felt my anomalous position, which I feared would be only too obvious to them, that the eyes of strangers could not fail to notice the difference between me and a loved and honored wife. To my shame it would be plain to perceive, that neither of us was happy, that there was no affection for me upon his side, and, without any previous knowledge of the circumstances, would draw their own inferences very derogatory to one or both of us. I wondered at his message, situated as we were, with respect to one another, that he would think of my appearance, neglected as I had been, before strangers. But he did not know, he meant it differently, his feeling was not like mine, and most probably he intended to show me that—that he was but treating me as he would any other lady. He so little regarded me as connected with him in any way, that he failed to perceive others would not think thus; then he did not know me, having the poorest opinion of me, I knew, for accepting such an offer as was made when I permitted myself to be led to the altar.

I had to go over a retrospect of the past to nerve me up to the effort, before I could venture upon exposure by going down, feeling it as keenly as I did.

When the dinner bell sounded, I timidly took my post and stood at the head of the table, awaiting their entrance. It sounded like a vast throng as they came in, Alfred preceding them to perform the necessary introduction.

"Mrs. Chauncey," he said briefly and coolly, while I was too much embarrassed to be startled at his first recognition of my right to that appellation; bowing my drooping head, as Melissa told me one of the gentlemen said, like a lily on a stalk, and blushing as I felt I did, to welcome my—my husband's friends. They bowed in return, and I had to run the gauntlet of many pairs of eyes as they took their places. Several of the older gentlemen came up and courteously took my hand.

"Most fortunate has the son of my old friend been," said one, an elderly gentleman of the "old school." "Alfred, I congratulate you."

"And I, and I also," exclaimed two or three others.

The blood that stained my face now was painful in its heat. I glanced at Alfred. To their congratulations he uttered not one word; he could not dissemble, nor would he stoop to such hypocrisy, and with an air of uneasiness he attempted to draw their thoughts in another channel. Persistently they rallied, as they thought, the bashful young husband, and were unmerciful in their jesting. My head sank lower and lower, till I wished that the floor would open and swallow me.

"Why, would you believe it, madam," exclaimed a young man with a bold, rakish looking countenance, "that this Alfred has actually become so domesticated, so wedded to his home, we cannot draw him away from it? He never leaves it for his old friends, and has become the most sedate married man I know. Not even will he come to visit me, who used to get him out of all sorts of college scrapes. Ungrateful, is he not?"

"More probably he got *you* out," returned one of the gentlement, laughing, "you were bad enough to get yourself into trouble as well as your friends."

"That's the way with these married men," replied the first, with a shrug of his shoulders, "get very virtuous, put on a long face, and eschew their early companions. Alf, I thought, would have better taste. Mrs. Chauncey, I am sure, would not wish to exert an influence so deleterious to his old chums and associates."

Glancing at Alfred, I perceived that he could scarcely control himself. An angry red spot burned on his forehead, and his compressed lips might have shown them, that they were treading upon dangerous ground. With kindly meant badinage a facetious old gentleman continued it, without noticing the effect of his words. But I discerned, or felt rather than saw, that several of the guests were watching us with curious eyes, and looking from Alfred to myself with amazement; then interchanging meaning glances.

My position was becoming unbearable; it was as if I were seated on red hot coals, and I thought that the dinner never would be over.

After a while, to the intense relief of both, the jesting ceased; it had become evident to every one that it was painful, to their host particularly, and embarrassing to me. The gentlemen seated near addressed to me several remarks, and as the one on my right was quite pleasant and intelligent, I became interested in his conversation, at times almost forgetting my painful position while listening to his amusing anecdotes; like lulls in a violent attack of pain, that steep suffering for a moment in forgetfulness—alas! only to be reäwakened afterwards by the shock and thrill of its return.

Seeing me disposed to conversation, the wild young man I have spoken of, who was seated at my left hand, attempted to make himself agreeable, or rather tried how disagreeable he could be to me.

Eyeing Alfred curiously and keenly, he appeared satisfied with the inference he drew from his survey, and turned to me with more familiarity than he would have done to an *accepted* Mrs. Chauncey. Putting his impertinent face nearer mine, he said significantly:

"You must find it quite lonesome here for so young a lady."

I murmured some reply, I scarce know what, about having always lived in the country and being used to it.

"Chauncey has no business to bury you here in this way. I shall remonstrate with him."

"No—oh! no!" I exclaimed in my simplicity, believing his threat to be a real one, instead of a device to draw me out.

"Why not?" he asked, fixing his bold eyes on my face.

"Because I love this place and desire no other, nor want to go anywhere else."

"Yes, but that delight of traveling together to two young married people, as I imagine—unfortunately I am a bachelor myself, though the sight of my friend's happiness makes me quite envious and disposed to follow his example. Happiness," he repeated, bending nearer, "in securing you."

My eyes drooped beneath his, and a burning indignation fired my heart at the liberty he was taking; a liberty he presumed to take with one whom he plainly saw was unprotected; while I felt all the more severely that I had no husband, as they believed Alfred to be, to resent his impertinence.

"He guards you too exclusively," pursued my tormentor, relentlessly. "He ought to permit his friends to have the pleasure of your society also. I, at least, shall claim the privilege. When I heard of his marriage, I had no idea of the sweet, delicate lily he was hiding from us in his lonesome country place."

What could I do or say to rid myself of his impudent familiarity? But when he said,

"You will permit *me* to come, regardless of the jealous Chauncey," drawing still closer and whispering in a tone that was unmistakably improper, indicating plainly that his design was to see how far he could go, I raised my eyes with a look that sent his head back farther than it had been before, and kept himself at a distance that he fully understood I wished him to remain.

"What's the matter, Thomas?" asked a gentleman who had observed the whole, as I could perceive by the expression of his eye. "You look crestfallen."

"I was merely reflecting, sir," replied Thomas, curling his lip, "upon the ways of the world generally, and the affairs of my friends in particular."

"A most exemplary state of mind," remarked the gentleman, sarcastically, "I hope it produces suitable amendment should you cast your eyes within."

"It teaches me, sir," retorted Thomas, with flashing eyes, "to profit in many things by example."

"Yet more exemplary. A fine result of self-culture, is he not, Mrs. Chauncey?"

"However that may be, I think we stand upon equal ground, which I will soon take occasion to show you," exclaimed Thomas, compressing his lips with restrained passion, while his eyes looked venom at his cool tormentor.

Here the old gentleman I have spoken of thought it time to interpose.

"Come, Thomas, come Griffeths," he said softly, "remember where you are," and he looked at me.

They both glanced towards me, then as the teasing gentleman ceased his unpleasant style of conversation, out of consideration—I suppose—for me, peace was restored, apparently, and the general conversation was resumed.

All this had been unperceived by Alfred, who was engaged with those immediately around him, and was too distant to hear what had been spoken in a low tone on both sides, so he knew nothing of this little incident.

I left them after dinner, and went about my household duties, as usual, trying to lull in constant activity that gnawing pain at my heart.

Late in the afternoon, I was told that the gentlemen wished to bid me adieu, as they were about to depart. I went in the drawing-room where but two or three remained, the rest having gone to the porch or dispersed about the lawn.

"Good bye, dear madam," said the gentleman of the old *regime*, taking my hand and pressing it to his lips, "may your life be a long and happy one."

Something choked my throat, but with a strong effort I forced back the tears that were rushing to my eyes. I was afraid that he perceived my emotion, for he turned away as if from motives of delicacy, while another approached to bid his adieu.

Others came in for the same purpose. Alfred was out there with them and did not approach the parlor while I was in it. I did not see young Thomas again, but as he left I heard him say to Alfred,

"Good bye, Chauncey; you need'nt be so devoted to your wife that you can't come and see a fellow. There's time enough yet for the honeymoon to wear off.

Alfred gave a fierce stamp of his foot. "No more of this," he said passionately, "I cannot stand it."

All else was drowned in the noise they made as they rode off with their dogs and horses, leaving but the echo of their presence as their horns mellowed in the distance. Alfred immediately disappeared, having positively declined their urgent invitation to join the party, as had been his wont in time gone by.

I felt more desolate than ever, and my lonely, neglected state became vivid as it had never been before. Hitherto my love for him had fed my heart with living fire, and the pleasure of being near him, of having the opportunity, if not the power, to soothe him in trouble, had sustained me. Now there was a reäction. I had miscalculated my strength, and began to need love ln return. Must I go on thus,—I asked despairingly,—working for him, day after day, and yet to have nothing but polished coldness in return?

I saw but little of home. My mother was absorbed in my old duties as well as her own. Though she kept a seamstress now to help her, yet "it is not like you, Mary, for all your poetry and sentiment," she said affectionately to me.

And I—oh! I could not bear to leave him when he was at home, and when absent, my wearying anxiety for him must be borne alone.

I could not visit my home in the state of mind I then was.—Mother questioned me about this —her parental interest at times overcoming the reserve I had endeavored to establish between us on the subject—and tried to learn from me the state of affairs between my nominal husband and myself. I could tell her nothing, and quickly showed her with all the respect due to my mother, that about him my reticence must remain unbroken.

So passed the days as I lived my lonely life there in busy cares for him, a book my sole recreation when there was nothing more I could do and my self-appointed tasks were completed. My forte, however, was in working, not reading. With that restless misery gnawing at the heart, I could fix my mind upon mental enjoyment but rarely. Apparently so near, we were separated in reality by thousands of miles, for I grew no nearer to him. So wrapt was he in his own gloomy thoughts when in my presence, or merely polite with a coldly finished polish, that I could not thaw that icy surface; the same awe yet sealed my lips and made me appear so ignorant and awkward when he was by. How long? how long? I sighed.

(TO BE CONTINUED.)

CICERO'S ORATION FOR MARCELLUS.

ONE may be excused for turning to Ancient Literature. It is allowable to be lotus-eaters when we can neither bear, nor amend the present.

This oration has, by some admirers of Cicero, been, as we think, over-praised, while by others it has been set down as spurious. We may consider the question of its genuineness settled by the weight of critical authority. The internal evidence might, of itself, satisfy us. The art, the elegance, the dexterity, the copiousness, the swell, the ornament, the egotism of the great Arpinian are all here; nor are there wanting some of the loftier notes of patriotism and high philosophy that sound so grand in the Philippics, or so elevate us as we listen to the defence of Archias. On the other hand, it cannot be classed with the best of his speeches. It was in fact an impromptu performance, though he afterwards wrote it out carefully. The fatal defect in it is the narrowness of the subject. It is a panegyric, and to praise a fellow-man can never give sufficient scope to genius. A very great man, however, was he who was the subject of this praise. Cæsar had a great brain, a great heart, and very wide views—great faults too, unquestionably, the greatest being ambition. Cicero says in his oration, that the act for which he was there lauding him, was the greatest of his life, and gives several fantastic reasons to prove it. This was not true. Cæsar did not think so, nor did Cicero, nor does anybody else. His act was magnanimous, but not so magnanimous as the conquest of Gaul, or the battle of Pharsalia.

Marcellus, as consul, had been from the first a violent partisan of Pompey, and was in arms against Cæsar, at Pharsalia. Justly supposing that his conduct had compromised him too deeply to allow any expectation of reconciliation, he had retired into voluntary exile at Mytelene. Cæsar allowed him to remain unmolested in his chosen retreat. After some time his friends, at Rome, exerted themselves to procure his return, and in a full assembly of the Senate, a near kinsman of his, supported by all the Senators, implored Cæsar to recall him. Cæsar at first assumed severity, and complained of the resentment that Marcellus had ever manifested towards him, but concluded by saying that he would not oppose the desire of the Senate, and declared Marcellus to be forgiven and restored to all his honors. This was a very handsome act on the part of an old heathen, with wolf blood in him, living in Rome fifty years, and more, before Christ.

Hardly in Washington, in the middle of the 19th century, do we find, after the close of a revolution, a more christian spirit animating the bosom of our own statesmen. Cæsar had not read the text, "I say unto you, love your enemies," nor the commentary on it, "if thy brother offend against thee seventy times seven, thou shalt forgive him," nor had he learned at his mother's knee, nor had he repeated many a time in church the petition of the Lord's prayer, "Forgive us our trespasses as we forgive those who trespass against us." Nor had his ancestors come over in the Mayflower, nor landed at Plymouth, nor burned witches, nor enjoyed the benefits of the Common School System, nor belonged to Temperance and Abolition Societies, nor caught the spirit of Progress, nor learned the philosophy of Humanitarianism. Indeed he had not enjoyed any such special religious advantage as would justify him in saying, "Stand by thyself, I am holier than thou." It would be hasty to infer any thing about the christian character of Cæsar, because he manifested a spirit which, as is well known, is a characteristic of Christians in modern days. His magnanimity was due, I am inclined to believe, not to the fact that he was a great ante-dated Christian, but because he was a great man. Great brains and great souls were capable of acts of magnanimity, even as far back as 2000 years ago. Little minded men may be Senators and other functionaries, but magnanimous they cannot be—to offer no other reason—there is a philosophical impossibility in the way.

Another faculty for magnanimity possessed by Cæsar, was bravery. "Brave as Julius Cæsar" has long been a comparison used by people of dull imagination, just as "tricky as Grant" will hereafter serve the same class of speakers and writers. Men who are not brave, cannot be magnanimous; in fact they are styled pusillanimous. Nor can men behave by force of will. It is recorded in history that there was once a man that could not help being afraid of buck shot, and of another, who upon a certain occasion exhibited as much terror at the sight of a cane, as if he had been an immediate descendant of the martyred Abel.

Cæsar, however, was brave, and so when the idea was suggested that he might be in danger from these former enemies whom he was so freely pardoning, he put it down by saying, "*Satis diu vel naturæ vixi vel gloriæ.*" This, though Cicero does style it *præclarissimam et sapientissimam vocem*—sounds a little boastful, but Cæsar was accustomed to let off from time to time these Brobdignag epigrams, some of them have imposed themselves as sublime upon astonished critics—witness the famous *veni vidi vici*, and "*Quid times? Cæsarem vehis.*" Other great Captains have had the same tendency—Alexander, Bonaparte, &c.—A. B. C. I have no doubt that, with a little thought, I could, if I had time, illustrate the whole alphabet in this way. The letter P illustrates itself without a thought. Pope—not the Holy Father, nor the Poet of Twickenham, but the hero who kept his quarters (he modestly called them *head* quarters) in the saddle, and wrote his dispatches, some of the later ones at least, *currente calamo*—with a running pen.

It would not do to require that all men should come up to the imperial standard. If every man is to be persecuted till his persecutor can truly say—"*Satis diu vel naturæ vixi vel gloriæ,*" we fear cruelty would not soon come to an end. What American statesman, for example, (we regret that our limited knowledge of history so restricts our illustrations) would be inclined to say "I have lived long enough for myself," (so Cicero interprets the word *naturæ.*) It is the general opinion that many of them have lived quite too long for other people, but for themselves they would hold on to life, as a distinguished Secretary does to his office, *per fas aut nefas.* And as to having lived long enough for glory! If life is to be prolonged for them to this period, the final cataclysm will come upon them, still living, and still filled with bitterness.

That we may not give undue praise to Cæsar, it must be remembered that he was well established in power. Pompey was dead and buried, except his head, which had been cut off and burned, and the after campaign in Africa had settled the expiring struggles of the party under Cato and the other leaders. Had it been otherwise—had he known that in a few months, say the November following, the battle of Pharsalia was to be fought, the condition of it being to him, as Cicero says in his oration for Ligarius, victory or ruin—and had the result of the African affair been still doubtful, Cæsar's example and Cicero's eloquence might have been lost to the world. It is quite fine to observe how skillfully Cicero appeals at once to Cæsar's sense of duty and his love of praise. Towards the conclusion of the oration he says: "Upon you alone, Cæsar, depends the restoration of all things which you see in ruins around you, wrecked by the storm of war. Law must be set up again, public faith restored, licentiousness restrained, industry encouraged, and the wild recklessness of the times checked by wholesome laws. In a civil war so great, in the fury of feeling and the clash of arms, the loss by the Republic, whatever might be the issue of the contest, of many things which contributed to its glory and its stability, was unavoidable, and each side did in the heat of the conflict, what in peace it would have been the first to condemn. Now all these deep wounds are to be healed, and you only have the power to do it."—When we read this passage, how thankful should we be that, after a struggle not dissimilar, our condition is so different from that depicted by the orator who was at the same time a profound statesman, and accurately acquainted with the condition of the Republic. That the prosperity of our land has nowhere been affected, that law reigns supreme—and that its tribunals, from the *Pie-poudre* courts to the Supreme Court of the United States have never been assailed by a triumphant faction—that public faith is not suspected, and that public and private morals are pure beyond any period of the world's history, while the humanizing influence of Christianity sways in all places, from the smallest hamlet to the Capital of the nation—that the Constitution of the United States was so strong that it resisted every shock of arms—and that the Republican form of Government in America has been found to be so perfect a machine that the management of it can, with the utmost safety, be entrusted to emancipated blacks. And further, that the Supreme Legislature of the land has no need of a hint from a Cicero, living or dead, as to its duty, seeing that its whole energies are devoted to the grateful task of causing all traces of exasperated feeling to disappear. "*O fortunatos nimium sua si bona norint.*"

Cæsar was willing, doubtless, to do his duty *cæteris paribus*, but as the sound of the trumpet to the war-horse, was the word glory to his ear. Cicero knew this well, and was not likely to forget it, having, in fact, himself, a similar affection of the auditory nerve. So he discourses to him after the following fashion:

"If the result, O Cæsar, of your immortal works shall be, that having overcome all your adversaries, you leave the Republic in its present condition, where will be your glory—that glory which is the illustrious and widespread remembrance of great men, who have deserved well of their fellow-citizens, their native land, and of all mankind? Your soul, never content within the narrow limits of this mortal life, has ever burned with a desire for immortality. This fleeting breath is not what we call life. That is life—real life—which the memory of all ages will keep green, which posterity will cherish, and of which eternity itself will be the guardian. Have a care of this. Posterity will never forget the Rhine, the Nile, the ocean, the empires you have gained, your innumerable battles, and incredible victories. But if the State is not rehabilitated by your wisdom and your arts, your fame may be wide-spread, but solid, it never can be. Have regard then, to the sentence of those who, in years to come, will pass judgment upon your deeds—a judgment, perhaps, more impartial than ours, since it will be without prejudice. And even, if, as some unworthily suppose, it will matter little to you then, what men think of you, at least it behooves you so to act now that oblivion may never tarnish your praise."

Skillful orator, and noble man, moreover. For in his own bosom glowed the aspiration for immortality which he sought to arouse in the heart of his imperial auditor.

Well, Cæsar and Cicero have long had better opportunities than we, or Shakspeare, or Gray, of knowing what is posthumous honor, and whether "flattery can soothe the dull, cold ear of death;" but whether he can hear it or not, many ages have said, and many ages yet to come will repeat the saying, that it was a noble act, and well-done of Cæsar to lay aside his personal animosities and throw by-gones into the rubbish of the past, that he might magnanimously restore Marcellus, unconditionally, to his place, and to all his honors in the Senate. He did not even require an oath. Ironclads, whether in war or in peace, are an invention of modern genius, and christian morality.

And what obloquy would be justly awarded to the transaction, had personal animosity or unworthy fear checked the impulse of magnanimity!

No very great issues were at stake, nor any wide-spread consequences likely to ensue from the decision either way. No State was to be overthrown, had malevolence ruled his bosom. No institutions would be destroyed. No Roman community would be surrendered to Gauls, or Carthagenians. No crime against nature would have been committed by interfering with the relations established by the Creator, between different races of men. Cæsar had too much sense, not to say conscience, to do anything like this. Had he repulsed Marcellus it could hardly have been called a crime so much as a meanness that would sensibly have lessened the distance between him and the men who have been found in all periods, except our own, who were infinitely little in everything but a temporary power to do injury, and the boundless malevolence with which they exercised that power.

It is sad to remember that

Cæsar's pardon was unavailing to Marcellus. He set out on his return, but before he reached Rome, he was assassinated by one of his own attendants. The miserable resentment of a hireling frustrated the magnanimity of an Emperor. Still, the glory of the act will ever belong to Cæsar's name, and the moral of it will remain, if ever there should be found persons in power to whom it will apply. S. L. C.

ON THE HEIGHTS.*

WE have here a book of note, if we are to judge of its merits from the manner of its reception by the reading world of Europe, into many of whose languages we understand it has already been translated. It is presented to American readers in the usual handsome style of the publishers, whose *imprimatur* it bears, and its graceful appearance is quite beyond that generally awarded to works whose very external dress is apt to suggest a hint of an anticipated ephemeral existence.—This book, on the other hand, has a substantial look, as if it was a foregone conclusion, that it is destined to long life in company with the unquestioned occupants of the carefully-selected library,—not to be thrown aside, after a single reading, with other literary lumber, as 'only a novel.'

Before we say anything of the merits of the work itself, we must be allowed a few strictures, as to the translation. It has the air of having been made by one to whom English is a foreign tongue: we cannot otherwise, account for the singular grammatical errors, the unidiomatic expressions and the unaccustomed constructions. "Fanny Elisabeth Bunnétt" is a name we see frequently associated with translations, and we have been disposed to think that she is a German or French lady, employed by the Leipsic publishing house (Baron Tauchnitz's). However this may be, she does not give us pure, unadulterated English; and we constantly feel the trammeling influence of the stiff rendering as a barrier to our fuller enjoyment of our author.

Auerbach is not familiarly known this side of the water. Indeed we are not sure that any of his works have been heretofore given to the American reading public, though he is quite a voluminous and popular writer. Of his many books, "The Black-Forest Tales" are the most widely known, perhaps, and the most appreciated by his countrymen.

"On The Heights" is a book *sui generis*;—unique even among German novels. While all through its pages, the author holds persistently to his ulterior purpose of

---

* "On The Heights"—a Novel, by Berthold Auerbach. Roberts Brothers. Boston.

making of his story, a web into which he may work his speculations in regard to human life and human destiny—much in the same way that Lessing uses his "Nathan The Wise"—he nevertheless embroiders thereon, character and scene and incident—German legends, quaint traditions, domestic peculiarities and the thousand beautiful and wondrous phases of Alpine life, with as careful a fidelity to nature as even old Denner practiced. This is one of the greatest charms of the book.

A regular, professed novel-reader, who devours stories simply for the story, "as men smoke cigars"—might pronounce the action too slów: and perhaps there would be some truth in the objection, especially in reference to the earlier portiôn of the book, but there are not many pages that do not show a richness in minute philosophies, that would make any thoughtful reader unwilling to practice much elision.

The experience of the fresh, simple, unworldly-wise, yet clear-visioned peasant woman, Walpurga, when suddenly summoned from her mountain home to the royal palace, as wet-nurse to the crown-prince, is most tenderly and skillfully narrated. The struggle between the two opposing systems of life—nature's *naive* simplicity and art's unreal blandishments—is most truthfully wrought out: and the manner in which the pure and sturdy Alpine flower managed to exist, unspoiled and unwithered, amid the choking heats of the royal conservatory, is, in itself, an artistic study.—The peasant-wife's caressing pity for "the poor Queen who knew so little of the world out yonder"—according to *her* ideas, is, at times, very amusing. The chattering of the foster-mother with the baby-prince is as sweet as the chirping of birds. One would think that only a woman's intuitions could have suggested them.

The heroine of the book is the "Countess Irma," upon whose history and fate the interest of the story hinges. The interweaving of these two most skillfully contrasted lives—Walpurga's and the Countess'—the reflex influence of each on the other, and the moral lesson forced on the reader's attention, (all the more effective, in that the author seems unconscious of attempting to convey any such lesson) are all very admirably done.

"Irma's Journal" (Book Seventh) is the kernel, the heart's core, of the work, however. It might be called a series of prose sonnets,—so compact and terse and finished are the disconnected sentences—full of lofty thought, abstruse speculation, rich, suggestive fancy, and fine poetic imagery. The whole gist of "On The Heights" is wrapped up in this Seventh Book; and it contains more vigorous, incisive thinking, set forth too in poetical diction, than many a modern volume of poems can boast. Take a few passages selected at random.

"That Redeemer is yet to come, who will consecrate labor and the working-day."

—"Liberty and work—these are the noblest prerogatives of man."

—"The Arabians wash their hands before prayer: but in the desert where there is no water, they wash their hands in sand and dust. So it is:—the dust of work purifies."

—"It is not joy, nor repose, which is the aim of life. It is work, or there is no aim at all."

—"What will the world say?"—they ask in the palace: "What do people think?"—the peasant asks in his solitude.—"There lies our whole chain of slavery."

—"Man alone lives far into the night: *how* far is the measure of our degree of civilization."

—"To have once been on the extreme brink of death, only one step more, and a leap—this makes life easier: no unhappiness can now befall me."

—"We hear the rain fall, but not the snow: Bitter grief is loud—calm grief is silent."

"He who hasn't been away, doesn't come home."

—"So long as one can say, "Father" and "Mother," there is a love on the earth which bears one in its arms: it is only when the parents are gone, that one is set down on the hard ground!"

—"To a father, when his child dies—the future dies: to a child, when his parents die, the past dies."

—"The most mysterious thoughts are like a bird on a twig: he sings; but if he sees an eye watching him, he flies away."

We might multiply excerpts indefinitely, but sufficient have been given, by which to judge of the flavor of the whole.

We lay down "On The Heights" with an utter demur against many of the philosophic and religious opinions of the author. He says beautiful and true things about art: but he would make art fill, in the cultured mind, the place that religion does in the minds of the mass. The people, he complains, "live entirely without art—they have nothing to bring the other life before them, but the Church." So, in the absence of the former, he is content to accept the latter for them. He owns that our modern culture cannot take the place of religion, because "religion makes all men equal,—culture, unequal:" But he believes there will, some day, be a right and true culture that will equalize all men.

In these views, lies a deep-seated error, to which it is well to have our eyes open,—an error to which a literary class of our immediate day is committing itself to a dangerous degree. We Southern people, it is true, have not much temptation, at the present juncture of affairs, to sin in this particular direction, inasmuch as the struggle for simple existence is likely to be stern enough to blot from our minds, all remembrance of the refined leisure which this finished culture imperatively demands: *we* are surely being "purified by the dust of labor!"

Another fault we have to find with the teachings of our author, is his thorough pantheism: and were it not that it is set forth in rather too vague and transcendental a form to work a very decided impression upon mere ordinary readers, we should la-ment the popularity of the work.

And there is a yet graver error to be pointed out and rejected, as aimed at the very corner-stone of our holy Christian religion, namely: The possibility of the sinful, unaided soul, by the omnipotence of its own supreme will, *to expiate the past*, and to work itself, through its innate power, into a condition of *absolute freedom and purity*—so that the wine of life shall run crystal-clear, utterly and forever separated from the lees of human weakness and wrong doings;—the old philosophy of Paganism reproduced again, in one of its thousand Protean forms.

Yet we have in the *Grandmother*, a picture of simple, unquestioning peasant-faith, which it is refreshing to look upon, which, however, is quite consistent with the author's theory of 'a religion for the people.' There is not a sweeter character in the volume—so German—so strong—so full of a rich, rude poetry—so wholly natural—so wise in the deepest life-experiences!

We feel that we have very inadequately characterized this remarkable book; and that our examination of it has been much too cursory; and we reluctantly dismiss it, realizing it to be one of the most deep-thoughted and suggestive books (with all its speculative and theological errors) that has, for a long time, fallen into our hands.

MARGARET J. PRESTON.

JOHN SMITH, ESQ.

CHAPTER I.

ELLEN CLARDY swung herself to and fro on the gate, keeping time to a merry tune with the easy grace of childhood, but her violet eyes were fixed toward the sunset with the earnest look of a woman. A youth of frank, healthful appearance came up through the garden and paused to watch her, smiling as he watched. His name was John Smith. There was a pretty picture before him against the brilliant western sky, which threw yellow shafts of light through her brown hair, and touched each feature with a mellow tint of rose and gold. Ellen was pretty and sweet; pretty like a spray of white ash that grows slender and fine, sweet as a brier rose on a dewy morning, and her voice had the freshness of a glad valley stream. Brightness, daintiness and grace marked her attire, from the peasant waist, with scarlet lacings, to the fluted lace at her throat and hands; from the top of her head, with its knot of bright ribbon, to the sole of her foot that hung from the gate, touching the ground as she moved to and fro, with the toe of a silver buckled little slipper. To an artist it was a study—to a lover, a shrine!

When the song ceased, John called her name, startling her into a cry of surprise, as he twisted a long jasmine vine round and round her neck, head, waist and arms, stirring and bruising its yellow bells. Then he stood admiring her graceful efforts to disentangle herself, hearing her laugh and scold, seeing her aglow with pleasure, until he wished they might stand forever thus, with no sound save her voice and the subdued lullaby of nature, as she hushed the day to sleep.

A slender, heavy-bearded young man, gotten up in the most exquisite style of cheap romances, broke the stillness by riding past in a quick canter. It was Hugh St. Clair, who gave an expressive glance, a smile, and an elegant salutation, as he reined in his horse to a gait better adapted to display the figure of the rider, and disappeared, leaving a good impression. Ellen's face was red, but John's grew white, for the sky had grown grey and he knew the reflection went up from her heart.

"John," said she abruptly, "why cannot you and Mr. St. Clair like each other?"

"Because both of us like you too well, I suppose," replied John recovering his color. "Which do you like best, Nell?"

"Which?" echoed she, "why both, of course!"

"You absurd child! Which could you spare most easily?"

"Neither."

"Pshaw! If one or the other had to die, and you had the word to give, which name would you call," asked he excitedly, "his or mine?"

She looked troubled and tearful.

"Never mind, Nelly, dear, you are almost weeping, it was such a foolish question."

He spoke tenderly as he took her hand, believing she loved him. She felt it in his touch, manner and tone, and spoke resolutely.

"But I will mind, John, I must tell the truth."

He carried her hand to his lips and bit the tips of her fingers one by one—an odd caress of his she had known for years. He began it when she first sat alone, and her hand was about the size of a great-coat button. She was wont to receive it playfully, but now it was withdrawn as she continued, "We have known each other so long, John—"

"Ever since we were little children," added he.

"Yes, we are like brother and sister"—he shook his head as she went on—"and it would almost break my heart to part with you, it would be so hard, so hard, John!" He took the other hand and held both close to his breast. "But—I would have to call your name!"

"To live?"

"Oh John, dear John!" she sobbed out, "I could not bear to call his name, for him to die!"

"You mean, you mean," said he hoarsely, "oh tell me what you mean!"

"That I love Hugh St. Clair."

He dropped her hands as if they were heavy weights, stepped away quickly and leaned against the gate with folded arms.

She spoke again, but he heard nothing save those words; they had deadened every other sound and darkened the world to him.

At sixteen Ellen floated in an atmosphere of dreams, where she was the heroine and Hugh St. Clair the hero of all the trashy novels she had devoured—that sensational style of fiery delineations of inconceivable passions of love, jealousy and despair, which in spite of a wise system of State taxation, are still hurled among us. Many a night she fancied herself in the attitude of the thinly clad young ladies on the title page of "Frank Leslie's Illustrated," borne through a terrible tempest by an infuriated lover, dishevelled tresses streaming upon the wind, with her hands crossed in meek submission to the decrees of Fate, above the wild heart which demands immediate elopement with a scoundrel, lest it break!

To marry a man like plain cousin John—true, he was not her cousin, but they had been reared together and learned to love each other as if they had been cousins—it would never do in the world! Why they had eaten hominy out of the same oven and with the same spoon in Black Mammy's house many a time; she remembered distinctly when he quit wearing ruffles and took to collars, and when uncle switched him for going in swimming on Sunday. As for his memory, doubtless it was better, he could tell her how she looked when she was shedding teeth, in fact he had been her first dentist himself.—She loved to laugh over those old times; she loved him dearly but could not marry him—it was so unromantic. John was so prosaic, there was nothing dashy about him—he never created a sensation—never drank or swore. He smoked a little, and read more than heroes generally, but his hair was light and short. As for his moustache, it was as yet by no means conspicuous, and bid fair to be yellow—decidedly yellow; while Mr. St. Clair's was raven black. Poor John could only whistle, and Mr. St. Clair sang divinely! Last but not least was a fact for which he might be pitied, but certainly not blamed; as he had no voice in the matter of his christening, they called him John Smith!

She pronounced the name, "John Smith," and put her hands to her ears—but "Mrs. St. Clair!" Ah, that was so '*distingué*'—she accepted him.

CHAPTER II.

Two hours after her interview with John at the gate, her affianced was demanding an account of the conversation. He made some fierce threats, in a heroic style, and she, after the manner of the heroine in the last sweet story in "Godey's Lady's Book," retorted in indignant innocence. They quarreled until he relapsed into stern silence, and she into proud regret. Sarcasm and reproaches alternated until her penitent head sank on his shoulder and two small tears saturated her handkerchief. When it was all over, and the reconciliation had followed with its usual amount of tender blandishments, he asked who gave her the flowers she wore in her hair.

"John," answered she timidly.

"Who gave you those in your bodice?"

"You did."

"You are a coquette!" exclaimed he angrily, placing his hands on her shoulders, and pressing them against the lattice until a sharp nail pierced her flesh and spotted the muslin sleeve with blood.

"Answer me, do you love me?"

"I do."

"Then give him up."

"I have done so."

"You shall cease speaking to him. I command you to do so"

She was afraid of him, and bit her lips silently.

"Do you hear me, Ellen?" continued he, "If you ever speak to him again, we part. Promise!"

She hesitated a moment, saw the light from the parlor window shine on his malignant face, considered it the sublime frenzy of the grand passion, and promised to pass cousin John as a stranger. Hugh was then all she could wish. They returned to the parlor where he kissed the wounded shoulder, wiped away her tears, and sang,

"Thou hast wounded the spirit that
loved thee,"

to her heart's content.

That night she leaned out of her window to gaze, in rapture, at the moon, and abandon herself to her happiness. The realization of her ideal of a dark browed lover with the tenderness of a Romeo, and jealousy of an Othello, had come, and she would have been very happy, if she had not heard a step on the stair-case which reminded her of her promise. Poor cousin John! She wondered if he would say good-night as he passed her door, and go whistling to his room. He passed firmly by without pausing.

"It is well," thought she, "my promise would have been broken had he said good-night."

In the morning she was schooled to meet him without a word whom she had met nearly every morning of her life.

"Good morning, Nelly!" said John cheerfully.

She looked toward him, paused and turned away.

"Perhaps," thought he, "she did not hear me, I will try again."

"Good morning, Nelly!" She heard then, for her face was flushed to the edge of her hair. He looked steadily at her a moment, and understood her desire. It was the last time she saw him for five years. The next meal there was a vacant chair at the table—Ellen was there but ate nothing. Poor cousin John!

CHAPTER III.

Accident, or the hand of Providence threw a better influence about the womanhood of Ellen Clardy. The accident was that great blessing in disguise, *the blockade of the South.* Did the few friends from whom we were separated look pityingly upon us? Did we seem shut out from the light, imprisoned in darkness?—What an error! To our isolation we owe the development of the vast resources of the South, the industry of her men and women, the spirit of earnest endeavor, the pride of independent labor, the dignity of pursuit, and a social, moral and spiritual elevation.—Such are the fruits of sacrifice—then tell us not we fought in vain! We wear flushed cheeks, and conquer rising tears, but we neither blush nor weep for shame; for true Southrons have lain in the fiery furnace, and bear the ring of good metal within their souls. Not the least of our laurels do we count the elevation of Southern Literature.

The first year of the War, Ellen Clardy missed the visits of Harper, Frank Leslie, Godey and Peterson, and read the old numbers over again; then in desperation for something to read, borrowed the *Ledger* and Mrs. Southworth's novels. In the earnest life that Southern women lived, these palled upon her taste. The next year she enjoyed 'Debit and Credit,' it made her a worker, 'Les Miserables,' a thinker; so thinking and working together, she awoke from her old dreams. About that time a copy of Godey's Lady's Book crept through the lines and found its way to her. Therein she found something to this effect: "There is an innate refinement in the character of the Northern Ladies which can never be attained by a Southern woman, even through association and education, in consequence of the coarse manners which result from their peculiar institutions." She was a Southern Woman, and proud of the title; so she laid down the book, quietly made a bonfire of all such trash to be found in her possession, and placed that last crowning insult on the summit of the pile.

Her lover came down from his ideal height, step by step. The spell was finally broken by a falsehood. He raved, of course; and strove by an outburst of temper, and an imperious will, to force her back into his power, but she was firm.

"I am no longer a silly dreamer," said she, "I have conquered myself."

"It was a dream then," returned he quickly.

"Yes, a dream of an overwrought brain, warped by pernicious reading, and idleness."

"What are your objections to me?"

"You have a jealous disposition"—Perfect love casteth out fear. "You are cruel—you shot your horse last summer to intimidate me."

"Anything else, my brave and fair one?" asked he derisively

"Yes. I thought I loved you then, for I attributed your violent emotions to love of me, and was flattered by it."

"It *was* love! I would sell my honor for you, Ellen!"

"That is it, Mr. St. Clair; that is my reason for this step. I cannot become the wife of a man who would sacrifice a principle for my sake! He must hold his honor as sacred as my own."

"What have I done?"

"Ask your conscience—I am not your accuser, except in this—*you told me a falsehood*, and wronged a man who is brave and quick to resent a wrong, but will spare you for my sake."

"Then you forever refuse me?"

"I do!"

"Is there no remnant of past love to reproach you with broken faith?"

She smiled as she replied, "I would be untrue to you and to myself if I married you; I would not wrong any man thus. Your affection for me has not ennobled you, nor has the hope of mine made you a better man. It is an infatuation—-forget it."

So much for good reading and hard work. She felt very free when he left her, and would have been quite happy, but—poor cousin John!

One by one of Ellen's admirers were rejected, until it was said she would never marry. When she grew sad and quiet some one said, "Ah, she is setting her cap for our minister!" When the minister's sermons grew eloquent in denunciation, the young men said, "He has met our fate."—There was a rosewood box on a small workstand in her room; the key of it lay in her bosom. What did it contain? Ah, that was the secret! She must tell it herself.

CHAPTER IV.

John Smith came home after the surrender of Lee's army with a scar on his face and a star on his collar. The fatted calf would have been killed, and a ring put on his finger; but, alas! the calves in that section had all been slain, and the rings had rolled northward, so there was nothing left but a welcome. This was hearty enough. He was grateful for it, but Ellen labored under a difficulty of breathing which annoyed him.—There was an uncomfortable lump in his own throat, which his aunt endeavored to cure. He poured her remedies in the fire when that worthy lady turned her back upon him, but remained in his room twenty-four hours, reading with his book upside down. Twenty cigars were lighted during the time, half of them at the wrong end. Ellen understood the case sooner than he did, and laughed, sang and danced about the house in an unfeeling manner. She was very annoying to a sick man. He resolved to go to Brazil, but would show her before he left how calmly he could speak of the past; that he cared as little for her as she did for him. One evening he saw her from his window trimming the roses. It was a good opportunity; so he left the house, and walked leisurely down that way, cutting the air with a spray of spirea held in his hand. Nothing was easier. He dashed boldly at the subject.

"Ellen, do you remember how I used to dress your hair? Let me dress it again."

The spray was trembling when he wound it about her head, but it is a slender plant, and nods to the softest breath of spring.

"Yellow jessamine was your favorite then."

"It is still." Both voices were low and unsteady.

"What a fool I was the evening that"—

John was no coward—the boys in the ranks called him "steady and stout," while he wore "the grey"—but here he came to a halt and left the field in confusion. However, he rallied and recovered his position, facing Ellen and the roses. An old soldier ran from a little woman behind a breastwork of flowers and a battery of smiles, playing on him! But it came her turn to tremble before his resolute advance, so she bent over to examine the roses with the air of a professional gardener. There were some incoherent remarks made about the health of "Lady Banks," that year, and a fear expressed that "Louis the Fourteenth" was backward; to which he appropriately replied, as follows:

"Ellen, I thought I had conquered myself, or I would never have returned. I will go away again." She turned white. "You are not looking well, have I offended you?"

"No, John—I want to ask your pardon for refusing to bid you good morning five years ago." She spoke quickly and walked away from the spot, he following. She gave him no time to tell her she was forgiven—they were already at the gate—the same little gate on which she used to swing.

Her hand was on the latch, but it was fast. He leaned against it, and she looked up in his face as he spoke.

"Tell me, did you love St. Clair?"

"I did not."

"Have you ever loved?" Her eyes fell.

"Yes, John."

"I am a fool again! Forgive me, I had no right to ask." An April drift of light and shade crossed her face. The latch clicked, and he held the gate open for her to pass through. She made a movement forward, hesitated, and looked timidly in his eyes.

"When you see me again, I shall be more of a man," said he, looking away from her.

"Oh, John, why don't you ask the name of him I love!"

"Tell it, I can bear it." She stepped lightly back and whispered close to his ear, so close that her breath warmed his cheek—

"John!"

Still looking away, lest sight might break the spell, he asked again the name, and she answered again—

"John!"

"Ellen, could you marry a man like me? A common man!"

"Common?" echoed she almost indignantly, "common indeed! Why, John, I have never seen a man like you!"

"I am disfigured."

"Oh, John, hush! That scar is a patent of nobility, a badge of honor—look at me, I am proud of it." He looked, and saw that he was a man—every inch a King in her eyes; and she saw that to him she was the dearest woman in the world. Standing thus together, it seemed to both that the little venture that went down with the setting sun so many years ago, had anchored a fleet of golden argosies upon the sky, and the stars came out to clap their hands for joy!

CHAPTER V.

They were married. The bride had told her husband often why she loved him; but it never sounded old in his ears. He asked her again when the wedding was over, and she was more explicit than ever. So it was a charming new story.

"How did you learn that you loved me?"

"By contrast. When Hugh was jealous, I remembered one who would have trusted me to the end of the world. When he shot his horse, I thought of one who splintered the leg of a mocking bird and brought it home to me in his bosom. When he told me a falsehood, I thought of one who loved the truth and never swerved from it. Ah, John, how could you love me when I was so unkind?" Her lips quivered as she thought of that morning greeting she never returned. What if she had never heard his voice again!

"You had your faults, Nelly, and I had mine. I hoped we could help each other to mend them." His smile lifted the shadow.

"You have no faults, you dear one!" Those were earnest, worshipful eyes set upon him.

It is a hard thing for a man to tell a woman not to idolize him, when she insists on doing so. She stood at the back of his chair—her arms around his neck, and her hands locked together on his breast. There was tenderness given for tenderness, smiles for smiles, but his face wore a serious expression. He took a Bible from the table and turned the leaves over slowly. The bridal veil enveloped both as she leaned forward to read where he pointed. "Thou shalt have no other gods before me." Her hands were unclasped, and she was lifted around in his arms to hear him read on to the end of the commandment. Then he spoke in a firm but gentle tone: "Power is sweet to every human being. Its gratification is increased by the idolatry of those who love us until we become overbearing and exacting. Thus, many men, who truly love their wives, become their tyrants. Help me to guard against this, my darling!"

"You could not be a tyrant, said Ellen, unwilling to see a shadow of wrong in her abundant love.

"I asked you to help me guard against it, will you?"

"Yes."

"From this tyranny," continued he, "proceeds selfishness; from selfishness, servitude. True marriage is not a state of slavery. I do not wish my wife to be my servant in any capacity whatever. The idea is revolting to a lover, it should be to a husband. Habitual selfishness alone could demand it

—when I want a servant I will hire one."

"But dear," said Ellen, "you would not have me regardless of the comforts of your home?"

"No, but I wish no system of sacrifice instituted therein—where there is work to do, we will work together—where there is pleasure, we will enjoy it together also. If our burdens are grievous to be borne, we will help each other—the heavier burden borne by the stronger."

"Ah, yes," added she, "I see your meaning, you would have us co-workers, hand to hand, heart to heart, aiding and comforting each other—such a wife, with God's help, I intend to become."

"Then there will be perfect peace in our home. *I conceive the true spirit of marriage to be the toil of twain as one, in the exercise of every gift for mutual happiness, which redounds to the glory of God!*"

"These are serious reflections, and my bride wears too sad a face for our bridal day—you are not frightened, Nelly?"

"Oh, no, it is a solemn thing, but you are with me, and God is with us both—I am not afraid!"

"Then smile again, or I shall forget the dignity of my position as a married man, and become a teasing boy—I'll pull down your hair, I'll steal your slippers off your feet, I'll toss you to the ceiling like a baby, if you do not immediately smile for your tyrannical husband! There! That will do very well,—now laugh aloud or I will proceed to open this mysterious box."

"Oh, you prying fellow! Hands off!"

"My curiosity is on the increase; gratify it, or I'll light my cigar and smoke in your room. I'll color your laces with nicotine!"

"Guess then!"

"Some trophy of the War?"

"No!"

"A bunch of faded flowers?"

"No!"

"A package of letters tied with blue ribbon, perhaps?"

"No, you are not good at guess-work; you are the most stupid husband I ever had in my life—they are mementoes of my love."

"False woman, and you have preserved them until now!" exclaimed he, in playful reproach, as she took a small key from her bosom and opened the box. There was a mocking bird's wing lying on top.

"Do you remember the bird you gave me, John?"

"With the broken leg?"

"Yes; when the poor thing died, I kept this wing."

"I told you to cure the little sufferer and set him free."

"But he died."

"What is this then? Pot-hooks and hangers, as I live! Ha, ha! Fine specimens truly. Here is Hogarth's line of beauty!"

"You need not laugh, sir, you set the copies yourself—and marked them in pencil for me to trace over."

"I humbly beg pardon—now you will certainly permit me to laugh at this," said he, holding up a well-worn child's boot, with the red top half torn off—"what little ragamuffin's boot is this? you odd-notioned woman!"

"It belongs to the boy who used to climb trees for yellow jasmine for my hair."

"How did you come by it?"

"I put it away the day you lost the mate on the river bank, to keep uncle from making you wear one boot to school." He laughed at his wife's odd treasures, but appreciated them as she continued, "I put those things away while you were gone, because I was afraid you might never come back home."

"And you loved me all that time?" asked he fondly.

"Yes, John, dear, and I am so glad to know it by these simple signs! So glad to know my heart was true all the time, and only this crazy head went wandering. If you ever have cause to be jealous of my thoughts, it will be of those truants that slip off from our happy present to those dear old times."

"And you never regret that—that dream?"

"Yes, I regret its follies, but rejoice that it is over. I am awake now, and so happy!"

"But your ideal? You are sure you don't mind my light hair?" asked he suppressing a smile.

"Why, John, I like it!"

"Ha, ha! Love is not blind, but I am sure he wears glasses—nor my yellow moustache?"

"No!"

"Nor my large mouth?"

"That is benevolent!"

"In the way of kisses, very! As hereunto attested."

"Well, Ellen, there is one thing you do not like, and you must own it, with your usual candor. I shall not mind it at all, on the contrary, I agree with you perfectly—that is your objection to my name."

"John, I like it, I do, I declare I do! You need not laugh! It sounds honest, rugged and strong; and I like it because—"

"I won't laugh any more, finish your sentence."

"Because it is my husband's name, and he invests everything about him with his own sturdy manliness."

Thereupon followed a demonstration decidedly foolish, a fashion we laugh at, but must revere, since it bears date of the day when Adam kissed Eve in the garden of Eden.

"Ah, dearest, should I ever realize the highest and best within me, the merit will be yours.—God's best gift to me has been my own true wife!"

N. B. The wedding was a very private affair, nothing striking about it, not even a tone. What was the use of a grand display? The sum total of the matter was, that a beautiful girl named Ellen Clardy found something to admire, esteem and love, in a young man who signed his name—"John Smith, Esq."

LIME AS A FERTILIZER.

HAVING been frequently asked the value of lime as a fertilizer, and requested to state its specific uses in the economy of the farm, I propose to sum up the best established *practical* results derived from science, and confirmed by the experience of the most judicious authorities on the subject.

Lime is a substance familiarly known to all our farming communities, and is everywhere valued for its varied and important applications—so valued that some have regarded it "the basis of all good husbandry;" and even so excellent a judge as Prof. Johnston declares it to be "the most valuable and most extensively used of all the mineral substances that have ever been made available in practical agriculture."—A fertilizer that can claim such a high encomium from such a source, deserves to have its merits better understood—its nature, its modes of action, its practical results more thoroughly comprehended. We propose to confine our remarks to such points only as are applicable to carbonate of lime and its derivatives, such as quick lime, slaked lime, &c.

In the form in which it is usually offered in the market, and in which, therefore, it is most generally available for the farmer, lime is a caustic alkali, (burnt lime,) and this caustic quality is the main cause of its activity and efficiency in the service of the skilful agriculturist. The food we eat is not in a condition to nourish our bodies as it comes in its crude state from the harvest field—it must be cooked, masticated, and even when swallowed it cannot be taken up by the blood, and distributed through the system for the nourishment of our bodies, till it has been acted on by the gastric and other juices—it must be "digested." So with the plant; its food, too, must, in some sense, be cooked, masticated and digested, before it can be taken up and assimilated by the living organism.

Caustic lime is the cook that prepares the food, and the gastric juice that digests the nourishment for the plant. But while this digesting operation is, perhaps, in the great majority of cases where lime is artificially applied, its most important function, it must not be forgotten that this is not its only office; lime is not only the cook that prepares other food for the growing crop, but is itself essential to the nourishment of the plant, entering into its composition, constituting an important part of its inorganic elements, besides performing other valuable offices to be discussed as we proceed.

These general statements are sufficient to suggest the nature and character of the work which lime accomplishes for the practical farmer, and to show, in a general way, the foundation of its great reputation as a mineral fertilizer. But let us descend to particulars.

There are five modes of action by which mineral manures may profit the growing plant when applied to the soil.

1st. They may themselves become food for the growing crop.

2nd. They may digest and prepare the food already in the soil.

3rd. They may absorb gaseous fertilizers from the atmosphere, and retain them for the future use of the plant.

4th. They may destroy or neutralize substances in the soil which are poisonous or injurious to the crop.

5th. They may improve the mechanical condition of the soil.

Some mineral manures perform one of the offices, and some another, but lime accomplishes them all.

In regard to the first mode of action, chemical analysis settles the question; it shows that lime is present in the ashes of all our field crops, and that in some of them, as clover, peas, turnips, &c., it is a principal ingredient. Hence lime, if it be naturally deficient, may be usefully added to the soil simply as a food for the crop, and, if wholly wanting, its addition becomes an absolute necessity, as no crop could be matured without it.

In regard to the second point, lime may be considered as a specific; the most important service which it generally renders to the plant, when applied in large quantities, is the digestion and preparation of other manures, which, though found in the soil, are not in a condition to be absorbed by the roots, and thus made available, for immediate use.

By its caustic and alkaline properties, lime facilitates the decomposition of all vegetable and animal matters, liberating their nutritive elements, and converting insoluble, into soluble compounds, thus rendering them capable of being absorbed and appropriated.

Even the inert mineral masses of the soil do not escape the digestive action of lime: felspar and other minerals containing the silicates of potash and soda, more readily surrender, in the presence of lime, their treasures of potash and soda; and these alkalies in their turn help to convert the insoluble into soluble silicates, and thus supply to our cereals the elements that support their stems, enabling them to bear up against storm and wind; it is the absence of this soluble silica, which lime assists in digesting, that often causes our grain crops to fall to the ground before they are fully matured.

As to the third point, the absorption of fertilizing elements from the air, lime, both directly and indirectly, by its own action, and by its pulverizing effect upon compact soils, exerts a highly beneficial influence. True, it does not, like plaster of Paris, absorb ammonia directly from the atmosphere, but what is quite as much to the farmer's interest, it converts the ammonia which may be forming in the soil, into nitric acid, and thus fixes its valuable elements so as to prevent escape into the air. Moreover, we have the highest authority for saying that when organic matter is decomposing, in the soil, ammonia is generated by absorbing nitrogen from the air, and thus, as we have seen that lime promotes this decomposition, it promotes also, the formation of these most valuable manures from atmospheric elements.

In the fourth place, it is well known that lime will counteract the injurious acids, both organic and inorganic, which collect in damp soils where much vegetable matter is decomposing, and which render the land sour and unfavorable to successful cultivation. It is of the nature of an alkali, like lime, to neutralize these acids and make these sour lands sweet and mellow. Lime also decomposes and counteracts the injurious sulphates of iron, of magnesia, and of alumina, all of which sometimes abound to the serious injury of every variety of field crops, and often disappoint the hopes of the industrious laborer.

In the fifth place, that lime affects the mechanical constitution of the soil, would be naturally inferred from what we have seen of its power to decompose the earthy matters which contain the valuable mineral elements of the soil.

Lime, by pulverizing the solid particles, renders the land more loose and friable, at the same time that it liberates the valuable stores of nutritious matter locked up in them. By its chemical action it makes stiff and heavy clays more light and porous, while its mechanical effect is to render more compact the texture of looser soils.

Lime is thus the busy agent of the farmer, collecting, pulverizing, elaborating, digesting whatever it can find in air, earth or water, and diligently exacting tribute alike from the animal, vegetable and mineral kingdoms, for the use and support of the growing plant: it is not only itself a food, but it also acts as a digester, an absorber, a neutralizer and a mechanical improver. What more could be expected from a single fertilizer? This surely is a great deal, but it is not all.

Among the effects of lime Prof. Johnson enumerates several particulars in which it modifies even the character of the vegetation.—For instance, it alters the natural production of the soil by its tendeney to extirpate certain coarse grasses which infest some localities, and prevent the growth of richer and more nutritive kinds. "It kills," he says, "heath, moss, and sour and benty grasses, and brings up a sweet and tender herbage, mixed with white and red clover, more greedily eaten, and more nourishing to the cattle. Indeed all fodder, whether natural or artificial, is said to be sounder and more nourishing, when grown upon land to which lime has been abundantly applied." It is said also, that it "improves the quality of almost every cultivated crop:" all kinds of grains, peas, turnips, potatoes, &c., are found to be more suitable for food when grown on well-limed soils. It is claimed that it also "hastens the maturity of the crop," causing the small grains to mature from ten to fourteen days earlier on limed soils than on those unlimed. The quantity of lime necessary to accomplish these results when applied to cultivated lands, depends upon so many conditions of soil, climate and cultivation that no general rule can be given.

We learn from experiments carefully conducted in England, that "the quantity of pure lime contained in the crops produced upon one acre during four years rotation amounted, on an average, to 242 lbs." This gives us about 60 lbs. per acre, actually removed from the soil every year in composition with the vegetable matter, and which was necessary to its growth and healthy development. We thus see how much of this element may be needed for the actual *nourishment* of the plants, and how rapidly soils, not abundantly supplied by nature, must become exhausted of this essential ingredient, if it be not artificially applied.

Under such circumstances lands, which otherwise might be highly productive, may become sterile and useless.

But this statement only includes the lime necessary for a single one of the five uses specified above, and that one ordinarily demanding a less quantity than either of the others. If to this be added the amount sufficient for all the other purposes, we may appreciate more fully the quantities sometimes profitably employed in countries where agriculture is carried to the highest perfection. According to Bossingault "soil which is without a considerable proportion of the calcareous element, never possesses a high degree of fertility."

A simple calculation will show that where no lime is present in the land, it will require about 400 bushels per acre to give the small proportion of only one per cent. of lime for a depth of 12 inches below the surface.

Few soils are thus wholly devoid of lime, and much smaller quantities will suffice for all the purposes of agriculture. Bossingault informs us, that, in England, clay lands receive the large amount of from 230 to 300 bushels of lime per acre, and lighter lands from 150 to 200 bushels. This must be but once for a term of many years. In France the amount applied is greatly less, about 60 or 70 bushels per acre, at intervals of seven or eight years. Johnston tells us that in Great Britain a dose is on an average from 7 to 10 bushels, per acre, a year. In Flanders, where agriculture has achieved its greatest triumphs, the quantity used is not so large, only 10 or 12 bushels every three years.

In this country the experience is similar to Europe.

A practical farmer in Schuylkill county, Pennsylvania, writes: "The quantity (of lime) depends on the kind of soil and after-treatment. Heavy clay can bear 100 or more bushels to the acre, while, on light soils, from 50 to 80 bushels will answer very well." Another report from Chester county, Pennsylvania, says that, "lime is mostly spread on the sod at the rate of 30 to 60 bushels to the acre, once in each course of crops," and to show the practical results, it is added, "nearly all our land for miles around, was formerly worn out old fields, which would produce nothing, but the application of lime unlocked the hidden treasures of the soil and rendered available, as food for plants, the inert organic matter which it contained. This, accompanied by judicious cultivation and proper rotation of crops, has entirely changed the appearance of our neighborhood. Scarcely an old field is now to be found." Hon. T. G. Clemson, who was formerly connected with the Agricultural Department of the United States Government, remarks that so small a quantity as a bushel to the acre has produced good effects.

Governor Hammond, of South Carolina, one of the most successful, as well as intelligent planters the South has ever had, was accustomed to boat lime, in the condition of shell-marl, twelve miles up the Savannah river, for the use of his plantation, and apply it at the rate of 200 bushels per acre. The writer has witnessed on his light, sandy, pine lands, thus limed, a yield of 38 bushels of corn to the acre, while the same kind of land in an adjacent field, not limed, would scarcely average 10 bushels.—These statements show, at once, the importance of lime as a fertilizer, and the marked difference in the quantity which experience has shown to be best suited to the soil and climate of the several countries mentioned, and points out the necessity for a thorough understanding of the whole subject, in order to a judicious application of it. To apply to the loose and sandy soil of Flanders, the 200 or 300 bushels, per acre, which the Englishman finds desirable on his compact clay lands, or on his cold and tenacious heath meadows, would be a sad mistake.

Enough has been said to show that, comparatively, large quantities of lime are found to be useful in the experience of all these countries, where scientific agriculture has successfully worked out the highest practical results; but each individual must reflect for himself upon the principles involved, and upon their application to his particular case. It may be said, in a general way, that larger portions may be profitably added to stiff and heavy clays, than to light and sandy localities—to wet and marshy lands, than to dry and mellow regions, to deep rich loam, in which vegetable matter abounds, than to poor and exhausted fields. Indeed, as the primary object of using lime is to digest the organie substances already present, rather than to act as food for the plant, there being generally enough for that purpose naturally in the soil, it becomes a point of the first importance to have this organic matter abundantly present, and wherever this condition is fully met, as by the roots, grass and leaves of freshly cleared ground, or by green manures ploughed in, or by barn-yard composts, we may confidently use the lime with a liberal hand, but if these conditions be not complied with, damage and disappointment will follow, instead of the rich rewards anticipated.—More lime, also, may be safely applied in cold, than hot climates, and to land subject to deep tillage, than where ploughing is always shallow: for it is plain that a less quantity will suffice to supply the soil, if only four inches deep, than if it be ploughed 12 inches. Wherever, then, a system of high culture is proposed, both theory and practice suggest that we begin at first with a heavy liming, proportioning the quantity to the quality of the soil, and especially to the amount of organic matter it contains, and that this be followed at the close of every rotation of crops, embracing a period of several years each, with lighter limings. The Flemish rule, which gives the smallest quantity of any of the examples quoted above, requires 10 or 12 bushels, per acre, at the close of every three years, making an average of 3 or 4 bushels annually. This in Flanders yields the best results for the investment. In France and England, experience has indicated a much larger amount.

It need scarcely be added that the ultimate net profits of liming must depend, among other things, upon the cheapness and facility with which lime can be procured at the required locality.

All these points must be carefully weighed, if we would accurately balance the account of loss and gain.

But one thing is certain, that we of the desolated South are hopelessly ruined as an agricultural people, if we do not now avail ourselves promptly of all those artificial aids which are applicable to our case, and which have combined to make other countries agriculturally great.— The same practical wisdom, energy and earnestness which have made the marshes and sandy plains of Flanders the garden of Europe, can convert the abused and wasted regions of the South back again to even more than their primeval fertility and beauty.

The mode of application, like the question of quantity, depends much upon circumstances.

If the application is to be made to clay or boggy and peaty lands, or to such as have large supplies of inert vegetable matter, the lime should be slaked quickly and applied immediately, in a caustic state. When it is required on lighter lands, it should be "air-slaked," or allowed to slake slowly and spontaneously, by absorbing moisture from the atmosphere, as this gives it in a finer powder and somewhat milder form, and therefore, less liable to injure the tender herbage. But for general purposes, especially where the soil is light and poor, it is best that the lime should be well composted with rich vegetable mould, or such decayed vegetable matter as may be available: in this form it can be more regularly scattered, and its caustic power being somewhat masked in the compost, it is less liable to do injury, at the same time that it acts more promptly and efficiently upon the growing crop; this increased efficiency in the composted state is due to the fact that the digestive processes which lime ordinarily carries on in the soil, have already begun in the compost heaps, thus offering food for ready absorption. On this account, too, the longer it has been in this state the more fertilizing it becomes. It may be added also, with beneficial results to composts of *fresh* animal matters, as it so controls the fermenting process as to cause the valuable elements to form compounds which are not subject to evaporation, while, if lime had not been present, these same elements would have entered into combinations which are highly volatile and liable to escape: it should never be mixed, however, with animal manures which are *already decomposed*, as it expels the gaseous fertilizers existing in the mass before the lime is added. When properly composted with vegetable or animal matter, lime may be applied just as any other rich manure directly to the growing crop, whether it be tender grass, or clover, or grains of any kind: but if it is to be applied in the condition of slaked lime it will not produce its full effect at once upon the soil, and, therefore, as long an interval as possible should intervene between its application and the planting of the crop which it is intended to benefit—as, for instance, in the early fall for the benefit of winter and spring grain.

Some authorities, as Waring's Elements of Agriculture, and the American Muck Book, by Browne, with much plausibility, urge the use of a "lime and salt mixture" as containing more valuable qualities, both for manuring and digesting, than lime itself. This mixture is obtained by slaking fresh burnt-lime with water thoroughly saturated with salt, using the materials in the proportion of three bushels of lime to one of salt. The lime decomposes the salt, giving us chloride of lime and carbonate of soda, both valuable agents in promoting the fertility of the soils. To secure the more perfect combination of the lime and salt, the brine should not all be applied at once, but at intervals of a day or two, in order to give time for the changes to take place more thoroughly; and even after the slaking is completed, ten or twelve days should elapse before the mixture is used. There can be no doubt of the value of this compound, especially in cases where salt would be a desirable manure on its own account.

For evident reasons lime, when intended to benefit the land generally, should always be as evenly distributed, and as thoroughly incorporated with the soil as possible: it should not, however, be ploughed in very deeply as it has naturally a constant tendency to descend in the soil; and because, also, while near the surface, it is more easily reached by the air, which is essential to those digestive functions which constitute its chief value.

When quick-lime is added in large quanties to soils naturally wet, and which have not been sufficiently drained, the lime may form into a mortar, and become hardened to such a degree as to obstruct the free passage of water and air, as well as of the roots of the plants. Under such circumstances, of course, the lime would be an injury, and the remedy for the evil, thorough draining. On soils which are light, dry and poor in vegetable matter, a heavy application of pure lime would also prove injurious by rendering the land too open, and by its chemical effects causing the crop to "burn" as it is called.—In each of these cases, if the lime be added in a well composted state, all the evil consequences are at once averted, at the same time that additional supplies of warmth and nourishment are given to stimulate the growth of vegetation. Indeed, the opinion is maintained by some that lime may be indefinitely added without injury, provided we, at the same time, proportionally increase the organic elements of the soil.—Whether this be correct or not, it is certainly true that what is ordinarily spoken of as the exhausting effect of lime, is only the effect of the larger crops which it causes the soil to yield, and which, of course, requires more of the elements of the soil for its growth and maturity—what is needed under such circumstances is not less lime, bnt more organic food. It frequently has happened that even so valuable a fertilizer as lime has been wholly abandoned in particular localities in consequence of unskilful applications, or hasty inferences from partial experiments. Of course where nature abundantly supplies the soil with this important element, artificial additions would be waste of time and money. So, in like manner, when lime is applied, as in some parts of England, at the rate of from 40 to 60 bushels to the acre at the end of each rotation of crops, embracing a period of 4 or 5 years, it would be no argument against the moderate use of this agent, if after a lapse of years, these large additions should produce no sensible effects whatever in consequence of the soil having become fully saturated.—And, again, the time which is required for uncomposted lime to take its effect upon the soil is a fruitful source of discouragement and often of the abandonment of this valuable fertilizer. An experimental farmer, reporting his results for the first year writes, "I applied 100 bushels (of lime) to the acre on a corn stubble and planted again in corn, but saw very little profit to the crop."—In reference to the same soil and the same liming at the end of the third year he writes: "For the past two seasons I have mowed the finest of grass." Lime, though a most efficient and valuable fertilizer, is slow in developing its finest results—indeed it scarcely exhibits fully its true character, unless when applied in the composted state, till the second or third year after its application.

Lime is also distinguished for the permanence of its effects as a fertilizer. There is known to chemists a mysterious power called "disposing affinity," for the want of a better name, by which one substance while in the presence of another, is induced or influenced to enter into combinations which it would not form in the absence of the influencing body. This is the nature of many of the changes brought about in the soil by lime, and it is by virtue of this disposing power that it continues to act and retain its peculiar qualities as a fertilizer. The permanence of its action is further increased by its slight solubility; at the ordinary temperature it takes about 750 pounds of water to dissolve one of lime even in the caustic state, and still less can be dissolved after it has been acted on by the carbonic acid of the air. Thus it remains for a long time in the soil performing its important offices. It is said to produce sensible effects upon the crop after the lapse of 20 or 30 years, and some insist that a good supply, once added to the soil, never wholly ceases to be felt. This persistence in the effects of lime is a high merit, and one which insures to the farmer, sooner or later, if judiciously used, an ample interest upon his investment.

We have already seen that when lime is to be applied in the slaked condition, except in the case of stiff clays or rich vegetable mould, it should be slowly "air-slaked," because, in the latter case, it is not only more completely pulverized, but also of a milder character, as the caustic quality of about one-half of it is neutralized by combination with the carbonic acid of the air. As a labor-saving consideration, this slaking process should take place in the field, since, thereby, from one-fourth to one-half of the weight, and a large increase of the bulk, caused by the slaking, will be saved from transportation.

To effect this it may be piled up in heaps and covered with earth in the field, and left till it completely crumbles to powder: the covering of earth protects it from heavy rains which might convert it into mortar, and also from too free access of air which tends to change it back into the state in which it was before it was burnt. When prepared for distribution this may be accomplished by drawing it out from a cart into little heaps, from five to seven yards apart, and in quantities proportioned to the amount we desire to apply per acre, after which it can be evenly scattered. Some to accomplish the distribution more regularly, check off the land into little squares of convenient size, and apply a given quantity to each square.

Such is a general statement of the facts that seem to be best established in regard to lime as a fertilizer.

It may be useful, in conclusion, for convenient reference, to sum up the most important points of a practical character.

Lime, then, is useful to the farmer as food for his crop—as a digester of the animal, vegetable, and mineral manures in his soil—as an absorbent, indirectly, of valuable manures from the atmosphere—as a neutralizer of injurious acids and other poisonous compounds—as a pulverizer of his stiff clay soils, and as a general stimulant which improves both the quantity and quality of his produce.

The quantity of lime to be used depends on the character of the soil—on the abundance of organic matter—on the kind of cultivation—on the character of the climate—on the quantity already present in the soil, and on the cost of lime in the market where it is used.

The mode of application depends on the object chiefly aimed at. If to pulverize compact tenacious *clay* lands, the caustic, water-slaked condition is best;—if to act upon the *mineral* matter of lighter soils the milder, air-slaked form will do the work; but if to digest organic matter, or to serve the general purposes of a manure to enrich the soil and give it warmth and energy—to stimulate the plant and promote a prompt development, or whatever else may be deemed necessary, the composted state is greatly preferred.

Hence, every farmer should have his cattle-lots, and horse-stalls abundantly supplied with leaves, straw, grass and organic matter of every kind, to be trampled by his stock, and ultimately thrown into compost heaps with lime and vegetable mould, or peaty matter, which will absorb all the gases that might otherwise escape. The quantity of lime for these purposes need not be great. We have seen that, though in many cases large amounts may be profitably applied where it can be cheaply obtained, yet even very small quantities are highly useful, and experience indicates that these small quantities, frequently repeated, are more beneficial than larger amounts applied but once.

Let each farmer then do what he can, even if his efforts are confined to a few acres, for the time has come when our people must abandon the old system of extensive planting, and concentrate their time, energy, and means upon comparatively small areas of land, which, to be remunerative, must be stimulated to its highest capacity by all the appliances of science and art.

ARIEL.

"THE NEGRO: *Is he the progeny of Ham? Has he a soul? Or is he a beast? &c., &c.*"

When a quack comes into our cities, styling himself "King of Pain," and professing to cure all diseases, the simple are snared, and the wise—*laugh.* 'If he be a humbug, why not expose him?' ask the credulous of all doubters. 'The multitude flock to him, and if he be an impostor, the community will suffer, and it is the duty of our physicians to protect us, by exposing his false pretensions. Besides, he is making hundreds of dollars, where they make but one.' 'All true, but *cui bono?* the labor would be lost, for the easily duped are not likely to be influenced by argument.'

So we felt, when requested to review that shallowest, and most brazen of all quack effusions—"Ariel." But, it is urged, though the multitude of the duped will not be convinced, yet some may have their eyes opened to the true character of this disgraceful production. And, therefore, we make the attempt,—albeit, as one would shrink from dissecting a putrid carcass, so we shrink from running our pen through this farrago of corruption, folly, blasphemy, conceit and impudence. We will notice

1. His argument from Color. All Adam's descendants are white: but the negro is black: therefore not descended from Adam. Let us try this formidable weapon, and see how it cuts. Adam's descendants are white: but Indians are red; and as red is not white, as well as black is not white, therefore, Indians are not descended from Adam. But, *per contra*, Adam, he tells us, signifies "red;" the name denoting the complexion. Therefore, his descendants are red. And therefore Indians, and other red races, are the sole descendants of Adam. Again. The universal characteristics of negroes are "black skins, kinky-heads, flat noses, and thick lips," and yet, such is their beauty, that it has produced tremendous results! "that kind of beauty, that once seduced the sons of God, and brought the flood upon the earth"!

Again. The negro was in the Ark. But only 8 souls were in the Ark—Noah and his family. And as the negro is not descended from either of the sons of Noah, he must have been in the Ark, not as a soul, but as a beast.—But how is it proved that the negro is not descended from either of the sons of Noah? It is conceded by all that he did not descend from either Shem or Japhet. And it is argued, that neither did he descend from Ham. How? In this way. First, Ham himself could not have been a negro.—Neither his name nor the curse pronounced upon him proves it. The name *Ham* does not, primarily, signify *black*, but granting that it does, yet the *name* could not determine his color. Why not? Because if it does, then Shem's and Japhet's names must also describe their color. This is his argument from the *name.* But as the color of Shem and Japhet was the usual, normal color, there was no reason why *their* names should describe their color; whereas, on the supposition—*and we make the supposition solely for the purpose of testing the worth of his argument*—that Ham's color was not the usual color, then there would be a propriety in *his* name describing that abnormal color. His argument from the *curse* is as worthless as that from the *name*—although it be admitted that neither name nor curse, in itself, proved Ham to be a negro. The curse upon Ham could not, he says, have blackened his skin, kinked his hair, and flattened his nose, because the curse on our first parents, the curse on the serpent, the curse on Cain, the curse of Jacob on Simeon and Levi, did not "blacken the skin, kink the hair, and flatten the nose!" So that if the *same results* do not follow *all* curses, that follow, or are said to follow, *any one* curse, then they do not follow this last, at all! Accordingly, as Adam, when said to be cursed, did not, like the serpent when cursed, crawl on his belly and eat dust all his days, so it is clear he was not cursed at all! Again. He says that Ham "could not have been turned into a negro, for accidently seeing his father naked. Tremendous judgment for so slight an offence!"—This argument, if good for anything, would be equally good against the curse on Ham, or Canaan, to be "the servant of servants" for the crime of which he was guilty, exposing the nakedness of his father;—and is thus a reflection upon that God who inspired the curse of Noah. Having seen the character of his reasoning on Ham's name and curse, let us now see, secondly, his argument against the negro being among Ham's descendants. We know, says he, where Ham and his descendants went, what countries they peopled, and where they may be found at this day, and they all belong to the white race, with long, straight hair, high foreheads, high noses and thin lips, &c. He then endeavors to trace the course of two of Ham's sons, Mizraim and Canaan, but passes by the other two, Phut and Cush, the latter of whom is the father of the Cushites, (rendered *Ethiopians* about forty times in our English Bible,) to which stock the negro race belong: "Can the *Cushite change his skin?*"—"*Cush* shall soon stretch out her hands to God." "I will make mention of Rahab and Babylon to them that know Me: behold Philistia and Tyre, with *Cush;* this man was born there," &c. The infidel Gliddon himself says: "Kush, barbarian country, perverse race, being the Egyptian designatory name and title of *Negroes.*" The Cushite, or Negro, then, is the descendant of Ham. But, says Ariel, once white, always white: Ham himself was white, and therefore all his descendants *must be* white; and so we find them, everywhere, *all* having long, straight hair, high foreheads, high noses and thin lips! Indeed! Then this is more than can be said of all *Shem's* descendants or *Japhet's* either! Mr. Buckingham informs us, that the Arabs, near the Jordan, where the climate is intensely hot, have dark skins, flat features and coarse hair; and in the Hauran beyond, he found a family with negro features, a jet black complexion, and crisped hair, of whose genuiue Arab descent he could have no doubt. And Rozet says, that in Algiers there are many Arabs as black as negroes, and yet preserving all the characteristics of the Arab race. Bishop Heber was surprised to find natives of India as black as African negroes. And an American Missionary, Mr. Rankin, states that one in six of the natives of Hindostan are as black as a full-blooded African. The Jews in Cochin and Malabar are so black as not to be distinguished from the other inhabitants. Ethiopians, according to the Greeks, denoted both an Asiatic and an African people. Homer speaks of them as a divided race of men, living in the extreme East and the extreme West, (Odyss. 1, 23-24,) and Herodotus distinguishes the Eastern Ethiopians in Asia from the Western Ethiopians in Africa by the straight hair of the former, and the curly hair of the latter. He says: "The Eastern Ethiopians have their hair straight: those of Africa have their hair more crisp and curling than other men." "The Egyptians were of the opinion that the Colchians were descended from the troops of Sesostris: to this I myself was always inclined, *because they are black, and have their hair short and curling.*' "The circumstance of the Egyptian Priestess being *black*, explains to us her *Egyptian origin.*" The Egyptians *all white*, says Ariel. "The Priestess being *black*, explains her *Egyptian* origin," says Herodotus! In the recently opened tomb of Shishak, King of Egypt, B. C. about 970, there are found in his depicted army exact representations of the genuine negro race, both in color, hair and physiognomy. At a meeting of Anthropologists at Paris, a few months since, M. Quatrefages, one of the most eminent French savans, observed: "All travelers who have lived in countries where only the negro race dwelt, have remarked that sometimes children were born of paler color less distant from the white type. This, said M. Quatrefages, is to be explained by the influence of original white ancestors, whose type reappear exceptionally among their negro descendants. This re-appearance of the ancestral type is what is called *ativism;* and as black children are never found among the white races, it must be inferred, that if the negroes descend from the whites, the whites do not descend from the negroes."

We shall oppose, then, the testimonies of savans, historians, and intelligent travellers, to the reckless assertions of a bold ignoramus. We consider, for a moment,

2. His argument from Mummies. To demonstrate, beyond all doubt, that negroes are not the descendants of Ham, Providence, it seems, moved in an extraordinary manner, or inspired, the

posterity of Mizraim, Ham's son, to resort to an extraordinary thing, viz: embalming the dead, so that after ages might have ocular proof of the complexion of Ham and his children, and thus the slander of the parentage of the negro be forever rebuked! "No other nation, as such, then or since, embalmed their dead." "The people of Mizraim *alone*, of all nations of the earth, did so." "Millions of mummied bodies have been exhumed this century, but *not one negro* has been found among them." *Per contra*, the distinguished Hugh Miller affirms: "Negro skulls *of a very high antiquity* have been found among the mummies of the ancient kingdom of Egypt." Portraits of the negro are found on Egyptian monuments, and their skulls among the Egyptian mummies, as the eminent Dr. Morton in his "Crania Egyptiaca," shews. The museums of Europe demonstrate to be true what Ariel recklessly denies. So far from embalming being confined to one people, it is a fact well established, that the Romans, to some extent, embalmed; so did the ancient Peruvians, and the ancient inhabitants of the Canary Islands, and others.

But even Ariel feels that he has gone too far. He adds this note, at the end of his pamphlet: "Some few kinky-headed negroes have been found embalmed on the Nile, but they were generally *negro-traders* from the interior of the country, and of much later dates!" Kinky-headed beasts embalmed! Beasts trading in beasts, and trading with men! We consider

3. His argument from Ethnology. He tells us, that the sons of Mizraim, after settling Egypt, went to Asia, "which was settled by them," and "gave names to different parts of the country, which they retain yet." "The sons of Mizraim were Hind, Sind, Zeng, Nuba, Kanaan, Kush, Kopt, Berber and Hebesh; and that they founded, amongst others, the nations of Hindoos, and Turks, is unquestioned and undoubted by any intelligent scholar"!! For this wonderful information he refers us to the "Asiatic Miscellany," page 148, 4to. But the Asiatic Miscellany, page 148, 4to., gives us these words: "In the Rozit ul Suffa it is written that God bestowed *on Ham* nine sons, Hind, Sind, Zeng, Nuba, Kanaan, Kush, Kopt, Berber, and Hebesh; and their children having increased to an immense multitude, God caused each tribe to speak a different language; wherefore they separated, and each of them applied to the cultivation of their own lands." The Bible tells us that Ham had *four* sons, not nine, Cush, Mizraim, Phut and Canaan; and gives us also the descendants of Mizraim; Ludim, Anamim, Lehabim, Naphtuhim, Pathrusim, Casluhim, Caphtorim. And yet the dreams of an Oriental Fable are to set aside the teachings of the Word of God!

But this is not all. Not only the Hindoos, but the Saracens, the Scythians, the Turks, "the great Turko-Tartar Generals, Timour, Genghis Khan, Tamerlane, the chivalrous, the noble

Saladin, *all these were the children of Ham*"!! Now, his commentator, Adam Clarke, who is quite an authority with him, would have taught him better. "Magog, says Clarke, supposed by many to be the father of the Scythians and Tartars, or Tatars, as the word should be written; and in Great Tartary many names are still found, which bear such a striking resemblance to the Gog and Magog of the Scriptures, as to leave little doubt of their identity." So, likewise, Calmet: "Magog, son of Japhet, and father as is believed of the Scythians and Tartars, a name which comprehends the Getœ, the Goths, the Samaritans, the Sacœ, the Massagetœ and others. The Tartars and Muscovites possess the country of the ancient Scythians, and retain several traces of the names Gog and Magog." The Turanian stock, to which the Tatars, the Turks, belong, is a branch of the Japhetick, as the learned Bunsen shews.

In order to prove the impossibility of the negro being the descendant of Ham, that worthy and his posterity are exalted by Ariel to the highest pitch, so that the curse is transferred virtually to Shem and Japhet, they being made "servants of servants" to the illustrious Ham! "Ham—the maligned and slandered Ham—*governed and ruled the world* from the earliest ages after the flood, and for many centuries, and gave to it all the arts and sciences, manufactures and commerce, geometry, astronomy, geography, architecture, letters, painting, music, &c., &c.!!" Ham-All-ogy! We find even some Divines believers in this Ham-all-ogy, ascribing all the learning and wisdom of ancient Egypt to the children of Ham. It would be well for such to ponder the following facts: "There can be no doubt," says Robinson's Calmet, "that Egypt was *peopled from the East.* We find Egypt peopled in the days of Abraham, and governed also by a Pharaoh. There is reason to think that the posterity of Shem transmigrated into Egypt. Appearances indicate that the first Pharaohs of Egypt spoke the language of Abraham, Jacob and Joseph; and that Jehovah, the God of those Patriarchs, was not unknown to them."

The *Hyksos*, a warlike shepherd race, entered Egypt *from the East* about 2,100 Before Christ, overpowered the country, and held it for 511 years. In so long a period, how greatly must the character of the country have changed, under the dominion of a foreign race!—The learned Encyclopœdia of Herzog has this significant statement: "The primitive language of Mizraim is now fully supplanted by the Arabian, just as its people also, by a long-continued intermixture, and by a subjection of nearly 1,200 years, under a *second* Hyksos dominion, has become almost entirely Semitick." The language and the people of Ham almost entirely supplanted, in Egypt, by those of Shem!

So much for the Ethnology and Ham-all-ogy of Ariel. The negro cannot be the descendant of Ham, says he, for if he were, "he would be our social, political and religions equal." Are all the descendants of *Japhet* our social, political and religious equals?

(TO BE CONTINUED.)

THE HAVERSACK.

On the retreat from Dalton, and a few days after the death of General Polk, General Johnston walked out alone to the skirmish line, during a lull in the firing, in order to ascertain, as far as practicable, the position and strength of the enemy. He came upon two soldiers in such earnest conversation, that they did not hear his approach. One of them was a bronzed veteran of many a hard-fought field. The other was a raw recruit, one of the "new issue," as the phrase was. The veteran was laying down certain great principles in morals, and discoursed after this manner:

"Now, Jim, you've got some notions about serving your country, and thinking about nothing but your country. That's all well enough, but I tell you a fellow may as well look out a little for himself. Yesterday, I put my rifle to my shoulder and drew a bead on a Yankee, when I saw that he was too little, and his clothes would'nt fit me. So I waited till a fellow of about my own girth showed himself, when I took a sure aim upon him and *here's his boots!*"

The old reb's patriotism was about on a par with that of the loyal worshippers of the best Government the world ever saw. With all their love of country, they have managed "to look out a little for themselves," and have got in as Collectors, tax-gatherers, internal revenue kites, or vultures of the Freedmen's Bureau. The evidences of shoddy, but patriotic wealth by which they are surrounded, bring up the old reb's exclamation, "here's his boots," yea, and the booty too.

W——, of Harrisonburg, Va., was as brave and true a soldier, as he is an accomplished gentleman. But Nature has given him very long and slender legs and it was not always possible to get a pair of pants, in the Quartermaster's scanty supply, of sufficient length for these attenuated extremities. One day, he drew a pair of pants, which were two feet too short, and as he passed by a line of soldiers, they seemed to be a good deal attracted by the appearance of the protruding appendages. One fellow gazed so earnestly at the gallant W——, that he became offended, and said to the impertinent gazer,

"I hope that you will know me next time."

The man made no answer, and W—— stalked on indignantly, when he heard his tormentor remark,

"That must be a powerful brave man to venture out in the war on such a par (pair) of legs."

Rev. E. C——, near Washington, D. C., tells an incident of a retreat of the army of our Northern brethren, after one of the great disasters in Virginia. He heard a demoralized squad of blue coats recounting their adventures and misadventures, when one of them said,

"Well, boys, there are only two persons on the earth or under the earth, I fear, and they are Stonewall Jackson and the Devil!"

We would say editorially, to the speaker on this interesting occasion, it is well that children do not always inherit the terrible qualities of their parents; otherwise you would have to fear Stevens, Stanton, Bingham, and many other legitimate sons of the numerous family of the latter individual, named above.

Soon after the firing upon, and driving back of the Star of the West, in Charleston Harbor, in 1861, two negroes were overheard talking about the event, in the cars between Branchville and Columbia.

Tom. Whar you bin, Jim?

Jim. Down dar in Charleston trowing up de fortification.

Tom. Was you dar, when dey bin fitin'?

Jim. Speck dis child was just thar, and no whar else. De Yankee ships, he come in monstrous, saucy like. Den our boys, dey shoots at 'em, when the big ship cut dirt and run. Ky, how he run!

Tom. Was you skeered, Jim, when dey was shootin' de big guns?

Jim. Skeered? Bless the Lord, no. *Dey was shootin' toder way!*

There are a great many brave people after the manner of poor Jim, when the shooting is the other way. The Jacobin rebels who never faced a Southern foe, are now fierce and warlike, when the shooting is all in their own hands, and no balls are thrown back.

The Rev. Mr. D., of Harrisonburg, Va., gives the next anecdote:

In the summer and fall of 1861, it was the misfortune of quite a number of young men, who wore the grey jacket, to be stationed for many weeks upon Valley Mountain in West Virginia. Nobody who was there can ever forget how the rain poured down day and night through all those dreary weeks, and how the only "tap" for the poor soldier was the water, which fell upon those everlasting hills. "Rations were scanty and corn meal the order of the day." Surgeon C., of the 21st Virginia regiment, was sitting at his tent door on one of those bleak, gloomy days, wondering if the rain would never cease, wondering if we would finally succeed in whipping the Yankees, when a Tennessee lieutenant came along looking the very picture of woe. Rumor said that the lieutenant was too fond of his cups, when at home, but here he was of necessity a member of a Total Abstinence Society. The Doctor, a wag in his way, and at all times ready and willing to beguile an idle hour with chat, calls in the lieutenant and enters into a conversation with him.—The subject uppermost in the minds of soldiers naturally came up, and the length of the war and its probable results were fully discussed.

"Well, lieutenant," said the surgeon, "after this much experience in the army, what do you think of war?"

The lieutenant looked out on the falling torrents, and visions of a cosy room at home, and decanters and glasses passed before him, heaving a deep sigh, he answered:

"I am no military man, doctor, and therefore am not able to express any opinion upon military matters, *but I regard the war as the most gigantic temperance movement the world ever saw!*"

An Ex-Chaplain, now residing at Shelbyville, Tennessee, gives the anecdote below:

On the campaign in West Virginia, the infantry were fond of cracking their jokes at the expense of the cavalry. They insinuated pretty plainly that the cavalry had to be brought on by degrees and gradually made accustomed to fire-arms by first popping caps, then putting in blank cartridges, and finally allowing balls to be slipped into their rifles.

Capt. N., now living in Winchester, Tennessee, tells how he was victimized by the infantry. He was riding by Donelson's Tennessee brigade of infantry with a long clanking sabre, when he was accosted by a little fellow in the ranks, who was carrying a knapsack almost as big as himself,

"Mister, I'm most dead toting this knapsack, it's powerful heavy, it is, Mister, *if you'll tote it for me, I'll let you pop one of my caps!*" B.

From Winchester, Va., we get an anecdote of one of the bravest men who ever breathed the breath of life:

THE EXILE'S ROMANCE.—There is no man, however practical and prosaic, who is not moved when he is brought face to face with some of the grand scenes of Nature. In proof of this, I will relate an actual occurrence. Two years ago, I visited Niagara Falls with a distinguished Confederate General, now an exile—one whose name would recall a hundred battle-fields. Now, though the General was a superb soldier, he had never been accused of poetry and romance, and I was curious to see what effect Dame Nature would have on his unromantic temperament. He and I went under the Falls to get a better view, and it was while impressed by the sublime spectacle there presented that I watched him most particularly. For five minutes neither of us spoke. The romance in the General's nature had been stirred up at last. He stood silent and thoughtful, his eyes beaming with lustre as they used to beam in the days of battle; his whole soul seemed to drink in the glorious picture. Suddenly, above the roar of the Falls, I heard his shrill voice, "Oh that that old water-fall could be turned over to the other side and sweep off the whole Yankee Nation.—What a blessing for humanity it would be!" T.

It seems from this anecdote that nature inspires men in different ways, but we still see the truth of the maxim, "the ruling passion strong in death."

Many of our Trans-Mississippi

readers have never heard the anecdote of General Milroy, U. S. A., and John Arnold's cow, and we therefore repeat it, though it has often been told, and rather because it is necessary to the full understanding of a recent adventure of the same distinguished soldier.

While the notorious General was in command, at Winchester, Va., he issued an order for the seizure of rebel hay, fodder, corn, &c. A party of soldiers came to carry off a small hay rick, belonging to one John Arnold, a poor man, but true as steel in his love for the South. His daughter went to Milroy to beg for the hay. That chivalrous soldier answered.

"You shall not have it, unless your father will take the oath."

"That he won't do," replied the spirited girl. The colloquy took something of the following form:

Gen. Milroy, U. S. A. "Take the oath and keep the hay."

Miss Arnold. "Can't take the oath and the cow will starve this winter without the hay."

Gen. Milroy, U. S. A. "Let her starve, the rebellion must be suppressed."

Miss Arnold. "Well, General, if you expect to suppress the rebellion, by starving John Arnold's cow, you may, and be hanged to you!"

The great soldier took, as his head-quarters, in Winchester, the elegant mansion of Mr. Logan, and during his occupation, Mr. Logan's spoons and piano disappeared in a mysterious manner. The man of much booty, however, was roused up one morning with the pleasant intelligence that Ewell and Early were upon him. Mounting a swift horse, he retired with something like the speed of Schenck, from Vienna, or Lew. Wallace from the Monocacy. Years rolled by, John Arnold's cow lived, but the rebellion died. Milroy returned to the scene of his former glory, but the piano and the spoons returned not. Milroy, the great military chieftain, thought he would become Milroy the great orator and statesman, and he made a speech to the people of Winchester, advising them to accept the mild, just, and equitable measures of Reconstruction proposed by the patriotic Congress of the best Government the world ever saw. The people of Winchester came to hear Milroy, and Milroy was compelled to hear the people of Winchester. The speech had some interruptions and comical interludes.

Milroy. "I am more accustomed to fight than to speak."

1st Auditor. "Where's Ewell."

2nd Auditor. "Hurry up, General, Early is coming."

Milroy. "Congress in its wisdom has proposed certain measures as conditions precedent to your restoration to the glorious Union."

3rd Auditor. "What measures has Congress taken about John Arnold's cow?"

4th Auditor. "What measures for the restoration of Mr. Logan's piano?"

5th Auditor. "Has Congress said anything about restoring Mr. Logan's spoons?"

Amid pleasant inquiries of this

sort the noble Milroy struggled on. The rattle of squibs around him, however, *did* tell upon his nerves. He would raise both hands above him and atttempt to articulate, but no words would come. At length a broadside came, which brought him down as well as the house. An Irishman, on the extreme edge of the crowd, cried out in a clear, distinct voice, which was heard above the uproar, "faith, Gineral, we've had enough of yer spaach, now bring out Mrs. Logan's piano and play us a tune!"

Maj. G., of Staunton, Virginia, gives an anecdote of Stonewall Jackson:

After the first battle of Fredericksburg, the General was riding with one of his Division commanders past an encampment at Corbin's Neck. The weather was horrible, and the men, without tents and with but few blankets, were stretched upon the ground, trying to keep warm before the log fires. The General's companion was deeply impressed with the suffering of the soldiers, and said with much feeling, "poor devils, poor devils." General J. instantly correcting him, said, "call them suffering angels."

This was the opinion held of the Southern soldiery by Jackson, the man of prayer. Butler, the man of spoons, and the old negro-traders of the South, call them traitors.

The sister of a distinguished cavalry general sends us the following anecdote from Vicksburg:

After the fall of New Orleans my brother-in-law and family found a refuge in Jackson, Miss., where, purchasing a cottage in the suburbs, he made an effort to surround his family with the comforts of home, and to be in a measure self-subsistent, provided himself with cows, horses, poultry, &c. Feeling the war was to be of some duration, he also purchased supplies which he hoped to last him for a year or two.—Quietly settled there, of course one of the most intense anxieties was to learn "the news." Every day the newspapers were eagerly devoured, or refugees questioned by the ladies of the family; and the outrages of the yankees, the burning and sacking of houses, the equipping themselves in ladies' clothing, tearing and destroying children's and babies' clothes were recapitulated to my brother-in-law. He being a man full of chivalry and tenderness towards women and children listened, but with an evidently doubting spirit, or would sometimes laugh at our credulity. But at last, on that memorable 14th of May, 1863, Gen. Grant made his appearance, with his army, at Jackson. Believing, as did almost every one, that it must be a mistake, that the yankees were not coming to Jackson, my brother-in-law remained until the lest moment, until shell were falling almost in the yard, when, being just outside our fortifications, he had to hurry his family into the carriage, in a hard rain, and leaving everything, took refuge in town, where there was at least safety from shot and shell. Three days afterwards, when the yankees had finished their work of burning and pilfering, and set their faces towards Vicksburg, my brother-in-law went out to look and see what was left to him. Not a vestige of any thing movable remained; his wife's and children's clothes were gone or torn into ribbons, the house was stripped, the provisions gone, except half a barrel of sugar, which was polluted by them. An old negro man, who remained faithful, reported they had several times set fire to the house, which he extinguished; they had washed their feet over the cisterns, letting the water run into them, and killed every living thing except one hen, which had escaped by hiding in the grass, and about fifteen chickens of from a week or two to a few days old, which were the remains of a hundred and fifty of the same ages. These were all trying to follow the old hen, who, under the circumstances, must have had a yankee cross in her, as she was pecking at them, while they were shying around with a truly orphan air. As he looked around upon the desolation I asked him what he thought of the yankees now? He gave a glance around and said, "I don't believe there is a man living *damned enough liar to tell the truth about them!*"

EDITORIAL.

THE English satirist called the Radical of the French Revolution monkey-tiger—at one moment engaged in fantastic tricks and the next lapping up blood like water. The epithet was eminently applicable to the Jacobin of France, but may be applied with still more pertinence to the Jacobin of America. The French Jacobin drank toasts and sang songs in honor of liberty, equality and fraternity, and then ordered a few hundred thousands to be shot, a few hundred thousands to be drowned, and a few hundred thousands to be beheaded. The American Jacobin sings songs about John Brown's soul, and is as playful as a young ape, till the time comes for decreeing the utter ruin of ten States, and the lingering death of four millions of negroes. The war shut us off from a practical acquaintance with the American Jacobin, during the administration of the man, who went to Washington's bosom from Ford's Theatre, but we learn that the American Jacobin, for all that period, was alternately engaged in murder and monkey tricks.—He could be seen with pious care draping church—steeple and pulpit—with the beautiful "flag of the nation," and then with soft step and humble mien, he would ascend the ornamented pulpit and pray to a God of mercy to afflict the South until husband and father could see despair in the eyes of his wife and hear the wail of starvation from the lips of his children. At one time, in a playful mood, he would insert secular songs in hymn books and political speeches in volumes of prayers; then he would incite to house-burning, pillage and plundering, and even to starving prisoners.—The monkey and tiger were so equally divided in his nature that it was impossible to say whether the Jacobin did more foolish things or more wicked ones. But it was always noticeable that his fun and his jokes ended invariably in blood.

There is, since the war, the same nice adjustment of monkey and tiger in the Jacobin rebel of America. With inimitable humor, he declares that life and property are insecure in the South. So far the monkey. But this "little joke" is accompanied with certain measures which to execute requires the ferocity of the tiger rending his victim. One of the monkey tricks to amuse the public is a heavy appropriation for a burial corps, whose duty it is to provide suitable coffins, graves and head boards for the Irish, German, English, French, Spanish, Italian, Indian and African soldiers, who gave their lives "to save the life of the nation." But while this patriotic clap-trap deceives no one, and only suggests that these men need not have died, and would not have died, had the monkey-tiger never lived, there are thousands who remember the tiger-cruelty of forbidding any record to be kept of Confederate graves at Baltimore, so that their friends might never reclaim their dust.

The same curious blending of monkey and tiger seems to characterize all the acts of the Jacobin rebels. Childish frolic is followed by blood-thirsty acts. Puerile, undignified amusement is the prelude to the most fiendish acts of oppression. Thus the frivolous, absurd charges trumped up against the President appears to be only the fun of a set of half-grown boys, but they meant the overthrow of the Government of our fathers, and the striking down of two of the coördinate departments of the Federal system. Thus we fancy we hear the hand-organ playing, and see the monkey dancing and picking up coppers, when the Chicago Convention playfully and jocosely says, "this Convention declares its sympathy with all the oppressed people, who are struggling for their rights!!" It is a rich and racy joke, and was doubtless hugely enjoyed by the humorous gentlemen, who perpetrated it. But we see the crouching tiger gnashing his teeth, as well as the monkey dancing round the hand-organ. This sympathy with the oppressed means Freedmen's Bureau and its swarm of unclean animals.—It means degradation of the white race and exaltation of the black. It means military domination, garrisons of soldiers every where, unequal taxation, favoring the rich and grinding the poor. It means the persecution for all time of as brave and as noble a people as the sun ever shone upon. It means the turning into a wilderness the fairest portion of the land. It means the total destruction of all the products of the South, upon which the prosperity of the whole nation depends.—

It means the erection of a huge centralized despotism, which shall dictate to the people what religious worship they shall observe, what amusements they shall enjoy, what food they shall eat, what clothing they shall wear, and what fluids they shall drink. It means intolerance in all things, crushing out all semblance of opposition in speech and thought to "the party of great moral ideas."

These immaculate men are just now in a sad strait. They have been tinkering at the work of reconstruction for three years, when it could have been accomplished in a day, by justice and magnanimity. Now when the grand work has been accomplished, they do not know whether to approve or condemn their own labor of three years. They are doubtful whether they can trust the negroes, still more doubtful whether they can trust the old nullifiers and negro-traders, who manipulated the loyal Conventions.—These old rebels betrayed the loyal North, then they betrayed the rebellious South, then they betrayed Mr. Johnson, who gave them posts of trust and honor. May they not betray the saints next fall, when the Democracy will be sweeping everything before them. Ah! there is danger, there is danger!

Another thing, too, is alarming. The Constitutions framed in these Fetich Conventions, by negro-traders, bankrupts, swindlers, and adventurers, have in all of them an element of repudiation. They show plainly the *animus* of the loyal men of the South, and it is not a very amiable one in the eyes of the loyal North. The beginning of repudiation will be like the letting out of the great waters—a small leak at first, but soon overwhelming the whole land in a sweeping flood. Let it once start in the South, and the payment of the national debt will be the easiest job imaginable. The Jacobin rebels have had their fun over the negro orgies at the South. The hand-organ played, and the monkeys danced. With profound gratitude to the Author of all good, we venture to predict that the tiger part of the play will never take place. The great Democratic party has looked on with profound disgust at the farce. It will step in and forbid the tragedy.

It is impossible for the Editor of this Magazine to have a newspaper controversy of a personal character, with Mr. E. A. Pollard, however ardently he may desire the distinction of being thus noticed. The *author* of a pretended history could be exposed in these columns without impropriety, but it would be undignified to allude to the *man*. The February number, which pointed out the blunders, misrepresentations, and slanders of the so-called history of Mr. E. A. Pollard, contained no personalities about that individual himself, save that having occupied a bomb-proof during the war, and never having seen a battle-field, he was an unfit person to describe all the hundreds of battle-fields of the war. He has replied to this number in a very scurrilous article in the New York *News*, full of personalities as gross as they are untrue. If he were as well known everywhere as he is in his native State, and especially in Richmond, where he has longest resided, it would be useless to repel his slanders, his own character does that sufficiently. But as he is not thus well-known, it may be proper to show how very unscrupulous he is in private matters, that the world may see how wholly unfit he is to play the part of the historian.

In this article, Mr. E. A. Pollard says: "But seriously, no one knew better than D. H. Hill, at whose procurement, and from whose affectionate supplies of information the writer consented to make a memoir of his deeds, and include it in his book, (Lee and His Lieutenants.) Until these persuasions, he had decided to omit the hero of Bethel from his list of biographies."

Now, Mr. E. A. Pollard *knew* that this was wholly untrue. He first sent me a circular asking information about my early life, and of the battles I had been in, &c. I did not notice the circular at all. He then wrote himself, repeating the substance of the circular, and urging me to give the desired information. To this letter, I replied, declining to give him any incidents in my life, and politely, but firmly forbidding him to incorporate my biography in his "Lee and His Lieutenants."—Nor did I, for a single moment, suspect that it was there until after the publication of the book. The pretended historian, who is so regardless of truth in matters of personal, and therefore, subordinate, importance, is not to be entrusted with the momentous interests of a nation. The Confederacy deserves to have a man of truth as her annalist.

Spite of the "affectionate supplies of information" given to Mr. E. A. Pollard, he calls me a "female school-master." This was intended as a disparagement and an insinuation that there was something unmanly in the calling of a teacher, though he knows very well that Stonewall Jackson, Rodes, and very many of the bravest officers in both armies had made teaching their vocation. My self-constituted biographer ought to have known too, that my connection with a school was with the one, over which Lee now presides, and that I was never a teacher in a primary school, whether male or female. However, as Lee, Meade and Stonewall Jackson have been associated with schools *in time of peace*, the world will hereafter regard the position of a teacher as honorable as the bomb-proof, which Mr. E. A. Pollard occupied *in time of war*.

In one sense of the word, Mr. E. A. Pollard has received from me "abundant supplies of information." As Editor of The Land We Love, I have collected sketches of Confederate Generals, and numerous anecdotes and incidents of the war, which Mr. E. A. Pollard has appropriated bodily, article after article, page by page, word for word, without asking my permission, without quotation marks and without any acknowledgment whatever, of the source from which he got them!! If the supplies have not been "affectionate," the appropriation of them has at least been so!

The Cincinnati *Enquirer* and Louisville *Courier* exposed Mr. E. A. Pollard's gross plagiarism from Duke's "Life of Morgan." Colonel Henry K. Douglass exposed a like theft of an article of his in the *Old Guard*. But the most stupendous, wholesale plagiarism, ever perpetrated in the literary annals of the world, is the stealing of Mr. E. A. Pollard from THE LAND WE LOVE. It is monstrous, and unprecedented in the vast amount stolen, monstrous and unprecedented in the shameless and bare-faced manner in which it has been done. Let the reader compare the sketches in THE LAND WE LOVE, of Polk, A. P. Hill, Cleburne, and Price, with the same in "Lee and His Lieutenants," and then let him notice that all the anecdotes of Lee, Early, &c., have been taken out of the *Haversack* of THE LAND WE LOVE, and he will form some idea of the character of Mr. E. A. Pollard. The question is submitted to the candid reader whether the man, who is so unscrupulous in regard to taking that which belongs to another, would have any hesitation about misrepresenting the facts of history. It is the more unpardonable, because committed by the man, who had so grossly slandered me in his pretended history. It is adding theft of property to attempted theft of character.

In "Lee and His Lieutenants," and in this article in the *News*, Mr. E. A. Pollard sneers at my literary claims. However mortifying this unfavorable opinion of the great plagiarist may be to my self-love, I will frankly forgive him, if he will only promise not to borrow any more from my literary productions.

Mr. E. A. Pollard bravely says of himself "as to any personal care in the matter, he has never feared critical attacks, with pistols or without pistols. Wise or otherwise," &c. The world has never been disposed to honor the man, who boasts of his own courage. I have been in two wars and in as many engagements as Mr. E. A. Pollard has years upon his head, and yet I have never felt that I had any right to boast of that quality. Still, I have had grace given me to stay under fire till each fight had closed, while my observation was that the few bullies and braggadocios in the army left just before or just after the firing began. Most of this class, however, got into bomb-proofs and never heard the whistle of a ball, contenting themselves with growling and barking at all, who were going to the front.

Mr. E. A. Pollard frankly acknowledges that he *writes* for money. No fair-minded man can object to this. The objection is that he *slanders* for money, that he has produced a book, which Confederate officers of every grade, from the highest to the lowest, and Confederate soldiers of every arm of the service, have pronounced a libel upon history.—Mr. E. A. Pollard cannot name a single respectable Confederate, who will declare that the book is worth the paper upon which it is written. But nothing can be said by any one half so damaging as the acknowledgment made by Mr. E. A Pollard himself that it was produced in five months.—The editorials of the Richmond *Examiner* were pasted together with the sensational letters of army correspondents, and the medley was called the history of the "Lost Cause!"

But to the matter in dispute. Mr. E. A. Pollard stated in his pretended history that a dispatch from Gen. Lee at Frederick, Md., and directed to me was thrown down by me in a fit of passion and thus fell into the hands of McClellan. I pronounced the allegation a slander and demanded proof from an eye-witness. So dramatic an incident must have been seen by some one, or else it could not have been reported without making up a fabrication from beginning to end. Any Court of Justice in the world would pronounce the allegation a slander, if it was not proved by an *eye-witness.* Now what proof does Mr. E. A. Pollard bring up? He quotes from an English book and an English magazine! Whether he quotes correctly or not I do not know. This is all upon which to base as gross a slander as ever was uttered! Did the writer in the book or in the magazine witness this petulant act of throwing down the dispatch? No, they got it from American sources, of course,—from the sensational army correspondents or from Mr. E. A. Pollard in his bomb-proof at Richmond.

I deny that I threw down Lee's dispatch and demand the proof of an *eye-witness.* I could, with as much justice, be charged with being engaged in the John Brown raid.

The matter, however, need not rest upon a simple denial. The Adjutant of my Division, Maj. J. W. Ratchford, makes oath that no order came to us at Frederick from Lee direct. This living witness ought to know as much about the matter as Mr. E. A. Pollard or the English writers.

Gen. McClellan states that a dispatch from Lee and directed to me was found near Frederick. There is no doubt whatever of the truth of the statement. But I deny that it was thrown down by me in a fit of passion, or that it was lost by my carelessness, and I demand the proof for either of these allegations.

In the article referred to I had occasion to expose either the ignorance or prejudice of the pretended historian. I showed that he had omitted to mention my Division at Cold Harbor though it was one of the four heavily engaged, and there were but four. I showed that at Seven Pines, he gave Longstreet the credit of taking Casey's works, when my Division did it, and Longstreet had not a single man engaged. I showed a flat contradiction of Lee's Report of Malvern Hill and a suppression of a part of Lee's Report of Sharpsburg. I showed that he had falsely charged me with contumacious conduct at McLe More Cove and the proof was a statement from that peerless soldier, P. R. Cleburne. The story was a sheer fabrication out and out, and I appeal with confidence to Bragg, Buckner, Hindman, any and all of the Army of Tennessee that it was never heard of till Mr. E. A. Pollard's book came out.

It is idle to attempt to follow up so unscrupulous a man in any new slanders that he may put out. His last one is of misconduct, at Chickamauga. He *knows* that this is untrue.

One more specimen of his utter unscrupulousness, and I am done. He says that I attribute his unfairness to jealousy of North Carolina troops. There is not the slightest hint or intimation of such a thing in my article! The division, whose services Mr. E. A. Pollard ignored, was composed of troops from Virginia, Georgia, Mississippi, Alabama, and North Carolina. My corps had not a single North Carolina regiment in it! Mr. E. A. Pollard has taken the trouble to make a statement, which is foolish, as well as untrue. I will not attempt to keep up with his future slanders. He may next connect me with the assassination of Mr. Lincoln. I feel sure that he is harmless, however malignant. The American people will not respect the zealous advocate of the war, who crept into a bomb-proof when the bullets began to fly, snarled and snapped while there, alternately at Mr. Davis and Mr. Lincoln, at Confederates and Federals, and then crawled out when the firing was over, to make money, by stealing the property and defaming the character of Confederate soldiers.

BOOK NOTICES.

ANTE BELLUM. SOUTHERN LIFE AS IT WAS. By Mary Lennox. Published by J. P. Lippincott & Co. Philadelphia:

This volume is gotten up in Lippincott's usually beautiful style, and the contents are free from all immoral *isms*.

THE EMPLOYMENTS OF WOMEN. A CYCLOPEDIA OF WOMAN'S WORK. By Virginia Penny. Walker, Wise & Co. Boston:

This book supplies a want which has been felt for a long time.

It seems sad to think that women should ever be compelled to earn their own living. God made one sex physically strong—the other weak—but here, as in other things, extremes meet. In barbarous nations, women are almost on a level with beasts of burden—in those cities, such as Paris, which boast of the highest degree of civilization, the condition of women, *en masse*, is scarcely any better. It is not a law of Nature that women should "eat bread in the sweat of her brow"—that curse was only pronounced upon man.

But the cry for "work," comes

from all parts of this once happy land. "Give us work or we perish," is the heart-rending wail which arises from the homesteads of the South, where plenty once reigned. The husbands, fathers, brothers, and sons lie in the graves to which they were sent by their *dear* brothers of the North, and the broken-hearted widows and orphaned children must struggle for existence. We can only endeavor to assist them in the struggle, and comfort them with the thought that it is better to be Abel than Cain. At the South, agricultural pursuits engrossed the greater portion of the population, and now, in the present condition of things, there is neither agriculture nor manufactures suitable for the feeble strength of women and children. Still, there are some articles which can be manufactured at home, with a little instruction, and which, although the profits be small, will keep the wolf from the door. Straw plaiting, for instance, is light and easy work, and Virginia Penny tells us that "in 1855, 6,000,000 straw hats were made in Massachusetts, giving employment to *ten thousand of her people.*" Rye straw is the kind generally used. It is cut, soaked in water and dried. The plaiting is mostly done in farmers' families. Philadelphia is said to spend $6,000,000 annually in the manufacture of straw goods. Some of the straw plaiters earn from $4 to $5 a week. They work at home.

The manufacture of willow ware,—baskets, &c., is another occupation suitable for women and children. For the finer kinds of basket work, some practice, and a set of tools will be necessary. The tools cost $5, and will last a life-time.

Willow grows abundantly in many portions of the South, and baskets, &c., of all kinds command a much higher price than at the North. "A German woman asked $1.50 for a basket she had paid fifty cents for making—at that rate her profits were considerable. I met a German boy, with baskets, who said he could make from 75 cents to $1 a day by his work."

Virginia Penny calls attention to another branch of industry which might suit Southern women—bee culture. She says "most of the honey used in the United States, is collected in the South. In keeping bees, there is no expense. The hives can easily be made at home, or purchased at a comparative trifle. Their food they seek themselves. In many of the rural districts of England, the bee mistresses earn a living by selling honey. A new species of bee that build in trees instead of hives is about to be introduced by Government from Paraguay."

Canning fruit, and making preserves and pickles, for sale, is another profitable branch of female industry. An extensive public manufacturer writes to our authoress, "I employ women in packing pickles and all goods of this kind into glass—making jellies, jams, &c., bottling syrups, &c. The employment is *healthy*—so much so, that I have known invalids to regain their health." This may be accounted for in the same manner that the well known sugar house cure is—the fumes of the boiling jellies, syrups, &c., resembling those of the sugar house.

Virginia Penny deserves the gratitude of the public for this suggestive book.

LIST OF ADVERTISEMENTS.

Charlotte Female Institute,	Charlotte, N. C.
North State Washing Machine,	" "
Rock Island Manufacturing Company,	" "
Armstrong, Cator & Co.,	Baltimore, Md.
Baltimore Weekly Gazette,	" "
Bevan & Sons,	" "
Bickford & Huffman,	
Burrough Bros.,	
Butler Bros.,	
Brown, Lancaster & Co.,	
Canfield, Bro. & Co.,	
Samuel Child & Co.,	
Cortlan & Co.,	
W. Devries & Co.,	
Dufur & Co.,	
Gaddess Bros.,	
Thos. Godey,	
Grover & Baker Sewing Machine.	
Jno. D. Hammond & Co.,	
Howard House,	
Wm. Knabe,	
Lord & Robinson,	
W. G. Maxwell,	
Alexander McComas,	
Patapsco Guano Company,	
R. Renwick & Son,	
Rhodes & Co.,	
Rosadalis,	
H. Sanders & Co.,	
Shipley, Roane & Co.,	

Chas. M. Stieff,	Baltimore, Md.
R. Q. Taylor,	" "
Noah Walker & Co.,	" "
Washington University,	
Wilson, Colston & Co.	" "
Tiffany & Co.,	New York City.
Traphagen, Hunter & Co.,	" "
Claxton, Remsen & Haffelfinger,	Phila., Pa.
Collins & McLeester,	" "
M. Walker & Sons,	" "
Dunbar Female Seminary,	Winchester, Va.
Greenbrier White Sulphur Springs,	"
Piedmont Insurance Company,	"
Rockbridge Alum Springs,	
Southern University Series	"
Valley Female Seminary,	Winchester, "
Owen House,	Washington, D. C.
S. W. Owen,	" "
Holt, Murray & Tarleton,	Mobile, Ala.
Mobile Sunday Times,	" "

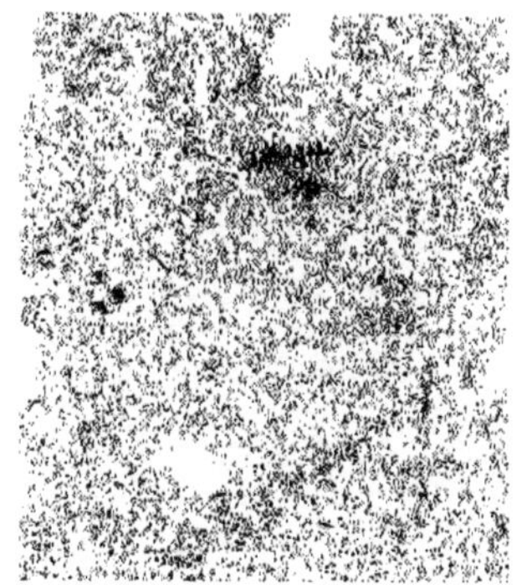

Yrs truly
Turner Ashby

THE LAND WE L[illegible]

No. IV. [illegible]

[illegible]

We learn from Mr. Avirett's charming book* that Gen. Ashby was born at Rose Bank, Fauquier county, Virginia, on the 23rd October, 1828, being the third of six children. Mr. Avirett thus speaks of the home of the General, and [illegible] of the Ashbys, [illegible] blackened ruins, [illegible] a beautiful eminence [illegible] eastern base of the Blue [illegible] in what is most ap[illegible] called the Piedmont country, [illegible] was surrounded by wild and picturesque scenery. At the foot of the eminence on which it [illegible] and in full view, ran Goose Creek, a dashing, sparkling mountain stream, just breaking away from the mountains above, among which it rises. These mountains were filled with deer and wild turkeys, ever tempting the boys to indulge in the invigorating sports of the field.

"The father of General Ashby was the man of all others who would exercise a powerful influence over his children; but when Turner was just beginning to take on character, in his [illegible] year, the father was called upon to pay nature's greatest [illegible] and the remains [illegible] his [illegible] [illegible] from any [illegible] mother, he learned his [illegible] character, and [illegible] parental views and were reflected in his subsequent life. The study of [illegible] when he [illegible] regard [illegible] fell [illegible]

* The Memoirs of General Turner Ashby, By Rev. [illegible] Avirett. Baltimore: [illegible]

Yours truly,

[illegible]

THE LAND WE LOVE.

No. IV | AUGUST, 1868. | Vol. V.

SKETCH OF GENERAL ASHBY.*

We learn from Mr. Avirett's charming book that Gen. Ashby was born at Rose Bank, Fauquier county, Virginia, on the 23rd October, 1828, being the third of six children. Mr. Avirett thus speaks of the home of the General, and his characteristics in youth and early manhood :

"'Rose Bank,' the homestead of the Ashbys, (now a heap of blackened ruins,) was situated on a beautiful eminence, near the eastern base of the Blue Ridge, in what is most appropriately called the Piedmont country, and was surrounded by wild and picturesque scenery. At the foot of the eminence on which it stood, and in full view, ran Goose Creek, a dashing, sparkling mountain stream, just breaking away from the mountains above, among which it rises. These mountains were filled with deer and wild turkeys, ever tempting the boys to indulge in the invigorating sports of the field.

"The father of General Ashby was the man of all others who would exercise a powerful influence over his children; but when Turner was just beginning to take on character, in his sixth year, the father was called upon to pay Nature's greatest and last debt, and his remains were followed to the grave by his sorrowing household. Colonel Ashby had been an officer in the war of 1812, and during his military life had kept a diary, which was the constant companion of his son Turner, as soon as he was able to read. From it, more than from any other source, save his mother, he learned his father's character, and many of the parental views and traits were reflected in his subsequent life. The study of this diary taught him, when he became an officer, to regard and treat his privates as fellow-beings entitled to love, respect, and sympathy.

* The Memoirs of General Turner Ashby, By Rev. James B. Avirett. Baltimore : Selby & Dulany :

"Upon the Colonel's death, the whole charge of the household devolved upon the mother, who, by nature and education, was fully equal to this responsible trust. Mrs. Ashby, in whom a taste for literature and flowers predominated, soon collected a fine library, and by persevering industry and care covered 'Rose Bank' with a profusion of flowers and rare shrubbery. But whilst she was careful to make their home as beautiful and attractive as possible, she by no means neglected the cultivation of the minds and hearts of her children. She took care to employ good teachers in her family, and whilst their minds were cultivated under all the happy safeguards of home, was not less careful of their physical education; her boys were taught, like the young Medes in the days of Cyrus, to ride, to shoot, and to speak the truth. As a child, Gen. Ashby was not promising in appearance, being small of stature, and inheriting the dark complexion of the Greens, through his mother. In his habits, he was retiring and reserved, grave and thoughtful, but with a manly and unselfish spirit, ever ready to stand up in defence of the weak, or to resent an injustice done either to himself or to his sisters or brothers; his devotion to his mother was unbounded, and he always considered the honor and interests of each member of his family as his own. He was fond of books, and generally preferred history. It was the custom of Mrs. Ashby to gather her household around her, and pass the evening in reading some well selected volume, the group passing the book from one to the other, thus heightening the interest and increasing the general benefit.—It has been mentioned that Mrs. Ashby afforded her children every advantage of education within her power. It has been a custom in many families in the South to employ teachers from the North, and among those thus employed at 'Rose Bank,' was a brother of Judge John C. Underwood, of evil fame and name. As the children grew older, they were sent away to school, but so admirably had the mother succeeded in making home and its pleasures attractive, especially to Turner, that she found great difficulty in inducing him to remain abroad. His local attachments were very strong, and no Swiss peasant ever loved his mountain cot more ardently than did this young Virginian his own 'Rose Bank.' At length, Mrs. Ashby placed him at school at Major Ambler's, in the neighborhood, where he became very fond of his teacher and schoolmates. His generous, unselfish disposition soon won him the admiration and affection of the band of noble youths here at school, among whom may be mentioned the Amblers, Striblings, and Marshalls, and there grew up a friendship which was as unfading as the laurel on the neighboring mountains. One of these very schoolmates, in a letter to the writer, says: 'General Ashby, as a boy, was remarkable for his contempt of danger, and his freedom from the vices common among boys; he was never known to swear, or to use profane language. His contempt of danger was exhibited nearly every day; whenever the creek was swollen by heavy rains, he might be seen in it, breasting the torrent above the waterfalls, where a failure would dash him to pieces on the rocks below; whenever a colt was found too wild and vicious to be ridden by any one else in the neighborhood, it was his pleasure to mount and tame him. In combats with his schoolfellows, whilst he was always brave and stubborn in the fight, after it was over he was always ready to forgive and forget.'

"Richard, his younger brother, was his constant companion, and the boys were taught at home to love each other very tenderly. Turner, as the elder, would watch over his brother with almost maternal care, would side with him in all his difficulties, and, if it came to blows, would insist upon fighting for him, though Richard would object to this, as he thought himself fully able to fight his own battles. In the formation of his character, happily blending gentleness with manliness, (but another name for chivalry,) his sister informs the writer that when he would return from school, he would take great pleasure in joining the girls in their in-door sports, kindly arranging their playthings and doll-houses with his own hands, and 'was always doing some kind act to make us love him.' At an early age, a singularly pleasing trait of character was developed—perfect unselfishness. A little incident in the life at 'Rose Bank' will illustrate this. Turner, indulging his boyish taste for pets, had managed to secure a wolf, which soon became very fond of him. Soon, perceiving that 'Lupus' was the terror of the children in the neighborhood, he gave up his pet, determining that his little friends should not be alienated from him by any selfish indulgence.

"Among the earliest tastes which he developed, was that of a passionate fondness for horses, and he liked to have the entire control of his own. As he scarcely remembered the time when he could not ride, so upon growing older he became marked as the best and boldest rider among a circle of youths all of whom were good horsemen, whether trial of horsemanship were made at the tournament, hurdle-race, or fox-chase.

"It will be borne in mind that the Cavaliers, who settled Virginia, faithfully transmitted to their posterity, among much that was noble, some objectionable tastes and customs. Among them, few were more unobjectionable than fox-hunting; aside from the waste of time and neglect of business consequent upon its indulgence, it was healthful, invigorating, and free from many of the worst features of other kinds of sport common in the South twenty-five or thirty years ago. Young Ashby was very fond of the chase, which frequently led him many miles from home. As a gentle, unobtrusive lad, he is still remembered by the older persons residing in Fauquier, but better by the younger as the singularly daring and fearless rider who led the hunt, ever as glad to welcome the ringing notes of the hunting-horn, awakening the echoes of the hills at early dawn, and summoning its lovers to a day of sport, as he was to catch the first notes of the reveillé, in later days, summoning him to combat and to glory."

We refer the reader to the deeply interesting book itself, and will give only one more extract, that which describes the death of the illustrious soldier:

"We fell back slowly before the advance of the enemy, and halted some three or four miles from Harrisonburg for the purpose of resting the tired infantry. The command 'Rest!' had scarcely been obeyed, when we were startled by the rattle of small arms and the yell we knew so well came from Ashby's boys in the headlong charge. A few minutes sufficed to tell the tale. The first prisoner brought to the rear, a private soldier, in reply to our interrogations, said, Percy Wyndham had met the man he had so long sought, and he didn't think he'd care about seeing him soon again, 'for,' to use his own language, 'we've been smashed all to flinders.' Prisoners were now brought in in numbers, and among them the redoubtable Wyndham himself, whose chagrin at his mishap, I shall long remember. Ashby had been entirely successful in his repulse of Wyndham's attack. It was, perhaps, two hours after, that orders came for three regiments of infantry to retrace the steps they had taken in the morning, and we felt sure from the command being accompanied by General Ewell in person, that some serious work was on hand. The regiments selected were the Fifty-eighth and Forty-fourth Virginia, and the First Maryland.

"After moving through the woods for some distance, we were met by General Ashby, when the command was halted, and two companies of the 1st Maryland thrown forward as skirmishers under the immediate eye, or, I may say, command of Ashby. The reserves followed closely, and, in half an hour, three or four shots announced that the enemy was near. The 58th was ordered up and soon became hotly engaged. The fire of the enemy was very deadly, and the 58th recoiled before it. Ashby was everywhere, encouraging and animating his men, until at last his horse was struck by a bullet and went down. Springing to his feet, and waving his sword over his head, he rushed forward, calling to his men to follow. He had not taken half a dozen steps, when he fell, pierced through the body by a musket-ball, and died almost instantly. No dying words issued from his lips, and the last command he was heard to give was, 'Forward, my brave men!'"

STONEWALL JACKSON.

When the rage of the North sent her myrmidons forth,
And Virginia—proud mother of States!—
First chosen for pillage, saw homestead and village
Succumb to the pitiless fates,
With a comet-like dash, with a lightning-like flash,
Eclipsing her own radiant story,
In Jehovah's dread name, wreaking vengeance he came—
Her youngest-born scion of glory.

'The foe-men! where are they?' This alone was *his* parley,
As o'er mountain and torrent he flew;
No ice could delay him, no darkness dismay him;
Starved, thirsting, yet sterner he grew;
He paused not to slumber, he recked not of number;
But, a cloud on the hurricane's breath,
He flashed out the fire of God's scathing ire,
And gave thee rich banquets, oh! Death!

What deed that he dared not? what peril he shared not?
Intuition her torch held to light him.
Relentless chastiser, sententious adviser,
To discover the foe was to fight him.
Of the wisdom that lies in the night and the skies
He took counsel, with knee to the sod.
His devices he bared not, for favor he cared not,
Since he held his commission from God.

MANASSAS! yet white to the awe-stricken sight,
With thy bones like a glimmering pall!
RAPPAHANNOC! still lost to the blustering host—
Ye blood-deluged battle-fields all!
Bear, bear into story with your own crimson glory,
So long as the ages revolve,
The name and the fame of that spirit of flame—
The man of undaunted resolve!

Still northward we'll bear him, and a grave we'll prepare him,
In the face of the foe he ne'er fled.
With the calm of the blest he'll take his deep rest,
Though invasion should sweep o'er his head.

But if the blue heaven be suddenly riven,
And thunder, announced by no gleam,
Should his cannon resemble, and the pillagers tremble,
The grim sleeper may smile in his dream!

Savannah, Ga. H. R. JACKSON.

COMPARATIVE GENERALSHIP.

BUT let us come to the promised sketch of Grant's campaign. He himself is reported to have said to an English gentleman, since the war, that though he had often been said to have been beaten, he had to be beaten for the first time yet. So it was stated by a correspondent in an English newspaper. We think he is mistaken. We think it can be shown that he was not only beaten on more than one occasion, but that he was very well aware of the fact.

At Belmont, for instance, when his forces were three to one, he was routed, pursued several miles by our troops, who tracked his men the whole way by the arms and knapsacks they had thrown away, by the dead and dying strewn along the line of flight and by the capture of his surgical head quarters, where they found a yard full of blankets, coats, knapsacks, and wounded men, with the surgeons attending them, and he was followed to his very boats, on which his men tumbled heels over head, and rushed to the opposite side to get out of fire, with so much tumult that guards with bayonets were placed to keep them off lest they should sink the boats. Even in their boats they had to run the gauntlet of a heavy fire from our sharp-shooters on the bank for more than a mile.—If that was not a defeat, Bull Run or Waterloo was not.

His next appearance was at Fort Donelson, in February 1862. Sidney Johnston, lying at the Bowling Green with 23,000 men, detached 11,000 of them to Fort Donelson, on the Cumberland river, built there to guard the approach to Nashville. The whole garrison, after reïnforcement, was about 12,500 strong. Grant appeared before it with 30,000 men, and attempted, in vain, for several days, to carry it by storm. Our forces were successful in repelling every attack made by the enemy, who were reïnforced every movement. Before the affair was over, Grant had before the place, eighty-two regiments, which must have contained, in the aggregate, 60,000 men, at a moderate calculation, and a naval force stronger by many degrees, than the whole combined fleet of the Confederate States. The place at last surrendered, our total loss, in men, was about 5,500, more than half had escaped, and we killed and wounded double that number. The Northern prints, with a characteristic regard for truth, stated our loss at 15,000, two thousand more than we had in the fort, and headed their columns with these figures, in type an inch long.

General Sidney Johnston retreated to Murfreesborough, and from there marched to Corinth, to unite his forces with those of General Beauregard, at Corinth. To these were added two divisions of General Polk's command.—Several regiments from Louisiana, and some troops from Mobile, which increased Gen. Johnston's command to about 35,000, were all admirable troops. About the first of April, Grant crossed the Tennessee, and took post near Pittsburg landing. He had given his enemy five weeks to rally, and he had, as we have seen, taken advantage of it. Why he did this, we do not know. It may have been military, it certainly was not *Napoleonic*, nor was it after the *Stonewall Jackson* fashion. Neither of these officers would have given Johnston a moment to rest, far less five weeks. If Jackson had been a Federal officer, and had had in his hands an army of 50,000 men, on the day of the surrender of Fort Donelson, Johnston and Beauregard never would have gotten together. But so it was, about the first of April, Grant lay at Pittsburg landing with 50,000 men, and was writing letters every day to Buell to hurry up, from Columbus, with the 35,000 or 40,000 under his command. Johnston resolved to attack him in that position, before Buell could come up. He was, unfortunately, one day later than he expected to be, having been unavoidably detained by horrible roads, horrible weather, and the tangled forest country he was obliged to pass through.—However, he attacked him on the 6th of April, a little before sunrise, carried one position, made him retreat to another, carried that and made him retreat to a third, carried that, and swept everything before him, taking nearly all his guns, of which he had 108, when he, himself, was killed. General Beauregard assumed the command, and continued the battle until the enemy was driven, on the run, to the very brink of the river, thousands of men sheltering themselves under the banks. A single push, and the whole mass would have been precipitated into the river, when the troops halted. The river, which would have been greater destruction had he been vigorously attacked, proved his salvation as it was. His whole army would have broken into an irretrievable rout, had they been able to fly, but the river prevented them. Towards the end of the action, Buell's army began to arrive. During the night, it all came up. Beauregard had complete possession of Grant's camp, retained it all night, and had the mortification of seeing his troops dispersed all over it, in search of the enormous wealth with which it was loaded. In vain did he attempt to rally them as the morning approached, to resist the attack which he knew that the enemy, reïnforced by 35,000 men, would be sure to make. As morning approached, he got all he could into line, which, after his losses of the day before, were not 20,000 men. The enemy were now upwards of 60,000; more than three to one. Yet, he fought this mighty force for six hours, and retreated in safety to Corinth, carrying off his wounded, his prisoners, a large part of the cannon he had captured, and a considerable portion of the spoils. This shameful defeat, the Yankee Press, and the Cabinet at Washington chose to call a great victory, and, by way of keeping up the spirits of their party, the President proclaimed a general Thanksgiving day. No occurrence of the war demonstrated more palpably than this battle, the great superiority of the Confederate troops ; for the Federal troops were all western men, not Yankees, and the western soldier is a very different man from the Yankee soldier.

General Grant's next exploit was the capture of Vicksburg. In that city there were 27,000 troops in all, from the beginning of Grant's operations away up the river, to its surrender, a period of eight or nine months, and he had, himself, at the time of that surrender, 120,000 men before it! So, at least, said Minister Adams, in an official speech which he made to the English Secretary of State for Foreign Affairs (Lord Russell) by direction of Secretary Seward. We are confident, that either of the great Captains to whom he is advantageously contrasted in the article, which has drawn forth this comment, would, with such an army, have taken Vicksburg in at least six months before it fell, and so would Stonewall Jackson.

In the fall of the same year, 1863, Grant defeated Bragg near Chickamauga. The soldiers of Bragg were between 40,000 and 50,000, those of Grant about 120,000. Bragg's army was thoroughly demoralized, and almost in a state of disorganization. They were, of course, easily defeated. But Grant, with characteristic slowness, seems to have made no use of his victory. His enemy was allowed a whole winter to reörganize and recover. Had Stonewall Jackson been in his place, that army would have been captured or destroyed, in one week after its defeat.

We now come to the campaign of 1864, against Lee, in Virginia. At the commencement of this campaign, Grant had with him on the Rapidan, 160,000 men.—Stanton telegraphed that he reinforced him twice between the Wilderness and James river; once with 45,000 men and again with 40,000; that is with 85,000 in all. Lee's whole force was 47,000 men, not one-third the number Grant had with him at the Wilderness. This enormous disparity of force induced Grant to believe that he could sweep his adversary out of his path as the whirlwind scatters the leaves of the forest. In the assurance of an easy and early triumph, he wrote to one of his correspondents, "I shall fight it out on this line if it takes me all summer." That is, I will sweep Lee out of my path, and march straight to Richmond.— His object, no doubt, was, to break through his line, turn him off towards the mountains, and having thus cut him off from his resources, pursue him and destroy his army at leisure, while Butler or a detachment sent from Washington took possession of Richmond. While he was thus calculating, and preparing to crush Lee, that officer anticipated him, and attacked his centre at the Wilderness with inexpressible fury. The battle raged for several days, during which he was unable to move Lee one inch from his position. Finding all his efforts vain, he withdrew his army by a flank movement, which would have been fatal to it but for its vast superiority of numbers, enabling him to keep in position a line quite equal to Lee's in number, and thus to mask the movement taking place behind it. It was the very movement which the Russians attempted at Austerlitz, and which caused the destruction of their army, and the loss of the campaign. But the Russians were only superior to the French by one-fifth. They could not, therefore, interpose an army equal to Napoleon's, while they were manœuvring in the rear with another of double the size. Napoleon could see what they were at, and attacked them while they were executing the manœuvre. Frederick attempted the same thing at Hochkirchen, and got his army destroyed by it. Marmont tried the same manœuvre at Salamanca, and was badly beaten in consequence. But Grant could do it with safety, because he could make a curtain of a force equal to Lee's while he manœuvred behind it. His loss was enormous. It was said, at the time, that it reached 50,000 men, and we have no doubt it did.— He left Lee standing where he stood at the beginning of the battle. He left an enormous number of dead on the field of battle lying unburied. And yet he claimed a victory, being the first victorious general that, so far as we know, ever marched off leaving his unburied dead strewn all over the field as thick "as leaves in Vallambrosa."

Grant filed off towards Fredericksburg, in hopes to get between Lee and Richmond. But his route was circuitous, and Lee had the interior line. He was, throughout the campaign, operating on the chord of an arc. He anticipated Grant, and got before him by a shorter route at Spotsylvania Court House. Here the whole thing was to be tried over again. Grant had probably received the first installment of his reinforcements, 45,000 men. His line, therefore, was still 150,000 strong, while Lee had lost heavily at the Wilderness, and could not have had more than 40,000 men. Three days' fighting preceded the tremendous battle of the 12th in which Grant was repulsed in all his attempts, and lost upon a moderate calculation, 40,000 men. Lee's loss was also heavy. The division of General Edward Johnson, occupying an advanced position, was deprived of its artillery on the night of the 11th. The General ascertaining that he was to be attacked by an overwhelming force, about two o'clock, sent a first messenger to reclaim it, and from that time, messenger after messenger. It came back after the fight was over, just in time to fall into the enemy's hands. In the meantime, Johnson's division, 7,000 strong, was attacked by Hancock's corps, of 30,000 men. They made a desperate resistance, but were overpowered, and the greater part taken or dispersed; the General, himself, being among the captured. Sure now of victory, the enemy pushed on only to be repeatedly repulsed, with a slaughter never equalled in any engagement fought in this country. It was stated that Grant lost 40,000 men on that terrible day, and he made no impression whatever on Lee. Lee's loss also was considerable. In all, he had lost during the campaign, at least 12,000 men, which reduced his force to 35,000. Before they came again in contact, at Cold Harbor, Grant had received a fresh reinforcement of 40,000 men, raising his numbers again to more than 150,000.

Grant finding he could not move Lee out of his tracks, again moved off by his left. Lee again faced him on the Pamunkey, but he did not evince the same ardor there, and after a not very hot engagement he again moved off by his left. Lee was ready for him at Cold Harbor, and there repulsed him with prodigious slaughter. It was said he lost on this occasion 30,000 men. But he still had 120,000, while Lee had but 35,000, and was too weak to follow him, when filing off again to his left he crossed the Chickahominy at Long Bridge, and passed over the James with the hope of surprising Petersburg.—Lee again anticipated him and joining Beauregard, who held Butler "bottled up" at Bermuda Hundred, his whole force, after receiving a reinforcement of two or three thousand from Breckenridge, was now 50,000 men.

This campaign, on the part of Gen. Lee, is one of the most brilliant recorded in history. It resembles, more than any other, that of Napoleon in 1814. The same use of the *interior line* was made by both, both moving upon the chord of an arc, and each compelling his adversary to move upon the circumference. The object of Napoleon was to prevent the several armies of his enemies from uniting, which he was enabled to do by moving on a short line, while they moved on a longer, so that he could attack the first of them which came to the place of union before the others could get up. The object of Lee was to keep between his enemy and Richmond, which he always did by moving on the short line. Actually before him—confronting him on the several fields of battle—were, from first to last, 245,000 men, while 47,000 were all that he had from first to last. We have here stated the losses of the the enemy, as they were reported at the time, and as we believe them to have actually been. Of course, the enemy make a very different statement. Gen. Halleck advised that their generals should be instructed to claim a victory on all occasions, and none of them ever neglected that duty. Their official reports are quite as trustworthy as the stories of the Baron Munchausen, but not more so. Suppose Lee to have had 160,000 men at the Wilderness, and Grant 47,000. How long would the latter have stood before him? Not one hour. Besides these, Hunter was operating on one flank with 30,000 men, and Butler, with 30,000, on the other. In all he had 305,000 men to contend with, at a time when, even after Breckenridge and Beauregard had joined, he could not muster more than 50,060. Suppose he had been at the head of 300,000 men. He would have planted the Confederate flag upon the roof or steeple (if it have any steeple) of Faneuil Hall, in less than a month. The detachment of 14,000 men, under Early, soon reduced his force to 36,000 men, and with this little force he confronted Grant, with an army 150,000 strong (including Butler's) backed by a naval force that was strong enough to have sunk both the fleets that fought at Trafalgar.*

It is very rarely that statements upon military questions, coming from opposite sides, differ so little. We are convinced, however, that we are nearer right than the World. That Grant had at least 143,000 men with him, at the opening of the campaign, that is, at the battle of the Wilderness, is, we think, certain. That Lee had but 47,000 men there, is also certain. That Grant had, in point of fact, 160,000 men, was stated at the time, upon evidence which we believed to be incontestable. But let it stand as it is stated by the World, and what immense glory does it not reflect on Lee and his men. Lee was reinforced by Breckenridge, Finne-

* This article was written in January last. The accuracy of its statements has been wonderfully confirmed since that time by the *New York World.*—That Journal has been publishing a severe scrutiny into the military pretensions of Gen. Grant. In its issue of June 9th it says:

"We have already shown the respective forces and losses of Generals Grant and Lee between the Rapidan and James, and, as prefatory to some further historical light on General Grant's soldiership, reproduce them.

"Grant, on assuming command May 4, 1864, had of effective men besides the reserve, when he crossed the Rapidan, 125,000.

"Lee at the same date had an effective force of 52,000.

"Grant's reinforcements up to the battle of Cold Harbor, June 3, were 97,000.

"Lee's reinforcements up to the same date were 18,000.

"Grant's total force, including reinforcements, was 222,000.

"Lee's total force, including reinforcements, was 70,000.

"Returns to their respective Governments showed that when both armies had reached the James, June 10, the number of Grant's army that had been put *hors du combat* was 117,000.

"Up to the same date, the number of Lee's men who had been put *hors du combat* was 19,000.

"The two armies then met in front of Petersburg.

"It will be seen that Grant's total force, including reinforcements, was 152,000, and his loss 98,000 in excess of Lee's, or that, with a force outnumbering his opponent's three to one, this bungler lost every other man in his army, while Lee lost but two out of every nine, or, to put it still differently, that Grant lost just six thousand men more than one and a half times Lee's entire army. That Grant succeeded is true, but a general would have accomplished the same result with less means and less loss."

gan, and a division of Longstreet's corps, which had been operating in North Carolina. So far from reaching 19,000 we are confident that they did not exceed the half of that figure, all told. It will be seen that we understated Grant's reïnforcements. Instead of 85,000, they were 97,000.

After all, Grant would never have succeeded but for the operations of Sherman in Georgia and South Carolina, which destroyed the last remaining resources of the Confederate army, and rendered desertion the only alternative for starvation. To that officer far more than to Grant is due the reduction of Richmond and the consequent subversion of the Confederacy. How the North can exult in such a triumph is difficult to conceive.

It has been pretended that Grant *always* intended to occupy the position around Petersburg. His own words prove the reverse. "I will fight it out on this line, &c." "This line" was not the way to Petersburg, and that was not his object. Richmond was his aim — Richmond "by this line" not by way of Petersburg. The road to Petersburg was by Old Point Comfort and Norfolk. He could have taken it, and arrived at the position he afterwards occupied, without fighting a battle. He took it finally, after he had been beaten in every battle, because he found it impossible to take it in any other way. He was *driven* to it. Every thinking man in the State was on thorns, throughout the war, about Petersburg. They saw that it was the true strategic point.— That once in the possession of the enemy, Richmond must fall, because he would have possession of all the roads that communicate with the South. They marveled at the stupidity of the enemy, which forbade them to see so plain a fact. Was it great generalship to lose upwards of 100,000 men for a purpose which might have been obtained without loss?

There has been no end to the eulogies bestowed upon the Russians for their defence of Sebastopol. What was it compared to Lee's defence of Petersburg.— They were fully equal in number to their enemies; nay, it may be well believed, greatly superior; for they relieved each other in the trenches, every twelve hours, as regularly as if on parade. Their camp was always plentifully supplied. They had a profusion of arms, ammunition, military stores and hospital supplies of every description. The marvel is, not that they held out so long, but that the place was ever taken at all. Lee, for many months, defended a line extending from the Chickahominy to Hatcher's run—fifty miles long, against an enemy whose force, and numerous reïnforcements had swelled to 180,000 men, fought a number of successful combats, and was never beaten until a severe winter, combined with hunger and destitution had thinned his ranks, and demoralized his troops, to such a degree, that though he had been reïnforced, in the Autumn, by what was called "the new levy," (that is, by men who were none less than 45 years of age,) yet on the day when Grant, at the head of 180,000 men made the final assault on his lines, he had but 35,000 troops to defend them. Thirty-five thousand, from the Chickahominy to Hatcher's run.

Such are the exploits, that in the opinion of this writer, place General Grant above Cæsar and Napoleon! Posterity will think very differently. The truth cannot be hidden. When the world reads the story of Confederate superiority of numbers, and compares it with the number of souls ascertained by census to have existed in the Confederacy, they will laugh the falsehood to scorn. It will see how all Grant's victories were gained. It will place Lee, not Grant, on the immortal roll in company with Alexander, Hannibal, Cæsar, Frederic, Napoleon and Wellington.

THE DECAY OF RELIGION IN THE SOUTH.

For generations the people of the Southern States had occasion to observe the nature of the negro there; and none know the negroes but those who have lived among them. The study of their history in other lands and under various conditions only confirmed the conviction that since the origin of the race there never existed any negro population enjoying a condition of equal physical and moral well being, or one so far advanced in civilization and religious development, and the people of the Southern States challenged their enemies to refute the assertion.

Not that they imagined the negroes, as a body, to be either Christians or civilized. They knew that both Christianity and civilization make slow progress, especially among a rude people of a low order of intellect. A nation of Christians never yet was, nor will be, nor has true civilization ever penetrated through the whole mass of a nation.

Are we guilty of an absurdity in speaking of the civilization and Christianity of slaves; and of expecting progress from those whom we keep in fetters?

When God has not directly revealed his designs, we can only infer them from the observation of his works. From the characteristics of each part of his creation we must infer its use, although we may not discover all the purposes of its Creator. Who doubts that the horse was made for draft and the saddle? or the sheep to furnish wool, or kine to furnish milk, butter and cheese, and both to furnish food for man? Who doubts that the dog, with his domestic habits, his strong affection, his incorruptible fidelity, his unceasing vigilance, was designed for the companion, the friend, the servant and sentinel of his master? See the common hen, contrary to the wont of the feathered tribe, hanging around man's dwelling, and laying her eggs almost daily for his use; her mate with his clarion-noted clock sounding the hours of the night for every homestead. Are not all these fulfilling their destined end? And do not these very characteristics lead to the multiplication and improvement of their race?

May we not reason thus as to the higher order of beings? Can we avoid contrasting the negro with the white man, who, go where he will, becomes the ruler? or with the red man now dying out from this continent? or with the Malay race in New Zealand, Tahiti and elsewhere on the Pacific, fading away before the influx of European settlers? In these cases the mere contact of races seems fatal to one of them. The colonists in this country not only bought African slaves, but reduced many of the Indians to slavery. The negroes throve and multiplied, the Indians died out. We can find only here and there a trace of them where they had mingled their blood with the blacks.

We know best the history of the negro in this country, but his history elsewhere, as far as it is known to us, corresponds with it. From his history we infer that God has given him a tendency to thrive and multiply in a condition of servitude, under which other races die out, and has given him little propensity to shake off that servitude. But in freedom he has shown a tendency to deteriorate and die out, in countries where other races were thriving and multiplying rapidly. May we not then infer that the servile condition of the negroes in the South was not contrary to the will of God? Nor is this contradicted by God's revealed word, which, so far from prohibiting human slavery, strongly inculcates the relative duties of the master and slave.

But where are the four millions of negroes which the sun shone upon in the South in 1860? Until disturbed by the Northern invaders they continued to thrive and multiply in every part of the Confederacy. But the decree of freedom was to them 'the beginning of the end.' We foresee that in taking the census of 1870, the United States government will order that no record be made of distinctions in color or race, under the plea that all are citizens, all free and equal, while the true object will be to hide from the world the fearful gap, freedom and Northern rule are making in their ranks.

The people of the Southern States felt that they had a civilization, and a political and social organization, from which not only they themselves, but their slaves drew countless blessings. They saw that these blessings could only be preserved by breaking off all connection with their faithless and usurping confederates. No class was more enthusiastic in the cause of Secession than the clergy and the more devout portion of the community. We witnessed but a feeble indication of this spirit, while listening to a devout minister of the Gospel teaching his lisping infant to pray for President Davis as the champion, not only of political, but religious rights. In what war have the clergy taken a similar part? We see a Bishop, without one word of censure from his brethren, taking high command, leading armies into battle, and perishing at the 'cannon's mouth.' We see a clergyman of the same church, at the first outbreak of the war, drilling his raw artillerists, himself point the field piece on the foe, while with the roar of the cannon he mingles pious ejaculations to his God. We see others leading their regiments of horse or foot into the fight—but examples multiplying around us soon become innumerable. Many crowd into the ranks of the volunteer army; many rise to commands and prove worthy of them. Others, withheld by their views of professional propriety from actually bearing arms, eagerly seek the posts of regimental chaplains, and are seen in the field assisting the wounded, or kneeling by the dying, as devoutly calm under the enemy's fire, as in their pulpit or closet at home. Many who had lived a priest's life died a soldier's death. Nor did these clerical warriors represent a party in the church. In the seven States which first formed the Confederacy, we know hardly a native clergyman who opposed Secession, few who did not approve of it.

For to numbers in the South, the war of Secession was a holy war; and General (Stonewall) Jackson was the worthy representative of this class. Few recluse devotees are more absorbed in a religious life, than he was even in the most active part of his military career. His was the spirit of Judas Maccabeus aroused in defence, not only of political right, but religious truth.

Yet, patriotism did not, in the South, usurp the place and assume the garb of religion—political sermons, so common at the North—discourses from the pulpit designed to produce a political effect, were hardly known in the South. Few of the most punctual attendants at church ever heard one. No communion table was seen draped with Confederate banners, in rivalry with 'the stars and stripes' as used at the North. No congregation chanted a national anthem, in place of a hymn to the Almighty, in answer to the 'star spangled banner' given out from the pulpit and shouted rather than sung by the choir and congregation of the Northern 'church militant.' The religious manifestations in the South contrasted strongly with the fanatic politics, which pervaded and over-rode the religion of the North.

Let no one imagine that we hold up to admiration each regimental chaplain in the Confederate army. With some neither the service of God or their country was the ruling motive. There were gross blunders in the official appointments made in this, as in every branch of the service. But the conduct of the clergy generally, and of the devout and zealous members, of both sexes, of all branches of the Church, proved that Secession did not find support only in the ambition of politicians, the worldly calculations of mercenary men, and the passionate and thoughtless impulses of hot and heady youth.

It is foreign to our purpose to trace the manifold blunders which, from the beginning of the war to the end, did more to ruin the cause of the Confederacy, than the arms or the policy of its enemies. We will consider what effect the circumstances attending the ruin of his country may have on the minds of the Southern man.

The effects of emancipation on the negroes first attract his attention. They have been pictured as a people cruelly oppressed—conscious of their wrongs, and only kept down hitherto by the strong hand—as true prisoners, as galley slaves or the inmates of a penitentiary. The fetters are knocked off, the bolts withdrawn, and the prison doors thrown open. What now is their conduct? Does it indicate the feelings engendered by a long course of wrongs? When we remember that this people lately numbered more than four millions, that in some parts of the country the blacks were three, five, and even ten to the whites—that agents were busy among them filling their minds and turning their heads, with dangerous counsels and impracticable hopes—how rare were the instances of violence, outrage, or even disrespect to the whites, especially to their former masters. In what multitudes of cases did they seek employment as freemen, from him who so lately held them as slaves. The instinctive sense of their own inferiority told them that there was nothing unnatural in their former condition.

It had been said that by a system of compulsory toil for another, they had been prevented from laboring for their own advancement. What is the history, not of their industry, but of their indolence? The greater part of them have shown little more providence than cattle turned out to pasture.

Where among them do we see the effects of their, at least, partial training in Christianity and civilization? With few exceptions, the most devout negroes celebrated their freedom by at once abandoning the congregations of whites, with which they had long connected themselves. They seek to escape from the restraints imposed by the proprieties of Christain worship and the presence of others of superior education and race; and to find in assemblies of their own people, opportunities which they instinctively crave for a boisterous and sensuous expression of their devotional impulses. The indulgence of this yearning after religious excitement soon produces extravagances utterly incompatible with Christian humility.

Its influence on the women not seldom led them to assume the prophetic character, and their inspired ravings, when they had any meaning, were utterly subversive of Christian truth. The suddenness and universality of this religious movement, in deserting the churches they had joined, was well expressed, in few words, by a clergyman of the Episcopal Church, who, although a native of England, had, in the midst of a negro population, devoted almost a life time to their religious instruction. "On the triumph of the Northern arms becoming known to the negroes, I saw the labors of thirty years perish in thirty minutes."

Their civilization clave to them no longer than their religion. They put off both as easily as their clothes. The writer of this article, being absent from his plantation on service, when his neighborhood was occupied by the enemy, requested a neighbor to ascertain what was the condition of his negroes. His friend soon gave him the required information, laying particular stress on one feature. 'You would no longer recognize the family relations among your negroes. There have been so many exchanges of husbands and wives that few households are in the state in which you lately left them.'

Yet for thirty or forty years, at least, especial pains had been taken to impress on these people the sanctity and permanence of the marriage tie. This was one of the speediest results of freedom even here, where the negroes remained on the plantation. In many cases, they deserted their old homes to seek their fortunes elsewhere, with a view, not of making, but finding a living. In so doing, they often disencumbered themselves of such impediments as wives, husbands, and children, throwing off, with the obligation of personal service, all domestic ties. This improvidence, and their neglect of a parent's duties, have been followed by a fearful mortality among the children, who, indeed, in the days of slavery owed their preservation chiefly to the master's care.

The destiny of the negro in the Southern States is becoming daily more manifest. For the inertness and improvidence of his unchangeable nature, proved by his history in every age and every land, plainly point it out. The negroes emancipated in the West Indies, indeed, however low they may sink into barbarism, may not become extinct. They have found a new Guinea and Angola there. Protected by a climate as hostile to the white man as propitious to the black, they gather rather than earn a subsistence from the almost spontaneous produce of the soil; and a subsistence, that they may exist to enjoy the *dolce far niente*, the luxury of indolence, is all they ask. But on the adjacent continent, life is not existence merely, but a struggle, under adverse conditions, requiring some thought, industry, self-denial, all so much wanting in the negro—an unceasing struggle which becomes hopeless, when it has to be maintained in contact, and often in conflict with a superior race.

Many a Southern man, led by his knowledge of the negro to this conviction as to their destiny, is startled at the reflections which force themselves upon him. Has God permitted the exodus of hundreds of thousands of these people from a country, one of the most barbarous, perhaps the most unimprovable on earth, where they were the slaves of barbarians like themselves? Did he permit their transportation to another land, where, although still in bondage, civilization and Christianity were within their reach? Has he multiplied their numbers fifteen fold in little more than a century, permitted their progress in civilization, and opened to many of them his revealed word? Has he made them the instruments for reclaiming from the wilderness vast territories, both continental and insular, of matchless fertility, and incalculable utility to man,—regions on which he has stamped a climate rendering them irreclaimable by the labors of any other race?—Has God done all this only that these millions of negroes entering, or within the pale of civilization and Christianity, should, through the results of a political convulsion, in which they took no part, suddenly relapse towards barbarism, lose sight of the cross of Christ, and, throughout the greater part of these wide territories, hasten to extinction? What better can now be hoped for in a large portion of these Southern States, than that, when, like the red man, the black shall have passed away, they may become pastoral and half-civilized regions occupied by the degraded remnant of what was once a free and high spirited people, cut short in their rapid progress towards an eminent position among the nations of the earth?

But this is, or has been, the Southern man's country, his home, endeared by every tender tie, hallowed by many glorious memories, watered with the blood of his brothers, who gave their lives for its defence. He may be forgiven if he is staggered at the unveiling of its coming fate.

He has seen the enemies of this, his country, the mass of them utterly regardless of God's law, and the political rights they had covenanted to respect, making war upon it in the name of religion and humanity. The smouldering ruins, the wasted fields, the herds slaughtered in wantonness, the plunder laden trains—all proved their object to be not mere conquest, but robbery and devastation. He has seen them triumphant, and pushing their success to the very ends they began by disavowing.

He now sees the Northern champions of universal liberty and equality, while carefully excluding the negroes among themselves from all political or social equality *with themselves*, yet striving to give them in the South dominion over their former masters, while these very negroes are perishing from off the face of the land.

He finds himself in a country cursed of God and man; and, prompted by his convictions of retributive justice, he looks around him and into his own heart to find the cause of this condemnation of himself, his country, his people, and the lately subject race. Looking back with scrutinizing eye on the great struggle through which he has lately past, he can repent of nothing but the blunders which led to the ruin of a righteous cause. He looks back upon sacrifice after sacrifice, great, numberless and heart-rending, made by millions of his people from the purest motives—and behold! each noble sacrifice draws after it the penalty of crime.— Whatever were their sins as a people, he can find, in the result of the late conflict, nothing but triumphant wrong in the North, and nothing but unmerited ruin and misery in the South.— Whatever their natural sin was, he sees them trampled upon, by God's permission, by a far more sinful people. The result is good to none, evil to all.— To the North loss, to the South ruin, to the negro *extermination.*

Bewildered in mind, he is yet more puzzled by the conduct of many of the clergy, whose patriotic zeal and sacrifices he can never forget. When, in the ruin and humiliation of their native State, he joins them in the public worship of God, he now hears all of the ministers of one branch of the church, and many of the others praying for a government which their congregations know only through its tyrannies, and calling down the blessings of God on magistrates whose whole authority is founded on usurpation.— Not a word is breathed to indicate that those, whom they pray for, stand in especial need that God should touch their guilty hearts, and move them to repent and seek pardon for their sins against God in their crimes against men. How strange the effect produced by hearing the minister praying for the prosperity of a government on Sunday, when he and nine-tenths of his congregation would think it a blessed day's work could they destroy it on Monday.

The clergy urge the example of St. Paul praying for Nero!— as doubtless he did—for his conversion and repentance as a sin-burdened man—not for his long life and prosperity as a blood-stained tyrant. Often as we are urged in Scripture to forgive our enemies, we are no where urged to forgive the enemies of our country, to the utter forgetfulness of that country's wrongs.— Let not the professing Christian forget how strong is now the temptation to abandon honest convictions under the plea of religious duty; how easily a base subserviency to his wrong doers can cloke itself under the garb of Christian forgiveness of injuries to the utter confounding of our sense of right and wrong. Ask yourself this question: After suffering the wrongs that we have experienced at the hands of our enemies, with the knowledge we now have of their true character, had we succeeded in breaking the yoke, would the most Christian spirit among us have failed to look upon them as enemies, not to be injured, but to be ever suspected, watched and shunned? Was there ever occasion calling more loudly for obedience to the injunction 'Let him be unto thee as a heathen man and a publican.' The contagion of iniquity must be shunned.

Such a construction as many of our clergy have practically put upon the text 'the powers that be are ordained of God' is a caricature of Erastianism worthy of the 'Vicar of Bray.' Those who thus teach need fear persecution from no tyranny in power, upholding, as they do, whoever gets the upper hand. Had the late unhappy Emperor, Maximilian, received the support of the Mexican nation, and, in the confusion and exhaustion produced among us by the war of Secession, had he reöccupied Texas as a Mexican province, every clergyman and congregation there would have been bound in Christian duty, on the principles acted on by many since the conquest of the South, to acknowledge allegiance to him, and pray for the prosperity of the sovereign and government thrust upon them at the point of the sword.

A prompt and frank admission that might makes right, that in every worldly undertaking failure or success manifests God's anger or approval; a return to the faith and practice of our Gothic forefathers, who, after overrunning and re-peopling Western Europe, had recourse in their law-suits to duels between the plaintiffs and defendants, and relied on the issue as the judgment of God, could not more confound our natural sense of right or wrong.

If we may judge from men's public acts and professions, too few in the South, and the clergy as little as any class, have rightly distinguished between a Christian resignation to God's will, and a forced submission to the power of an earthly conqueror. Prisoners in body, as every Confederate became, crowds seem to have yielded themselves prisoners in mind, and denying their deepest convictions, became the ready and apparently willing instruments in each measure devised by their conquerors to complete their ruin and deepen their degradation. It is vain to deny that many in the South feel degraded in their own esteem, not from the result of the war, but by their own conduct since the war. Tempted to recantations of principles and to pledges of allegiance by hopes, deceptively held out to them, of preserving some remnant of political or proprietary rights, many have allowed themselves to be made the agents in uprooting the very foundations of their own State. And they have not gained by their subserviency the semblance of a security for any right. They forgat that they were dealing with a people whom it is impossible to trust without being deceived. Many, even those who had displayed most valor as soldiers, have shown little of the spirit of martyrs, rather to suffer than to do a wrong. Yielding up their conviction of right, they have shaken hands with the slayers of brothers, fathers and sons, not doubting the justice of the cause in which they fell, but because that it is lost.

No man can look earnestly upon life without seeing that in this world wrong often prevails over right. Indeed, while we have abundant indications given to us that there is a rule of right for our guidance, the breaches of it, and the prosperity attending them, are so many and startling, as to lead us to look forward to a life hereafter in which all wrongs will be redressed. The destruction of earthly hope and trust often drives the believer closer to his God. It often arouses the unconverted sinner to look upon life as a state, not of enjoyment, but probation. But we have no reason to rely on material ruin and moral degradation, as the means of regenerating a whole people.

Every great revolution, which shakes society to its foundations, tends violently to unsettle the firmest seated convictions, and leads many to doubt what they have hitherto held as sacred and indisputable truth. There is much in this world to bewilder us. We see that evil exists and know not why; that it is often triumphant; and yet we can find many proofs that it is offensive to God. The instructed yet humble minded Christian is ever ready to exclaim, 'The ways of the Almighty are past finding out.' Even in the ages of heathen darkness, gifted men, guided by no revelation but that which God had stamped upon their hearts, have recognized the nothingness of human wisdom in all attempts to weigh the counsels or measure the plans of the Deity. Man knows but one spot in limitless space; he experiences but one point of endless time; he sees but one flash of the all pervading glory; and, could he gaze upon the whole expanse of the material and moral universe, he might not comprehend its relations. As the Creator, God has not opened to us his counsels, while, as the Redeemer, he has made known only his will.

But this is a skeptical age, in which men are loath to search for the solid ground on which they may build up a Christian's faith; while they are open-eyed and open-eared to every difficulty in reconciling God's Word with their dim and narrow views of nature, man, and the course of this world's events; proudly requiring God to lay open all his counsels, before they will obey that which he enjoins.

The doubts and contradictions that beset the human mind engendered of old a creed, embraced by many philosophers, and well expressed by the Roman poet of that school—

"Far, far from mortals and their vain concerns,
In peace perpetual dwell the immortal Gods;
Each self-dependent and from human wants
Estranged forever."

In thus teaching that the Deity exists not for man, they indirectly denied the existence of the Deity. This creed of unbelief has never died out, and evil influences often propagate it far and wide.

When the Southern man surveys the immense tropical and adjacent regions of the Western continent, in which the soil admits not of tillage by the white man's hand, from the malignant effects of a climate which is yet more benignant to the negro than that of Africa itself; when he recognizes the productive powers of these regions, running to luxurious waste, enlarging, not the realms of civilization, but of an African barbarism; when he thinks of their measureless capacity to supply the wants and elevate the condition of untold millions, not only those who might dwell upon the soil, but yet vaster multitudes throughout the remotest regions of the earth; when he remembers that the peculiar capacities of the negro, guided and controlled by the skill, forethought and energy of the Caucasian race, have more than demonstrated the practicability of this happy result; when he contrasts the almost certain future with what might well have been, and beholds how much is thus cut off from the possible expansion of the civilized and Christian world, may he not be tempted to adopt the creed of Zoroaster, and recognize in all that he beholds but one vast field for the perpetual struggles between Ormuzd and Ahriman, the Principle of Good, and the Principle of Evil, and conclude that in his quarter of the world, Ahriman has permanently gotten the upper hand?

The mass of mankind cannot look beyond the local and temporary circumstances which surround them. They mould their conviction upon them. Standing amidst the ruins of his country, with the evidences of a perishing civilization around him, and triumphant wrong lording it over him, realizing the weakness, folly, and faithlessness of many to whom he had looked for guidance and example, is it strange that, here in the South, many an unregenerated man, many an unconfirmed believer should find it hard to resist the doubts that crowd upon him? Doubt of the possibility of human rectitude—doubt of the unvarying and eternal nature of right and wrong—doubt yet more horrible—of the justice and benevolence of God!

It is, perhaps, not in the power of the whole people of the South to reverse the decree of material ruin and desolation past upon their country. But how far the conduct of professing Christians may have tended to its moral degradation, let each one ask his own conscience, and whether it acquit or condemn him, let him recognize the multiplied evil tendencies of the times, and with true Christian zeal labor to counteract them.

"LACON" AND ITS AUTHOR.

PROVERBIAL wisdom is universally popular; but, few of those who have given to the world a wise saw, or a proverb, have credit with the learned, still fewer, with the masses. Many a man has a bit of wisdom from Rochefocauld which he produces on all occasions, to his own satisfaction, and the edification of his friends, without having heard that such a man as Rochefoucauld ever lived; and it is surprising, on looking over "Lacon," to find how many newspapers are enriched from its pages, without the slightest acknowledgment to its author; probably, most often, from inability to assign the authorship.

The author of "Lacon," the Rev. Charles Caleb Colton, was an off-shoot of that combination of Church and State, which has done so much to bring discredit on the Anglican church. The following anecdote will illustrate to what class of ministers he belonged, and also serve as a key-note to one phase of his character, by no means the worst. Contrary to the opinion of smokers in this country, he thought his cigars should have a certain degree of dampness, and to secure this, he used to keep them in a little dark place under the pulpit, because it imparted the exact degree of dampness required; he did this instead of wrapping them in a cabbage leaf, which he thought a poor substitute for his little pulpit cuddy. One naturally thinks in this connection of fox-hunting, card-playing, wine-bibbing parsons, and the Rev. Caleb will not be found to "disable" the judgment.

He was chosen a fellow of King's College, Cambridge, in 1801, and was presented by his college to the perpetual curacy of Tiverton, Prior's Quarter, Devonshire; there he lived and flourished, after his kind, for many years.

"Lacon, or many things in few words," is the only work of any enduring fame that he gave to the world. He wrote, besides, "Hypocrisy, a satirical poem," "Napoleon, a poem," with strong English views of Napoleon; "Modern Antiquity," and others, none of which have sufficient of Attic salt to preserve them from oblivion.

In manner, he seems to have been kind, agreeable, and sociable enough, to win for him warm friends among those who knew him intimately and were not repelled by his principles. He made no personal pretence to religious sentiment, and cannot, therefore, be charged with hypocrisy, though, unfit as he was, he entered the pulpit and won the gown. A man of his talent could not but preach with great force, and it is said, that at times he would be as eloquent as Demosthenes in praise of Christian virtues. Indeed, in a mass of apothegms, drawn, generally, from the darkest and weakest points in human nature, some gems occur that illustrate the best. It would be difficult to put the point more strongly than in this, for instance: "Sincerely to aspire after virtue, is to gain her, and zealously to labor after her wages, is to receive them. Those that seek her early, will find her before it is late; her reward also is with her, and she will come quickly. For the breast of a good man is a little heaven commencing on earth; where the Deity sits enthroned with unrivalled influence, every safety from danger, resource from sterility, even subjugated passion, 'like the wind and storm fulfilling his word.'" Or this: "Vice stings us even in our pleasures, but virtue consoles us even in our pains." The following also comes strangely from a man who made a cigar case of his pulpit: "In pulpit eloquence, the grand difficulty lies here; to give the subject all the dignity it so fully deserves, without attaching any importance to ourselves. The Christian messenger cannot think too highly of his prince, or too humbly of himself. This is that secret art which captivates and improves an audience, and which all who see will fancy they could imitate, whilst most who try it will fail. '*Sperat idem, sudat multum, frustraque laborat ausus idem*;'" which, being freely rendered means, He that undertakes it will have his trouble for his pains.

I must make an exception to the remark that Colton made no personal pretence to religious sentiment. Although he would, on Sunday, make the most irresistible appeals to the consciences of his hearers, and "the next day gallop after the fox with a pack of hounds, fish, shoot, or fight a man, in company with sporting blacklegs, bruisers, dicers, *et hoc genus omne;*" he, on one occasion, enacted the role of "When the D—l was sick," &c., without being the sick man himself. The circumstance is striking and I will give it in the words of one of his biographers: "Among Colton's sporting companions was a very abandoned Devonshire squire, who had squandered a fine fortune, and beggared his family, by his extravagance and dissipation. Becoming sick, and his physicians having assured him that a speedy death was inevitable, he dispatched a messenger for Colton, and demanded of him an acknowledgment of a fact, which he said all parsons' lives declared, 'that their religion and all religion was a lie.' This Colton refused to do, wherefore the dying wretch, in a paroxysm of rage, called down curse after curse upon the head of the conscience-stricken parson, and immediately expired. Language cannot describe Colton's horror; he returned home and shut himself up in his chamber; on the following Sunday, he preached upon the uncertainty of life, and in a most impressive manner discoursed upon the dreadful realities of death, judgment and eternity, closing his sermon with a solemn declaration that he had seen the error of his ways, and was resolved to lead a new life. His reformation, though of longer continuance than the morning cloud, was not lasting. Three, four, five months of exemplary conduct and then came the first symptoms of declension, in the shape of the parson's grey horse harnessed to a dog cart, with his gun and brace of pointers, in charge of a groom, the whole 'turn out' for starting, and waiting at the entrance of the churchyard, on Sunday evening, the last night of August, to carry the parson, so soon as service was over, to a celebrated shooting ground, five and twenty miles off, that he might be on the spot ready for the irresistible first of September."

Colton was essentially an adventurer and a gambler. He is said to have written a tract in which it is shown, beyond the possibility of a doubt, that when in gambling, the chances are in the slightest degree against a man, he must in the end be ruined. A fact which has been forced on most persons, who have tried it. After writing this tract, he went and laid down his last thousand pounds upon the rouelle. He won, he doubled his stake and won again, and went on doubling and winning until he broke the bank; but went back the next evening and was ruined himself. He attempted money-making in various ways. In Paris he was "a horse dealer, then a wine merchant, and then again a picture dealer." It is said that he won within a year or two £25,000. By gambling and speculations he lost all he made; and writes thus in "Lacon:" "The gamester, if he die a martyr to his profession, is doubly ruined. He adds his soul to every other loss, and by the act of suicide, renounces earth to forfeit heaven." He is not the only man

> "Who never said a foolish thing
> And never did a wise one."

Perhaps his most discreditable mode of "raising the wind" was that adopted in Paris, as his other resources failed him. He extorted money from the wealthy Islanders who visited Paris, either by black mail or begging. On one occasion, when he heard that the Duke of Northumberland was in Paris, at the coronation of Charles X., he immediately said that "the Duke is on my ground and must pay me contribution money." He made a touching appeal to His Grace by letter, who sent him an order for 25 Napoleons. Then, rather shabbily dressed, but bedizened with a great profusion of watch chains and other jewelry, of which he was extravagantly fond, he presented himself to the Duke's banker. "The latter," to use the words of his biographer, "struck with the brilliant decorations of his otherwise half genteelly dressed visitor, and supposing that he was some eccentric son of wealth and nobility, bowed him, with most obsequious grace, to his private cabinet, and waited to hear his brilliant visitor's business.—When it was told the banker replied: 'Can it be possible, s-i-r? You are not the Mr. Colton, s-i-r, mentioned in His Grace's order?' 'The arrived petition, s-i-r, can't be yours?' 'Let's see,' said C. 'Yes, that's it; but the Duke has made a trifling mistake: in his note to me, he promised me £25, but you can rectify that little error.' The banker, however, refused to pay more than 25 Louis to the clerical beggar, whom the Duke's note described as a *distressed, sick, suffering clergyman.*"

Some very discreditable cases of levying black mail on his countrymen are told of him; but he was not always successful, as he was balked in such an attempt by the nerve of the Duchess of St. Albans.

The shores of America were honored by the presence of this clerical adventurer. Before he went to Paris, he visited this country to get rid of troublesome creditors, in 1824. He landed at New Port, in Rhode Island, is said to have spent some time in New York, and to have written articles for the New York papers; thence he went to Charleston, South Carolina, where he must have created a good impression, as he was highly spoken of in the "Southern Literary Journal."—It is supposed that he spent about two years in this country, after which he went to Paris.

With regard to the book which we have before us, it has been said, "That few works have appeared for the last fifty years, which contain more original thoughts happily expressed." Those apothegms, which give the name to the book, are mostly too long to enter much into the proverbial sayings of the world, but they do enter largely into current literature. "Lacon" is also largely embellished with pointed and appropriate anecdotes. The author's knowledge of mankind was not altogether, though to a great extent, "an acquaintance with his weak points, his infirmities, hypocrisies and short comings."—He says in his preface, which is very trenchant, "Should my readers think some of my conclusions too severe, they will, in justice, recollect that my object is truth, that my subject is man, and that a handsome picture cannot represent deformity." Alas! that it should be so; but is there not enough truth in the statement, to make us feel that there is at least some excuse for an author to say severe things? Unfortunately, the standard of principle, as well for religion and politics as business, is lamentably low. We can speak for our own country, let these laconics tell the story of the country where they were inspired. From these many lessons of worldly wisdom may be learnt, or learnt without them, forced upon men by their daily intercourse. But we are happy to know that they are not of universal application. A few men can be pointed out, here and there, *rari nantes*, whom it is not necessary to *watch* in our business transactions. It is deplorable for a country when such maxims enter largely into business operations; or when they are justified by the conduct of professed Christians, or properly characterize the motives of political leaders. In the opinion of a large portion of our people, Walpole's estimate of the corruptibility of mankind, seems to be taken for granted; but we will still believe that the "faithful man" can be found.—With all due honor be it stated that Walpole himself refused £60,000 to interfere to save the Earl of Derwentwater, when under sentence of death. Whether the great minister boasted his own virtue, I cannot say. The standard of proverbial wisdom is vastly lowered since the Son of Sirac told us that "A wise son maketh a glad father," and "That treasures of wickedness profit nothing." Now, I have mistaken this generation very much, if from one end of the country to the other, one does not hear "sons" commended more as "*sharp*" or "*cute*" boys (atrocious idea) than recommended and taught to be wise ones. The italicized words are the key-notes of American education. Solomon counsels caution against securityship, carelessness, dealing with a slack hand, &c., but tells of fidelity, diligence, liberality, and the "memory of the just." To adopt Solomon's proverbs would be to force us to adopt a different standard of success than that which we practically propose to ourselves.

"Lacon" is truly "many things in few words;" the author touches on every imaginable subject; he writes *de omnibus rebus, et quibusdam aliis*, and throws light on all. In such a mass of apothegms, anecdotes and good things, it is difficult to make a selection. Somewhat at random, I will select a few, avoiding the longer ones, and those that are of a more argumentative character; and one of the very best is one of the first I find. "Men will wrangle for religion, write for it, fight for it, die for it, anything—*but live for it.*" Does not the following tell the story of "Stonewall" Jackson's life and success?

"Secrecy of design, when combined with rapidity of execution, like the column that guided Israel in the desert, becomes the guardian pillar of light and fire to our friends, a cloud of impenetrable darkness to our enemies." The following apothegm is generally accepted as true. "Times of general calamity and confusion have ever been productive of the greatest minds. The purest ore is produced from the hottest furnace, and the brightest thunderbolt is elicited from the darkest storm." What, then, must be thought of the state of a country whose purest ores and brightest thunderbolts are such as Thadeus Stevens and B —— Butler, after passing through such calamity and confusion? The morals of the following must be left to the casuist. "The sun should not set upon our anger, neither should he rise upon our confidence. We should forgive freely, but forget rarely. I will not be revenged, and this I owe to my enemy; but I will remember, and this I owe to myself." What do the advocates of *The Code* think of this? "If all seconds were as adverse to duels as their principals, very little blood would be shed in that way."

The following is commended to every body South of the Potomac, and especially those who live in the track of Sherman and Sheridan: "Murmur at nothing, if our ills are reparable it is ungrateful, if remediless it is vain. A Christian builds his fortitude on a better foundation than stoicism; he is pleased with every thing that happens, because he knows that it could not happen unless it had first pleased God, and that which pleases him must be best. He is assured that no new thing can befall him, and that he is in the hands of a father who will prove him with no affliction, that resignation cannot conquer, or that death cannot cure." The following anecdote is told in connection with Erasmus' doubts as to whether he had the courage to become a martyr. "Had he been brought to the stake, and recanted in that situation (which no one believes he would have done,) I question whether he would have found a better salvo for his conscience, than that of Mustapha, a Greek Christian, of Constantinople. This man was much respected by the Turk; but a curiosity he could not resist, induced him to run the hazard of being present at some of the esoteric ceremonies of the Moslem faith, to see which, is to incur the penalty of death, unless the infidel should atone for the offence by embracing the faith of Mahomet. Mustapha chose the latter alternative, and this saved his life. As he was known to be a man of strict integrity, he did not escape the remonstrances of former friends, to whom he made this excuse for his apostacy. '*I thought it best to trust a merciful God with my soul, than those wretches with my body.*'"

The following, among others, does not show as high an appreciation of the gentler sex as the author would probably have had, if he had been a better man. "If you cannot fill a woman with love of you, fill her above the brim with love of herself; all that runs over will be yours." Of wit, he says: "Wit, however, is one of the few things which has been rewarded more often than it has been defined. A certain Bishop said to his Chaplain; what is wit? The Chaplain replied, 'The Rectory of B—— is vacant, give it to me and that will be wit.' 'Prove it' said his Lordship, 'and you shall have it.' '*It would be a good thing well applied,*' rejoined the Chaplain." He does not say whether he was rewarded.

The following is too good a repartee to be passed over; it is found in an observation on Voltaire. "Voltaire, on hearing the name of Haller mentioned to him by an English teacher, at Ferney, burst forth into a violent panegyric upon him; his visitor told him that such praise was most disinterested, for that Haller, by no means, spoke so highly of him. 'Well, well, *n'importe*' replied Voltaire, 'perhaps we are *both* mistaken.'"

The recent war has furnished an opportunity to test the truth of this. "An Irishman fights before he reasons, a Scotchman reasons before he fights, an Englisman is not particular as to the order of precedence, but will do either to accommodate his customers. A modern general has said that the best troops would be as follows: an Irishman half drunk, a Scotchman half starved, and an Englishman with his belly full." As we, of the South, are now the subjects of governmental experiment, the two following will have a home bearing. "Of governments, that of the *mob* is most sanguinary, that of soldiers most expensive, and that of civilians the most vexatious;" and, "Despotism can no more exist in a nation, until the liberty of the press be destroyed, than the night can happen before the sun has set." Colton might have learnt a lesson of inconsistency, had he remained long enough in our *favored* land, which would have made him drop this axiom, or amend it with an exception.—In a note, our author quotes the following from Sir Wm. Drummond, which, as a proverb maker, he must have envied with his whole heart. "He that will not reason is a bigot, he that cannot reason is a fool, and he that dares not reason is a slave." The following quartette shall close my excerpta. "The excesses of youth are drafts upon old age, payable with interest, about thirty years after date." "An act by which we make one friend and one enemy, is a losing game; because revenge is a much stronger principle than gratitude." "When the million applaud you, seriously ask yourself what harm you have done; when they censure you, what good!" "The keenest abuse of our enemies will not hurt us so much with the discerning, as the injudicious praise of our friends."—Which reminds us of "He that blesseth his friend with a loud voice, rising early in the morning, it shall be counted a curse to him."—Prov. xxvii. 14. Blatant praise surfeits. Aristides was ostracised for having such friends.

Apothegms, anecdotes, illustrations might be selected *ad infinitum*, but my limits, and possibly the reader's patience forbids. It remains only to tell what became of this unfortunate man, who wrote so wisely, and acted so unwisely. "For a number of years," writes a biographer, "he had suffered a great deal from a complaint, for the cure of which, the knife of the surgeon was indispensable. The disease grew worse, and Colton, going to Fontainebleau, sent for his friend, Maj. Sherwell, and without divulging his intention of committing suicide, said that he must either die by the crisis of the complaint, or risk dying under the operator's hands. He made his will, made Maj. S. acquainted with his wishes, and after chatting pleasantly, bade him good-night and retired. It afterwards appeared, that about midnight he applied a pistol to his head, and by his own hand terminated his existence. He died Saturday, April 28, 1832."

A few days before his death he wrote a short poem which closed with the following stanzas:

"Devouring grave! we might the less deplore
  The extinguished lights that in the darkness dwell,
Wouldst thou from that lost zodiac one restore
  That might the enigma solve—and doubt, man's tyrant quell
To live in darkness—in despair to die—

Is this indeed the boon to mortals given?
Is there no port—no rock, nor refuge nigh?
There is—to those who fix their anchor hope in Heaven.
Turn then, O man, and cast all else aside;
Direct thy wandering thoughts to things above;
Low at the Cross bow down—in that confide,
Till doubt be lost in faith—and bliss secured in love."

THE SYSTEM OF ENGLISH GANG LABOR.

HARDLY had the cry of indignation been hushed at the horrible developments of suffering and ruin perpetrated upon children engaged in manufactories, when the same *Commission* was called upon to expose still more flagrant abuses, prevailing among agricultural labors in certain parts of England, at the details of which indignation can only be equalled by the surprise and pity aroused. Were the facts gathered by any private individual, or proclaimed under the sanction of a political party, people would be ready enough to question their truth. But the work has been done by a Commission of Parliament,* men who would conceal rather than declare a national disgrace. And who, at least in the impartiality that has marked their proceedings, deserve a nation's gratitude.

It is not necessary now to draw comparisons—rather let us state facts. Right or wrong, the leaven of English abolitionism has, as far as the Anglo-Saxon race is concerned, destroyed the institution of Negro Slavery, but the fearful truths of the Report above referred to are, enough surely to make men wonder if England was really in earnest when abolishing slavery, and enquire whether, among certain portions of her laboring classes, a system has not grown up to which negro slavery ranked as freedom.

Abuses among the English people are usually examined into by a Commission. This Commission reports to Parliament, and generally a law, if necessary, is framed to suit the facts evolved. Early in 1867, the Commission completed their report, and not until then did Englishmen realize the horror of the terrible abuse that had crept in among them, which now rests as one of the darkest spots on the escutcheon of a free country.

This evil is known as "the agricultural gang system," and is confined, almost exclusively, to the counties of Lincolnshire, Huntingdonshire, Cambridgeshire, Norfolk, Suffolk, and Nottinghamshire, as also to portions of

* See Report of the Children's Employment Commission, 1867.

Northampton, Bedford and Rutland.

An organized gang consists of (1) a gang master, (2) a number of women, (3) a number of children of both sexes. They variously contain from ten to forty persons. About twenty being the usual number. There are two species, (a) private and (b) public gangs. The evils that attend them both, are similar in kind, but the evidence rather goes to establish the fact that public gangs fare better than private ones, i. e., those hired, maintained, controlled, and worked by the farmer himself.

As was said before, the gang consists of three elements, the master, women and children.—These enter into the composition of the organization in no regular proportions, but the number of each depends upon the character of labor for which the gang may be engaged, and upon the capacities of the various localities for supplying either women or children.

The question naturally arises, in what operations do they engage, and during what portion of the year are they employed? Agriculture in England demands a large array of women and children, and it would not be overstating the truth to say that three fifths of the field laborers are women and children. There is a great deal of light work they perform as quickly and as perfectly as men, while their services cost the farmer not half what other labor would. The women and children clean the fields, pick up stones, top and pull turnips, set plants, hoe potatoes, weed the grain, spread manure, gather the crops, etc. In most places the gangs are busy throughout the whole year. Winter and summer, it is toil alike. If they become cold, wet, hungry, weary, the gang master allows them hardly a moment's rest before in his own words they must "go in again."

The most important consideration is the character of the persons controlling and working in these gangs. Many of those composing the gang are adepts in every species of crime and wickedness. This would matter not so greatly if young children year by year were not added to the organization, who in turn are cast loose upon the world, after having served an apprenticeship of six or seven years, amid scenes from which it would be impossible to come forth without having lost shame, virtue, honesty, and every principle elevating to humanity.

The gang master collects together a number of women and children, and engages with a farmer to work by time, or the job. In the larger number of cases these men were found to be totally unfit for the control of children and women, being men who did "catch work," who the farmer was unwilling to receive into his regular employ, "men of indolent and drinking habits, and in some cases of notorious depravity." With such men as their leaders and masters, it could hardly be otherwise, than that the members of the gang should reflect their moral character.—The report is bad from beginning to end, yet no sadder truth is established, than that the young adult women are the most degraded and depraved of all the persons employed.

Little children begin to labor in these gangs at five, six, seven, eight and nine years of age.—While the parents sometimes kept their smaller ones at home, in very numerous cases they made "the employment of the younger children a condition upon which they let the older ones go." As the period of labor ranges from eight to fourteen hours per day, it is not difficult to comprehend how destructive are the effects of a system upon the constitution, which demands so lengthened a service from children barely able to walk. Yet all this is true with a still further terrible fact that the children, in addition to eight or fourteen hours' toil as the case may be, are compelled to walk a distance of two, three, four, five, six, seven and even eight miles, each way.—Rarely if ever has such misery been depicted as that unfolded in the leaves of the Commissioners' investigation. We quote an instance or two lest the reader should accuse us of exaggeration:

"A gang master employing children, and having had some as young as six and seven years, used to take his gang to two farms six and seven miles, and two or three times, a distance of seven and eight miles." Again,

"Elsewhere a woman, whose children began young, some before seven years of age, says: 'Mine have gone four, five, six and seven miles,' and adds 'that the little ones, even those getting seven cents a day had to go.'"

It is nothing wonderful then that the children are overcome with fatigue, and that death frequently results from the mere physical prostration and weariness incidental to such cruel and barbarous treatment. Day after day these little ones drag their weary limbs along. If exhausted, they must "go in again." If disposed to play, or indulge in a pleasant word with their neighbor, a stroke from the whip or stick of the gangmaster is the response to that little exuberance of spirit in beings, whose lives are worn away and sacrificed to the rapacity and greed of their heartless employers. But let the report speak.

"A little boy five years old used to be carried home from his work by the other children, and elsewhere, you see the big ones come dragging the little ones home, and sometimes taking them on their backs when over-tired." Another mother says of her little boy, "that he had been six miles, and further, to work, and had come home so tired that he scarcely could stand, and that they had also had to send out, late in the evening, to look for him, and had found him dropped to sleep in a cowshed."

The profits of a gang master rarely exceed the wages earned by an ordinary farm hand. They are gang masters chiefly because they cannot get other employment, whether that inability arises from age, misfortune or misconduct. Their profits are principally made by "piece work," for in certain operations, the amount of labor to be done can be approximated sufficiently, to render its performance a matter of contract. It is here that the capabilities of the gang master for utilizing the services of his gang become apparent. It is his object and his interest to make the women and children perform the greatest amount of labor in the least possible time, and how he succeeds by promises, threats and blows, the investigation abundantly attests

"When work is taken by the piece, it is generally said to be harder than at any other time.—The poor children, young as they are, always know whether it is piece work or not, as they say 'when it is piece work they are not allowed to stop one moment to rest.'"

It is the ordinary practice among the gang masters to carry a whip or stick, not so much for use, they say, as to exert a salutary impression upon the children by the presence of such an instrument. Yet instances are recorded in the evidence, and cases have come before the magistrates repeatedly, in which it appeared, the whip was used far more effectively than for purposes of mere fright. Who is to restrain the gang master? He is independent of the employer—bound to him only in the matter of wages, and still worse, the farmers, in the treatment of their own gangs, and in their encouragement and connivance at the abuses of the system, are proven far worse than the gang masters themselves. The children are entirely under their control, and complaints are useless, where, as it frequently occurs, the parents are dissipating in idleness, the gains purchased by the physical and moral destruction of their offspring.

"A mother, whose boy had never complained, says, that on hearing from others of the gang master's 'flogging him,' I looked and found bruises on him from it.—It would be, as I was told, for standing up, or looking about or something of that kind. I did not notice it for fear of making him disobedient. Another mother testifies, that 'one of my girls complained that the gang master had hit her with a spud, but I told her no doubt it was her own fault.'"

Sometimes, the children were cast into the water, at other times held up by the back of the neck and the chin until nearly insensible. Again, knocked down, or kicked, or beaten with hoes and spuds, (straps,) etc. Such, then, are the means of punishment employed by a depraved, irresponsible gang master, upon children whose parents are unwilling to protect them, and who, alas! are unable to protect themselves.—The interest of the gang master, it is evident at a glance, is ever opposed to the well being of the child. Slavery at least prompted the master to protect and preserve the health of a slave, but gang labor, with most of the evils of slavery, adds this one, that the person in whose charge the laborer may be, cannot hope anything from the pecuniary interest of the employer. A redundancy of population will always insure the needed supply of children.—The gang master may destroy them as he pleases, by excesses of toil, it matters not, others will fill the places of those who have been disabled—or worse—killed outright. The pittance of eight or twelve cents a day will always tempt parents, whose wages are barely sufficient to support themselves, or who may be willing to make victims of their children, to their own sloth and rioting.

The gang system previous to 1868 was largely on the increase. The excuse pleaded is scarcity of labor. But this cry is very much like complaining that one has no family after driving off all his children. In the portion of England cursed by the operations of the gang system, no doubt laborers on the farm are scarce, but it is because landlords have removed and refuse to build farm cottages. And will the reader know why? The answer is obvious; to prevent an increase of the *poor rates*. They have driven the working men out of the parish lest they should become paupers, and thus increase taxation for local purposes, and now reëmploy them in gangs at a much less remuneration than they could do otherwise, without the least possibility of their increasing the parochial roll of pauperism. Forced to leave the farms, the laborers must press into the villages outlying the farming districts. These become "cities of refuge" for the surrounding country, and willing or unwilling, into these dens of infamy, filth and vice, the peasantry must congregate. Farms containing from 150 to 200 acres have not a single resident laborer. All being drawn from the towns and villages in the vicinity, coming out by day and returning at night.

The Commissioners sum up the objections under three heads.

1. The moral effects of herding together a number of women and children, especially when under the control of such men as usually constitute gang masters.

2. The interference with education.

3. The exposing children to such an excessive amount of hardship and suffering.

A system morally, socially, and physically bad, cannot have much good said in its favor. Every individual examined bore unqualified testimony as to the demoralizing tendencies of the gang system. The mere mingling of the sexes in such employment would naturally lead to fearful results, but how much more terrible when under the control of men, who themselves are of the lowest and most sensual type. The older women and children corrupt the younger ones, whenever they become members of the gang, and soon educate them in all the vice and wickedness, they in their turn had acquired under it. Obscene language, oaths and curses are the ordinary styles of expression. With forty persons in a line, the gang masters, even if desirous, would be unable to repress such proceedings. The districts, in which the gang system is found, show a wretched state of morals—no less than three, four, and even five times the usual ratio of illegitimacy being registered. Returning from the fields, the gangs are free from all restraint whatever, and so low and brutal have they become, that no respectable person, can, without insult, encounter them.—Ninety-five per cent. of them never enter a church, and in ignorance and humanizing qualities they are but little better than the natives of interior Africa. A minister testified that during a missionary life in Africa, he had "never seen such shameless wickedness."

From the very nature of the system, it must act as an absolute bar to even an acquisition of the elements of an education. A large majority of the children enter the gangs previous to their ninth year, an age too early for any progress in, or lengthened retention, of knowledge. The work is too continuous to admit of alternating labor and schooling, and even if a month now and then was given, the influences of the gang have rendered the children too rude and intractable to profit from any short lived advantages.

Yet the educational side has another phase. The farmers are opposed to the introduction of schools. The more ignorant and brutal the people, the more easily are they retained for agricultural services. Not ashamed of introducing and continuing such a system, the farmers hinder as far as they can, all efforts for the improvement and elevation of the children and their parents. One went so far as to say, "that he would sooner give $50 to close a school than $5 to keep it open." Another, "We don't want schools, we can't get servants as it is."

In some places, attempts have been made to set in operation "a half time system," by which the children should work half the week, and attend school the remainder, but so far the efforts of those interested have been unavailing. With parents and employers averse to education, nothing can be done by individuals.—The only preventive is to enforce the majesty of law. And from present indications, compulsory education ere long will put an end to the dreadful evil of gang labor.

The physical hardships and suffering are almost incredible. The duties required are especially injurious to women and children. Carrying stones, and pulling turnips are very trying on the spine, and such labor has tended to treble the rate of infant mortality. The mothers, in order to make the children sleep, drug them with opium, and this must be added to the long list of horrors, which renders the gang system odious in the eyes of a civilized people. A mere statement of facts is all that is necessary. The evils direct and indirect arising out of such a state of things are innumerable. In truth, the whole system has not one ameliorating feature, not one redeeming phase to soften the ruin and misery consequent upon its practice.

To meet the shameful and degrading facts brought to light, by the efforts of the Commission, a law was enacted, which went into operation on the 1st of January, 1868. It decrees that no child, under eight years of age, shall be employed in a gang, that no female shall labor with males, that no gang-master shall employ females, unless there be a gang-mistress employed with him; that every gang-master or mistress shall be licensed by two Justices of the Peace, which license shall be in force a period of six months, its issuance to cost twenty-five cents, and in no case, to be held by the keeper of a Public House. It also provides that the license shall state the distance, to which the children may be carried for work.

Such are the provisions for the eradication of an evil, unexampled for virulence in the annals of English history. Whether it will answer the end proposed, remains to be seen. The disease has been gently dealt with. The moral difficulties have been but slightly remedied, while the physical are left almost untouched. With parents, farmers, and gang-masters conniving at the practice, the enforcement of the law will be a matter not easily accomplished. Every lover of the human race must rejoice that the evil has attracted attention. The system had advocates indeed: but the voice of the people, beyond the districts interested, was unanimous for the interference of the law. Time alone can determine the efficacy of the prescription. The diseased branches may have been lopped off, but the vigorous root will send them forth again. Englishmen deal slowly and cautiously with political evils, yet they generally deal surely. However thorough and earnest may be one's dislike of the nation, all must give them credit for acting promptly, and the Commissioners for exposing, thoroughly, this practice, so disgraceful and brutalizing to humanity. The gang system is, comparatively, modern, having existed no where, more than sixty years. Yet in its short term of life, it has already reduced to the level of barbarism, thousands who might otherwise have been prosperous, happy, and enlightened.

THE FIRE-FLY.

'Tis in the lazy, summer hours
The bees are humming 'mid the flowers,
The painted butterfly's at rest
Upon the lily's spotless breast;
Deep in the rose the fire-fly lies
Awaiting evening's darkened skies,
Breathes in its perfume, sucks its dew,
And gathers strength to soar anew,
When darting through the dusky air
'Twill sparkle here and twinkle there.

Just so amid life's flowers, I lie—
Am neither bee nor butterfly—
For in these sunny hours, I find
That, like the fire-fly, my mind
Will always darken if I rest
Too long on pleasure's perfumed breast,
And brightest shines, when on the wing
And feeling work a glorious thing,
It gathers truth e'en from its doubt
As darkest clouds white snow give out.

So, I but sip the rose's dew
That wasted strength I may renew,
And sparkle with a twinkling light
Ere twilight deepens into night.

MARY BAYARD CLARKE

THE DICKENS' DINNER.

BY T. C. DE LEON.

MR. DICKENS has "been," he certainly has "gone," and there are many who declare admiringly that he has most emphatically "done it."

Several months since, this writer had occasion to review "Mr. Dickens' Readings" in this magazine; and to refer to the wild orgy of boot-licking indulged in by a set of super-servile flunkies. But he then tried to do full justice to the earnest purpose—no less than to the great mental grasp and peculiar humor—of the first writer of his school.

As then predicted Mr. Dickens' tour through the country was one long and steady ovation. A few rabid newspapers spattered his back with mire, as soon as it was turned; but the great majority licked his boot with a slimy osculation that must have been infinitely more disgusting to him. The more respectable journals, however—and to their great credit be it spoken—were firm and fixed in their declarations of appreciation from first to last. They spoke plainly and honestly of the strong reasons, the American people had to mistrust the hand that had so scourged them before, now that it was so cordially offered to their grasp; but spoke, too, of the very good reasons for that same scourging and gave a warning note for the future.

But despite the snarling of the one, and with little heed for the warning of the other, that potent American Sovereign—the People—rose with one accord to welcome Charles Dickens. They not only "gave him their hands," but—unlike the constituents of Pericles—they held in them goodly sheaves of the "money of the the realm."

If the great humorist saw any peculiar appropriateness in the color of the offering, that certainly did not cause its rejection.

The people welcomed Mr. Dickens of their own free will; the people saw him, heard him, and thrust their greenbacks upon him; and finally—when all else was done, the accredited representatives of the people—the Press—fed him.

For some time, this latter process had been in contemplation, Mr. Dickens himself. unlike a coy young lady, listening to the wooers and "fixing the day" with prompt celerity.

The committee, who invited him to the banquet, was supposed to represent the country; but unless the great city of New York has adopted the favorite axiom of the *Grand Monarque*, it could hardly be said to do so. But the guest accepted it in that light, believing ignorance to be bliss and that there was no folly like losing a good dinner. At last the day arrived.

Delmonico's famous saloon and his no less famous cooks were put under contribution. The rightest right hands in his employ were bid to exercise all their cunning; and the most secret nooks of his cellarage were ransacked for libations fit to pour on such an occasion.

The busy note of preparation and the nose-some steam of close-completion penetrated even into the hungriest nooks of the great Bohemia. Wild eyed men, with long hair depending lank upon greasy collars, blinked in the unaccustomed sunlight, and trod upon each other's unblacked boots in the eager rush before the Secretary's door. But, though, Delmonico might open no sublime Porte, the laws of Grand Turkey (pardon the pun) were inexorable as the Medes; and only two hundred favored and famished penmen were permitted to invest fifteen dollars each, and then *receive an invitation* to the feast.

When the evening came, though the dinner was fixed for the unusual hour of five, the anxious two hundred were prompt beyond precedent. Conversation, broken by many false alarms and frequent eager glances towards the door, killed the time until the appointed hour. Then the tale was complete, except the anxiously expected guest.

Five minutes passed; ten, fifteen—yet no Dickens appeared.

The parlors were filled with, perhaps, as bright a set of men as could be collected between walls. The great guns of disquisition, the columbiads of argument, the mortars of monthly literature, the small arms of paragraphing, and the pop-crackers of reporting—all these were there—arranged *en barbette* for the grand Salvo to the Field-Marshal of the Pen. But as the evening of doubt settled down over what was to be the grand field—one by one the loud reports of the columbiads fell into silence; the mortars grew black; the small arms ceased to crackle, and even the pop-crackers lost their fizz!

In plain English, Mr. Dickens was late, very late—and every one of his two hundred hosts began to look very blue, and to feel very hungry.

A runner, swift of foot as the sons of Atalanta, was dispatched; then another, and another.—Vague rumors of every conceivable mishap went round the room in uneasy whispers; and every member of the Bohemian Congress offered his own resolution.

It is a fact, worthy of note, that there was no movement to impeach Mr. Dickens!

Perhaps the diners felt the eyes of Delaware were upon them.

Finally, cloudy doubts vanished, and the sun of Dickens shone upon the great two hundred; albeit the foot of Dickens was in a flannel shoe, while he leaned upon a friend and a stick. There was a subdued buzz of welcome, but it was understood the guest was too sick for formal introduction; and—Bohemia behaving itself pretty well on the whole—the dinner began.

There are no better dinners in the world than can be gotten up in America; New York dinners are perhaps the best here; and it is probable Delmonico's are the best in New York.

Therefore, all the details of the feast, eating, drinking, and appointment—which must be taken for granted—were all that could be desired; and more than one guest declared that a more appropriate and excellent dinner, of the kind, was never seen on either side of the Atlantic.

The guest of the evening sat at a centre table, at the head of the great saloon, with the British flag draped above his head. He was flanked by Mr. Greeley, of the *Tribune*, who presided, and by Mr. Raymond, of the *Times*.

Seven other tables ran across the room, so arranged that almost every one might see the lion of the occasion. Then there was fast and furious mastication—violent thrust of fork, and fierce lunge of knife: there was popping of corks, gurgling of fluid and chinking of glass:—and then, all was still.

Everybody—even who had not

heard of them before—has, by this time, read Mr. Dickens' American books; and everybody, of course, remembers the *New York Sewer*, the *Rowdy Journal*, and Mr. Jefferson Brick, as therein described.

It may have been because of their peculiar fitness to heap coals of fire upon his head!—it may have been because "the whirligig of time brings in strange revenges;"—but it has been more than once guessed that the President of the Evening was the Editor of the *Sewer*; and that Mr. Raymond was the original of Jefferson Brick!

It is rather sad to think that the unities were not kept up; but Mr. Bennet, who figured as the man of the *Rowdy Journal*, was absent;—some said from persistent and long-suffering indignation; others because of a misfortune in his family, not to be mentioned here.

When the cloth was withdrawn, Mr. Greeley made some pertinent remarks to introduce the toast to the Guest of the Evening.

To this, Mr. Dickens—though suffering most fearful twinges of gout, and being besides, as hoarse as the raven of his own *Barnaby Rudge*—responded in an earnest and sincere speech, happily put, and with not enough humor to lessen its reality. He spoke of the pleasure his visit had given him; of the vast changes even in manners, and morals; of Progress, with the big P; and of his early mistakes and misrepresentations of the country.

While he did not personally "take it all back," from Mr. Greeley and Mr. Raymond, he yet said plainly in effect that they did him very proud indeed to let him eat their dinner; he did not state any objection to doing so frequently; and it was believed—by one or two ardent and sympathetic young nobles of Bohemia, present—that had Bennet, *pére*, been present, Mr. Dickens would have embraced him, offered to kiss his cheek and proposed to write for the personal columns of the *Herald*.

In regard to his two American books already written, Mr. Dickens cried *peccavi* in a voice broken by pledges and promises not to write another. But he stated that he would hereafter give up his own paper—or part of it—to a continuous vindication of America and Americans; to a sort of running fire of "taking it all back." He moreover promised to write—and to make his sons and their sons to the third and fourth generation—write appendices to the two American books; and he drew a beautiful picture of the cordial and unweaned love of the Britisher for the Yankee; of the perfect accord of sympathy, of taste and of thought between the two.

Now, seriously to speak, all due allowance should be made for a man who has been boot-licked and lionized—puffed and enriched—dined and wined. But even under these circumstances there is a flavor of Buncombe about the farewell speech that may give us a suspicion, that many things in his America became him more than the leaving it. We can readily appreciate that—seen through the magnifying glasses of fifty, things look very different from what they did to the piercing, but superficial glance of twenty-five. Whatever we, at home, may think of our present men, manners and morals—as viewed by the light of Charles Sumner and Ben. Butler, rather than that of Henry Clay and John C. Calhoun; by that of our up-town churches, our stock markets and our absconding tellers, rather than by the hard-fisted cant of Penn and the Puritans—it is natural to understand that the surface seems improved to a stranger.

We have more brown fronts and are addicted to cleaner linen; we wear our hair shorter, and are given to a more generous use of the fork; and we have G. A. Rs. and K. K. Ks. in secret instead of bowie-knife fights in public. On the surface, we are perhaps smoother and cleaner than ever before; but what a seething and foul mass of festering corruption underlies that surface, one must perhaps be in it—if not of it—to appreciate.

It is natural then, that with a calmer judgment weighing the best of everything, as it was presented to him; and with his heart warmed by adulation, real appreciation and pecuniary success, Mr. Dickens should have sung his palinode. We can feel that he really meant what he said; and can even honor him for a full and frank confession of an error of his youth.

But it may strike us that the promise to *write up* America in his particular journal will, perhaps, be as evanescent as the bubbles that broke in his wine that night; and could we suspect the great author of being—like his own Jerry Cruncher—"an honest tradesman," there would seem an admirable advertisement for new editions of the American books in the promised appendices.

But the most absurd—and seemingly the most insincere-thing Mr. Dickens said was about the American in England.

The native Britisher thinks that every other nationality is far beneath his own—and none so immeasurably far as the American. Once he pitied and despised "the blasted Yankee." Now he looks on him with a fierce loathing—with contempt not unmixed with fear.

The conventional American, he still considers a long-haired creature, with jack-knife, yellow waistcoat and dress-coat at breakfast; and—whatever travel and association may have done in individual cases—what the *national* opinion of the Yankee is we can find by easy reference to a file of *Punch*; to the leaders of the *Times*; to the Alabama question, or to any well thumbed copy of "*Martin Chuzzlewit!*"

But I have wandered so far from the dinner it has grown cold.

After Mr. Dickens, the "New York Press" was toasted, for the after dinner sentiments,—like those of Charity—began at home. Mr. Raymond—*not* in the character of Jefferson Brick—responded in a sensible and condensed speech. Then there were given *seriatim* the Weekly, Monthly, Boston, Philadelphia, North-western, South-western, Southern and all the other presses.

There were responses, long and short, scholarly and flippant—smelling of the lamp and again of bread-and-butter. Long before they were half over, Mr. Dickens retired from the scene with a pain in his toe—but let us hope, with peace in his heart.

He will eat no more dinners with us for the present; but, for the sake of literature, we should hope he eat many another hearty one elsewhere,

"And good digestion wait on appetite."

One fact about the dinner reflects great credit on all concerned. Two hundred men dined together, with unlimited wine and sitting far into the night; yet, I have not heard that one of them showed he had taken a single glass too much.

One fact may interest your readers. When the order of the dinner was shown to Mr. Dickens, he made but one comment:—

"I am *very* glad the Southern Press was not omitted."

When that toast was offered, Mr. Greeley, in a few happy remarks introduced Mr. Edwin De Leon—the Editor of the *Southern Press* in the days before the flood—as "its genealogical representative;" and he briefly responded with a statement that the South had ever appreciated the Guest of the Evening; and that he hoped the press of the two sections, "so long dissevered, discordant—belligerent"—might now reünite in the great work of peace and good will towards men.

Such was the Dickens' Dinner; or rather, such was Mr. Dickens at the dinner.

That there was some sincerity in the utter recantation he made, seems proven by the fact that, next evening—after his last reading in America—when untoasted, undined and unwined, he said, substantially, the same things in the self-same matter.

THE OLD MAN'S "YESTERDAY."

BY EDWARD A. JENKS.

"Was't yesterday? Yes, 'twas yesterday!
  It must have been yesterday morn:
I stood on the bank of the River Ray,
  Where the squadrons of martial corn
Their silken banner had just unfurled
  To the breeze, by the singing stream,
When a vision of beauty, all golden-curled,
  Grew into my waking dream.

"'I know it was yesterday,—for now
The rustle I seem to hear,
As the tall corn parted right and left,
And a voice rang soft and clear,—
'Wait, Willie, wait! I am almost there!
I said I would grant your wish,—
So I've made a line of my golden hair,
And am coming to help you fish!'

"Yes! (why do I doubt?) it *was* yesterday—
For I see the soft tassels there
Sunning themselves in a worshipful way
In the light of her yellow hair,
While her voice rings merrily over the corn,—
'Oh, Willie! come help me through,
For I am "the maiden all forlorn,"
And my feet are wet with dew.

"'And you know I'm coming to help you fish—
But you'll think me a silly girl,
For I haven't a bit of bait—but wait!
I'll bait with a tiny curl!
And, Willie, say—do you think they'll bite?
And then, what shall I do?
Must I pull and pull with all my might?
But I'll wait, and look at you!'

"Ah, me! ah, me! *was* it yesterday?
It seems but a day ago!
Yet three-score years of yesterdays
Have whitened my head with snow
Since we sat, in that sweetest of summer-times,
I and my beautiful May,—
Coining our love into wedding chimes,
On the bank of the River Ray."

Memphis, Tennessee.

MARY ASHBURTON.*

A TALE OF MARYLAND LIFE.

CHAPTER X.

THE mail was generally brought in, while we were at breakfast, when Alfred would glance over the letters and papers with a gloomy, and abstracted air, then throw them down impatiently as if weary of the sight of them; or, if it was a letter from his father, retire with it to his own room.

One morning—shall I ever forget that day?—the papers were brought in as usual and placed beside his plate before he came down.

He picked up several, glanced his eye over their contents, took another, looked over that, when his eye falling upon a section of a column was arrested suddenly by something.

"What is the matter?" I exclaimed, alarmed out of all my awe, for ghastly as death, I thought he would fall.

I ran to him, but before I could reach where he had sat a second ago, he was gone,—gone, I knew not whither, out from the house, stricken by some additional calamity.

Too frightened and trembling to stand, I sank down by the paper and took it between my palsied fingers, afraid to see what might meet my eyes as it had done his. In his violence he had torn the sheet, so it was easy to find what had caused his sudden and terrible emotion.

* Continued from page 241.

Yes, she was married now,—had been united for two days to a man who, it was to be hoped for his own sake, was as vain and heartless as herself; and this had caused his sudden paleness and departure. Poor, suffering Alfred! it is for this woman that you are throwing away your youth and existence. Well, she was married—and to Moloch, her god. The world would flock to her standard, and its denizens vie with one another in doing homage to her beauty, while the heart she had crushed was bleeding like a wounded stag.

Enough of her!—I threw the paper away. Did a sensation of selfish relief mingle with my sorrow for him? I can only say that it was natural if it did; but intense anxiety banished it at once as the fearful effect of the news we had just received flashed upon my mind.

Where is he? where had he gone? I cried out aloud. If his grief was such before, what will it be now?

"Where has your master gone?" I asked of Tom, whom I met at the door.

"I don't know 'zactly, madam, I think I saw him go through the park into the woods."

To do what? I asked myself in a frightened whisper.

He did not return that day nor the next.

I neglected my usual occupations, for I was too wretchedly uneasy to fix my mind on any one thing, and wandered about the house and grounds looking for nothing, thinking of nothing, but his return. The servants seemed to be aware that something more than usual was the matter, though I strove to hide my uneasiness from them, and they had a hushed, scared look that the whole place appeared to wear as well as they.

On the evening of the second day, I could stand it no longer. I did not know what his anguish and despair might lead him to do. Wandering about the house with the hope of meeting him on his return, to his room repeatedly to see if he could have come back without our knowledge, till in the evening my uneasiness framed itself into words, and simply telling Melissa of the news, I took her with me to the woods, frightened out of the awe in which I had stood of him, and the fear of intruding upon his solitude, into so bold a step. We walked and walked, but saw no one there.—Twilight fell, then darkness, but he was not to be seen. Anxiety shaped itself into every imaginable evil, and suffering intensely I was obliged, when I could see no longer, to return home.

Every sound that night I imagined to be his footfall in the passage leading to his chamber.—But the morning came and he was not there, so I ascertained by the door ajar, and the silence that reigned in his apartment. I opened it wide and saw that all was as he had left it two days ago, a solemn hush upon it that told of greater desolation than in any previous absence.

With bitter disappointment I descended the stairs and passed another wretched day. The evening came again. I wandered about the grounds in restless misery, unable to conceive where his hiding place might be.

I was in the garden at dusk, pacing the walks in all directions, when I perceived a tall, dark figure stealing by a side door into the building.

It is he, I cried, in one respect my anxieties removed, and I hurried to the house as fast as my trembling limbs would take me. Ascending to his door, I found it closed and locked, so I knew that he was within.

That night when all was dark and silent, save one heavy footfall, resounding like the march of death throughout the house, I stole to the door and seated myself as was my wont, upon the sill, there to grieve for him, and with him, while I listened to his passionate tread, heavier than before, and the groans that seemed to rend his heart in twain, and that went like a dagger into mine.

It was maddening, to sit there motionless, with no power to comfort, to hear such agony without the privilege of attempting the slightest alleviation. I could not be nearer, he would not let me comfort him, and all that I could do, was to weep at his threshold, be one with him at least in grief and suffering.

How little he knew who was at the door! who would have flown to weep with him since she could not comfort.

The woman that bore his name, the poor heart that his father had plucked for him as a wild primrose, whose fragrance he deemed to be unworthy of his acceptance.

I lay there for hours, chilled and cramped, yet I could not leave him, listening to his movements and trying to gather from them his state of mind.

He paused in his rapid, irregular, movements, and I heard him go to his desk, open it, and busily engage himself with something for a moment.

A rapid step,—the report of a pistol,—a sudden fall. Oh! God! he had killed himself.

I did not shriek, for horror sealed my lips, but I beat wildly against the door, shook and beat till my hands bled. It was fast locked—oh! I must get in!

Should I call the servants and expose his shame to them before I could do anything for him? Remembering that the roof of the piazza ran below his window, and that I had heard him raise the latter, I ran into the adjoining apartment, got out of the window on the steep roof, clung by the ledge till I reached that nearest his room, found it open and climbed in.

The moonlight was streaming in on his upturned face where he lay, weltering in his blood, shed by his own—oh! horror—his own hand. A pistol lay a few inches from him, soaked in gore, and the dark stream oozed noiselessly from a wound in his breast.

Was he dead? With a stifled cry in my heart, an anguished appeal for help to the only One who was witness, with me, of this scene, I knelt to see. Not now—not now, oh! God! I cried, not from *this* to take him, not in his sin. Oh! grant that life be there still. Do not kill me too.

I put my ear to his lips, my hand on his gory breast. Yes—oh! thank Him, he still breathed. Afraid to utter the cry of thanksgiving that arose to my lips, for fear that the next moment would dash away the last hope, I set to work. I had some difficulty in getting at the wound, fearful as I was that moving him might accelerate the life stream that flowed from his side. But carefully unfastening the vest with my trembling fingers, I tore open the shirt which was perforated in two places by the pistol balls.

It was not directly in his breast; the ball had taken a lateral course and was embedded half way to the arm pit, instead of striking at the heart where he had aimed it. An ugly, horrid wound it was, but I was thankful that the blood did not flow from a mangled heart. From this there might be hope. I tore a sheet up and bound it quickly, staunching it as well as I could.

No time was to be lost. Wiping up the blood around him with a sponge and disposing him as decently as it was possible to be done, I unlocked the door and hurried away for a physician to be summoned.

The apartments of the house servants were over the kitchen, except that of Melissa who slept in the attic; and it was to arouse his old nurse that I hastened for the purpose. I was up the steep, and narrow stairs at almost one bound, and ran along the dark passage to her door.

She was in a deep sleep when I entered the room, snoring spasmodically, with her yellow turban half on and half off, her mouth open to its utmost extent. I had not taken time to search for a candle, but could see quite distinctly by the moonlight flooding the little room, under the green and white paper blind which was partly rolled up.

"Melissa!" A loud snore was my only answer. "Melissa!" I shook her gently, but she still slept that deep sleep peculiar to many of her race. "Oh! Melissa, wake up." This time I shook her so energetically that it had the effect of partially arousing her.

"Hey! what is it?" she cried, starting up and looking stupidly around her.

"Up, up," I shook her again, "your young master wants you."

"Missey's that you? Good Lor! how you did frighten me! Oh! missey, what's the matter?"

"Your young master is sick," I replied as collectedly as possible, so as not to alarm her out of all self-control. "Go as fast as you can and tell one of the boys to be off immediately for Dr. Green."

Bewildered, frightened, she had hardly the sense to understand me, but comprehending from my manner the need of the utmost celerity, she hurried on her frock and ran to the servants' quarters as I urged her, while I returned to Alfred.

He was as I had left him, except that the deep stain of the bandages told of his life-blood still ebbing away. In an agony of impatience, I listened for the trampling of a horse's feet, proving that Melissa had been successful in her errand, and that speedy succor might arrive. The time seemed interminable before the welcome sound was heard, and a rapid galloping in the lane told me that the messenger was off at last.

When I heard Melissa's steps returning in the passage, I went out to meet her and said,

"Remain outside till I call you."

"Mayn't I see him, my honey darling, my poor sick child?" she cried in a tone of deep injury.

"No," I replied imperatively, as I reëntered the apartment, closing the door, noiselessly, after me, for I feared that her self-control might desert her, completely, at the first view of him, horrible sight as it was, and she would utter some exclamation that would precipitate the catastrophe before the doctor could arrive.

I seated myself on the floor at his head, just raised it a little to put it in my lap, bending over him to catch his faint breathings, and feel that he yet lived. He lived, but so cold and clammy were his hands, so like death. I took one in mine and chafed it between them, and smoothed up his wild, tangled hair from his forehead, then looked down on the white, upturned face, for the first time, beginning to think,—though thought was dangerous then, and wild thrills of horror ran through me as the scene, with its full meaning, forced itself upon my awakening senses.

What I felt and suffered during that time I cannot tell. While watching and waiting, sitting there with his head pillowed on my bosom, the hand, that I had never dared to touch but as a stranger, lying so helplessly in mine, his life fast ebbing away, counting the minutes as if they had been hours; with old Melissa curled up against the door outside, no sound disturbing the intense, oppressive quiet but her breathing, there fell, as it were, great scales from my eyes.

Suddenly it came to me with full force, my sin in worshipping the creature of the Creator. He whom I had deemed perfection, as incapable of error, was, after all, very fallible, very sinful, had committed that most awful crime of taking the life that God gave him. He was no longer a hero in my imagination, a star of purity and perfection, but a frail, perishable mortal, subject to sin as the worst of us,—and of such sin!

His sufferings had been long and terrible, the deep furrows on his forehead showed what his mental anguish had been; but then the mercy and love of God were great too,—could he not have cast his weakness upon Him and thus gained strength for support under blasted, earthly hopes?

He had been no professor of religion, yet his life had almost borne testimony against the transforming power of the latter in its pure and perfect morality. Now how fallen! The morality of the world will do in the sunny smiles of prosperity, but let adversity come, and the boasted bulwarks are swept away, the creature lies there subject to be tempest-tost of passion, no sustaining God to keep him steady in the paths of right.

Thus lay Alfred Chauncey—and I, who had worshipped him as an ideal of beauty and excellence, that no mortal had ever equalled,—was undeceived, saw my error as I had never seen it before. It was not love nor admiration I felt at that moment, but an intense pity and shame for his miserable weakness. So weak! to take his own life. Poor boy! poor boy! I felt towards him like a mother to an erring, sick child; all my awe gone just then, and nothing but the tenderest pity and sorrow for him, while I silently prayed that he might live, at least, long enough for repentance and a fitter preparation for meeting One into whose presence he had attempted so suddenly to rush.

As I said before, I had to respect where I loved, and my adoration of him had originated in his fancied perfection. All my hero-worship was now gone,—nothing but flesh and blood after all—the fallen, broken clay idol dashed to pieces at my feet.

My heart sickened, I felt as if we were both so weak and sinful, the worshipper and the worshipped, as if we lay under the same ban.

Ah! no, I had not been guilty of self-murder; my crime had been that of idolatry,—elevating a creature to the place of the

Creator; but awakened at last to its power and extent—fearfully awakened.

I felt his hand growing colder, but the bleeding had ceased as I saw by the fresh bandages, which were unstained as yet.

An hour passed thus;—two hours, oh! when would the doctor come? There was nothing I could do for him, but to sit patiently and hold his head.

I had always felt myself so inferior to him—not in a worldly point of view, or in social position, for the power of such vulgar distinctions I did not acknowledge where true refinement and mental culture should meet, but I felt myself unequal in so many things. He was exceedingly handsome, and I thought myself so plain; he so graceful and elegant in manner, I so nervous and awkward. Then compared to his high mental attainments, what was my poor little knowledge? When I had heard him conversing with others I felt my ignorance so deeply, yet more my want of power to express myself, which a dearth of intellectual intercourse had prevented me from acquiring. We had many thoughts in common; ideas that I had heard him express with such grace and fluency had been mine also, but we had never interchanged them, therefore he knew nothing of my abilities or attainments. Now the awe was gone—awe of the poor bleeding object, wounded by his own guilty hand—God forgive him, I prayed tearfully—oh! come what grief may, I could never do that. The poor form with the little light struggling in it—a helpless human creature. The elegant, the gifted, what was his beauty or his grace to him at that hour, which the trembling of his fingers had prevented being his last on earth?

Will he die? I pressed my cheek to his forehead; it was warming a little. He never moved nor spoke; the stern frown yet furrowed his brow, as if even in unconsciousness the resolution to die remained firm. I smoothed again the long, wavy hair, and taking up one of the curls pressed it sorrowfully to my lips, for the memory of what he had been, of what I had been wont to consider him. So I sat thus and watched him as he lay, the work of his own—ah! can I say it?—wicked hand.

Will the doctor never come?—From a torturing agony of impatience I relapse into the calmness of despair, and growing hopeless I waited for the end.

Carriage wheels at last. With difficulty repressing a start of relief, I called Melissa. She went to meet the physician and I soon heard them coming up stairs. I gently moved his head from my lap and placed it on a pillow, hid the blood as well as I could that his eyes might not be startled by the sight of the deed at once, then went out softly to meet Dr. Green, enduring such shame at the thought of his exposure to another.

"What is the matter with your husband, madam?" asked the physician, a portly, handsome man of middle age.

"His pistol went of and wounded him in the side," I answered without meeting the doctor's inquiring eyes, and turning to Alfred's door with him.

"Is it *that* that's the matter with him?" exclaimed Melissa; "what'll become of my poor child?"

I felt the doctor's searching gaze, but he entered without making any further remark at the time.

He was an old family physician, had known us all from infancy, so I minded him less than I would have done a stranger, yet my lips writhed to speak the horrible words, and gasping for breath I could hardly articulate. Praying for strength, I took his hand as I led him in and looked him beseechingly in the face.

"Oh! doctor, his sufferings have been terrible. Indeed, indeed they have. In a fit of desperation, he—he hurt himself."

Without a word, with compressed lips, the doctor advanced with me to the prostrate figure.

"Is it possible!" he exclaimed, then, without saying more, he proceeded to work.

"Tell me, sir," I asked breathlessly, "there is hope?"

"Yes," he replied, after a rapid examination, "there is hope. Thank Heaven he has not killed himself, though he was within an ace of it, and will be a dead man yet before dawn, if every care is not taken."

Melissa had come in now, an abrupt warning from the doctor having silenced her cries and lamentations.

How shall we get him in bed, doctor?"

"Can't do it, madam. You'll have to fix a mattress on the floor till the blood is stopped and the ball extricated. *That* will be a job."

We arranged a bed for him as we could, when the doctor had dressed his wound, and with the help of the man who had gone for the latter, and who was called in for the purpose, placed him upon it with great difficulty.

A pool of blood lay where he had been.

"Oh! Lor! oh! Lor!" groaned Melissa, as she wiped it up, "that young marster should see such a day as this!"

During all this time, Alfred had not regained his consciousness, but lay still in a deathlike stupor.

When the doctor left me, day was far advanced.

"Now rest, my dear madam," he said compassionately, "you can do nothing at present."

"*Rest?*" I echoed, and shook my head as if the subject was not even worth talking about.

Rest? For days and weeks, by night and day I sat by his bedside, anticipating every need, living but for him, almost sleepless; unconscious of fatigue, want of rest or sleep, my post was there.

His life hung upon a thread, for delirium and brain fever succeeded the first stupor from loss of blood. The deep mental suffering of months, the frequent exposure by day and by night in the wet and cold, long vigils and fastings from food, then that last—oh! I cannot speak it now!—had done their work, and that terrible struggle began between a naturally fine constitution and these contending causes of extreme danger.

(TO BE CONTINUED.)

PERSONAL RECOLLECTIONS OF EMINENT MEN.

Mr. Preston's first visit to the White House.—I was not yet 18. My father thought it was desirable for me to see somewhat of my own country before going to Europe, and decided to send me to Washington City, where Congress was then in session. He gave me letters to Mr. Madison, and others, but put me under the special care of his friend and kinsman, General B. My reception by this gentleman was cold, stiff and formal, but not deficient in what are called the substantial kindnesses; that is, he was willing to do the useful, but was not at all capable of doing the graceful. He professed his willingness to serve me, said he would introduce me to the Hall, advised me to take my lodging in his mess, and said, if I chose, he would introduce me to the President: although he, himself, was a Federalist, he offered to go with me the next day to present my letter.

My imagination was much dilated with Washington and Congress. The war was in progress. Clay, Calhoun, Cheves and others filled the public attention, and contested the public admiration. My heart bounded as I looked upon these gentlemen, not indeed as I looked upon my icy Federalist. Next morning, however, I drifted with this iceberg to the President's house, with thronging notions of magnificent scenes and illustrious characters. I was very painfully impressed with the approaching introduction. I was very raw, I doubt not very awkward. I and my conductor proceeded in the hack in utter silence, the General not uttering one word. The appearance of the house and grounds was very grand; there was a multitude of carriages at the door, many persons were going in and coming out, especially many persons in gaudy regimentals. I followed the stately old Sachem with a sort of awe. Upon entering a room where there were some fifteen or twenty persons, Mr. Madison turned towards us and said: "Good-morning, Gen. B." The General said, presenting his victim, "my young kinsman, Mr. Preston, who has come to present his respects to you and Mrs. Madison." The President said to a servant, "Tell Mrs. Madison, General B. and young Mr. Preston have called to see her." The President was a little man with a powdered head, having an abstract air and a pale countenance, with but little flow of courtesy.—Around the room was a blaze of military men and naval officers in brilliant uniforms. The furniture of the room, with the brilliant mirrors, was very magnificent.—The General and I stood, until I felt it was awkward; while we yet stood, Mrs. Madison entered, a tall, portly, elegant lady, with a turban on her head and a book in her hand. She advanced straight to me, and extending her left hand, said: "Are you William

Campbell Preston, the son of my old friend and most beloved kinswoman, Sally Campbell?" I assented, I suppose. She said, "Sit down, my son, for you are my son, and I am the first person who ever saw you in this world. Mr. Madison," said she, "this is the son of Mrs. Preston, who was born in Philadelphia." The President shook hands with me cordially. "Gen. Wilkinson," said she, addressing a gentleman who seemed to have been dipped in Pactolus, "I must present this young gentleman to our distinguished men—Capt. Decatur, Mr. Cheves—and yet, after all, you would as soon be presented to the young ladies," said she, turning to three, who entered at this moment—"Miss Maria Mayo, Miss Worthington, and your kinswoman, Miss Sally Coles. Now, young ladies, this young gentleman, if not my son, is my protegé, and I commend him to your special consideration.—With you, he shall be my guest at the White House as long as he remains in the city. This, General B., I have the right to do, for while you are his father's kinsman, I am his mother's kinswoman, and stand towards him in the relation of a parent." All this was performed with an easy grace and benignity, which no woman in the world could have exceeded. My awkwardness and the terror, which had risen in my bosom, on entering the fine house—all suddenly subsided into a romantic admiration for the magnificent woman before me. With something of a romantic turn of thought and expression, I said,

"If General B. thinks fit to be divested of the trouble of my guardianship, it will, of course, be very agreeable to me to be subject to the Providence of Mrs. Madison." Turning to a servant, she said· "Paine left us this morning, and his room, next to Mr. Coles', is vacant, that is for Mr. Preston. Now, Mr. P. you are at home."

Thus suddenly and strangely domesticated, in the President's house, I found myself translated into a new and sort of Fairy existence.

Edward Coles* was private Secretary to the President, a relation, a thorough gentleman, and one of the best natured, and most kindly affectioned men, it has ever been my good fortune to know. He was an inmate of the house, as were Miss Mayo, afterwards Mrs. General Scott, and Miss Coles, afterwards Mrs. Andrew Stevenson. These ladies were experienced belles, now used to reigning over, and swaying a multitude of willing subjects. They soon turned me to account, made me useful as an attendant, were entertained by my freshness, perhaps amused at my greenness. I rode with them, danced with them, waited on them, and in a short time, they created, or developed in me a talent for thread paper verses, on which they levied contributions. When I met Mrs. Scott, in New York, in 185— she gracefully, and even touchingly, alluded to one of these half extempores, which, with the tact, that made her so admired, she had remembered for thirty years.

*Afterwards first Governor of Illinois.

Being thus domesticated at the President's, and regularly appointed *Cavalier Servante* to two belles, I was swept into a current of fashionable dissipation without being subject to much excitement about it, or regarding myself as aught, but a looker on. The country was in the midst of the agony of the war. Mr. Madison's position was painful and difficult; his labors were incessant; his countenance was pallid and hard; his social intercourse was entirely committed to Mrs. Madison, and was managed with infinite tact and elegance. He appeared in society daily, with an unmoved and abstract air, not relaxing except towards the end of a protracted dinner with confidential friends, after he had drunk a quantity of wine. Then he became anecdotal, facetious, a little broad, occasionally, in his discourse, after the manner of the old school. His most confidential companion was a Mr. Cutts, a kinsman of his wife, whom Gen. Jackson afterwards removed from office. This gentleman habitually recounted to the President, over a glass of wine, the news, gossip and *on dits* of the day. Mr. Madison listened with interest to his details, frequently interposing questions in a dry, keen way and, as it seemed to me, directing his inquiries more to personal matters than to things of real importance. He showed more interest in hearing about General Marshall, as he called the Chief Justice, than in regard to any one else, frequently asking, "what does General Marshall say about such and such matters?" For the diplomatic corps (I forget who they were,) he habitually, and somewhat ostentatiously, expressed the most thorough contempt. Mrs. Madison told me, the necessities of society made sad inroads upon his time, and that she was wearied with it to exhaustion. As she always entered the drawing-room with a volume in her hand, I said, "Still you have time to read?" "Oh! no," said she, "not a word; I have this book in my hand—a very fine copy of Don Quixote—to have something not ungraceful to hold, and if need be, to supply a word of talk." She was always prompt in making her appearance in the drawing-room, and when out of it, was very assiduous with household offices. She told me that Mr. Madison slept very little, going to bed late and getting up frequently during the night to write or read, for which purpose a candle was always kept burning in the chamber. When not in company, he habitually addressed Mrs. Madison by the familiar epithet of Dolly, under the influence of which, the lady, and on no other occasion, relaxed the deliberate and somewhat stately demeanor, which always characterized her.

As to the graver matters which stirred the minds of men at that exciting period, I was too young to comprehend them, or to be much interested in them. I was a gay young man, favorably received and considered in consequence of being in the White House, and a pet of Mrs. Madison, she being universally beloved and admired. When I knew her in after life, widowed, poor and without the prestige of station, I found her the same good-natured, kind-hearted, considerate, stately person that she had been in the heyday of her fortunes. Many of her minor habits, formed in early life, continued upon her in old age and poverty. Her manner was urbane, gracious, with an almost imperceptible touch of Quakerism. She continued to the last to wear around her shoulders a magnificent shawl of a green color. She always wore a lofty turban, and took snuff from a snuff-box of lava or platina, never from gold. Two years before her death, I was in a whist party with her, when Mr. John Q. Adams was her partner and Lord Ashburton mine. Each of the three was over 70 years of age.

My gay residence in Washington, which my father considered a part of the education he had prescribed for me, certainly put out of my head any serious thoughts of continuous study, and gave me a very decided turn for gay society. I, however, was soon thrown by him into a comparatively solitary way of life, at least removed from the fascinations of fashion and dissipation. Having flashed and floated along this bright current for four or five weeks, I returned to my remote village of Abingdon, Va., making the journey of four hundred miles on horseback, thus having time, during the solitary ride through the mountains, to recover from the gay and excited scenes through which I had passed.

SHEEP HUSBANDRY.

We wish to present to the farmers and *ci devant* planters of the South, some reasons for adopting a more extensive system of sheep husbandry;—and to endeavor to account for the failure which has attended such efforts heretofore. Our small experience in raising sheep has taught us three things in regard to them.

1st. They can subsist upon a less quantity, and cheaper quality of food than any other domestic animal.

2nd. They enrich the pastures in which they are kept, sooner, in proportion to their size and number, than any other animal.

3d. They destroy coarse herbage and noxious weeds, as if by magic, and induce the growth of tender, nutritious grasses.

When we add to this, the fact that in those portions of the world where the most enlightened system of agriculture prevails, and where farming lands are valued at $500 per acre, a farmer's thrift is estimated by the number of sheep he keeps in proportion to his number of acres, we must believe that we are very blind to our interests, in neglecting this branch of rural industry as we do. The planters of the South have never evinced any want of intelligence and energy in producing paying crops. The great commercial value of their crops of rice, cotton, and tobacco, enriched not only the South, but the whole nation. And we believe that now, even upon the wreck of their whole former system of industry, the same intelligence and energy, which enabled them to contribute so largely to the civilization and prosperity of the world—keeping up the busy whirl of millions of spindles in Great Britain, France, and Northern United States,—will be but turned into a new channel after the present depression has passed away. It is true that agriculture, at present, in the South, is at the lowest ebb. It is so hard a life, and the profits so small, that none but those, who have no other resource, are willing to engage in it. Yet, as thousands really have no other resource, their land being their only possession, we should endeavor to bring the wisdom of a "multitude of counselors" to bear upon the subject, in order to give them such advice as will, if followed, lighten their labors and increase their profits. That agriculture can, and does, pay handsomely even since the war, has been too clearly and practically demonstrated by Mr. David Dickson and others, to admit of a doubt. Yet, the majority of farmers, relying upon bountiful Mother Nature, do show frequently an amount of thriftlessness, which would ruin any other business but that of the farmer. We would say that a grocer, who stored his cheese in a rat-infested cellar, and his sugar and salt in a leaky roofed ware-house, had no right to complain if he were ruined. Yet, we listen with grave sympathy to the aggrieved farmer who mourns over the ravages of dogs among his sheep, and who declares it impossible to raise sheep because the dogs *will* kill them. He would consider it almost an insult if you were to reply, "You cannot raise corn either, for the cattle *will* destroy it."

If he retains his temper, however, he will say, "I have good fences around my corn fields, which exclude cattle."

Ah yes, here common sense comes into play. If he thought it worth while to go to the same expense to protect his sheep that he does to protect his corn, we would hear no more of the one being destroyed by the dogs than the other by the cattle. And the interest of half the money invested in fences would provide shepherds for all the sheep in the country.

A well known agricultural writer says: "Strange as it may seem, the greatest investment in this country, the most costly production of human industry, *is the common fences*, which divide the fields from the highways and separate them from each other. No man dreams that when compared with the outlay for these unpretending monuments of art, our cities and our towns, with all their wealth, are left far behind. You will scarcely believe me when I say that the fences of this country cost more than twenty times the amount of specie that is in it." Were the interest of half the amount invested in fences, put into the wages of shepherds and food for sheep, the produce of the country could be increased ten fold. If a farmer, who is allowing a flock of 300 sheep to wander unprotected around his neighborhood, were to take one hand out of his crop, and allow him to devote his whole time to the care of the sheep, he would lose thereby the produce of twenty acres of land. Say this twenty acres would yield 200 bushels of corn, valued at $250. But his gain would be as follows: In England, according to Stephens, 300 sheep will manure sufficiently one acre of land in one week.—When an English farmer says that an acre is sufficiently manured, he means that more than that quantity would be injurious. They value the manure thus given per week at £3, ($15.) Therefore these 300 sheep will bring to the highest degree of fertility 52 acres of land annually—valued at £156, ($780,) as compared with the cost of commercial manures. Subtract the $250 which your shepherd would have made in the culture of corn, and $150 for winter food for your sheep, and you have a surplus of $380. But this is only the beginning. The next year you may count on this 52 acres yielding at least forty bushels where it yielded probably ten previously, and this is a gain of thirty bushels per acre, or 1,560 bushels in the aggregate—$1,950 in value.

I have estimated the winter food at 50 cents per head, although in South Carolina it was formerly estimated at 20 cents per head.—When the Norfolk breed of sheep was popular in Norfolk, England, their winter food was estimated at 5s., ($1.25) per head, while in Sussex, where the South Down breed was the favorite, the winter food was estimated at only 3s., (75 cents) per head, and this great difference was decided to be owing entirely to the difference in the breed. Our winters are much shorter, and we think 50 cents per head a fair estimate. In Saxony, where sheep husbandry is carried to great perfection, the quantity of hay considered necessary is calculated to be one-thirtieth part of the weight of the live animal per day. In summer the sheep, at the South, require no food, but only the constant care of the shepherd, to protect them from dogs, and to be regularly folded at night, on the lands undergoing the fertilizing process. They must also be regularly supplied with salt. During the last century, the number of sheep kept in England has nearly or quite doubled. Her agricultural progress keeps ahead of that of France, just in the proportion that her number of sheep (per acre) outnumber those of France. Omitting Scotland from the calculation, England keeps three sheep per acre to one kept by France. But the French are gaining rapidly upon their English neighbors, under the guidance of the most extensive of European farmers—the emperor Napoleon, whose practical knowledge of agriculture is carried out into results so successful that we expect to hear the admiration of his subjects find expression in the soubriquet of "Métayer Napoleon," as the English formerly lovingly denominated their George III. "Farmer George."

Lieutenant-Governor Stanton, of Ohio, says in regard to sheep raising in England:

"One thing that struck me very forcibly was, that all farmers testified that sheep raising was absolutely indispensable to successful farming; and that without them the whole kingdom would, in a few years, be reduced to barrenness and sterility. It is in this view, that I regard sheep raising in this country as more important to the ultimate and permanent prosperity of the country, than on account of their profits. Whatever else may happen, we cannot permit the virgin soil and these beautiful fields of ours to be reduced to barrenness by the time they pass into the hands of our children and grandchildren. The fertility must be preserved at all hazards, even at the expense of present profit."

We have been considering the value of sheep husbandry merely as a means of enriching our lands, and upon this advantage we will continue to dwell, although Bakewell, the great English farmer, scorned this idea as much as a Southern planter would have scorned the idea of raising cotton on account of the fertilizing qualities of the cotton seed. But we are so far behind our English friends in farming—not in planting—that we must not attempt to overtake them at a single step. Let us enrich our lands first, and then we can, like Bakewell, talk of the fineness of the fleece, and the flavor of the mutton.

As an instance of the intelligence and energy of a Southern planter, even under the most adverse circumstances, we will again refer to Mr. David Dickson, of Georgia. He takes the agricultural position at the South, which the late Earl of Leicester recently occupied in England, and makes his piney woods land yield at the rate of 2,700 pounds cotton per acre, by expending $17 per acre in bone dust, guano, and plaster. (See *Southern Cultivator*, March 1868, page 87.) Let us suppose the case of two young farmers located in Mr. Dickson's neighborhood, and determined to follow his example in expenditure upon their lands. We will suppose each to have $4,000 in bank stock, the annual interest of which they determine to devote to the enrichment of their lands. The first closely follows Mr. Dickson's footsteps, and lays out his $400, per year, in commercial manures at the rate of $17 per acre, extending over something less than 24 acres. He acts wisely, but might he not do better still. His neighbor puts $750 of his capital into sheep, (at $2.50 per head) leaving $3,250; the interest of which he devotes to purchasing food for them, and paying his shepherd. He manures "sufficiently" in the English sense of the word, 52 acres in the course of a year, more than double the amount manured by his neighbor, and still has his wool and the increase of his flock;—which latter items, however, we have agreed not to take into consideration. Let us simply consider the fact that the one enriches 52 acres, while the other does not enrich quite 24. The purchaser of commercial manures is sometimes imposed upon by dishonest dealers, but the owner of the sheep runs no such risk. We do not wish to discourage farmers from purchasing commercial manures, however; on the contrary, we cite Mr. Dickson's success with them as an inducement to use them; but we wish, also, to convince our friends that if a corn field is worth a fence, a flock of sheep is also worth a shepherd. Where farmers own too small a number to justify the employment of a shepherd, let them form a coöperation society, and put their sheep together, or better still, let them sell their sheep to those who have capital enough to take care of them. Although most farmers assign the ravages of the dogs, as the reason of their failure in sheep raising, yet, a few assert that even if this difficulty were removed, the deficiency of pasturage would be an insuperable objection, and that we cannot raise the large root crops upon which the flocks of England, France, and Germany are chiefly fed. This objection comes from farmers, who are not willing to purchase food. It is probably true that our climate and present system of labor will prevent the culture of roots as a field crop, but there is no such difficulty with clover. Any land which will produce 15 bushels of corn per acre, will, if deeply plowed, and well pulverized with a roller, bring fine and abundant crops of clover. Where sheep are pastured for any length of time, the grasses best suited to them, spring up naturally—it seems as if God's blessing followed the innocent creatures since Abel's day: and that they, above all other created animals, were formed for the special service of man. Abel, of course, did not use his flock for food, as animal food was not permitted at that time, but they, no doubt, abundantly repaid his care, in destroying the thistles and noxious weeds which sprang up in obedience to the curse, and in promoting the vigorous growth of the "trees for meat," which God had appointed for their sustenance.

"At an agricultural meeting in Boston, one of the speakers remarked, that on a tract of land which was overrun with wood box, briars and other shrubs, he turned one hundred and fifty sheep. At that time a cow could not have lived on the whole tract. The sheep were kept there several years, and so killed cut the wild growth that the tract now affords good pasture for fifteen cows."

Sheep are Nature's landscape gardeners. They cut the grass, which grows green and tender under their enriching tread, with their small, clipping teeth, as short as the finest bladed English scythe would do;—and although they will nibble roses and shrubbery a little, they do them no material injury, unless forced to by starvation. Neither will they injure the bark of young fruit trees, unless other food is denied them; and it is asserted that canker worms are never found in orchards where sheep are folded. In the old world, "stock" and "high" farming are synonymous terms, and the stock consists principally of sheep. They are suited to the extreme of civilization, and to the simplicity of primitive habits.—They are found around the park gates of the European prince, and around the hut of the New Zealand emigrant;—on the torrid plains of Africa, and in the snow-bound valleys of Iceland. Wherever man finds a home, his faithful, woolly friend accommodates itself to his surroundings—furnishing food and clothing for himself and his little ones, and enriching his lands. We will close by a description of the general management of sheep farms on the Pampas of South America.

"The farmers usually divide their sheep into flocks of a thousand each. In a very few instances a flock is permitted to grow to the size of two or even three thousand, and is kept up to that number. But the prevailing rate of increase being about thirty-three and a third per cent., a flock of a thousand, having doubled itself in three years, is, at the end of that time, divided into two. In this way flocks continue to be multiplied until, in some cases, two hundred thousand sheep may be seen feeding on a single farm. If flocks are allowed to exceed a thousand or fifteen hundred each, the proportion of loss in lambs is largely increased. The annual loss in lambs has heretofore been from *ten to fifteen per cent.*

"There is no necessity of feeding, summer or winter. One man, assisted by a small boy, can do all the work essential to the care of a large flock. The ordinary conditions of agreement between proprietors and shepherds are few and simple. If the shepherd's compensation for his services is to be an interest in the flock, the customary stipulations are that he shall bear the expenses of superintending and shearing; shall take from his charge meat sufficient for himself and his family, and shall receive one-third of the yearly increase, both of lambs and wool. On the other hand, the proprietor furnishes pasture, pens for folding, and a dwelling house for the shepherd's family. The contract is generally made for three years. At the end of that time the shepherd has a fine flock of his own, and is able to commence business for himself—he is an independent *estanciero*, with a career open to a handsome fortune."

HELEN ASHLEY

OR,

THE REFUGEE AT HOME

CHAPTER I.

" While the perfumed lights
Stole thro' the mists of alabaster lamps,
And every air was heavy with the sighs
Of orange groves, and music from sweet lutes,
And murmurs of low fountains that gush forth
I' the midst of roses."

[*Bulwer's 'Lady of Lyons.'*

It is night. The moon is shedding her soft radiance over one of the many fair and luxurious homes to be found on the sea-coast of South Carolina. Though as late in the season as October, the evening is very warm, for the charming Indian summer lingered on, as though loath to leave such fair scenes to the cold domain of winter. As yet, the Ice-king had sent no herald of his approach, and the noble mansion, the majestic oaks, the smooth green lawn, and the blue water of the river, all smiled calmly in the clear moonlight.

Mrs. Ashley, the mistress of this peaceful home, had been left a widow at the early age of twenty-one. At her husband's death, the care of a large property and two little children devolved upon her. With all her sweet and gentle manners, Mrs. Ashley possessed much strong good sense; which she now showed in the management of her property and children. The eldest, our sweet Helen, proved an easy charge; and even for Charlie, wild and head-strong as he was, Mrs. Ashley feared little, for, surely, with so warm and generous a heart, he could not go far astray.

Very fair and bright was Ashley Hall, on that soft October night. The stately mansion was brilliantly lighted, and the many forms, flitting joyously about, in the parlors, on the broad piazza, and even on the lawn, speak it a gala night. And well it may be, for on that day sweet Helen Ashley has completed her seventeenth year, and the proud and happy mother has invited her friends, for many miles around, to celebrate the commencement of her only daughter's young ladyhood.

In the luxurious drawing-room, the centre of a group of matrons, sits Mrs. Ashley. Reclining in a large arm chair, the crimson back of which sets off her stately form to the greatest advantage, she does the honors of her elegant home, with the easy gracefulness of the high-born Southern lady. Her face is still beautiful, for she has seen scarce thirty-five summers, but her rich dark hair is almost hidden by the widow's cap, put on for her young husband fourteen years before, and worn ever since. She still wears her weeds, too, and would be greatly hurt were any one to hint at her making a change. At the moment we see her, she is speaking to a tall boy of fifteen, whom she calls, "my son." That is Charlie, with his large bright blue eyes and glossy curling hair; so like the handsome young father, he cannot even remember, sleeping under the dark cypress, in the quiet family burial-place, by the river. The boy's cheek is flushed with dancing, for, although so young, his early wit, saucy gaiety and beautiful dancing, make him the chosen partner of many a fair belle several years his senior.

But where is Helen, the gentle queen of these gay revels? Not in the dancing room, not in the parlor, not even in the lawn.—She has not been seen for the last half hour, and more than one comment has been made on her absence. But Charlie says, in reply to his partner, pretty Minnie Claire's exclamation of "Where can Helen be," "Oh, I suppose she is somewhere with Allan St. John. I see he has disappeared too."

"Now, Charlie, do you know that is a match I cannot understand? I wonder Helen fancies him, he seems so cold and proud, while she is so merry and warm-hearted."

"But Allan is not cold," returned Charlie eagerly; "and as for being proud, why I like that. Has not a Southern gentleman a right to be proud? I tell you what, Miss Minnie, I, for one, am as proud as Lucifer."

"Oh, Charlie," laughs Minnie, "I did not think you would allow such a thing. You men are getting so bold in your wickedness. I don't know where it will stop."

Charlie colors high at her laughing words, but answered merrily.

"I know I'm not a man yet, Miss Minnie, and that's well for you. If you find me so irresistible at fifteen, what *would* be the state of your heart if I was twenty-five? But this is a charming waltz. Will you dance?"

"Well, as you just said I found you irresistible, I suppose I must;" and turning from the cool piazza, they again sought the dancing room.

While we leave them to enjoy the waltz, let us ascertain if Charlie is right in his suggestion that "Helen is somewhere with Allan St. John."

On one side of the lawn, sloping down to the river, lay a beautiful flower-garden; on the other, a thick grove of orange trees, planted in regular rows, three abreast, with gravel walks between. They were a magnificent sight, particularly at this season, with their golden fruit gleaming in the moonlight, among the rich, dark leaves.

There indeed we find Helen, and with her, St. John. They are standing still, and by the light of the friendly moon, we can see them distinctly. How very lovely Helen is, in her snowy dress, with necklace and bracelets of pearl. Her rich brown hair is drawn simply back from her temples, and fastened behind in a large knot, very low on her neck, its only ornament a white rose with its dark green leaves. Her liquid brown eyes are veiled by their long lashes, as though afraid to meet her companion's earnest gaze.

And most worthy was St. John to be the lover of that gentle girl. Tall, and strikingly handsome, with a grave, earnest face, now lit up with passionate love, he stands beside her. One arm is around her waist, her hand is clasped in his, and as we draw near, his low, musical voice is whispering,

"In two years, my darling, your mother says you shall be mine. It seems a long time to wait, but I fear not, for I know and feel that your love will never change."

And her sweet voice answered: "Change! Oh, Allan, I could not live without your love!"

And here let us leave them, happy in their love and trust.—Leave them in their bright, sunny home, their young hearts filled with hope, and apparently no cloud in their fair sky. No cloud, did I say? Alas, the little cloud, "no larger than a man's hand," is rising, and soon, soon will it burst over that devoted land.

It was early in October of '60. To Southern ears I need not repeat the dreadful tale of all that the next short year brought forth. The proud heroic patriotism, the noble self-devotion, the dauntless courage; and oh! the bitter tears, the costly life-blood that bought our victories; the deserted homes, the woe and desolation, are engraven on the heart of every liberty-loving Southerner.

CHAPTER II.

"Come let the burial rite be read—the funeral song be sung!—
An anthem for the queenliest dead that ever died so young—
A dirge for her, the doubly dead, in that she died so young!"

[*Edgar A. Poe's "Lenore."*

The two years which Mrs. Ashley had stipulated should pass before the marriage of her daughter, are over. The day, to which Helen and St. John had looked forward so eagerly and confidently, had at length arrived.

Let us hasten to beautiful Ashley Hall, to witness the gay revels there. As we near the place, we do indeed hear sounds of merriment, but can those loud voices, and that coarse laughter proceed from the polished and high-born guests, who were wont to grace the noble old mansion. We pass through the broad oak avenue and observe with wonder how neglected is its appearance. By a sudden turn we come in front of the house. Without pausing to notice that the lawn is overgrown with weeds, the beautiful flower-garden a ruin, and even many of the orange trees cut down, our gaze is riveted on the house itself. On the piazza, in the parlor, lounging in the luxurious chairs and on the sofas, are scattered groups of dirty, half-dressed, negroes. One of them is even striking on the piano, while others dance to the uncouth sounds. Can this be the home of the Ashleys'? Alas, it is now in the hands of our cruel and vindictive foes, who have abandoned it to the negroes.

We turn with horror from so revolting a scene to seek the noble family, now driven into exile and poverty.

Far away, in one of the upper districts of South Carolina, there is a small and sparsely furnished cottage. In one of the rooms, on a low couch drawn near the window, lies a young girl. In that worn and pallid face, we can scarcely recognize the once blooming Helen. The rounded, graceful form is wasted to a shadow, and the wistful, brown eyes retain nothing of by-gone-days, save their gentle, loving softness.—Their brightness has been dimmed by bitter tears, and sorrow and suffering have almost entirely quenched the hope that once shone so purely in their liquid depths. The beautiful hair is still drawn back as of yore, and you may plainly trace the blue veins in the fair temples. Beside her sits her mother. In spite of the close cap, you see that sorrow has thickly streaked her hair with grey. The stately form is bowed and the face is worn and weary.

And why is St. John absent from his promised bride, now that she is ill, in poverty and exile? Alas! he has fallen, one of the many victims on the altar of freedom. He rests where he fell, on the bloody field of the second Manassas. A simple cross marks the place of his grave, raised by his comrades, that he may, at some future day, be moved to his island home. On the cross his name is cut.

"Private Allan St. John, Palmetto Guards, 2d Regiment S. C. V."

Yes, with all his talent, wealth and aristocratic birth, St. John died a private. Possessed of neither a military education, nor peculiar military skill, he sought no office, but was content to die with no higher title than that of being a gentleman private; yet, methinks, no purer, nobler name can be borne in such a struggle for liberty. For his country, and for her alone, he fought; and no thought of self mingled its alloy with the pure gold of his patriotism.

A few short months after the date of our last chapter, when South Carolina called upon her sons to rally around the walls of Sumter, St. John hastened to join the patriot band under the command of the gallant and lamented Captain Cuthbert. As a member of the Palmetto Guards, he fought until death laid him low. A few weeks after his fall, his place in the company was supplied by

Charlie, then scarcely seventeen. The boy had long been anxious to join the army, but, on account of his youth, his mother had hitherto refused her consent. Now, however, when he heard of the death of his friend, his almost brother, and saw his sister's anguish, he passionately implored his mother to hold him back no longer. And she, seeing it was best, yielded up her treasure to her country's service. He had not been in Virginia more than six weeks, when he was summoned home to his sister's death-bed. That evening was the earliest time, possible, on which he could arrive, and mother and sister were both anxiously watching for him. They had been silent for the last hour, when Helen spoke.

"Mother, if Charlie does not come to-day, I shall never see him again; for I feel that I shall not live until to-morrow. To-day was to have been our wedding day, you know; and I feel it shall be yet. But, oh, mother, we never thought it would be in Heaven."

She paused, then softly repeated,

> "Nearer my Father's house,
> Where the many mansions be;
> Nearer the Great White Throne;
> Nearer the jasper sea.
> Nearer the bound of life,
> Where we lay our burdens down;
> Nearer leaving my cross;
> Nearer wearing my crown."

"Mother, do you remember how we used to sing that at home? It was Allan's favorite. I recollect his telling me once that Heaven never seemed so near to him, as when he sang that. Now, I am going to my Father's home, and oh, how I thank him that Allan will be there to meet me. Do you know, mother, on the night that I was seventeen, I told him in the dear old orange grove, that I could not live without his love; and you see I was right.— My Father saw I was a poor, weak creature without my Allan, and so He is taking me to him. Do not cry so, darling mother. Have you not taught me that 'to live is Christ, but to die is gain?'"

"My child! my child! How can I give you up? You, who have been my comfort, through so much of sorrow and affliction. Help me, oh God, to say 'Thy will, not mine, be done!'"

"But, mother, you will have Charlie here, and two children in Heaven, with father. Surely you, who have always lived so near to God, will not find it hard to think your treasures are with Him.— Oh, mother, dear mother, let me go home!"

Her voice ceased, and drawing her mother down to her, she strove to kiss away the blinding tears. So absorbed were they, that the opening of the door disturbed them not, and Charlie stood some seconds in the room, before they were aware of his presence. In an instant, however, he was clasped in his mother's arms, and she was kissing him with all the passionate fervor of a mother's love for an only son.— When she released him, he turned to his sister, but, shocked at the change a few weeks had wrought, he could only throw himself down beside her in an agony of uncontrollable sobbing.

She held him closely, kissing again and again the cheek already embrowned by his few weeks' exposure to the hardships of a soldier's life. At length, his mother, fearing the excitement would prove too much for Helen, drew him away till he could regain composure.

The sun was slowly setting.—Still on the couch by the window lay the dying girl. But now she was supported in her brother's arms, and her pale cheek rested on his grey jacket. Softly she spoke:

"Mother, Charlie, will you sing, 'There is rest for the weary?'"

They complied: and sadly the strains of that sweet hymn sounded in the chamber of death.—When it ceased, she said,

"Thank you, oh thank you. How sweet it it to know that

'Pain nor sickness there shall enter,
Grief nor woe my lot shall share.'

"And, mother, you and Charlie will join us there, 'in the Christian's home of glory;' will you not? But, oh, it is so hard to say good-bye, even though I know it is only for a little while. I wish I could have seen our dear, dear country, our beautiful sunny South, free once more; but God knows best. One more kiss, mother, dearest; and now you, Charlie, my own kind brother, my darling soldier boy. Mother, Charlie, if it is ever in your power, let Allan and me rest together in the old grave-yard at Ashley Hall, beside dear father."

She paused a moment, then added,

"I feel weary, but Charlie holds me so nicely, and I like to think the grey jacket in which Allan died, and which you wear, my darling, is to be my last pillow. Mother, will you and Charlie sing once more for me, 'Nearer my Father's house?' I feel very, very near now."

The weeping mother calmed herself and commenced; and ere long Charlie's voice joined hers. When the hymn was ended, Helen still lay with her eyes closed and a peaceful smile on her lips; but there was a change, which made her mother start and bend more closely over her. Raising her head, she whispered softly,

"She is with Allan, Charlie.—Our darling is in her Father's home of rest."

Another year has passed and the little cottage is empty. Beside Helen's grave is another, for Mrs. Ashley is with her daughter. And Charlie? On the blood-stained field of Chancellorsville, where the captain fell, he so passionately loved and admired, another martyr in our sacred cause, the boy soldier yielded up his young life. The shock proved too much for the fading strength of Mrs. Ashley, and, one short week afterwards, she joined her husband and children in the land where "the wicked cease from troubling and the weary are at rest."

THE HAVERSACK.

THE Provost Marshals of "the best government the world ever saw" had a jolly time of it, during the struggle for emancipating "the man and brother." Loyalty was a good paying virtue in that charming period, and no one knew better how to make it pay than a certain German Provost Marshal in Baltimore, whose love for the old flag intensified every day, as his pocket-book swelled larger and heavier.

A friend gives the following scene in the Provost Marshal's office of the truly loyal Maj. B.

A neat, well dressed recruit has just been brought in, and the truly loyal official sees a fine opportunity for patriotism and green-backs.

SCENE 1ST.

Maj. B. Vat's your name?

Recruit. John Jones.

Maj. B. Vell, John Jones, has you got von vatch?

Recruit. (Pulling out his watch) Yes, I have a splendid one.

Maj. B. (Affecting surprise.) Vell! vell! Py tam. John Jones has von vatch in his pocket! von vatch in his pocket! Vy, John Jones, py tam, you know having vatches is giving aid and comfort to the enemy. Vy, John Jones, py tam, you know te rules and te regulations of te army say dat no soldier shall have te vatch.

John Jones. (With astonishment.) How does carrying watches give aid and comfort to the enemy?

Maj. B. Vell, looks here, tere is one million of soldiers in te grand army. Suppose all te soldiers has te vatch, and suppose tere be's von big battle and te rebel vips our man and take ten tonsand prisoners, ten he get ten tousand vatch, and he send te vatch to Nassau and he puy te powder, and te gun and te cannon. Vy certainly, John Jones, vearing te vatch is giving aid and comfort to te tam rebel. Here, Clerk, take John Jones' vatch and give him five tollar in green-back for him.

John Jones. (Angrily.) I gave a hundred dollars in gold for my watch. I won't give it up.

Maj. B. You von't give up your vatch! John Jones, py tam, you von't obey te rules and regulations of the army. Sergeant of te guard! take John Jones to te guard house, gives him pread and vater five tays, and pring me his vatch.

(Exit Sergeant with prisoner and return again with watch.)

SCENE 2ND.

(Enter Sergeant with a dirty, ragged, seedy recruit.)

Maj. B. Vat's your name?

Recruit. Bill Smith.

Maj. B. Vell, Pill Smit, has you got von vatch?

Bill Smith. (Pointing to his rags.) I am a pretty looking fellow to carry a watch, ain't I?

Major B. (with great surprise.) Vat, Pill Smit, you a soldier of te grand army of te best government in te vorld, and not have a vatch! Py tams to hell! Pill Smit, you disgrace te old flag! How you specks to be te sentinel on te Potomac mit no vatch in te pocket? How you know ven te relief come? Te rules and te regulations of te army say all soldier must have te vatch, and all Provost Marshal must keep tem and give to te soldier vat don't have em.

Here, Clerk, give Pill Smit a vatch, and take fifty tollar out of his pounty money.

Bill Smith. (Angrily.) I don't want a watch, never had one in my life. You shan't have my bounty money.

Major B. Ha! ha! Pill Smit, you like te tam rebel, you von't obey te law? Vat says te rules and regulations of te army?— Every soldier shall have te vatch to support te dignity of te government. Sergeant, take Pill Smit in to te guard house, gives him pread and vater till he buys te vatch.

(It is almost needless to say that in a few days, Bill Smith sees the necessity of supporting the best government the world ever saw.) R. Q. T.

Our friend T. omits the best part of this anecdote. He was telling the story, one day, in a crowded saloon, 'mid the hearty laughter and cheers of all present, when a hand was laid upon his shoulder, and looking around, he saw the veritable Maj. B. himself.

"Ah," said he, "T. you tells a story tam vell. I vants you in our Club. I sends in your name. I asks tem to vote for you. Come, let's take von drink."

A friend gives us an anecdote of another Baltimore worthy, one truly loyal S.

The first invasion of Maryland created quite a stampede here.— The hero of Vienna blockaded the streets with tobacco hogsheads. The city bells were rung one night, and there was hurrying to and fro of brave men, the wild tramping of furious horses, the rolling of hogsheads on the streets, the shouts of drivers and the braying of donkeys. Altogether there was a scene of disorder and confusion in the streets, scarcely inferior to that in the brain of our frightened commander. The din and uproar reached the ears of the loyal S. on the outskirts of the city, who was remarkable for the hatred and bitterness with which he always spoke of "that rascal Lee and his ragamuffins." He came to his door in rather an unpresentable night dress and inquired of a passer-by what was the matter.

Stranger. Nothing much, only Gen. Lee's army is in the city, and they are ringing the bells for joy.

S. (Shivering and stuttering with fear.) Gen-gen-er-er-al Lee in the cit-cit-y?

Stranger. That's all.

S. Will you-you-see Gen-er-al Lee?

Stranger. Yes, I expect to call upon him.

S. (Recovering himself.) Well, my good friend, tell the General to send to my house for anything he wants. It will give me great pleasure to aid him and his gallant soldiers. I always did like the General!

The suppleness of the loyal S. would qualify him to be an admirable Fetich Governor, in any one of the "States lately in rebellion."

Maj. G., of Staunton, Virginia, gives an anecdote to show the appreciation of the Christian character of General Jackson by the soldiers of the A. N. V.

The Major attempted to cross a bridge near Gettysburg at which there was an infantry guard.—He was stopped and told that he could not cross the bridge without a pass. Gen. Jackson had then been dead some months, but the Major, without thinking of it, drew out a general pass which had been signed by him, a year before his death. The soldier on post examined the pass attentively, and then returning it to Major G. said:

"You can't cross this bridge; the name on that paper is good to pass you into Heaven, but not over this bridge."

An old reb at Adairsville, Ga., who lost a foot in the war and had its place supplied by a very bungling workman, calls our attention to a grievous mistake of Shakspeare. The illustrious poet says that "there's a divinity that shapes our ends rough hew them as we will." Old reb thinks that the "hewing" of the new foot was "rough" enough, but he is not able to discover any "divinity" about the rough carpenter, who did it!

The next three anecdotes have been sent to us from Mobile, Ala., by D. W. L., late of the 3rd Alabama, a regiment that fought with a gallantry on *every* field, which was excelled by no other regiment in the service:

During the occupation of Tupelo, Mississippi, by the Confederate troops, under Price, after Bragg had gone on his famous raid into Kentucky, a favorite officer of "Old Pap" was taken very ill, and his death pronounced inevitable by the attending surgeons. While the sufferings of the gallant captain were at their height, General Price called upon him to condole with him, and comfort him in his last moments.

General Price. Can I do any thing for you, my dear friend?

Captain. (Faintly.) Nothing.

General Price. Have you any messages for friends?

Captain. None, all my effects are disposed of, and all my relations and dependents provided for.

General Price. Can I not, in some way, add to your personal comfort?

Captain. Do you think I'll die?

General Price. The physicians pronounce your case hopeless. What relief can I afford you in this critical period?

Captain. (Very faintly.) Have me sent to Meridian. I think that I can leave this world with less regret from that point than from any other in the Universe!

There were among the last called out regiments for the field, an undue proportion of officers, who, not endowed by nature with the brightest intellects, had attained to manhood without having passed through a very rigid system of birch discipline, and in consequence of that neglect, were very partially educated, and in some cases could not distinguish between a muster roll and a sermon. They were, nevertheless, "clever fellows," as the term is generally used, not deficient in courage and popular qualities. In fact, they generally owed their elevation more to this turn for popularity than to any other cause. Of this class was Lieutenant G. of the — Alabama regiment, though it must be confessed that he could "read writin'". Soon after his regiment had been mustered into service, and were in camp, waiting orders, schools of instruction were opened in each company. Hardee's Tactics became the order of the day, and no one was more diligent in his studies than Lieut. G. Finally, the day of examination came, and the captain of his company began the examination of his hopeful lieutenant. After taking him through the "school of the soldier," and "the school of the company," which the lieutenant understood pretty well, *under the circumstances*, the captain went into the more complicated "school of the battalion." In this branch of tactics, the lieutenant was completely at sea—could make no head-way at all. The instructor finding his patience fast ebbing away under the stupidity of the pupil, marked on a piece of paper, the position of "company A" in the regimental line, and the posts of the several file-closers, designating them by name, as Lieutenant G., Sergeant B., Corporal C., &c., &c.

Then supposing a case in which a certain movement would be required, the captain asked "what would Sergeant B. do now?" The lieutenant had been completely bewildered by the diagram and the contemplated movement, but brightening up at the question, he replied, "Why Sergeant B. would do his whole duty, for he is every inch a soldier and a gentleman!"

Lieut. G. was recommended to resume the study of Hardee's Tactics.

Editorially, we would remark upon this anecdote, that though the Fetich legislators are as much bewildered in the mazes of legislation as was the poor lieutenant in the intricacies of tactics, yet we cannot recommend them to *resume* the study of honor, honesty and decency, for all that has been a sealed volume to them.

Everybody who took a hand in the affair (or rather a *foot* in it we should say) remembers Gen. Bragg's campaign into Kentucky. It was fraught with many hardships and privations, and, at the time, regarded an immense affair, "a big thing." On arriving at Bardstown, Col. B., of an Alabama regiment, was seated around the mess table, and each member thereof related some incident of the march coming under his personal observation. With the exception of Lieut. Bart. O. it so happened that every member of the mess was a mounted officer, while "Bart" had tramped the whole distance on foot. When a lull occurred in the conversation, the Colonel remarked,

"Well, boys, I am glad it is over, I'm glad that we have a chance at last to rest, but with what enthusiasm will we, in years to come, tell these stories over to our children, and how proud will we all be to tell of our trials, privations and hardships on this memorable march into Kentucky."

"Yes," says Bart, who had been a quiet listener to the Colonel's pretty speech, "You'll all tell of it and be mighty proud of it, but not a durned one of you will recollect to tell that you walked all the way on horseback!"

Miss M. L. M. sends from Lake Village, Arkansas, the next four anecdotes:

Soon after the Conscript Law was passed by the Confederate Congress, Captain Slack was appointed enrolling officer for the Parish of Claiborne, with orders to have its provisions duly executed. His manner of execution was the reverse of that suggested by his name, and created quite a lively sensation among the "bomb-proofs," who, finding the pointed arguments of his muskets irresistible, moved rapidly, and in a right line towards the front. Not long after his arrival, my sister had occasion to visit an old lady, whose son was notoriously of the peace persuasion. She soon missed his familiar presence, and the following conversation occurred:

"Mrs. —— where is John?"

"Gone to fight for his country, child."

"Indeed! I thought he was one of the exempts."

"Lor, honey! Cappin Slack don't know no exempts. The other day I see his men a galloping down the road, I hollered to John they war comin' and told him the chimbly was a good place. 'Twarnt no use, though, they found him quicker than a cat does a mouse."

"Well, Mrs. ——, what did John do?"

"Do! Why he come down and *'listed like a man.*"

[We hope that John will give us the history of his "Lost Cause."]

During the time that Allen occupied the Gubernatorial Chair of the State of Louisiana, he issued an order requiring all men, young and old, to organize into companies of minute men, whose duty it was to drill and be ready to assist the regular Confederate forces in case of State invasion. On one occasion the minute men, of Bienville Parish, had been ordered out to serve a mock campaign of a week's duration. As they came "marching home again with gay and gallant tread," the whole command was halted in front of a log cabin to permit an old man to go out of the ranks. Forthwith there issued from its doorway, a numerous progeny of Confederate tow-heads, joyfully crying:

"Yonder's daddy! yonder's daddy!" "Hush! hush! children," said the fond father, softly, waving them back with his hand! "I want to see if the old woman will know me with my soldier clothes on."

After the failure of the first gun-boat expedition against Vicksburg, and the subsequent departure of the fleet for the "Land of Egypt," it was deemed advisable by the War Department to take advantage of the lull in hostilities and send over to the troops of the Trans-Mississippi department a portion of the arms so gallantly won by their brothers in arms on the glorious battle-fields of the "Old Dominion." The 31st La. regiment, then newly organized, was ordered to Milliken's Bend to receive and guard the military supplies, as they should be forwarded. Sick, poorly clad, and badly armed, they were no match for the two thousand Yankees, backed by the whole gun-boat fleet, that swooped down upon them without warning, in the wee small hours of a midsummer night. A retreat took place only surpassed in celerity by that of the Federals at Bull Run, and other *runs* where they bore off the palm for speed. The route of retreat (for as many as followed the route) passed by my mother's house, and in spite of our alarm and sympathy, it was impossible to resist a smile at the ridiculous flight of the discomfited "Rebs." One handsome lieutenant, making a graceful bow in acknowledgment for the refreshments provided, bade us not be alarmed, and while promising to return and defend us, made rapid strides towards the back gate. A lady who was present called out that she hoped, when we next heard from him, he would be occupying a less equivocal position *with his back to the field and his feet to the foe!*

While the pursuit was still hot, a Federal officer of artillery dashed up to a neighbor's house and demanded the surrender of concealed Confederates. The lady of the house came to the door, and told him there were no soldiers on her premises. He ordered a search, and while it was being executed, he launched into an insolent diatribe against our boasted Southern chivalry, taunting her until forbearance ceased to be a virtue. She bade him respect her sex, and said, "Those flying grey coats will yet teach you the useful lesson." A prophecy that was literally fulfilled a few months later at the engagement of Chickasaw Bayou, where the gallant 31st Louisiana met the same Federal troops face to face, and won a glorious victory, blotting out forever the opprobrious epithet gained in their former encounter of the "31st fast foot."

The same day a soldier fresh from "der Fader Land," and a member of an Illinois regiment, while lounging on the banquette in front of Mrs. R's. house, was assaulted by a belligerent calf.—Turning around to defend himself, and looking askant at Bully, he exclaimed: "Hein! you Secesh too?" and rapidly decamped from a neighborhood, where opposition to Yankee invasion was so strikingly developed.

———

From Laurens C. H., S. C., we get an incident of gallantry in a private soldier. Such incidents should be preserved, and we are always glad to record them:

On the morning of the 18th of September, 1863, Kershaw's S. C.

brigade was ordered to charge a breastwork of the enemy at the Armstrong House, in front of Knoxville, Tennessee. Colonel Nance's 3rd S. C. regiment was in the centre, and had to pass over about five hundred yards of open plain, under a heavy infantry fire. The works were charged and carried. During the charge the fire was deemed too hot for the "litter corps" to keep up with the line, and private James Dorroh, (Co. G.,) of the litter corps, seeing a man wounded in the leg, and unable to get away, rushed forward, and picking him up in his arms brought him off the field. Later, this gallant soldier was killed in one of the battles around Petersburg, Va.

From Liberty, Texas, we get a letter from two old rebs, who sign themselves "unreconstructed."

We send you a few odd bits from our haversack to replenish yours. If you like the offering and your "war-bag" is low, we we will send you more; first assuring you that they are true.—One of us went out in May, '61, with the gallant 15th Mississippi, the other in '62, with the 29th Mississippi, two years of his military life, he spent in that charming abode, Rock Island, Illinois. There are but few remnants left of our once proud and glorious regiments, and the war-bronzed veterans find it harder to "live for Dixie" than to "die for Dixie."

The prisoners at Rock Island, Illinois, in '64, whiled away many weary hours in drawing, their imaginations, aided not a little by the rumors which reached them, of the movements of Lee and Grant. One daring artist drew a picture of Grant skedaddling with the seeming velocity of Pope, followed by one poor, frightened looking Yank, while Gen. Lee, alone with a "forty pounder," was bushwhacking them from behind trees. The sketch was tacked up on a tree in a conspicuous place. One evening, two Federal officers were walking around the enclosure, and paused to comment upon this evidence of rebel impudence and skill;—a ragged prisoner, (name unknown,) who had been caught, a few days before, in the act of escaping from that *pleasant* (?) abode, bearing his cross—a ball and chain attached to his leg—stood in rather close proximity to the connoisseurs, one of whom turned round and asked roughly,

"What do you want here?"

The reb's eyes twinkled, but he answered demurely enough—

"*I came to bring Gen. Lee some ammunition, sir.*"

Three members of company D, 1st Mississippi cavalry, E. G——, Mc. K—— and E. J—— went out "hawking," while in Georgia, in 1864; but as the sequel will show, it proved to be "hogging" instead of "hawking." They stopped hard-by a comfortable farm house, and not wishing to disturb the inmates (so considerate were they,) kept as quiet as possible. A gun went off and the nicest hog in the lot breathed his last. Silence was on the lips, but grief was in the hearts of the gallant cavaliers, lest the nerves of the ladies should be disturbed.

E. G., on guard in advance of the rest, saw an old woman coming towards him, not exactly in the majestic style of Milton's Eve. There was more haste than "grace in her movements," and if there was "Heaven in her eye," it was the kind of Heaven to which old Thad. and the loyal Governors of Dixie will go with free tickets. E. G. hurried forward to meet the old lady before she would reach the gap in the lot, through which his comrades had to escape with the unfortunate victim of the fatal shot.

"Don't be alarmed, madam," said E. G., in his blandest tones, 'nobody is hurt.'"

Old Woman. Nobody hurt? ain't there a hog killed?

E. G. Only a ha-r-k.

Old Woman. A hawk! you lying rascal, it is a hog.

Again, E. G's. lips attempted to get out the word hawk, but again he only stammered ha-r-k, chicken har-k, madam; but at length recovered sufficiently to explain "it's only a chicken hawk the boys have been shooting." The explanation came too late, and the enraged dame rushed to the gap. The boys were brave (they belonged to the cavalry,) but they were glad to drop their hawk to escape that terrible tongue.

E. G., poor fellow, had to bear the whole brunt of the fire from the feminine battery, and the no less unpleasant allusions so often afterwards made to "har-k, har-k."

G. P. M.

Four or five members of company H., 5th Mississippi, while lying in the trenches around Atlanta, in 1864, had a brief respite one day from the annoying shot and shell. We had got a large lot of biscuit, and expected to have a fine time of it, in enjoying the unusual banquet. But "human hopes oft deceive us." While we were sitting a là Turk, on a blanket, pitching into the biscuit, and old Tommie R—— a long, lean specimen of rebeldom was stretching out his bony arm for the biggest one in the pile, a minnie took off a piece of his head as big as a five dollar Confed. note, and pitched him over upon our stock of biscuits. Geo. H—— jerked at him, and cried out, "damn it, boys, don't let the old man bleed on the biscuits!"

F. J. M.

In the good old days before the Abolition war, "pot liquor" was quite an institution upon Southern plantations, for fattening and developing young negroes. It was the liquor or water, in which cabbage, beans, &c., had been boiled with bacon, and when mixed with corn bread or mush, it made a very healthful diet, of which the little darkeys were inordinately fond.

J. T. M., of the 6th Mississippi, rode up to a house, in Georgia, one very cold, rainy day, in the hope of getting something warmer than water. The halloo of M—— was answered by the coming to the door of a good dame of the cracker school of society.

M——. Madam, I am almost frozen. Is there any spirits in your house?

Old Lady. No, indeed! our

house is jist as free of ghosts as any in this country. I never seed but one sperrit in my life, and that was long before me and the old man up and got married.

M——. Madam, you mistake me. I meant to ask if you had any liquor in the house.

Old Lady. I'd like to know how you'd raise little niggers without liquor. I has a pot full allers on hand. Wait a bit and I'll get you a ladle full, thouten that dratted hound has drunk up all on it. I se'ed him gwine out a lickin' his chops a minute ago. Wait a bit and I'll see.

M——. Thank you, ma'am, I am in a hurry. F. J. M.

R. H. D. sends the following anecdote from St. Louis, Mo

In December, 1861, when a part of the army of the Potomac was in quarters at and around Dumfries, Dr. Estill and myself, Surgeons of the "old 3rd brigade," were requested by Capt. Imboden to visit his battery for the purpose of examining a young man, who had been convicted of desertion on the battle-field of Manassas.—The youth, as stated, belonged to a highly respectable family, was well educated, and had borne a fair character for bravery and general good conduct. When we arrived at the camp, the Captain remarked that the penalty of being shot as a deserter would have to be summarily executed, unless some very good reason could be shown for his reprieve; and we were conducted immediately to a tent, in which he was confined. The boy's appearance was that of a healthy, fine looking youth, about 19 years old, writhing under the pain of disgrace, and greatly depressed by the near approach of his awful doom. We entered into conversation with him, and found him to be very intelligent, and perfectly free in the confession of his guilt. On being asked the reason of his desertion at so critical a time, he remarked that, while the battle was going on, he was suddenly seized with such trepidation and *blindness* that he fell unconsciously on the ground, where he remained till his comrades had passed on.—Finding himself alone, and being still so frightened, that his heart was painful and seemed ready to burst, he made his escape from the battle-field, as best he could. In reply to our questions, he stated that his heart had never failed him before that time, but that it had given him much trouble since. We bared his chest, and on a careful examination, found his heart most palpably laboring under organic disease, sufficient to incapacitate any man to withstand the shock of battle.

As we passed out through the door of the tent, we observed, sitting on a camp stool near the captain, a well dressed, delicate lady in black, weeping, with her head leaning forward, and her face covered by a large veil, exhibiting all the signs of intense grief. I knew at once who she was; and I hastened to say to the captain,

"This man is laboring under organic disease of the heart, and it is well known and admitted that no man in that condition can stand the shock of a battle."

The captain paused a moment and said, "If that is your opinion, gentlemen, his life is spared."

Instantly, the lady sprang to her feet, shrieked, and cried out, "God bless you, sir, forever!—You have saved my darling, my *only* child!"

A gallant and esteemed colonel of the late so-called sends from Warrenton, N. C., a noble incident of unselfishness:

Among various attempts to escape the blandishments of that "delightful summer resort," Johnson's Island, a party of some twelve or fifteen dug down through the floor of one of the rooms, and after reaching a depth of ten feet, struck off at right angles, until they had bored beyond the fence, and then worked up until they had reached the surface. It was the labor of a month or more. On the day of the night selected to carry into execution their design, a heavy rain fell and almost filled the horizontal tunnel. Upon trial, however, it was proved that they could manage to keep their noses above water, and they accordingly commenced their exit. After three or four had gotten out, it came to the turn of a Captain Cole, of Arkansas, (I regret that his given name has escaped me,) a tall, athletic man, who proved too tight a fit for the hole, or rather the hole for him. He, however, succeeded, by Herculean efforts, in wedging his head through the outer opening, when he stuck fast, unable to get forward or turn back. In this condition, drenched to the skin, he remained, on a cold, chilly night, from 10 P. M. until reveillé the next morning, when he called to the guard to come and dig him out. On being asked by the commandant of the post, why he had not sooner given the alarm, and had himself extricated, he replied that he considered it dishonorable to betray those who had gone before in order to save himself. It should have been stated, likewise, that when released from his uncomfortable situation, he was barely able to stand and could not use his legs for sometime thereafter. W. J. W.

Greeley tells of a grim joke practiced by the truly loyal upon the negroes, whom they love so dearly. It seems that the immaculate Stanton, the honest Freedmen's Bureau and others of the moral-idea party, have robbed the negro-soldiers of a million and a half dollars of the bounty money belonging to them!

If the statement came from any other source, than honest Horace himself, it would be pronounced a "Copperhead lie."

It is no longer doubted that enormous frauds have been perpetrated in the Second Auditor's office, in the payment of bounties to colored troops, and there is every reason to believe that the government has been swindled to the extent of $1,500,000. It appears that certain clerks in the Second Auditor's office in the Bureau of Colored Troops, and in the Freedmen's Bureau, entered into a conspiracy, and that papers for whole regiments have been forged, presented, and paid.

[*N. Y. Tribune.*

The colored troops fought nobly and the Rads stole characteristically!

The "little joke" upon the negro deserves to be embalmed in the Haversack.

EDITORIAL.

THE delicate attention shown to the negroes during the recent election, in Arkansas, is in very pleasing contrast with the boorish want of consideration for their convenience and comfort, in the other nine States, "lately in rebellion." The mandate went out from the Head Centre of all the Loyal Leagues, that each negro should be required to vote three times throughout all that region, once known as the Southern States. The loyal whites in Arkansas, (lately nullifiers, negro-traders and Yankee haters,) made a noble provision for the accommodation of their colored brethren, in the shape of a perambulating ballot-box, which traveled from precinct to precinct, gathering in the colored votes from the corn-fields, the hedges, and the high-ways, and returning often enough to allow each "man and brother" to deposit his three votes without loss of time, without bodily fatigue and unnecessary waste of loyal green-backs. This was "neat and appropriate," but what a rebuke it is to the loyal men in the other districts! Why did'nt Joseph E. see that the thing was done equally *brown* in Georgia? Why was the worshipper of Mr. Calhoun so neglectful of the interests and the feelings of his black allies in North Carolina? Why were the other leaders of "the party of great moral ideas" in Alabama, Florida, Mississippi, Texas, and Louisiana so indifferent to the well-being of their friends? In "the name of justice, liberty, and humanity," (See telegram on Mr. Johnson's impeachment,) we protest against this heartless negligence. In the delinquent States, the poor negroes could only give their three votes by marching on from county to county, like John Brown's soul. They lost time and money by this management, and in addition, had much personal annoyance and inconvenience. These things ought not so to have been. Let there be an improvement in the Fall elections. Let not the other nine States be behind Arkansas in courtesy and kindness to that race, which fought so nobly to save the life of the nation.

But as we have been pardoned by the President's Proclamation of general amnesty, and are "just as good as new," it may not be presumptuous in us to give a suggestion to the truly loyal leaders in the five Districts. We think that the Arkansas scheme can be improved upon, and that the negroes can be spared even the trouble of going from the field to the ballot-box by the road-side. Let a careful estimate be made of the majorities required at each election precinct, and let the loyal managers of the polls be instructed to report these majorities, and thus save the negroes the trouble of voting at all. This simple expedient would have saved Alabama and Mississippi to the glorious Republican cause. It is true, Alabama has been redeemed, but redeemed in such a way as has reflected seriously on the honesty of the men, who so freely gave up Irish and German lives to "revenge the insult to the old flag of the nation." Mississippi is, perhaps, lost forever, when our artless plan would have saved it. It was Solomon himself who said, "great men are not always wise," but it is seldom, indeed, that we have to record so remarkable an instance of want of tact, management and cunning in great rulers, who are untrammeled by the usual restraints of honor and honesty.

The Boston gentleman, who, some months ago, gave us the interesting incident of the battle of Winchester, writes to us under recent date that if Sumner, Phillips & Co., had been hung as high as Haman, years ago, it would have been better for the whole country. As Boston is a super-loyal city at this moment, and we belong to a State lately in rebellion, it may be disloyal in us to dissent from this frank opinion of the Boston gentleman.

Some of the loyal Governors are quite exultant over their success in manipulating the negro vote. His Excellency, Governor Brownlow, has recently announced his intention to see to it that the rebels have town lots in hell. It has long been suspected that His Excellency was a Director in that underground Institution, but not until lately has he given official notification of the same, over his own signature. His Excellency, Gov. Holden, has declared his willingness to give free passes to hell or to Connecticut, to all North Carolinians, who are dissatisfied with the present order of things. The association of ideas is very suggestive, but is scarcely loyal. It looks like one of the Governor's old outbursts of hatred against Yankeedom. We hope that His Excellency will sign the free passes with the pen he used in signing the Ordinance of Secession, and which he promised to preserve in his family forever. It would console the poor exiles, too, to have a copy of his beautiful poem on Mr. Calhoun. Could he not have it set to music, so that they might console themselves with the song as they sit down by the rivers of Babylon?

We ventured to hint some months ago that the time would come, when the Republican party would become distrustful of their Southern allies. It *does* look queer that men can be true to that party, who have despised all the obligations imposed by birth and education, and who have stultified all their previous history. It is not unreasonable for the Republicans to have some misgivings as to the future fidelity of these men.

The Cincinnati *Gazette* gives out gloomily, its apprehensions of the steadfastness and reliability of Southern loyalists.

"We are soon to have the Southern States readmitted under the present reconstruction—Virginia, Texas (and probably Mississippi) alone excepted. The Republican party has hitherto calculated upon great political gain from this admission. The leaders are now far less confident. It must be confessed that neither the fruits of reconstruction, nor the promises from the other States are especially encouraging.

We have one rebel State back again—Tennessee. Before she had been finally restored, her delegates to a National convention gave us Andrew Johnson. Since, her Legislature has given us Senators Fowler and Patterson.

Yet these are men of high character, compared with those now coming up from the South. There are whole delegations to the House from large Southern States that do not contain one man as reputable in private life, or as respectable in ability and experience as Senator Fowler.—There are plenty of them for whom Senator Patterson may stand as the type. 'God only knows what we are to do with these creatures,' exclaimed one of the leading members of the Republican party, and one of its most prominent Congressmen.—'They seem to be without character at home; they have not very much hope of retaining their hold on their districts after the first election; and a good many of them are sure to go in for making the most they can out of their positions while they have them.' Perhaps the Congressman was severe in his judgment; but there is no doubt that the feeling among many of the leaders grows to be that in seeking for Republican strength at the South, we have got a very large elephant of very uncertain disposition on our hands."

This is a very sorry picture, it must be confessed. But the Republicans ought not to be unreasonable. In looking out for elements of strength at the South, they wisely or unwisely ignored the antecedents of those, who wept at the sight of the old flag. They were, with rare exceptions, old negro-traders, life-long nullifiers and Yankee-haters, who hailed emancipation and the restoration of the Union with such unbounded enthusiasm. The Republicans did not ask them what have you been? but what are you now? Are you base enough for our present purposes? And the renegades replied, "we are!"

Now we think that the Republicans are unreasonable in raising any doubts about this statement. Its frankness should not excite any suspicions of its truthfulness. The Republicans need not have any fears, that, these men are not ready and willing to do any thing dishonest and disreputable that may be imposed upon them.—They will be as true as steel to the Republicans as long as they remain in power, and can pay them well. After the Fall elections, the Southern loyalists will be fierce in their denunciations of the Radical party and violent opponents of negro suffrage.

Nor should the Republicans expect too much. Renegades are proverbial for zeal and want of stability. Let the party of great moral ideas purify themselves and thus set a pure example to the old nullifiers and negro traders. Ben Wade gives this opinion of the reckless expenditure and corruption of his own party.

"We cannot stand this frightful system of public expenditures. Its effect is demoralizing upon every branch of the Government; and, besides, the people are heavily pressed by taxes, and won't stand it much longer. We must economise—everywhere, if possible, but especially at the points of our greatest expenditure—the army and navy. Then I believe there's another thing we've got to do. The party can't live without it; and what's more important, the country can't prosper. *We must stop this outrageous system of fraud and peculation. The Government can't stagger under it much longer.*"

It is supposed that honest old Ben, after thus exposing the wickedness of his colleagues, swore a score or two of oaths, partly to give emphasis to his declarations and partly to illustrate the principles of the party of great moral ideas.

Don Piatt, a truly loyal Republican, of the straitest sect of haters of Democracy, does not compliment his colleagues any more than does honest old Ben. Hear the Don:

"We could have survived a blunder great as this is, had it come alone, but it is the concluding act of a long series. Through the unsettled condition of a country suffering from civil wars, *we have developed more rascality than any organization ever called into existence. We filled the offices with thieves and their pockets with stealings. We have organized rings, that in turn create officeholders and control the Government. Men go in poor and come out rich.* For one dollar paid to the Government from hard earned taxes, hundreds stick to the dirty fingers of official scoundrels. We have whisky rings, Indian Bureau rings, manufactures' rings, railroad rings, land jobbing rings, and internal rings. From the lowest official up to Senators and Cabinet officers, the taint of corruption runs, until the people dazed and confused confound the right and listen with indifference to the threats of exposure.

At the end of a fearful war, the people had a right to expect that the expenses of the Government should be brought back, at once, to a peace footing. They demanded a reduction of the army to what it was in 1860; that the useless monitors should be sold for old iron; that the hundred thousand thieves, called office holders, should be dismissed, and the appropriations cut down to a reasonable expenditure.

The people have expected that in our hands reconstruction at the South would progress with reasonable speed, and that unhappy region be restored to a state of quiet and prosperity. The expectation might not be reasonable, *for the blind bigotry that hurried us into a bloody war has developed a hate that, with stupid fury, casts aside all social and legal restraint.*"

This is pretty satisfactory evidence that the people are right in their determination to turn out a party so utterly depraved and unprincipled. But the testimony of *The Revolution* is still more conclusive. This is a thoroughly loyal paper, full of love for the negro and hatred of slavery and the Southern people, and therefore up to the Republican standard of patriotism. Mrs. Elizabeth Cady Stanton is the Editor, and Miss Susan B. Anthony, Proprietor of this loyal and patriotic paper, and the testimony of these distinguished and enterprising ladies is overwhelming against their colleagues and coadjutors. We will give a few extracts from the only number we have seen, dated May 14, 1868.

"The party now in power is the most corrupt and dangerous that has ruled this nation from the foundation of the Government, and although its effort for the last eight years has been simply to perpetuate itself, yet it has succeeded in making the American people believe that the life of the nation depends upon its success."

This is from the gentle Mrs. Cady herself, and our Southern training does not permit us to utter one word in opposition to the opinion of the lady. Gentle being! we will not differ with you! The amiable Editor (we use big E, and the masculine termination, as grammatical and appropriate) has no very exalted opinion of "the greatest captain of his age." She says in reference to the nomination of Grant: "A man to govern this nation in the most critical period of its history, who cannot govern his own appetites. We have drunkenness and sensualism enough in high places already. If we would exalt the moral tone of this nation, let our young men just coming on the stage of action, see that vice and weakness disqualify a man for the highest honors of the American people." Very sensible, Mrs. Cady. But who would have thought that the moral-idea party would take up such an individual and seek to exalt him to the highest office in the gift of the nation?

A male writer for the same paper (for even the *Revolution* cannot dispense with the rougher sex) says: "Were the average of the people at large as brusque and brutal as Congress is, society would not be tolerable, if indeed it were not absolutely impossible." What would one of the five Kings think of such a sentiment from a Southern editor? Would it not be regarded as rank treason and rebellion?

But hear him again: "Surely the knaveries and swindlings practiced in, and around, the national capitol, afford some pretext for the not more culpable frauds of the whiskey rings and other great and unrighteous monopolies elsewhere." If the national capitol is really such a cage of unclean animals, (and who can dispute such loyal testimony without being rebellious?) it cannot be sinful to wish to see the beasts driven out.

We will give one more extract from the lovely and frank-spoken Mrs. Cady:

"*The New Slaveholders in the United States.*—American citizens are just beginning to suffer from the High Art Swindling system of slavery, by which 'their bodily toil and the fruits thereof' are taken from them and 'made the property' of government officials and other thieves, national bank men and bond-holders at home and abroad. Three hundred thousand slaveholders before the rebellion lived luxuriously on 'the bodily toil and the fruits thereof' of about four millions colored people called 'slaves.' Since the rebellion, five hundred thousand government officials and other thieves, national bank men and bondholders live luxuriously on the 'bodily toil and the fruits thereof' of thirty millions of white people called 'free.'—Everywhere, throughout the United States the people are in a straitened condition. They are suffering from the want of money. They work harder than ever, they economize more than ever, and yet they are poorer than ever. Every kind of business is unsatisfactory. Only the few very rich are pleased. The interests of the many are subservient to those of the few."

The State Treasurer of North Carolina under the new régime is an old negro trader, distinguished years ago for his brutality to his slaves. Men of his calling and character are now filling the highest offices in their respective States. What do they think of the opinion of slavery expressed by their loyal sister? What do they think of her calling five hundred thousand government officials by the unsavory epithet "thieves!" Frankly, they respond: "Sisters, we are loyal; as it is in the General Government, so we will make it in the State Government. In our humble way, we will imitate the great leaders of the nation."

A whisky spring has been discovered in Nodaway county, Mo., which contains 32 per cent. of alcohol. The friends of General Grant propose to erect him a summer residence in the neighborhood of the spring.

The *Copperhead*, a very able and sprightly paper, published at Ottumwa, Iowa, tells a good story of one Loughridge, a loyal M. C., or would be M. C. from the 4th Congressional District in that State, who, when drafted, got off on the plea that he "had no teeth and could not bite a cartridge."—The Southern Congressmen should eschew the company of the toothless patriot, lest "evil communications corrupt good manners." They can chew any thing, the iron-clad oath, their previous history, their professions of undying hate to the North, their pro-slavery rant, &c.. &c. But their speciality is "eating dirt."

Harrisonburg, Va., and Louisville, in the county of Kentucky, received charters of incorporation from the State of Virginia, in the same year. Louisville has got somewhat ahead of Harrisonburg.

It is, probably, not fair to expect men of genius to be confined to strict rules of grammar in their speeches and writings. The *poetic license* is tacitly extended to them, as well as to the sons of song. Still, even the most gifted orators and statesmen are expected to make themselves intelligible, and are sharply criticised when they have failed to make themselves understood. Now, who has been able to understand the closing sentence of Gen. Grant's letter of acceptance? The first captain of his age says:

"Peace and universal prosperity, its sequence, with economy of administration, will lighten the burden of taxation, while it constantly reduces the national debt. Let us have peace."

What is nominative to "will prolighten?" Do you answer "peace and prosperity?" What then does the "it" refer to in the next line? There is a plural something, which is to lighten the burden of taxation, and there is a singular something, which is to reduce the national debt. Will some loyal grammarian explain what it is all about? In the preceding clause to the one under consideration, the General says: "I always have respected that will and always shall." Will the same loyal scholar explain what the "shall" refers to? Does he mean to say that he always "shall have respected it?" If not, whose grammar has he used? "Let us have light," as well as "peace."

"I would rather be right than President," was the grand sentiment of Henry Clay, and it will live in the hearts of the American people, as long as they are capable of appreciating nobleness of soul. Some twenty years ago, Hon. W. L. Sharkey, of Mississippi, became a candidate for the office of Chief Justice, (which, in that State, is in the gift of the people) and was warmly supported by the lawyers. An attempt was made to excite a prejudice against him, on the ground that he was the lawyers' candidate. He met the charge boldly and said, "that nothing could gratify him more than to believe that he was the first choice of his legal brethren. He would rather be beaten with the support of those, who knew him best, and could best judge of his qualifications, than to be elected without their votes by men of other callings and professions, who were not so competent to pronounce an opinion upon his fitness for the Bench."

Tried by the standard of Clay and Sharkey, what valuation can be put upon men, who have attained power and place through the votes of the ignorant, debased and depraved? Would they rather be right than have office? Not one of them will be so shameless as to make such a claim. Would they rather be beaten with the support of those, who know them best, than be elected by those who are not capable of judging their qualifications? Not one of them would be so reckless, as to make any such pretence of decency and self-respect. Not one of them has received the support of the virtue and the intelligence of their respective States. Not a single reputable man has voted for any one of them. With an insane greed for office and its emoluments, they have been willing to gain their ends, by cutting themselves adrift forever from respectable people and entering into alliance and fellowship with the most beastly and besotted of the human race.

A terrible rebuke has been administered by General Charles P. Stone, of Massachusetts, to these miserable Southern renegades, as well as to the carpet-bag emissaries from the North, who would disgrace the civilization of Congo and Guinea. General Stone had been offered the nomination of State Senator from three counties of Virginia. In declining the nomination, he says:

"I should lose my self-respect

did I accept a public trust not freely offered, and climb to office by reason of the present peculiar condition of public affairs.

While, by its Constitution, our country claims to be a free Republic, resting upon the consent of all the whole people, no voluntary act of mine shall appear to admit that it is not one—and it would be apparent, should I now be selected from among my peers for the trust in question, that one strong point governing the choice is my mere ability to freely take an abominable test-oath, which disgraces the proposed Constitution of the State, rendering ineligible large numbers of the most honorable and most trustworthy voters and tax-payers within its limits.

I can never accept office under such conditions."

General Stone was a gallant and distinguished Brigadier in the Federal service, and yet he pronounces the Reconstruction measures to be infamous. He ought to be as good a judge of what is loyal and what is not, as the old nullifiers who betrayed the Union, (according to their present views) then the Confederacy, and finally the trust and confidence of Mr. Johnson. The difference between him and them accounts for the difference between his conduct and their misconduct. *He* is a high-toned gentleman, who "would rather be right than be President." *They*—must have office at all hazards.

An exchange tells of a pleasant little chat between Gen. Butler, U. S. A., and the Hon. Mr. Bingham, who was so prominent in the hanging of Mrs. Surratt.—Gen. B. called Bingham "*a lady-killer.*" Blushing at the compliment, the Honorable gentleman replied: "Well, General, if you really have all the female apparel and jewelry, which you are said to have, you must have quite *taking-ways* with the ladies!"

There are several things in the article on the causes of "Decay in Religion at the South," from which we totally dissent. It is unquestionably the duty of the "five districts" to submit to the will of the conqueror with what fortitude and cheerfulness, they can summon to support them in this dark hour of trial. Nor need the writer of that article begrudge the prayers that are offered for our rulers. They certainly need praying for, and if they can be improved thereby, no reasonable man ought to object. We think, too, that Mr. Manigault is mistaken in regard to the insincere professions of attachment to the government once sought to be destroyed by those, who now pray for its peace and prosperity. There is no evidence of insincerity, or inconsistency in the truly good men of the South, who never wished for the destruction of the United States Government: all they wanted was to establish a nationality of their own, unmolested by the interference, the slanders, the wrong-doing and the corruption of the party of hate and ruin. They failed in their effort, and now acknowledge their failure with manly resignation. The arms-bearing portion of the South have sworn to submit in good faith and they have been true to their pledges. The most law-abiding and conservative people of Dixie are those, who fought most faithfully and zealously for the dear Southern cross. A distinguished Federal General said to the editor of this magazine, that the most trust-worthy and reliable men, whom he had found in a three years' residence in the South, were those who had worn the grey. He has associated with him several, who lost arms and legs in our noble cause. The honorable men, who once wore the grey, have just as much faith at this hour in the truth and righteousness of that cause, as when McClellan was hurled back from Richmond. Father Ryan, in the *Banner of the South*, has beautifully and eloquently expressed the sentiments of the honorable men of his section:

"The surrender of the sword is no argument against the causes which drew it from the scabbard. Shot and shell do not reason—they slaughter—and slaughter, be it more or less, is only slaughter—it is no argument for or against the rights of those, who kill or are killed. Bullets may mangle flesh—spill blood—slay men—but they can never reach the vital principles, for which men contend.—These principles are beyond the range of muskets and cannon.—Battle-fields may be the burial-places of men—never of rights.—Above the smoke and storm of battles, unaffected by victory or defeat, calm, and immovable, Justice sits on her eternal throne, and in her eyes is right and right forever—wrong is eternally wrong—and trampled right is grander than triumphant wrong. From the decision given against us in the court of battle we there appeal; and these decisions we carry up to the high court for reversal. This, and this alone, was settled by battle—that we were the weaker party. We had less brute force on our side and we were obliged to yield to the superior strength of our assailants. The armies and government of the Confederacy were but the mortal flesh and blood of an immortal cause."

God rules in the armies of Heaven and among the inhabitants of earth. All that the high-toned men of the North expect of their brave antagonists at the South, is the acceptance in good faith of God's will manifested in the defeat of the Southern arms. They want no hypocritical tears at the sight of the "dear old flag." They want no hollow professions of Unionism, concealed so carefully during the long years of war that wife, nor children, nor confidential friends could ever discover it.

A few men at the South wished the *destruction* of the United States government, and sought to compass their object during a quarter of a century, breathing out threatenings and slaughter during all that long period against Abolitionists at home and Yankees across the border. They are the same men, who wept tears of joy at the sight of "the flag of the nation," and embraced its lovely folds with such affectionate ardor. They are now loyal governors, treasurers, judges, &c., all over the States lately in rebellion.

The *Norfolk Virginian*, edited by the poet and scholar, James Barron Hope, gives a truthful, but humiliating view of the kind of literature supported by the Southern people. It says:

"We see upon our streets, in our shops, in our offices, in our cars, on our steamboats—everywhere, pictorial papers, printed mainly in New York, which are eagerly bought; while the *Land We Love*, the *Banner of the South*, and numberless other meritorious publications, are supported only by a small class of our people. This is a humiliating reflection, but nevertheless true.—Our people prefer the spread-eagle literature and the leg-pictures to the inspirations of our poets, or the best reflections of our thinkers. But bad as the pictures are, the 'literature,' commonly so-called, is infinitely worse. We find them all filled with "sensations' of a licentious character. Sands and Dumas have lent their sensuous coloring, without a gleam of their genius; and the Cardinal Sins are assiduouly taught both by text and illustration. Not only do these papers corrupt the public morals, but they perpetually affront the mind of a Southern reader, by indulging in the most reckless partisan statements in the interests of the Radical party."

We have been at some pains to ascertain the relative support given to Northern and Southern literature at the South. The statistics are truly wonderful. Excluding political, agricultural and religious papers, and confining our examination strictly to literary periodicals, quarterlies, monthlies and weeklies, we have found that the ratio of Northern to Southern was 8 to 1, where Northern literature was least taken, and 240 Northern, to one Southern, where the Northern was most patronized. The city, where the proportion is so great against Southern literature, is preëminently a Southern city in feeling and principle. If any one is inclined to question the accuracy of this estimate, let him go to his own Post-Office and let him see the kind of reading matter sold by the news-boys on his own streets. He will see how little support is given to Southern literature, and he will discover, moreover, that what comes from abroad, is of the most corrupting character; pandering to low sensualism, or devoted to the propagation of some infidel scheme, or gotten up to libel and vilify the South, or crammed with statistics of crime, or given over to a namby-pamby sentimentalism. Christian parents purchase and take home to their families these vicious and demoralizing periodicals, and never seem to feel that they are thereby poisoning the minds, and corrupting the hearts of those, they love as their own souls. They would carefully guard their children from evil company, not reflecting that the reading of impure and wicked books and papers is at once the most subtle and dangerous form, in which sin tempts the youthful mind.

A Hard Case.—The Rev. Mr. Ferree, agent of the Freedmen's Bureau at Leesburg, Va., has been dismissed from office for pocketing certain fines and fees, which belonged to the Freedmen. It seems a hard case, a very hard case, for the Reverend gentleman to be punished for discharging the legitimate duty of the Bureau.

We have long thought that the

very best service, that the Southern people could render the Democratic Party, would be the collecting of the statistics of the fines imposed by the Bureau throughout our unhappy section. Let the Democratic Club or Association of every county in each of the Southern States get accurate and authentic information of the fines extorted from the whites, and then ascertain, so far as practicable, what disposition has been made of these funds. If one dollar, out of a thousand collected, has been given either to the negroes or reported to Gen. Howard, we will frankly acknowledge that the officials of the Bureau are a hundred fold more honest, than we now believe them to be.

On the 17th day of December, 1862, Gen. Grant, then commanding the Department of Tennessee, published, at Oxford, Miss., an order banishing all Jews out of his Department. The following is a copy of the order:

General Order, No. 11.

The Jews, as a class, violating every regulation of trade established by the Treasury Department, also Department orders, are hereby expelled from the Department within twenty-four hours from the receipt of this order by post commanders.

They will see that all this class of people are furnished with passes and required to leave; and any one returning after such notification will be arrested and held in confinement until an opportunity occurs of sending them out as prisoners, unless furnished with permits from these headquarters.

No passes will be given these people to visit headquarters for the purpose of making personal application for trade permits.

By order of Maj. Gen. Grant.

JOHN A. RAWLING, A. A. G.

Official—J. LOVELL, Captain and A. A. G.

Gen. Grant seems not to be aware that the time has passed, when the Jews could be roasted alive as a pleasant pastime, and when a needy king or a hungry feudal lord could stretch a Jew upon the rack and extort from him gold and silver to replenish his empty coffers. Nor does "the first captain of his age" seem to be aware that "this class" and "this people," so contemptuously alluded to, have produced the greatest warriors, statesmen, poets, scholars, financiers and diplomatists. He himself might have studied with profit the campaigns of Joshua, David, and Judas Maccabeus. Will it be worth while to tell him that Lord Chatham read the writings of Isaiah, the Jew, as the best preparation for a forensic effort? That Milton, Dante, Calderon, Pope, Byron, Tennyson, and hundreds of lesser poets have drawn their most beautiful imagery from Hebrew poetry?—That the common law system of the civilized world is founded upon the code of Moses, the Hebrew leader? Washburne may reply for him that these Israelites were inspired men. *That* only heightens the insult to the race. They were inspired, *because* they belonged to the chosen people of God—the people selected (accord- to the General's own faith) to bring forth the incarnate Deity. If not profane, it is certainly in bad taste, in a Christian to sneer at the lineage of Peter, Paul and

John, and the Redeemer, whom he professes to worship.

But leaving out the religious and inspired element in the Jewish history, there is still a brilliant list of illustrious names, which have shed lustre upon the Jewish annals. As the worldly maxims of Solomon are admired, quoted and acted upon, by nations ignorant or regardless of his character as a man of God, so the genius and the deeds of eminent Jews have been extolled by thousands, who knew not that they were commending the talents and the exploits of "this class of people." Unless the name distinctly points to Hebrew origin, it is not suspected to belong to a Jew, and as the Israelites have adopted, in very many instances, the prominent names in the land of their abode, and, possibly, of their nativity, their lineage is lost sight of. Thus few suspect that Neander, the eminent historian of the Christian Church, was a Jew by birth: that Salvator Rosa, the celebrated painter, was a Jew; that Meyerbeer, the great composer, was a Jew, and that Hassan, the astronomer, was a Jew: but all recognize the Jewish origin of Rachel, the tragedian, and Moses Ben Ezra, the poet, because their names indicate their race. The *National Quarterly Review* justly remarks:

"Only a few of the literary and scientific men of the present age who are Jews, are known as such. Some of the most learned critics and comparative philologists of France and Germany are Jews. It is only those who have characteristic names that are known to the public as belonging to the persecuted and despised race to which belonged David and Solomon, Paul and John the Evangelist, nay, Jesus Christ himself. But had we no Jewish men of genius but Moses Mendelssohn and Salvator Rosa, they should be sufficient to awaken kind feelings in favor of their brethren. This is particularly true of Mendelssohn, who is one of the greatest metaphysical and philosophical writers of modern times, and whom no offers or inducements could induce to abandon the faith of his fathers. It is, however, equally true of the astronomers Stern, Beer, and Slonimski, and of the mathematicians Sklow and Witzenhausen. There are no Orientalists of the present day superior to Oppert, Weil, and Dernburg; no anatomist superior to Hirshfield; no physiologist superior to Valentin; how few composers have given us sweeter music than Meyerbeer? and how few have shed more lustre on the genius of tragedy than Rachel?

The Polish and German names of some of these persons have concealed the race to which they belong. So it has been with the Arabic names of Hasdai, the mathematician, Menahem the lexicographer, and Abulmalud, the grammarian. So the Spanish name of General Marquez, who fought so truly and bravely for Maximilian, has given the impression that he was a Spaniard and not a Jew. Thousands have read the books and tales of Grace Aguilar, without dreaming of her being of the Jewish race. Twelve of the Professors of the University of Berlin are Jews by birth. The diplomacy and the monetary affairs of the Courts of Europe have been largely controlled by Jews for more than a century, while the name of the diplomatist or the financier has given no clue to his lineage.

For the benefit of those, who speak flippantly of "this class," we will mention some Jews, who have been quite as illustrious as the scorners themselves: Eusebius, the historian; Philo, of Alexandria, a prodigy of learning; Judah Cohen, the friend and counselor of Frederick; Raschi, the traveler and scholar; Reuchlin, the philologist, (if we mistake not;) Orobio, the philosopher; Maimonides, to whom Spanish literature is so much indebted, and from whom Spanish writers have borrowed so freely; Moses Mendelsshon, the "Jewish Socrates," and friend of Lessing; Salvator Rosa, the painter; the Rothschilds and Heine, the great bankers of the world; Disraeli, the author; Sir Moses Montefiore, the philanthropist; Prof. Bopp, Maurice Myer, Rapaport; Isaac Leeser, Judge Cardozo, &c., &c.

It may be well, too, to remind the scorners that the Premier of "the Kingdom upon which the sun never sets" is Disraeli, the Jew. The London *Spectator* says of him:

"The brain ought to rule the body, and Mr. Disraeli's elevation to the avowed chieftainship of the Tory party seems to us, therefore, not only natural, but right. He has for many years found them ability, lent them eloquence, secured them organization, been in fact the centre of their whole nervous system, and it was fitting that his mastery should be publicly acknowledged, that the man, who has re-made the House of Commons, should first essay to use the mighty machine he has constructed. * * With a birth, which of itself aroused prejudice, without a relative, without an acre, obviously a rhetorician, and presumably hungering for place, in the teeth of a fire of criticism such as hardly ever has been poured upon any public man, he has fought his way step by step up the ladder of power, has used dukes and earls as stepping stones, and compelled two generations of men, 'acred up to their lips, consolled up to their chins,' to recognize in the 'adventurer,' who failed in his first speech, the 'kinless loon' without a shilling, their inevitable chief."

It may be well, too, to remind "the first captain of his age," whom his admirers pronounce to be greater than Hannibal, Cæsar, and Napoleon, that Napoleon Bonaparte was the first French ruler who removed the civil and political disabilities of "this people." Grant may be greater than Napoleon, but he is hardly so magnanimous. At the very time he was speaking so contemptuously of "this class," Russia, Austria, Prussia, the Netherlands, France, England, Spain, Portugal, Italy and Sardinia were enrolling illustrious Jews in the order of nobility.

Old Thad., the brain of the Republican party, has shown a spirit of intolerance against the Jews equal to the persecuting zeal of General Grant. He has published a lengthy letter on Finance full of insinuations of frauds and peculations on the part of the Jews. The *Jewish Messenger* thus comments on it:

"*Thaddeus Stevens on Finance.*—Mr. Stevens being aged and on the verge of the grave, may be pardoued extravagances of statement and childish garrulity, but while he possesses the power of writing a four column letter on finance, he is certainly strong enough to explain, if facts permit, the innuendoes against the Jews as contained in his pronunciamento on the National Debt and kindred subjects.

The day for open accusation of the Jews that they are counterfeiters of the currency, clippers of coin, enemies of the country, one might justly suppose had passed away with the fagot and the Inquisition. It is contrary to the American spirit to indulge in invidions calumnies directed against a creed or confession. Mr. Stevens has no right to charge upon the Jews any share in the national bankruptcy, as he would denominate it, or to insinuate that, while the government securities depreciated, and articles needed for war advanced, the Jews were the men that made money out of the country's necessities."

OUR ADVERTISEMENTS.—The schools in Winchester, Virginia, are located in one of the most beautiful, picturesque and healthful regions in the world, among a brave, patriotic, and high-toned people. We know, of our personal knowledge, that the Principals have the high qualifications required for their station, scholarship, ability and moral worth—the whole adorned by genial and sincere piety.

Baltimore is a sacred city, with the impoverished people of the South. It has done more to relieve the want, wretchedness and suffering of this distressed section than all the other cities of the Union combined have done. The charity, too, of this benevolent city has been as gentle and quiet as the dew of Heaven. It has been accompanied with no Beecherian display of superior goodness and insulting allusions to the sins of the sufferers. The mountebank Pharisee of Brooklyn ushered in his few crusts and coppers, with a deafening roll of drums and clangor of gongs. Baltimore has given noble donations without the left hand knowing what the right hand did. Every consideration of gratitude should induce the Southern merchant to patronize a city, so refined and delicate in its generosity. When prosperity shall again visit our unhappy region through a wiser and more magnanimous system of legislation, the South should remember the true friend she had in her hour of sorrow and humiliation. Baltimore is an importing city, and our merchants have only to visit it to learn for themselves that they can purchase there on as fair terms, as any where on the continent.

To Missouri Subscribers.—Our St. Louis Agent failed in business, in arrears to us some thirteen months. We learn that he had taken subscriptions in various parts of the State, for which we are responsible. Subscribers sending in their names will have their claims made good.

REPUDIATION.—A RHYME FOR THE TIMES.—This is a campaign pamphlet of 29 pages, by N. C. Kouns, of Fulton, Missouri.—Mr. Kouns is a true poet, and his pamphlet deserves great success. Price, 25 cents per copy, or $15 per 100.

ARIEL.*

4. His argument from Creation. Gradation marks all the works of God. In the animal creation, from the lowest of each species, we ascend the scale to the highest. Thus, cat, cougar, panther, leopard, tiger, lion. Also, ass, donkey, mule, horse. So too, "in philosophic harmony with this order," we have "monkey, baboon, ourang-outang, gorilla, *negro!* the noblest of the beast creation!" "The difference between the negro and these other beasts is very slight, and consists mainly in this one thing: the negro can utter sounds that can be imitated; hence he could talk with Adam and Eve, for they could imitate his sounds. *This is the foundation of language!!*"—Language came then from beasts, and beasts taught it to men! This being so, *negro* should cap the climax, and man be located between negro and gorilla! As conversation is no more than imitation, parrots converse with men, and men converse with beasts!

The theory of "connecting links," held, for the most part, by pretenders to philosophy, has been exploded by science. Professor Guyot says, that facts prove "that there is an impassable chasm between the mineral and the plant, between the plant and the animal, between the animal and man." The microscope proves the truth of the inspired declaration, that "God hath made of *one blood* all nations of men to dwell on all the face of the earth." The blood of the different varieties of the Human Race, including the Negro, has been examined by the microscope, and its decision is, that their blood *is one and the same*, whilst the blood of *animals* has, by it, been proved to be different. Physiology also shows, that whilst the blood of one man, including that of the negro, may be transfused into the veins of another, to preserve life, the transfusion of the blood of an animal into the veins of a man, will cause death.

"The greatest naturalists in all ages," says Dr. Bachman, "however diversified may have been their views in regard to Christianity, regarded all the races of men as composed of one species. Among these were Linnæus, Leibnitz, Buffon, Humboldt, Blumenbach, Cuvier, &c., the lights of the world, who studied all the departments of nature.—And who are on the opposite side? Virey,—who pronounces the negro 'undoubtedly a distinct species from the beginning of the world,' and divides mankind into two species, the white and the black, and suspects a certain fraternity between the Hottentot and the baboon—Desmoulin, Borey, Broc, Dr. Nott; men whom the world of science has never admitted into their ranks as naturalists." To make up what is lacking in weight, the name of Agassiz is thrown into the same scale with these sciolists, and he is regarded as the Oracle whose sentence settles all controversy. But, like some

* Continued from page 273.

other oracles, his utterances are not consistent. For example, we have, at one time, the following deliverance from him: "Whilst the lower animals are of distinct species in the different zoological provinces to which they belong, man, notwithstanding the diversity of his races, constitutes *one only and the same species*, over all the surface of the globe. In this respect, as well as in so many others, man seems to us to form an exception to the general rule in this creation, of which he is at the same time the object and the end." "Man is everywhere *the one identical species*, yet several races, marked by certain peculiarities of features," and these "differences in the physical constitution of man" are ascribed to "*varieties of climate, food, modes of life and customs.*"

At another time, we have the following deliverance from him: "The different races of men are descended from different stocks." At another time, the following: "He believed in an *indefinite* number of original and distinctly created races of men."

Let those, who appeal to Agassiz as a decisive authority, reconcile, if they can, these antagonistic opinions;—and when they would give us an oracle, give us one who at least does not deny himself.

The "prognathous skull," (projecting lower jaw,) which is said by some to be characteristic of the negro, is yet exhibited by only a portion of the natives of Africa; some even of the black nations have an erect face, prominent forehead, and fine features. The facial angle of the European is 80 deg., Kalmuck 75 deg., Negro 70 deg., whilst the facial angle of the Ape is shown, by Owen, to vary from 30 deg. to 35 deg. The conformation of the Chinese and Peruvian heads is as distant from the Grecian or Caucasian type, as that of the Negro. We consider

5. His argument from the Negro not being made in the Image of God. "We read in the Bible, that God said, Let us make man in our own image; which is equivalent to saying, We have *man* already, but not *in our image*; for if the negro was already in God's image, God could not have said, now let us make man in *our* image." "Whenever Adam and his race are spoken of in the Hebrew Scriptures, invariably his name has the prefix, *the* man, to contradistinguish him from the negro, who is called *man* simply, and was so named by Adam."—The negro taught Adam *language*, and now Adam returns the service, and gives a *name* to his instructor, and calls him *man!*—"By inattention to this distinction, ('man,' and 'the man,') made by God Himself, the world is indebted for the confusion that exists regarding Adam and his race, and the negro."

The distinction being so important, and the neglect of it having produced so much mischief, let us therefore, by all means, acknowledge it—provided it be true. Is it then true? must be the first inquiry. Accordingly, we turn to the Hebrew Bible, and find that in the following passages where 'man' is used, the prefix *the* is wanting. And as, according to this distinguished scholar, in all such passages, '*negro* (who is a beast,) is meant, we shall therefore, substitute 'negro' for 'man':

Gen. 1:26. "Let us make *negro*, (or *beast*,) in our image!!" (no prefix here.)

Gen. 6:3. "'My Spirit shall not always strive with *negro*, (or *beast*.")

Neh. 6:29. "They sinned against my judgments, which if a *negro* (or *beast*) do, he shall live in them."

Job 11:12. "Though *negro* (or *beast*) be born like a wild ass's colt."

Job 14:1. "*Negro*, (or *beast*) *that is born of a woman!* is of a few days, and full of trouble."

Ps. 8:5. "What is the son of *negro* (or *beast*) that Thou visitest him?"

Ps. 36:7. "O Lord, Thou preservest *negro*, (or *beast*,) and beast."

Ps. 36:8. "Therefore the children of *negroes* (or *beasts*) put their trust in Thee."

Ps. 45:3. "Thou art fairer than the children of *negroes* (or *beasts*.")

Ps. 68:19. "Thou hast received gifts for *negroes*, (or *beasts*.")

Ps. 73:5. "Neither are they (the wicked) plagued like other *negroes*, (or *beasts*.")

Ps. 86:6. "Blessed is the *negro* (or *beast*) whose strength is in Thee."

Prov. 16:1. "The preparations of the heart in *negro* (or *beast*,) are from the Lord."

Prov. 20:27. "The spirit of *negro* (or *beast*) is the candle of the Lord."

Prov. 27:19. "As in water, face answereth to face, so the heart of man to *negro* (or *beast*.")

Prov. 28:23. "He that rebuketh a *negro* (or *beast*,) afterwards shall find more favor than he that flattereth with the tongue!"

Eccle. 7:20. "There is not a just *negro* (or *beast*) upon earth, that doeth good, and sinneth not."

Eccle. 8:1. "A *negro's* (or *beast's*) wisdom maketh his face to shine!!"

Ezek. 3:17. "Son of *negro* (or *beast*,) I have made thee a watchman."

Ezek. 11:4. "Prophesy, O son of *negro* (or *beast*.")

Hosea. 6:7. "But they like *negroes* (or *beasts*) have transgressed the covenant."

Micah. 6:8. "He hath shewed thee, O, *negro* (or *beast*) what is good. And what doth the Lord require of thee, but to do justly, and to love mercy, and to walk humbly with thy God?"

Mal. 3:8. "Will a *negro* (or *beast*) rob God?"

What an accomplished Hebrew scholar!

Other passages could be adduced, but these are abundantly sufficient to signalize the ignorance and impudence of this shameless upstart.

(TO BE CONTINUED.)

LIST OF ADVERTISEMENTS.

———o———

Bankers & Brokers—Wilson, Colston & Co.,	Baltimore Md.
" " Brown, Lancaster & Co.,	" "
Books & Stationery—Claxton, Remsen & Haffelfinger,	Phila., Pa.
Clothing—Noah Walker & Co.,	Baltimore, Md.
" Shipley, Roane & Co.,	" "
Druggists—Burrough Bros.,	" "
Dry Goods—W. Devries & Co.,	
Fertilizers—B. M. Rhodes & Co.,	
" Patapsco Guano Company,	
Grain Drill—W. L. Buckingham,	
Guns, Pistols, &c.—Alexander McComas,	" "
Hagerstown Mail—Dechert & Co.,	Hagerstown, "
Hotels—Owen House,	Washington, D. C.
" Howard House,	Baltimore, Md.
Importers. Hardware, &c.—Cortlan & Co.,	" "
" Hats, Furs, &c.—R. Q. Taylor,	" "
" Ribbons, Millinery, &c.—Armstrong, Cator & Co.,	"
" China, Glass, &c.—Samuel Child & Co.,	" "
India Rubber Goods—W. G. Maxwell,	
Insurance—Piedmont Insurance Company,	Va.
Marble Works—Bevan & Sons,	Baltimore, Md.
" " Gaddess Bros.,	" "
Manufacturers. Pianos—Knabe & Co.,	" "
" " Chas. M. Stieff,	
" Cedar Ware, &c.—Lord & Robinson,	" "
" Furniture—Thos. Godey,	
" " R. Renwick & Son,	
Organs & Pianos—H. Sanders & Co.,	
Patent Medicine, Rosadalis—Dr. J. J. Lawrence,	

THE LAND WE LOVE.

No. V SEPTEMBER, 1868. Vol. V

GEN. PRICE'S REPORT OF THE MISSOURI CAMPAIGN, 1864.

General:—I have the honor to make the following report of my operations in the late expedition to Missouri. I regret to state that the report is meagre and incomplete, for the reason that Maj. Gen. Marmaduke and Brig. Gen. Cabell, who bore so honorable and conspicuous a share in the greater part of the expedition, were captured before its close and are prisoners in the hands of the enemy: whilst Maj. Gen. Fagan, who commanded the Arkansas troops, composing a large part of the forces engaged, has as yet been unable to make any report nor have any been received from the subordinate commanders. In conformity with the letter of instructions from Gen. E. Kirby Smith, dated 11th August, 1864, I made immediate arrangements for a movement into Missouri, as concluded upon in my interview and conference with him upon that subject, with the cavalry force in the District of Arkansas, then under my command, being promised, in addition, the brigade of Louisiana cavalry, commanded by Col. Harrison, estimated at 1,500 strong. At the same time, information in full detail of the proposed movement, of the route to be pursued, and of the probable time when it would be made, was, without delay, sent by me to Brig. Gen. Shelby, who then commanded in North East Arkansas, with instructions to make an attack when in his judgment he should deem advisable, upon Du Vall's Bluff and the railroad between Little Rock and White River, in the possession of the enemy, and by diverting their attention, enable me to cross the lower Arkansas and unite our forces without danger of failure. These instructions were carried out in full by Gen. Shelby, and resulted in an attack upon the railroad, terminating in the most complete success; over 400 Federals captured, 300 killed and wounded, 6 forts taken and destroyed, 10 miles of railroad destroyed, as well as vast quantities of forage, &c.; full particulars of which are contained in Gen. Shelby's Report accompanying. This exploit was one of the most brilliant of the war, and cast additional lustre upon the well earned fame of that gallant general and the officers and men under his command. It was part of the plan concluded upon, that I should cross the Arkansas river about the 20th of August, with the troops under my immediate command, but from delay in receiving the necessary ordnance stores, I was unable to do so. Finally, the required complement was received on the 27th, and on the 28th of August, I was relieved from the command of the District of Arkansas, and crossed the Ouachita river. On the 29th, arrived at Princeton, where the divisions of Fagan and Marmaduke were, and assumed command of all the cavalry in the District of Arkansas, according to the instructions of Gen. Smith above referred to. In the mean time, owing to the delay in starting, I was of the opinion that the enemy had become informed of my intended line of march, and concluded to cross the Arkansas river at the most feasible point north of Little Rock and south of Fort Smith, taking into consideration the probable means of obtaining forage and subsistence.

On the 30th, I took up my line of march in the direction of Little Rock, and arrived that afternoon at Tulip, a distance of 9 miles. Colonel Harrison's brigade had not yet arrived, but as I could wait no longer, I left instructions, at Princeton, directing him, if he should arrive there within three days, to follow on and form a junction with me, giving him information of the route I should take; but in case he did not reach Princeton, in that time, he should then report to the commanding officer of the District of Arkansas. Colonel Harrison did not take part in the expedition.

On the morning of the 31st, I resumed my march in the same direction as on the previous day, and continued on the same until within 7 miles of Benton, when I diverged to the left, taking a North-west direction, sending Major General Fagan across the Saline river to make a demonstration towards Little Rock, and to protect my right flank. On the 5th September, he joined me, bringing up the rear. I reached Dardanelle, on the Arkansas river, a distance of 167 miles from Camden, on 6th September. The country, through which I had passed, was hilly, and in some parts mountainous, sparsely settled, but plenty of forage and subsistence was obtained. The Arkansas being fordable at this point, on the 7th I crossed and marched to Dover, a distance of 14 miles. Major General Marmaduke, with his division, and part of his train, had already crossed before my arrival, thus covering the crossing of the remainder of the army.

At Princeton, verbal and written communications had been sent to Brig. Gen. Shelby, apprising him of the changes of route, and directing him to join me at Batesville. But up to this time, I had received no information from him of his movements or position. I resumed the march in the direction of the last mentioned point. Major General Fagan with his command marching along the Springfield road, and Major General Marmaduke, and Head-quarters train, the Clinton road; taking separate roads on account of the scarcity of forage, and to rid that section of country of deserters and Federal jayhawkers as they are termed, (*i. e.* robbers and murderers) with which that country is infested. These bands, however, dispersed and took refuge in the mountains at the approach of the army; several were killed and a few taken prisoners. Arriving at Little Red river on the 10th, and still without information of the position or movements of General Shelby, I dispatched an officer of known skill and daring to communicate with him, directing that he should unite himself with the rest of the command at once. On the 18th, I arrived at a point on White river, 18 miles above Batesville, and received information that Brigadier General Shelby was at Powhatan, about 64 miles North-east of Batesville, and on the selected route to Missouri. I adopted the town Pocahontas, as the point of rendezvous, and directed Major General Marmaduke, with his own command and train, and that of Head-quarters, to march to that point direct, while I proceeded to Batesville, and thence to Powhatan. Major General Fagan, with his division, who had arrived at Batesville, marched to Powhatan on the left. I arrived on 13th September and found General Shelby with part of his command. Reached Pocahontas the next day, and then the remainder of Shelby's command reported, including the brigades of Jackman, McCroy and Dobbins. In fine, the whole army was concentrated. The country over which I had passed was rugged and mountainous in the extreme, and had damaged the transportation to some extent, but it had been, or was on the point of being repaired, and on the other hand, by adopting the routes marched over, sufficient forage and subsistence had been obtained.

The towns and villages, through which I had passed, had been robbed, pillaged, burned, and otherwise destroyed by the enemy, and were nearly deserted by the former inhabitants; in fact, the whole country presented but a scene of desolation.

Upon arriving at Pocahontas, I proceeded to organize the army, which was completed on the 18th, as follows:

Fagan's division, commanded by Major General J. F. Fagan, composed of Brigadier General W. L. Cabell's brigade, Colonel Slemmons', Colonel McCroy's and Colonel Dobbin's brigades, Cols. Lyles' and Rogan's commands, and Captain Andrews' battalion.

Marmaduke's division, commanded by Major General J. S. Marmaduke, composed of Brig. General Jno. B. Clark's and Colonel Freeman's brigades, Col. Kitchen's regiment, and Lieut. Col. R. C. Woods' battalion.

Shelby's division, commanded

by Brigadier General J. O. Shelby, consisted of Colonels Shanks' and Jackson's brigades, and Colonel Coleman's command.

Having determined to invade Missouri in three columns, Gen. Fagan with his division was ordered to march to Fredericktown, Missouri, by the way of Martinsburg, Reeves' Station and Greenville. * Major General Marmaduke, with his division, was ordered to march to the vicinity of Fredericktown, Missouri, to the right of the route to be followed by Fagan's division, as above designated; varying from it 10 to 30 miles, or as near within those limits as might be practicable, on account of the roads and forage. Shelby, with his command, was to march to the vicinity of Fredericktown, by a route to the left of Gen. Fagan's, varying from 10 to 20 miles, as nearly as practicable, on account of roads and forage. Head-quarters to march with the centre column. At Fredericktown, the three divisions were ordered to form a junction. A map of the route to be followed was furnished each of the division commanders. The most stringent orders were issued against straggling and pillaging, under the severest penalties, and the division commanders were earnestly enjoined to use their utmost endeavors to have the orders carried into effect in every particular, and without delay.

On the 19th of September, the army marched in the order above designated, and on that day, I entered Missouri, with 12,000 men, only 8,000 however, armed, and 14 pieces of artillery; and on the 24th of September, reached Fredericktown, Missouri, with the centre column. Brig. Gen. Shelby was in the advance, passing, in his route, through Doniphan and Patterson. Whilst Major General Marmaduke, whose route was by Poplar Bluff, Castorville, and Dallas, had not yet come up. On the 19th, before Brigadier General Shelby reached Doniphan, news of the arrival of the army having been received, a force of the enemy, composed of a part of the Federal, Missouri, 12th cavalry, then occupying the place, withdrew, first setting fire to the town, which was consumed, and retreated to Pender's mills (burning the houses of citizens as they passed) where they were overtaken the next day, and routed with a loss of a lieutenant and 3 men killed, 4 wounded, and 6 prisoners, besides several horses and small arms; our loss 2 killed and 5 wounded.

On the 22nd, Brigadier General Shelby attacked the town of Patterson, but the garrison having received information of his approach, hastily evacuated the place, with a loss of 28 killed and several wounded; also a telegraph battery and operator captured: no loss on our part.

On the 25th, I remained at Fredericktown awaiting the arrival of Marmaduke's division, which came up that evening within 8 miles of the place. Gen. Marmaduke, on his route, had a few skirmishes with the Federal militia, killing and wounding 4 and capturing 11. Col. Jeffries, of Marmaduke's division, had, before the arrival of the army at Pocahontas, been sent with his regiment to Bloomfield, Mo., which the enemy evacuated on his approach, killing a number and capturing arms and six wagon loads of army stores. He rejoined his brigade (Clark's) on the 24th: detached again on the 25th, he attacked, and by a gallant charge, drove the enemy out of the town of old Jackson—for particulars see Brig. Gen. Clark's Report. I received at Fredericktown, satisfactory evidence that the strength of the enemy at Ironton was about 1500, and that the Federal General A. J. Smith, was camped about 10 miles from St. Louis with his corps, composed of about 8,000 infantry, on the St. Louis and Iron Mountain Railroad. I immediately ordered Brig. General Shelby to proceed at once with his division, by way of Farmington, to a point on the St. Louis and Iron Mountain Railroad, where there were then five bridges in close proximity to each other, to destroy the railroad there and the bridges, and after effecting that object, to fall back in the direction of Ironton and Pilot Knob, which would effectually prevent Gen. A. J. Smith from reinforcing the garrison at those places, which I would attack and take with the divisions of Major Generals Fagan and Marmaduke. Gen. Shelby proceeded to the point indicated and performed the duty assigned him, in the most complete and effectual manner, destroying the splendid bridge at Irondale as well as the three mentioned, tearing up miles and miles of the track, burning the ties, rails, &c.: for full particulars reference is made to his Report accompanying. On the morning of the 26th, being rejoined by Maj. Gen. Marmaduke with his division, I proceeded at an early hour with his and Fagan's divisions, in the direction of Ironton and Pilot Knob, at the same time sending forward a portion of Fagan's division to take and hold a difficult pass, in that direction, between two mountains, within 3 and 4 miles of Ironton. This was effected rapidly, and with success. That evening, I sent forward the remainder of his division, leaving his train at St. Francois creek, where forage could be obtained for the animals, and where I encamped for the night with the rest of the command. That evening, Gen. Fagan drove in the Federal pickets at Arcadia and took position before the town for the night. Next morning, he drove the enemy from Arcadia, where they abandoned a very strong position, through Ironton, where he also took a strong fort, in a most gallant and brilliant manner. The enemy took refuge behind their fortifications at Pilot Knob. Having received such information as appeared to be perfectly reliable concerning the character and strength of the fortifications, as induced me to believe that the place could be taken without great loss, I accordingly directed Maj. Gen. Marmaduke to take possession of Shepherd's Mountain, which was west of the fortifications and completely commanded them. This was most satisfactorily accomplished, and his artillery placed in position on the mountain. Maj. Gen. Fagan formed on the South and East. Skirmishing took place all the day, and firing of artillery from the enemy until 2 P. M. when a charge was ordered and made in the most gallant and determined manner: officers and men vieing with each other, in both divisions, in deeds of unsurpassed bravery—charging up to the muzzles of the enemy's cannon. Where all acted as heroes, it would seem almost invidious to make any exception; but I must be allowed to call attention to the courage and gallantry of General Cabell in leading his men to the assault, having his horse killed under him within 40 yards of the fort. But the information, I had received in regard to the strength of the fortifications, proved totally incorrect. Our troops were repulsed, and it being too late to renew the assault, they were withdrawn beyond reach of the enemy's guns, and preparations were made for a renewal of the assault on next day. I had dispatched a courier, on the morning of the 27th, to Brig. Gen. Shelby, informing him of the proposed operations, and directing him to rejoin the main army to assist in the attack, and on the evening of the 27th, another courier was dispatched, informing him of the capture of Arcadia and Ironton, and of the repulse at Pilot Knob, and of my design to renew there the attack on the following morning, and hoping that the courier would meet him on the way, instructed him to join me, as also the route to pursue. Neither of these communications, as it appears, was received by Brig. Gen. Shelby, who, having heard that there was a force of the enemy at Potosi, had left the railroad and marched to attack them at that place, which was captured by him with its garrison of 150 Federals, arms, &c. The depot of the railroad at that place, with seven fine cars, were also destroyed: for full particulars reference is made to the accompanying Report of Brig. Gen. Shelby.

The enemy at Pilot Knob, on the night following the first attack, evacuated the fort, blowing up the magazine, leaving in my possession 16 pieces of artillery, a large number of small arms, a large amount of army stores, consisting of bales of blankets, hundreds of barrels of flour and bacon, quantities of coffee, &c. After destroying the artillery, which I could not take with me, and distributing among the troops such of the stores as were needed, I moved my command 12 miles on the road the enemy had retreated, sending Marmaduke forward in pursuit, in command of his own and Shelby's divisions, which had rejoined the command. Untiring pursuit was made night and day, but it was not until the evening of the following day, that he was overtaken, owing to the natural difficulties presented by the country over which the enemy retreated. Major General Marmaduke, who was in advance, fought him until an hour before sunset, when Shelby was thrown in front, and the fight continued until dark. The enemy having thrown up fortifications during the night, it was deemed not advisable to renew the attack, and the forces were withdrawn: the particulars in full are contained in accompanying Reports of Brigadier Generals Shelby and Clark.

My loss in this effort, I cannot give, as I have no Report from Fagan's division, but the loss in Marmaduke's division, was 14 officers and 80 men killed and wounded. The loss in Fagan's division was, doubtless, greater. Whilst at Ironton, receiving information that the Federal forces exceeded my own two to one, and knowing the city to be strongly fortified, I determined to move as fast as possible on Jefferson City, destroying the railroad as I went, with a hope to capture that city with its troops and munitions of war. I arrived at Richwoods on the 30th, having passed through Potosi. Lieutenant Christian, whom I had sent to the Mississippi river before I left Camden, for the purpose of obtaining gun-caps, joined me at this place, bringing 150,000. Lieut. Christian is a most energetic and efficient officer, and deserves especial notice. Major General Fagan sent 300 men to DeSoto to destroy the depot, which was effected and the militia, who had gathered there in some numbers, at the same time was scattered. At the same time, General Cabell was sent with his brigade to cut the Pacific railroad, east of Franklin, which he did effectually, also burning the depot in that town. On the 29th, Colonel Burbridge and Lieut. Colonel Wood were detached by Major General Marmaduke, and sent to Cuba to destroy the depots on the Southwest branch of the Pacific railroad, at that place, which they succeeded in doing. The divisions of Marmaduke and Shelby tore up several miles of the Southwest branch of the Pacific railroad. For full details, see Reports of Brigadier Generals Clark and Shelby. Lieut. Col. Wood, of Marmaduke's division, destroyed the important bridge over the Moselle. These two divisions were sent forward in the direction of Union, which was captured by Brig. Gen. Clark, killing 32 and wounding 70 of the Federal garrison. On the 2d of October, Clark's brigade took possession of Washington, without opposition, and destroyed the Pacific railroad bridge about two miles from that place. On the 3d, a train was captured at Miller's station, with a large amount of clothing and 400 Sharp's Rifles. On the same evening the town of Hermann was taken possession of, after a slight opposition, (the enemy abandoning a 6 pound iron gun) by Clark's brigade: for particulars see Report of Brig. General Clark, with the accompanying report of Col. Green. On the 4th of October, Maj. Gen. Marmaduke sent 400 men, with one gun, under command of Lieut. Colonel Wood, to destroy the Pacific Railroad Bridge over the Gasconade river, which he effected. Linn was captured with 100 prisoners and as many arms by a portion of Shelby's division. On the 6th, Brig. Gen. Shelby sent a force under Col. Shanks to destroy the bridge over the Osage, on the

Pacific Railroad, which was successfully accomplished. A passage was there forced by him across the Osage, six miles below Castle Rock. The enemy disputed the passage warmly, but in vain. In this action, the gallant Col. Shanks received a severe if not mortal wound, and was left in the hands of friends to be cared for: he afterwards fell into the possession of the enemy and is reported to have since died—a loss greatly to be deplored. He was ever foremost in battle and last in retreat; his death would be regretted by all who mourn the loss of the good and the brave. At the same time Col. Shanks forced the passage of the Osage as stated, Col. Gordon, of the same division, forced its passage at Castle Rock, and the division bivouacked that night 7 miles from Jefferson City. On the next morning, Maj. Gen. Fagan was thrown in front with his division, and on the march came upon the enemy 5 miles from Jefferson City, in large force. A hotly contested battle immediately ensued, but the enemy was gradually driven back to Moscow creek, when being reinforced they again made an obstinate resistance, but were finally routed and forced to seek shelter in their entrenchments, Fagan occupying the heights in full view of the city. On this occasion, Maj. Gen. Fagan handled his troops with marked skill and ability, under my own immediate observation. Night approaching, I determined to move my forces two miles south of the city, where water and forage were abundant. Did so, and encamped for the night. I had received positive information that the enemy were 12,000 strong, in the city, and that 3,000 more had arrived on the opposite bank of the river, by the North Missouri railroad, before I withdrew to the encampment selected: whereupon, I gave immediate instructions to Brig. Gen. Shelby to send a sufficient force to burn the bridges and destroy the railroad west of Jefferson City, in the direction of California, the county seat of Moniteau county, and after a consultation with my General Officers, I determined not to attack the enemy in his entrenchments, as they outnumbered me two to one, and were strongly fortified, but to move my command in the direction of Kansas, as instructed in my original orders, hoping to be able to capture a sufficient number of arms, to arm my unarmed men, at Booneville, Sedalia, Lexington and Independence, places which I intended to occupy en route. The next day, I accordingly marched towards Kansas, and was followed by General McNeill who made an attack on my rear guard, Fagan's division, but was easily repulsed. Gen. Shelby's division constituting my advance, reached California on the 7th, having sent a portion of his command to destroy the Pacific railroad which it did, track, bridges, &c.; passing rapidly on to Booneville, he by a rapid charge drove in their pickets and the garrison took refuge in their entrenchments. Brig. General Shelby disposing his forces in such a manner as to prevent the arrival of reinforcements, awaited until his artillery could come up. In the meantime, propositions for the surrender of the town were made to him and accepted. Accordingly, the place, its garrison, stores, &c., were delivered into his hands: for particulars, reference is made to his accompanying Report.

I followed on with the divisions of Major Generals Fagan and Marmaduke, and camped, on the night of the 8th, 14 miles from Jefferson City. On the 9th, marched through and beyond California, making 26 miles.— On the 10th, arrived at Booneville with the rest of the command. My reception was enthusiastic in the extreme: old and young, men, women and children, vied in their salutations and in ministering to the wants and comforts of my wearied and war-worn soldiers. About 300 prisoners were captured at Booneville, with arms, ammunition and many stores, which were distributed among the soldiers. On the 11th, hearing of the approach of General McNeill, with a cavalry force, estimated at 2,500 men, for the purpose of attacking Booneville by the Tipton road, I selected my position about ½ mile from the river, and placed the divisions of Maj. Gens. Fagan and Marmaduke in line of battle to receive him. The enemy attacked them, but was easily driven back, with loss and was pursued, by a portion of Fagan's division and Jackman's brigade, a distance of 21 miles from Booneville, with heavy loss, in spite of an obstinate resistance, and the ruggedness of the country over which the pursuit was made.

For full particulars of the action, so far as his own troops were concerned, see Report of Colonel Jackman, accompanying.

Captain Anderson, who that day reported to me, with about 100 men, was sent to destroy the North Missouri railroad: at the same time, Quantrell, with the men under his command, was sent to destroy the Hannibal and St. Joseph railroad, to prevent, if possible, the enemy from throwing their forces from St. Louis in my front. These officers, I was afterwards informed, did some damage to the roads, but none of advantage, and totally failed in the main object proposed, which was to destroy the large railroad bridge in the edge of St. Charles county. I moved that evening from Booneville to Chatteau Springs, on my proposed route, a distance of 11 miles, having recruited at Booneville 1,200 or 1,500 men, mostly unarmed.— That night, receiving information that there was 5,000 stand of arms stored in the City Hall at Glasgow, I sent Brig. Gen. Clark, of Marmaduke's division, with his own brigade and 500 of Jackman's, with orders to cross the river at Arrow Rock and attack the place, the next morning at daybreak and capture it. At the same time sending Brig. General Shelby, with a small portion of his division, and a section of artillery, to attack the town at the same hour from the west side of the river, to divert the attention of the enemy, and protect their advance under cover of the fire from his artillery. Owing to unforeseen difficulties in crossing the river, Brig. Gen. Clark was unable to commence the attack for an hour after Brig. Gen. Shelby had engaged them. The place was surrendered, but not until the City Hall was destroyed and the arms consumed by fire. However, we obtained 800 or 900 prisoners, 1,200 small arms, about the same number of overcoats, 150 horses, one steamboat, and a large amount of under-clothing.—This enterprise was a great success, effected with but small loss on our side, and reflects great honor on all parties concerned.—The prisoners were paroled, such of the ordnance and other stores as could be carried were distributed and the remainder with the steamboat burned. For particulars, reference is made to the accompanying Reports of Generals Clark and Shelby. In the awards of praise contained, the commanding General cordially concurs.

On the night of the 13th, encamped at Mr. Marshall's, marching 14 miles, and on the next day to Jonesboro, 8 miles, where I was joined by Gen. Fagan, who had been left behind at the Lamine. I then ordered Brig. Gen. M. Jeff. Thompson, then commanding Shelby's old brigade, to take with him a force of not less than 800 or 1,000 men and one section of artillery by Longwood and thence to Sedalia, and to attack the Federals at that place, if he should deem it prudent and advisable. This order was promptly and completely carried out by Gen. Thompson; the place, though strongly fortified and well garrisoned, was carried by a bold and daring assault, and fell into our hands with over 200 prisoners, who were paroled, several hundred stand of arms, many pistols, and wagon loads of goods suitable to soldiers. Reference is made to the accompanying Reports of Generals Shelby and Thompson. The latter withdrew on the approach of a large force of the enemy.

On the 15th, I reached Keisus, having passed through Marshall, marching 17 miles, where I remained two days, awaiting Gen. Clark, for whose safety I began to entertain fears, inasmuch as information had been received that the enemy were on my left flank, and in my rear, in large force. Previous to the attack on Sedalia, the large and magnificent bridge over the Lamine, on the Pacific Railroad, had been destroyed by Lieut. Jas. Wood, of Elliott's battalion, who had been sent there for that purpose by Gen. Shelby. On the 17th, I received information that the enemy (Kansas troops) had entered Lexington on the 16th. On the 17th, I also received news of the capture of Sedalia by General Thompson. On the 18th, having been joined by Shelby's division and Clark's brigade of Marmaduke's division, I marched to Waverly, 22 miles.

On leaving Pocahontas, I had sent an agent of great intelligence and tact into St. Louis to ascertain the strength of the enemy at that city, with instructions to report to me, if possible, at Potosi. He was, however, so closely watched that he could not join me until I had passed that city: upon overtaking me he informed me that I would be pursued by 24,000 men from St. Louis and 15,000 from Jefferson City, which, with the force in my front from Kansas, he believed to be the entire force, with which I would have to contend.

I then abandoned my former determination to issue an address to the people, calling upon them to rally to me, as they were already pouring in so rapidly, that I knew I would not be able to proteet and feed them, and as it would require that my army should be kept together to protect them on a rapid and dangerous retreat from the State. At daybreak on the morning of the 19th, I moved from Waverly towards Lexington; General Shelby's division in the advance. Having received information that Gens. Blunt, Lane, and Jemmison, with between 3,000 and 4,000 Federals (Colorado, Kansas and Missouri Federal troops) were at Lexington, and fearing they might make a junction with McNeill and A. J. Smith, who were at Sedalia and Salt Fork, I made a flank movement to the left, after crossing Tabo, so as to intercept their line of march. The advance under Shelby met them at 2 p. m., and a battle immediately ensued. For a time the Federals fought well and resisted strenuously, but finally giving way, they were pressed by our troops, driven well past Lexington, and pursued on the road to Independence until night. That night, the enemy evacuated Lexington in great haste and confusion. Shelby's old brigade under Brig. General M. Jeff. Thompson, bivouacked that night in the suburbs of town, I encamped at Gen. Shield's, 3 miles south of Lexington, marching that day 26 miles. On the morning of the 20th, I moved west, in the same direction as before, to Five Creek prairie, 22 miles, where I encamped. Information was received that the enemy had fallen back to the Little Blue. On the 21st, I resumed my line of march to the Little Blue on the Independence road; Marmaduke's division in the front, whose advance soon came upon the enemy's pickets who, being driven across the Blue, burned the bridge as they crossed. A ford ½ mile below the bridge was seized by our troops, and Marmaduke's division crossed it. His advance, Col. Lawther's regiment, soon came upon the enemy who were strongly posted behind a stone fence, in superior numbers. Lawther's regiment was driven back and hotly pursued by the foe, when they were reinforced by Col. Green with 150 men. A fierce engagement ensued with varying success. Col. Green contesting every inch of ground, when Wood's battery arrived and the enemy gave way, but being reinforced again renewed the attack. Just as the ammunition of our troops engaged, who still manfully resisted with success, the far superior numbers of the enemy, was about to become exhausted, Col. Kitchen's regiment arrived. Again the enemy was repulsed and fell back to their former strong position.—Hearing of the critical condition of Gen. Marmaduke's division, I had sent orders for Shelby to move rapidly to his relief.—

He accordingly hastened with his division to the scene of action, and arrived there at the time the enemy had taken refuge in their first position; an attack was made upon them; a furious battle followed; the enemy was forced from his position and retreated. Gen. Shelby now taking the lead, drove them in a stubborn running fight on foot (his men having been dismounted) for 2 miles, and beyond Independence. For full particulars of this fight, reference is made to the Reports of Generals Shelby and Clark, and to that of Col. Green, accompanying the latter. In this action, Gen. Marmaduke acted with distinguished gallantry, having not less than two horses shot under him. Gen. Clark, of his division, also exhibited great skill and bravery, whilst Col. Green, by the manner in which he handled his regiment against vastly superior forces, flushed with success, beating them back with his handful of men, contesting every inch of ground until assistance came, as well as by the personal courage exhibited by him, justly excited the admiration of his superior officers. Fagan's division, under my orders, supported Gen. Shelby, but was not immediately engaged. Encamped that night in Independence, marching 26 miles, the troops being engaged most of the time.

On the evening of the 21st Capt. Williams, of Shelby's division, who had been sent on recruiting service, rejoined his command with 600 men, capturing on his route the town of Carrollton with 300 prisoners, and arming his entire command. On the morning of the 22nd, I left Independence. The enemy had fallen back to Big Blue on the Kansas City road, to a position strong by nature, and strengthened by fortifications, upon which all their art had been expended; where they had been joined by General Curtis and his forces, thus increasing Blunt's army to between 6,000 and 8,000 men. Receiving this information, I determined to advance on the Santa Fe road, with Shelby's division in front, detaching Jackman and sending him on the Kansas City road to engage the enemy, then skirmishing with the pickets. Gen. Shelby crossed the Big Blue with the remainder of his division, meeting some opposition from the enemy, which was soon overcome. After crossing, he engaged the enemy to cover the crossing and passage of the train. Gen. Thompson with his brigade, except Gordon's regiment, pressed the enemy to near the town of Westport, when he was ordered to fall back to the Blue. Colonel Gordon, with his regiment, who had been detained to guard the left, soon became engaged and was sorely pressed by overpowering numbers; when he was rejoined by Jackman, and gallantly charging, they repulsed the enemy, pursued them some distance and inflicted heavy loss upon them; also captured a 24-pound Howitzer. A large force of the enemy came out from Westport, and a fight ensued, the enemy endeavoring to regain the lost gun. They were sternly resisted and finally the arrival of Gen. Thompson and night, stopped the combat. Reference is made to the Report of Gen. Shelby for particulars. Two flags were also captured and presented to me on the battle-field by Captains McCoy and Wood of Gordon's regiment, who had taken them with their own hands from the enemy. In the meantime, other forces had engaged me in the rear. Having received information that other bodies of the enemy were pursuing me, I had directed pickets to be placed at the Little Blue, to give notice of their approach.—This had been done by General Fagan, and being advised on the morning of the 22d that the enemy had attacked and driven in his pickets, he dispatched General Cabell to drive back the enemy, which he did; but on his return, coming through Independence, the enemy struck Cabell in flank, cutting off 300 or 400 men and capturing 2 pieces of artillery. Gen. Marmaduke's division which formed the rear became engaged with the same enemy, half an hour before sundown. The division was then about two miles from Independence, the advance of the enemy was checked by our troops, who then fell back ½ mile to a new position, which the enemy attacked with increasing fierceness, driving our troops steadily back until a late hour at night, and in almost impenetrable darkness.

For particulars reference is made to the accompanying Report of Gen. Clark.

I encamped that night on the battle-field, near Westport, in line of battle, having marched 12 miles, the troops constantly engaging the enemy, the whole distance. On the morning of the 23d, I took up my line of march and soon discovered the enemy in position on the prairie. The train had been sent forward on the Fort Scott road. I had instructed General Marmaduke to resist the advance of the enemy, who was in his rear, if possible, as he was on the same road as the train. Gen. Shelby immediately attacked the enemy, assisted by Gen. Fagan, with two brigades of Arkansas troops, and though they stubbornly resisted and contested every point of approach, drove them six or seven miles into Westport. In the meantime, Gen. Marmaduke who was to my right and rear, being attacked by an overwhelming force of the enemy, had to fall back, after a most strenuous resistance, his ammunition being exhausted.

For full particulars reference is made to Report of Gen. Clark.

Being at that time near Westport, and in full view of Generals Fagan and Shelby's commands, I received information that my train, which was in front and on the right of the Fort Scott road, was threatened by some 2,000 or 2,500 of the enemy, moving in a line parallel with the Fort Scott road. I immediately directed Gen. Fagan and Gen. Shelby to fall back to the train as soon as they could do so with safety, which I would attempt to defend until they arrived. I immediately pushed forward to the front of the train with my escort, and there formed in line of battle the unarmed men who were present to the number of several thousand; throwing my escort and all the armed men of Tyler's brigade forward as skirmishers, the whole not amounting to more than 200, to the front of the enemy, and directing Gen. Cabell, who arrived soon after, to hold the crossing of the creek on my left,, sending forward at the same time for a portion of Col. McCroy's brigade, which was in advance of the train, and on his arrival found him in line of battle on the left flank of the enemy, which caused the enemy to fall back a considerable distance on the prairie. In the meantime, the rear and flank of the commands of Generals Fagan and Shelby, by the falling back of Gen. Marmaduke, were uncovered, and the former, in attempting to rejoin me, was attacked by a large force of the enemy, but with the aid of Col. Jackman and his brigade, who acted so heroically and skillfully as to receive the thanks of Gen. Fagan on the field, the enemy was repulsed. Gen. Shelby, in attempting to obey my instructions, was attacked in the flank and his command thrown into some confusion, but he rallied, repulsed the enemy and joined me that evening, as did also Gen. Fagan. Full details of this are contained in the accompanying Reports of Gen. Shelby and Col. Jackman.

I encamped that night on the middle fork of Grand river, marching 24 miles, the troops having been engaged with the enemy nearly all day. The number of the enemy's troops engaged that day exceeded 20,000 well armed men, whilst I did not have 8,000 armed men.

On the evening of the 24th, I moved with the command on the Fort Scott road to the Marais du Cygnus, where I encamped, having marched 33 miles; no enemy appearing. During the night, I received information from Gen. Marmaduke, who was placed in charge of the approaches in front, that the enemy was threatening his pickets, and upon consultation with Gen. Marmaduke, we were both of the opinion that the enemy was marching upon our right by Mound City, on a road parallel to the one on which we were. We were strengthened in that belief by a dispatch, which had been captured from the commanding officer (Federal) at that place, to his scouts stationed near our then encampments; stating "that he would be largely reinforced that night, and he wanted a sharp look-out for my army, and he wanted the earliest information of the route on which I traveled, and the direction." I also learned at a late hour that night, from some recruits who joined me, and had traveled 15 miles on the route I had come, that no enemy was in my rear.

On the morning of the 25th, I resumed my march in the same direction as before, and thinking from the information received the night before that if I should encounter the enemy, it would be in my front or on my right flank.

Gen. Shelby's division composed the advance, Gens. Fagan and Marmaduke brought up the rear. Col. Tyler's brigade to the right of the centre of the train, 400 yards. Shelby's old brigade to the right of the front of the train,

400 yards, and Col. Jackman's brigade to the immediate front. On reaching Little Osage river, I sent forward a direction to Gen. Shelby to fall back to my position in rear of Jackman's brigade, for the purpose of attacking Fort Scott, where I learned there were 1,000 negroes under arms. At the moment of his reaching me, I received a dispatch from Gen. Marmaduke, in the rear, informing me that the enemy, 3,000 strong, were in sight, with lines extending, and on the note Gen. Fagan had endorsed he would sustain Gen. Marmaduke. I immediately ordered Gen. Shelby to take his old brigade, then on my immediate right, and return to the rear as rapidly as possible to support Gens. Fagan and Marmaduke. I mounted my horse and rode back at a gallop, and after passing the rear of the train, I met the divisions of Gens. Fagan and Marmaduke retreating in utter and indescribable confusion, many of them having thrown away their arms. They were deaf to all entreaties or commands, and in vain were all efforts to rally them. From them I learned that Major General Marmaduke, Gen. Cabell and Col. Slemmons, commanding brigade, had been captured with 300 or 400 men and all their artillery—five pieces. Gen. Fagan and several of his officers, who then joined me, assisted me in trying to rally the armed men without success. I then ordered Gen. Shelby to hold the enemy (who were pressing their success hotly and fiercely) in check, if possible, at the crossing of the Osage, until the train could be placed in safety—which he succeeded in doing for several hours. I again formed the unarmed men, numbering several thousand, in lines of battle on the prairie beyond the river. Gen. Fagan in the meantime had succeeded in rallying a portion of his forces and assisted Gen. Shelby in again holding the enemy in check upon the prairie, and in front of the immense lines of unarmed men, until night when I withdrew. The train having reached the Marmiton, 10 miles, I then overtook it, having marched 28 miles. On the next morning, after destroying many wagons with broken down teams that could not be replaced, I moved at two o'clock, there being but little forage in the neighborhood of my camp. We marched over beautiful prairie roads 56 miles and encamped at Carthage, on Spring river, the nearest point where forage could be procured, as I was informed by Generals Fagan and Shelby, who earnestly desired me to reach Spring river, as no forage could be obtained short of it. The Federal prisoners I had with me became so much exhausted by fatigue that out of humanity I paroled them. For full report of this action see the several Reports of Generals Shelby and Clark, and other accompanying Reports.

On the next morning at 9 o'clock, after giving the men and animals time to rest and feed, I resumed the march and camped on Shoal creek, 22 miles. During the march, a number of desertions took place among the Arkansas troops and recruits. No enemy having appeared, the morale of the troops had much improved.

On the 28th, I marched towards Newtonia, Gens. Fagan and Marmaduke's divisions, the latter now commanded by Gen. Clark, in the rear, and Gen. Shelby's in the advance. On approaching Newtonia, our advance was discovered by the Federal garrison, who commenced to retreat. On seeing this, Shelby's advance attempted to intercept them, the distance they had gained was too great for this to be effected. They succeeded, however, in killing the Federal Capt. Christian, a notorious "Bush-whacker," noted for his deeds of violence and blood.

After passing over the prairie 4 miles beyond Newtonia, Gen. Shelby encamped in a skirt of timber; the other divisions passed beyond and encamped in the positions they were to take in the march of the following day. Ere long our scouts brought information that the enemy was crossing the prairie in pursuit of us. Preparations were at once made to receive him, and at 3 p. m., Gen. Blunt, with 3,000 cavalry, made a furious onslaught on our lines. He was met by Shelby, supported by a portion of Fagan's command, a short but obstinate fight ensued, when Gen. Blunt was repulsed, and driven 3 miles, with heavy loss. This was the last we saw of the enemy.

For full particulars see Gen. Shelby's Report.

The army marched that day 26 miles. On the 29th we marched 26 miles and encamped on Sugar Creek, 5 miles south of Pineville, passing through that town. On the 30th and 31st we reached Maysville, near the Arkansas line, marching 43 miles. November 1st we reached Boonsboro', or Cane Hill as it is commonly termed, marching 17 miles. Then information was received by Gen. Fagan, from Col. Brooks that he had the town of Fayetteville, Arkansas, closely invested, having forced the garrison within their inner fortifications; and asking for men to enable him to take it, as this was a place of importance to the Federals, and its capture would be of great advantage to the cause. Upon Gen. Fagan's earnest solicitation, I ordered a detail of 500 men and 2 guns to be made to him for that purpose, which was furnished by General Shelby under command of Colonel Elliott, the guns from Collins' battery. The expedition started to Fayetteville, formed a junction with Col. Brooks, but before the place could be taken, the approach of Gen. Blunt, with a large cavalry force, caused the siege to be raised, and Col. Elliott rejoined his command. Our march from Illinois river to Cane Hill, was over a bad road, rough and hilly, rendered worse than usual by constant rain: in consequence, much of the stock became worn out and was abandoned on the route. On the 3rd, I remained in camp, the weather very bad, both snowing and raining during the day. I there received information that the Federals, at Little Rock, had been greatly reinforced by a portion of Gen. Canby's command. And as it was necessary that I should here adopt the line of march I should pursue on my return to Arkansas, to District Headquarters or elsewhere, as I should be directed, I determined not to risk the crossing of the Arkansas river between Fort Smith and Little Rock, on which route I could not procure subsistence, forage or grass, in anything like sufficient quantity; but decided to cross through the Indian country, where beef at least could be obtained, which would subsist my men for the few days it would require them to march, until they would meet supplies, even if no salt or breadstuffs could be procured, whilst some grass could be obtained for the animals. In addition, the route across the Arkansas river below Fort Smith, would be over a hilly and mountainous country that the stock in its present condition would be unable to travel over, whilst through the Indian country it would be over level plains traversed by good roads. Again, by taking the route below Fort Smith, I would expose my army to be destroyed by a joint attack from forces detached from the heavy garrison there, acting with large forces from Little Rock, which could be easily spared, and which would, in all probability, take place, as information of my adopting that route would certainly reach them, and the slowness with which I was compelled to move would give them ample time to make all preparations. I furthermore came to this conclusion, from the fact that it coincided with my instructions, in the propriety of which, my own judgment fully concurred. Colonels Freeman, Dobbins and McCroy were ordered to return with such of their men as still remained, with their colors, to the places where they had raised their commands to collect the absentees and bring them within our lines during December, if possible.—And on the 4th of November, I marched with the balance of my command through the Indian territory in the direction of Boggy Depot. On the 13th, I reached Perryville, a distance of 119 miles, when I met three wagons with supplies, and encamped, remaining one day to rest and recruit my men. I had marched carefully and slowly, stopping to graze my stock whenever an opportunity offered. On the 14th, Gen. Shelby, at his request, was left behind on the Canadian to recruit. On the 20th, Cabell's and Slemmons' brigades were furloughed. On the 21st of November, I arrived at Clarksville, where I received an order from Gen. Magruder to march to Lanesport and there establish my Headquarters. I arrived there on the 2nd of December, having marched 1,434 miles. The march through the Indian country was necessarily a severe one, especially upon the stock, many of which died, or became worn out and were left. The men, in some instances, hungered for food, but never approached starvation; nor did they suffer to the extent that other of our soldiers have cheerfully endured, without complaint, for a much longer time, during the war. At all events, I arrived in the country where food and forage could be obtained in abundance, bringing with me all the sick and wounded, and all my command with which I entered the Indian country, except those who voluntarily straggled and deserted their colors. To enumerate, specially, the names of the officers who distinguished themselves for skill and courage, would swell this Report beyond all reasonable limits. Therefore, as to all but General Officers, and those who acted in that capacity, I must simply refer to the accompanying Reports, heartily concurring in the meed of praise awarded to such officers as are thus enumerated by their immediate commanding officers.

Gen. Fagan, commanding the division of Arkansas troops, bore himself throughout the whole expedition, with unabated gallantry and ardor, and commanded his division with great ability.

General J. S. Marmaduke, commanding the division of Mississippi troops, proved himself worthy of his past reputation as a valiant and skillful officer, and rendered with his division great service. His capture was a great loss to the service.

General J. O. Shelby, commanding the division of Missouri troops, added new lustre to his past fame as a brilliant and heroic soldier, and without disparagement to the other officers, I must be permitted to say that I consider him the best cavalry officer I ever saw. The services rendered by him, and his division, in this expedition are beyond all praise.

General Cabell bore himself as a bold, undaunted, skillful, officer. Impetuous yet wary, he commanded his brigade in such a manner as to win praise from all. I regret that from want of Reports from their several commanding officers, I cannot do justice to this, as well as the other brigades of Arkansas troops. Gen. Cabell's capture was a great misfortune, and his place will be difficult to fill.

General Clark, true to his past fame, bore himself with undaunted courage and bravery, as well as skill and prudence. His brigade was most skillfully handled.

Colonels Slemmons, Dobbins, and McCroy (the first of whom was captured,) acted throughout as brave, daring, yet prudent commanders, and are each entitled to great praise.

Colonel Jackman, through the whole expedition, won for himself great honor for the services he rendered as have been herein enumerated, and for which the whole army awarded him the highest praise.

Colonel Freeman proved himself to be a brave and energetic officer, but as his men were mostly unarmed, they were unable to render the same brilliant services as other brigades that were armed.

Colonel Tyler, who was placed in command of a brigade of new recruits, for the most part unarmed, deserves great praise for the success with which he kept them together and brought them within our lines. He deserves especial mention for the cool gallantry he displayed in charging the enemy with them at an important juncture, thereby greatly aiding in saving the train from destruction.

My thanks are due to my staff officers, for their untiring energy and unremitting attention to their duties during the entire campaign; their zeal and devotion cannot be too highly commended by me.

In conclusion, permit me to say that in my opinion, the results flowing from my operations, in Missouri, are of the most gratifying character. I marched 1,434 miles, fought 43 battles and skirmishes, captured and paroled over 3,000 officers and men; captured 18 pieces of artillery, 3,000 stand of small arms, 16 stand of colors, (brought out by me, besides others destroyed by our troops who took them,) at least 3,000 over-coats, large quantities of blankets, shoes, and clothing, many wagons and teams, numbers of horses, and great quantities of subsistence and ordnance stores. I destroyed miles upon miles of railroad, burning depots and bridges. Taking this into the calculation, I do not think I go beyond the truth in saying that I destroyed, in the late expedition to Missouri, $10,000,000 worth of property. On the other hand, I lost 10 pieces of artillery, 2 stand of colors, 1,000 stand of small arms, whilst I don't think I lost over 1,000 prisoners, including the wounded left in their hands, other than recruits on their way to join me, some of whom may have been captured. I brought out with me over 5,000 recruits, and they are still arriving daily. After I passed the German settlements, in Missouri, my march was an ovation; the people thronged around and welcomed us with open hearts and hands. Recruits flocked to our flag in such numbers as to threaten to become a burden instead of a benefit, being mostly unarmed. In some counties, the question was not who should go to the army, but who should stay at home. I am satisfied that, could I have remained in Missouri this winter, the army would have increased 50,000 men.

My thanks are due Lieut. Col. Bull, my Provost Marshal General, for the able, energetic, and efficient discharge of his duties.

I have the honor to remain,

Your obd't servant,

[Signed.] STERLING PRICE,

Maj. Gen. Com'd'g.

Brig. Gen. W. R. BOGGS,

Chief of Staff.

Shreveport, La.

JULIA JACKSON.

[*Portrait in November number of "The Land We Love."*]

A child's face. Softly shadowed, sweetly serious—
  And lovely with the shade of Thought which lies
On chiseled lip, on arching brow imperious,
  And in the deeps of glory-haunted eyes.
'Tis like a vesper-chant, serene and holy—
  Some reverential and harmonious hymn—
An avé floating solemnly and slowly
  Through forest cloisters in the twilight dim.

'Tis not the face of fairy, or of angel—
  Better—'tis human—its expression tells
A noble sire here left a bright evangel
  By which to read Life's hidden oracles.
As though through that young spirit, pure and tender,
  He poured clear teachings, otherwise untold,
And childish brow and eyes retain the splendor
  Of thought and feeling in their noblest mould.

That blank, white page about thee! Lo! 'tis peopled
  With glorious images, and scenes of dread—
New "Cities of the Silent" strangely steepled
  With marbles rising o'er the hero Dead.
And round thy small feet lie the thousand furrows
  Where Southern soil is ploughed with Southern graves,
While o'er them—pilgrims of eternal sorrows—
  Bend pallid mourners, weeping fallen braves.

In dim perspective stretch the War's red surges,
  Armies in glittering, long, embattled lines,—
And the quick ear is filled with swelling dirges
  Wailing through old Virginia's sounding pines.
Before the battle-blast the banners quiver,
  And battle-thunders crash along the sky,
While, like the rush of some imperial river
  The "STONEWALL" legions sweep to victory!

Forms of the mighty, who with names historic
  Passed bravely forward in procession grand,
Mightiest among them, stately, stern, and Doric,
  Thy father,—passing to the Silent Land.
Lone legacy of one who stands immortal,
  Crowned in the temples of Eternity—
When that great spirit entered glory's portal,
  Thou wert an orphan;—ah! and *so were we!*

Thank God!—(Alas! that we should praise the Giver
  For bitter, bitter blessings, such as these!)
Thank God! *in victory* he passed the river,
  And sought the shadow of eternal trees!
Passed—ere the dire DISASTER, fierce and torrid,
  Rained on us blight from burning, brazen skies,
To brand the cross on Manhood's haughty forehead,
  And quench the flash in Woman's haughtier eyes.

Passed—ere he saw Virginia 'neath the lashes
  Of Tyranny, sit stolid—yet disdain
To own she hides, with robes of dust and ashes,
  The slow, sad wasting of a mortal pain.
Passed—ere all freedom in the dust lay leveled—
  Or ere he saw in ruins—tempest-tost,
A nation's liberties lie scorched and shriveled—
  The "Cause" for which he battled, labelled "*Lost.*"

WE wander in the darkness. Half-astounded,
  Stunned with a mighty sorrow:—we can know
Nought of God's purpose for us—cloud-surrounded,
  We only grope in blinding mists of woe.
But *he* beholds God's purpose, clearly shining
  Beyond our clouds, instinct with mercy's dyes,
As when the Day-king gloriously declining
  Leaves golden love-gifts on the sunset skies!

Forest Home, May, 1868. L. V. F.

THE SUEZ CANAL

BY T. C. DE LEON.

Now that the Caterers for our mental diet, both in Europe and America, devote themselves almost exclusively to the preparation of over-spiced messes of Sensation—little time is allowed for the solid middle-course of reason; and the majority of book bolters are reduced to a morbid state of mental dyspepsia that loathes all healthful food and retains the froth alone.

Few of these are cognizant what pleasant bits of fancy cling round the most rugged rocks of fact ; that flowers, bright-hued and delicate, cluster thick along the dusty-high-road of traffic. Few of these care to discover that, as "Truth is stranger than fiction," so all great enterprises undertaken for the good of mankind possess an intrinsic poetry—a richly colored Romance of Reality.

Both from its location amid the time-encrusted remnants of oriental poesy—the very scenes of those wonderful prose-poems that delighted our childhood in the Thousand-and-One-Nights —and from its own power of producing such, there is a peculiarly romantic atmosphere hanging over the Suez Canal.

The overland route to India has ever been food for almost unlimited imaginings. Leaving the steamers of the P. & O. Company, at Alexandria, the tourist would mount a donkey that, for size, appearance and obstinacy, might have been a lineal descendant of Ali-Baba's friendly beast; followed by a donkey-boy who might have just stepped from the page of the Fairy Tale, he threads the narrow streets crowded with water-carriers, foreign merchants, the running *sices*—dotted by bazaars with sleepy looking Turks smoking the unfailing Latakia, and bordered by dingy houses, in any one of which Scheherazade might have been born.

There is an all-pervading atmosphere of the unchangeable past that it seems profanation to dilute with the thriftful air of to-day. There are by-ways of the long-ago that we feel should never be trodden by the hot hoof of Progress.

Leaving the old town for a still older seeming one, the traveler is soon whirling across the sands on the Cairo railway. Where lately only the desert-born steed flashed by and only his neigh echoed, now the iron horse thunders along —blowing his sooty breath into the eyes of Memnon, and sending his fierce snort into the caves of the immemorial past.

From Cairo the transit across the Short Desert to the Red Sea was formerly made on camels; the high hats, the prim coats—strangely uncouth among the flowing draperies of the Orient—with the inevitable cigars and brandy-flasks of Cocaigne, doubtless appearing to the caravan attendants a strange and often repeated nightmare, from which they must sometime awake.

Can we imagine the feelings of the good Caliph Haroun al Raschid, had he wandered so far as Cairo in one of his lonely night walks and seen the Alexandria train rattling into the depot!—What would have been the dismay of Sinbad, the Sailor, had he beheld a prim English spinster—in all the glory of a Balmoral, Sandwich-box, Aquæ-scutum cloak and Pork-pie hat—dismounting from her camel and stepping upon the puffing, snorting sea-monster that now revolves its paddle-fins in the waters of the Red Sea!

Later, the demands of increased travel and transportation caused lines of huge Vans from Cairo across the Short Desert; and these drawn by six splendid horses, made the transit in some thirty hours.

Strange changes were these, wrought by enterprise and perseverance over the time-honored traditions of a whole race; but stranger still are the triumphs Science wedded to Capital will yet achieve over the very course of Nature herself. She will weigh and calculate—ponder with knotted brow, and cypher with rapid pen—and lo! the waters of one sea shall be taken in the hand of man, carried across the sands of the desert and poured into the basin of another.

And with these waters will be borne the huge ships that float upon their bosom—bearing distant nationalities together, and causing Time himself to stand still in the lessened duration of the transit.

Such is the great mission of the Suez Canal, conceived in the brain of one great thinker, and soon to be born in the full maturity of its usefulness.

About the year 1846–7 there was attached to the French Consulate, at Alexandria, as *Eleve-Consul*—a sort of *attaché*, the next in the line of promotion, a young Frenchman of excellent family, fine person and high cultivation.

This was Ferdinand de Lesseps, the father and leading spirit of the Suez Canal Company.

The Vice Royalty of Egypt was then held by Abbas Pacha, the most crafty, bigoted and cruel of the descendants of Mehemet-Ali, whose grandson he was. The throne of Egypt descended to the eldest male of Mehemet's line; therefore, the successor of Abbas, on the event of his death, would be, not his son, but his uncle, Saïd-Pacha, one of the younger of the sons of Mehemet.

This young Prince, then in Alexandria, was as remarkable for his progressive ideas and energy as he was for his high culture and European tastes.

It is customary for many of the Eastern Princes to have their education perfected by the most accomplished tutors of the European Continent; and it is not unusual for these men, domesticated in Turkey, or Egypt, possessed of influence over their Sovereigns and wedded to the combined luxury, laziness and power of Oriental life, to become citizens of the countries where they reside so long. The dignity of *Bey* may be conferred upon them ; and more than one fez covers to-day the uncropped head of the European. By changing their religion and embracing the Code of Mahomet, they may even be elevated to the dignity of the *Pachalic.*

The tutor of the young Saïd was a Frenchman, of great accomplishments, named Köenig-Bey; and he had imbued the mind of his pupil with an admiration for the culture of Europe and a love for her accomplishments that had remained with him until the time of which we write, and in fact until his death.

No wonder that the fascinating address and polished cultivation of the young *Elève-Consul* first attracted the Pacha, and finally retained him, to such very great advantage. The friendship of the Son of Ali was genuine, and he proved it by his works in after years; but the influence of the Frenchman was equally great and was also proven as well.

In '48 the merit of M. de Lesseps was recognized by his government by his appointment as Minister to Rome; but he belonged to the progressive liberal party of France, and gradually came to be looked upon with some suspicion by his paternal Foreign Office. In the political agitations, convulsing the whole of Europe, M. de Lesseps sympathized strongly with the Roman Revolution. He protested against the occupation of the Holy City by the French troops; and, upon the protest being disregarded, resigned his Commission in disgust and left the diplomatic service.

Restless, of active intellect and quick of conception, he returned to Egypt just after the Accession of Saïd to the Vice Royalty of Egypt in '54. Abbas-Pacha had verified the proverb of curses coming to roost, and had violently ended a life of violence at the hands of two agents of his equally black-hearted sister—Nezlé Hannam.

On his return, M. de Lesseps was at once admitted to his old footing with the New Pacha. He also became connected with Mougel-Bey, a French engineer of great distinction, long resident in Egypt, in charge of the *Barrages* of the Nile.

These are the great National works of Egypt, consisting of an immense dam, (or back-water) and bridge near Cairo, to keep back the flow of the current to a certain depth for purposes of irrigation. Commenced under Mehemet-Ali, continued under Abbas-Pacha and Saïd-Pacha,—and having cost already, over three million pounds—they are still unfinished under Ismaïl.

Mougel-Bey, both from his ability and long experience, was thoroughly conversant with the nature and characteristics of the country.

M. de Lesseps conceived—and after consultation and discussion with the French engineer—put into shape the plan of that gigantic enterprise which his unexampled skill, energy and audacity have pushed so near to completion.

This was none other than to connect the waters of the Mediterranean with those of the Red Sea, by means of a ship canal, capable of allowing passage to the largest ships. This duct was to be cut directly across the Isthmus of Suez, at its narrowest part, a length of some 92 English miles; and—so said its sanguine progenitor—its completion was to revolutionize the whole trade of the world, diverting to it the whole traffic now passing around the Cape, and lessening the water passage to India to less than one-fourth its present duration.

If any one will take the map and trace upon it the line of the present overland route, they will see that the Peninsula and Oriental Co's. steamers leave Marseilles and connect at Alexandria with the Suez railway. This great work is almost entirely the result of English energy and engineering; and in its completion, numerous fortunes have been made, and many constitutions ruined by the omnipresent subjects of Her Majesty. It passes to Cairo—crossing the Nile over a splendidly constructed bridge, some sixty-five miles above Alexandria—and thence to Suez.

Until the completion of the road the transit was made by the vans and caravans mentioned above.

From Suez the route by steamer is down the Red Sea to Aden—thence through the Arabian Sea to Bombay.

This route is the property of the Peninsula and Oriental Steam Navigation Co: and—while it is of almost incalculable money value to its owners—lessens the transit to India to twenty-four days instead of ninety to one hundred occupied by the steam route around the Cape. By the latter route sailing vessels take from four to six months.

It was urged that the completion of the Canal would not only shorten the time of the overland route some three days, but would be very much cheaper and more convenient, as it would save all trans-shipment and handling of cargoes.

Great as was the idea, it is but justice to M. de Lesseps to say that the skill, energy and audacity with which it has been engineered—both in a financial and in a scientific point of view—is in no degree below the conception.

Its infancy was wholly entrusted to the hands of the Ex-Diplomat who—skillfully using his personal access to the Pacha—sounded him on the subject. The Pacha said the project was a dream—there was no more substance in it than in the mirage of the desert—and he could not, at first, be induced to do any thing but laugh at it.

But M. de Lesseps was not the man to be discouraged by trifles. His indomitable energy saw in the Pacha's ridicule, only the seeds of stronger adhesion when that should be changed to faith. Gently, but steadily he persevered; and finally the Turk ceased laughing. But the profits to the Egyptian government of the railroad and transit to Suez, *via* Cairo, were annually immense—and he hesitated long before he would consider a project that would take annually millions of pounds from his coffers. But Saïd-Pacha was that rare thing for a Turk—an ambitious man;

and whatever may have been his belief as to where his body would go, he still desired to leave behind him a name that would live forever.

The temptation had never been offered to Monarch to build a more magnificent and lasting monument to inscribe his name on; and M. de Lesseps so worked upon the susceptibilities and the ambition of the Viceroy as to gain his favorable consideration.

The United States Consul General, Mr. DeLeon, and the Dutch Consul General, Mr. Renysennear, both encouraged the idea and urged upon the Pacha to give it his sanction.

The British Consul General at that time was Sir Frederick Bruce, who so lately died, while British Minister at Washington. He opposed the scheme with all the influence he could bring to bear upon Said, for two reasons.

First: English prestige in the East has always been a sore spot in their Foreign Office, and the Suez Canal would not only diminish this—by breaking up the control of the immensely valuable railway transit which she controlled, but it might also imperil her possessions in India by opening so direct, short and easy a route for the passage of transports and war-vessels.

Secondly: Immense sums were made by the army of Railway contractors and engineers under Mr. Stephenson, the celebrated English engineer, out of the Pacha's Railroads; and the sensibilities of his pocket are always more readily touched than any other in John Bull's organization.

Besides these reasons—or rather forming a part of both of them the English government felt that the completion of the canal, should it prove a success, would tend to an immediate revival of the Mediterranean ports, such as Trieste and Marseilles; and this would injure British shipping interests, while it tended directly to the advantage of French and Continental.

With this combined pressure upon him, Sir Frederick Bruce worked with a will against the project. Mr. Stephenson also—after what should have been careful calculations—made an elaborate report in which he stated the whole affair to be a natural impossibility, *because the level of the Mediterranean was thirty feet below that of the Red Sea.* Subsequent experiments have proven beyond question that *the difference of level is less than thirty inches!*

Whether this error goes to prove that science is sometimes unreliable, or only that capital is mightier than science, none may tell; but, in any event, the Lion desired to put his paw upon the egg before the enterprise was hatched, which would probably be, in its maturity, such a very ugly and dangerous rival.

The French Consul-General, M. Sabatier,—whatever may have been the grounds for his course—was so lukewarm in his support as to injure, rather than aid the project. But this reticence cost him his position a little later—he being recalled through the influence of M. de Lesseps.

When Saïd-Pacha was first approached upon the subject of the grant, he was asked for no pecuniary aid. All that was asked was his permission to cut the canal, and the cession to it of certain lands lying upon it. Upon this foundation, M. de Lesseps was to form a great Inter-national stock company, do the work with foreign capital, and indirectly do a great good to Egypt by directly conferring a great boon upon the civilized world.

Influenced by his inordinate ambition even less than by the magnetic energy of M. de Lesseps, Saïd made the grant on these conditions; adding a clause that promised M. de Lesseps full power to *corver*—or press to compulsory labor on his work—his *Fellah* subjects. These *Fellahs* are the drudges of the land, an abased and oppressed native population about on a par with the *peons* of Mexico.

With this valuable basis, M. de Lesseps went to work more actively than ever for the second step, the formation of his International Stock Company.

In '55 he procured the thorough examination of the proposed route by a Commission of Engineers from the different countries of Europe. Their report was, that while difficult, there was nothing in the plan to prove an insurmountable obstacle; and further armed with this, the tireless projector called for subscriptions to the Stock.

At first they poured in rapidly, but the virulent opposition of the British press at home, and of Sir Frederick Bruce at Alexandria, frightened off the heavy British capitalists upon whom he had, in great part, depended.

A less determined man might have been staggered at this. Not so with M. de Lesseps. He merely shrugged his shoulders, said in effect—"You will not let me make it International—then I will make it National!", and went to work harder than ever.

As I have said, he had been looked upon by the Government with some suspicion for his republican leanings; but he is a cousin of the Empress Eugenie, and through her gained the ear of the Emperor. This done, the work was accomplished.

The press of France resounded with praises of the Canal; M. de Lesseps himself started a paper devoted to its interests and called *Le Journal de l' Isthmus de Suez;* French capital poured in—with some Dutch—and finally in 1859, the Company was formed with a capital of $40,000,000.

How much of this immense sum was actually paid up, or how much was allowed for in the bonus of stock, it is impossible to say; but it is certain there was full enough cash to break ground and push the work with vigor.

But for partial stoppages—which cannot be set forth at length in an article like this—the work would have been completed before this time. Even with them—and with the added National jealousies and delays they produced—it has been pushed with a rapidity unequalled in any great work of the kind.

The original dimensions of the canal were to be 92 miles in length, 330 feet in width, with a depth of 26 feet below low water of the Mediterranean. This would allow the passage of the largest vessels—and would permit them ample room to pass each other. Sailing vessels could be towed through by tugs.

The canal was to cut the Isthmus of Suez at its narrow part, and to traverse the Short Desert. This, contrary to the generally conceived idea, is not loose shifting sand—like that of the Great Desert—but is a gritty, gravelly soil that yields a sharp edge to the spade, and retains excavation made in its surface. The general elevation of the Isthmus above the level of the two seas does not average more than six feet—with a general tendency downwards to the Mediterranean; and the only elevations—and those of inconsiderable extent—are not over thirty feet in height.

It is an old idea that the two seas were once united, and that the Isthmus was thrown up by some convulsion of nature; a theory which has some support from the general formation and composition of the soil, and its variation from that of the other desert. It has the remains of very ancient canals and aqueducts still clearly traceable; and one of these—said to have been built by Necho or Darius—forms a portion of the line of the present canal. From this it would seem that the idea of connecting the seas—or, at least, of facilitating connection between them—is not entirely new; and it is said that the First Napoleon had meditated, at one time, the inception of such a work.

The canal enters the Isthmus at the Gulf of Pelusium, on the Mediterranean side, and extends directly across to Suez—on the gulf of the same name—on the Red Sea end.

This gulf forms the North Western arm of the Red Sea, and runs up—with an average breadth of some 35 miles—between Egypt and the Peninsula of Sinai for some two hundred miles. At its head stands the town, some 78 miles due East from Cairo. It is situated in the desert, and its supplies of good water and vegetables have to be brought from a distance.

It is noticeable here, too, from the formation of the shore, that indications of deeper water once having come nearer inland are frequent. The water now is so shallow that only the lightest craft can be brought to land; and though the roadstead, some two miles below, is good, all unlading and lading has to be done in lighters.

Suez, before the inception of the great enterprise, had probably two thousand inhabitants. It was partially walled, and mounted a few guns for defence. Now, it has increased its population to nearly double, and the air of antiquity has, to a slight extent, been rubbed off, by friction against the rougher characteristics of the newer world outside.

Since work on the canal has been vigorously carried on, the whole face of the Isthmus has changed—and a population new and strange has sprung up, bringing with it towns, habits and enterprise of another state of being to that obtaining before.

The limits of one article will not contain more than a mention of the singular effect of a little Europe, transported bodily, and set down in Africa; nor will they allow an allusion even to the means and machinery by which the great results already obtained, have been wrought out of the sterile sands of the Desert.

Such was the inception of the Suez canal: such was the man who made it—a lasting monument to energy, skill and perseverance: and such are the main features of the country through which it passes.

Even unfinished as it is, M. de Lesseps may point to it with reverence and pride and truly exclaim—"*Exegi monumentum ære perennius.*"

MARY ASHBURTON.*

A TALE OF MARYLAND LIFE.

In his delirium, I often heard her name. He called upon her wildly, beseechingly. "Adèle! oh! Adèle! how I loved you! She was very beautiful," he would murmur, "the loveliest of earth's creatures. To see her in a ball-room—here she comes—she comes. I would go to her, but,"—a dark shade would come over his face—"she looks so coldly and haughtily upon me. She does not love me. She does not love me, and another claims her." The shade would grow very dark then, and he wildly clutched the bed-clothes in his hand. "I saw her,—saw the bride. Very lovely she was with the diamonds glistening on her forehead. Methinks they turned to adders, and stung her, for when she saw me they seemed to turn and writhe and burn in her dark hair. I heard them say 'the bride,' and I knew whose bride. She was to have been mine, but,"—here he opened his eyes and fixed them full on mine,—"though she liked me a little less than gold and diamonds, she liked me not so well, and so sold herself to what she loved, set Moloch up in her temple and fell down and worshipped him. And yet I gave my love to her.—My life was nothing.—How madly I loved her! yet she threw it away, my devoted love for the dross of the earth. And this after so many promises, so many declarations of mutual love. I believe in nothing—will never believe again. After her, whom can I trust?" he asked piteously, while I took his poor hand and bowed my tearful face over it, my heart wrung with sorrow for him.

Sometimes, in delirium, he would toss his arms about so wildly that I feared the wound would bleed afresh, but fortunately his great weakness from loss of blood, prevented his moving

* Continued from page 336.

to a more dangerous extent.

It seemed like a dream to me that my time had come at last,—that I who had looked up to him at such a distance, to such an inaccessible height, was now permitted to be so near him,—that he should at last be so dependent upon one on whom he had scarcely bestowed a thought. To moisten his parched lips, smooth the disordered hair, dress the wound, that sent such shudders through his enfeebled frame, with soft, tender touch, perform all the duties of nurse, wife, mother, all in one, was *her* privilege now whose love he had not noticed or desired, while she whom he would have chosen, who was ever present to him in the ravings of delirium, was far away in the midst of worldly pleasures which she was enjoying with another, who had the power of gratifying her selfish inclinations.

I wondered if he would ever notice me, welcome my appearance as a relief from the tedium of suffering, and regard me at least with gratitude.

That he should care for me save as a friend, I never dreamed, considering that his heart, like mine, having bestowed its affections upon but one object, could never love again. A scathing fire had passed over his heart and consumed it; he had none to give me. I was not humble now, for was he not dependent on me, under Providence, for life itself?—No, self was lost in him and for the time he was but as an infant in my hands.

His sufferings were very great; wild fever raged in his veins and his hollow eyes glowed as with fire. Kneeling by his bedside, I bathed his hot hands often with my tears, or raised his head upon my shoulder while I applied the cooling moisture to his lips, my old nervous diffidence forgotten for the time.

Had he been conscious and could have followed my movements about his sick room with those searching dark eyes of his, I could not have been so self-forgetful, and should still have been awed by his gaze.

Day after day passed thus,—my rest was obtained in a few snatches of sleep at his bedside; yet I did not feel wearied, for anxious excitement prevented my obtaining the rest that they urged upon me.

Mother came often to inquire for him and offer her assistance, but I rejected the latter and permitted no one to enter his room but the physician and the nurse.

When the ball was extracted—I pass that scene over, for I cannot dwell upon it—the wound commenced healing slowly, and gradually the fever left him, but in a state of such utter prostration, that it required all the natural vigor of his constitution to sustain the feeble spark of life that remained in his body.

When the fever was gone, consciousness began dimly to dawn upon his brain, the wild delirium and dangerous tossings ceased, and he lay as quiet and weak as an infant, unable to move a single member.

I shall never forget the strange sensation upon seeing him in his right mind, that it was Alfred himself once more.

He had been asleep, after a gradual subsidence of the fever, and I sat by watching him and delighting in his regular breathing, till I grew drowsy myself from fatigue, and finding that I could no longer resist its influence, I retired to the next room and lay down. I could not sleep long, for I had lost the power of suspending action and thought for only a very short time, so rising from my couch for the first time since his illness, I arranged my dress. Then with a neat, clean wrapper and smoothly braided hair, I returned to his room, taking with me some early spring flowers that Rose had procured for me from the garden, arranged them in a vase by his bedside, and freshened up the apartment as I moved noiselessly about, dusting the various articles of furniture on which the dust had remained undisturbed for weeks.

When I had done, I seated myself in the easy chair by his bed, with my Bible in my hand, enjoying the delicious fragrance of the flowers which I had not noticed for so long a time before, while the psalm that I was reading refreshed me with even greater sweetness, as it expressed, beautifully, just what I wanted to say.

I was leaning thoughtfully over it, when a slight movement of the sleeper caused me to raise my eyes.

Alfred was awake,—his eyes were fixed full upon me, with a look too languid for wonder, yet with an expression nearer to that than any other

Those hollow, vacant eyes,—vacant because too weak for thought—they shocked me like an electric thrill when I looked up and met their almost meaningless gaze; as when one sees a corpse unexpectedly open its eyes from the trance that had been confidently deemed to be death.

Rising from my seat, I took a powder that was to be given when he awoke, and tendered it to him to see if he would notice it. He made no attempt to extend his hand to take it, but still kept that look fixed upon my face. To my great relief, Melissa entered at that moment, and seeing the proffered glass, went up to him with officious remonstrance.

"How now, young marster, won't you take your medicine from the kind mistress that's did everything for you?"

Upon that, he languidly turned his hollow eyes around and attempted to take the glass from me, but his arm immediately fell down, and he sank back with closed eyes.

"Let me help you," I said softly, and passing my arm under his head, I raised it with one hand while I applied the draught to his lips with the other.

Without further hesitancy, he drank the mixture and then I laid his head gently on the pillow, smoothed and cooled by Melissa again. He sank hack and closed his eyes, apparently, as if exhansted, but when I looked up, some moments afterwards, that gaze was again fixed upon my face as if he had made it a subject for languid study.

It made the shy blood mount there again and creep nervously in my veins, so I busied myself in a corner of the apartment where he could not see me, till I grew more reassured and did'nt mind it quite so much.

He lay so quiet, more as if dead than alive, while life struggled back in his frame, the spark of vitality feebly warming it again and bringing him back from the chaos and annihilation he had endured during the past year. Would hope ever thrill his heart's pulsation again, restore the buoyancy of his step and make life an object with happiness and usefulness?

I hoped and prayed so, kneeling where he did not see me, and beseeching in tears that he might repent and become a better man, that he might not be restored from the dead—-oh! fearful thought!—only to commit the same violent deed again, to lay guilty hands on the life that God's infinite mercy had restored to him. It could not be, I thought. Surely he had been raised up from his fearful peril, the pit of darkness and destruction into which he had almost plunged, for a nobler end, and the same hand that had saved him from such an eternity, could now rescue him from it hereafter.

I would often meet that look of his, when busied about his room, following my movements with the same languid interest, but he turned his eyes away upon perceiving that I was conscious of his gaze, as if aware that it was embarrassing to me. Yet I mastered my shyness so well as to treat him as my patient, and even to assume authority over him when he seemed too listless to take the proffered nourishment or allow the necessary medicines to be given him.

Nothing but an utter listlessness characterized the first stage of his convalescence. He did not speak for a day or two except in reply to some questions about his sensations at the time, and then only in monosyllables in a dry, hollow tone that I could hardly believe it to be his voice.

As he grew a little stronger something of his old gentle nature returned to him, and his unselfish consideration for others.—"Thank you," he said feebly one day as I bathed his forehead, then sank back with those wearily closed eyes. "You are very kind," he said another time when I performed some other little office about him as nurse.

I cherished these expressions with heartfelt joy and thankfulness; they formed a sufficient reward for all my care,—the knowledge that he felt grateful and kindly towards me for it, though ever so feebly.

I permitted nothing, as far as I could, to remind him of his sickness and its cause, keeping the bandages and applications out of sight, as well as everything like medicine, except such as I was obliged to have around me, while I pleased myself in exercising my taste and ingenuity by disposing flowers and delicate white drapery around his room till it looked less like a sick room than a lady's bower. Dr. Green would come in and say sometimes—

"Surely, Mrs. Chauncey, you have time for everything."

"It is inclination, doctor," I would answer, "I love these things; flowers and sunshine are my delight."

"So it would seem. You have been the sunshine of this young man's life anyhow, and I'd like to see him up to reward you for your care, and take care of you, for I shouldn't wonder if you were down after this."

I treated his prophecy with indignation, feeling rather new life in me just then than a lack of it, for I had something to animate existence, and an object to live for at present.

So Alfred grew better, so slowly that the stages were almost imperceptible, but that wanness left his cheek and some expression came back to his eyes, while the furrows passed from his brow and a peaceful look, almost of boyish innocence, came over his features.

He was exceedingly handsome as he lay asleep, his fine, regularly cut features, and curling hair that tossed above his forehead as if carved in *bas-relief* from the pillow, than which they were scarcely less white, the cleanly cut forehead with the straight, delicately defined eye-brows, and the long lashes that lay upon his cheeks in a silken fringe; I loved to watch him as he slept in this quiet way, and rejoiced in the peace that had stolen over those exquisite features at last.

When the hollow look left his eyes, something of the light of gratitude stole into them for my care.

When I sat up late to give him his medicine at the appointed hour, he said thoughtfully,

"You must be very tired. Go and rest, I insist upon it."

I gently resisted and maintained my place.

"I am not worth this trouble," he said with a dreary sadness that sent the tears to my eyes, "why don't you leave me?"

"Do you think I'd leave you?" I asked with tearful reproach.

"Yes, they have all left me." He turned away and drew the covering up on his shoulders, as he closed his eyes with that heart-broken look that went so pitifully to my heart. Ah! that was the worst thing I had to contend with, that dreary loss of self-respect and sense of being forsaken by both God and man. How to arouse him from a sense of moral degradation, to give him a place once more among his fellow-creatures? Alas! my weak hand could do nothing, but I prayed and trusted in Him. Like a mother to a poor, sick, fretful child, my heart melted in tenderness and pity for him as I looked on the wreck of what he had once been. Would he ever arise from that bed to assume his manhood once more? I turned sickened from that other picture of unresisted passion swaying him as before, to result again in the same wicked, unlawful deed.

So I wept bitter tears as I watched that dreary, dreary look on his tired face, the tender heart whose love for him had crushed it so long, bleeding cruelly to see it there.

Rising from my seat, I took a glass of wine and a teaspoon in my hand and approached him that I might do something to arouse him from that state it pained me so to see.

"Mr. Chauncey," I touched his hand.

"Ah! what is it?" He started and turned his head.

"Take a little of this wine for me, won't you?"

"I am tired and sleepy," he said with a slight fretfulness.

I bent over him and smoothed back the hair from his forehead. "It will do you good if you are tired," I said.

He opened his eyes and looked me in the face, then held out his poor, thin hand for it, but it was too feeble, and fell down beside him on the bed.

"Will you let me give it to you?" I took the spoon and put some between his lips. He took it and seemed refreshed, then half smiled as he said:

"You are so kind. Yet why should I be grateful?"—then sighed so sadly as the sudden light faded from his face.

"That you are getting better—will soon be well again," I answered as cheerfully as I could, and arranging his pillows.

"Getting better?" he echoed, opening his eyes and looking at me again. "Why should you wish to save me? I was in the jaws of death, on the brink of eternity. Hell gaped open before me, a gulf of liquid fire leaped to receive me, when an angel's hand snatched me from destruction, and I awake to find my body still here, my soul vacant. I cannot think; evil has departed from me. A vacuum possesses my mind. I am surely dreaming. Was the angel real? Am I saved?"

"Saved by God's mercy," I answered softly. "See how He loves you. He has preserved you for himself, and intends you to be his always now."

"*I?* His? What does Perfection want with me, a guilty, fallen creature whom He forsook also."

"No, no, He did not," I said earnestly. "See what he did for you when you thought He had forsaken you entirely. How could He have been kinder than that?"

"I was deprived of all I loved," he went on as if recounting his wrongs to himself, "life was a blank, existence a misery. Why should I live when I had no object for so doing? how could I live when every breath I drew was an agony beyond endurance?"

"To live for? oh! so much! I will not say now, for you are too weak to think about it, but—do you know the Saviour?"

"The good know Him," he replied with a slight curl of the lip. "I presume you do. What has He to do with me?"

"Oh! Mr. Chauncey, His sufferings were greater than yours."

"And had a Godlike nature to sustain Him."

"Such support have we through him. When you fully know Him and love Him, you'll feel differently. I know you will. Life won't be a blank then, for with Him urging us on, giving us our tasks and appointing the reward which he holds in heavenly places for our encouragement—oh! it will seem short for so much to do."

I spoke so earnestly and enthusiastically that he caught something of it, and the eyes were brighter that gazed me so searchingly in the face, while I was too much carried above self to flinch from that examination now.

"*You* feel so," he said, "it does *you* good. The fruits of your belief I see in your conduct."

I might have answered that it required no religious exertion to minister to *him*, but I said nothing to this, only,

"I *want* to be kind to you."

He smiled painfully. "Poor child, yours is a heartless, thankless task,—restoring a life that was thrown away, bestowing your pains and infinite care upon a poor creature, who has hardly feeling enough left in him to be grateful. But be sure, Mary, (how strangely my name sounded from his lips) that for you I feel the nearest approach to gratitude I am capable of, and that is more than I can say of any other creature."

He had called me "Mary," had expressed a warmer feeling for me than any other human being. I had my reward then, no longer worked for nothing.

He was sometimes a little peevish and fretful, as all sick persons will be, but when I appeared, he would instantly become patient and submit without a murmur to what he had declared before to be of no use.

Thus it came to pass, — so gradually, I know not how, it seemed quite natural,—I lost my shyness sufficiently to be almost myself with him, and he submitted to my nursing and authority quite patiently, would take the most nauseous draughts at my hands, and permit no one else to do what I could.

(TO BE CONTINUED.)

A SERENADE.

Sleep, Dearest! sleep,
My heart will keep
Its vigil till yon star be low;
And though it set,
Love, faithful yet,
Will but the brighter, steadier glow.

Dream, Sweetest! dream,
And let it seem,

While tender fancies charm thy rest,
That he who waits
By thy closed gates,
Is ever fond, if never blest.

Wake, Darling! wake,
For true-love's sake
Show thy sweet face at lattice-bar,
The star has gone,
The vision flown,
But Love outwatches dream and star.

New Orleans, La. J. D. B.

MR. DICKENS AND HIS "DEBT OF HONOR."

It will be fresh in the memory of our readers that the recent departure of Mr. Dickens, for America, was signalized at New York, the port of his embarkation, by a banquet of quite peculiar interest, significance and *éclat.* Two hundred gentlemen of the press of the United States, claiming him as a *confrère* by reason of his service in early life as a reporter for the *London Morning Chronicle,* entertained him at dinner. The *cuisine* was Delmonico's, the wines were choice and of the proper temperature, the utmost good-feeling reigned at the board, and Horace Greeley presided: altogether, it was a grand success. Mr. Dickens was, indeed, an hour behind the time in consequence of an inopportune attack of the gout, so that the journalists grew hungry in the halls of reception, and, when the cloth had been removed, the eloquence was undoubtedly less of the epi—than of the Po—grammatic sort; but the long delay neither gave rise to mutiny nor spoiled the soup, and the speeches were received with the loudest demonstrations of applause. And then the two hundred editors went home and gave, each in his own way, two hundred accounts (be the same more or less) of the entertainment; wherein they duly set forth the names of all who sat down, the bill of fare, the orations and the decorations, the jokes of Mr. Greeley, and the music of the band, omitting, probably, nothing whatever that lent attractiveness to the occasion.

While we should have been reluctant, at the time, to say anything ungracious of hospitality so generous and so artistic, we could not help thinking that the banquet would seem to have been designed not altogether as a tribute to the genius of Mr. Dickens, and that a suspicion of the kind must have occurred to him, long before the hour of his leaving the table, at moments when his toe was tranquil and his mind at ease. Mr. Greeley said with good reason that the opening line of the great epic of New York's great bard—Walt Whitman—"I celebrate myself," expressed the dominant purpose of the evening; and evidently Mr. Dickens was only cajoled into accepting the dinner that an opportunity might be presented for a glorification of the American press, which should be graced by his presence. It does not appear to have struck any one of the two hundred that Mr. Dickens was not indeed one of themselves, wholly identified with journalism, though it has been more than thirty years since he quitted journalism forever; and that the fame which they so complacently claimed for their own order belonged to the mere newspaper press, almost as little as John Bunyan's to the tinkers, or Shakspeare's to the scene-shifters. The long succession of toasts, therefore, in honor of the daily, weekly, monthly press, North, South, East and West, N.E., N.N.E., N.W., N.N.W., S.E., S.S.E., S.W., S.S.W., (it is noteworthy that the *English press* was wholly omitted from the list of compliment) must have inspired him with some little weariness with the calendar and the points of the compass, and with much wonder at the wide geographical diffusion of the editorial class in the United States. But this wonder could not have failed to give way to amusement, that might have tickled even podagra in its felt buskin, at the clever suggestion that the works of Charles Dickens were written for the exposition of New England ideas in general and Boston notions in particular; and when a frantic provincial orator declared that the works of Charles Dickens were valued by the American people next to the Bible itself, amusement in its turn must have yielded to disgust.

But the significance of the Dickens banquet lay not in the celebration of itself by the press of the United States, nor yet in the good feeling that undeniably prevailed at the festive board; but in the amends voluntarily made by the illustrious guest, as a farewell peace-offering for all the hard things he had said of America in his *American Notes* and *Martin Chuzzlewit*. Mr. Dickens, indeed, retracted nothing contained in those two wretched fictions, but he gave hearty utterance to the favorable impressions made upon him by the America of to-day, and promised that every future edition of *American Notes* and *Martin Chuzzlewit* should contain this tribute by way of appendix. The promise has been kept, and a late number of *All the Year Round* pays the "Debt of Honor" by publishing the Postscript hereafter to accompany the works in question.

We shall presently quote this Postcript for purposes of comment, but before doing so, we may be indulged in a word or two concerning the enthusiasm that was manifested at the New York dinner, and the kindly reception that was everywhere extended to Mr. Dickens on his second visit to the United States. The reconciliation of hearts that have been long estranged, is always a pleasing subject of contemplation to the well-regulated mind, and where much has been given up, on both sides, he must be a cynic or a churl who would disparage a consummation so desirable. But it may well be doubted whether much undue credit has not been given to the American people, for generosity and magnanimity, in the free pardon they extended to the most obnoxious of their satirists. The generation, which Mr. Dickens so mercilessly caricatured in those too unhappy books, has passed away. The lapse of twenty-eight years might well have healed the wound inflicted upon the pride of a more sensitive and a more stable people. In the older communities of the world, where society remains substantially the same from age to age, the memory of the wrong might possibly have rankled still in the breasts of the descendants of the immediate victims, just as Thackeray has never been forgiven for the *Irish Sketch Book*. But the Americans of 1868, at least in the Northern States, are another people from the Americans of 1840. Mr. Dickens on his second visit addressed a new audience, the majority of whom had little or nothing to forgive, and with whom forgiveness consequently required small exercise of magnanimity. Moreover, Mr. Dickens came ostensibly, not as a tourist to see what wonderful progress the United States had made in a quarter of a century, but as a showman with his little entertainment to make money. His Readings were a novelty, and a people who are fond of novelties went to hear them, as they go to see and hear every new thing. It was a fair bargain, and both parties were pleased. The public came with its two dollars, and the showman came with his Justice Stareleigh and his Sergeant Buzfuz, and his table and the rest of his characters and properties. Making due allowance for the disappointment felt and expressed in individual cases, the public considered that to spend an evening in this way with the great master of English fiction, was worth the money, and thus became a generous public, when, had Mr. Dickens not given his Readings at all, it would have remained an apathetic one. The pecuniary result was so satisfactory to the great master of English fiction, that it insensibly modified his views of the country at large, and changed from *jaune* to *rose* the medium through which he surveyed every thing that came under his observation. Thus it was natural that Mr. Dickens should have repaired to the dinner at Delmonico's in the best humor consistent with a sharp attack of the gout, and as the two hundred editors resorted thither in the best possible humor to celebrate themselves, the good feeling of the occasion, however gratifying to contemplate, was only what might have been reasonably expected. Where so many good things were provided, and so many pleasant things were said, the most saturnine of journalists might have been mollified. If the no longer youthful Mr. Jefferson Brick and the now venerable Colonel Diver had faced Mr. Dickens (as who shall say they did not?) they might have condoned the crime of the author of *Martin Chuzzlewit* against themselves in their favorite champagne. Indeed, we can almost fancy we hear Col. Diver speaking for himself and his War Correspondent, thus characterize the reigning *bonhommie*, "Behold in this, Sir, a Spectacle of Magnanimity worthy of the Leaders of Human Civilization." Such a manifestation of good feeling is indeed quite delightful, but we do not see in it anything of that real magnanimity which, like Charity, vaunteth not itself, is not puffed up.

With regard to the *amende honorable* of Mr. Dickens, it is just a little curious that he himself should have overlooked the true nature of his offence, and that it should not have occurred to him that no correction, of the unfair picture of the American society given in *Martin Chuzzlewit* and the *American Notes*, could possibly meet the case at all. The picture *was* unfair, because it withheld all the more favorable traits, while it exaggerated all the weaknesses and vices of the American people and character. That these weaknesses and vices did exist, though in less degree than was represented, most intelligent Americans are now prepared to admit. But the fullest retraction of the slanders in these books could not excuse Mr. Dickens for having written them; still less can praise of the Americans of the present day excuse him. The unpardonable sin of Mr. Dickens was that, true or false, these books were acts of gross ingratitude to a people who had lavished upon him a hospitality, without a precedent for its cordiality and its profusion. True or false, these books should never have been written by the man whom America, foolishly yet generously, had delighted to honor. The universal American home had been his home for the time, and it was a poor return, indeed, for the kindness of a whole people to cover them with inextinguishable ridicule.

It may have been true that the interesting members of the Norris family of New York bored Mr. Dickens, in the person of young Martin Chuzzlewit, with snobbish inquiries concerning individual personages of the British nobility, but it was wholly indefensible in Mr. Dickens, having been their guest, to tell of it in a manner to bring upon the miserable Norrises the derision of Great Britain. Herein lay Mr. Dickens' grievous fault. He does not seem to recognize it, and therefore he cannot see that no tribute he may now pay to the American people can atone for it. But we recognize none the less the manliness and magnanimity of his remarks at the New York Dinner, embodied in the Postscript just published in *All the Year Round.* They were made of his own free will, at a time, the very eve of his departure, when he had nothing to gain by them, when fine words would sell no additional tickets for his

Readings, and when America could do nothing more for him, except grant an International Copyright. We would not imply by this exception that Mr. Dickens had the matter of the Copyright in his mind in the promise he gave and has so faithfully kept. We believe his tribute to the American people of the present day to have been wholly unselfish and sincere, as it was frank and manly, and as it was also (in our judgment) of no real value whatever.

To establish this latter proposition, it will be necessary for us to quote Mr. Dickens' testimonial, and this we do from a recent number of *All The Year Round.* Here it is:

"A Debt of Honor.—Desiring to record in this Journal, in the plainest and simplest manner possible, certain words publicly spoken by its Conductor on a recent occasion, we present the following extract from the latest-published copies of *American Notes* and *Martin Chuzzlewit.* It is entitled,

"Postscript.

"At a public dinner given to me on Saturday the 18th of April, 1868, in the city of New York, by two hundred representatives of the Press of the United States of America, I made the following observations among others:—

"'So much of my voice has lately been heard in the land, that I might have been contented with troubling you no further from my present standing-point, were it not a duty with which I henceforth charge myself, not only here but on every suitable occasion, whatsoever and wheresoever, to express my high and grateful sense of my second reception in America, and to bear my honest testimony to the national generosity and magnanimity. Also, to declare how astounded I have been by the amazing changes I have seen around me on every side, — changes moral, changes physical, changes in amount of land subdued and peopled, changes in the rise of vast new cities, changes in the growth of older cities almost out of recognition, changes in the graces and amenities of life, changes in the Press, without whose advancement no advancement can take place anywhere. Nor am I, believe me, so arrogant as to suppose that in five-and-twenty years there have been no changes in me, and that I had nothing to learn and no extreme impressions to correct when I was here first. And this brings me to a point on which I have, ever since I landed in the United States last November, observed a strict silence, though sometimes tempted to break it, but in reference to which I will, with your good leave, take you into my confidence now.

"'Even the Press, being human, may be occasionally mistaken or misinformed, and I rather think that I have in one or two rare instances observed its information to be not strictly accurate with reference to myself. Indeed, I have, now and again, been more surprised by printed news that I have read of myself, than by any printed news that I have ever read in my present state of existence. Thus, the vigor and perseverance with which I have for some months past been collecting materials for, and hammering away at, a new book on America, has much astonished me; seeing that all that time my declaration has been perfectly well known to my publishers on both sides of the Atlantic, that no consideration on earth would induce me to write one. But what I have intended, what I have resolved upon (and this is the confidence I seek to place in you) is, on my return to England, in my own person, in my own Journal, to bear, for the behoof of my countrymen, such testimony to the gigantic changes in this country as I have hinted at to-night. Also, to record that wherever I have been, in the smallest places equally with the largest, I have been received with unsurpassable politeness, delicacy, sweet temper, hospitality, consideration, and with unsurpassed respect for the privacy daily enforced upon me by the nature of my avocation here and the state of my health. This testimony, so long as I live, and so long as my descendants have any legal right in my books, I shall cause to be republished, as an appendix to every copy of those two books of mine in which I have referred to America. And this I will do and cause to be done, not in mere love and thankfulness, but because I regard it as an act of plain justice and honor.'

"I said these words with the greatest earnestness that I could lay upon them, and I repeat them in print with equal earnestness. So long as this book shall last, I hope that they will form a part of it, and will be fairly read as inseparable from my experiences and impressions of America.

CHARLES DICKENS.

MAY, 1868.

As a general proposition the weight of testimony, the impartiality of the witness being conceded, depends upon the opportunity the witness has had for accurate observation of the matters concerning which he testifies.—With regard to Mr. Dickens, neither upon his first nor his second visit to America, was he an impartial witness. In 1840, he came to secure an International Copyright and failed. In 1867–'68, he came to make money, and succeeded beyond his most sanguine expectations. Both the failure and the success disqualified him as a fair, not to say as a dispassionate, critic of American society. But giving him the fullest credit for impartiality, he certainly had no means of forming an intelligent opinion of the social, moral, and intellectual condition of America, upon his recent visit. The extent of his journeyings was extremely circumscribed.—The state of his health and "the nature of his avocation here" enforced upon him, as he tells us himself, a privacy which he honors the American people for respecting. He had no glimpse of the domestic life of the country outside the little æsthetic circle of poets, publishers and philosophers of Boston. He did not give the New York Norrises of the period the chance of asking after their dear friends, the Marquess and Marchioness, or how the Gold Fish was getting on in the Grecian fountain of the well-remembered conservatory. He attended no public entertainments but his own. He did not go to church, for the reason, as was happily suggested by some wag of the daily newspapers, that he felt no interest in American politics. In short, he saw nothing but what could be seen out of the windows of railroad cars, inside fashionable hotels, and from the platforms of lecture halls. The testimony of such an observer, as to the social, moral and intellectual condition of a great country, is surely of no importance whatever.

But the value of Mr. Dickens' testimony to the wonderful improvement wrought in twenty-eight years upon the American continent, can best be judged by a comparison of certain aspects of the United States in 1840 and in 1868. Unquestionably, there has been a vast augmentation of material wealth since 1840. There are more miles of railroad now than then, and we have seen an immense increase in population, more than a reduplication of the national resources, and a considerable advance in the comforts and luxuries of life. Mr. Dickens could not therefore help observing, from the railroad car and the omnibus, "changes in the amount of land subdued and peopled, changes in the rise of vast new cities, changes in the growth of older cities almost out of recognition." All this has been in conformity to the general law of physical progress in newly settled communities, the law of emigration from over-crowded nationalities to regions where land is plenty and labor well paid. The same development has been witnessed in a comparatively greater degree in the Australian colonies. We have been purged since 1840, it is true, by a national convulsion, of the damning sin of slavery, which, upon the occasion of his former visit, gave Mr. Dickens such constant disquietude. But in the effect of emancipation and enfranchisement upon the blacks themselves, and upon the general condition of the Southern States, Mr. Dickens felt so little interest, that he did not go into the military departments, to ascertain it. We do not censure Mr. Dickens for this indifference to the state of things in the fairest and alas! the most desolate portion of the country, because that region lay quite beyond the field of his operations. He was well aware that the only class in the South who could enjoy his Readings, had no money to spend in such literary entertainments. "No pay, no preach;" *point d'argent, point de Suisse* is necessarily the motto of all public performers. Leaving the South entirely out of view, however, as a vast district in which, from the very nature of things, we could not look at this moment for progress in its unreconstructed political condition, we turn to the "changes moral" of which Mr. Dickens speaks, "changes in the graces and amenities of life, changes in the Press," and would soberly ask if these changes have not been changes rather of deterioration than of improvement.—Where, indeed, has Mr. Dickens found improvement? Is it in the tone and personal character of the national legislature? Let us take Massachusetts as the State of largest development, as the model of American commonwealths, if, indeed, we may not mourn that "the name of commonwealth is past and gone" in the new order of things. In 1840, Daniel Webster sat in the seat now occupied by Charles Sumner in the Senate, and John Quincy Adams was the venerated head of the delegation in the House of Representatives—a position now assigned, by general consent, to Benjamin F. Butler. Is this a change for the better?—Has the improvement been discovered in society? What mean the numberless peculations, robberies, defalcations, homicides, conjugal infidelities, nameless bestialities committed by people of the highest social position during these past twenty-eight years, and constantly increasing in frequency out of all proportion to the increase in population, and immeasurably beyond Mr. Buckle's law of average? Crimes by bank presidents, doctors of divinity, members of Congress, peccadilloes of clergymen's wives, scandals of Senators' wives, sins of the saints and prostration of the "polished corners of the temple?" What mean the whisky frauds, the extent of whose guilty gains no man may compute—frauds which colossal conspiracies have been formed to promote and to defend, as if the product of the illicit distillation were an elixir to bless instead of a poison to desolate the land? What means this gigantic swindle of a Gettysburg Asylum Lottery, endorsed by the journal of the largest circulation in America, commended officially by the Postmaster General and the Chief Commissioner of the Internal Revenue, and allowed to close its doors upon the thousands of its victims without even so much as an inquiry into its getting money under false pretense? What means the vile "Personal column" of the *New York Herald*, with its shameless assignations carried on openly through the branch Post Offices of our largest city? And what significance are we to attach to the crowds that for two years have attended the performances of the *Black Crook* and the *White Fawn*, abominations which, in 1840, would have been put down by the police? Do these things indicate an improvement in the moral tone of society? Or shall we say that the applause with which the *Cancan* itself has been nightly received by the fashionable audiences of the French Theatre of New York, indicates a healthful "change in the graces and amenities of life?" Perhaps Mr. Dickens only meant by this pretty phrase that the manners of such of the Americans as he had met on his second visit were less boorish, and the vice of the republic had lost all its evil in losing half its grossness. Tobacco spitting has diminished, perhaps, though the stained marble stairway of the national Capitol would not warrant the belief.—People, especially in Boston, do not put the dinner knives in their mouths as in 1840, and the general use in Massachusetts of the silver fork for carrying food to its proper receptacle may have been one of the happy results of General Butler's New Orleans Proconsulate. We do not know.—But it surely cannot be that in the "changes moral" Mr. Dickens refers to a supposed improvement in the religious aspect of the country. All Christian men bitterly deplore the schisms of the church, and the world laughs in scorn at the bickerings of religious sects, and asks, in the words of the heathen poet, how it is that such resentments can inflame celestial minds. The growing spirit of irreligion is shown in nothing more strikingly than in the general disregard of the

Sabbath day. In the city of New York, three journals of wide circulation and influence are issued continuously all round the year, while the Sunday papers proper are notoriously among the worst emanations of the press. It may even admit of a doubt whether the very services of the sanctuary have not shared the universal demoralization in political preaching sustained by a people, who, having driven Shakspeare from the stage, evince a strong desire to banish the Bible from the pulpit. Let us look at the press. "Changes in the Press," says Mr. Dickens, "without whose advancement no advancement can take place any where." Assuredly no one can deny that there has been great advancement in the activities of the press since 1840, nor can we say that this has been wholly mechanical. Many well-known journals at various points publish daily an amount and variety of matter, which would have staggered the most energetic editor of a quarter a century ago. The printing presses of that time would not have thrown it off, nor would the circulation of the most prosperous paper have justified the expense. To this extent, indeed, the progress has again been in the line of physical development. But the universal extension of the magnetic telegraph under seas and across continents, bringing us into instantaneous communication with the ends of the earth, has necessitated the employment of a larger amount of talent in the editorial staff of the leading journals, and the demand for sharp, rapid, pungent paragraphs upon the topics of the hour has produced a class of writers which did not exist in 1840. Never before has it been so important for the press to "catch as she flies the Cynthia of the minute."—What happened the day before yesterday has already passed into the domain of ancient history. It might be questioned whether the enterprise and cleverness which comments at a run upon the most momentous as upon the most trivial matters of daily occurrence, turning out with equal facility a leader upon the smash of a railroad train and the fall of an empire, has not been purchased at the expense of all calm and thoughtful discussion. But we will let this pass. We will admit that the press of 1868 displays more energy and, if you please, more ability than the press of 1840. But does it also display a stricter observance of the truth, a loftier independence, a greater regard for the "graces and amenities of life?" Is it not notorious, without reference to individual cases, that the advocacy of the press may be purchased for any purpose, no matter how demoralizing or flagitious? All right-thinking men concede (what, indeed, there is no attempt, even in thinnest drapery or in modest periphrasis to conceal) the impudicity of the ballets and the dialogue of the *White Fawn* and the *Belle Helène*; yet if a dramatic critic but dare to hint at the immoral nature of these entertainments, he is immediately assailed as a "prurient prude," and cited as one of those nice people of whom Dr. Johnson spoke as having very nasty ideas. Does this not hint at money judiciously employed, if only in profuse and liberal advertising, to get the press on the side of the managers? It is not necessary to our purpose, in this contrast, to make more than a passing allusion to those beastly hebdomadals, the legitimate offspring of the immodest drama, which under the names of *The Last Sensation*, *The Town*, etc., etc., have been sold by the hundred thousand throughout the land, for fairness demands that we should deal with the best and purest, rather than the lowest and vilest, of the American press, and with daily, rather than weekly publications. Reference has already been made, incidentally, to facts connected with the daily press as indicative of social demoralization and the growing spirit of irreligion; to the "Personal Column" and to the issue as well on Sunday as on the other days of the week, of three journals of established reputation. But coming more directly to the independence of the press, how many papers of the country are there not in the pay of the Whisky Rings, how many have not been bought by a share in the proceeds, to uphold swindling Lottery schemes advertised in the sacred name of patriotism, how many "money articles" are not prepared in the interests of the "bulls" and "bears" of the Stock Exchange? As for "the graces and amenities of life," it will suffice to cite one line, and that the running head of an editorial article in a leading journal, to show how the Press of 1868 has improved in its consideration for decency and urbanity. It comes from a journal which sets itself up as a model of good manners. It appeared singularly enough the very week of the banquet, and was written singularly enough by the eminent journalist who presided at the banquet, and sat on Mr. Dickens' left hand—Hon. Horace Greeley. It runs simply, "HORATIO SEYMOUR AS A LIAR." We submit that this is enough to prove that the "change in the press" has not been beneficial since the days of Buckingham and Halleck, and Joseph Gales.

Does any one suspect that this gloomy view of the social, moral and intellectual condition of the Northern States has been inspired by the petty feeling of sectional prejudice? We would ask him to read the following paragraph from, perhaps, the ablest and most independent of the weekly journals of New York City:

"Hitherto we have been, substantially speaking, a happy, even-minded people, of whom a very large proportion have been firm believers in the doctrines of Christianity, contented with simple pleasures, addicted to domestic life, and having little taste for violent "sensations" of any kind. The changes that have come over us are great and significant. The bitter sorrows and anxieties of a long civil war, followed, in the North at least, by an epoch of violent speculative excitement, attended by extravagance of living and a widely-spread passion for sensual pleasure, have made our country any thing but the country of ten years ago. Life now, to be tolerable, must be spiced with condiments of the keenest and most titillating sort. Each fresh gratification quickly palls, and new devices must constantly be brought forward to stimulate the jaded sense. The theatre is radiant with voluptuous images, and thousands swarm nightly to gloat on the female charms their clouds of gauze scarcely affect to conceal. Gross pictures are hawked about the streets, and obscene books are offered to boys and greybeards alike in the exchange and market place. The newspapers strain every nerve to outstrip each other in the astonishing, the preposterous, and the extravagant; and those from whose occasional exhibitions of care, thought, and scholarship we have learned to hope better things seem of late to have abandoned themselves to the worst spirit of the hour and to have plunged bodily into the coarse vortex of sensation. Even the pulpit yields to the vulgar tendencies that mar nearly all less sacred things, and the most influential and successful preachers are men who in a purer and more cultivated age would be simply laughed down as greedy and sensual charlatans. The artificial and highly colored, in contradistinction to the true and the natural, are producing in every direction their legitimate effect. We see on every hand false views of life usually ending in bitter disappointment, minds and bodies prematurely broken and withered, a horrible lust of money as the sole genuine good of life, a prevalent infidelity—spreading everywhere in sympathy with parallel conditions to those of France at the time of her revolution—and, in a word, every promise of social decay and ruin unless the baleful progress of things is arrested by powerful reformatory agencies, signs of which are unhappily not yet apparent."

So speaks the *Round Table* of New York, a paper from which it is surely not disloyal to quote.—The picture is, indeed, darker than we should have dared to draw, but its fidelity, alas! cannot be gainsaid. We have no satisfaction in dwelling upon it. Far pleasanter were it to believe, if such belief were possible, that the Northern States, to whose hopes and destinies we are bound by ties which it was vainly attempted to sunder, were steadily moving onward to a higher development of the race than has yet been known; to dream of a happy and not distant fulfillment for them and for us of that noble ambitiou which the poet imputes to King Arthur in founding the Round Table of old romance—

> "To serve as model for the mighty world,
> And be the fair beginning of a time."

But flatteries like those of Mr. Dickens will rather retard the day by blinding men to the true condition of affairs, and it is certain that there is small hope of a higher culture and a purer Christianity for a people who already believe themselves the wisest, best and greatest of mankind.

SOCIAL REMINISCENCES OF DISTINGUISHED NORTH CAROLINIANS.

No. I.

THE HON. FREDERICK NASH.

Lord Macaulay in his admirable essay on History, compares the historian to a portrait painter.

"Any man with eyes and hands," he says, "may be taught to take a portrait. The process up to a certain point, is purely mechanical; if this were all, a man of talents might justly despise the occupation. But we could mention portraits which are resemblances, but not mere resemblances; faithful but much more than faithful; portraits which condense into one point of time, and exhibit at a single glance the whole history of turbid and eventful lives—in which the eye seems to scrutinize us, and the mouth to command us—in which the brow menaces, and the lip almost quivers with scorn — in which every wrinkle is a comment upon some important transaction."—The simile strikes us as more appropriate to the biographer than the historian, who represents in his picture, not the history of one eventful life only, but the leading incidents of many lives.

Biography is often to History what Grotius defines equity to be to law, "a correction of that wherein the law (by reason of its universality) is deficient." And the best historians, such as Macaulay and Alison, do not hesitate to refer frequently to the biographies, sketches, and memoirs of the men and women of the age of which they are writing, for material out of which to construct their histories; just as the painter, who wishes to represent some striking event in the life of a great man, or the history of a nation, seeks carefully for correct likenesses of the individuals concerned in it; and, while he gives full play to his imagination in their grouping and posture, will, if he be a true artist, take no liberties with their faces and figures, but transfer these in as exact and life-like a manner as possible, to his canvass.

The greatest minds have not thought it beneath them to write biographies, yet one of the weakest of men has given to the world the best biography ever written, simply because he possessed quick observation and a retentive memory, and did not hesitate to record, for the benefit of posterity, the most trifling remarks and actions of the great Dr. Johnson.

But there is another art—or rather trade--for as not even talent is required to excel in it—much less genius, it cannot properly be called an art—which we value highly, not only because it gives us good likenesses of distinguished men, at a price within even the limited means of most ex-Confederates, but because by it the real artist is frequently enabled to re-produce, with life-like correctness, the features of the dead on which he never looked when living. But for a coarse and poorly executed photograph of the great Stonewall Jackson, the true artist, William Garle Brown, could not have preserved to the world that face, the representation of which, by the hand of genius, it is only necessary to look upon to be at once convinced of the fallacy of the statement, too often made by those who knew him but slightly, that though a great general, his was but an ordinary mind.

The writer of these social reminiscences of distinguished North Carolinians, offers them to the readers of THE LAND WE LOVE, not as finished portraits, but as simple *cartes de visite*, and if any one of them shall assist a real artist to paint a truer and more lasting picture, or aid the future historian of the State to place in a more worthy or conspicuous position any one of her sons, they will not have been written in vain. Like the lover, who painted his mistress asleep and awake, standing and sitting, and yet lamented that he could not reproduce her in each new posture and dress, the people of North Carolina are ever eager to hear something more of her history; and many of them would value more highly a common photograph of one of her distinguished men, whom they had personally known and esteemed, than a finished engraving of a much greater man, whom they knew only by reputation.

Among those, who have sat in the high places of the State, though some may have been better known and more admired abroad, none have been more highly esteemed, or more sincerely beloved at home, than the Hon. Frederick Nash, who succeeded the Hon. William Gaston on the bench of the Supreme Court, and was, for six years out of the fourteen that he sat there, Chief Justice of the State of North Carolina.

A native of the town of New Berne, which also gave birth to John Stanley, William Gaston, George E. Badger, and Francis L. Hawks, he was worthy to be the friend and associate of these gentlemen, all of whom are well known to have been men calculated to elevate the moral, and adorn the intellectual tone of the the circle in which they moved. There was a courtly dignity and a polished grace of manner about the New Berne gentlemen of that day, which distinguished them even then. In the first settlement of a country, the sea board is always far in advance of the interior in cultivation and refinement of mind and manners. In no States is this fact more noticeable than in Virginia and the Carolinas, where the first permanent settlements were made by men of standing and wealth in their native country, and not by mere adventurers. The men of "thews and sinews," were the pioneers, who went further inland and became agriculturists: as the country was gradually settled, they were followed by the "men of mind;" but most of the large grants of land held by the younger sons of the nobility, direct from the crown, were located near the sea-board, and there their descendants may still be found, in many cases residing on the land granted to their ancestors, which has never been either bought or sold.

Born in the palace of the old colonial Governors, an edifice said to be superior to anything of the kind in the United States, shortly after his father, Abner Nash, Esq., succeeded Richard Caswell, as Governor of the State, something of the air and manner of the aristocratic régime of General Washington hung round Judge Nash all his life.

Small in stature, and remarkable in his appearance only for the exquisite neatness and appropriateness of his dress; plain, unpretending and simple in his manner, and modest in the extreme, he yet showed at a glance that he was born, as well as bred, a *gentleman*. To no one was that noblest of all appellations, "Christian gentleman," more peculiarly applicable, for his gentility came, not from acquired graces, or the polish of education, though he was by no means deficient in this last, but from the innate purity and beauty of a character which rudeness, or even roughness of speech or manner, seemed unable to approach near enough, to ruffle or excite. The ancient Greeks adorned their homes with statues and pictures representing men and women of exquisite grace and beauty of form and feature, because they believed that the physical development of a people was heightened by the constant contemplation of such objects of art. The moral, mental, and social characters of men and women are undoubtedly influenced by the examples around them. And in the present day, when something of the rudeness and freedom of the camp has insensibly crept into our drawing-rooms, tinging the manners of our young men, and blunting the sensitiveness of our young women, a contemplation of the dignified ease, and social graces of their grand-fathers and grand-mothers, cannot but be advantageous to them. At an age when most susceptible of life-long impressions, many of the sons of our most polished gentlemen, have been for months, not only away from the refining influences of home, but thrown into the closest contact with the roughest, and most unpolished of men. And their mothers and sisters during their short, and unfrequent furloughs and leaves of absence, thought more of clothing the outer, and solacing the inner man, than of polishing their manners.—There is a great deal of truth in most of our copy-book sentences, and in none more than "Manners make the man."

Genius is a gift and cannot be acquired, but any young man of fair abilities and good character, may, by application and attention to business, fit himself to become Chief Justice of the State, and be called to fill that position, but they are few, indeed, who could do it as Judge Nash did.—When he was elected to the Supreme Court bench, a gentleman speaking to an intimate friend of his, who was also a lawyer, expressed a regret that a more brilliant man, and one better known out of the State, had not been chosen to succeed Judge Gaston. His reply was: "Nash is by far the best person to fill the position, for his high moral worth, and strict sense of justice is such that his decisions would have great weight with the bar of the State, even if his legal learning was less than it is: he has not the genius of Mr. Badger, or the profound legal knowledge of Mr. Winston, both of which are remarkable, but he has qualities which better fit him to be a Judge of the Supreme Court than either of these gentlemen."

He was a man of the strictest integrity, and utterly without deceit or duplicity of any kind, simply because he never felt the need of them in his own case, and would have scorned to use them for another.

"Just was his word, in every thought sincere,
He knew no wish but what the world might hear."

Seldom taking the lead in conversation at those social gatherings of the Raleigh bar, which were enlivened by the sparkling wit of Judge Gaston, the playful humor of Governor Manly, the intellectual elegance of Mr. Henry, and the brilliant conversation of Mr. Badger; there was yet something in the glance of his eye, the smile on his lip, and the quiet retort which he ever had ready for the witticisms of others, which showed him at once to be neither a common-place nor a dull companion. Hospitality was a leading feature of his character, and no where did he appear to better advantage than in his own house, where he loved to gather around him the young people of both sexes, though he was the most partial to the society of young girls, and made himself more agreeable to them than many nearer their own age could have done. The daughters of his intimate friends, many of them, called him "Uncle Nash," and even those, who did not so address him, almost always spoke of him by that affectionate title among themselves; a fact which goes far in itself to prove the gentle amiability of his disposition, which, with his playful good humor, made them feel that the interest, which he expressed in them, their occupations and amusements, was real, and not assumed for their gratification.

"That's just like Uncle Nash," said one of them once to his friend, Mr. Winston, who was reading aloud to her the diary of Mrs. Margaret Roper, in which she so beautifully portrays the character of her father, Sir Thos. Moore. "So it is," was his reply, "the likeness never struck me until you mentioned it, but their characters are not dissimilar, although their minds are of a different order."

Although Sir Thomas was a Catholic, and Judge Nash a Presbyterian, both held to their religious belief with the same unwavering tenacity, and one would have died for it as bravely and coolly as the other did. Campbell, in his lives of the Lord Chancellors of England, gives an extract from a letter of Sir Thos. Moore, to Peter Giles, of Antwerp, which is a charming picture of the private life of a public man: Judge Nash might have sat for the portrait, for, not only did he spend his leisure hours in the same manner, but used frequently to speak in similar terms of the duties of the head of a family, and regret that he had so little time to give to them.

"For while the greatest part of the day is spent in other men's affairs, the remainder must be given to my family at home; so that I can reserve no part of it to myself for study. I must gossip with my wife, and chat with my children, and find something to say to my servants; for all these things I reckon a part of my business, unless I were to become a stranger in my own house; for with whomsoever either nature, or choice, or chance, has engaged a man in any relation of life, he must endeavor to make himself as acceptable to them, as he possibly can."

Judge Nash not only endeavored to make himself acceptable to all with whom he came in contact, but he also endeavored always to find in them something acceptable to him: and if there was a good, or agreeable trait in a person otherwise unpleasant, it seemed to be always the first thing that caught his attention. He was very near-sighted and used spectacles all his life, he frequently spoke of this defect with regret, but said he missed seeing many disagreeable, as well as some, pleasant things.

On one occasion, something was said in his presence about the freckles on a certain lady's face, greatly impairing her beauty.—"See there now," he said in his quiet, quaint way, "there is something I have gained by being near-sighted, for although I looked at her through my spectacles, I never discovered a freckle on her face, which struck me as being a remarkably pretty one." A few moments after, a young girl, whom his indulgent kindness had rendered affectionately saucy in her manner to him, made a true, but rather harsh, comment upon the character of a common acquaintance. "My dear," said he mildly, "I think you must be mistaken, I knew him well, and never saw anything of the kind in him."

"No, Uncle Nash," was the saucy reply, "and you will have to get spectacles for your mind as well as for your eyes before you can see what is disagreeable in a person, unless it conceals something good, and then you look right through the bad, and only point it out to show us the good that it hides."

He *had* spectacles for his mind as well as his eyes, for he looked at every one through the medium of that charity which "thinketh no evil;" and was, to the day of his death, remarkable for the child-like unsuspiciousness of his character, Though deeply and fervently pious, he had neither the asceticism nor the worldly prudence of the Puritan: this latter trait of character being generally quite as prominent in this sect as the former, and only yielding to it when their stern uncompromising religious prejudices intervene between them and their prosperity and comfort. He left most of the pecuniary management of his family affairs to his wife, who was a woman well fitted to be a helpmeet to such a gentle and amiable character, for her lady-like refinement, which rendered it impossible for her ever to shock his taste, covered a strength and energy of mind and disposition, on which he felt he might rely in any emergency. He used to tell of his once buying some napkins of a peddler, and taking them home to her, supposing she would be delighted with his excellent bargain.

"Are they not nice, my dear?" he asked when, after looking at them, she laid them down without remarking, as he had thought she would, on their quality.

"Oh yes, they will do very well for the children," was the evasive reply.

A little crest-fallen he said, "Well, I suppose I'am not a good judge of dry goods, but these were so very cheap, that they were a real bargain, though they are not quite so fine as you usually get them."

He then named the price he had paid, and Mrs. Nash, raising both hands, exclaimed:

"My dear Mr. Nash, you did not pay *that* for them."

"Yes, my dear; was it too much?"

"Just fifty cents in the dozen more than I gave for the last set of company napkins that I bought," replied Mrs. Nash, unable to restrain her laughter, on discovering how he had been taken in.

"Since then," he used to say, "I have confined myself entirely to my own department, and left my wife to manage hers without my help, which is more of a hinderance."

When attending court in Raleigh, he always staid with Mrs. James F. Taylor, to whom he was most warmly attached, and who returned his affection with the devotion of a daughter. She had known him from her childhood, being herself a native of New Bërne, and the adopted daughter of Judge John Lewis Taylor, at whose house Judge Nash visited intimately. Judge Gaston, who was the brother of Mrs. John Lewis Taylor, also made Mrs. James Taylor's house his home during his visits to Raleigh, after the death of his brother-in-law, and it was a joyful event to the children of their friends, who attended the school kept by Mrs Taylor, when either of them arrived. Both were remarkably fond of children, and loved to sit on the porch and watch them at play, during the half hour in the morning before, as Judge Nash used to say, "both of our schools open." Judge Gaston entered heartily into all their sports, and would frequently gather them around the steps and tell them stories, or teach them new games; he wrote more than one song for their May-day celebrations, and used to drill the speakers, at the coronation of the queen, for days beforehand, and took a lively interest in the dance round the May-pole, which he always attended, besides adding, in a more substantial way, to their enjoyments, by producing from his pocket, papers of sugar plums for distribution among them. On one occasion, hearing Mrs. Taylor speak of Judge Battle's children, as "the little Battles," he said gravely to her, "Don't you think, Eliza, it would be more correct to say the 'Skirmishes?'" As long as these children attended Mrs. Taylor's school, they were familiarly known by this sobriquet. Judge Gaston and Judge Nash were intimate friends from their earliest youth, until death separated them. Judge Gaston, who was full of real Irish wit and humor, always had some joke on his more quiet friend, who was, not, however, without his occasional revenge, instances of which would be related by Judge Gaston with as much zest as though they turned on another.

The *entente cordiale* between lawyers of the same bar is generally more perfect, than that existing between gentlemen of any other profession. They are fairly pitted against each other in the Court-House, where they fight out their battles, and, as there is nothing personal in these contests, they come from them to the social circle with the feelings of boxers who have laid aside the gloves, and only enjoy each others society the more for the previous encounter of their intellects: their jokes conceal no sting, and their witticisms seldom or never wound. This was especially the case with the Raleigh bar of that, day, and the entertainments given by the resident lawyers to those attending the Superior Courts of Wake, and the Supreme Court, were marked by an unusual flow of intellectual good things. A witty lady visiting one of these gentlemen once, said in allusion to one of these parties where she had met Mr. Badger, Mr. Hogg, and Mr. Hawks, who was then a lawyer at the North Carolina bar, and, had he continued in the profession, would doubtless have distinguished himself as much in it, as he afterwards did in the ministry; "that she could not have believed it possible she would so highly enjoy the society of the beasts of the field and the birds of the air."

Judge Nash and the Hon. Jas. Iredell, on one occasion, when riding the circuit together stopped for the night at the house of a brother lawyer. As the day had been both wet and cold, their host prevailed on them as soon as they entered, to take a glass of brandy and water. Fatigued with his journey, Judge Nash was even more quiet than usual, while Gov. Iredell, being a younger and more robust man, was, after a cup of coffee and a hearty supper, uncommonly brilliant in conversation, and persisted in asserting that Judge Nash, who happened at that time to be driving a young and rather wild horse, did it from a desire to cut a dash, adding that he must certainly be a descendant of the celebrated Beau Nash, and would be seen before long coming out in the dress of his great relative. Judge Nash bore his witticisms for some time without retort, at length rising from the sofa on which he was sitting, he said quietly: "I have one advantage over you, Mr. Iredell, at any rate, for my liquor never stops at the end of my tongue, but mounts at once to my eyes and makes me sleepy, so I will bid you good night."

A good companion to this anecdote is one related by a gentleman of Raleigh, when Judge Nash was a Superior Court judge. It was just after the completion of the Raleigh and Gaston Railroad, and the first train of cars that passed over it was expected to arrive about 8 or 9 o'clock in the evening. Curiosity to see an engine in motion carried a number of persons to the depot, near which was a small house, occupied by a man named Caleb Malone, who had been indicted for selling liquor without a license, and was to be tried the next week. Two gentlemen standing near this house, the door of which was open, heard Malone's wife urging him to go out and see the train arrive. "Lord bless you, Betsy," was his reply, "I hai'nt got no heart to think about injines and sich nonsense, for I hearn tell today as how Judge Nash rides this here cirket, and if I's fotch up before him on that there in-dite-*ment* for selling liquor, I hai'nt got a grain 'er chance of gitting off, and he a Presbyterian and a te-totaler too."

His amiable disposition never affected his decisions as a Judge; of him it might truly be said, "the cause which he knew not he searched out;" but judgment was to him "a robe and a diadem," which he wore only when duty required, and gladly divested himsel of. He early entered on the duties of public life, for at twenty-two he represented his native town in the Legislature; and at twenty-six was elected a trustee of the University of North Carolina, and during the whole of his long life, took a lively interest in its prosperity and success. Shortly after his marriage to Miss Kollock, he removed to Hillsboro,' where he ever afterwards resided, and where his memory is still cherished by all who knew him. He was mercifully gathered to his fathers before the beginning of the late war, and thus spared the pain that his kind heart must have borne, had he lived to witness its horrors; as well as the mortification he would have experienced in the present degradation of his beloved State. He attended the Synod of the Presbyterian Church, which was held in Newbern, the autumn before his death, and, having looked once more on the scenes of his youth and early manhood, returned to the home of his married life, where in the bosom of his family, this good and faithful servant "entered into the joy of his Lord."

His death, like his life, was calm and peaceful, many of his old friends gathered around his dying bed to take a last farewell of one so universally beloved, and of whom it may truly be said—

"Calmly he looked on either life, and here
Saw nothing to regret, or there to fear."

CECIL.

BY I. M. PORTER HENRY.

In memory of my brother, who died about sixteen years of age, in the Confederate States Army.

Here where thy young feet rest, I bring
My simple gifts of flowers and speak
My simple words of love. God willed that thou
Should cast the burden of thy life
With bloodless hands, before His Throne, and thus
With manly mien and woman's innocence,
Thy soul passed on, "unspotted from the world."
Ah hadst thou stayed, thou wouldst have loved me Here;
But thou art gone, and love me There!

When I am near thy grave, I would not hear
Grand martial airs, nor tramp of feet,
Nor rolling drum—nay, I would ask the bird
In yonder sighing oak, whose shadow almost clasps
Two brothers in its arms, to sing aloud
For thee and him. Poor little tender-heart!
It hides away from tearless pain—I wish
'Twould sing and sing and sing, until the world
Grew full of Love, as Heaven is of Joy!
Ah hadst thou stayed, thou wouldst have loved me Here;
But thou art gone, and love me There!

I often wonder, gentle boy, if thou
And he who sleeps so near, have not clasped hands
In Heaven for me and mine!
Both died as strong men die; both fell as Princes fall
In warfare grand!
Alas, *he* fell at sword-point, stained the earth
With blood of Southern prime!
But thou wert young—the angels pitied thee,
And stayed the arm of Death
Until a mother cradled her poor boy—
Her poor, tired boy to rest.
Ah hadst thou stayed, thou wouldst have loved me Here;
But thou art gone, and love me There!

I weave for him this laurel green, sweet Bays,
And Ivy crowns, full blown Magnolias white,
And crimson blooms that tell of Southern growth
In flushed maturity; but slender fashioned flowers,
These pale Blush-roses, Hyacinths, Snow-drops,
And nodding Ash, I bind with shoots
Of tender green, that tell me of thy youth.
Ah hadst thou stayed, thou wouldst have loved me Here·
But thou art gone, and love me There!

Then sweet-lipped Violets I find, that fold
Imperial hues above their scented hearts,
And count them, one by one, to give each brother
Flower for flower, in sweet dividing.
Both clusters then I kiss, and bind with these
Dark strands, thy mourning sister's hair.
Long, tender messages of love I send
By them to Heaven, and in my simple Faith
They comfort me with dreams, of how two brothers,
Hand in hand, look down on me and smile.
I know that far off land is fair; but oh,
Forget me not! Still give me love for love,
It is the fairest, sweetest thing I cast
Upon thy grave; the heaviest, saddest thing
Is this hot tear!
Ah hadst thou stayed, thou wouldst have loved me Here;
But thou art gone, and love me There!

Greenville, Ala.

THE EMPRESS OF THE FRENCH.

The history of the Empress is invested with an almost romantic interest. She was born at Granada, in Spain, in May 1826. Her father, the Count Montijo, was of an old and noble family, and by marriages at different periods, allied to some of the most illustrious names of Spain. Among them are those of Guzman, Fernandez, Teba and Barras. Her mother, though also born in Spain, was the daughter of a Mr. Kirkpatrick, for some years English Consul at the Spanish seaport of Malaga. He was descended from an ancient Scottish family of Closeburn—still in existence, but without their property.

Though educated principally at Madrid, she spent some time at school in England, and traveled a great deal with her mother, under the name of the Countess de Teba.

She was never, so far as I have been able to learn, considered remarkable for talent, but was always admired for her personal grace and beauty, and won much affection by her affable manners, and her uniformly amiable character. As is but too common with the attractive women of certain classes of society, she is said to have had a dash of coquetry, but possessed an under-current of deep, strong feeling, rendering her capable of very ardent attachments. And she is said to have had one disappointment, which rendered her for some time almost desperate. Nor was her heart less sensitive to other trials bearing upon her affections. A few years since, her sister, the Duchess D'Alba, died at her residence in Paris, which event affected the mind of the Empress with such violent anguish as to make her, for some time, quite inconsolable. Whenever she had occasion to pass her sister's home —situated within view of the Champs Elysées, which is the principal drive leading from the Palace of the Tuileries, her paroxysms of grief were so violent that the Emperor, in order to destroy the association, decided to purchase the property, and had the structure taken down; an incident which reflects rather pleasingly on the character of this singular man in his domestic relations.

But to return. Her mother, sometime a widow, removed to Paris, where she resided for a series of years. With means comparatively limited, she had no little difficulty, it is said, to keep her daughters in that circle of fashion, to which they naturally aspired, and to which their rank entitled them.

To effect this object, she incurred considerable indebtedness, which the Emperor is stated to have generously liquidated after his marriage to her daughter.

He is said to have long admired a grace, beauty and wit, which indeed were the admiration of all who knew her.

Being, however, desirous to form an alliance with some of the crowned heads of Europe, by which he would strengthen his position and gratify the French people, he probably entertained no serious intentions towards her, until his proposals to the various courts had been rejected.

The brief and stormy reign of his uncle, with his sad fate, was still too vividly remembered to incline them to risk so intimate an alliance with one, who was at first naturally regarded as indebted for his elevation, not so much to his ability, as to the brilliant fame of Napoleon Bonaparte.—His remark, after the successive failures, is well known. He did not care, he "would now marry to please himself, but the time would come when they would regret it."

What regrets may have since been experienced by any of the parties, it might be difficult to ascertain, but the rejected suitor has, for years, been established in a power at home, and wielded an influence abroad, which is the marvel of the nations. His marriage to Eugenie Marie de Guzman, took place at Notre Dame, in January, 1853. The event had a happy celebration, in being made the occasion of granting an amnesty to four or five thousand political prisoners.

It was, however, very displeasing to the French people, whose inveterate pride was deeply wounded by what they regarded as rather a parvenu connection for the head of the nation.

There is in the palace of the Luxembourg, a splendidly executed painting, representing the ceremony. The figures are almost life-size, and include, besides the bridal party and officiating priest, several of the spectators.

The bride, attired with elegant simplicity, looks almost angelic in her exquisite and delicate beauty, her eyes cast to the floor.

I was told by a gentleman who was present, that she was pale and much agitated, owing, probably, to her knowledge of the general discontent prevailing in the city at the marriage. At first she was silently received by the populace—it is said there were occasional hisses even. But her uniform amiability and affable manners gradually overcame prejudice, and won her a place in the hearts of the people. Nor is this popularity, which may be said now to be almost universal, the result of merely amiable manners. Commendable as these may be, it is founded upon qualities still more substantial and creditable to the Empress. Her benevolence has been variously manifested. Those, who have regarded her merely as the leader of fashion, may be surprised to learn that some of those very fashions originated in efforts on her part to relieve the manufacturers of those fabrics. I will select one instance from several, which have been related to me.

On one occasion, when the manufacturers of embroidered muslins were in much distress in consequence of the little demand for them, they sent a deputation to wait upon Her Majesty. She received them kindly, heard their complaints, and immediately sent in orders for some of their most expensive fabrics. In these she made her appearance at the first party—at the next, almost all the ladies were attired in the same, and very soon the numerous orders quite relieved the manufacturers.

This is ennobling fashion, if such a thing can be done, but at the same time, is no excuse for those, who to adopt it must make too large draughts upon a light purse, and perhaps add to the labors and mental anxiety of a father, or a husband, who may be already overtaxed with both.—But her benevolence has been manifested in a yet more noble manner. She has devoted both time and means, largely, to the indigent, the sick, the poor, and the orphan. She has not hesitated to visit hospitals, where cholera prevailed in its virulent forms, walking through the wards and speaking cheerful and encouraging words to the poor sufferers. It is related that these visits have sometimes been followed by a surprising number of immediate convalescents. Making due allowance for exaggeration, it seems not altogether incredible, when we reflect how much the physical condition is often affected, by an entire diversion of thought into some pleasant channel. It would be no little matter to poor, friendless inmates of a hospital to have a personal visit and kind words from Her Majesty, with all that winning manner for which she is remarkable. The orphan poor have had her especial attention.

Her first public efforts in this way were during the absence of the Emperor, in the Italian war in 1859. Having been invested temporarily with the regency of the empire, she made personal visits of inspection to various places. Among these, she found an Orphan Asylum, under the patronage of the Government, so miserably conducted, that, by virtue of her authority, she immediately broke up the establishment, and had the children dispersed in homes, which promised both comfort and an opportunity to learn some useful trade. The first near view I had of the Empress, during a sojourn of several weeks in Paris, last Autumn, was at the presentation of prizes to the Orphans of the Industrial Palace. This commodious and handsome edifice, erected for the first universal Exhibition is situated on the Champs Elysées, in the midst of attractive grounds.—It has been, for sometime, devoted to the use of a large number of orphans, who assemble there daily, and are taught many things, both useful and ornamental, which they may afterwards turn to good account in providing for themselves. They are neatly clothed, and appear bright and cheerful. Of this commendable Institution, she is the especial patroness, and once a year there is a public presentation of rewards to such of the pupils as have been particularly diligent, or excelled in any of the arts. At such times she is always present, accompanied by the young Prince, who, happily, seems to be her companion generally in her benevolent missions. On this occasion the bright expression of his face, and the spirited clapping of his hands indicated a more than passive interest in the events of the day. Not only was the spacious building filled, but thousands of people were assembled in the grounds. These circumstances naturally endear the Empress to the people, and perhaps her popularity has done as much to strengthen the Emperor upon his throne, as a matrimonial alliance with any of the crowned heads of Europe could have done. There are, as usual, captious persons who insist that these efforts all spring from a desire for popularity. It is more agreeable to take a different view, and seems not unreasonable, considering the uniformity of her course during a long series of years. Still a most attractive looking woman at the age of forty-one, much of her beauty consists in that very lovely expression of countenance, which makes the beholder feel that she derives a real pleasure from doing good. At all events, whatever may be the motive, we must rejoice that it has been the source of great benefit to those who most needed it. Her example may be a useful one. Active benevolence seems to be the peculiar and appropriate field for woman. It is a pleasure which the humblest may enjoy, and when her influence is extended by the possession of superior position, wealth or intellect, it should find its noblest outlet in those works which afford relief to the suffering in body or mind. Even the blandishments of a pleasing manner are not to be disregarded. They are grateful to all, and where it is only an appropriate expression of a kindly nature, seldom fails to win its way to the heart of the most careless or the most obdurate.

S. B. H.

THE HAVERSACK.

We have all heard of the man, who found Napoleon, Arkansas, "such a refreshing place," because he was allowed to get battered and bruised to his heart's content in "a free fight," in that hospitable and kind-hearted town. An ex-captain of the so-called sends us the counterpart to this story from Bellevue, Alabama:

Private Cushman, of the 5th Alabama battalion, a gallant son of Erin, was known as one of the best soldiers in the command. He never missed a battle in which his company was engaged, never straggled, never missed duty on account of sickness, never asked for a furlough and was in every way a faultless soldier, except that he would occasionally "get a brick in his hat." He was offered the first "furlough of indulgence for meritorious services." He answered, "what do I want with a furlough? Jist let me go away for a day or two for me health. I have a bit of a wakeness in me stomach, and a wee drap would be afther doing me good." He went to Richmond, invested all his Confederate "promises to pay" in the stimulant he loved so well, and came back, when his funds were all exhausted, with blackened eyes, a swelled nose, a mashed up face, and the general appearance of a used-up rebel. "I'm hearty as a buck now, me honey, all the wakeness is gone out of me stomach, and I'm ready for another turn at the bloody Yanks." He served to the close of the war most gallantly, without ever having been sick or wounded.

Confederate soldiers were never at a loss for expedients to cross the sentry line, when there were prospects of good foraging in the neighborhood. Private M., 5th Alabama battalion, became quite distinguished in this species of strategy—or stroll-ology. His dark skin enabled him to practice a trick upon sentinels, who did not know him, with almost unvarying success. With a canteen, or some cooking utensil in hand, he would walk across the sentry-line with the most unconcerned manner. When halted, he would seem very much surprised and exclaim, "what, you doesn't stop black folks, does ye?" The sentinel would say, "why, you are not a nigger are you?" "O, yes, I is, I belongs to Capt. Porter of the 5th Alabama battalion." "Go ahead, nig."

Would that the difficulty of discriminating between negroes and white men had terminated with the war. But it is more perplexing now than then. Some, who seem to be of the Caucasian race, affiliate with, associate with, and vote with the African. They ought to belong to Capt. Porter or some one else, and have free passes across the line.

Oxford, N. C., tells of a devoted and patriotic North Carolina mother:

When —— N. C. regiment was stationed at Wilmington, a young lad from R—— county deserted that command and went home. He arrived at night, knocked at the door and his widowed mother, *all of whose sons were in service*, opened it—the ruddy pine light showed her youngest born, Absalom, the son of her old age, standing without. Now the good widow had been informed, a few days before, that no furloughs were granted, and suspected something was wrong. Repressing the mother's instinct to clasp him in her arms, and holding the door so he could not enter, she said:

"Absalom, have you a furlough?"

"No, mother, I have not."

"You have deserted your colors, then."

Yes, mother, I have," and was going on to excuse himself when she cut him short with

"Stop, Absalom, there is no excuse for deserting your country's cause. You cannot enter this house. Your father was a brave, true man. He built this house with his own hands, and no deserter shall enter it. Go to the kitchen, sir, and I will send supper and bedding out to you. In the morning, you must return to your company."

Absalom retired to the kitchen. How that mother's heart yearned towards her boy that night, God alone can ever know. In the morning she came to see him, impressed him with the error of his course, and then made him join her in prayer to the Almighty to forgive him the crime, he had committed against God and his country. After this, she dismissed him with a letter to the colonel of his regiment. Absalom promptly delivered the letter, and according to a request contained in it, was let off with a light punishment. He afterwards made a good soldier, and was with the regiment at the final surrender.

The boys in camp said Absalom's mother "impressed him with the error of his course" by means of a hickory. This Absalom stoutly, and I believe, truly denied.

Talk of Spartan mothers after this! W.

The gallant colonel, who sends us this, has not given the subsequent history of the young man. We are sure that his Spartan mother would rather have heard of his death in battle, or even of his being shot as a deserter, than for him to become one of the loyal Fetich.

Our next two anecdotes come from a young lady at Dover, Tennessee, who signs herself an "uncompromising rebel." What has become of Brownlow's "mcclish?" Why have they not hunted up this fair rebel? Are they getting disloyal? But let her speak for herself.

Mrs. W——, of Huntsville, Alabama, during the occupation of that place by the United States forces, was compelled, in order to prevent destruction of property, to "play Union." She was sitting in her parlor one day, talking to a Federal officer, when her little boy, six years old, came in. "How-de-do, buddie," said the officer, taking him on his knee, "is your ma Union or Secesh." "She's Union—*to get along*," innocently replied the little fellow.

We would say to our young rebel friend that we had just such a case in old North Carolina. A man, who had been a life-long Nullifier, turned "Union just to get along." But as there was no little boy to betray him, President Johnson thought that he was in good earnest and appointed him to an important office. But he betrayed Mr. Johnson just as he had done the Union and the Confederacy—all "to get along!!"

After a Federal raid on P——, West Tennessee, an old citizen of the town was seen walking very hurriedly up the street. "Where are you going, Mr. A., in such a hurry," asked a gentleman on the sidewalk. "The d—n Yanks have been to my house and eat everything on the place, and I am going up town to *get a lick of salt to give me a relish for water*," was the reply.

The last anecdote showing the mild manner, in which the war for the Union was carried on, brings out in strong relief the cruelty of Wirz, at Andersonville, who was so brutal as to give

Federal prisoners no better rations than Confederate soldiers had.

Carrollton, Missouri, tells of some of the freaks of the loyal militia in that severely oppressed State.

In the summer of 1864, the local militia became so oppressive as to provoke bush-whackers to retaliate. We were visited by one Capt. Anderson, better known as Bill Anderson, of Centralia notoriety. In addition to the local force, several companies were organized to kill, capture, or head-off the redoubtable Bill. Whenever he was known to be on the tramp, these companies were ordered to rendez-vous at a certain point, and they were sure to be too late to meet him. This occurred so often, as to excite a faint suspicion that the loyal and true men had a decided aversion to the sight of the rebel Bill.

On one occasion, however, a Mr. K——, a jolly son of the Emerald Isle was ordered out. He came on an old horse well-packed with blankets, bedding, eatables, cooking utensils, &c., and with a long shot gun on his shoulder. As he passed by a neighbor's house, he was asked where he was going.

"Jist gwine to take a bit of a hunt," said K——.

"What are you going to hunt?" asked the neighbor.

"Somat, I don't want to find," replied Emerald Isle.

What is that?" next queried the neighbor.

"Faith and it's that bloody ribil Bill Anderson!" A. C. B.

Col. H. K. D., of Stonewall Jackson's Staff, sends an anecdote of "old Jubal" from Hagerstown, Maryland:

In January, '65, I left the army about Petersburg, on a short furlough, for the purpose of standing beside several of my fellow-officers, who were bent on marriage, in spite of the disjointed times. In my trip I visited Staunton, the Headquarters of "Old Jubal," and the remnant of the gallant little army of the Valley. The day after my arrival, being a a bright Sunday morning, Gen. Early surprised his staff by announcing his intention of going to church, requesting their company. It was a novel suggestion on the part of the commanding General, and chiefly for that reason, I fear, it met with a ready assent. I think the congregation of the Episcopal church was somewhat astonished at the entrance of Gen. Early and his large, characteristic staff—among whom were some gentlemen, whose piety much resembled that of their chief.

The sermon was a good one, earnest and impressive—the General and Staff devout listeners.—Toward its conclusion, where the exhortation usually comes in, the clergyman closed his book emphatically, and raising his right arm, with emphasis exclaimed:

"Suppose, my Christian friends, that those who have laid for centuries in their graves should arise now and come forth from their quiet resting places; and marching in their white shrouds should pass before this congregation, by thousands and tens of thousands, what would be the result?"

"Ah!" exclaimed old Jubal in

a stage whisper, "I'd conscript every d—d one of them."

It was an unfortunate suggestion on the part of the preacher, for Gen. Early remembered the great host of Sheridan and his own little band, and he would, willingly, for reinforcements, as Gen. Grant said, "have robbed both the cradle and the grave." And such is our natural depravity, that I have forgotten the text of that day, and all of the sermon, except what was pinned to my memory by that irreverent *mot* of old Jubal.

H. K. D.

Bayou City, Texas, gives the next two incidents:

Captain C—— of company H., 5th Texas, had a most remarkably loud voice—which, in battle, could be distinctly heard above the din and clangor, repeating the various commands. Before writing a single line more, let me here record for the reader's benefit, that a braver, cooler, and more gallant officer never went into action, and this we all knew and appreciated. It is told on the Captain that at "Gettysburg," in in one of the charges, the men were rapidly approaching a rock fence, and he being infused with a sudden amount of either patriotism or generosity, cried out in his loud voice, "*ten dollars to the man that first leaps that stone wall.*" And at break-neck speed ran company H. for the stone-wall—a new and unworn Confederate, "new issue," of the $10 print filling their imaginations. The one most fortunate was Sergeant Keys, but just as he was in the act of throwing the remaining leg over the wall, Captain C's. voice was again heard, "*hold on Sergt. Keys, file-closers not included.*" The pith of the affair is this. Men can be cool under danger—and the Captain, besides being cool, repented of his generosity, or his promise, when he saw that it would cost him an X, and his wits prompted the above rebuke to Sergt. Keys, for as next best to Keys, came the whole company.

If you ever meet the Captain, don't mention Sergt. Keys and that stonewall.

Every soldier is well aware of the confusion and demoralization a panic among troops will cause, even though they be soldiers as brave, renowned and fearless as Napoleon's "Old Guard"— Men lose self-possession, second thoughts take wings, and a few moments may change an army that was a machine, into a vast, ungovernable mob. The following incident, of which "Hood's Texas brigade" were the heroes, has invoked a laugh every time my mind has recurred thereto, and deeming it able to bring a smile upon the countenance of others, I repeat it.

On Lee's march from the vicinity of Richmond, in 1862, on his way to the plains of Manassas—where we afterwards met him of "Head-quarters in the saddle," we were frequently called upon to tax our limbs with forced marches. On one occasion, we had been marching for 20 hours, night approached as we were nearing the boundaries of Fauquier county, and still we were informed that we would have to continue our march, until a late hour of that night. Thus wearied, it is not surprising that at every momentary halt, the men would fall down in their tracks asleep, and even enjoy a "snooze" while standing. On one of these halts, the hour 10 p. m., the men as usual sank down, and were in a dreamy sleep. Just ahead of our command was a wagon train, the head of the column halting at the foot of a hill, its sides covered with stones, and the last wagon halting immediately upon the brow of the hill. Thus stood affairs, the men lying and standing along the road in a fitful sleep, down came an empty barrel from off the wagon on the hill, rolling down the hill over stones, making a most terrible racket. "*Yankee cavalry*" screamed the first sleepers, the cry was taken up, ran down the lines, and away scampered the men through pine bushes, rolling and tumbling over each other. Your correspondent "followed suit," and found himself with three others endeavoring to make his way over a pine bush. Order came, and we resumed the march. R. C.

The concluding incidents have been furnished us by an esteemed Ex-Chaplain, now at Lexington, Virginia:

The dislike of the private soldiers for Quartermasters and Commissaries was well nigh universal, and frequently did great injustice to worthy officers and gentlemen. The ragged jokers of our army never neglected an opportunity of making a hit at these officers, and many were their practical jokes at their expense.

When Lee's weary boys were hurrying on to reinforce Beauregard, at Petersburg, in '64, they passed a spot near the city in striking contrast with the dusty roads. A beautiful grove shaded the green yard of a stately mansion, a cool spring gushed forth from the hill-side, and it seemed indeed an oasis inviting to repose. The attention of the men was called to a large placard, bearing the inscription: "This yard has been selected as Head-quarters of Maj. ——, Q. M. of —— division." Many jests were passed about the Q. Ms. always contriving "to make themselves comfortable," when a ragged Confed. stepped from the ranks and wrote in large characters under the inscription, "Maj. —— will *hold his position at all hazards.*"

The men used to call shot or shell that passed over head and went far to the rear, "*Quartermaster hunters.*" Upon one occasion, at Petersburg, during a severe artillery fire, a gallant fellow with more humor than prudence—jumped upon the parapet, and pointing to a shell then passing over, exclaimed: "A little more to the right, a little more to the right, the Quarter-masters are *down behind that hill.*"

During the battle of Cedar Run Mountain, General Ewell got off a grim joke at the expense of a gallant Q. M. Seeing him at some distance, the General called out, "I say!—you man with the fine clothes on, come here." The order was obeyed and the old veteran asked: "Who are you, sir, and what were you doing there?"

"I am, sir, Capt. ———, Q. M. — Virginia regiment. I was only looking at the progress of the fight."

"Good Heavens" exclaimed the General, in well feigned astonishment—"who ever heard of a Quartermaster on a battle field? But since you are here, sir, I'll make you *useful as well as ornamental*," and thereupon he sent him with a message to Gen. Jackson, who was to be generally found during an engagement, nearer the post of danger than was pleasant to a non-combatant. The gallant Quarter master carried the dispatch, and brought back old Stonewall's reply, but says that he suddenly remembered that he had to see after his train and never went near Gen. Ewell during a battle again.

———

A certain Commissary of high rank used to ride a splendid charger, whose white tail and mane showed clearly that they were familiar with soap and water. As he passed some troops one day a ragged (if not dirty) private called out in stentorian tones: "Look, boys,—look at that horse's tail and mane. Thar is whar all of our soap is gone to, that's the reason we got no soap at the last drawin'"

EDITORIAL.

THE great danger now at the South is that the manhood, the independence, the integrity of the people will be destroyed,—a calamity, which the truly noble and high-toned at the North would deplore as much as we would ourselves. Every thing has been done to debauch the moral perceptions of our unfortunate section. We have seen treachery rewarded, wickedness triumphant, the honorable thrust down, the base elevated, honesty despised, successful villainy applauded, consistent adherence to principle crushed to the earth, sleek subserviency raised to posts of honor and power. We have seen culture, refinement, and virtue regarded as crimes, while ignorance, coarseness and vice were commended. We have seen the high-born reduced to beggary and the obscure rolling in luxury. We have known family names covered with obloquy, which had been revered for generations, while the vilest and meanest of mankind were suddenly transformed into honorable governors, judges, congressmen, mayors, aldermen, &c. All this is calculated to upset all previous convictions of the immutability of right, and to awaken the fear that honor is but a name, virtue a myth, and principle a folly. This appalling state of the public mind is fearfully aggravated by the false standard, which has long existed in America, viz: that success is the true criterion of merit. The millionaire has been honored though he made his fortune by fraud, peculation and knavery. The demagogue has been honored, who attained his position by appeals to the low instincts and passions of the mob. The lawyer has been honored, who succeeded in clearing the guilty by brow-beating and confounding the witnesses, or by some adroit legal quirk. And so in all the departments of human effort, failure has been construed into an evidence of weakness, and success has been regarded as indicative of superior ability. We have not stopped to inquire whether the failure was owing to uncontrollable circumstances, or to an unwillingness in the unsuccessful man to do a low and mean thing. Nor have we asked in regard to the fortunate individual whether fortuitous causes had not been in his favor, and whether he was scrupulous in the use of the means to advance his ends. The American people simply look at the *result*, and praise or blame as that result has been brilliant or otherwise.

The effect of this false system of reckoning is mischievous and only mischievous, when applied to individuals. It is absolutely monstrous, when applied to nations. We are now having the absurd doctrine thrust upon the South that our cause was wrong because it failed. Almost every page, certainly every chapter, of profane history demonstrates the falsehood of this teaching. The very men, who are loudest in proclaiming this hideous standard of right and wrong, acknowledge that their cause failed in the old world and that they sought a refuge from persecution in the new. Plymouth Rock is a perpetual monument of the failure of Puritanism in England. Will the descendants of the Puritans admit that their ancestors were sinners because of this want of success? Will they pretend that the mongrel, barbarous, and idolatrous nations, who desolated Palestine and scourged God's people, were more righteous than those they oppressed? Was the great Teacher of Christianity successful in his day and generation? He was denied by one disciple, betrayed by another, and deserted by all. Of the vast crowds, who attended his ministry, three women alone were faithful to him, when he died a death of shame and torture. His spotless life was a failure, according to the detestable maxims of these modern reformers. But we will draw an illustration from a man, whom they reverence a thousand fold more than they do the lowly Nazarene. Will the Tyngs, Cheevers and Beechers of the loyal North admit that the cause of the horse-thief and murderer, John Brown, was wicked, because the old villain perished upon the gallows? Have they not sung in Christian Churches and on the Lord's Day, "John Brown's soul is marching on?" If his death did not prove him a sinner, why does the death of the Confederacy prove the unrighteousness of the Southern cause?

When the Poles failed to preserve their nationality, did their want of success prove them greater sinners than the monsters, who partitioned their territory? Upon what principle, do these pretenders affect sympathy with Greece, Ireland, and Crete? Does not failure indicate the frowns of Heaven against the struggling nations? The loyal North ran wild in its enthusiasm over Kossuth and oppressed Hungary.—But Kossuth and his compatriots failed more ignominiously than Jeff. Davis and his Confederates.

La Vendée contained the purest, best and bravest population in France. Alison says of this people: "They were gentle, pious, charitable and hospitable, full of courage and energy, with pure feelings and uncorrupted manners. Rarely was a crime, seldom a lawsuit, heard of among them . . Religion, as might naturally be expected with such manners, exercised an unbounded sway over these simple people. They looked up with filial veneration to their village pastors, whose habits and benevolence rendered them a faithful image of the primitive Church." They were attached to the old order of things, they loved their country and their religion, they were devoted to their king, faithful to their wives, tender to their children, honest and upright in all their dealings.—Such principles could not fail to make them odious to the Jacobin leaders, and a ruthless war was waged against them. The skill and courage of their leaders, Lescure, La Rochejaquelin, Bouchamps and Cathelineau availed nothing. The dauntless heroism of their troops availed nothing against overwhelming numbers, superior discipline and more efficient equipments. Thurreau was sent against them, and anticipated by seventy years the fiendish policy of Sherman and Sheridan. "He formed twelve corps, aptly denominated *infernal columns*, whose orders were to traverse the country in every direction, isolate it from all communication with the rest of the world, carry off or destroy all the grain and cattle, murder all the inhabitants and burn down all the houses. These orders were but too faithfully executed ; the infernal columns pierced the country in every direction ; their path might be traced by the conflagration of villages, their footsteps known by the corpses of the inhabitants." (Alison, vol. 1, page 271.) We will digress here a moment, to remark that Sherman showed no originality in his "march to the sea." He but adopted and pursued the policy of Thurreau, whom the whole world execrates.

La Vendée was conquered and desolated. Her great leaders perished in battle. From a fourth to a third of her people died on the field or were butchered in cold blood. The infamous Barere announced, "La Vendée is no more; a profound solitude reigns in the Bocage, covered with cinders and watered with tears."—There is probably not a man living so lost to truth and decency, as to contend that the slaughtered Vendéans were more wicked than their Jacobin butchers.

The South was the La Vendée of the United States. Her conservatism, her love for the Constitution, her attachment to the old usages of society, her devotion to principles, her faith in Bible truth—all these involved her in a long and bloody war with that Radicalism which seeks to overthrow all that is venerable, respectable and of good report. Every student of history must have been struck with the resemblance of the South to La Vendée, both in the principles for which they fought and in the fate which befell them. It was a struggle with both for conservatism against lawlessness, infidelity, irreverence towards God and man, *radicalism*. Both gained prodigious victories, both exhibited miracles of courage and constancy, and both—failed utterly and hopelessly. If the failure of La Vendée be not construed into a token of the Divine displeasure, the misfortunes of the South ought not to have a different interpretation.

In all conscience, it debauches the public mind enough to see villainy triumphant and virtue oppressed. Save us from the dreadful doctrine that the triumph of the villain proves him to be a favorite of Heaven, and the suffering of the virtuous man shows that God is his enemy.—Away with this monstrous teaching which history and experience alike demonstrate to be false, and which the Bible utterly condemns. It is a sore trial of faith to see thieves rolling in luxury and honest men in rags. It is a sore trial of faith to see the hypocritical renegades in power and true men crushed to the earth.—Even David, the man of God's own heart, was startled by these things, and found it hard to preserve his unwavering belief in the over-ruling Providence. Even he compared the wicked to the green bay tree, the most flourishing of the trees of the East. But David looked again and the wicked had "passed away, and lo he was not: yea, I sought him, but he could not be found." The wisest of men has said, "the lying tongue is but for a moment." It is not possible that the mean creatures can long remain in power, who have reached their present height by falsehood in thought, falsehood in words and falsehood in deeds. The proverb says that "every dog must have his day;" and that is to be expected in the summer solstice, but we trust that the *dog days* will be short, and we look forward hopefully to the *shortening* days of November.

Our young men have a sad spectable presented to them.—They see worming, squirming, wriggling, writhing, twisting, crawling, fawning renegades become governors, judges, congressmen, presidents of railroads, mayors, aldermen, &c., &c. A voice seems to come from these loyal dignitaries to our ambitious youth, "be vile like us and you too shall have your reward!" Let none of noble instincts listen to these dulcet notes of syrens (whining of curs?), but let the ingenuous youth reflect rather that "the name of the wicked shall rot" while "the memory of the just is blessed." The fortunes of Washington were at a very low ebb, when Arnold was rewarded for his treachery, with ten thousand guineas and a high command in the British Army. But the loyal traitor is despised throughout the world, while the rebel, who was true to his own people, is revered by the whole human race. Gen. Hampton, in commending the example of Washington to the young men of his country, thus eloquently alludes to this disastrous period:

In these days, when justice is forgotten, honor laughed to scorn, truth scoffed at; when the foundations of the great deep of morals are shaken to their center, and when falsehood and perjury are disguised under pleasant names, we may well call on our young men, in whom lies the future hope of the country, to mould their being from the noble model presented by his. Let them learn from the study of his history that truth was the firm basis on which his great character was formed; and let them remember that, if the devil is the father of lies and of liars, no true excellence of character can be attained where the corner-stones are not truth and honor. When Rome could apply the epithet "*mendax*" to Greece and speak of "lying Greece," the land of Aristides and Socrates was but a subjugated province, whose people were slaves.

Follow as closely as you can in the footsteps of our great countryman; and though it may not be given to you to reach that grand height to which he soared, you can at least, like him, walk through life in the path of duty, and be supported as he was, in the hour of death, by that blessed faith which springs alone from the faithful discharge of every duty to one's country, to his fellow-man, and to his God.

Greeley says that the Republican party is the representative party of American ideas. Let us see how this is: Butler, with his spoons, represents honesty; Bingham, with Anne Surratt cowering at his feet, represents chivalry; Thad., with the "lady and sister," represents chastity; honest Ben., with his oaths, represents reverence; Boutwell, with his "hole in the sky," represents science; *Colonel* Wilson, with his champagne bottles at Centreville, represents strategy; Gen. Schenck, reconnoitering in a railroad train at Vienna, represents progress in the art of war; Gen. Banks represents improvement in the Commissariat; General Burnsides, with the New Berne (N. C.) pianos, represents music; General Sherman, with his bummers, represents charity; Gen. Sheridan, burning barns and mills, represents Ceres, (excuse the gender;) Gen. Grant represents eloquence; Grant, Pére, with mule and monkey, represents history; Mullins, of Tennessee, represents the spread-eagle; Beecher, with his novel and theatricals, represents theology; Tyng and Cheever represent brotherly love. Truly a representative class of loyal worthies!

But not content with such a display of representatives among the great leaders of the party, they have appointed 500,000 moral lights in the shape of loyal officials, which should dispel the darkness of ignorance and the gloom of rebellion. The gentle, lovely and accomplished Mrs. Cady Stanton tells us, that these 500,000 officials are all thieves! We would not for the world be so deficient in courtesy as to differ with this charming lady, even if our experience was different from hers. But it isn't! Estimable lady! we believe you to be a model of truth and a miracle of frankness! May your shadow never be less!

We have hitherto mentioned the distinguished honor, which our city (?) had bestowed upon her in an address delivered by Hon. W. D. Kelley of Philadelphia. His audience was intensely small, but select, composed of different races and colors; all, however, of kindred souls and kindred tastes. The Judge gave a glowing picture of the wondrous fertility of the Southern soil and of the vast mineral wealth of our *F*etich-ridden section. He was particularly ardent in his admiration of Alabama, perhaps his admiration was somewhat fired by his warm reception at Mobile.—We don't know certainly how that may have been, but he is reported to have said:

Alabama has more natural wealth than all the New England States together. Alabama abounds in iron, while New England is without any, save a little bed of ore on the borders of Connecticut and Massachusetts, so small that it would scarcely be noticed, amid the broad veins of heaven enriched Alabama. She has no coal, while coal and limestone in immense deposits lie in close proximity to your beds of iron ore. New England can grow but little wheat, corn or rye—so thin and sterile is her soil in many places, that her people sow rye, not for the grain, but for the straw to manufacture into hats and other articles, and so wide apart do the stalks grow, that at the proper season, children find employment in plucking it stalk by stalk, and laying them down perfectly straight, that those who are to work them into fabrics may have them at their greatest length. In my dear Pennsylvania, it will be late in August, before the wheat is ripe, but yours in favored parts of the State is now (the spring) ready for the sickle.

Now it is a little remarkable that all these enthusiastic eulogies upon the vast resources of this region come from the very men, who are inaugurating a system, which is fast turning it into a desolate wilderness and is driving out of it all the respectable people, who can raise the means to get away. The persistency of these eulogists in a course of conduct, which they *know* can have no other result, is well calculated to raise the suspicion that their object is to get rid of the owners of the soil, so that they themselves may come in and take possession. We earnestly hope that they have had no such design, but they could not have taken a more effectual course to bring about this end. There are thousands here, who believe that these men have devised a systematic and well-considered scheme to make the lands of the South worthless, that they may get them for a trifle, or for the simple occupation. There has not a single emissary of the party of hate and ruin visited the South, who has not gloated over the richness of the lands. This uniformity of sentiment among all their orators does look like they had been casting greedy and covetous looks upon these fertile fields. History often repeats itself. An incident similar to this took place 2,800 years ago.

A certain king wished to buy a vineyard from one of his subjects, and he was willing to give a fair price for it, (here the parallel fails.) But the subject replied, "I will not give thee the inheritance of my fathers." Then the king became very sad and was "heavy and displeased," after the manner of the pure Thaddeus when impeachment failed. But the wife of the king was a strong-minded woman, and she devised a scheme by which the vineyard of the rebel could be got very cheap, yea, without costing a farthing. The man was a rebel against the wishes of his sovereign, and had no right to life or property. (See letter of Gen. Sherman in elucidation of the law of nations.) So they killed him and the joyful king went down to take possession of the beautiful vineyard. But the terrible prophet of the Lord met him and said: "in the place where dogs licked the blood of Naboth shall dogs lick thy blood, even thine." And the prophet said of the strong-minded woman: "the dogs shall eat Jezebel by the wall of Jezreel."

Now, the most instructive part of this true story is this: the dogs which licked the blood of Ahab, and the dogs which ate the flesh of Jezebel were *their own dogs*, which they had fed, trained and caressed. Just here the story has a fearful resemblance to what we now see going on. These covetous Ahabs and these covetous Jezebels (for there are strong-minded women among them,) are feeding, training and caressing a breed of renegade dogs, which are more ferocious than those which craunched the bones of the miserable woman by the wall of Jezreel. The first act in the tragedy, the murdering of Naboth has been played, the last act may come in its season.

Blackwood's Magazine ontains the views of J. Q. Adams in opposition to coërcion of Sovereign States. Would the old man eloquent have changed his opinions as easily as did Mr. Lincoln?—Who knows?

"The indissoluble link of union between the people of the several States in this Confederation," said John Quincy Adams, President, and son of a President, "exists, after all, not in the *right*, but in the *heart*. If the day should ever come—may Heaven avert it!—when the affections of the people in these States shall be alienated from each other, when the fraternal feeling shall give way to cold indifference, or collisions of interest shall fester into hatred, the bonds of political association will not long hold together parties no longer attracted by the magnetism of conciliated interests and friendly sympathies; and *far better will it be for the people of the disunited States to part in friendship from each other*, than to be held together by restraint. Then will be the time for reverting to the precedents, which occurred at the formation and adoption of the Constitution to *form again a more perfect union by dissolving that which could no longer bind*, and to leave the separate parts to be united by the law of political gravitation to the centre."

The writer in Blackwood adds

this comment upon these views of Mr. Adams:

Happy would it have been for all America if the North had been of this opinion in 1861. Happy will it be for them now if such sentiments shall animate the majority, on whichever side it shall declare itself.

It is probably not generally known that the only Theological Seminary for colored people in the whole United States is in the *town* of Charlotte, N. C., which some jocular persons got incorporated as a *city*. A characteristic incident has taken place in this young seminary. A loyal student, inflamed with the desire to imitate other loyal personages of eminence and renown, put his hands in the pocket of a fellow-student and Butlerized his pocket-book. He was taken to the head-quarters of loyal men, the county jail, and at this writing, is in durance vile. Be not discouraged, emulous youth! your loyal conduct will make you an immense favorite with loyal men everywhere.—Our loyal Judge, who so recently left the Maine penitentiary, will hail you, in a double sense, a "man and *brother*." It would be a graceful and appropriate thing in our Fetich Chief to pardon you, and appoint you chaplain in ordinary to our loyal Legislature.

WANING LOYALTY.—A fractional piece of currency valued at twenty-five cents has come safely to our office, all the way from Owensboro, Kentucky. This is the first evidence we have had of flagging zeal on the part of the loyal Post Office officials. We hail the auspicious omen with unqualified delight.

OUR ADVERTISEMENTS.—We feel it to be a duty to call attention to the *home* schools advertised in this magazine. Washington College, with its illustrious Head and able Faculty. The Virginia Military Institute, enshrined in our hearts by Stonewall Jackson's connection with it. The teachers there are all men of thorough scientific attainments, but we think that we make no invidions distinction when we note the fact that Maury and Brooke have a world-wide reputation.—The Institute, we believe, furnished more distinguished officers to the Confederacy than any dozen Colleges of the South combined.

The Medical College of Virginia, at Richmond, is well worthy of the patronage of the South. The University of Maryland is entering upon its 61st Session.—In addition to all the advantages afforded by the more Northern Colleges, the students have the benefit of the refined and cultivated society of Richmond and Baltimore, and association with ladies and gentlemen of congenial tastes and sentiments.

Washington University of Baltimore has a Faculty composed entirely of Confederate Surgeons, all gentlemen of large experience and extensive reading.

It is a little remarkable that the University of Pennsylvania, with its intense Radicalism, is better patronized by Southern students, than conservative Jefferson College, numbering among its distinguished Faculty, Prof. S. H. Dickson, so long and favorably known at the South.

Davidson College has the largest building and the best endowment in the South. Its Faculty is inferior to no other in this section, and now that the loyal Fetich have closed the University, we hope to see this meritorious Institution have the patronage it so richly deserves.

ARIEL.*

6. We consider his argument from the Fall of Man. The wonderful discovery is made that the Fall of Man was occasioned by the *Negro!* who was Adam's Tempter in the Garden of Eden! "The intelligent cannot fail to discover who was the tempter in the Garden of Eden. It was a *beast, a talking beast*, a beast that talked *naturally*. God called it a beast 'more subtle than all the beasts the Lord God had made.' As Adam was the Federal Head of all his posterity, as well as the real head, *so was this beast, the Negro, the federal head of all beasts and cattle, down to creeping things.*" *! !*

This being so, then these consequences follow: 1. As Federal Headship implies not only intelligence, and intelligence of the highest degree, but also moral responsibility, and therefore presupposes personality, moral agency, then of course the Negro being a federal head, must also be a person, moral and responsible, and therefore has a soul, and is no beast. 2. The intelligence of this federal head of the beasts, the Negro, proved to be superior to the intelligence of Adam himself, the federal head of men!—3. The curse pronounced upon the *Negro*, who was the Serpent, the Tempter, was, that *he should go upon his belly, and eat dust all the days of his life! !* He was not to eat *his* bread in the sweat of his brow—*he doesn't do it now!*—for that was the sentence passed upon Adam's race; nor were negro women in sorrow to bring forth; but both were cursed above all cattle, and were to go upon their bellies, and eat dust all their days!! 4. As the Bible teaches us, that the *Devil* was Adam's Tempter, and really says nothing of the shape of the Tempter, then the Negro is the Devil, and the Devil is a beast! 5. Although Adam had dominion given him over *all* the beasts of the field, yet the Negro, a beast, and the federal head of all beasts, got dominion over him, and so "all beasts and cattle, down to creeping things" in their federal head, the Negro, got dominion over Adam's race! Thus Adam's race fell under the

* Continued from page 378.

power of the Negro, the Tempter; so that the people of the South now have *precedent* for their condition—which is the just and natural one—viz: *under the power of Niggers!!* And into this condition the whole country is bound to come. So that, the sooner the Radicals manufacture *another* "Constitutional Amendment," recognizing *Nigger Federal Headship*, and *Nigger Dominion*, the sooner will be better "the best government the world ever saw!!"

7. We consider his argument of the Negro causing the Unpardonable Sin. "The crime of amalgamation, or miscegenation of the white race with the black—*mere beasts of the earth*—is" he says, "the most awful crime that man can commit in the sight of God"—"all, all the crimsoned crimes of earth, or within the power of man's infamy and turpitude to commit and blacken his soul, are as nothing on earth, as compared with this"—"this unforgivable sin"—"cannot be forgiven by God, *never* has been forgiven on earth, and *never will be*"—"cannot be propitiated by all the sacrifices earth can make or give." That amalgamation should involve social degradation and loss of caste, on the part of the superior race, is right and proper. But that it is a *sin unpardonable, of itself*, and, therefore, that the parties are doomed, necessarily, to inevitable damnation, *even though united, formally, by marriage*—is a piece of most monstrous folly, to assert. According to this dogma, every one who was *once* guilty of this sin, is infallibly damned!—For there is no repentance and no forgiveness, for it. Every mulatto, then, is the sign of the Unpardonable Sin! the token that the white parent is certain of damnation! And as the Law of God required, that "If a man lie with a beast, he shall surely be put to death; and ye shall slay the beast"—and in some States this is also the law—then, the white, and the black, and the mulatto, must all be put to death!

Again. It seems that not only the human race are guilty, but that also "mere beasts of the earth" are "involved in the same *sin*," "*moral criminals* in the sight of Heaven"—although they have no souls! We consider,

8. His argument of the Negro originating profanity, idolatry, and demon-worship. "Then began men to call upon the name of the Lord." "These *men* who then began to call upon the name of the Lord, were *negroes*—the "men" so named by Adam, when he named the other beasts and cattle. This cannot be questioned." "That the calling was profane, is admitted by all our ablest commentators and Biblical scholars, as may be seen by reference to their works. See Adam Clarke. The Jews translate it thus: 'Then men began to profane the name of the Lord.'" Now, in the first place, the word "men" is not in the Hebrew at all! Properly rendered, the words are, "Then it was begun to call upon the name of the Lord." This is death to his theory. In the second place, "the calling on the name of the Lord" is *not* admitted by all the ablest commen-

tators and scholars, to be profanity. A bold ignoramus only would have ventured such an assertion. The great majority of commentators and scholars condemn this view.

Calvin says: "It is a foolish figment, that God then began to be called by other names; since Moses does not here censure depraved superstitions, but commends the piety of one family which worshipped God in purity and holiness, when religion, among other people, was polluted or extinct."

Pool says: " 'To call upon the name of the Lord;' to worship God in a more public and solemn manner. Some render the place thus: 'Then began men to profane the name of the Lord.' But this seems neither to agree with the Hebrew phrase, nor to suit with this place, where he speaks of the posterity of Seth; who were the holy seed, and the only church of God then in the world." Even Adam Clarke, to whom Ariel particularly refers, holds the same view with Pool. And this is one of many proofs, that no dependence whatever can be placed upon even the quotations of this scribbler. Clarke shews what his opinion is by these words: "As the followers of God, at this early period, found it indispensably necessary to separate themselves from all those who were irreligions and profane, and to make a public profession of their attachment to the truth; so it should be so now." He refers the opinion, originally, to the Jewish Doctors, that the words signified "profaning the name of the Lord." Most of them, he says, held that view. But on examination, we find, that great difference of opinion existed even among them.

Onkelos, the Chaldee Paraphrast, renders it, "Then began men to pray." But the Chaldee in the Masorites Bible says: "Then in his days, the sons of men left off from praying in the name of the Lord."

In the third place, even if the word "men" were in the Hebrew, and if the word "call" means "profane," how could *beasts* "profane the name of the Lord?"—Neither worship, nor the abuse of it, profanity, can be predicated of a creature that has no soul.—Again. He tells us, "that the law of God, that 'no man having *a flat nose* shall approach unto his altar,' includes the whole negro race, and expressly excludes them from coming to His altar, for any act of worship!" If all flat noses are excluded, then many white men are flatly excluded! And also, every one blind, lame, broken-footed, broken-handed, crookbacked, every dwarf, every one with a blemished eye, or any blemish, are, by the same law, excluded! But it is the flat-nosed man "*of Aaron's seed,*" that is specified! See Leviticus 21:17, 18. But if it be forbidden to negroes to engage in an act of worship, what will Ariel make of the following passages? which, according to his canon of criticism, must refer to negroes, as, in each, "men," not "the men," is found: where the prefix "*the*" is wanting, he says, the reference is always to negroes:

"Let us make *negro* in our image."—"The preparations of the heart in *negro* are from the Lord."—"Blessed is *the negro* whose strength is in Thee."—"Son of *negro*, I have made thee a watchman."—"He hath shewed thee, *O Negro*, what is good. And what doth the Lord *require of thee*, but to do justly, and to love mercy, *and to walk humbly with thy God?*" Again: He tells us, that if the negro be left to himself, "to the worship of demons he will go. *Not so with Adam's children.*" And yet the Bible tells us, that "the Gentiles sacrificed to devils, and not to God." 1 Cor. 10:20; and that *even the Jews* sacrificed, not only to idols, but "to devils, and not to God"—Deut. 32:17; yea, that they did even "sacrifice *their sons and their daughters to devils!!*" Ps. 106:37.

9. We consider his argument of the Negro causing the Flood. Miscegenation again, the curse of the old world! Only one man kept himself pure. Noah only "was perfect in his generation." 'Generation' should have been translated 'genealogy.' "Any English scholar will see at once, that, to make sense, it should have been *genealogy*. 'He was a preacher of righteousness, the husband of one wife.' The 'righteousuess,' then, that Noah preached, was *anti-amalgamation!* Keep your genealogy pure! Keep clear of the negro, and the one thing needful is accomplished, multitude of sins are covered, and Heaven is secured! But the "sons of God" would not heed the anti-amalgamation Gospel. They *would* marry the "daughters of men." "These daughters of *men* were *negroes*, and these sons of God were the children of Adam and Eve." "God determined to destroy the world by a flood, for the crime of amalgamation, or miscegenation of the white race with that of the black—mere beasts of the earth."

Now, to these silly vagaries, we reply: 1. That if he understood the Hebrew tongue at all, he would have seen that while in our version the same word, "generations," occurs twice in the verse quoted, "These are the generations of Noah: Noah was a just man, and perfect in his generations, and Noah walked with God," in the Hebrew, two widely different words are used. The first is *tohldoth*, which signifies also *genealogies*—"these are the *tohldoth*, generations, or genealogies, of Noah." The second is *dohr*—"Noah was perfect in his *dohr*"—which *never* signifies *genealogies*. It comes from a verb, signifying *to move round in a circle*—hence, *an age*, *a generation*, the *revolving period or circle of human life*. In order that "any English scholar may see" what "sense" it will make, to "translate it, *genealogy*," we cite the following passages, where *dohr* occurs, and instead of "generations," the proper rendering, we will give Ariel's substitute, "*genealogy:*"

Deut. 32:5. "A perverse and crooked *genealogy*."

Deut. 32:20. "A very froward *genealogy*."

Ps. 24:6. "The *genealogy* of them that seek Him."

Ps. 33:11. "The thoughts of His heart to all *genealogies.*"

Ps. 49:19. "He shall go to the *genealogy* of his fathers."

Ps. 90:1. "Thou hast been our dwelling place in all *genealogies.*"

Ps. 145:4. "One *genealogy* shall praise thy works to *another.*"

Prov. 30:11. "A *genealogy* that curseth their father."

More than a hundred similar passages could be quoted, but "any English scholar" will, doubtless, be satisfied with these.

2. As to the "daughters of men being *negroes,*" it is sufficient to kill this interpretation outright, to state that, in the original, the words are "daughters of *the* men:" the prefix "*the*" occurs: and according to Ariel, this invariably denotes *Adam's race.*— "The daughters of the men," then, were the children of Adam, and not beasts.

10. We consider his argument of the Negro causing the Confusion of Tongues, and the Dispersion of the Nations. "It appears from the Bible," says he, "that Nimrod was not entirely cured, by the flood, of the antediluvian love for, and miscegenation with, negroes." "Nimrod's hunting was not only of wild animals, but also of *men*—the negro—to subdue them under his power and dominion." "It was Nimrod that directed the great multitude that assembled on the Plain of Shinar. This multitude *were mostly negroes.*" "These Babel-builders *knew that they were but beasts.*" "The Confusion of Language *was confined to those there assembled.*" All this being so, then these inferences follow:

1. If these Babel-builders were beasts, then they were *most wonderful beasts* to build such a City and Tower! But he forgot all this, afterwards, when he tells us, that "the negro builds nothing for ages to come, but like any other beast, his building is only for the day." Surely, the Tower of Bable was a wonderful structure, an illustrious proof of human genius! If these builders were negroes, there is no evidence that they were "directed" by Nimrod, or any one else. They certainly went at their work with a wonderful *vim.* There was unity of purpose, and great concert of action, and their aim was certainly *very high.* They said, "Let us build us a city and a tower, whose top may reach unto heaven, and let us make us a name." Ambition, enterprise, skill, perseverance, genius, certainly characterized these builders; and if they were beasts, they were most wonderful beasts, rather ahead of men now-a-days!— And if they were negroes, they were wonderful negroes, such as are not now to be found on earth!

2. If "the confusion of language was confined to those there assembled," who were "negroes"—who "knew that they were but beasts"—then, variety of languages is characteristic, exclusively of negroes, or beasts, and *not of Adam's race.* Cousequently, this variety of tongues proves that those among whom it obtains are negroes, or beasts! But it obtains amongst Whites. Consequently, Whites are Blacks, or Beasts! It is nonsense, too, for Missionaries to go to foreign

lands, and acquire the language of *beasts*, in order to save souls, where there are *no souls* to be saved! For the variety of tongues was a curse upon *beasts*, and as the Bible tells us that "the Lord did there confound the language of *all the earth*," then all the earth is made up of *talking beasts*, and the race of Adam is extinct!!

But the Bible plainly shews us who the Babel-builders were.—"The Lord came down to see the city and the tower, which the children of *the* men builded."—The prefix "the" is found here; so that, according to Ariel, "the men" denote the children of Adam. Thus, this most unfortunate, suicidal rule of his, is perpetually cutting the throat of all his theories! Again: The Bible plainly tells us, from whom the nations were descended, that were divided after the flood: "By these were the isles of the Gentiles divided in their lands; every one *after his tongue*, after their families and their nations." "These are the sons of Ham, after their families, *after their tongues*, in their countries, and in their nations."—"These are the sons of Shem, after their families, *after their tongues*, in their lands, after their nations." "These are the families of the sons of Noah, after their generations, in their nations; *and by these were the nations divided in the earth after the flood.*"

STUDIES IN THE BOOK OF PSALMS: Being a Critical and Expository Commentary, with Doctrinal and Practical Remarks on the Entire Psalter, By WM. S. PLUMER, D. D., Author of "The Bible True," "The Grace of Christ," &c., &c. Philadelphia: J. B. LIPPINCOTT & CO.; Edinburgh: A. & C. BLACK, 1867, pp. 1,211:

This generous volume has evidently been the product of many years of love and study, running parallel with the many other labors of the same prolific mind and pen. And the work selected to be done—a Commentary upon the Psalms for the whole Church—is one of the noblest and needfullest in religious literature.

The Book of Psalms has long been as the conduit of the Pool of Siloam to the people of God; whither all the springs from beneath the Temple sought their way, to reach the light. All the aspirations of a worshipping, praying, exulting, weeping world have found a voice here, and its weariness and sorrow have come hither for solace and refreshment. The shadow of the earthly Zion, and the sunbeams of Divine compassion and promise, alike fall here. These "Studies" are a sort of "Porch" beside the Pool, where we may linger, and steep our hearts in its healing and invigorating waters, and catch the voice of many others, rejoicing in its sweet fulness.

And while it is not quite clear to us that the venerable author's plan is, in one respect, presently to be named, the very best for his own purpose; his book is so rich in its selections and compilations, and so abundant in wise and pithy remark, that it remains, by far, the most valuable aid to the study of the Psalms, outside of the Sacred Word itself.

That fault, in our judgment, is one of *excess.* The Commentary proper is a vast mosaic. The preface contains quotations from fifty-three uninspired authors, and some of them are quoted more than once. The study of the first Psalm quotes twenty-five such authors, some of whom have not contributed to the preface. How great the temptation is to this excess, we will be better able to imagine when we learn that nearly a century ago, *more than six hundred* commentaries on this Book were enumerated, besides those included in expositions of the whole Bible, and those devoted to particular Psalms!

The result of this excessive accumulation of expositions is, not only that one is often left in doubt, which one of the many is the true account, but also that an air of uncertainty is cast over the exposition as a whole. A superficial and partial reader would get an impression that the Book of Psalms was a kind of debatable ground—an impression utterly at variance, of course, with the experience of Dr. Plumer, and of all devout and loving hearts.

Waiving this one objection, there is everything to praise. The English of the "Studies" is of the very best for its purpose; terse, forcible, translucent; usually simple, but not afraid of a "hard word" that is necessary to the thought; dignified throughout, and as quaint, at times, as unaffected dignity may be; while occasionally the fervidness of the language verges upon declamation without actually reaching it.

The "Doctrinal and Practical Remarks" come in for the larger share of this praise. They are often rather apothegms than "remarks"—pointed, shrewd, proverb-like. Thus, that common weakness of Church members of the masculine gender, their professed inability to take part in social prayer, is hit off with the saying—"it is a bad thing for a Christian to be possessed by a dumb devil."

Here is a pithy caution: "all other flattery would be harmless, if we did not flatter ourselves."

And here, a pregnant formula: "in the end it shall infallibly be seen that he who serves God is the only wise man."

We commend this book, therefore, as an inexhaustible treasury of instruction in one of the very most precious portions of the one Divine Book. Let all who would dig deep there, and drink deep, avail themselves of this aid.

A. F. D.

BURKE'S WEEKLY, Macon, Ga.—This is, we believe, the only attempt at the South to afford a weekly paper to boys and girls. It is most admirably done, and we know how eagerly the lads and lassies in one family look forward to the expected feast of good things.

THE LAND WE LOVE.

No. VI. OCTOBER, 1868. Vol. V.

SKETCHES OF THE CAMPAIGN OF 1864.

Walker's Division—Retreat up Red River—Battle of Mansfield.

SKETCH NO. 1.

BY COLONEL T. R. BONNER, 18TH TEXAS INFANTRY.

"A thousand glorious actions that might claim
Triumphant laurels and immortal fame,
Confused in clouds of glorious actions lie,
And troops of heroes undistinguished lie."

[*Addison's Campaign.*

To make some record of their endurance, prowess and bravery, is due both to the surviving soldiers of the Trans-Mississippi Department, as well as to the memory of their gallant companions in arms, who so fearlessly met their death in the camp and on the bloody field.

In giving a few desultory sketches of those movements and scenes which came under my immediate observation, and "which I saw, and of which I was a part," I shall attempt to pen only their brief outlines, and those incidents more immediately connected with Walker's division of the army, to which I had the honor to belong. I shall be content if I can but impress more deeply upon the memory, the toils, hardships and glories of our gallant army, and incite others to record their certain recollections, for the benefit of the future historian.

Though vanquished in the final result—though the principles for which we fought, and for which our comrades died, seem to be forgotten in the blind passions of the hour—yet we have the proud satisfaction to know that our defeat was accomplished by a brave and overwhelming foe; and they must, and ever will do us the justice to say, that they "met a foeman worthy of their steel."

On the 13th day of March, 1864, the renowned infantry division of Major General Jno. G. Walker, composed exclusively of Texans, and which then numbered about 5,000 effective men and officers, abandoned its winter encampment near the town of Marksville, Louisiana, and commenced the memorable retreat up the Red River valley, before the exulting and boastful army of Gen. Banks. This division was composed of three brigades, the 1st consisting of the 8th Texas infantry, commanded by Col. Overton Young, the 18th Texas infantry, Col. W. H. King, the 22d Texas infantry, Col. R. B. Hubbard, and the 13th Texas, dismounted cavalry, Colonel A. F. Crawford, and commanded by Gen. T. N. Waul. The 2d brigade, commanded by Gen. Horace Randall, consisted of the 11th Texas infantry, Colonel O. M. Roberts, the 14th Texas infantry, Col. Edward Clark, the 28th Texas, dismounted cavalry, Col. Eli H. Baxter, and Lieut. Colonel Gould's battalion, dismounted cavalry. The 3d brigade, commanded by Gen. Richard Scurry, consisted of the 16th Texas infantry, Col. George Flournoy, the 17th Texas infantry, Col. G. W. Jones, and the 16th Texas, dismounted cavalry, Col. Fitzhugh, and the 19th Texas infantry, Col. R. Waterhouse.

On the day after our departure from Marksville, Fort De Russey, situated on the bank of Red River, three miles from that town, was surrendered, with its garrison of 400 Texans, after a brief and futile resistance to a combined land and naval force of the enemy. This garrison was composed of detached companies, one from each regiment of Walker's division, and commanded by Lt. Col. Bird, of the 14th Texas infantry. Nothing was saved from the fort, except two large 32-pound Parrot guns, which, by order of Gen. Taylor, commanding the District of West Louisiana, were removed before the arrival of the Federal forces, and accompanied our division on its retreat. These huge guns, transformed into field pieces, and each drawn by a *dozen yokes of oxen*, presented such a novel appearance, that when first seen by our troops, they created no little merriment. A witty soldier, incited by the comical idea of artillery drawn by oxen, exclaimed, at the top of his voice, "here goes your *Bull* battery;" and by that appellation these pieces were afterwards known during the entire campaign.

For several days after our retreat commenced, we were closely pressed by the land forces of Gen. Banks. His cavalry sometimes dashed upon the rear of our column, and as our command consisted of infantry alone, our duties were necessarily much more arduous than they would otherwise have been. In addition to heavy guard and picket duties, we were sometimes compelled to march during the whole night. About the 20th of March, we were joined by the infantry division of General Alfred Mouton,—composed of one brigade of Louisiana troops, (Mouton's brigade) and one brigade of Texans, commanded by the French Gen. Polignac,—and by the 2d Louisiana cavalry, commanded by Col. Vincent. On the night of the 23d of March, we bivouacked in the piney woods near Carrol Jones', a wealthy free negro, about 35 miles west of Alexandria, which city had already surrendered to Gen. Banks.

Notwithstanding the gloomy weather—the violent storm of rain and sleet which fell while we were at this point, every thing betokened the greatest activity, and the prospect of stirring scenes was brightened every day.

Gen. Richard Taylor had taken the field in person, and had immediate command of our little army. The Missouri and Arkansas infantry, under General Churchill, had been ordered from Gen. Sterling Price's army, of Missouri and Arkansas, to reinforce us, and the renowned cavalry division of Gen. Thomas Green, was on the march from Texas, and daily expected to arrive. The foe, encouraged by our continued retrogade movements, were becoming bolder, and even more daring. Our troops, accustomed to retreat,—owing to the vast territory over which we so often marched, extending from lower Louisiana to the Arkansas River, and the rapidity with which the enemy could concentrate his forces on the large streams which penetrated these two States,—calmly obeyed their leaders, and confidently awaited the result of coming events. Walker's division, unlike many other troops, in the service, had so often advanced and so frequently retreated, owing to the causes already stated, that to do either, had become to them alike a matter of indifference.

But while in the camp near Carrol Jones', an event occurred which spread a momentary gloom throughout our little army. The splendid cavalry regiment of Col. Vincent, which had so recently joined us, was posted, under direction of Gen. Taylor, as advanced pickets, on the Alexandria road. While the infantry were enjoying their quiet slumbers, the first for nearly two weeks, a large detachment of Federal cavalry, guided by some citizen traitor, made a circuitous march during the night and attacked Col. Vincent's command in the rear, capturing nearly 400 men, besides the guns and men of Capt. Edgar's Texas battery of artillery. In consequence of this severe loss and the non-arrival of the expected troops from Texas and Arkansas, Gen. Taylor declined making a stand at this point, which had been previously contemplated. We immediately recommenced the retreat, which was continued to four miles beyond Mansfield on the road to Shreveport.

In the meantime, that magnificent body of cavalry, known as "Green's old division," and two or three other brigades of Texas cavalry, all under command of that illustrious hero and chieftain, Gen. Tom Green, had arrived, and were daily engaging the enemy, chastising him whenever he ventured to make a dash upon our slowly retreating columns. The whole country, far and wide, was aroused to the highest pitch of excitement. The inhabitants all along the route of our retreat, were hurriedly quitting their homes, and flying before the approach of the invader. Consternation and alarm everywhere prevailed among the citizens. Old men shouldered their guns and came to our assistance from the interior of Texas. Notwithstanding every effort had been made by our leaders to collect as much available force as possible, to meet the impending danger, yet the great distance of the troops' in Arkansas, and the want of facilities for transportation, the advance of the Federal Gen. Steele through Arkansas, who had already crossed the Ouachita River, driving before him the army of Gen. Price, and intending to form a junction, about the middle of April, with General Banks, at Shreveport, prevented the concentration of more than about 10,000 men at Mansfield. The army of Gen. Banks, in our immediate pursuit, was composed, as we have always understood, of the 19th army corps, with the 16th corps in supporting distance.—Besides these two corps, Admiral Porter, with an immense flotilla of gunboats and transports, had ascended Red River to within about 40 miles of Shreveport. But with his apparently inadequate force, Gen. Taylor here resolved to give battle, and to this end every preparation was made on the night of the 7th of April.

The sun of the 8th as it rose majestically in a cloudless sky, presented to the view of the astonished inhabitants of Mansfield, the divisions of Walker and Mouton marching proudly back to meet that foe before whom they had so long retreated. As we passed through the streets of the beautiful town, they were thronged with fair ladies—misses and matrons—who threw their bright garlands at our feet, and bade us, in God's name, drive back the Yankees, and save their cherished homes. As their cheerful songs of the Sunny South fell in accents of sweetest melody upon our ears, we felt that we were indeed "thrice armed," and though greatly outnumbered, *would* drive back the foe. Alas! how many brave hearts which thrilled with patriotic emotion that morning, as we marched with flying banners through the town, were stilled in death before the last gleams of that day's sun rested upon the field of carnage! How many strong men, as they listened to the voices of those maidens, and thought of their own loved ones at home, had ceased to think, or speak, or breathe, before that day had gone!

At 12 o'clock, our division, in consequence of the near proximity of the enemy, after marching, and countermarching, and manœuvring, formed its line of battle in the edge of a large field about four miles from Mansfield, immediately on the right of the road leading to Fort Jessup. The division of Gen. Mouton occupied a similar position on the left of the road, and half a mile from it. The intervening space between the two divisions was filled up with several batteries of artillery, some of which were in position on an eminence a few hundred yards in front of the the main line. The cavalry of Gen. Green, except that portion then skirmishing with the enemy, had been dismounted and occupied the left of our line. Here we remained, inactive, for about three hours, awaiting the expected attack of the foe, during which time, the firing of our cavalry skirmishers became each minute clearer and more distinct.

This calm before the storm—the period which immediately precedes the conflict, when it is apparent that the deadly contest is near at hand—is more trying than even the battle itself. Unsustained by the reckless excitement and wild furor of the actual strife, the strongest mind must then shudder at the fearful thought that a few short moments more may usher the soul into eternity!—Fondly, Oh! how fondly do we then recall the homes and dear ones far away, and the heart grows faint and sick with the thought that, perhaps, for the last time, these associations rush upon the memory! In such a moment the hero is lost in the man!

Suddenly, at about the hour of half past two o'clock, we were aroused from our momentary reverie by the rapid firing of the artillery, followed in quick succession by the loud, long volleys of small arms, on the left of our line, which plainly announced that the work of death had indeed commenced. The division of the brave, but now lamented, Gen. Mouton, numbering less than 3,000 men, had attacked a superior force of the enemy in strong position. For 20 minutes the echo of their guns swelled upon the breeze, and for 20 minutes an awful feeling of intense anxiety and suspense filled the minds of the troops not engaged in the conflict. The firing ceases—in a few minutes a courier comes dashing over the hill —the dispatch is handed to Gen. Waul—the moment is an anxious one, fraught with eagerness to learn, yet dread to hear the result. But soon the spirit-stirring word of "victory" is conveyed to us from the General—Mouton had attacked the foe, and though he himself had fallen, and many of his daring soldiers had shared his fate, yet they had borne the banner of the "stars and bars," again to victory. Soon a column of 1,000 captured federal prisoners and 6 pieces of artillery, marching towards Mansfield, confirmed the glorious tidings. Then did our long pent up suspense give way to the wildest emotions of joy. As the welcome notes of triumph passed from regiment to regiment down to the right of the line, a shout of exultation, loud and long, echoed and re-echoed far over the field, bearing congratulations of success to our victorious comrades, and foreboding a repetition of defeat to the astonished foe.

This was the turning point of the whole campaign, and to the indomitable courage and glorious success of this first charge of Mouton's division may we safely ascribe that series of brilliant achievements in the valley of the Red River, which shed such additional glory upon the Southern arms. Just at this critical period defeat would have been ruinous. But now our division, animated with the reckless exuberance of feeling produced by unexpected success, was anxious to be led into action, and as the command "By the right of companics to the front" rang out loud and clear upon the evening air, every man moved quickly off with confident and determined step. Passing through the large field in our front, then through a skirt of timber and into another field, we beheld the enemy in position on the opposite side. Here we formed by companies into line, and passed Gen. Walker, the idol of his division, and with a shout of defiance marched steadily forward. The enemy greeted our coming with a perfect shower of leaden hail, from both artillery and small arms, but we dislodged them without firing a gun. 'Twas a sublime, yet appalling spectacle to see those noble men of Waul's brigade, while their comrades were falling mangled, bleeding, dying, press on, and still on, with a steady, unwavering step, and fill up their broken ranks, at the quick, stern command "Close up! close up!" Their determined resolution to conquer gave an irresistible power to their advance, and the astonished and amazed Federals fled in confusion. Then arose again that shout of triumph. It was answered first by Randall's, then by Scurry's brigade, and soon the whole cavalry force of Gen. Green took up the strain, filling the earth and the air with the unearthly yells of nearly 10,000 victorious Texans. The movement had been simultaneous and successful along the entire line.—Everywhere the enemy had been routed and disorganized. Urged on by the excitement of victory, we pursued the flying foe, killing where they dared resist, and capturing them by hundreds. Their officers rallied them again and again, but as often as they paused were they compelled again to retire.

They finally succeeded in making a stand at a field 7 miles from Mansfield. Here, for a short time, a stout resistance was made, and a desperate conflict ensued. But it was to no purpose. We rushed upon them and again they fled. This momentary stand, however, gave time for the formation of a large Federal reinforcement, consisting of the 16th army corps. Entirely unconscious of the arrival of these fresh troops, which were formed at the upper edge of the field, their lines extending far over the hills on either side of the road, we pressed on after those we had already defeated. By the time we had passed half way through the field, which enclosed a large peach and plum orchard, our flying foemen had taken shelter behind the line of their reinforcements. Then came the terrible shock. Volley after volley resounded from the hill, and shower after shower of bullets came whizzing down upon us. It was utterly impossible to advance, and to retreat beneath the range of their long guns seemed equally desperate. Never shall I forget that moment, and what soldier that was there can ever cease to remember the "Plum Orchard" fight. We lay down, arose again, and then involuntarily sought such shelter and protection as the ground afforded. Encouraged by their leaders, our brave men attempted again and again to charge, but human fortitude and human bravery were unequal to the task. Even Napoleon's "Old Guard" itself must have quailed before that terrible fire. The very air seemed dark and hot with balls, and on every side was heard their dull, crushing sound, as they struck that swaying mass, tearing through flesh, and bone, and sinew. The position of our line could have been traced by our fallen dead.—Within a few short moments, many a gallant spirit went to its long home.

We were compelled to retire. As soon, however, as we reached the timber, the men were rallied, and though the sun had gone down behind the hills, and night was fast closing upon that bloody scene, still it was resolved to make another effort to take the hill. Again the line was formed and the order given to charge. Right gallantly did we commence the task, but the enemy were fully prepared for our reception and reserved their fire until we had advanced to within 100 yards of their position. Then their rifles belched forth a bright red sheet of flame along their whole line, lighting up the expiring day with an unearthly glare, while the thunders of 10,000 guns resounded through the heavens, and seemed to shake the earth to its very centre. For our wearied and almost exhausted troops to oppose such fearful odds with success, was utterly impossible, and the attempt to dislodge the enemy from his stronghold, proved as unfortunate as it was ill-advised. Many a brave man, for there were no craven hearts in this last charge, whose life might have been saved to his country and his family, was slain in this vain attempt to drive the enemy. Had the battle closed when we first received our check in the orchard, no page in the history of the war would have recorded a more brilliant Southern victory than that of the battle of Mansfield. As it was, much of the prestige of success gained in the day, was lost in the blood of the fearless, undistinguished heroes, who fell in this deadly night charge.

Having retired from the contest, unpursued by the enemy, our broken regiments were again reformed. Waul's brigade, placed in line of battle across the road, occupied during the night, the front of our army, only 300 yards from the enemy's line. The remainder of our infantry forces, "watch-worn and weary," truly slept upon their arms, and silence—save the moans of the wounded and the groans of the dying—soon fell upon that field where late was heard the din and crash of battle.

Thus commenced and closed the memorable battle of the 8th of April. If we except the Louisiana brigade of Mouton's division, it was fought by Texans alone. We were sorely repulsed at night fall, still we justly claim it as the greatest victory of the Trans-Mississippi Department.—But though glorious, it was dearly won. Among the killed, I cannot refrain mentioning the names of the young and gifted Lieut. Col. James W. Raine, of the 8th Texas infantry, and Col. James R. Taylor and Lieut. Col. Noble, of the 17th Texas infantry. These were personally known to the writer, and no truer spirits died in defense of the Land we love. The remains of the lamented Col. Raine, have been removed, by his father, to Kentucky, his native State, since the war. Besides these from our own Texas, there were Cols. Armand and Beard from Louisiana, besides many other officers and men from both these States, who, though gallant and brave, rest to-day in unknown graves.—Though their names are forgotten, yet their glorious deeds will live in the hearts of our people, as long as we shall continue to cherish the principles for which they contended.

Col. Wilburn H. King, of the 18th Texas infantry, a native of Georgia, was severely wounded during the last charge of this battle. His skill as a regimental commander, and his daring intrepidity on this occasion, led to his promotion as a Brigadier General, which position he held with credit to himself and benefit to the cause, until the termination of the war. It is impossible for me to make individual mention of all those who, that day, sacrificed their lives upon the altar of our country; but many a once happy Texas home now mourns the loss of some brave soldier who, that night, slept in death upon the sanguinary plains of Mansfield.

TRANSITION.

"BRILL-ON-THE-HILL," ALA.

How soon will end the summer days!
Though thick and green the forest leaves,
Already Autumn's golden haze
About the woods and hilly ways
A veil of tender radiance weaves.

Oh! what is in the Autumn sun,
And what is in the Autumn air,
Makes all they shine and breathe upon,
Ere yet the summer days are gone,
Look so exceeding sweet and fair?

E'en weeds, that through the summer rain,
Grew wanton, and o'er topped the flowers,
—Rude children of the sunburnt plain,
Bud out and blossom, not in vain,
Around the summer's faded bowers.

For long ago the violets fled,
The pansy closed its purple eye,
The poppy hung its uncrowned head,
And on the garden's grass-grown bed
The lily laid her down to die.

No more the roses bud and blow;
The few late beauties that remain
Are tossed by rough winds to and fro,
And all their fragrant leaves laid low,
And scattered by the latter rain.

Like some old limner's quaint design
The sunlight's checkered play doth seem,
And through the clusters on the vine,
As through a goblet filled with wine,
Soft, shimmering sparkles gleam.

The red-checked apples thickly grow
About the orchard's leafy mass,
But when they hear the tempest blow
Through twisted boughs they sliding go,
And hide within the tangled grass.

No more the partridges' whistle rings;
The dove her plaintive cry has ceased—
From tree to tree, on restless wings,
The mock-bird flits, but never sings;
The west-wind rocks an empty nest.

All harmonies of Summer fail!
The vaulting insects cease to sport;
The songs of bees alone prevail,
The wingéd traffickers that sail
From flowery port to port.

Upon the hills and in the fields
A few pale flowers begin to blow,
A few pale buds the garden yields,
A few pale blooms the hedge-row shields;
Summer consents not yet to go.

Oh! yellow leaf amid the green!
Sad presage of the coming fall,
Soon where your withered tint is seen
Shall Autumn's gorgeous banners screen
Th' incipient ruin over all!

Though sadly to ourselves we say
'The summer days will soon be o'er,'
Yet who may tell the very day
Whereon the Summer went away,
Though closely watching evermore?

With sailing clouds the heavens teem,
That beckon like impatient guides,
And like the gliding of a stream,
Like thoughts that mingle in a dream,
The summer into autumn glides.

She goes! and leaves the woods forlorn.
For grief the birds refuse to sing;
Bare lie the fields that laughed with corn,
But of each garnered grain is born
The certain promise of the Spring.

KAMBA THORPE.

CHICAGO, one of the two wonders of America, is on the western shore of Lake Michigan, about thirty miles above its southern extremity.

The Chicago River flowing into the Lake here, forms the only harbor to be found from the mouth of St. Joseph's River, in Michigan, to Milwaukee, Wisconsin, a distance of two hundred and fifty miles, which can afford protection, or wharf room, to a score of vessels at a time. This is the true secret of Chicago's greatness. Without this sluggish gash in the Lake shore, she would have remained to this day a little prairie village; with it she is—what she is. Any man, even without the gift of prophecy, who knew anything of agriculture, or the vast producing capacities of our Western territories, must have foretold the immense advantages of her situation and the greatness of her future.

Long before the exigencies of war had caused the erection of Fort Dearborn, on the site of the present city—long before the gleam of the white man's musket menaced the Indian in the hunting grounds of his ancestors, nature had lavished upon this spot her most benignant influences.

Millions of acres of the most fertile lands in the world, where Ceres herself might hold her celestial court, radiate from it on every side save one, and on that one is the best harbor on the whole of our five great Mediterrean Seas. Nothing remained for man to do, but to gather up the gifts so profusely showered upon him.

But if Chicago was thus geographically fortunate, the Pontine Marshes could not have been more inhospitable than the location in itself. The shore is but a few feet above the level of the Lake, and the greater portion of where Chicago now stands was formerly under water for half the year. Fort Dearborn might have been described as a block house with a sea of water on one side, and a sea of mud on the other, and no man ever attempted to traverse the latter during the winter months, except on horseback. The geological formation was a black, slimy ooze, furnishing about as secure a basis for building as soap-suds, and this was for many years the greatest drawback to the prosperity of the city.

It was overcome at last, and in a manner which furnishes a remarkable illustration of the genius and indomitable energy of the people: but of this more anon. When we understand the situation of Chicago we will be better prepared to take up its rise and progress. The Chicago River, which is in reality but an arm of the sea, extends inward in a direct line from the Lake, for about three-fourths of a mile, and then branches off into two streams running in opposite directions. The letter T may be taken as a rough sketch of the harbor, the base resting on the beach.

Thirty miles of wharves now line this stream, and give Chicago one of the most commodious harbors in the world. Scarce a shipping house in the city but has its back door opening on a wharf or basin of its own.

The mouth of the inlet was once choked up with a sand bar, but in 1834 a timely freshet swept it away, and subsequent dredging has rendered it deep enough for the largest vessels along its whole length.

In 1830 the population of Chicago consisted of four families, or less than twenty-five persons, excluding the garrison of the Fort, and the only vessel ever seen was the little schooner sent there twice a year by John Jacob Astor, for the furs collected by the Indians. Now upwards of four hundred vessels are frozen up during the winter months as securely as if they were on the coast of Spitzbergen, and her shipping aggregates 218,215 tons, while the population may be estimated at 230,000 souls.

The year 1831 may be taken as the nativity of the Chicago of today. During that year emigrants began to swarm in, and it soon became a brisk trading post with the Indians. These latter, for several years, hovered around the place and retarded its progress, while they corrupted traffic; but in 1835 they were moved off to the far West and the face of the Red man was seen no more within its precincts.

During this year (1835) the population increased to nearly four thousand, and then was inaugurated that watchword of Chicago, "corner lots." They were eagerly sought after, not so much for their then actual value, as for the confidence which her inhabitants felt in the future opulence of their city, and the historian must even say for the Chicagoans that, now, as then, this noble self-confidence and independence is the main-spring of their prosperity. No outside pressure has been required to stimulate their enterprise, and for their present they are indebted to themselves alone.

The general depression throughout the country in the year 1837 was a sad blow to Chicago.—Emigration was checked, business stagnated, and city property became an emetic to its owners.

Some of the richest men in Chicago, to-day, owe their wealth entirely to their inability to dispose of their lots at any price during that year of gloom.

But even then the day of her greatness was beginning to dawn, and from that time her sun has loomed steadily toward the meridian.

In 1838 was shipped the first bag of grain from what is now the largest grain market in the world, not even excepting Odessa. The growth of this trade has been one of the most marvellous facts in even this country of marvels, and to it, principally, Chicago is indebted for her present position in the commercial world. The table below shows its increase through successive years in the item of wheat alone.

YEAR.	BUSHELS.
1838.	78
1839.	3,678
1840.	10,000
1841.	40,000
1842.	586,907
1845.	1,000,000
1847.	2.000,000
1853.	1,689,798
1855.	7,110,270
1857.	10,783,292
1860.	16,054,379
1862.	22,902,765

The total shipment of grain for for the year 1867, may be estimated at 60,000,000 bushels.

Such figures need no comment, in themselves they read like a fable; but the end is not yet, the chronicler of 1900 will probably go up into hundreds of millions, if, indeed, he do not discard mathematics altogether. The facilities for receiving and distributing this vast quantity of grain have been brought to perfection in Chicago. Any one of the seventeen tall elevators in different parts of the city will unload and load a vessel with incredible rapidity. They are worked by steam. A vessel loaded with grain can come alongside, and in a few minutes the wheat or whatever it may be, will have gone a hundred feet into the air and down the opposite side of the elevator into another vessel, or cars, which will carry it to its destination. The situation of the city conduces to this in a very favorable manner. If the banks of the river were high as in St. Louis, or the water-level variable, the difficulties of this transfer would be very great.

But Chicago is also the greatest cattle market in the country, and the development of that trade has been no less astonishing.—Three thousand cattle were slaughtered, packed and shipped in 1839, and since then the strides have been gigantic. No regular statistics can be obtained for the successive years, but during the last three the number either killed or shipped alive, has averaged 300,000 per annum.

It is very difficult for the mind to conceive with accuracy of numbers, but comparatively easy to understand distance. If these 300,000 cattle averaged nine feet in length they would extend in a straight line, without any intervals, 511¼ miles, or computing five hundred pounds to the animal they would produce 150,000,000 lbs. of beef, which, sold in New York for 25 cents, would amount to $37,500,000.

Lumber too plays a conspicuous part in the traffic of Chicago. The immense prairies which stretch for hundreds of miles around the city, and which are rapidly being peopled, are almost utterly destitute of building material. This need, Chicago takes it upon herself to supply, and the vast forests which shroud the upper waters of Lake Michigan furnish an inexhaustible resource. Six hundred and fourteen millions of feet of timber were sold in 1866, and the yards extend for miles along both sides of one fork of the river. One house in Chicago can furnish anything in that line, from a pine board to a ready made village, and will forward, on receipt of price, to any part of the country, either cottage, church, court-house or towns.—These buildings are securely packed and can be put up in a very short time.

The mind, startled by these figures, naturally enquires for the causes of this unparalleled progress. They lie first in the natural advantages of the place, and secondly in the energy of its inhabitants. For years all the exports of Chicago were hauled into the city in wagons over miry roads and with incredible toil, but in 1836 was begun the canal which connects the Chicago River with the Illinois and the Mississippi. This canal, completed in 1848, opened to Chicago the wealth of an immense territory, and brought its produce into her markets.—The Chicago and Galena Railroad was also completed in 1850. Up to this time the Chicagoans had looked with a considerable degree of coldness upon Railroad enterprise, but when in 1853 this railway paid a dividend of 11 per cent. they were awakened from their lethargy, and began to realize the possibilities of their situation.

Since then their chief aim has been to extend their roads into every producing acre of the State, and so indomitable has been their energy that Chicago has, in a few years, become the greatest railway centre in the world.

The system of which she is the centre includes nearly 10,000 miles of track, and the whole State is reticulated with her roads.

It is computed that the average distance of the farms in Illinois from a railroad is only about seven miles. A passenger train reaches or leaves the city every fifteen minutes during the twenty-four hours, and at least two hundred trains arrive or depart in a day and night.

Here is the explanation of her growth. Here is the index to her prosperity.

Chicago collecting the wealth of such an immense territory could not be other than what she is. But her ambition rests not here. Ship canals, which shall connect the Mississippi with the Atlantic Ocean are projected, and this generation will probably see the enterprise inaugurated.

In short, everything which Science can aspire to, or energy undertake, or skill consummate, she has made the instrument of her progress, and on the banner nailed to the mast-head, and in the hearts of the people is inscribed the motto—Chicago Excelsior.

Having sketched the rise and progress of Chicago, we will now describe her as she is. Chicago will not impress the stranger as a beautiful city—there is too much monotonous level and too much smoke—but she has many and very great attractions. The buildings on the best streets are in general, large and fine, and some of the private residences on Wabash Avenue aré among the most elegant in America.

The public buildings are commodious and elegant, and the churches superb. Some of the latter soften the sterner lineaments of religion by encouraging social gatherings, and are provided with complete kitchen and restaurant apparatus, and contain suits of apartments in which the ladies of the congregation give entertainments twice a month.

Education is worshipped here as a tutelary deity. Colleges and academies are numerous, and the free schools are among the most ornate and durable structures in the city. Thousands of children irrespective of color, are yearly educated at these last. One of the most striking edifices is that where the Board of Trade meets. Here in a spacious room, ornamented with fine fresco paintings, the principal business of Chicago is transacted. From a thousand to eighteen hundred of the grain and lumber merchants assemble here every day to buy or sell, and to learn the prices current in the different markets of the world. In a very few minutes fortunes are lost or made, men are ruined or enriched.

The proverbial impossibility of building castles in the air has been falsified here, for Chicago has been raised twelve feet in the air and the earth built up to it. For years the quagmire on which the city was built reduced the inhabitants to despair. Planking was tried, but for half the year the wagons projected, from between the crevices in the planks, graceful jets of marshy ooze in every direction, and in very wet weather the thoroughfares floated about like pontoons. Ditching both sides of the streets was then tried, but it only made the matter worse, and at length Chicago was convinced that no resource was left but to raise the level of the city.

Three different grades have been established at different times, until now the city is elevated twelve feet above the Prairie. The huge Tremont House, one of the most massive hotels in the United States was raised bodily into the air and ten feet of earth thrown under it. Whole blocks of stores were raised at the same time.

The mythic conflict between Typhon and Osiris was here fought out once more, and again Osiris has triumphed, for nowhere will you find a better paved city than Chicago of to-day. In some places the old struggle continues, and you can get a sectional view of the successive strata, but the principal thoroughfares are excellent, and many of the streets are paved with that boon of metropolitans, the Nicholson pavement.

Owing to the peculiar shape of its harbor, Chicago is essentially a "City of Bridges." Every street, whether running North or South, East or West, crosses the river. The delay at these draw bridges is often prolonged and annoying on account of the numerous craft which ply in and out of the harbor. On some days, when the wind is favorable, a hundred vessels will be wafted in at once, and then transit is interrupted for hours. At such times long lines of vehicles extend up the streets on either side, and oaths and shouts wrangle in the air.

This is another obstacle which Chicago has set herself to overcome with her usual enterprise, and soon tunnels under the bed of the river will connect the opposite streets.

The suburbs are handsome and picturesque. The streets leading along the shore of the lake, as they get beyond the feverish turmoil of the business centres, wind among beautiful villas surrounded by luxuriant gardens. The smoke which envelops the city in a murky cloud extends not to these sylvan retreats, and the Genius of Repose broods over them with folded wings. It is to be hoped that red brick walls will never stare each other out of countenance across these now beautiful avenues.

It is proposed to encircle the city with a shady drive like the Boulevards of Paris, and I believe the work has already commenced. A great park is also in contemplation, of which one of our writers humorously remarks:

"It is not unlikely that the park will enclose a range of mountains, the loftiest peaks of which will pierce the air half a hundred feet; and up those giddy heights Chicago's boys will climb on Saturday afternoons, inhale the breath of liberty on the mountain-tops, and learn why Switzerland is free."

The city is supplied with water by a tunnel, which runs out under the lake two miles.

This triumph of engineering skill was completed during the past year, and thereby the water is insured to be cool and pure, uncontaminated by proximity to the foul slime of the harbor.

By an ingenious arrangement at the lake end the water is filtered as it pours into the tunnel.

When the work was finished, and before it was opened, the Mayor and Common Council, with some gentlemen of the press, went out to see the wonders of the deep from a submarine point of view. They were greatly relieved when, after groping for an hour by torch-light, they came safely to the surface in the midst of the lake far out from the land. The Chicagoans consider this enterprise one of the miracles of the age, and are inclined to think the Croton Aqueduct of New York comparatively an insignificant affair.

About four miles out from the city on the flat prairie, two feet below the level of the lake, are the famous "Stock Yards." Two millions of dollars have been expended here in the construction of a cattle market. The company owns nearly a square mile of land—three hundred and forty-five acres of which are already enclosed in cattle pens, and one hundred and fifty acres of these are being floored with plank.

This great "Cattle City" is laid out in streets crossing each other at right angles, the principal of which is called Broadway, and has accommodations for 75,000 hogs, 20,000 cattle, and 20,000 sheep. The facility with which immense droves of these animals are driven in and out is astonishing. The principal entrance and street is partitioned by fences into three parts—on the right are the droves going in, on the left those coming out, and in the centre walk the drivers. When the cattle are sold they are driven to the yards adjoining the railway and are weighed in passing *at the rate of thirty a minute.* Here they are placed on cars and shipped to their destination.

Nine railroads have branches connecting with this cattle city, and a canal to the river will soon be commenced. Here also is a large hotel of yellow stone called the Hough House, and near by another beautiful edifice, called the Cattle Exchange, in which is a telegraph office, which is constantly reporting the price of beef, &c., in the markets on both sides of the Atlantic. There is also a bank in the building which does a business of from one hundred thousand to five hundred thousand dollars per day, solely with these cattle men. With all this prodigious business a man might live in Chicago for a year without seeing or hearing a cow, sheep or hog.

Chicago has the reputation of being one of the most immoral and dissolute cities in America, but if depravity is more noticeable there, I fancy it is because she has not acquired the same dexterity in concealing it, which our older cities have attained.

The fabulous progress of the place, and the El Dorado ideas entertained regarding it, attracts a crowd of adventurers who would corrupt any place in Christendom, and as in all new cities vice makes a desperate stand for supremacy.

There is an anecdote to the effect that a Chicagoan dying recently, aspired to enter Heaven. St. Peter, at the gate, enquired whence he came, and being answered, "Chicago," said reflectively, "Chicago, Chicago.—No you don't—there's no such place. I never had an application from there before."

So the Chicagoans when they die, instead of going to Heaven, must rest content in the beautiful cemeteries near their city, of which there are five.

This city is the Paradise of discontented married men, for it is more easy to procure a separation than a wife, and the number of divorces during the past, bear a very respectable proportion to the number of marriages.

The good people of Chicago are very fond of amusements, and will sit in wretched theatres and see tragedy murdered, and comedy smirked with a patience perfectly marvellous. They have the finest building yet devoted to the Thespian Art, in the United States—the glorious Crosby Opera House—but they cannot yet support the Opera. Every attempt heretofore has failed, and one of the Chicago papers not long since said in disgust that, "The majority of the people don't know the difference between a symphony and a sardine." This has all the spice of antithesis which is often more forcible than truth, so whether it contains the latter is a superfluous inquiry.

The Press, that mighty lever of modern civilization, is well represented in Chicago. Six great dailies with seventy weeklies, monthlies and quarterlies supply the intellectual wants of the people, and a more able, high-toned, generous, and liberal Press is not to be found anywhere in our land.

In their hands we can leave the future of Chicago.

While the Press does its duty, no City, nor State, nor Nation, can retrogade—the march must ever be onward. *It* must educate the people. *It* must be the great conservator of the public weal, and as progress, without education, is a pyramid resting on its apex, the Press must ever be responsible for the permanent prosperity of the city; for *it* is the Palladium in which are deposited, as of old, the pledges of the City's safety.

TO ST. MICHAEL'S BELLS.*

JULY 4, 1868.

Oh bells! that your sweetest chimes ring out
So jubilant, and so gay,
Do ye well, to chime for a rabble rout,
For a negro holiday?
Of cannon that roared this day's salute,
Not a single gun was our's.
Our bells! could not you be sternly mute?
Need *you* hail the reigning powers?

Crushed in the foul Desolator's track,
Long, shattered you lay, and dumb,
From your treasured fragments conjured back,
Gladly we welcomed you home.
Shame, that you join in the glee to-day
Of those who trample us down!
Better that still in the dust you lay,
Of our burned and ruined town!

Cease! lest we loathe the silvery chime
We have loved so long and well.
Cease! bide ye your people's coming time,
In proud silence ev'ry bell!
Or if ye ring, thro' the still night air,
Oh! chime out a solemn toll.
Up, with each stroke, ye shall waft a prayer
For a hero's parted soul!

---

* Carried for safety to Columbia, broken to pieces there by Sherman's men, sent to England and re-cast, hung again in Charleston last year.

WAR-SKETCHES FROM THE LIFE.

No. 1.

DANCING UNDER SHELLS.

AMONG the strange varieties of the late War, I recall one which strikes me as specially unique.

I was in Charleston for some months in the winter of 1864, and attended several parties which the youth of the city found charming. One of these, I particularly remember. It was at a house just "out of range" of the Parrot shells, etc., with which the enemy favored us. The young officers of the 1st and 2nd Regulars, and the Light Dragoons, flower of our "chivalry," were those who most enjoyed these breaks in the monotony of war.

How we look back and number over the graceful forms in the brilliant artillery uniforms, or the privates in citizen's dress, equally of our first and oldest names! Ah! how do we think of the number now lying low around Petersburg, at the Wilderness, in the last sad fields of North Carolina! Who shall say their fate was not the brightest? Who of us would call them back to humiliation and despair? Rather let us remember them as they fell, at their brightest and their best. And the brilliant little parties of which I speak are glowing spots in my memory, for to those poor fellows they gave great pleasure, and their pleasures were few, hardships innumerable. It was a strange feeling to glance round at those officers, many of them mere boys in years, and remember how they had held Fort Sumter when the magazine was breached, and not an inch of the Fort bomb-proof. Held it when the suffering was so great that veterans from Lee's army begged to be relieved. Others of the dancers had been the heroes of Wagner and Gregg, others had shared the glory of Pocotaligo, where the foe were literally "ten to three." I cannot describe the mingled feeling of reverence and compassion, I, an older woman, felt for these noble boys!

The furniture of our party-room was droll. An ancient hired piano, all the odds and ends of chairs and sofas which were not worth removing, bare floor waxed for dancing, curtainless windows gracefully draped with ivy and evergreens generally, wood fires in the grates and very bad gas constituted the embellishments. But the musicians of the St. Cecilias had not forgotten their cunning, and the waltz and galop was as sweet as the richest salons. During the early part of the evening to which I refer, no shells came, but at supper-time our fun grew more funny. The game and oysters, eaten with pewter forks and spoons—(silver buried) out of all varieties of china (sets sent to Cheraw for safety!), the punch made of whisky, (Bee sale,) in soup tureens, and drank out of everything from tumblers to coffee-cups, seemed particularly exhilirating. Everybody sat where they pleased, and groups ate supper at all manner of small tables, growing merrier and merrier.—The enemy seemed to suspect something "was up," and began shelling furiously. The whole air was filled with the roar of huge Parrot shells, and the house trembled as each rushed in. We could hear the crash into a house and then the explosion of each within a square or so of us.

Then our fun reached its climax! It was madly delightful to think how we were enjoying ourselves while their impotent fury roared around us. A distinguished Colonel at my table remarked:

"If the roof of this house were taken off and by a magic reflector the Yankees could see us just as we are now, I think they would give up shelling in despair!"

So we drank another toast—to the shells of course—and forming into a glorious German, we danced and the shells roared, and we ignored them, except to dance the more gaily to their roaring, until the unfortunate band-master showed me his left hand cramped into an impossibility of longer performance. So our dance ended. Back to Fort Sumter, Moultrie, James Island, Battery Beauregard and the Lines, rowed and rode our heroes. The gallant creoles of "the Staff" took an easier trip to head-quarters, and the belles retired to dream of the various combinations of grey, red, blue, and buff, and to wake late next morning under a firm impression that the shelling had ceased as soon as their heads were laid on their pillows—an error their late partners might have very truthfully corrected.

Oh happy, youthful hearts! which of ye beat so lightly now? Gone the high hopes, vain the noble courage, the uncomplaining fortitude, all in vain! No! not in vain! We have the undying memory of great things borne and done, and it is God's decree no heroic act is done in vain, even though our eyes cannot see its end. We failed—it was His will—but we are the nobler for the struggle, and we struck for the right, right manfully—the end was not our's to rule.

THE CHANGE.

So you are married. Well I'll not complain,
  Or with reproaches greet the new-made bride;
Or urge the fullness of my love. 'Twere vain
  To argue from it, and him by your side.
But tell me why, on one soft summer night,
  In voice that mingled with the murmuring pines,
You bid me love, and said your heart's good might
  Was in its love, and strong in its confines?
And you did tell me watch the fleecy cloud
  That floated listless in the blue above;
And said how like the silent, pearly crowd
  Of vapor was to woman's tender love;
For they were bright and golden-edged when
  The warm-lipped sun kissed their moistened cheek;
And come in purple for the joy of men,
  Cleanse the impure and emulate the meek.
And oft a dainty bit of paper told
  The history of a heart within a page—
The facile pen spoke earnestly and bold,
  And wailed my absence as a woeful age,
And on some like Patchouly-scented sheet
  You urged me softly come to you again
With open heart your own full heart to greet—
  To speak the love whose silence gave you pain;
That you had taught your soul how very sweet
  It was to love and to be loved by one,
Who gave no artful words arranged to cheat
  A confidence. And said your soul was won,
While every "P. S." held within its space
  A well wrought love, epitomized in word:—
And yet I cannot see in your calm face
  The danger that I trustingly incurred.
Your eyes are grey but truthful in their gaze,
  And hold a day-full of benignant light,
While over all your countenance there plays
  A well expressed emotion of delight.
But now, methinks that *you* have proved untrue,
  It is an easy thing to love another,
And any well instructed heart can do

As you have done—forget an absent lover.
Farewell grey eyes—no light of yours is mine;
And rosy lips, you owe me not a kiss;
For me no more a loving light will shine,
Or there recall th' once beguiling bliss.
And smooth white hands no more th' electric touch
Will send my heart full throbbing to my throat;
And soft-toned voice whose wooing power was such
That Love swore fealty to its primal note:
Good-bye to these and each associate grace
And all that Love distinguished in your mien.
I hope no dream will shadow out your face
To fill my slumbers with its faithless sheen.
I hope no inconsiderate memory may
Retain concealed within some sacred nook,
When faithful spirits nightly kneel to pray,
The still remembrance of a word or look,
To bring when years have placed a waste between,
And I forgetting deem myself forgot,
A vision of the Past whose lovely sheen
Shall fill my soul and light the lethean spot.
The years were long and man uncertain:—true;
But less perfected hearts beat still the same;
And prayed that He might lead us safely through
And bring the loved ones, loving home again.
Through four long years their souls were with the Grey,
Whilom, the God of Battles, pierced their heart,
And bade us yield the Flag, the Cause, the Day—
Of cherished love they gave no single part.
But you were fain to drop a single tear
For our great loss, and turn to sunny life,
To strangely counsel with a growing fear,
And make yourself the victor's radiant wife.

Memphis, Tenn. HENRY P. PARR.

GEN. LEE AT THE "WILDERNESS."

BY R. C——, OF "HOOD'S TEXAS BRIGADE."

IN reading the February number of "The Land We Love," your correspondent read with unfeigned pleasure the able article under head of "*The Lost Dispatch*," which was a partial criticism upon E. A. Pollard's "Lost Cause"—a work that assumes the glorious task of recording truthfully the deeds and experience of Confederate arms, but which, in fact, prostitutes its pages to abuse of our late President, and in giving incorrect, unfair and impartial statements of both actors and their acting. In "The Lost Dispatch" the position is well taken that the *true* history of our late struggle will be the labor of that historian, who dilligently collects from every source possible, the information oral and written which those who were actors are able to give, and upon this data of fact build, in an honest and impartial manner, the glorious historical structure which is to tell future ages and generations of the gallant struggle which the Southern people made for their liberty and independence. From the Field Marshal to the humblest private in the ranks, each has a rich store of information—and as a thousand mountain rills go to form the deep and fast rolling waters of a majestic river—so will these varied and multifarious sources, from whence will flow the correct history of our late war, have to be consulted before truth can place her seal upon any writing that assumes to be a history of the Confederate States upon land and upon sea.

An humble participant in the late war, I take upon myself the liberty of seeking in your columns a brief space for the purpose of mentioning and preserving from error, an important incident of the late contest—which deserves to occupy one of the brightest pages upon our country's history. I come prepared to state what I saw and what I heard, and not what was reported to me through many mouths—I shall be brief—for were my pen able, no ornamentation from it, could add to the glory and grandeur of the main fact that I shall state.

That Gen. R. E. Lee exposed his life during the battle of the "Wilderness," May 6th, 1864, is generally known to the Southern people—but the truth of the affair has never, to my knowledge, been given—I have read accounts, both in prose and poetry, of Gen. Lee's noble conduct on the eventful 6th of May—but however near to the truth of the case—and were written, perhaps, by some who "snuffed the battle from afar," and gathered their records from those who fled the face of danger—the truth is this.

In the fall of 1863, Gen. Longstreet, with two divisions of his corps, (Hood's and McLaws') was ordered to Georgia to reinforce Gen. Bragg. This we did, and participated in the battle of "Chickamauga," after which we were ordered to Knoxville, Tennessee to lay siege to the place, and which was done without success.

In the latter part of April 1864, Gen. Longstreet found himself and corps in the vicinity of Bristol, on the Virginia and Tennessee line. About May 1st, 1864, we took up the line of March, and were transported to Cobham station, on the Virginia Central Railroad, near Charlottesville. At this place new clothing, guns, bayonets, ammunition and ample provisions were issued to our corps, and we were reviewed by Generals Lee and Longstreet. At that time our corps contained only the two divisions that Longstreet took with him to Georgia. During our stay in Georgia and Tennessee, Gen. Hood was made a Lieutenant General, and Major Gen. Field assigned in his place. Maj. Gen. McLaws was removed and Brig. Gen. Kershaw, of South Carolina, made a Major General in his stead, and my old brigade, "Texas," was placed under Brig. Gen. Jno. Gregg, of Texas—vice Brig. Gen. Robertson removed.

We took up the line of march from Cobham station about the 2nd or 3rd of May—which, I now forget—and continued on a steady march until the night of the 5th, going into camp about 7 or 8 p. m. Late in the evening of the 5th we heard the report of cannon, and were informed that we were near Gen. Lee's army. We did not know at the time that the grand battle of the "Wilderness" had begun on the 5th, and merely deemed the report of cannon "a feeling of the enemy's position." At this time, as I had been for several months, I was acting on Gen. Gregg's staff as courier—and in a position to see and know all that I have, or may hereafter relate.

By 3 a. m., on the morning of the 6th, the long roll beat, the men were aroused, under arms, and the march soon began. We moved steadily on, though rather at a rapid pace, with the "Texas Brigade" leading the van of Gen. Field's division. By daylight, or perhaps a little later, we had reached the turnpike known as the "Fredericksburg Turnpike." By daylight the boom of cannon, and the distant rattle of small arms, were borne upon the breeze, and knowing that the two armies were immediately facing each other, we recognized that a grand battle had begun, and we would soon be called upon to act well our part. Reaching the turnpike, we took the direction leading to Fredericksburg, and before going very far not only was our speed accelerated, but Gen. Kershaw's division (the other division of our corps) occupied the pike side and side with us, and thus situated, the two divisions moved rapidly down the pike in the direction of the firing —the men of separate commands mingling one with another.—

When moving down this pike, the sun rose beautifully, but to the notice of all had a deep, red color, and the brave Gen. Gregg, upon seeing this, remarked to those who were riding near him, "there is the sun of Austerlitz"—a prophecy that found verification ere it sunk to rest among the sombre shades of night. The nearer our steps led us towards the firing, the din of battle became louder and more terrible.—Faster and faster our columns moved on to the scene of conflict, until we were almost at a double-quick. Directly horsemen came dashing to and fro; aids were cantering about; ambulances containing the wounded went flying to the rear; litters with their unfortunate burdens were moving towards the hospitals; stragglers without number were flocking back with tales of distress, annihilation and defeat—all these signs betokened that bloody and desperate work was going on, and that too not many yards distant. A half mile more, and by 6 o'clock, we found ourselves upon the scene. Both of our divisions mingled together in one mass upon the turnpike.—As a part of this narative, I will give the situation of affairs as we found them upon our arrival at the scene, and a short or imperfect idea of the ground.

The position where we found ourselves upon being halted, was near the brink of a hill which gradually sloped down for the distance of 200 yards, where immediately began the dense undergrowth known as the wilderness. The turnpike led over and down this hill and continued on into the wilderness. Immediately at the turn of the hill, where the turnpike or plank-road passed, hasty breastworks were partially constructed and under construction; and along these were strewn a body of stragglers that had been rallied, as well as some half dozen pieces of artillery that were playing upon the dense wilderness below. Near this hasty defense we fonnd, upon our arrival, our loved commander-in-chief, Gen. Lee, Gen. Longstreet, their staffs, and body-guards. I have often seen Gen. Lee, but never did I see him so excited, so disturbed—never did anxiety or care manifest itself before so plainly upon his countenance. If I mistake not he was almost moved to tears—if in error, others share it with me, and his voice was anxious and tremulous. And well, kind reader, may his anxiety have been great. The evening before, Gen. A. P. Hill, with the divisions of Generals Wilcox and Heath, had met the enemy upon the ground before us, and night found them victorious. That night, (May 5th,) supposing the enemy demoralized and fleeing, they placed their pickets but a stone's throw in advance of the line of battle, and laid aside their accoutrements and arms, at least such is my latter day information. But be this as it may, they were attacked next morning, at break of day, unawares, and unprepared, and ere many blows were struck, the great body of Gen. Hill's two divisions were in full flight—and an overwhelming and victorious enemy had only a handful of brave souls who dared stay their advance. On they came, and by 6 or 7 a. m., at which time our corps (Longstreet's) came upon the scene, the enemy were not far from the hill before described—and unless checked would soon possess it, be out of the wilderness, and prepared to strike us a death blow.—The other division of Gen. Hill's corps, (Gen. Anderson's,) for some reason, had not arrived as soon as was expected. Here let me say that if in aught written I have done any injustice to the brave men who composed Gen. Hill's corps, it is not so intended. That their conduct on that day was natural from the circumstances, we cannot deny. I will also state here, that since that battle, I have learned that when our corps set out that morning, (May 6th,) at 3 a. m., we were on a flank movement, and that Gen. Hill being attacked and routed, the flank movement was abandoned in order that this position might be relieved.

As we stood upon this hill, Lee excited and in close consultation with Longstreet—-our batteries thundering into the Wilderness below, the roar of musketry from the undergrowth below—our men retreating in a disorganized mass, and the Yankees pressing on and within musket shot, almost, of the hill upon which stood our idolized chief, indeed was an exciting time, and the emergency called for *immediate* and *determined* action upon the part of the Confederate General. Lee was equal to the hour. Action must *not* be delayed, for in less than five minutes the enemy would be upon the hill. Longstreet's corps as it then stood in one mingled mass upon the plank road, could not be thrown in, and time must be allowed for it to reform, and place itself in line of battle. The cannon thundered, musketry rolled, stragglers were fleeing, couriers riding here and there in post-haste, minnies began to sing, the dying and wounded were jolted by the flying ambulances, and filling the road-side, adding to the excitement the terror of death. The "Texas brigade," was in front of Fields' division—while "Humphrey's brigade" of Mississippians led the van of Kershaw's division. The consultation ended. Gen. Gregg and Gen. Humphrey were ordered to form their brigades in line of battle, which was quickly done, and we found ourselves near the brow of the hill, Gregg on the left—Humphrey on the right. "Gen. Gregg prepare to move," was the order from Gen. L. About this time, Gen. Lee, with his staff, rode up to Gen. Gregg—"General what brigade is this?" said Lee. "The Texas brigade," was General G's. reply. "I am glad to see it," said Lee. "When you go in there, I wish you to give those men the cold steel—they will stand and fire all day, and never move unless you charge them." "That is my experience," replied the brave Gregg. By this time an aid from General Longstreet rode up and repeated the order, "advance your command, Gen. Gregg." And now comes the point upon which the interest of this "o'er true tale" hangs.

"*Attention Texas Brigade*" was rung upon the morning air, by Gen. Gregg, "*the eyes of General Lee are upon you, forward, march.*" Scarce had we moved a step, when Gen. Lee, in front of the whole command, raised himself in his stirrups, uncovered his grey hairs, and with an earnest, yet anxious voice, exclaimed above the din and confusion of the hour, "*Texans always move them.*" Reader, for near four years I followed the fortunes of the Virginia army, heard, saw and experienced much that saddened the heart or appealed in one form or another to human passions, but never before in my lifetime or since, did I ever witness such a scene as was enacted when Lee pronounced these words, with the appealing look that he gave. A yell rent the air that must have been heard for miles around, and but few eyes in that old brigade of veterans and heroes of many a bloody field was undimmed by honest, heart-felt tears. Leonard Gee, a courier to Gen. Gregg, and riding by my side, with tears coursing down his cheeks and yells issuing from his throat exclaimed, "I would charge hell itself for that old man." It was not what Gen. Lee said that so infused and excited the men, as his tone and look, which each one of us knew were born of the dangers of the hour.

With yell after yell we moved forward, passed the brow of the hill, and moved down the declivity towards the undergrowth—a distance in all not exceeding 200 yards. After moving over half the ground we all saw that Gen. Lee was following us into battle—care and anxiety upon his countenance —refusing to come back at the request and advice of his staff. If I recollect correctly, the brigade halted when they discovered Gen. Lee's intention, and all eyes were turned upon him. Five and six of his staff would gather around him, seize him, his arms, his horse's reins, but he shook them off and moved forward. Thus did he continue until just before we reached the undergrowth, not, however, until the balls began to fill and whistle through the air. Seeing that we would do all that men could do to retrieve the misfortunes of the hour, accepting the advice of his staff, and hearkening to the protest of his advancing soldiers, he at last turned round and rode back to a position on the hill.

We reached the undergrowth—entered it with a yell, and in less than 100 yards came face to face with the advancing, triumphant, and sanguine foe--confronted only by a few brave souls who could only fire and yield their ground. The enemy were at least five or six to one of us, and death seemed to be our portion. With only 15 or 20 paces separating us, the contest waxed hot and deadlier. We gave a cheer and tried a charge, but with our handful of men our only success was to rush up to them, shoot them down, and shove them back some 10 or 15 yards. For 25 minutes we held them steady—not a foot did they advance, and at the expiration of that time more than half of our brave fellows lay around us dead, dying and wounded, and the few survivors could stand it no longer. By order of Gen. Gregg, whose manly form was seen wherever danger gloried most—I bore the order to the 5th and 1st Texas, to fall back in order.

After retreating some 50 yards, a most deafening yell was borne upon the breeze, and ere we were prepared to realize its cause, Gen. Longstreet's corps came sweeping by us, reformed, and reinforced by Gen. Anderson's division, and with a valor that stands unrivaled swept everything before them for three long miles—driving, in that long charge, the yankees from four different lines of breastworks that they had thrown up in their rear. The "Battle of the Wilderness" was won—all other fighting by the enemy that day and next was to prevent defeat from terminating in destruction.

The object, reader, of the advance made by Gregg and Humphrey, was to hold the enemy in check, to give Longstreet time to reform his corps. We accomplished our object.

The "Texas Brigade" entered the fight 673 strong. We lost in killed and wounded over 450.—Did we or did we not do all that men could? Gen. Gregg entered the fight with at least 12 commissioned and non-commissioned on his staff. Of these, several were killed, some wounded, and only two horses untouched. Gen. G's. horse was pierced by 5 balls—each creating a mortal wound—though he rode him until we fell back—sent him to the rear where he died.

My task is finished—and I have only to say if there ever lived a brave, fearless, unflinching and noble soldier—if ever there breathed a pure and honest patriot, he is to be found in that mouldering dust of a certain coffin in Hollywood cemetery, which contains the remains of Brig. Gen. Jno. Gregg, who fell near Richmond, Va., Oct. 7th. 1864, one of the best, the truest, the noblest men that Texas ever claimed.

MARY ASHBURTON.*

A TALE OF MARYLAND LIFE.

To brighten him up and dispel all gloomy visions from his mind, I assembled everything that was bright about the house in his room. A gayly embroidered easy chair, with deep red roses and startlingly blue morning-glories, was transferred from the parlor to his bedside, a lively rug decorated the fire-place in which crackled and spurted a brisk, cheerful fire, while even the golden goblet, its brim crowned with a chaplet of violets and rich purple heartsease, was summoned from the parlor to

* Continued from page 413.

do him honor, and placed upon a dainty little table beside the chair. Everything looked bright and tidy. I wore the most cheerful dresses I owned myself; even the servants must always appear nicely clad in dainty white aprons and neat dresses. I had trained the few servants that I had kept about the establishment so well, that affairs had gone on almost as usual during my absence in the sick room. Father had everything in the best order out of doors, and mother had come over expressly to attend to the vegetable garden; so that fine beds of peas and lettuce greeted my eyes on my first descent among such sublunary matters.

Alfred's room was a source of never-ending wonderment and delight to our good doctor when he would come in, and his feelings always found vent in some delicately kind expressions of encouragement. Doubtless he knew much of our previous history, the strange circumstances under which we had been married, Alfred's mad love for another, and his total neglect of the woman whom he had married out of pure pity for his father's broken-hearted sorrow. I could see by his manner that he appreciated our relative positions, endeavoring in an unobservable manner to improve that I occupied. For instance: he would say,

"Why, my dear sir, how *much* better you look this morning. It is all Mrs. Chauncey, I know. Waiving all pretensions to skill in her favor, I am a mere cipher in comparison to her."

To this, for a long time, Alfred would make no reply. It seemed to sadden him yet more, and I understood his feeling—at least, I thought I did—a sense of obligation where he did not wish to feel it, and the inadequateness of the cause for obligation, in proportion to its burden, the restoration of a life he did not prize or care to sustain. At that time he took scarcely any notice of the doctor, giving such slight answers to his questions that the latter had some difficulty in obtaining the necessary information.

But this gradually changed; his countenance softened, so did his manner. One day when I entered the room after a brief absence, I found the doctor quite confidential with him, and some pleasing topic appeared to be the subject of conversation, for they both looked towards me, the doctor with his kind smile, and Alfred with a light of welcome in his eyes.

"Your patient is better, madam," said the former, "I have been trying various restoratives. See that they are carried out," he added meaningly.

"I hardly think I have failed to execute any of your orders, doctor," I replied smilingly, "at least I do not remember to have done so."

"No, no, madam, I have perfect confidence in your judgment and memory both, I assure you. But I want to get this young man strong again, and have been offering him every inducement to get well as soon as possible that my poor brain could think of. It is time your care was approaching an end and he was growing independent of you."

This time Alfred's face did not darken as had been its wont when the doctor mentioned my connection with his restoration, and he looked kindly towards me as he said sadly yet without gloom,

"I am not worth her care, doctor; it is a pity it should have been bestowed upon so worthless an object."

He sighed and turned away as if he had sealed his fate, and to be the object of kind solicitude filled him with nothing but shame, each act of kindness but making him feel the more that it was undeserved.

"Worthless?" exclaimed the doctor apparently quite indignant, "what are you talking about? The world has need of you, my boy. Be up and see if it don't. I only wish I could have your vote next fall to put that confounded rascal, Jones, out of place. Besides," he continued, seeing that Alfred did not warm to politics, "There is much to arouse and animate you, as you will see when Providence first, Mrs. Chauncey next, and I last, will have got you down and about again.

The doctor would talk thus to his languid patient, trying by every kind means in his power to arouse him into life again, or a desire for it, the greatest difficulty of all and that which most retarded his recovery.

I never left him long; but one day when I was busy about some housekeeping duty in another apartment, Melissa came in with her breathless, agitated manner.

"Wont you please come to Mars. Alfred, madam?

What's the matter?" I asked, not so much alarmed as I might have been, for I was accustomed to Melissa's excited manner, "I left him quiet a few minutes ago."

"Nothin' at all, madam, nothin' at all. But he woke up and looked 'round startled like, and then seemed disappointed like, and axed where you was."

"Did he tell you to come for me?"

"No madam, but I knowed as how he wanted you, for when I axed him if I must call you, he said, 'no, no, don't disturb her,' but I knowed he did want you, and come to tell you."

I put the finishing touch to what I was doing, and then returned to him with a new joy in my heart, sending the light to my eyes and the color to my cheeks, I felt, as I timidly approached him.

"Did you want me?" I asked, smoothing his pillow or doing some little office or other as a relief to the shyness that stole over me just then.

"Did Melissa go for you? She should not have done that. You have kept yourself so constantly in this sick room that it is better for you to be away. Go again, do not stay here; it must be so tiresome to you."

"Oh! no, I *want* to stay," I replied timidly, "I only went out to attend to something while you slept, and was coming right back when Melissa came for me."

"You are very kind," he said with that only expression of gratitude he then used to me, a look of shame causing him to turn his eyes away from me. "Of all the world you did not forsake me. Is it that there is still good in it—that there is a merciful God in heaven?"

"Yes, yes," I replied earnestly, "there is good in all things, and the world is not so dark after all. Then God has made the earth very beautiful. Look at that sky beyond, framed in the tasselled fringe of the curtains above the basket of fruit, (I had set a basket of Malaga grapes and oranges in the window that the light might stream in over them and play on their bright, mingling colors) that bit of white cloud sailing before the March wind like a dropt plume from an angel's wing; at those white and purple violets in that gold cup, and do you tell me that God does not seek to make His children happy?"

"But the flowers fade, dark, stormy days come too, and the wind and the rain beat away the beauty from the earth and the light from the sky," he answered gloomily.

"So they do," I replied cheerfully, then quoted a line from a favorite little poem,

"Behind the clouds the sun is still shining."

"But the stormy days make the bright only the more beautiful by contrast, to be welcomed and enjoyed but the more intensely.—Then they clear away the horizon, dissipate sickly vapors that might be arising, the wind blows away the clouds that may be accumulating much more heavily, and the rain washes sky and earth till they come forth fresher and lovelier than ever, the flowers sweeter, the sky bluer than before."

He looked at me for a moment, then turned away sorrowfully.

"And I have been through such a storm, is it not so? Is the sun to shine, are the flowers to bloom again for me?"

"By God's mercy," I answered softly. "If not here, at least in heaven."

He turned his head again and glanced towards me.

"What do *you* know of life's storms—you who have never felt them, who have been all your life sheltered in your innocence and ignorance of the world by your own native oaks?"

I did not answer but turned my face away, and my hair falling down my cheek as I did so, he could not see my emotion.

"Your task, poor child," I heard him say in a changed tone, "I pity you for. I should not have said that last, for life must be very disagreeable to you under such circumstances, and I—" here he paused a moment, then added, "there *is* good on the earth—at least in you—; whether above it or not I cannot tell. In my dark moments I doubted the existence of a God. Now I think there must be."

I turned my eyes to him with the unshed tears still in them. "Oh! Mr. Chauncey, how could you doubt Him so? You did not pray to Him for strength, or He would have revealed Himself to you, I know. He has been so tender and merciful that you will soon learn to know and love Him, I am sure."

"Be it so then," he answered wearily. "The pride of intellect has departed from me; my mind is like a blank sheet on which I am too weak to trace characters of thought."

"A sheet on which the finger of God will write in characters of love with the knowledge of Him and His word illuminating the page," I answered cheerily.

That wan smile that sickness gives to the features passed over them, then he closed his eyes as if to sleep, but the expression did not indicate that repose he appeared to be seeking, and looked more like thought, as his brow was yet slightly knit, and the muscles of his lips tremulous.

CHAPTER XI.

His weakness continued a long time; such a weariness had taken possession of body and mind, and the effort to live so much of an exertion that strength seemed to have left him forever. He was very taciturn, would spend hours in silent thought, his head raised upon the pillow, with the thin hand clasping the forehead, and his dark eyes either cast down or fixed upon some object far away. At these moments I approached him hesitatingly, for some of my old awe would return, and I feared to break in unwelcomed upon his train of thought. Yet, upon turning and seeing it was I, a light would unconsciously break over his face, and a half smile play upon his lips. "My kind, gentle nurse," he said one day;—then many times afterwards.

I wondered what these fits of abstraction could mean, and feared that he was thinking of his lost love, so sad was the expression sometimes upon his features.—However, it comforted me to note that it had nothing of the wildness of despair in it, and appeared to be rather the revolving of some deep subject for thought than the anguish of jealousy or remorse.

One day I sat near him a little retired, so that my figure was not the first object his eye would rest upon in that direction. I heard him move and saw that he had changed his position so as to see me.

"What are you reading?" he asked.

"The Bible," I answered reverently, and resumed my reading.

"You seem to be much engrossed with it. What is it that pleases you so?"

"It all pleases me," I replied simply, "it gives me life and strength."

"To perform your present thankless task, I presume?" he questioned, and looking at me with searching eyes.

"We need but little support where our own feel ——" here I stopped as I felt the blood mounting to my face, then continued rapidly, "if you loved it, I think you would feel very differently; it promises so much help and support in trouble."

"Let me hear it then and see," he answered gravely.

I selected one of the Psalms, because they are so soothing to a sick ear, choosing the twenty-third for the first, then pausing when done to see if he had listened.

"That is very sweet, indescribably so," he said, "read more of them."

I read him several, then as the evening was far advanced, I closed the book and seated myself by a window to look out upon the great red sunset. For many weeks I had not cared to look upon my greatest source of pleasure, the fading or dawning landscape, but this evening the old enjoyment came back with the keenness of a long denied relish.

The sunset clouds were in full glory, sweeping, rolling in full blazes of yellow and purple and crimson on the far off horizon, while through the reddened dusk, through the soft twilight of the room, seemed to float the music of the versicle, "Like as the dew of Hermon which fell upon the hill of Sion."

It appeared to have been a lullaby to Alfred, for he slept when darkness had blotted out the redness from my view and I had turned to look at him again, as he did all that night, awaking more refreshed than he had been yet in the morning.

Upon first opening his eyes he turned them as if seeking for something. If they sought me, I was not far off, for they soon rested where I sat, very near with some little piece of woman's work in my hand.

"You look so much better," I said, going to him with a tray that I had arranged for him upon awaking.

"I feel better," he said in a whisper, "but so weak. Yet there is a new sensation, a desire long lost, to eat and to live."

I called Melissa, and we propped him up while he partook, to my intense joy, with some appetite of the breakfast I had prepared.

When I had smoothed the coverlet and the pillow and had laid his head gently back upon the latter, he said,

"Would it be convenient for you to read to me?"

"With the greatest pleasure," I answered, "what shall I read?"

"Did you sing me to sleep last night?" he smiled faintly, "I fancied you did. Read to me from the same book; it soothed me so and fell like music on my senses."

I took the Book and read from the Gospel of St. John, the raising of Lazarus from the dead.

"As a child," he remarked when I had finished, "I was taught from that Book for the historical information it would give me, and as a part of my education, and if mentally impressed with the beauty and truth of its doctrines, they never touched me with the meaning of the words coming to me now. A revelation of infinite mercy appears to open upon my limited comprehension. Is it your reading?" he asked with a grave smile.

"Oh! no," I answered with earnestness, "it is God appearing to you through His Word."

"And you hope, though you

do not say so, that I will hearken to His communications."

"Yes, indeed;—for that I have prayed ever since your sickness."

His face became very thoughtful, but after a few moments he asked again,

"Then your kindness and care proceeded from a sort of missionary feeling towards me, as if I were a subject for tracts and conversion? You bestowed on me only a part of the kindness you feel for every one else?"

"'Oh! Alfred!" It was the first time I had ventured to call him by his christian name, and it burst from me now involuntarily, while I felt my face crimsoning at my boldness, and he searching into it so intently. I was pained and embarrassed beyond measure, still he had no mercy.

"What does 'oh! Alfred' mean?" he asked with some earnestness.

I gave him no answer, of course, and drew away from him to a remote part of the room. Mine had been a silent, suffering love—it should never be intruded upon him till he sought it. He must read a stronger feeling than mere philanthropy in my confusion, but I did not dare to look up.

These Bible readings led to the perusal of other books, and I searched the library for suitable volumes. He preferred poetry to the more solid standard works, and we soared with Milton and Dante (in a translation) and many other old authors whose sublimity of conception ever strikes you with fresh wonder and admiration.

"Byron?" I asked one day smilingly, "will you have him for a companion to-day?"

"No," he replied, "I do not want him. He would be rather unwholesome nurture for a sick mind. Give me more healthy, nutritious food. Him I devoured when a stripling, though rejecting his grossness with disgust. Get something else."

I had tempted him with Byron purposely, and was rejoiced at his rejection of that most magnificent, most unhealthy of poets; so I selected the "Fairy Queen," making his grave face almost expand at times into a smile at my queer pronunciation of the quaint old English.

When he could sit up, I had one of the most luxurious easy chairs from the parlor wheeled into his room, and arranging it with cushions satisfactorily to myself he was placed there, his languid head reclining upon a pillow. My own seat was by the window between the curtains; and with a vase of flowers beside me on the sill, occupied with books when he desired me to read, or work when he was tired of listening, I passed hours near him thus.

Resolving never to intrude myself or my affections needlessly upon him, when I thought he could do without me, I would withdraw at times and busy myself elsewhere.

"You have been gone very long," he said to me reproachfully one day as I reëntered his apartment after having left him for rather more than an hour comfortably arranged in his easy chair with books and all I thought he could want about him.

"Did you wish for anything during my absence?"

"Yes, I wished for *you*, Mary. You do not know how very lonesome I am when you are gone.—However," he added, changing his tone, "do not let me confine you longer to this dull room. You have done infinitely more for me, than I deserve already, and it is shamefully selfish in me to desire more at your hands."

I took my seat and work immediately.

"You wish to be out in the bright sunshine," he said with an invalid's nervousness. "You brought in roses in your cheeks as bright as those in the garden. Go, then, my kind, gentle Mary, and recruit yourself in the open air."

"I would rather be here," I replied without raising my head.

"Would you rather be here?" he repeated with something like pleasure in his voice. "Then there is some one who does not care to leave me." His tone saddened as if old memories swept over him and he knew that I was all that remained to him.

From that time I understood that he did not wish me to leave him, that he was lonesome when I was away, so I stayed by him, took my work in there, and busied myself where he could see me.

But this did not deceive me,—even my heart's trembling hope could not make me regard these instances of interest in me as love. I knew that sickness and convalescence make great changes in us, that the childish dependence we feel in the hour of suffering and weakness is lost in returning health and strength; as, looking back in our maturity, we wonder at the feelings of childhood, and marvel that we could ever have been children. I might be to him as a sister, a friend, but nothing more. To love me after the brilliant Adéle was impossible I knew.

CHAPTER XII.

Days and weeks passed thus. My father attended to the property agreeably to my request, and never had it returned better harvests than when under his skillful hands; while mother was extremely kind with her assistance in-doors, so prosperity smiled about us while I was in my dear one's sick room.

Our readings went on while Alfred slowly regained his strength. Sometimes he would take his pen and write for hours, at other times sit there in quiet thought. Often upon my return to his room after a brief absence, I would find my little Bible in his hand, and he engaged in searching out my reference marks, once or twice laying it down upon seeing me, with some trifling observation, and smiling at my marginal notes. My opinions, however, I steadily maintained, feeling myself there to be his superior, for however great his intellectual knowledge of the Book might be, I knew that mine was from the heart not the brain, that it had adapted itself to my poor understanding as it would not to those who sought it in earthly wisdom. At least, such was my humble faith, so I firmly combatted his sentiments which, I believe now, he uttered partly to bring me out.

When we had been reading for some weeks,—at first in his weakness and pain he had listened in silence,—we would pause and speak of the various characters and incidents described in our book, or he would make some remark calculated to draw me forth, so that, unconsciously, I frequently lost myself in admiration of the subject, warming into enthusiasm as I dilated upon what was congenial to my tastes and sentiments.

Turning to him for his opinion one day, I caught an expression of delighted surprise upon his countenance, which speedily recalled me to myself, and caused me to stop in the midst of my enthusiastic eulogy.

"Go on," he said, "you refresh me like a shower upon a dry, thirsty land with your fresh, original thoughts."

"You didn't know that I loved books?" I said half playfully, half in earnest.

He sighed as he answered, "I had many things to learn about you, and every day teaches me to expect yet more." *Gratitude* teaches you, I thought; as a friend he can discover in me qualities greater than he had supposed me capable of possessing.

So he grew stronger day by day, very slowly and imperceptibly, yet improving nevertheless, able to stand and to walk about the room, or to sit, unsupported, by the window. The wound was healed, though the scar—alas! remained to tell its fearful story, and the debility resulting from the illness and loss of blood.

One day when I had been gathering fresh flowers in the garden, I returned to his room, and disposing of my hyacinths and wall-flowers, I went softly about, thinking of many little things I intended to do for him, and doing all I could to promote his comfort for the present.

It was evening, a lovely May evening, and he sat by the window in his easy chair, looking handsomer than he had done since his illness, in a dressing-gown of rich colors falling loosely about him, the lingering sunbeams shooting across his wavy hair, till it brightened into threads of gold, across his forehead where the blue network of veins told of his sickness and suffering.

He was silent as in thought, with his head supported on his arm which leant upon the arm of the chair, the shadows growing longer about him as eve advanced. He asked me to read a little. I took the book we were engaged upon at the time, and drew my seat near, when he said,

"Not there, will you take this?" It was a low stool at his feet. "I do not want to place you so humbly," he added, smiling slightly, "but I want you near."

With my heart beating strangely, I took the seat there as he wished, feeling the sunlight glow upon my hair too, and it seemed to envelope us both in one golden haze. As I was searching for the lost place in the volume, he said,

"Never mind the place, Mary; it will soon be dark."

The book fell from my hand.

and lay unheeded on the floor.

'Life seems very different to me since I knew you, Mary."

"Why so, Alfred?"

"Do you think that a man can be so far lost as that the daily intercourse with a good woman will have no effect upon him?"

"Do you think that I could watch you day after day with all your loveliness of disposition and unselfish devotedness, ministering to me in my lost, despairing hour"—here his voice broke down—"like an angel of kindness and consolation, yet remain unmoved? Could I be constantly with you and not learn to love you?"

My drooping head was turned away from him, while my heart beat to suffocation. Was I dreaming or waking?

He took my hand and pressed it in his. "My dear, guardian angel," he said, "you do not know how I have learned to love you. I had a wild, mad passion," he sighed as he spoke, "it led me into horrible sin. But since my illness, and companionship with a good woman, the old things seem to have passed away and all things to have become new. My old self appears to have departed in the hours of suffering, in which mental anguish far outweighed the physical; when a gentle hand laid its cool, soft touch on my burning forehead and a low, sweet voice whispered consolation in my ear, strengthening me to endure a life which I believed to be robbed of all motives for continuance; when an earnest voice prayed for me at my bedside at the times you supposed me to be unconscious, and an angelic countenance was raised in supplication, bringing the return of prayer in peace to my wearied soul, old as I was in disappointment and sorrow, if young still in years. So, Mary, peace has stolen into my bosom again. The memory of my passion is now as but a dream. It was rather adoration,—delirium,— than love. In her place has stolen the sweet face and pure, fresh heart of my jewel."

The disengaged hand clasped itself tightly over my face, while the sobs of happiness that swelled to my throat choked my utterance.

"Oh! Mary, if I were but worthy of your love, if your pure, angelic heart could but feel for me as I do for you, I might be happy once more."

Still I said nothing.

"You say nothing," he said reproachfully, "you cannot love me then, and I only grieve you by this acknowledgement."

I turned my face then, and it must have been glowing with the long suppressed love I had borne him, for he took both my hands and bent his head towards me.

"Is it so?" he asked eagerly, "can you like me?"

"As I like myself, only far better,—as a part of my nature, of my existence, I like you, Alfred. Do you think that I would have married you when I did if I had not loved you, humiliating as the circumstances were?"

"Love me?" he repeated, mute with surprise.

"How else could I have married you?"

"I thought—" he uttered confusedly.

"I know what you thought;—that an ignorant country girl, too void of sensibility and delicacy to be alive to the painful position she would occupy, from motives of vulgar ambition consented to marry you unsought, and thus, in spite of coldness and repulsion upon your part, pushed herself on you with the aid of our respective parents."

He was silent to this.

"What else could you think?" I said smiling, and much reassured myself at his confusion.

"Never mind what I thought. I thought nothing in my days of madness and folly. I know now of a very lovely woman, who has been the source of unspeakable comfort to me, and whom I love with the respectful devotion of maturer years."

"A brother's love," I murmured turning away.

"Not so," he exclaimed impetuously, "why will you doubt me, Mary? You asked me why you married me,—let me hear it from yourself. You did so because—"

It was very hard to answer him then, particularly as he seized both my hands more firmly in his grasp and bent his head to search into my downcast eyes, while my face glowed as if it had been on fire.

"Because—?" he repeated impatiently.

"Because, Alfred, I loved you."

I felt his hands tremble as they held mine. "How could you?" he asked in a low tone.

The gathering twilight gave me more boldness. I did not tell him all, for reserve even then forbade my letting him know of the wild delirium of unsought love, of my mad jealousy of my brilliant rival, and of those years of hopeless, despairing sorrow.

One thing I told him, and more eloquently than when my stammering lips had confessed my love;—that was, that when I knew him to be in deep suffering my own anguish had been little less, how I had longed for power to comfort, had prayed for him, little thinking in what form that power would come; and that when it did come, I had willingly, though in so humbling a manner to woman's pride, accepted the post.

"*I* am humbled now," he said in a low tone. "Then, Mary, when the world was dark,—God's heaven a black abyss engulfing me,—when I stood in a wilderness as desolate as Hagar's, bitterly warring in my heart against every creature; and everything human or divine arrayed, as I believed, against me, you came as an angel from Him and rescued me from a worse than death. It was to your unselfish devotion—how earned I know not—and so purely, delicately shown—that I owe my salvation from— " he shuddered.—"What do I not owe you? what *will* I not owe you, my Mary? I will go from this sick room—God helping—" he reverently bent his head—"another man, every energy spent in endeavor to retrieve the past and profit to the utmost in the future. If I can but make myself worthy of one whom I have the honor and happinoss to call my wife, I shall be something yet, Mary."

Was *he* talking in this strain to

me? I could not believe it—that the patient love of years had its fruition at last;—that with his arm thrown around me I was sobbing out my happiness upon his shoulder.

The next morning when father came and sent up some message to me about the business of the day, Alfred said,

"I wish you'd ask him up. I should like to see him."

With a pleased smile I ran down to meet father and deliver to him Alfred's message.

"Humph! so he wants to see me, does he?" was father's characteristic reply. "Glad he's coming round."

When I reëntered Alfred's room with him, the former arose and received him with a very different air from what he had ever done before.

"Glad to see you looking so well, Mr. Chauncey," spoke father, after giving him a look of examination.

"Oh! I hope to be out of this room and from under your angel of a daughter's care before long, when I shall be able to relieve you of the charge you have been burdened with so long."

"Happy to hear it," replied my father, "it has been about almost too much for me,—yours and Mary's affairs and my own. It would be a blessed thing, indeed, to see you about again."

They entered into a long conversation about the farm, the prospects for harvests and so forth, while I stitched away in trembling happiness by the window; sunbeams pouring in around me over the flowers, between the curtains; sunbeams in my heart, flooding my life, as the more tangible ones did the room, and sent every object swimming in its lustre.

Loved at last! A song of thankfulness gushed forth in my heart, and transformed the pale, timid creature into a new being, fitter to mate with him.

His bride at last, and loved best of all the world!

In the first impulse of joy, I had hasted away and thrown myself at the feet of my heavenly Father, there to pour forth my happiness and gratitude.

As I sat there, too happy at seeing them thus together to listen to the dry statistics of weather and crops, the door opened and mother was ushered in.

She looked hesitatingly about her as if uncertain whether to enter or not, with her basket in one hand, her chicken bonnet in the other. "I was told Mr. Ashburton was here," she said.

"Come in, madam. I am glad to see you," said Alfred, rising and going to meet her. "Take this chair," and he pushed his own easy chair towards her.

"No, on no account, Mr. Chauncey," she replied in wondering confusion, and seated herself uneasily on the edge of a cane-bottomed one, bonnet and basket still in hand.

"Let me relieve you of your basket, mother." I took it from her and was going to remove the bonnet too, but she resisted the latter.

"I just come to bring Mr. Chauncey some jelly I made yesterday, thinking he might like something from home."

"I thank you," returned Alfred, smiling," I have profited very much by your skill already in your instructions to your daughter. You made her as great an adept in that line as yourself, didn't you? At least it has seemed to me lately that no hand could be as skillful as hers in anything she undertook."

"Yes," replied mother, only half understanding him, and looking from one to the other in amazement, "she was a smart child enough at such things, though the moment she was through, she was at her books. I often wondered how she contrived to do both, for I was always of opinion these book-learned people didn't know much else."

"Well, that old belief was completely disproved in your daughter's case," observed Alfred with another smile, "and I have the rare happiness of possessing one who can unite intellect and domestic talent without making the one interfere with the other. If I can but make myself worthy of her, my dear madam, and repay her care by taking, in my turn, the best care of her, it will be all I seek or wish in this world."

He took my hand and drew me near him, while tears glistened in the eyes of all;—even father brushed away a drop with the cuff of his rough working coat. They understood then that Mary's love had won its reward, and that she was dear at last to the heart of the man whom she had served so long and so hopelessly.

THE END.

WESTMINSTER ABBEY.

THE first time we entered Westminster Abbey was during Divine service. The pews were filled, and as we joined a group standing a little to the right of the entrance, I directly perceived just above us, the monument to William Pitt, so intimately connected with American history. It was surmounted by his statue, with extended arm and earnest face, as in the attitude of speaking. It awakened a thrill in my mind, and the long past seemed to become a living reality. At that distance we heard little of the service, but as I stood in that venerable building, and glanced at one and another of the monuments and statues of the illustrious dead of other ages, the emotions awaked by it were indescribable. The solemn tones of the organ reverberating through the ancient arches, seemed truly the music of other days, and the words, "I believe in the resurrection of the body and the life everlasting" were deeply impressive and full of meaning. We gradually approached until near enough to hear distinctly the latter part of the sermon. It was scriptural and earnest, inculcating strongly the duty of diligence, self-consecration and self-denial in the work of Christ—daily striving to follow that example of active usefulness and benevolence, which the Master himself had given: to accomplish which he happily impressed upon them the necessity of an unceasing reliance upon the aid of the Holy Spirit.

It was just what we would wish to hear in such a place, and from a clergyman of the established Church of England.

I felt it a pleasing introduction to what is one of the most interesting memorials of successive centuries, not only in England, but perhaps in all the world.

We afterwards made a second visit to it in the week. The building is in the form of a Latin cross, and as we passed slowly down the aisle, crowded with the monuments and statues of the celebrated, of widely-varying periods, the impression is one of solemn magnificence. Founded in 616 by King Sebert, it was altered and added to in successive reigns, but received the finishing embellishments by Sir Christopher Wren in the beginning of the 18th century. Here are memorials, comprising alike statesmen, philosophers, military commanders and bishops, with representatives of every branch of literature.

Perhaps no portion attracts so general interest as the Poet's Corner, appropriated to the monuments and relics of poets and literary men. Here is a crowding of noble names familiar to every reader, as Cowper, Campbell, Johnson, Addison, Milton, &c., as well as others whose works are little known at the present day. My eye caught the bust of Macauley, just to the right and a little behind the elegant monument to Addison. I went near to enjoy a close observation of the finely-sculptured features of this attractive writer, and after some little time, glancing at the floor, found myself standing on a marble slab, which covered his remains. I quickly stepped aside, feeling almost as if I had committed sacrilege. These slabs are of dark color, and exactly on a level with the stone floor. Perhaps no one takes a step in this Abbey, which has for centuries been the cemetery of distinguished persons, without walking over some one. But they utter no complaint.—There they have been resting quietly, some of them, for several centuries, indifferent alike to praise or blame; their spirits, if happy, only so because they exercised in life that faith in the merits of the Saviour, which is alike the privilege of the humblest intellect. But we love to linger among these tombs and monuments, and reflect that those, whose memories they perpetuate, are yet living, most of them, we trust, a higher, more glorious life, in the light of that "eternity which still begins where computation ends." They did their work, and the work of the historian and poet, rightly directed, is a noble one. They have done much to extend and elevate the range of thought, and to purify and ennoble the feelings. They made all the phases of nations and of human character, all the forms and resources of nature subservient to their large and fertile minds. While their labors have encircled their names with undying fame, they have sent forth an influence, which is still felt from the palace to the cottage.

Afterwards we went with a large party into the old chapel at the eastern extremity of the Abbey, and appropriated almost exclusively as the burial place of sovereigns and princes. We were conducted by a guide through the various compartments of this very ancient structure. Here are the tombs of kings and queens extending back to the eleventh century. Some of them are surmounted by figures in recumbent position, which are often peculiar and repulsive, but a few are beautiful as works of art. There were the tomb and monument of the faithful queen Eleanor, erected by her devoted husband, Edward the First. We were gratified to see the beautiful monument to the unfortunate Mary, Queen of Scots, built by order of James the First. He has been accused of much neglect of his unhappy mother, and it is pleasant to see even a partial contradiction of this charge in this beautiful memorial in this venerated place. It far exceeds that of her inveterate enemy, Queen Elizabeth, and indeed is equaled by very few in the crowded chapel. A life-sized statue of her with well-chiseled features rests full length upon the summit of the monument. Here are aged and mouldy representatives of many noble and some very unfortunate families of England.—A tomb of a niece of Cromwell was pointed out to us, and the place where once rested the body of Cromwell himself. After the restoration it was taken up, and consigned to utter oblivion, no one having the slightest idea where it was removed. But it is unnecessary, and would be tedious to the reader to enumerate all which are interesting to an observer. We must not, however, omit to mention those of the hero of Macauley, William III., and his queen, Mary, which are simple in construction, but we loved to linger around them.

The stone work in some parts of this division is so elaborate and so delicately traced as to be truly marvelous. At one point we had a splendid view of the long aisle, extending 180 feet, the beautifully stained circular window in the western transept, just then lighted by the rays of the evening sun, shed a mellowed and many colored light upon the columns, arches, and singular sculpture.

We saw the ancient, oaken and rather unsightly chair, in which all the monarchs of England are seated when crowned. Here Queen Victoria received the solemn badge of empire. It seemed almost the value of a crown, almost enough to crush a sensitive spirit, to come into that dismal place, so old and mouldy, so filled with the tombs and monuments of the dead, and sit in that old chair, which seems in itself almost a sepulchre of centuries, take there the solemn oath, and have the head encircled, with what indeed glitters resplendent with rare and costly jewels, but which, in all the responsibility and publicity it brings to the wearer, may be as the band of iron or a crown of thorns. Surely at such an hour the thoughtful mind would need a firm reliance on that wisdom and strength which cometh only from above.

Under this chair is the dark stone on which the kings of Scotland were crowned for many centuries, and which was captured and brought to England by Edward I.

It was some relief to emerge at length from these dreary wanderings among the long past, through an iron gate into the Poet's Corner again. Just as we entered, the sun shone brightly through an upper window, illuminating all that hallowed place, bathing the statues and monuments in a soft and pleasing radiance. It seemed a visitant from another world to tell of the glorious immortality of those whose bodies rested there. Just opposite was the statue of Addison, with a countenance at once so thoughtful and serene.—We thought of his last message to his infidel friend, that he "wished him to come and see how peacefully a Christian could die." It was the farewell visit of the evening sun—lingered just a little and was gone. But it was pleasant to know, that at least once every sunny day, this resting place of the great and the good is irradiated by his beams.

S. B. H.

PARIS.

THE PARC MOUCEAUX.

ONE of the most beautiful spots in this city of beauties, indeed, it is almost warrantable to say the one of greatest attraction, is the Parc Mouceaux. Possessing not the vast size, and long drives, and walks which greet the eye at every turning in the Bois de Boulogne, and whose far extending vistas, shaded by the large trees which, from either side, entwine their giant arms overhead in green luxuriant arches, as though Nature, and not Man, had exerted her power to form at once a sheltered, cool, and agreeable retreat, where the freshness of the forest seems transported to the middle of the great city, nor the stiff, artistic appearance of a modern garden, with its beds of flowers at such regular distances, and trimmed trees, and vines, so mathematically exact,—it yet combines them both, losing the faults of the one in the beauties of the other, the immensity of the first, in the comparatively small dimensions of the second

It was first planted in 1778, by the care of Philippe d'Orléans, father of King Louis Philippe, then Duc de Chartres, and occupies the spot where an ancient village stood,—Mouceaux, Mouceau, or Mousseaux,—from which it takes its name—prior to that period, to the North West of Paris.

The site was at first arid and barren, devoid of all that could make it interesting, but being confided to the skill of Carmontelle, he made a delightful English garden of it; conducted to it water in abundance; raised temples, obelisks, tombs, grottoes, kiosks, a fort in ruins, a fire pump ; created jets of water, fountains, and cascades. It was then a beautiful proof of what man could produce from Art and Nature combined, and is, to-day, a miniature of the vast and luxurions promenades of the Bois de Boulogne, of the Luxembourg, and the Tuileries, and a place of pleasure and resort.

After the death of Philippe d' Orleans, the National Convention ordered that it should cease to be exclusive, and become a place of public utility, and hence made of it a promenade open to all, established games, and balls there. For a time it was much frequented, but because of its distance from the centre of the city, it was soon abandoned by seekers of pleasure. When the Restoration was effected, Louis XVIII. restored the Parc to the family of Orleans, in whose possession it remained until the promulgation of the Presidential decrees of 1852. Since this epoch it was only accessible through the permission of its guardian, M. d'Arboussier. After the death of the Duchess of Orleans, the property was ceded by the heirs, to M. Emile Périére, and finally, in adopting the project of the Boulevards Malsherbes and Mouceaux, the city of Paris itself came into possession of a part of it, in order to appropriate it to use as a public walk, after it had suffered numerous and radical transformations.

The garden may be approached by three principal entrances, one at the rotunda of the ancient Barriére de Chartres; the two others, specially intended for the circulation of carriages, are placed, one on the Boulevard Malsherbes, and the other on the Rue de Courcelles, facing the Avenue Monceaux, which, commencing at this gate, stretches down to the Arc de Triomphe, or Barriére de l'Etoile. These entrances at gates of different sizes, designed as much for carriage ways as pedestrians, are ornamented with magnificent iron railings, surmounted by the arms of the city of Paris, and the seal of the Emperor. The doors themselves are hung on pilasters of the Ionic order, topped by elegant amortessments. Two large arteries run through the grounds, ornamented here and there with handsome candelabres de gaz, and bordered with granite, while multitudes of other and smaller alleys cross each other in either direction, whose sides are garnished with a profusion of flowers, and the curiosities which the dismemberment of the Parc has let remain. Of this number are the river, the bridge, the grotto, the Naumachie, (a vast basin of an oval form, surrounded by columns of the Corinthian order,) the tomb, shaded by a large forest tree, and finally, the rotunda.—

This last monument, however, completely transformed, serves to-day as the habitation of the guardian of the Parc.

The Duc d'Orléans seems to have understood that the true plan of construction for a garden is to avoid those stiffnesses and formalities in the gardens of now-a-days, and presenting different views, and varying tableaux, to lure the eye on, and charm it with the changing landscapes, that move like the shifting scenes of some fairy opera. It was a place consecrated to pleasure, and hence its founder and first owner gave it the name of Folly. It frequently served as the theatre for incidents, which only the private recollections of the period can tell.

The principal pavilion, in which gathered the familiars of the prince, was of elegant construction, was afterwards used as a rendezvous to the sons of Louis Philippe, returning from the chase, and still exists in a part of the Parc not under the control of the State. It was in this Pavilion that Louis Philippe—Joseph, Duc d'Orléans, and Grand Master of the Free Masons, made his adepts undergo the fantastic, and sometimes apparently cruel proofs which preceded their reception into the order. Here also he passed his nights in wild play. A story is told on this subject to this effect: A young German came to Paris with large sums in his possession, was presented to Philippe under the double quality of a noble, and a libertine, and was admitted to Monceaux. He played, and lost, and the humor having seized him, he allowed familiar imprecations to escape him towards those whom the fatal passion for play had mastered.—A nobleman attached to the Duc de Chartres represented to the German that he should not speak thus before the Prince, his master. The too frank person replied unconcernedly that among cheats there were no princes. At this they fell upon him; he was stabbed while sitting, and as death followed, he was buried secretly in the garden. If, from those ultra mundane regions, the spirit of the player has been able to see what was passing here below, it ought to have been proud of the honors that have been rendered to its mortal covering, for there was raised to him a tomb, of the pyramid of which we see to-day but a fragment. From the writing in ancient characters on this tomb, we gather that it is an Egyptian pyramid; that its interior decorations are eight granite columns, buried in a row, with tops ornamented by Egyptian heads, sustaining a tablet of white marble, of granite, and of bronze. A rose work of bronze decorates the vault. Opposite the door opens a niche containing a green antique marble vasque, where is found seated on its talons, a woman of the most beautiful black marble, the head dress of whom, is a fillet of silver strings. In the angles are four niches, and in each censers of bronze. The entrance is closed by iron work, and the door has for ambages two Egyptian pillars supporting an antique green vase. Only a small number of confidants know what poor devil reposes there.

As a set-off, and perhaps as a palliative to this event of the tomb, the prince, who had, it must be admitted, certain generous sides in his character, had placed opposite, at the extremity of the bridge, a mill, by which reposed the habitation of the miller. This little house forming a dairy, was decorated in marble within, and the outside of a rustic style. Mme. de Genlis, governess of the children of the Prince, had placed there a young girl, a pretty villager, named Rose, married since to a young man whom she loved. The Duc d'Orleans contributed by his generosity to perpetuate the happiness of this young couple, to whom he gave six thousand livres as a memorial.

Nothing remains of all this today, but the bridge, which it was necessary to cross to reach the little isle of rocks, where is still found the cascade. The temple, the kiosks, the statues, have suffered the law of destruction.

The celebrated author of the "Liaisons Dangereuses," Chaderlos de Laclos, born at Amiens in 1741, produced his first literary works in the little theatre of Mouceaux. He was afterwards appointed Secretary Supernumerary to the prince, and soon becoming his intimate confidant, it is supposed he exercised a great influence over the conduct of the man who habitually admitted him to his counsels. To the Chevalier Laclos is attributed the compiling of those letters from the Duc d' Orleans to the King, where is found the germ of the ideas of '93. Laclos was one of the principal editors of a Jacobin journal, entitled "Journal des Amis de la Constitution," and he, in concert with Brissot, made the petition which provoked the assemblage at the Champs de Mars, where was demanded that the King should be judged. Prejudiced by these services against the Duc d'Orleans, he was arrested and confined in the house of Picpus, but from the bottom of his prison, he still continued to write, and composed there, some fugitive poems, which are destitute neither of spirit nor grace. Liberated in the 9th Thermidor, and appointed Secretary General to the administration of the Hypotheques, he was soon familiar with his new duties, but shortly after abandoned them for a military career. He was sent into Italy as general of a brigade, which he occupied with distinction, until finally, the fatigues and emotions of his active spirit hastened the term of his existence, and he died at Tarene, the 5th of October, 1803, entirely imbued with the material skepticism of the 18th century. His Ex-Master, the Duc d'Orleans, evinced the same kind of stoicism, in face of a much more horrible death.

A much pleasanter souvenir of the beauties of Monceaux, is the incident of the herb-gatherer, who crept in by stealth, seeking a certain plant which he had been told he would find there. Startled by meeting Mme. de Genlis, and her illustrious pupils, the botanist fled with downcast head, endeavoring to conceal his spoil. He had been recognized however, and the next day was given the key of a little door, by which he could come at his pleasure, without fear of surprise. This timid personage was none other than Jean-Jacques, who, like a shooting star, lights his period with meteoric brilliancy, and leaves his writings behind like a luminous trace.

The rock with its cascade produces an agreeable diversion among the artificial beauties of the harmonious horticulture scattered through the park. Placed at the center, not far from the spot where the principal alleys cross each other, it breaks with good effect the otherwise plane surface of the ground, and gives, exactly what is required, a glimpse of wild Nature, amidst the splendid vegetation with which it is surrounded. The rock itself is a work of art, but art so well concealed as to bear the semblance of Nature herself, as though in one of those mighty throes, to which the Earth in ages past, still unfinished, was subject, the volcanic fires had found an outlet here, and upheaving this memorial of their power, left it as a testimony of that terrible destructive force which the globe conceals within its bowels, and which one day or another may rend it asunder, and hurl the fragments into space, perhaps to the destruction of other worlds, and other systems. From its summit a mountain cascade leaps forth from an overhanging rock, and bounding in sparkles, and spray, from stone to stone as they project themselves unevenly in its course, falls into the little river below, and is borne along across the Parc, under the bridge, and finally into the Naumachie, a large oblong space, in whose centre is a little islet, where three large trees have sprung up at one end, while the other is covered with rushes and marsh grass. Under the rock is a sinuous grotto, from whose roof hang in pendants at various lengths, innumerable stalactites, seeming the work of centuries, as the water has filtered through the intervening stone, and produced this natural effect, like some subterranean cavern of the Alps or the Pyrenees. These stalactites have been brought here, one by one, but with so much ability and taste have they been placed, so perfect is the effect, that the hand of the constructer has left no trace of its presence.

Take it all in all, it is one of the most delightful little garden-parks imaginable, though by "little" must not be supposed a space less than ten acres in extent. To while away a morning hour under its waving, cool shades, within sound of the cascade's clatter, surrounded by blushing roses, and blooming exotics, the air filled with bird-song, no other place is half so pleasant. It is a little paradise, but like all things Parisian, it cannot be described; one must see them to know them.—As the Parisians say, "*Voir Paris, et mourir.*"

ORCHARDS.

ORCHARDING, as Evelyn quaintly terms it, consists in the care and culture of fruit-bearing trees. There are some reasons for supposing that this care and culture of fruit-bearing trees is man's natural occupation, just as a bee's natural occupation is honey-making or a silk-worm's natural occupatiou is silk-making. If we are, as Cuvier, the greatest of modern naturalists, believed, frugivorous animals, like the monkeys, then a man without an orchard is like a silk-worm without his mulberry leaf, or a nautilus without his shell. We do not presume to decide whether Cuvier was right or wrong, but his scientific conclusions certainly placed him on the poetical and artistic side of the question. Poets, from the days of the Greek Empedocles down to the days of the English Shelley, have loved to sing the praises of trees and tree fruits; and painters, like Claude and Salvator Rosa, literally revelled in their beauty. The tree is, in the vegetable kingdom, what man himself is in the animal kingdom, God's crowning and finishing work, and this is one reason for supposing that the former was designed for the special use of the latter—and for him only. Grasses and green herbs are placed within reach of the brutes, which they gather with their soulless faces turned earthward; but the tree of the field, which Holy Writ declares to be man's life, holds its fruit securely above their reach, and man gathers in his peculiar and luscious treasures with his face turned heavenward. Everything else we eat is shared by the animals of the brute creation—our fondness for flesh food is shared by the wolf, the dog, the cat, the lion and the tiger—all of our garden vegetables are placed, by nature, within reach of the browsing sheep and grazing ox, but a peach or apple tree may stand unprotected on the common, safe from the attacks of either.

Another proof that fruit was designed for man's special use is that it is the only created thing which we relish in its natural state. The herbs, which stock our vegetable gardens, and the flesh which comes from the butcher's shambles must go through laborious processes to make them fit for food. But with fruit, nature, in giving the finishing touches for our use, invests it with every charm to gratify our senses. When ready for our use, it assumes the most beautiful colors, blue, crimson, gold and purple, and rivets the eye of every passer-by. These colors are such as are seen at the greatest distance, and the rosy apple, crimson peach, purple grape and golden orange, while they nestle amid the green leaves which protect them from the sun, attract our attention from afar, and the love of the beautiful in our hearts responds to the appeal, and as we involuntarily draw near, a new charm meets the senses in the fragrance, which is another provision of nature appealing to our natural instincts. Then the fruit is just the size most convenient for us to handle, and its whole composition is exactly suited to our needs. Our winter fruit,—nuts, are provided with the oil necessary to generate animal heat, and the albumen which plays so important a part in furnishing muscular strength. The very prevalent idea that nuts are unwholesome, is true with regard to invalids—the most wholesome food acts injuriously upon a diseased stomach, but are exactly suited to the demands of a healthy human organization. Nuts, unlike summer fruits, are of a brown, inconspicuous color—because, we suppose, not designed for immediate consumption, but to be stored away for winter's needs.—They are provided with a covering which preserves them pure and fresh, for an indefinite length of time, and are just the most convenient size for handling, storing and eating.

While we do not carry our ideas on this subject so far as to eschew all animal food, like Shelley, but partake thankfully of our beefsteaks and mutton chops; still we must admit there are, in this connection, some striking facts. The human race we believe to have existed for six thousand years, and for one-third of this long period, animal food was not permitted by God, for it was only after the flood that permission to partake of it was given.

The great difference between the anti-diluvians and post-diluvians consists in length of life. The shortest life recorded before the Flood, was that of Lamech, who lived seven hundred and seventy-seven years. There had been no decrease of longevity up to Noah's day, for Noah himself lived nine hundred and fifty years, twenty years longer than Adam did, and only nineteen less than Methuselah lived. But immediately after the flood, and immediately after the *grant of animal food was given*, the decrease in the duration of human life commences. Shem's life was shorter than his father's by three hundred and fifty years. Yet Shem's life was longer than that of his own son, Arphaxad, by one hundred and sixty-five years. And so the diminution gradually went on until in Abraham's day, a hundred and seventy-five years was esteemed great length of life.

Another striking fact with regard to animal food is, that four thousand years of habitual use has not taught us to cease to shudder at the blood-stained flesh which constitutes our daily repasts. It must be disguised by cookery, both in appearance and taste—browned by fire—salted, peppered, spiced: without which, it is uneatable. Casper Hauser, when first released from his life-long imprisonment, was nauseated by the sight, taste, and smell of flesh food, and when, after long persistence, he grew accustomed to its use, he declined in health until his short and sad career was closed by death.

The relative positions which the vegetable productions of the world hold to each other seems suggestive. The esculent and other roots are placed under the earth—the grasses and green herbs are spread upon or near the surface of the earth, and the tree fruits are suspended above the earth.—The hog, peccary, &c., are furnished, by nature, with the means of reaching the first class of esculents—cattle of the herbivorous classes are furnished with the means of appropriating the second kind, and man and the monkey, his soulless brother, were created so as to subsist upon the third kind of food.

The highest order of monkeys, the gorillas, approach men very nearly in their anatomical structure,—but the one being endowed with mind and soul, is required to provide his own food by planting, "dressing and keeping" his Eden trees, while the other, being a brute, subsists upon the spontaneous productions of the earth.

Fruits and nuts are just of that degree of tender firmness in texture, which, in mastication, exercises the salivary glands and produces the amount of secretion necessary for digestion; while our flesh, herb and root dishes, are reduced by cookery to a soft (but not always a tender) moistness, which does not demand a full exercise of these glands; and the consequence is, imperfect digestion and tartareous incrustations upon the teeth.

In Germany the term for orchard is *baumgarten*, tree garden, and was it not Goëthe, the dear, grand old German, who, in eulogising some one, said, "*he understands trees?*" Eden itself was a tree-garden and Adam a tree-gardener. Trees, besides supplying us with food, protect us from the heat of the summer's sun, and the keen blasts of the winter's wind, and gratify, at the same time, our love of the beautiful.—We have only to fill our tree-gardens with trees bearing *both* the Eden characteristics, goodness for food and pleasantness to the sight, and arrange them in the natural landscape-garden style to make another Eden worthy to be the care of unfallen man. The most beautiful trees are the most valuable for food, as for instance, in our latitude, the Persian walnut, the black walnut, (the only tree mentioned by name in Poe's description of Arnheim, which is one of the most gorgeous dreams of beauty that ever filled a poet's head and heart), the chestnut, the pecan, the shellbark, the sweet acorned oaks of the south of Europe, mulberries of various kinds, the Swiss and Italian stone pines, with their sweet edible nuts, the strangely beautiful Salisburia, and the magnificent Araucarias. The tropics furnish ten to each one of ours, but still we have enough for all the purposes of the orchardist as well as the landscape gardener. Our usual orchard fruits, the apple, pear, plum and cherry, possess many beauties, and could be made entirely beautiful by proper cultivation, their ofttimes twisted and knarled trunks being the result of neglect and abuse.

THE APPLE being the most common and widely distributed of orchard fruits heads the list.—It is peculiar to the temperate zone, flourishing as far north as 60 deg., and ceasing as far south as the confines of the tropics. All the multitudinous varieties which we cultivate are supposed to have been developed by patient horticultural skill, from the common crab apple, which is a well known small thorny tree, bearing acid, worthless fruit. Scientific facts indicate that the apple and all its congeners appeared on the earth just before the creation of man, and as Hugh Macmillan believes that no thorns existed before the curse, "thorns also and thistles shall the earth bring forth to thee," the crab must have degenerated from the apple of Eden. Macmillan says that thorns are merely abortive efforts of nature to produce branches, and as nature made no abortive efforts before the curse, there were no thorns. The persevering efforts of man, in the sweat of his brow, has restored the apple, if not to its original excellence, at least to that degree of vigor that the thorns have disappeared, and the fruit is of inestimable value. The apple compares most favorably with more popular esculents in value as a nutritious article of food. It contains 17 per cent. of nutriment while the beet contains but 15 per cent., turnips but 4½, carrots but 10, and cabbage but 7½. Yet more labor is bestowed upon each of these crops than upon the apple. As to the amount yielded per acre it also takes a high stand. We have an instance of a single tree in Niagara Co., New York, producing twenty-six barrels of fruit.

Profit of Apple Growing.—"H. T. Brooks, Esq., at the New York State Fair, during one of the evenings' discussion, gave, among other evidence of the profits of apple growing, the following:

"A tree in Middlebury gave 11 barrels: four trees in LeRoy, 13 barrels each. Patrick McEntee, of Perry, took 14 barrels of Baldwin's from one tree, and sold them to A. W. Wheelock for $60. Mr. True, of Castile, took 15 barrels of Gilliflowers from a single tree. Enos Wright, of Middlebury, sold the product of two trees for $100. Two years ago Mr. Hammond, supervisor of Middlebury, sold the product of 33 trees of Northern Spys for $900. C. Cronkhite sold the apples on less than four acres for $1,500. He said that Edmund Morris, the admirable author of 'Ten Acres Enough,' who, by-the-by, with the usual consistency of preaching farmers, had added 13 acres to his 'Ten,' had told us of 20 apple-trees that paid their owner $225 one year. Here, said Major Brooks, is a story to match: Robert McDowel, of York, Livingston County, has 22 trees, grafted nineteen years ago to Dutch Pippins, Greenings, Russets, etc., standing 35 to 40 feet apart—his soil sandy loam, annually ploughed and cropped, being also heavily manured every year, and protected by woods on three sides. He sold from these trees, after reserving his culls, in 1865, 163 barrels of apples for $779.50.

"Prescott Smead, of Bethany, Genesee County, from six acres, on clay and strong clay loam, sold as follows:

1862................	750	barrels..	$2,370
1863........	590	" ...	1,700
1864	600	"	2,100
1865...............	810	"	4,500
1866...............	150	" ...	863
1867.(*estimated*).	600	" ...	3,000

"Add to the above, copied from

his income report (and reports of this kind are not apt to be overstated,) apples used in the family, and we have 100 barrels to the acre, and 2½ barrels to the tree *annually*, for the whole six years, paying $400 per acre every year for the whole term."

[*Horticulturist.*

If good winter varieties are procured, of Southern origin, they will keep through the winter months with far more ease than our usual vegetable winter stores, potatoes, beets, &c.,—and the only reason we can assign for the culture of the latter receiving more care and attention, is that they yield an immediate return, while the apple trees will require six or eight years to come into bearing. To be sure when the apples do come, they will yield for the rest of one's life-time without further trouble, and may be left a heritage to one's children, but—"it is too much trouble"—"we haven't the time"—"it won't pay!" are the foolish, and almost wicked, reasons assigned by some really industrious men, for neglecting these Eden trees. There are many hundreds of varieties of the apple, of which we can only notice a few, best suited to the South.

Of the summer varieties, there is the Red Astrachan, worthy of its Eden origin; beautiful to the eye, fragrant as the odors of Araby the blest, and luscious to the taste. Then the Julian, not inferior, but later. The Early Red Margaret is not so beautiful, but of high flavor. And the Indian beauty, Nantahalee, who may plume herself on having won the heart of Dr. Ticknor, who sings her praises in the following humorous and happy style:

"You've heard, I think, of the beautiful maid,
Who fled from Love's caresses,
Till her beautiful toes were turned to roots,
And both her shoulders to beautiful shoots,
And her beautiful cheeks to beautiful fruits,
And to blossoming spray, her tresses!
"I've *seen* her, man! she's a'living yet
Up in a Cherokee valley!
She's an apple-tree! and her name might be
In the softy musical Chewkee,
A long drawn—"Nantahalee!"
'Tis as sweet a word as you'll read or write;
Not *quite* as fair as the *thing*, yet quite
Sufficient to start an old Anchorite
Out of his ashes to bless and *bite*
The Beautiful 'Nantahalee!' "

Of the autumn varieties there are the Buncombe, (or Meigs) the Carolina Greening, the Disharoon, the Hamilton, the Taunton, Tuscaloosa Seedling, and Yopp's Favorite—all treasures, and each worthy of pages of praise, instead of a mere mention.

But it is the winter apples in which the most interest should be felt—winter being the season of scarcity; while in summer, so many other delicious fruits crowd themselves upon our notice that the apple is less cared for.

The kinds most popular in our Southern nurseries are, first, the Equinetelee, the finest of early winter apples, a large, luscious and high flavored fruit, and a vigorous and handsome tree of the pyramidal form.

The Holly is deliciously aromatic and sugary—yellow, with a crimson cheek, and the tree is of free and healthy growth.

The Mangum (or Carter) is a very distinguished and well known noble of the apple family, whose red, striped coat, and high flavored, tender and juicy character, are always welcomed warmly at the planter's dinner table.

Kittageskee and Cullasaga, Nickajack and Junaluskee are all distinguished countrymen of the beautiful Nantahalee, although, unfortunately, they never see her, for she comes with the roses of summer, and they with the holly berries of Christmas. Some tasteless Goth has given the most valuable of our winter apples the shocking name of Shockley. But it has acquired a princely reputation under this ugly name, and so let it remain to the end of time, the good and beautiful Shockley. Its flavor and size may not be *quite* equal to some others, but it is worth its weight in gold for its conservative principles—it was created a winter apple, and a sound winter apple it is going to remain, in spite of the disorganizing elements in apple society.—Let the persecutions of the radical frost be never so severe, and the warm dissolving breath of spring be never so seductive, it is going to maintain its ground, like a faithful sentinel, a sound conservative apple, until the Red Astrachan and Early Harvest come to relieve guard,and its duty is done. Let us plant them by the thousand in the desolate fields of the South.

THE PEAR will flourish in the same latitude as the apple, and the winter varieties are almost as easily kept. Trees have been known to produce twenty-five hundred pounds of fruit annually, and as forty-eight trees will stand on an acre (at the usual distance of thirty feet apart) this would be a yield of sixty tons per acre, a yield double that of the thirty tons of turnips of the English farmer. And then we must recollect the great annual labor and expense which the thirty tons of turnips costs the English farmer, and the little labor and expense which the sixty tons of pears costs the American orchardist. And also the fact that the pear contains 16 per cent. of nutriment, very little less than the apple, while the turnip contains but 4½ per cent. The varieties are very great, but the most popular at the South are as follows:

SUMMER VARIETIES.

"Beurre Giffard-Medium, showy appearance, and the best and largest of early pears. June.

Bartlett—Too well known to need any description.

Madeleine—Medium, melting, sweet, one of the earliest.

Ott's Seedling—Medium, melting and fine flavored, good grower. August.

Tyson—Above medium, juicy, sweet, fine flavored. August.

AUTUMN VARIETIES.

Andrews—medium, fair, melting and sweet, very productive. September.

Beurre Bose—Large, long, vinous, fine grower. September.

Beurre Diel—Large, or very large, rich, buttery, rapid grower. September to October.

Beurre Clairgeau—Very large, nearly melting, high flavor, one of the very best. Sept. to Oct.

Beurre Golden of Bilboa—Large, buttery and melting, high flavored. August to September.

Belle Lucrative—Large, melting, delicious, a fair grower, first quality.

Doyenne White, or *Virgalieu*—Medium, very good, a good grower and productive.

Marie Louise—Large, melting, first quality. September.

Seckle—Small, but excellent, well known as one of the finest of Fall Pears. September.

Sheldon—Large, round, melting, rich and delicious, handsome tree. September.

Urbaniste—Large, melting, buttery, good grower. September and October.

Beurre Easter—Large, roundish oval, melting, good, keeps very late.

Columbia—Large, melting, good grower and productive. Dec.

Doyenne D'Alencon—Large, oval, rich and melting, tree vigorous, and a late keeper.

Josephine de Malines—The very best of Winter Pears, rich, juicy, melting and good flavor, very productive, late keeper, poor grower.

Lawrence—Fine, melting, large, tree fair grower.

Winter Nelis—Medium, melting and buttery, rich flavor, tree a poor grower. October to December."

THE PEACH is next upon the list, and the beauty and exquisite flavor and size which it has attained under the hands of skillful and scientific horticulturists, induces the belief that we are indeed approaching the promised time when there will be 'no more curse,' and our fruits will be restored to the pristine beauty and goodness of Eden.

All over the South it grows like a bramble wherever a peach stone happens to fall. But these wildliugs are not "goot for much," as Professor Herder said of whortleberries—they only prove, by the ease with which they grow, and the tenacity with which they cling to life, how admirably adapted the peach is to our soil and climate. Hear Dr. Ticknor again, how his wit sparkles around

THE OLD PEACH TREE—WITH A MORAL.

"That old unsightly Tree!
What moral might it teach,
When it lately tendered me
A melancholy Peach?

Its roots in rifted clay!
  Its trunk to worm and sun!
Blown down and washed away
  Yet strangely living on!

The very utmost crest
  Of that unshadowed hill,
And not, from east to west,
  A rival pinnacle!

Beside a cabin, all
  As mouldered as itself,
With weeds upon the wall,
  And a " May-Pop " on the shelf.

Of man, or beast, the sole
  Successful speculation!
The harvest of a whole
  Plantation's desolation!

What moral might it teach,
  That old unsightly Tree,
As it tendered me a peach,
  Acidulous, tho' free.

'Twas thus the Peach-Tree said—
  'Oh! stranger! tell me why,
If this old Peach ain't *dead*,
  A Peach should *ever* die!'
But I only shook my head,
  And inly answered—' Why! ' "

The varieties are not so numerous as those of the apple and pear, but still more than could be crowded into any one orchard.—We have not space to enumerate even the best, but will pick out a few of the first water, the Koh-i-noors.

Hale's Early Red is ripe by the first of June, and is beautiful and delicious. Its blossoms withstand the effects of frost better than any other variety.

The Early Tillotson comes next in order, and then that splendid variety, the Honey. This is a large, oblong fruit, coming to a sharp curved point, color, yellowish white, mottled with crimson, flesh juicy, tender, of a peculiarly delicious, honeyed sweetness.—The stone has the same curious curved point as the fruit. It was originated by Mr. Lyon, of Columbia, S. C. Ripens the latter part of June and first half of July.

Grosse Mignonne–We wonder if Eve ever pressed her pearly teeth into a more delicious fruit than the Grosse Mignonne? Description unnecessary—it is found in all the Southern nurseries. Ripens early in July.

Amelia—Large and delicious.

Columbia—Very large, rich and luscious.

Green Catharine,—A beautiful and very productive peach of first quality.

The following are all splendid: Osceola, Chinese Cling, Duff's Yellow, Eaton's Golden, Flewellen, Indian Cling, Baldwin's Late, Mitchell's Mammoth, Nix's Late, Pineapple, White Globe and Heath.

THE PLUM succeeds well in the border States. In addition to its value as a summer fruit, many varieties are suitable for drying into prunes, and make a valuable and wholesome addition to the winter stores of the Southern housekeeper. The Plum is a very nutritious fruit, containing 29 per cent. of nutriment, while beef only contains 26 per cent.—pork 24 and veal 25. They commence ripening in July, and contimne until September. The best varieties for this latitude are considered to be the Blue Impera trice, Bradshaw, Columbia, Duane's Purple, German Prune, Green Gage, Yellow Gage, Imperial Gage, Laurence's Favorite, Wilde's Italian Gage, Morocco, Washington, Smith's Orleans, and Prince's Golden Gage.

CHERRIES are one of our earliest and finest fruits; they contain 25 per cent. of nutriment. Some of the best are Knight's Early Black, Black Tartarian, May Duke, Osceola, Coe's Transparent, and Early Purple Guigne.

THE APRICOT is also very valuable for its earliness, and is a wholesome fruit, even for invalids, and very nutritious, containing 26 per cent. of nutriment. The varieties celebrated here, are Breda, Moorpark, Orange, Early Golden, Schuyler's Large, Roman and Turkey.

THE FIG grows finely in the Gulf States, forming a small tree, very suitable for orchard culture. It is an exquisite fruit, both in a fresh and preserved state. The Malta, Brunswick, Pregussata, Black St. Michael, Marseilles, the White Ischia, Green Ischia and Nerii, are a few of the many varieties.

THE MULBERRY has received very little attention in this country, our ideas of its character being derived from the wild, sour fruit found in our forests. Downing's Everbearing is a very elegant tree, which deserves cultivation merely for its beauty. It originated in 1845 with Mr. Charles Downing, of Newburgh, N. Y. The fruit is of a purplish black color, and of a delightful, rich, sub-acid taste. Comes into bearing the third or fourth year, and the fruit increases in size as the tree acquires age. The black or Persian Mulberry (*Morus nigra*) has long been a favorite in England, and is one of the most healthy, and delicious fruits of its season. Although this tree matures early, it attains a great age. There is one in England, at Lyon House, the seat of the Duke of Northumberland, which is three hundred years old, and is supposed to have been planted by the botanist, Turner, in the 16th century.

OUR LIFE IN BOOKS.

NO. I.

Early Years.

THE markets exhibit so much to invite perusal, and the purses of our people contain so little to command luxuries of that description, that the question as to the influences in books to which we shall choose to subject ourselves, an interesting and important one at all times, becomes doubly interesting at the present time.

There does seem to be some truth in that beautiful theory, that there is an analogy between the different ages of the world, and the different ages of human life. The infancy of man appears to correspond to the infancy of the world, in its perfect simplicity, its objectivity, its want of abstract ideas—and its deep wanderings in dream and reverie upon the very borders of the celestial realms in which, also, wander those beings above man, good spirits and bad, who wish to look frequently over the walls into the terrestrial abodes. In this infancy of the world, stand forever its Garden of Eden, its Garden of the Hesperides, its Golden Age, its Arcadia, its Paradise of Iram, and all the dreams of the Young Earth and of the young human soul. As the early chapters of the Bible are first and earliest in human knowledge concerning those early ages of the world, so the subjects of which they treat, are the very foundation crystals around the source of life upon which the young, in a healthy state will love to muse in deep earnest ponderings, and questionings, and efforts, to solve difficulties. And the mind of a child near the fountain of its thinking life, will as certainly run upon the ORIGINES in the classic mythology as upon the ORIGINES of Holy Writ itself. If it is an ingenuous and finely touched spirit, it may be deeply interested in the scenes of Eden, and in the night-wrestlings of Jacob with God, and with the transplanted life of Joseph in Egypt, and with the deep and gorgeous romance of Moses, and the wild riddling, and the growing hair of Samson. But it will be as deeply interested in the labors of Hercules; and in the meeting of Paris with the goddesses on Mount Ida, and all its consequences; and in the "tale of Troy Divine, and in the house of Tantalus, the line of Laius, and in the grand witchcraft of Medea.

And wishing to judge for no other man, and in this matter allowing no other man to judge for us, we declare that we willingly allow the roamings of the minds of our children, in that deep dreaming season of early years, when the cravings of their spirits demand such things, not only into the deep, sacred and gorgeons romance of Holy writ, in which God is at the top of the trooping and glorious companies of ascending and descending celestials, but also freely to the Gardens of the Hesperides, where the golden apples grow; to the feast of the gods where one golden apple "to the fairest" was thrown in by the Goddess of Discord; to the vision from the Scæan gate of the fight around Troy; to all the glorious dreams of early Greece, and to all the iron grandeur of early Rome.

We also take the responsibility of permitting our children at this age, to read the FAIRY TALES; and have no idea their minds, by the high gift of God, haunted from day to day—(if black and panic TERROR be not wickedly thrown in by silly nurses)—by scenery and visions from "Beauty and the Beast," and from "Cinderella," will be half as much fitted for "treason, stratagem and spoil" as will be minds more puritanically trained.

And here, as one of the poets of England bids us "hold the good, and define it well, lest divine philosophy should be procured to the Lords of Hell," we venture to define what we mean by *puritanical*. We do not mean *pure*. We object to no modes either of education, or of morals, or of religion on account of their purity. And should, therefore, in all probability, deeply dissent from the reasons for which the wits of the courts of Charles Second detested puritanism. Nor do we admit that any right theory of morals or of religion, is any the worse in fact for being *right;* or that that practice is a fair subject for appeals to prejudice through the powerful odium of traditionary hard words, which is STRICT, in the sense of hearty, and faithful conformity, inward and outward, to strict right principles.

But we use the word puritanic in its historical, and not in its etymological meaning, to signify a scheme whose main-spring is *envy:* which hates human happiness through *envy:* which persecutes because it hates human happiness, which hates human happiness because it is itself unhappy, righteously, justly, necessarily, unhappy because God is just; which has no law but prejudice, and the power of the demagogue, which lives for and seeks, and believes in, no other courts of appeal, save and except new efforts to overwhelm the whole Temple of Truth in ruins, to prevent men from clearly seeing the ruined pillars and the crumbling arches of that temple which it has made. There is no doubt that the oracles of our Holy religion do contain precepts which command us to *deny ourselves*, to mortify our members which are upon the earth, and to bear a daily cross along the footprints wherein the holy feet of the Son of God have gone. And every just mind will see and admit the propriety of giving to those precepts their just full, fair, proper weight in any, and every theory of manners, morals, or religion. But we do not understand those precepts to be based in the *hatred* of human nature, but in the *love* of it. We understand that their foundation is laid in the fact, well known to the divine mind, that, by them, man may come to the highest, purest, most genuine and intrinsic happiness of which his nature is capable. They are simply the inculcated amputations of the soul, to deliver it from a far more deadly mortification—the gangrene of the Spirit itself. But the puritan view, fastens upon self-denial, and self-mortification, as *ends* and not *means*. It loves them for their own sake, especially when inflicted on others. The Book of Sabbath Sports in the days of Charles I., of England, was terribly detestable to puritanism for two reasons: one was that being *wrong in itself*, and a violation of the Law of God, there was a good ground for agitation against it; the other was that the green stomach could not well have borne to witness the happiness of the people dancing around the May pole, on *any* day of the week;—and much less on a day when the objection to it could be made good to honest Christian conscience. And we firmly believe that genuine puritanism—without the piety—existed just as much under the vermin-infested hair-shirts of Becket and Dunstan, as upon the sonorous noses and psalm-singing lips of Cromwell and his iron-sides;—and more in the wild heresies and virtual atheisms of Channing, Emerson, Park, Parker, and their followers, than in either.

We do not allege that these men and parties carried their sournesses into education, where we are now looking upon it. But they show what the thing is, in its developments.

The point involved in the question whether Fairy Tales are to be granted as food for the spirits of Christian children, is, whether the paths of correct and pure Christian morals are more apt to be trodden bravely and cheerfully by those to whom it is permitted to strew the margin of that way with flowers; than by those to whom, in order to beget low, silent pulses of the spirit, the way is kept forever apparent, and the eye bound to an incessant gaze upon it, in its most forbidding and unadorned appearance, with the careful exclusion of all influences to give hope and cheerfulness to the heart and vigor to the muscles of the moving feet, and also with the exclusion of the power of the sweeter and better, than siren call from before us, in the path of WISDOM and PRUDENCE walking arm in arm, saying "these are ways of pleasantness and peace." If there were not in religion any such precepts as self-denial and mortification of earthly lusts, upon which such things may be erected with a powerful plausibility, there would not be, and would not have been, half the danger that there has been and is, in asceticism, monasticism, and puritanism. But those things have been permitted to spring up on one side of the chariot of Redemption as it has moved over the world; while Lasciviousness, Revelry and Sensuality have held the opposite borders; that in them we might recognize the dangers of either coast, and see where runs, with angels hovering over it, the true road to heaven.

MABEL.

BY CLARA V. DARGAN.

"We are almost there now, m'am: You can see the end of the house between the trees."

I leaned forward, and looked out of the carriage window. Twilight was closing in, but through the dusk I caught a glimpse of white walls; and in a few moments we had passed the gates, and were rolling rapidly up the broad, gravelled sweep. It was a lovely May evening, and the air was laden with the perfume of flowers which grew in rich luxuriance around: but over all came floating the breath of heliotrope—Mabel's old favorite—and I saw, as the carriage drew up before the door, that it grew everywhere.—In plots either side of the steps—in marble urns upon the long, low piazza;—everywhere lingered that intangible, haunting fragranee. A sigh which was a half sob escaped me: I knew Mabel was not changed.

There she stood. How we met I scarcely knew—but neither of us spoke. Such long, sad years had separated us, that we were too full for words: I only felt her velvet cheek pressed to mine, and her faithful arms around me.—Presently she put me off a little and looked in my face.

"It is Dora," she said, "my Theodora—'the gift of God.'"

The familiar voice, so singularly sweet and plaintive—the utterance so low and clear—opened the sealed fountain. I clasped her closer in my arms and wept.

"Don't Dora! It is all over now. We will be happy together, and try to feel that the past is in the eternal past."

"*You* are not unfaithful, Mabel," I said, looking up at her.

"No, dear," she answered quietly, but a shadow crossed her face: "It is God's will that we should suffer. The sin lies in bemoaning broken idols."

The words fell upon my heart like a sudden conviction. Mabel saw it, and said no more; but she drew me gently down the long piazza, and opened a door at the farther end.

"This is your room, Dora, and I have chosen it for you because it is at once the pleasantest and most retired. But mine is next to it," she added, "or rather my sanctum; so you will not be lonely."

It was an exquisite little apartment. All the appointments were such as Mabel only could have chosen. The delicately-tinted walls, the gossamer lace that draped the couch—even the rose-colored lamp, which threw its mellowed light over all, bespoke that rare refinement and delicacy of taste which was an essential attribute of her character. She had not always possessed the means of gratifying it; and I knew so little of her present circumstances, that I looked around with an interest I could not disguise.

Mabel smiled. "Yes," she said, answering my thoughts, "I have all I desire—" and then, after a moment's pause, repeated, "*all* I desire."

"And your husband—"

"Is a noble and estimable man. I am indeed blessed in his affection."

The tone satisfied me, but the words did not.

We passed the evening together alone. I did not see Mabel's husband. He was off, she said, at a lower plantation, and would not return till the morrow. So we had ample time for reviewing the years which had elapsed since we parted. Only one subject was tacitly avoided; there are some wounds which will not bear re-opening, and I thought Mabel shrank from this. Once or twice some chance expression seemed to approach it; but my own griefs were yet too familiar to me, not to feel intuitively she also had suffered.

I met Col. Hayne the next day at dinner. He was a tall, well-made man, rather portly, and extremely dignified, but quite gray, and evidently twice her age. I glanced involuntarily at Mabel standing there, in all her grace and delicacy, robed in white, with the purple heliotrope resting against her ivory throat—and a sudden shock of disappointment rushed over me. A vision rose before my eyes of a handsome, spirited face I had last seen bending over her's with such unutterable tenderness. Had she forgotten it? Alas! I had learnt so many sad lessons of human falsehood that I had come to believe in nothing. Mabel was my only faith now: was she too like the rest? I could not answer.

It was about twilight when, coming into the drawing-room, I caught a glimpse of Mabel's white dress as she sat at the piano, with her head bent upon the rosewood paneling. She did not perceive me, and shortly after she raised her face and began playing. The rich, soft, painfully sad air throbbed through the gloom, and her voice rose with it. I remembered it was *his* favorite. Well might she sing "*Infelice.*" The tones were thick with tears, and my heart ached as I listened. I stole out of the room, and wept in the silence of my own chamber.

The days went on, and wrapped in her matronly dignity, it was in vain I strove to read Mabel's heart. I recalled the summer so long ago which we had spent together in a mountain village, where strangers flocked in search of fine scenery and pure air.—There we had met one who seemed to us—a pair of enthusiastic maidens—the personation of our ideal. They were betrothed—and I was suddenly called away from my own wild day-dreams by circumstances of a peculiarly painful nature. Far away upon a foreign shore I had afterwards lived a few brief months of happincss such as few can comprehend—for my capacity for an all-absorbing affection, unselfish and unstinted, was nature's most lavished gift. And yet it had proved the bane of my life. This passed—and yet I lingered among the scenes of my sorrow—alone, forgotten by all save this one true friend. At length I returned to my native land, and sought her: but in vain I searched for the lost clue to her history.

It was on Mabel's birth-night that I found it. As I entered the drawing-rooms, I saw her in the center of a group, under the chandelier—radiant in the pride of her peerless beauty: the exquisite features as still and passionless as if carved in marble—the eyes burning with an ever-changing opaline light, looking forward with that strange, yearning expression in which lay the subtle charm that had made Mabel Hayne the empress of a thousand hearts. She wore a robe of pearl-grey silk, embroidered with rose-buds, and a cluster of pink hyacinths in her soft, chestnut hair: but what were outward ornaments to her! She would have been regal in the simplest guise.

I watched her from afar. I heard the sound of her voice with its low, plaintive music;—I saw men gather around to listen to the unconscious eloquence which flowed from her lips;—I saw her move among her guests with that imperial grace which distinguished her every gesture: and I wondered if that calm face, so beautiful, yet to me so sad in its frozen loveliness—was the same I had seen five years before, flashing with every ennobling emotion—a face which made one comprehend those impressive words: "*He created man in His own image.*"

The guests departed and I sat alone in my room. A faint light streamed under the door which opened into Mabel's sanctum: I knew she was writing. I had heard her come in about a half-hour before—and I waited, hoping she would call me before she retired. But I waited in vain. After a while the light disappeared: I could bear it no longer—I rose and went in. All was dark, except where the moonlight streamed in at the open bay-window, and I saw Mabel was reclining on a couch within its recess.

"Is it you, Dora?"

I came and knelt down by her, while she passed her fingers caressingly over my hair.

"Brave, true soul! Do you believe me still, Theodora?"

"Mabel—Mabel. I *cannot* mistrust you—but what does it all mean?"

"I will tell you" she said—and there I heard the sequel to that sweet summer-idyl so long passed.

"September was closing when I left the mountains, to hasten home and prepare for my marriage. He, —— Gaston, came with me. When we reached F—, a lady, dressed in deep mourning with her veil closely drawn, entered the train, and took a seat near us. She, evidently, shrank from notice, but under cover of the dusk, steadily surveyed us; and then leaning her head against the window, seemed lost in thought. It was quite dark when we arrived, and Gaston left me in the waiting-room at the depot to find the carriage. I was sitting there thinking of my great happiness—I remember it seemed for the moment more than I could bear—when I looked up and saw the lady I had observed in the cars, standing before me. She threw back her veil; I never saw a face so grand and imposing. Her voice was steady as if under the control of a powerful will. She made no preliminary remarks—no excuses—but simply asked—

"Are you engaged to *him?*" with a slight gesture towards the door.

Something impelled me to answer in the same spirit: I saw she was terribly in earnest.

"I am."

"May God help you! You have committed your fate to a perjured, heartless man."

I looked up at her helplessly—I felt bewildered.

"You are a beautiful young creature," she went on, with a falter in her voice. "It is a pity you should come to such a sad fate—but it is mine too—and I did not deserve it. God help us both!" She paused a moment, and then thrust a worn letter into my hand. "Take it!" she said: "I have kept it two years and learnt the cruel words by heart. Do you learn them now before it is too late. Innocent little darling!" she murmured, with infinite gentleness—"it is a hard and bitter lesson, but we must all learn it sometime."

She bent down and kissed me as she spoke, and walked away into the dim shadows outside.—I heard a carriage drive off, as I sat holding the letter tightly in my hand—the only tangible proof that all this was not a hideous dream. I read it that night when I was alone. It was *his* letter—*he* had written it—a cold, formal announcement that he had been mistaken in the nature of his feelings towards her, and begged to be released from the engagement which existed between them. He considered it, he said, only honorable that she should not be left in doubt with regard to his intentions. I read it again and again—I could not deny it was genuine. Little Dora, we all have our own griefs; but oh, what is so hard to bear, as to *prove* the treachery of those we love?"

"I need not tell you of that long, dreary night. I sat there as one bereft of reason. My idol, so rudely torn from its pedestal, fell at my feet shattered—its beauty, its truth, its purity forever lost. No eye but that All-seeing and pitiful ever looked upon anguish such as mine: we must bear it alone, and alone I have ever borne it. When the gray dawn broke—that solemn hour when nature comes face to face with Jehovah—I fell upon my knees and prayed for strength. It was granted me; I saw the path which duty had clearly opened.

"That evening he came. Dora, when I saw his face—that face which so many women had loved—I felt one keen pang. But it was soon over. That fatal letter was before me in letters of fire. I hushed every heart-throb, and told him of it. It struck home—oh, it struck home! He could not comprehend me at first. He did not think I meant to give him up entirely; but when he did realize it—and he knew I was not a woman to waver—he reeled and almost fell. I thought I heard that weird voice saying: 'God help us both!' and in my heart the petition went up for him also—whose wickedness or weakness had caused so much misery. God forbid we should judge *which!*"

When he recovered, he tried to explain it. He called it a passing fancy, as men do—a fascination of the senses;—that he had admired her character and intellect, and imagined he loved her, till time and separation had proved its fallacy. But I could make only one answer—

"You deceived her."

And that was all, Dora. If any call me fickle, let them not dare to judge till they have read this page of my heart's history. I let him kiss me once more when we parted. It was the last—*last* time! I had loved him so dearly—and though my faith in him was utterly gone, I could not overcome in those few brief hours the affection I had lavished upon him for so many months. When he was gone, I thought life had lost all its brightness for me—and for four years, I lived in that memory alone. You know that little verse, the epitome of many a woman's story:—

"'Tis not the lover which is lost—
The love for which we grieve;—
It is the *price* which they have cost,
The memories which they leave."

Sometimes on a spring evening—such an evening as this, I sit and recall the beautiful romance which filled my life for six months: and after I have lived it all over, I turn to this book wherein I recorded my marriage vow to one who is truth and honor itself—whose slightest word is a sacred oath:—and when I close it, I say reverently:—

"Ah, what am I that God hath saved
Me from the doom I did desire;—
Aud crossed the lot myself had craved
To set me higher!"

She ceased, and there was a long silence. The moon shone full on her beautiful face, and I saw a tear glistening upon her cheek. Presently she rose, and saying—

"I have something here to show you," placed in my hand a small mother-of-pearl casket.

When I was alone, I opened it. There was a slip cut from a newspaper:

"*Killed at Fort Donelson, Feb. 13th, Capt. Gaston V. Moore, aged thirty-two. A brave soldier, a true patriot, an honorable gentleman.*"

It was enclosed in a small envelope, in which was a faded sprig of heliotrope; and on it inscribed:

"INFELICE."

"THE CEDARS,"
Union Point, Ga.

THE FUTURE OF YOUNG AFRICA!

"LABOR," says Degerando, "is the morality of the uneducated classes;" and in uttering this broad truth, the philosopher almost falls into a truism. Although with man, the great object of labor is the immediate and direct result—it is not so with God in his decree, "in the sweat of thy face thou shall eat bread." For labor is a training. The habit of labor implies a motive for exertion, the steady pursuit of a useful object, the acquisition of strength and skill productive of beneficial results, of a steadiness of mind and heart excluding frivolous and mischievous occupations. It is a defensive armor against the assaults of malignant and enervating passions. Labor is in a broad sense both morality and education.

When we inquire into the history of nations, we find that nothing more distinguishes one people from another than their relative aptitude for labor, and the direction they give to it. The amount of it is one of the best tests of civilization ; and one hour added to, or substracted from the daily industry of the working part of a nation, will make the difference between a rapidly progressing prosperity, and a condition of national stagnation and decay.

Many circumstances will influence the industry of a people. Want is the mother of labor. Where nature does most to supply man's wants, he least feels the necessity of supplying them by his own exertions. Where nature does little beyond making a measured return to systematic toil, there man learns to do most for himself. The gratification of his wants by industry stimulates that industry, and new wants spur him on to new exertions—he acquires skill, knowledge, arts, accumulates wealth and multiplies his resources. Where no amount of toil can force nature to increase her scanty gifts doled out with a niggard hand, man, with all his energies can never raise himself above the condition of the fishing, or hunting, or at best, the pastoral tribes.

We can thus, in a great measure, account for the habits and occupations of the people in the easy living climates of the South of Europe, and similarly situated lands, where the climate discourages arduous labor, while the soil readily supplies urgent wants. This, too, explains to us the greater energy and industry of the less bountiful and more exacting regions and more bracing climates further North. Beyond that, and cut off from the possibility of forcing production from barren nature—by any amount of toil, the Laplander is solely occupied with the care of his herd of reindeer, his only possible wealth. We may see in regions still more desolate and hopeless, as Greenland, and the frozen Siberian coast, man's life divided between arduous and hazardous enterprise in fishing and hunting, and absolute idleness and gluttony when success affords the means of excess. Although in this progress from South to North, we remark unmistakable differences of race among these people, we need not have recourse to that in accounting for the difference of their habits and pursuits.

Yet, it is evident that different races of men vary greatly in their propensity to industry, and in the skillful application of their labor. The fertile fields now yearly widening over this continent, teeming with productions for the maintenance of millions, were, for uncounted centuries, but the hunting grounds of a race, who had every opportunity of appropriating the untold wealth scarcely hidden in the soil. Yet, these people were capable of the occasional exertion of rare energies, and matchless endurance. We cannot but believe that the difference of race in the succeeding inhabitants of the country, has had much to do with the different conditions of this continent, in the 15th century, and now. Other lands and races afford corroborating testimony to this unequal propensity to labor among the races of men. We need but contrast the condition of New Holland with its handful of wretched Papuas—or New Zealand with its tribes of fierce and cannibal Malays, with their condition in the hands of the European colonists who have now crowded thither.

But the negro affords in this respect the most remarkable peculiarities. With a capacity for labor exceeded by few races, he has an indisposition to labor, rivalled by none. While in the only instance in which they have been known to thrive and multiply rapidly as a population—they were for generations subjected to a system of enforced labor, there has never yet been an instance of their spontaneously forming an industrious population. The Papua of New Guinea, and New Holland, an inferior variety of the negro, seems never to have got beyond the fishing and the hunting state. In the true negro regions of Africa wherever society has progressed beyond pastoral life the conqueror imposes the task on the vanquished, and the many are slaves to the few. It is possible that in the history of man's progress, all steady, systematic industry originated in enforced labor, exacted by the master from the slave. For in the earliest times known to us, and long after, we find slavery existing in every civilized country, and slaves most numerous in the most civilized. Thus Athens far exceeded Sparta in the number of her slaves. Perhaps it was thus that the tendency and aptitude to toil were first cultivated for generations in the race. But in the negro no such tendency has been developed, and the rare instances of systematic industry in the negro distinguish the individual among his people.

This aversion in the negro to systematic industry cannot be attributed to local causes. It has exhibited itself for tens of centuries in Africa, and kept the race almost on a dead level, raised but one step above the brutes. It reappeared in full vigor in the West Indies the moment that emancipation from slavery removed all external impulse to a life of toil. In both these instances we might attribute the negro's indolence to nature's bounty which there often gave food in return for the mere stretching forth the hand. But the previous emancipation of the negroes in the Northern States had been followed by the same results; idleness, improvidence, want and crime. On the emancipation of the slaves in the Cape Colony, at the southern extremity of Africa, slaves of two different races seem to have been set free; the indigenous African, and some Malays brought from the Southern peninsula and islands of Asia. These last have, in some measure, availed themselves of the boon of liberty, and seem actually to have improved their condition; while the negro sunk lower and lower into idleness, ignorance, and squalid want. The experiment now being so broadly tried in the South gives the strongest promise or rather confirmation of similar results.

The adult negroes of this generation have been trained to the systematic labor of civilized life, and they have been trained too to some of the wants of civilized man, their position, and association with a higher and more cultivated race have necessarily inculcated upon them some of the elementary principles and maxims, that control society and guide the conduct of responsible beings. And yet the moment the control of the master is withdrawn—as soon as the local and domestic government which was thus supplied is abolished—the negro population, without tumult, mob violence, or any of the symptoms which usually attend the sudden withdrawing from the populace of all habitual restraint—began gradually but rapidly to lose the habits, attachments, and ideas which lie at the foundation of civilized life. Doubtless their condition as slaves, while it in some respects counteracted, in others it encouraged their native want of forethought. Yet we think the former effect greater than the latter. Thus the bulk of negroes in the South, perhaps nine tenths, were employed in agricultural labor. Now to clear land, enclose and drain it, to plough, to harrow and sow, to till the crop through the summer, as is necessary with the summer growing crops of the South,—to harvest it in autumn; to undergo all this labor for a remote return, a provision for the wants of another year—is the especial exhibition of forethought, enterprise, and perseverance, that first stamped man as a provident being, capable of civilization. How did this example operate upon the negro? His lesson is ever half learned. We were long in the habit of watching the cultivation of a rice plantation, where after great labor had been expended during the winter in preparing the lands, a large gang of negroes would be employed from the end of March to the middle of May in sowing the crop. Numerous small but highly productive pieces and corners of land, outside of the fields, were allotted to the ne-

groes, one to each separately, as his own. But not a stroke of work would be done in them, until within a few days of the end of the sowing season, when the negroes, seized with a sudden fit of industry, would avail themselves, on finishing their regular tasks, of an hour or so of the sun's light, twilight and even moonlight, and in a few evenings dig, trench, and sow their own fields. A crop sowed so late need be hoed but once. Often have we asked one or other of the most intelligent of them, why they did not time their industry better. "If you began to sow your rice when I began, with three good hoeings you would make a full crop, and now you will make but half a crop." But Cuffee always gave us to understand that his arithmetic taught him that a half crop made by one hoeing was better than a full crop made by three.

This is characteristic of their aims, and their industry; the negro is easily content. Now content is a virtue when it teaches us to moderate unreasonable desires, and endure, without repining, unavoidable wants. But content is a vice when it leads to the indolent gathering of but half the good things placed by Providence within our reach; and when it leads to the slovenly performance of every duty, it becomes a crime.

On the emancipation of the negroes, multitudes, from having been satisfied with their lot, or from mere inertness, remained where freedom found them, engaging for wages and a maintenance to serve their late masters, or perhaps transferred their services to one of his neighbors. But while using, in a most wasteful manner, their own supplies and those of their employer, squandering their wages, and, if possible, running into debt, few had perseverance and industry enough to fulfill their engagements; and many, after having been maintained through the pinching time of winter, went off to avoid the more active and continuous labors of the spring; and lived like grasshoppers through the summer on what they could pick up. Those that staid seemed to lose all ability to do careful and thorough work. Thus, to recur to the rice plantations, no crop is more dependent on thorough drainage than this. Every field must be intersected by numerous ditches and drains, which must be kept clear of all obstruction. But as the rice does not grow in the ditches, no wages or inducement can make the negro undertake the labor of cleaning them out. All thorough tillage became equally impossible throughout the South; and farming enterprise, with free negro labor, has already ruined most of those who undertook it.

A large proportion, however, of the most active and enterprising negroes, when set free, at once rambled off in search of the living the world owed them. The negroes very generally, but very illogically, associated the idea of liberty and property as inseparable; and expected, now that they were free, to become, in some way, proprietors of houses and lands, and the means of cultivating the latter. Yet even the select few, whose character and intelligence procured them the occupation of farming lands, have generally shown the characteristics of the race; the smallest possible reach of foresight, an utter want of plan, slovenly tillage, neglect of all repairs, or a makeshift for present emergency. They hopefully aim at an easy and speedy way of attaining a remote end; and their half labor does not always produce the half crop which would content them. Yet these are the enterprising and provident among the race.

But the negro is a social being, and loves the town. On acquiring freedom, numbers crowded into the Southern cities, perhaps with no definite views. Being without means, they sought employments in which they might lead an easy life—content with small wages if the labor was proportionate to the pay. But nothing suits the negro so well as what may be called job-work.—His industry looks for prompt reward, and he will work very hard for some hours, or even some days, for the means of giving himself a prolonged holiday in which perfect idleness is the crowning enjoyment.

When compared with the white man, the most strongly marked trait of the negro, even beyond his constitutional indolence, and if not the cause of that indolence, yet inseparable from it, is his indisposition to look far ahead.—Had the poet, Young, known no race but the negro, he would have had little occasion to ask the question which he himself answers with so much point:

"Is it that things terrestrial can't content?
Deep in rich pastures will thy flocks complain?
Not so, but to their master is denied
To share their sweet serene. Man, ill at ease.
In this, not his own home, this foreign field
Where nature fodders him with other food
Than was ordained his cravings to suffice
Poor in abundance, famished at a feast,
Sighs on for something more, when most enjoyed."

But the negro is easily content—"Deep in rich pastures" *he* will not complain. Although capable of deep emotions, they do not last long. Care is not natural to him. Thought does not worry him. Nothing worries him more than to compel him to think. The negro has not thought enough to keep him awake, and has a most peculiar constitution. In our own excursions on a river far South, on leaving our boat for an hour of two, we have on our return, constantly found our negro boatmen asleep in the sun, with the thermometer at 112 deg. or 115 deg. and the shade neglected near at hand. The neighboring terrapins basking on that half-sunken log do not more enjoy their nap.

We have been told that on the freeing of the negroes in the

British West Indies, while on most of the islands they fast sunk into indolence, on one of the Bahamas it was not so. The island was small, the lands in few hands, and all under culture.—The negroes, when freed, had no where to go, not a foot of ground to stand on. The labor question was reduced to a simple proposition: work, or starve. They chose work; and may be working to this day.

But this is not the condition of the South. The country is new, wide and thinly peopled—with, in many parts, a decreasing population; and in its best days not a tenth of the land was under culture of any kind. Although neither climate nor soil is prolific of spontaneous bounties, yet a very little labor will supply the bare necessaries of life to an individual; and the negro is disposed to be content with bare necessaries. This is not favorable to the cultivation of systematic industry. A few hours labor in the day, a day or so of work in the week, a week in the month, and the laborer may enjoy the *dolce far niente* the rest of his time. But while this provides for all the wants of the adult negro, it is not that provident industry which maintains the family; and it is there that provident races display their forethought—looking forward through life to generations beyond. Under the system of servitude a punctual and often liberal provision for the necessary wants of the negro household—precluded all uncertainty and irregularity as to the means of sustaining life. Young Africa was sure of having his stomach filled, his back covered, and a shelter over his head, and was moreover taught betimes to make himself useful, and the household throve and multiplied wonderfully under the system.

But young Africa will have now to rely on his progenitors for maintenance and training. We do not think they will do for him more than they are doing for themselves. The parent not only begets the child, but often stamps his destiny upon him.

Young Africa has the prospect of a very irregular and uncertain maintenance, and rather rough treatment from the parental hand; for, except to the new infant, the negro is no tender parent. He will get also, a very thorough training in the art of frittering away his time. He may indeed, chance to fall into other hands, for the negro is often ready to lighten the domestic burden, by putting his child out to service at an early age. The boon of freedom to the negroes has been attended by an evident loosening of all domestic ties. An increasing number show an indisposition to bind themselves to fixed occupations and settled homes. Many of them are content with the most moderate, temporary, and uncertain provision against want.

There is no surer indication of the physical and moral condition of a people, than the rate of infant mortality; and rapidly as young Africa comes into the world, he has of late betrayed a greater propensity to die than to be born.

The future of Young Africa

turns altogether on the question whether any political, moral, or intellectual training can imbue his constitution with a propensity to forethought, and an aptitude for continuous, systematic labor. We see no prospect of such a revolution in his nature, and very little prospect of the experiment being tried. All the indications of history are, that civilization does not create races, but that particular races have created civilization, or at least, receiving it from some unknown source, have greatly modified it to suit their peculiar temperament. Thus the civilization of the Chinese, the Hindo, the Egyptian, the Jew, the Greek, the Roman, the Saracen, the Sclavonian, the Teuton, and the Celt, each varies with some constitutional peculiarity of the race. We have good evidence also, that some races, as the Indian of North America, and Malay of the Pacific, cannot receive civilization, but die out before it. And we have overwhelming proofs running back to the beginning of history, that the negro, far from dying out, becomes the servant of civilization, receiving only its lowest forms. Such civilization as he can acquire is received and sustained only by intercourse and contact with higher races; and his civilization grows and wanes with the increase or dimunition of that intercourse. He is a black mirror that reflects in dusky hues, with some distortion, the face of that civilization presented to it, and as it is withdrawn the image fades away.

There is a very large part of the South, in which it would be a mistake to suppose that the presence of a white population tends to exclude the negro, or the presence of a negro population to exclude the whites. In all those regions unfavorable to white field labor, it was the care, control and providence of the whites that multiplied the number of the blacks, and it was the productiveness of negro labor, so directed and controlled, that afforded employment for the skilled and professional labors of white men; and thus rendered possible the existence of a large white population.

The increase of a laboring and productive negro population increased the number of the whites by furnishing suitable and profitable employment for them; and this increase added in turn to the demand for negro labor and to the skillful application of it. Under the system that gave the control of negro labor to the whites the progress and prosperity of each race was based on that of the other, and the country went on continually to provide for the support of a larger negro and white population, increasing together, either of which would many times exceed that which it could sustain of only one race.—It is only in the absence of this control of the whites over the blacks that there is a tendency to the expulsion of one or the other race.

Upon these characteristics as laborers depends the status of every race of men. The whole history and philosophy of negro labor may be summed up in an anecdote. An English naval officer, on some emergency, landed on a remote part of the coast of Jamaica, with dispatches for Kingston. By an obscure path, through a wilderness teeming with fertility, he found his way to a wretched cabin occupied by a family of negroes. While inquiring the way further, he observed the squalid poverty of the inmates, and said to an old woman, the most intelligent of the group: "My good woman, I am astonished at the poverty of your household, when I see the fertility of the soil around the house."

"True, sir, the land is rich, but you forget that we have no slaves."

If, when, like Ephraim, he is joined to his idols, he be let alone, young Africa, true to the instincts of his race, will emulate and in time attain the barbarism of the old land.

THE HAVERSACK.

R. J. G., of Union C. H., S. C., gives a model letter from a young lady, whose sweetheart was in the 5th S. C. regiment, to President Davis, asking for a furlough for her lover to come home and get married:

Dear Mr. President:—I want you to let Jeemes ——, of company ——, 5th S. C. regiment, come home and get married.—Jeemes is willin', I is willin', Jeemes' mammy, she is willin', my mammy, she is willin', but Jeemes' captain, he ain't willin'. Now when we're all willin' 'ceptin' Jeemes' captin', I think you might up and let Jeemes come.—I'll make him go right straight back, when he's done got married and fight jist as hard as ever.

Your Affectionate friend, &c.

Mr. Davis wrote on the letter, "let Jeemes go," and Jeemes came home, married the affectionate correspondent of Mr. Davis, and returned to his regiment and did "fight jist as hard as ever."

Louisville, Ky., gives a dodging incident of the war. A similar anecdote was told at Monterey, Mexico, of Maj. Martin Scott, and no one enjoyed the joke more than the stout-hearted old soldier himself.

I was a member of the —— Tennessee cavalry regiment, and can vouch for the truth of the following, which I send to The Haversack:

In February, 1865, while Gen. Hampton's command was opposing the advance of Sherman's army, through South Carolina, Major D——, then commanding the regiment, was detached from the main force to guard a crossing on the Saluda River. Very soon after he had put the boys in positiou to defend the bridge, a heavy line of the enemy's infantry made its appearance along the opposite bank. After several minutes hard fighting, with small arms, the enemy brought up a battery of light artillery and directed a heavy fire upon the Major's command. While the shells were passing over and making a terrible noise as they clashed through the surrounding trees, he observed some of the more timid of his braves dodging and bowing as if to avoid the certain death to which they were so much exposed, and stepping to the front, a few paces, with sword uplifted, he shouted,

"What in the h—l are you dodging there for? Keep cool, I tell you, there's no use in it."

Just then a six-pounder passed close to the Major's head, and falling to the ground he crawled to a stump near by and finished his sentence, by exclaiming with great excitement,

"Unless—unless. I say, my good boys, unless they come like that one."

The Major and his command held the crossing until night-fall, when, owing to the movement of the Confederate forces they were compelled to withdraw.

"Long may they wave."

J. R. F.

The Major's experience in dodging must be of great service to him in this period of lowering the head and bowing the knee. But the loyal renegade can beat him a thousand to one at that game.

Richmond, Va., gives an incident of pretended modesty:

Modesty and Spy Glasses.—The soldiers, who were for any length of time, stationed on the James River, near —— Bluff, will remember quaint old Mr. Tugmuddle. He, with his numerous family of daughters, lived within a short distance of the river bank and very close to our camp—near where, in summer, the soldiers were wont to bathe. So near, indeed, that one day "Col. Cramp" received a visit from Mr. Tugmuddle in which T. took occasion to say:

"Sir, your soldiers strip and bathe, sir, right before the eyes of my daughters, who are modest young ladies, to whom the sight that they are daily made to witness is extremely offensive."

The Colonel, with gallantry, resolved and promised that the evil complained of should be remedied, and he stationed a guard, thereafter, on the bank to make the soldiers go further up the stream. But a few days elapsed when old "Tug" made the same complaint again.

That evening at dress parade orders, stricter than ever, were promulgated forbidding our boys to bathe nearer to old "Tug's" house than a certain point, about five hundred yards distant therefrom. Within a few days, however, old "Tug" came back with his old complaint.

"Why," said the colonel, "have my orders been disobeyed? surely your daughters can't see my men now—five hundred yards off!"

"Yes, sir, they *can!*"

"What! *see men bathing over five hundred yards off?*"

"But, sir," said 'old Tug,' "*my gals have spy glasses!!!*"

W. D. C.

An old friend sends from Mobile, Ala., an incident of Hood's campaign:

During the first day's disastrous fight at Nashville, as Hood's troops were falling back, they passed a house from which a young lady rushed out, and seized one of the regimental colors, and exhorted the men to rally around her. The minnie balls and shells were flying so fast, that the soldiers apparently thought that it was an inopportune time for devotion to the fair sex. She had many admirers, but very few attachés. Will some of our Nashville friends give the name of the heroine to The Land We Love?

T. C. C.

Could do Nothing for the Ladies.—When Hindman's division passed through Napoleon, Arkansas, in 1862, the men were ragged and dirty, even beyond the usual Confederate standard. The ladies saw in them, however, only their devotion to the South, and their effort to save us from the horrors of Abolition rule. They, therefore, received the ragamuffins with the utmost enthusiasm, bouquets were showered upon them, sweet smiles were lavished upon them, kind words greeted them everywhere. A hatless, shoeless reb passed along minus his pants below the knees. He seemed to be a special sufferer in the cause, and his appearance was hailed with an unusual demonstration of white pocket handkerchiefs. As he neared the groups of young ladies, who were waving their snowy handkerchiefs and their little rebel flags, they observed that he was red-headed, freckle-faced, horror of horrors! unmistakably and undeniably ugly to the last degree. Their ardor was damped, but they were too well-bred to show their disappointment, and the flags continued to wave, and the smiles still continued to be sweet. The reb halted in front of them, looked pityingly at them, and said in a melancholy tone,

"Ah! ladies, I can do nothing for you. I am not a marrying man, I have a wife at home!"

H. R. C.

The annexed anecdote comes from Fort's Station, Tenn., and we make but a single comment upon it, viz: "the horrors of Andersonville!"

Sometime in the fall of 1862, while the inmates of Northern prisons were suffering the fiercest pangs of hunger, a party of English travelers visited Camp Douglass. Before the party entered, we were ordered by the policemen, known by us as Uncle Billy, Old Red, and Prairie Bill, to clean our quarters and get ready for inspection. Everything was put in "apple pie order," and the Post Commander came in escorting his distinguished guests, who were profuse in their compliments of the well-swept walks, the thorough drainage, the clean quarters, &c., &c. Post Commander was quite a saint in their eyes, and his noble benevolence gave a still more atrocious character to the cruelty of Winder and Wirz. The visitors entered Barrack No. 5. They saw the sunken eyes and hollow cheeks of the prisoners. They looked upon Post Commander; he no longer seemed a pitying Howard. Just then Barrack No. 5 raised the cry, "bread, bread, bread!" Post Commander lost his benevolent smiles, his demure aspect; Post Commander was in a rage.—"Truth hurts worse than fiction." Post Commander was hurt, so were we, for we soon saw an order stuck up, "No rations will be issued to Barrack No. 5 to-day. Any one known to sell or give rations to No. 5 will be treated to a ride on Morgan's mare!"

Who will give the history of Morgan's mare?

H. H. F.

Greensboro', Georgia, tells how an "o'er smart youth" was "done for."

There was a cadaverous soldier belonging to the hospital at this place, who often contrived to get a stout dram of real old apple or peach (none of your Commissary stuff) by feigning to be suddenly seized with the chills. He would stroll to some gentleman's door, shake all over violently and beg to get a warm drink, lest his chill should terminate fatally. He had such a sickly, unhealthy look, that no one suspected the trick. And so he went on from day to day, getting his hot toddies, and abundance of sympathy from kind-hearted ladies. He was about to become that most hopeless and incorrigible of all nuisances, "a hospital rat," when his pleasant style of living was broken in upon by an unexpected incident. He had taken his seat, on this occasion, on the door step of a very shrewd, or a very benevolent, old lady, I do not know which, and there began to shake as though every bone would come out of his body. The tender-hearted lady coming to the door seemed but to aggravate the violence of the attack; he stammered out,

"'Most-froze-to-death-can-you-give-me-some-liquor?"

The compassionate eyes of the old lady took in the situation, and her orders were given with military precision.

"You, Jim, here's a poor soger a shakin' with the ager, you tote him in that thar room and put him in the feather bed. Lizy Ann, you run and git some hot bricks for his feet, and you Betsy Jane, make him some real, strong red-pepper tea, hot as pisin."

The orders were literally obeyed. Poor Tom ——— was smothered in a feather-bed in June, roasted with hot bricks, and drenched with fiery, pepper tea. But the prescription was admirable, he had no more chills. All the unhealthy humors in his body were effectually sweated out of him. Would that a similar treatment could be applied to the old nullifiers, and negro-traders, who are running the loyal machine at the South. What an awful amount of virulent puss would have to be expelled, before the patient got better!

Our next is from New Providence, Tennessee:

I send you an anecdote, which I think has never been in print. It occurred at Fort Donelson.

When Schwartz began to shell the position occupied by the 42nd.

Tennessee regiment and 8th Kentucky regiment, Capt. F. of the 8th Kentucky, sent his servant, a negro boy about 16 or 17, to the ravine back of the line of battle, where he might find shelter. After the fighting had somewhat slackened, the captain went to see what had become of his boy. He found him seated behind a big tree and apparently enjoying the shelling very much. When the captain came to him, he said: "I 'clare, masser, de Yankee shell ain't wort a cuss, some on 'em buss when he hit de ground, and some on 'em so no 'count he buss right in de ar."

W. G. W.

Our next comes from Lexington, Kentucky.

During the winter of 1863-'64, while the Confederate army was encamped around Dalton, Ga., the Commissary Department was supplied with beef from South Western Georgia and Florida, and to save trouble, the beef was killed and sent forward by the cars. The Kentucky brigade was encamped about a mile from the depot, and, like the rest of the army, was sometimes on short rations. But skill and strategy sometimes enabled them to supply the deficiency. Col. Cofer of the 6th Kentucky, was Provost Marshal, a rigid, strict, and just officer. But spite of his executive qualities, the boys would, sometimes, get ahead of him. As I said before, the beef was brought ready dressed on the cars, and the distribution to the several commands took place from the platform of the depot.

One morning, two or three of the Kentucky boys came along, and one of them, having his musket with him, mounted guard over the beef. The Receiving Commissary, seeing him walking on his post, thought that he was there by authority. Presently, the sentinel leveled his musket at a man, who had seized a large piece of beef, and threatened to shoot him, if he did not let it drop. The sentinel cursing the rogue, told the Commissary that he would take the offender to Col. Cofer. The Commissary assented, but as the prisoner started off with the beef on his shoulder, he told the sentinel that it had better be left behind.

"Oh, no," said the sentinel, "I want Col. Cofer to see exactly what he has stolen." The Commissary said,

"Very well, take it along then."

As the sentinel was some time in getting back, the Commissary stepped over to Col. Cofer's office, and learned that neither sentinel, nor thief had appeared there.—The meat had been *stolen* and the Commissary had been *sold*.

J. R. V.

The sentinel must have got his lessons before the war, from some of the party of great moral ideas. He feigned to be in the discharge of duty, when conniving at the stealing of the beef, and was very indignant at the theft of another. Isn't this exactly in the style of the moral-idea gentleman? What is the Freedmen's Bureau but a great thieving concern? yet, professedly a humane and benevolent institution in the performance of duty.

A former member of Pickett's division, now in Charlotte N. C., gives an anecdote, which has an instructive moral connected with it:

What he bet agin my old Rooster.—Just before my brigade was ordered to coöperate with Hoke, in the expedition of that gallant and accomplished officer against Plymouth, we were encamped on the Central Railroad, about 20 miles above Richmond. I was sitting in front of the tent of Commissary Sergeant D——, one of the boys in every sense of the word, witty, lively, and gritty. We had been chatting about one thing and another, and I was just about to leave him, when we saw an old countryman drive up in a little wagon, which had a chicken-coop in it, with one solitary old rooster, the only inmate.

Sergeant D. Halloo, old fellow, it is not worth while to take that old rooster back home. Let's trade for him.

Old Man. Well, you see, I'se sold them all, ceptin this old rooster, and my old woman, she told me to ax a dollar for him.

Sergeant D. A dollar for that old thing! I hain't seen a dollar since last pay day, a year ago. But I'll tell you what I'll do; I'll play seven up for him.

Old Man. Well, I don't care if I do take a turn or two at the cards.

Now, Sergeant D. had often bragged to me that he never lost a game of cards, and that if he could not beat any living man in playing, he could beat all creation at counting. (Just as loyal poll-holders always make the count on their side at elections.) A crowd gathered around to see the old man initiated in the mysteries of old sledge, and it soon became apparent that the old rooster was in a bad way. Sergeant D. was the victor; the old man sighed and said, "My old woman's rooster is gone and she hain't got the dollar nother." Off ran the Sergeant to make a chicken pie, kindly inviting me to come over when it was ready. The old man went off in none of the best of humors probably dreading the Caudle lecture he would get on his arrival home without the rooster and without the dollar.

We were still sitting there chatting, when the old man drove up again, saying:

"Whar is that feller what won my old woman's rooster?"

One said, "he is making pot pie of the old rooster, won't you come and help eat him?"

Another asked, "do you want to take another lesson at old sledge?"

A third hoped that the old man "had some more roosters to trade off."

A fourth inquired, "shall I tell Sergeant D. that you want to see him?"

"No, no," said the old man, "all I wanted to ax him was, *what he bet agin my old rooster, for I don't 'member that he sot up one dratted thing agin him!*"

And so it had been, the Sergeant had staked nothing, and it was a one-sided game all the time. J. R. P.

The moral of the story is obvious. The little game of Reconstruction played at the South had the stakes all on one side. But we will not envy our Republican friends. The old rooster they have won, in the shape of loyal governors, judges, &c., will make a very unsavory pot pie, and will offend the nostrils with an odor of tainted flesh!

H. F., of Holly Springs, Mississippi, relates a touching incident:

The writer was among the wounded at Perryville, and was carried thence to the hospitable town of Harrodsburg. Among the large number of wounded, was a boy, shot in the arm. He did not appear to be more than sixteen; and the nobleness and manhood which shone through his beardless face, prompted me to enquire his name. It was George Hamer, of the 24th Tennessee regiment, Maney's brigade. The little fellow's arm was badly shattered, and had to be amputated. The operation was performed by Dr. German, a gentle, tender-hearted Surgeon, who had been the family physician at little George's home. Chloroform was administered, and the operation performed. When the brave boy recovered from the effects of the chloroform, and saw the unsightly stump hanging where his arm had been, he cried as if his heart would break; but he presently recovered himself, as if ashamed of the weakness, and turning his yet dewy eyes upon the good doctor, said to him:

"Don't tell ma I cried, please, doctor."

And when the doctor promised, he grew quiet, and seemed satisfied. Since then, I have been told that this mother's darling died of his wound. What incident of old, chivalrous days is more touching and tender? or contains more of the true and gentle sublimity of courage?

The "Haversack" is always filled with interesting incidents, and anecdotes; but none of them, in my opinion, more deserving of record, and remembrance, than this I have undertaken to tell.

Memphis, Tennessee, sends an anecdote, which we think that we have seen before, but will repeat it that it may be preserved among the records of the late so-called.

On Gen. Bragg's celebrated march into Kentucky, the troops were often on half rations, though they had full marching to do.—One day, Gen. Hardee rode in rear of Cleburne's division and came across a foot-sore Irishman, who had straggled far behind.

Gen. H. Why are you not up with your regiment?

Emerald Isle. Me foot is sore wid the rocks, bad luck to them! me stomach is wake wid the half rations, and me back is broke wid the big knapsack.

Gen. H. All the other men are in the same fix and you ought to get along as well as they.

Emerald Isle. Will the Gineral allow me to ax him a question?

Gen. H. Certainly.

Emerald Isle. Didn't yer Honor write Hardee's Tactics?

Gen. H. Yes.

Emerald Isle. And ain't there an ivolution called double column at half distance?

Gen. H. Yes, there is.

Emerald Isle. And is there an ivolution called double distance on half rations?

Gen. H. No, certainly not.

Emerald Isle. Well, thin, if a great Gineral doesn't put down that ivolution in his Tactics, Patrick O'Donnahue is too good a soldier to go agin the Tactics of his own Corps Commander!

Gen. H. Patrick O'Donnahue shall ride the balance of the day. Come and get on this horse. My servant shall walk.

Emerald Isle. Long life to yer Honor! You always was a man of sinse!

We get the next anecdotes from Norfolk, Va.:

Believing that our gallant neighbors can appreciate a joke, even at their own expense, I send you one on a North Carolina soldier, which is strictly true.

A Virginia brigade was encamped near Hanover Junction, and Pettigrew's North Carolina brigade had to file past them. Of course, the boys began to "remark a few remarks," and to bandy jeers and home-thrusts, not always of the most delicate kind. Finally, the last straggler had apparently passed, and all the Virginians were about to return to their tents, when a small, bilious-looking, sallow-faced, tar-smoked, North Carolinian came dragging his weary way along. Chills had unmistakably marked him for their own. He was in none of the best of humors, and *noli me tangere* was plainly written in his eyes, and withal there was a defiant look, which seemed to say that 'twould be dangerous to trifle with him. Nevertheless, a bold wag determined to have his fun.

Virginian. (Mockingly.) Mister, what ridge-*ment* do you belong to?

Straggler. 'Blong to 52d Kliner, you ugly cuss, (cocking his gun) now say "Tar-heel," and I'll put daylight through you!

The obnoxious word was not said!

I was telling this anecdote to some of my North Carolina friends, when I got for my pains, a harder story on a raw recruit of a well- known Virginia regiment of cavalry. It seems that this recruit was put out on picket, all alone, on a pocosin on the Chowan River. The gloom and dreariness of one of these swamps would be unpleasant even to a veteran. They were too much for our recruit. He was shaky from the start, but for brevity, I must dramatize my story.

Owl up a tree. Whoo, a whoo, a whoo are you?

Raw Recruit. Don't shoot, I'm Sam ——, of Virginia cavalry. I surrender, don't shoot, don't shoot!

The following is said to be a true bill:

General Forrest was one day sitting in his tent in company with his A. A. General, when a long, lank, sallow-faced Tennessee Cavalryman rode up to the guard and announced himself the bearer of a dispatch. The sentinel silently pointed to the tent, and the Tennessean, nothing daunted, dismounted from his angular steed, and plunging his hand into the depths of a very greasy looking haversack, drew out the dispatch and proceeded to the tent; entering and seeing only two plainly dressed persons, he laid the paper on the table, merely remarking, epigrammatically, "'spatch for the Gineral." Having done this, he sat down on a stool, without removing his hat, and crossing his legs, commenced whistling an air well known in the army, viz: "If you want to catch h—l jest jine the cavalry, jine the cavalry." Occasionally he would sing the song instead of whistling it, keeping time always with his bare feet. More than once in the rendition of the monotonous yet otherwise forcible ballad, he would give the General a familiar and kindly slap on the back.

Presently the A. A. G. arose, and beckoning him to follow, advanced to where his horse was tied, and after giving him a bundle of papers, and scanning him curiously from head to foot, asked him if he knew that it was General Forrest with whom he had been so familiar. Butternut protested violently that he was not aware of the fact, and insisted on returning to "pologize." The A. A. G., curious to hear his apology, acquiesced. Whereupon they returned to the tent, when the cavalryman, lifting his hat with all the grace of a French Hussar, said:

"Gineral, you looked so uncommon plain just now that I took you for an orderly. If I'd knowed you I wouldn't have been so familiar. No offence, I hope."

Here he turned and commenced to retire, when, as if undecided, he stopped, and once more approached the General and laid his hand upon his shoulder (very respectfully, however,) and said:

"No offence, Gineral, I swar, but if you want to ketch hell, you jest jine the cavalry." J. R. R.

EDITORIAL.

THE readers of this magazine know that we have all along contended that peace could only be restored to this disturbed country, through the efforts of the soldiers of the two armies. True pluck and genuine manhood respect true pluck and genuine manhood. A permanent estrangement between brave men in the same country, is impossible. The brave conqueror will be generous and magnanimous. The conquered brave man will never be truckling, cringing, base and false.

At the South, we have seen the extraordinary spectacle of the fierce fire-eaters keeping out of the way of bullets; next, of their slandering and vilifying all who tried to do their duty in the war; and finally, of their allying themselves with the vilest of mankind to degrade and oppress the men, whose only crime was following their teaching. At the North, a still more humiliating sight was witnessed. There those, who hounded on others to fields of carnage, not only did not go to the front themselves, but actually grew rich upon the tears of the orphan, and the groans of the widow. Not content, when the war closed, with the bloated wealth acquired through the traffic in blood, they racked their ingenuity to devise new and strange methods of humiliating the foe, whom they feared to meet in battle. Three years after the last gun had been fired, they are found still rancorous in their hate and still unsated with vengeance. Through the thin disguise of love for the negro, whom their very soul loathes, may be seen their inextinguishable hatred of the South. The coward never forgives, the coward never trusts his adversary, the coward is incapable of anything noble and high-minded.—The coward, who whined like a puppy when the cane of a gentleman was laid upon his shoulders, will never consent to see a Southern gentleman upon the floor of Congress. The miscreant, who used his official position as an officer of the United States Army, to insult Southern ladies, and steal their jewelry and wardrobes, will never consent to any measures of Reconstruction, which will expose him to the hazard of meeting, face to face, the husbands, sons or brothers of the insulted ladies. Craven fear, as well as relentless malignity, make these poltroons the most remorseless oppressors. So, too, miserable, selfish fear of the negro, and fear of the Union power drove the fire-eaters, of the South, into the ranks of the loyal Fetich. The renegade Nullifier, and the malignant Abolitionist have allied together—the bond of union between them, being their mutual cowardice. No good can be expected from this unnatural junction of base spirits. The cowardly Northerner wishes the extermination of the race he hates and fears. The renegade Southerner has so forfeited his own self-respect by betraying his brethren, violating his conscience and stultifying his previous history, that he has become a mean and despicable thing in his own eyes. The sincere lover of his country must look away from these two degraded classes, and place his hopes of an enduring peace, and lasting prosperity in a cordial union between the brave men, who fought each other fairly and squarely.

It was, therefore, with inexpressible pleasure that we read of the cordial meeting between Northern and Southern officers in the grand Democratic Convention, in New York. That pleasure was enhanced a thousand fold, when in the long list of Northern officers, we saw not a single name, which did not belong to an honorable foe in the days gone by. Butler was not there to remind us of robbery, murder and slander of Southern women. Schenck was not there to recall tyranny and oppression. Sherman was not there to tell of "the ashes of Southern homes." Sheridan was not there to recount the mills and barns burnt in the Valley of Virginia. McNeill was not there to bring up the murders in Missouri. Burbridge was not there to bring up vividly the picture of the lads shot in cold blood at Georgetown, Kentucky. Burnsides was so far off that even with his own "powerful field glass," we could not see the New Berne pianos. Milroy was not there to remind us, in his small way, of John Arnold's cow and Mrs. Logan's spoons. So we read the list, and with no little emotion, said, "honorable men, all honorable men." Devoutly do we thank Heaven that it was so. We are glad, too, that General Blair, a soldier of courage and reputation, has been among the very first to proclaim the whole scheme of fraud, cruelty and iniquity to be unconstitutional, and therefore null and void. So far from having bitterness towards such men on account of their military career, we are profoundly grateful to them for their zeal to save us from the horrors of Hayti and Jamaica.

We believe that our own peerless Hampton spoke not only the sentiments of his own great soul, but those of all the true soldiers of the South. All are ready to join heart and soul with their late brave antagonists in the effort to resist a tyranny, which seeks not merely to subvert the government of our fathers, but also to upheave the very foundations of society. We are pleased to notice every where a growing fraternization between "the boys in blue" and "the boys in grey." The *Kentucky Yeoman*, edited by a distinguished soldier with an honored name, comes to us with an earnest appeal to the union soldiers. It is so appropriate that we copy it entire:

Of all men who may rightfully complain of the enormities of Radicalism, and who may rightfully denounce them, the Federal soldier has the best right and strongest grounds. We mean, of course, the patriotic soldier, who enlisted in the army to prevent a division of the Union and the destruction of the Constitution; who, accepting the solemnly plighted faith of the Government—that the war should be prosecuted for no purpose "of conquest or subjugation, nor for any purpose of interfering with the established institutions of any State, but simply to preserve the Union under the Constitution, with the dignity, equality, and rights of the several States unimpaired"—responded to the call for troops, as was the case especially with all Kentuckians.

They have a right to complain because they have been cruelly and shamefully betrayed by the authorities controlling the government. They enlisted to preserve the Union; their services were perverted into its destruction. They assumed the duties and risked the dangers of the camp and the battle-field to perpetuate the Constitution; their sacrifices and valor are made the means of its destruction. They enlisted under the solemn promise of the government that the "established institutions, dignity, equality, and rights of the States should be preserved," and find at the end of the contest, that they have been made the unwilling instruments of utterly destroying all these sacred boons. They enlisted to save to the Union ten States of white men, and find their success made to substitute ten colonies of negroes for those States.

We make an appeal to the honest, patriotic, gallant, chivalrous "white boy in blue," to ponder over these facts, and then answer us if he will longer sustain his betrayers. Remember the promises of the men who, claiming to be Union men, won your confidence, and look at their acts of shameless betrayal, then tell us, will you "lick the foot that kicks you?"

The heathen had a proverb, "the mills of the gods grind slowly, but they grind surely." A day of retribution will come for every evil deed. It is a fearful thing to fall into the hands of the Living God. In no case within our recollection has the retribution been so sudden and so summary as it has been upon the murderers of Mrs. Surratt. The *Republican*, of Lynchburg, Va., gives a statement, which ought to alarm the cowardly wretches, who are not yet sated with blood. Of the four witnesses against Mrs. Surratt, Baker, the principal, died unhonored, neglected, shunned and abhorred; Conover, the next in infamy, is in the Penitentiary; and the other two are undergoing punishment for crime. Preston King, who denied Anne Surratt access to the President, drowned himself in North River. Jim Lane, who supported King in his cruelty, shot himself in St. Louis. Stanton, who employed suborned witnesses and kept back the record of the trial from the President, is, probably, next to Butler, the least respected man on the continent.

We have seldom seen any thing neater and more conclusive than the annexed extract from that able Democratic paper, the *Watchman*, of Bellefonte, Pennsylvania:

Grant, Jackson and Clay.—It is certainly not very respectful to the memory of Jackson and Clay to associate their names and memories with the name of Grant, but, by way of contrast, the apparent disrespect will, no doubt, be excused. In his letter accepting the Radical nomination for President, Grant says:

"I shall have no policy of my own to interfere against the people."

U. S. GRANT.

Now, if you want to see the great difference between this man and the immortal Jackson, who was a statesman as well as a soldier, read:

"I say again, fellow-citizens, remember the fate of Rome, and VOTE FOR NO CANDIDATE who will not tell you with the frankness of an independent freeman, the principle upon which, if elected, he will administer your Government.

"That man deserves to be a slave who would vote for a mum candidate when his liberties are at stake."

ANDREW JACKSON.

Henry Clay was not, like Jackson, a warrior, but he was, like Jackson a great statesman. Do you suppose Henry Clay would vote for Grant, if he were alive to-day? If so, undeceive yourself by reading the following:

"If my suffrage is asked for the highest civil officer of my country, the candidate, however illustrious and successful he may be, must present some other title than laurels however gloriously gathered on the BLOOD-STAINED BATTLE-FIELD." HENRY CLAY.

A young lieutenant had to take a detachment of twenty men to the army. He said to them one morning, "hurry up, boys, we've twenty miles to go to-day." A jolly Patrick in the detachment replies, "faith and that's just one mile apiece; its nothing at all, at all!" This is no Irish Bull, there is true philosophy in it. Genial companionship *does* divide the distance on a tedious journey. Cordial coöperation *does* lighten the burden of labor. Sickness and suffering are relieved, if not made positively pleasant, by kind and sympathizing attention.

What we need at the South is to go to our work with shoulder-to-shoulder, mutually cheering, supporting and encouraging one another. We have but few friends abroad: let us befriend one another at home. Let us encourage our own schools and colleges, our own manufactures and work-shops, our own mechanics, our own scholars, our own enterprises in every department of human effort. When we have a glowing fire and bright lights at home, we care not how dark, cold and stormy, it may be abroad. Let us make our oppressed section bright and cheerful with mutual love and sympathy. We need not care then for the howls of the Jacobins without.

We do not know precisely the effect of Mr. Johnson's pardoning Proclamation, but we suppose that it makes us, who fought for home and fire-side, "bran new again," and as loyal as the loyalest in the land. But as the Proclamations, of the eminent person alluded to, have been generally over-ruled and made to amount to just nothing at all, we are very cautious in speaking of the dignitaries in power. It is, we presume, loyal and proper to quote themselves in condemnation of themselves. So we have given the opinions expressed by honest Ben Wade and frank Don Piatt and charming Mrs. Cady Stanton in regard to the waste, extravagance, folly and roguery of the "party of great moral ideas."—We suppose that it would be disrespectful, in one so recently made loyal by Presidential Proclamation, to question these authoritative opinions of the great leaders of Republicanism. We, therefore, assume them to be just and correct. And so in regard to the declarations of the gentle Anna Dickinson, who hates the South and Democracy as cordially as she loves Fred. Douglas and his race. We find an utterance of sweet Anna quoted in a highly esteemed exchange, the *Times*, of Selinsgrove, Pennsylvania. It is in these words: "Grant's whisky record is not half so infamous as his Indian baby record in California." Gentle Anna! this is strong language for a delicate and refined lady to use, and the subject is hardly becoming. But as your allies have expended their strength in violating the Eighth Commandment, (see statement of Mrs. Cady), you are right in expecting them to be more particular about the Seventh.

One of the most extraordinary things in this age of wonders is the trial of the Columbus, Ga., prisoners. A low wretch was murdered in a negro brothel in that city, and upon mere suspicion, some twenty young men, of the best and noblest families in that noble State, were arrested and thrust in a dungeon, whose horrors were scarcely inferior to those of the Black Hole of Calcutta. We find a Card from nine of these unfortunate youths, in our able contemporary, the *Chronicle and Sentinel* of Augusta, Ga. We make a brief extract:

The prisoners arrested in May were at Fort Pulaski before their removal to Atlanta. Their cells were as dark as dungeons, without ventilation, and but 4 by 7 feet. No bed or blanket was furnished. The rations consisted of a *slice* of *fat* pork three times each week, and beef too *unsound* to eat the remaining days. A piece of bread for each meal, soup for dinner, and coffee for breakfast, finished the bill of fare. An old *oyster can* was given each prisoner, and in this vessel both coffee and soup were served.

It may be said that the soldiers received nothing better, but these citizens were not soldiers, and their friends were able, willing and anxious to give them every comfort. Why were they denied the privilege? Refused all communication with their friends, relatives or counsel, they were forced to live in these horrid cells, night and day, prostrated by heat and maddened by myriads of mosquitoes. The calls of nature were attended to in a bucket, which was removed but once in twenty-four hours.

At McPherson Barracks we were placed in cells 5 feet 11 inches wide by 10 feet long. These cells were afterward divided, reducing their width to *two feet ten inches.* This is terrible, but true. Upon the arrival of the officer sent from Washington to investigate the arrests, the partitions were removed. Neither bed nor bedding was furnished for from two to five days. We were not permitted to see our friends, families or counsel until after memorials to Congress had aroused the whole country to the enormity of the outrage. Even after this, our LETTERS, breathing the affection and sympathy of a wife or mother, were subjected to inspection. The prison sink was immediately at our cell doors, and emitted a stench that was horrible.

At times, when some humane soldier was willing to transcend his orders, and give us a breath of fresh air to soothe our distended, bursting veins, we would ask him to close the door, preferring to risk suffocation rather than endure the intolerable smell.

During all this time we were ignorant of the charges against us.

Think of this horrible suffocation in the summer months in Georgia! Think of men being treated thus before conviction, before trial, before even they knew the offence with which they were charged!! Was any thing more infamous ever committed in the darkest days of the dark ages? Savages never did any thing half so atrocious. They burned at the stake or slew with the battle-axe the enemies taken in battle. But there is no record of their torturing those of their own tribe before trial and condemnation. That infamy has been reserved for our model Republic in the latter half of the 19th century!

Every device was employed and every cruelty practiced upon the negro witnesses to force them to testify what was required of them. Their heads were shaved, halters were put around their necks, cannon were trained upon them with the threat of blowing them to pieces. (Weep, ye hypocrites, over Uncle Tom's Cabin.) But not satisfied with this, a steam torture-box was invented.

We give a short extract from the Macon (Ga.,) *Telegraph*, a calm, dispassionate paper, bold in the denunciation of wickedness, but not disposed to exaggerate the enormity of that wickedness:

In conversation with one of the most eminent citizens, of Macon, yesterday, he assured us that Gen. Meade explained to him, in Atlanta, week before last, the whole modus operandi of this instrument of torture. Meade described it as a box sufficiently capacious to admit the victim, and then arranged for compression by screws, by which a force could be brought upon the prisoner sufficient to "squeeze the breath out of him." It was also provided with a steam apparatus, connected with the throttling box by pipes, and upon turning a fosset, jets of steam were thrown in, which added materially to the anguish of suffocation. This machine was applied to three of the witnesses—Betts, Marshal and a negro, with entire efficacy—the negro gave in in a moment, and cried out that he would swear anything if they would only let him out of that box.

The most remarkable part of this whole matter is, that all these outrages have been perpetrated by Gen. Meade, who has been hitherto regarded as a gentleman. It only proves how rapid must be the descent into crime and infamy of any one, who consents to become the tool of the Jacobins.

We are often surprised at the mistakes made at the North by those, who are not unkindly disposed to the South. Doubtless, we make similar blunders, and thus the sectional ill-feeling is kept up. The Philadelphia *Age* is usually well-posted, but it seems to be a believer in "the horrors of Andersonville," if we may judge by the extract below:

Mortality among Prisoners.—A communication made by Stanton while Secretary of War, but just published, shows that by the reports of the Commissary-General of Prisoners—

I. That twenty-six thousand four hundred and thirty-six deaths of rebel prisoners of war are reported.

II That twenty-two thousand five hundred and seventy-six Union soldiers are reported as having died in Southern prisons.

By this it seems that the actual number of deaths among prisoners was greatest at the North.—But as compared with the whole number of prisoners, the ratio was larger at the South:

The reports also show that two hundred and twenty thousand rebel prisoners were held in the North, and about one hundred and twenty-six thousand nine hundred and forty Union prisoners in the South.

These are the figures given by Mr. Stanton, and they are published to correct an account which, placing the deaths at the same numbers, made a different estimate of the prisoners actually held by the respective belligerents.

Now we are surprised that the *Age* did not detect the trick of Stanton and did not see why he should publish a second table of prison statistics after giving the first to the world more than two years ago.

Mr. Stanton's first report merely gave the deaths of the prisoners (substantially the same as in the last report) and the numbers held by each belligerent. He, evidently. had not calculated the ratio of the respective losses. But it was not long before the Copperhead and Southern papers showed that from Mr. Stanton's own figures, the ratio in Northern prisons, of those who died, to those who lived, was 1 to 7½: while in Southern prisons, it was but 1 to 11. So, if there were horrors at Andersonville, there were much greater horrors at Johnson's Island, Elmira, Fort Delaware, &c. This would never do! The whole world had rung with rebel atrocities and now the figures of the Federal Secretary of War proved greater atrocities at the North! A second report must be got up and the scheme was devised to make the Southern prisoners exceed by some hundred thousands the Northern prisoners held at the South. This ingenious plan was carried out by including in the estimate all the Southern prisoners captured at the forts, garrisons, &c., &c., of the South, most of whom were held but a few weeks, or paroled on the spot! This is the way the thing was done, and we charge that Mr. Stanton knew that his second report was calculated to produce a wrong impression, and that *he made it expressly to produce that impression.* We are sure that if the estimate of mortality is confined to a calculation among the prisoners held for six months, and over, the ratio of deaths among the Southern prisoners will be found greatly to exceed the ratio of deaths among the Northern prisoners.

There is this aggravated guilt, too, in the case of the Federal authorities. The North had the means to make the Southern prisoners comfortable. The South had not the means. Moreover, the Confederate authorities desired the exchange of prisoners, but Mr. Lincoln, at Grant's instigation, refused. It was believed that the South could not be conquered, if exchange went on, and so it was stopped.

It is very gratifying to our pride as an editor, and to our loyalty as one of the late rebels, to find that the great apostle of loyalty has come to entertain the same views that we have often expressed, viz; that the loyal Fetich cannot be trusted. Wendell Philips fears that the men, who betrayed the Union, then the Confederacy, then Mr. Johnson, then their neighbors and friends—may even take it into their changeable heads to betray the Republicans! Hear him, ye Fetich:

Congress brings the rebel States back into its halls; *not because any man considers them fit and ready, but to help Grant's chances of election.* In this sort of game, the Republican leaders have always shown themselves clumsy players, and we fear they are fated in this instance to find themselves at fault. Tennessee and West Virginia were brought in with the same plea—sagacious managers' idea of strengthening the party. But the Senators from these two States have been constant stumbling-blocks and checkmated impeachment at last. Present appearances indicate the same result in these lately admitted States. If their admission defeats Grant, we shall not be surprised. If Senators may be bought, why not Presidential electors? Bribery has become now a fixed element in our politics.

We look to see the action of the Presidential electors steeped in such corruption as will throw the impeachment market thoroughly into the shade. With Johnson in the White House it is a dangerous step to admit these seven States. *Unless carefully watched they will prove a serious danger to the loyal party.*

This peril is more specially imminent because the land has been left so exclusively in the hands of white Secessionists. The negro votes the Republican ticket at the risk of starvation, if not of life. Beside this the negro voters lack organization. They are just now especially liable to be deceived in their candidates. *The South swarms with adventurers and reckless speculators;* the most hopeful speculation just now, is by hypocrisy and bribes, to buy admission to the Senate or Electoral College. With the influence of the Administration on their side, success will not be difficult. *Such transition times as these are hotbeds of turncoats and traitors.*

If the cold North plants Rosses, Fowlers and Fessendens, what a four-fold crop of Burrs and Arnolds the tropic South will give us back! The Republican party has charlatans enough who plume themselves on being "practical men." The admission of these States is their boasted "practical statesmanship." In our view it is putting a knife into the hands of Northern and Southern rebels wherewith to cut the throat of the loyal party. Nothing but the persistent vigilance and activity of fanatics can avert that result. Statesmen—denounced as dreamers—must take up the stitches these blunderers who think themselves owls—are constantly dropping. Save us from conceited friends, and we risk the shrewdest enemies.

We know two books, which have taken whole paragraphs, pages and chapters from this magazine without saying so much as "by your leave, sir!" In after years, it may be thought that we have borrowed pretty freely from these books. So now, it may be thought that some of our expressions, months ago, about renegade Southerners, have been borrowed from Wendell Philips! So, too, our predictions, repeated so often, that the loyal Fetich could not be trusted and would desert the Republicans, seem but an echo of Mr. Philips' sentiments! But upon our honor, we have not stolen from the great apostle of Abolitionism. As we became more and more loyal, it was natural that our thoughts should fall into the loyal channel and finally that we should talk like this model of loyalty. We hope that this explanation of similarity of views and words will be satisfactory.

We wonder what Bullock, Abbott, Deweese, Scott & Co., think of the declaration: "the South swarms with adventurers and reckless speculators." We wonder what the old nullifiers and negro-traders, now among the loyal Fetich, think of this sentence: "such transition times are hotbeds of *turncoats and traitors.*" We wonder what they think of the sentence: "unless carefully watched, they will prove a serious danger to the loyal party." Oh! ye young converts to the stronger side, we wonder whether you consider Wendell a loyal man!

We have been so delighted with

Mr. Philips' plain talk that we do not like to make a carping criticism. But we would gently remind him that the "tropic South" did not bring forth Arnold and Burr. They were both born nearer "to hum."

BOOK NOTICES.

THE EMIGRANTS' VADE-MECUM, OR GUIDE TO THE "PRICE GRANT" IN VENEZUELA, GUAYANA. By Mrs. Mary Amanda Pattison, of Maryland. J. Wall Turner. Richmond, Virginia:

As every Southern citizen should have a home selected to remove to, in case our condition does not improve in this land, purchased by the blood of our fathers, we recommend the perusal of this little book, to every one. The authoress, Mrs. Pattison, resides in London, where she seems to be unwearied in her efforts to aid her Southern countrymen.

The grant to Dr. Price, of Virginia, of 240,000 square miles of land, by the Venezuelan Government, seems to have attracted very little attention among our people. Their ideas of a country only 8 deg. from the equator, consists, generally, of vague notions of a climate of burning heat, rank vegetation, malarious diseases, anacondas and boa-constrictors, poisonous reptiles, and unfriendly Indians. On inquiring into this subject, however, they will find that Venezuela has a healthy and delightful climate, cooled by the sea breezes on the coast, and by the elevation of its broad plateaux in the interior. These breezes and this elevation, while they moderate the heat of summer, have no influence in producing cold in winter, and so the temperature, the year round, is one of delightful moderation.—The scenery is grand and unique—comprising forests of the richest and most gorgeous tropical vegetation in the vallies,—and prairies, hundreds of miles in extent, are roamed by vast herds of cattle, and backed by snow-peaked mountains. The capital of the country, Ciudad Bolivar, contains about 15,000 inhabitants, the better class of whom are cultivated, intelligent and polished. The town is well and substantially built, containing many buildings of stone. Earthquakes are unknown. Our space will not admit of extracts from this charming book, but we hope our readers will all procure it from Mr. Turner, of Richmond, and read it for themselves.

THE RESOURCES OF CALIFORNIA. By John S. Hittell. W. J. Widdleton, New York:

California is another region to which the soul of the oppressed Anglo-Saxon, of the South, turns with longing from the Radical, bayonet-pointed, negro legislation and negro jurisdiction of our once princely political heritage. In California the lower races are not forced up from their proper level, and the civil rights of a race of freemen placed in their hands.

The country at first, when adventurers were pouring in from every quarter of the globe, was given to some extravagance in the administration of impromptu laws—but the worst instances of this kind, were mild in comparison with the horrors of Jamaica and Hayti. Their condition at present, is far better than ours in this respect ; for here, house-breaking and burglary are almost of weekly occurrence.

Their climate is healthy and delightful, and the soil is rich. They have some disadvantages, however—dust and drought in summer, and mud and freshets in winter. Their scenery is grand and beautiful, beyond description—surpassing that of Switzerland. Mr. Hittell says:

"The Helvetian Republic has, for hundreds of years, had the fame of possessing the greatest area of elevated land, and the largest number of great peaks within the limits of high civilization, but the newly discovered mountain region surpasses that of Switzerland. That country has only four peaks above 13,000 feet, and not more than 150 square miles above 8,000 feet, while California has 100 peaks above 13,000 feet, and 300 or more square miles above 8,000 feet.

"The 'Big Trees' were supposed to exist only in a few isolated groves, but are now found in extensive forests, with tens of thousands of trees along the Sierra Nevada." The principal agricultural products of California are fruit and grain, and these are God's best material gifts. Home is dear to the heart of the Anglo-Saxon every where, but no homes are so sweet as those nestling amid blossoming orchards and waving fields of grain. And when these homes are set, like gems, amid the lovely scenery of California, where snow-capped mountains tower on one side and verdant savannas stretch out to the horizon on the other; or where the waves of the Pacific break, with musical murmurs, upon the lengthened coast—our children may forget, although, alas, we never can, the land bequeathed us by our fathers, and who paid for it the precious price of toil and blood.

ABRAHAM PAGE, ESQ. A novel. J. B. Lippincott & Co., Philadelphia:

This is an interesting tale, naturally told; and the typography of the book is beautiful;—but we are sorry to see the writer taking ground against church organizations. A church can no more exist in this wicked world without an organization, than a man could exist in this natural world without a body.

Lightning Source UK Ltd.
Milton Keynes UK
UKHW01f1258200818
327506UK00005B/861/P